GEORGE BENTHAM

AUTOBIOGRAPHY
1800–1834

Portrait of George Bentham by Charles Leblanc.
Reproduced by permission of the Linnean Society of London.

GEORGE BENTHAM

AUTOBIOGRAPHY
1800–1834

edited by

Marion Filipiuk

UNIVERSITY OF TORONTO PRESS
Toronto Buffalo London

Published by University of Toronto Press Incorporated

Toronto Buffalo London

Printed in Canada

ISBN 0-8020-0791-0

Printed on acid-free paper

Canadian Cataloguing in Publication Data

Bentham, George, 1800–1884
  George Bentham : autobiography, 1800–1834

ISBN 0-8020-0791-0

1. Bentham, George, 1800–1884.   2. Botanists – England –
Biography.   I. Filipiuk, Marion.   II. Title.

QK31.B5A3 1997   581'.092   C96-931219-9

University of Toronto Press acknowledges the financial assistance to its
publishing program of the Canada Council and the Ontario Arts Council.

This book has been published with the help of a grant from the Humanities
and Social Sciences Federation of Canada, using funds provided by the Social
Sciences and Humanities Research Council of Canada.

To

JOHN M. ROBSON

(1927–1995)

sine quo non

Contents

Introduction

George Bentham (1800–84), whose life spanned most of the nineteenth century, is recognized by the scientific community as among the greatest taxonomists of his day, and is known to generations of botanical students as one of the authors of the monumental *Genera Plantarum*.[1] Outside the sphere of the natural sciences, however, he is little known, because his work was not, like Darwin's, the origin of a dramatic conceptual revolution. Bentham's quiet contribution to botany was nevertheless extraordinary in range, insights and precision, and his influence has been worldwide, particularly through the colonial Floras that he composed. The legacy of his labours therefore endures, and a financial endowment at the Royal Botanic Gardens, Kew, established in his will, has continued to promote his science in various ways.

Bentham's friend and collaborator, Sir Joseph Dalton Hooker, was the recipient of another legacy, a large collection of family papers and memorabilia, which included not only George's own, but those of his grandfather, his father Samuel, a brilliant naval engineer and inventor, and some of those of his uncle, Jeremy, the Utilitarian philosopher and law reformer. Hooker was frankly daunted by what Bentham had entrusted to him. As he confided to the botanist Asa Gray, "I have . . . a huge mass of his correspondence to deal with and a huger of his uncle's and father's, and am at my wits' end to know what to do with it all. . . . As for the botanical papers, they must be for some botanical authority to sort. Not for Kew, however—our hands are full enough of unpaid work. . . ."[2] Despite his impatience at the considerable nuisance value of the collection, Hooker ultimately acquitted himself well. The twenty-eight volumes of the letters and papers of George's elders, Jeremiah, Jeremy and Samuel, were sold in 1889 to the British Museum,[3] where they have provided rich materials for scholars in the flowering of Utilitarian studies during the past thirty years. As George Bentham had already given his extensive library and herbarium to Kew in 1854, and spent the rest of his very long working life there, Hooker's subsequent decision that Bentham's own papers should be retained in the Kew Archives seems both logical and proper.[4]

Along with the "huge" amount of botanical correspondence, and assorted essays, speeches and an occasional unpublished preface comprising the "botanical papers," the collection contains some twenty-five volumes of Bentham's journals and diaries, kept over a lifetime, and his "Autobiography," which in fact covers only the first thirty-four years of his life. This last document had also given Hooker pause, as he told Asa Gray:

I am puzzled what to do with his autobiography, which he left to me without further instructions than left me unfettered what to do with it. It is contained in about 700 closely written pages of his small hand, 4to, and goes down to 1883 [sic]. It was begun to please his wife, and continued to please himself, finally broken off by his illness. It is full of curious matter, and, to the like of us, is most interesting, but I am in doubt how far any considerable public would be interested.[5]

Hooker's assumption that the "Autobiography" would engage only botanical friends quite naturally reflects his professional bias, though he is indeed aware of all the "curious matter" that it contains. From the perspective of a later century, Bentham's account of his youthful experience is fascinating, both in its depiction of the era and as context for understanding his development as one of the great natural scientists of his times. It is also a rich source of material for students of utilitarianism and its adherents.

The account of his early years is, of course, primarily a Bentham family story. Now, with the appearance of the volumes of correspondence published by the Bentham Project at University College London, the *Collected Works of John Stuart Mill* and other scholarship, such as recent writings on naval history, there is a new wealth of information available about that remarkable group of individuals, the Benthams.

The Bentham Family

On the origins of his family, George himself does not dwell, pointing out in his opening remarks merely that the record "shows them to have been . . . Scriveners [in the City of London] . . . from the commencement of the seventeenth century" (1).[6] Later in the narrative he recalls with some amusement his dealings with a distant cousin, Mr William Bentham of Gower Street, a man of antiquarian interests, who was inordinately proud of being related to Thomas Bentham (ca. 1514–78/79), Bishop of Coventry and Litchfield. William had spent a rather large sum of money in adopting the bishop's coat of arms, only to discover, many years and bookplates later, that they were not the ones to which he was entitled (269). The connection with the bishop is, however, perfectly genuine; he is the common ancestor of the branches of the family that appear in the volumes of Bentham correspondence,[7] and the line of descent is traceable through his grandson, Francis, who established himself in London and died there in 1670. Francis had earlier been a draper in Stafford, and it may be his son and/or grandson, both named Bryan, who became "money scriveners," or pawnbrokers, lending at interest with the deposit of a security. According to John Bowring's account, it was the second Bryan, George Bentham's great-great-grandfather, who began to fill the family coffers. Bryan's son, Jeremiah (1684/85–1741), became an attorney, adding to his inheritance by investing his large savings in real estate, and his son, also Jeremiah (1712–92), George's grandfather, another attorney, "amassed a considerable fortune, principally by successful purchases of lands and leases."[8]

The record of his ancestry is of far less concern to George than the status and the stature of Jeremiah's two surviving children, Jeremy, born in 1748, and Samuel, born in 1757.[9] The early deaths of the many siblings in between and, in 1759, of their mother, Alicia Bentham, are a not uncommon story for the times, and had a not uncommon outcome in the strong bond of devotion between the elder and younger brothers. Father Jeremiah, recognizing that in Jeremy he had an "infant prodigy," and believing that "everything was to be done by 'pushing',"[10] enrolled him in Queen's College, Oxford, in June 1760, at the age of twelve, after five years at Westminster School. Less than three years later, in January 1763, he was admitted to Lincoln's Inn, a step that might have been, in his father's ambitious view, the first towards the Lord Chancellorship, but which rather inaugurated the son's mission as a critic of the system he was to study. If there was much that made him unhappy during the years of his formal education, Jeremy found genuine delight in scientific pursuits, especially chemistry and botany. He was, however, less than delighted with his father's second

marriage in October 1766, and moved into chambers in the Inns of
Court, where he continued to live until he inherited his father's house
in Queen Square Place in 1792.

Jeremy Bentham never practised law after being admitted to the Bar
in 1769, but that year was of great importance to him, as he began "to
get gleams of practical philosophy. Montesquieu, Barrington, Beccaria,
and Helvetius, but most of all Helvetius, set [him] on the principle of
utility,"[11] i.e., that the value of any thing or any conduct is to be judged
by the degree to which it contributes to the greatest happiness of the
greatest number of people. Applying this principle to the field of legislation, Bentham undertook a vast analysis of offences, classifying them
according to the ways in which they variously detracted from the well-
being of the community, his goal being to design a comprehensive code
of penal law. And the model he followed for the purpose was the one
that had impressed him in botany and medicine, in the work of Linnaeus, Sauvages and Cullen.[12] The specific method of analysis that he
adopted was that of "bipartition," dividing a logical whole into two
(and only two) mutually exclusive sub-classes, differing from each other
by a single characteristic possessed by one and not the other. These two
classes would then be divided again in the same way, and so on, producing an exhaustive analysis of the subject. The classifications that
resulted, addressed to the principle of utility, applicable to all mankind,
and in accordance with the psychological fact that only two things can
be compared at any given moment, would be "natural," rather than
"technical," i.e., artificial or contrived. Offences, for example, would better be defined and classified according to the various ways in which
they harmed the general well-being of society, as opposed to their existing arrangement in the strange categories that had emerged during the
chaotic development of the legal system, such as "felonies," "con-
tempts" or "misprisions."

The question of language is, of course, inherent in such an undertaking, and Bentham attacked the problem head on. There had been, in his
view, a flagrant abuse of language in jurisprudence (and elsewhere).
Falsehood often passed for truth when, in definition of such concepts as
"rights," for example, it was suggested that abstractions had some kind
of real existence; there was a corrupting influence in the use of legal fic-
tions, and of jargon that made the law the exclusive domain of the privileged few. On such abuses he made open war. He also had to find a
nomenclature suitable to the new classifications that he was himself producing, terms that would suggest the interrelation of the various parts

of the system, without creating a whole new language that would make his work incomprehensible. He was forced to compromise, on the whole, with the language Shakespeare spoke, but he coined many new words; for example, on the analogy of "eulogistic," he created "dyslogistic," to mean its exact opposite. This last word, though reported in the *Oxford English Dictionary*, has disappeared from common use, but some of Bentham's other word inventions—"international," "codify" and "codification," "maximize" and "minimize"—have fared rather better.[13]

Bentham's early published works expounding his theories and advocating thorough reform of the English law were the *Fragment on Government* (1776), in which he attacked Blackstone's views on sovereignty, *A View of the Hard Labour Bill* (1778), criticizing a scheme for the construction of two new prisons, and his major treatise, *An Introduction to the Principles of Morals and Legislation* (printed 1780, published 1789).[14] These brought him some international notice, local notoriety, and the friendship of Lord Shelburne, later Marquess of Lansdowne. If Bentham was still disappointing his father's ambitions for him, he had hopes himself, about 1780, of making his mark in the world through influencing Catherine the Great to adopt his principles (which he thought universally applicable to all nations) in her proposed reform of the Russian law.[15] It was at this time that his brother Samuel's aspirations and his own became actively intertwined.

Samuel, who had just turned two at the time of his mother's death, accepted his stepmother, the former Mrs Sarah Abbot, as Jeremy never could. In her published account of Samuel's early life, his wife Mary (George's mother) seems to be deliberately trying to set the record straight about this stepmother, when she quotes a letter (undated, but presumably written shortly after the marriage), from Jeremy himself to a cousin, commenting upon the happy report the cousin had received from the new stepson, i.e., Samuel.

It is with pleasure that I can confirm the favourable account you are pleased to say you have heard of my father's choice, and from the best authority, for such in that case is that of a stepson, who is but too often the last person to do it justice. . . . Since their marriage, she has ever behaved to me and my brother in the same manner (making an allowance for the difference of ages) as to her own children, whom she tenderly loves: they form a little triumvirate, in which, very differently from the great cabals distinguished by that name, there reigns the most perfect harmony.

Mary Bentham continues:

This is but a tribute justly due to a lady who has been mentioned in print in less flattering terms, and is moreover a proof that the bias of Samuel, which led him early away from home, did not originate in any discomfort experienced under the parental roof.[16]

Jeremy's solicited praise of his stepmother is, perhaps, faint, and it is clear that he felt himself to be outside the little "triumvirate" formed by Samuel and the two Abbot boys, Farr and Charles. The latter, who had a distinguished career as Speaker of the House of Commons until 1817, when he retired and was raised to the peerage as Baron Colchester, remained a close friend and confidant to Samuel, as is attested by George below (238, 245), and, if from a greater distance, lent his aid over the years to Jeremy as well.

Like his brother, Samuel attended Westminster School, and was destined for a liberal profession and the university, but he persuaded his father to allow him to pursue his talent for engineering, and was apprenticed to the best master-shipwright in the royal dockyard at Woolwich. He was allowed time to study "mathematics . . . chemistry, electricity, painting, grammar, especially of the French language, and many other subjects, besides those more immediately connected with naval architecture. . . ."[17] And, surely as a result of the influence of his brother, who had taken an active role in his education, he almost at once demonstrated a "bias" as an inveterate reformer and inventor of practices and machinery, their common aim being to apply truly scientific principles and methods to the improvement of their chosen field.

After completing his seven-year apprenticeship, Samuel spent two years more at the Naval Academy at Portsmouth, learning about the administration of the dockyards, and also went to sea as a volunteer in the fleet commanded by Lord Keppel. By the summer of 1779, he had completed his naval education, and was casting about for an appropriate position, when Lord Howe, First Lord of the Admiralty, apparently suggested that he should visit the maritime countries of northern Europe to study their facilities and practices in shipbuilding and maintenance.[18] The advantages of such knowledge and experience were made plain to his father, and his brother saw at once the possibility of Samuel's being able to promote his designs for legal reform abroad, particularly in Russia. Samuel himself was hoping to find opportunities for pursuing his experiments in naval construction and other manufacturing techniques, and for acquiring capital to finance some business venture when he returned to England.[19]

Armed with some seventy letters of recommendation, the indispensable social passports of the times, Samuel set off in August 1779 for Holland, visiting naval establishments there and in various ports in the Baltic Sea, and collecting yet other letters of recommendation for the next stage of the journey. He spent more than half of the year 1780 in St Petersburg, during which time he concluded that the only way he could successfully, and safely, carry out his plans for advancement was by securing some official rank in the administration. It was to qualify himself for a government post that he undertook a fact-finding mission of more than two years. He travelled both southward to the Black Sea, and eastward into Siberia, ultimately as far as the frontiers of China, exploring all sorts of possibilities for trading, and observing the practices in various manufacturing and mining operations.[20] On his return to St Petersburg, he employed all his courtier's skills in seeking a place, and was finally rewarded with an appointment, in mid-1783, as "Conseiller de la Cour," with the rank of Lieutenant-Colonel, and with responsibility for the operation of the Fontanka canal.

His fortunes improved again almost immediately when, not long after that first appointment, Prince Potemkin, the now all-powerful minister of the Empress, recruited his services for the development of a powerful fleet to be based at Kherson, on the Dnieper River near its mouth on the Black Sea. This fleet would protect Russia against the likely attempt by the Ottoman empire to reconquer the Crimea, which it had been forced to surrender in 1774 and which, after a brief period of independence, had been recently annexed by Russia. Bentham was settled on a tributary of the Dnieper, at Krichev, the centre of the vast estate that Potemkin had been granted by the Empress in 1776, from land acquired by the partition of Poland with Austria in 1772. The area was rich in timber, vessels could be floated down river to the naval base, and Bentham was given a free hand to introduce all the improvements that his designing mind could imagine, not only in shipbuilding, but in the considerable number of factories, related both to the ship business and to the local needs of the community, which he was given to manage—factories for making sail-cloth, rope, tools and utensils, pottery, glass, leather, and spirits. He took it all on with a will, ultimately working out an entrepreneurial arrangement with the Prince that made it more profitable to himself, and importing over time, mostly with his brother's help, a great quantity of technical works and a number of English assistants.

Jeremy himself paid him an extended visit in 1786–87, and personally
assisted with the agricultural experiments that were being conducted on
the estate farm, ordering from home "Miller's *Gardeners' Dictionary*,
Dossie's *Agriculture*, and various works of Arthur Young: *Annals of Agriculture*, *Essay on Hogs*, *Farmer's Guide*, and *Tour in Ireland*," and sending
to Lee, a nurseryman of Hammersmith, for "quantities of grass and clo-
ver seed, sainfoin and seeds of various vegetables. . . . An English strain
of potatoes with which the brothers experimented . . . proved very successful."[21] Among the assistants who joined the Bentham team was the
Scottish gardener John Aiton. Trained by his uncle William Aiton, royal
gardener at Kew, this young man, who had "extensive experience in
both botanical work and farming," would take charge of the projected
botanical garden; according to Jeremy, he was "a compleat master of his
business."[22] Jeremy also became very enthusiastic during his visit about
the plan Samuel had drawn up for a building that facilitated the central
supervision of the workmen, dubbed in Benthamite fashion "Panopticon," a plan that would subsequently engage, and long frustrate, the
brothers' combined ambitions.

When Turkey declared war on Russia in August of 1787, the issue was
control of the great bay in the Black Sea at the mouth of the Dnieper, and
Samuel was at once pressed into service at Kherson. He had already
constructed various vessels, notably a number of articulated boats
called "vermiculars," of shallow draft, composed of three to six separate
units closely hinged together, which could easily navigate the shallow
and twisting stretches of the rivers.[23] Now everything that would float
had to be armed, more ships had to be built, and it was Bentham who
organized the project over the following winter, as his friend Admiral
Mordvinov, in command of Kherson, was absent for much of that time.
Bentham put together a fleet which, though outnumbered by the Turkish ships, utterly defeated them, owing to yet another of his ingenious
engineering procedures. It allowed the Russians to mount heavy, long-
range guns, avoiding the perils of normal recoil on narrow boats by having one gun's recoil activate the firing of the next. Bentham commanded
a section of the fleet himself, emerging from the battle of 28–29 June
1788 unscathed, and a hero.[24] For his considerable services, he was
raised to the rank of full colonel, given the military order of Knight of St
George, with a gold-hilted sword of honour, and, later, a share (with
Mordvinov and another) in an estate near Kherson.[25]

Following this triumph (and the sale of Prince Potemkin's estate),
Samuel moved on to other fields. He took up a command in Siberia,

aimed at promoting trade between Kamchatka and the American coast, and between Russia and China; and promoting, too, the well-being of those serving in that remote outpost, he "established a school on the borders of China, for both men and boys of the battalion stationed there, on the principle of mutual instruction."[26] After two years in this rigorous environment, he obtained a leave of absence from Prince Potemkin, and set out for home in the spring of 1791, clearly expecting to return to Russia, since he left his personal belongings at his centre of operations in Tobolsk.[27] He travelled via Paris, where he stayed for three weeks, during a period of relative calm (though the revolutionary violence would soon break out once again), enjoying the society of

his friends the Duke de Richelieu, D[a]mas, the Count de Ségur, and many others whom he had known in Russia . . . still allowed to retain their rank and many of their privileges. He was furnished with a billet of entrance to the National Assembly, on the *last* occasion when the Count de Ségur had power to give him one, and was with the Duke de Richelieu in his box at the opera the *last* time that his Grace enjoyed it.[28]

It was then that he met Mme d'Andlau, daughter of the philosopher Helvétius, Count Chaptal the chemist, Jean Baptiste Say the political economist, and others, all of whom would prove firm friends to him and his family fifteen, and more, years later (27).

On his return to London, he found his brother Jeremy actively engaged in promoting the scheme of prison management that they had been developing earlier at Krichev.[29] If Jeremy's visit to Russia put an end to his ambition for the patronage of foreign sovereigns, it provided the inspiration for another grand design. The problem of "secondary punishments" in Britain had become a serious one a decade earlier, when the American War had terminated the practice of transporting convicts to that colony. Jeremy had already contributed to the debate in his *View of the Hard Labour Bill*, and had been writing extensively on penal law in the intervening years.[30] The plan he now submitted to government involved much more than merely Samuel's clever design for a prison. He proposed to become an entrepreneur in the prison business, contracting not only for the construction of the prison, but for the maintenance and employment of the inmates as well. He and Samuel would be in charge of a community of convict workmen gainfully employed in making a variety of products, using Samuel's inventions of manufacturing machinery. It would be a laboratory to test some aspects of Jeremy's theories about the proper operation of law as an instrument of social management, demonstrating whether a system that provided not merely punishment, but rewards and education in useful activities, would be the best method of dealing with most criminals. And it would turn a profit for the contractors. After protracted negotiations and ultimately insurmountable opposition from aristocratic members of the administration, he finally received some compensation from government in 1813 for the outlays he had made on the scheme (184n). Out of pocket and out of patience with governmental bureaucracy, he was radicalized by the experience.[31]

Samuel left the conducting of the unfortunate business to his brother, pursuing the technical side of the enterprise after his return home. He made a tour through the principal manufacturing centres of England, assessing the extent to which machinery was in use, and, in consequence, developed and improved the machines he had invented in Russia, constructing working models in shops at Queen Square Place, where he lived with Jeremy after their father's death in 1792. He obtained an extension of his leave of absence from Russia for this purpose, and he conducted a whole host of other experiments on all sorts of materials in the ensuing two to three years.[32] All these undertakings helped him to make a successful presentation to the Lords of the Admiralty on the modernization of the naval arsenals, and in April 1795 he was authorized to make an inspection tour to that end. His report resulted in his being appointed Inspector-General of Naval Works, a position that he himself defined, and which, by definition, was destined to be a difficult one.

The British navy was, at the time, under a dual system of control, the senior Board of Admiralty being specially concerned with the strategy and tactics of His Majesty's fleet, and the Navy Board with building, equipping and maintaining it. The day-to-day operation of the dockyards, therefore, was under the control of the latter body, and new projects might be initiated either at the recommendation of the Navy Board, or, more frequently, by its approval of a scheme that came from the yard officers. In practice there was little financial control of what was undertaken and virtually no long-range, systematic planning.[33] Bentham's friend, Earl Spencer, First Lord of the Admiralty, sponsored the creation of a new, independent position and department for him. Taking full responsibility himself (a principle in which he firmly believed), Bentham would report directly to the Admiralty, as he introduced improvements in the construction of vessels and efficiency in dockyard management. It was an arrangement that occasioned frequent opposition from the Navy Board, since a war was at that moment being waged with France, and a high level of performance, rather than change, was its first priority.

In fact, however, much was accomplished under Bentham's mandate. Lady Bentham's chapter headings, from which the following examples are drawn, provide a breathtaking account of the scope of his endeavours:

Invention of a Mortar Mill for Grinding Cement . . . Chemical Tests and Experiments on Ship Timber . . . Supply of Water . . . Precautions against Fire . . . Introduction of Steam Engines . . . Coast Defences . . . Alterations and Improvements in Plymouth Dockyard . . . Dock Entrances at Portsmouth . . . New South Dock for Ships of the Line . . . Steam Dredging Machine . . . Enlargement of Marine Barracks at Chatham . . . Improved Copper Sheathing . . . Success of the Experimental Vessels . . . Principle of Non-recoil in Mounting Guns . . . Principles of His New System of Management . . . Education for the Civil Department of the Navy . . . Changes in the Accountant's Office . . . Provisional Plan for the Education of Dockyard Apprentices. . . .[34]

Recent naval historians recognize that Bentham made a distinct contribution to Britain's naval power, and that by "introducing new technological and administrative ideas, [he] brought into the highly traditional world of the yards ways of thinking that broke with the past" and changed perceptions and procedures in the future.[35] The historians qualify his wife's report in several respects, however, stressing Bentham's reliance on the engineers Marc Isambard Brunel and Henry Maudslay for the actual production of the machines set up in the wood and metal mills at Portsmouth, and suggesting that his own personality was a major factor in creating the difficulties that he encountered.[36]

If it is true that a full assessment of Samuel Bentham's role in naval and engineering history has yet to be written, it is even more certain that his wife's part in his undertakings, and in the botanical career of their second son, George, remains virtually unexplored. Her account of her husband does nothing to aid the research; she merely notes her existence in a one-sentence aside to the account of Samuel's activities of 1796: "In October of this year he married the eldest daughter of Dr. George Fordyce."[37] Now, however, the Bentham *Correspondence*, George's "Autobiography" (and the comments of such third-party observers as John Stuart Mill and Asa Gray) reveal a truly extraordinary woman, intelligent and well educated, enterprising, courageous and "a very good botanist" in her own right.[38]

Lady Bentham's father, George Fordyce, and Jeremy Bentham had been friends for decades. As a medical student under William Cullen at Edinburgh University, Fordyce had developed a passion for chemistry and materia medica; and after graduating in 1758 he moved to London (a city with no centre for medical education), where he instituted a course of lectures the following year on chemistry related to medicine. If Jeremy Bentham's reminiscence is to be taken literally, he must have been among the first students: "I made acquaintance, before I was of age, with Dr. Fordyce, in consequence of his lectures on chemistry; and I once gave him and (Chamberlain) Clarke a dinner at Lincoln's Inn. Dr. F. was, I think, at that time, the only chemical lecturer, and was very poorly attended."[39] The course of lectures, however, ultimately proved very popular indeed. In 1764, Fordyce added two more subjects, materia medica and medical practice; and, according to the *Dictionary of National Biography*, "He continued to teach these subjects for nearly 30 years, lecturing on the three in succession from 7–10 on 6 mornings in the week the whole year through." He also became a very successful practitioner, at St Thomas's Hospital from 1770, publishing many treatises on medical subjects, and one on agriculture.

George Fordyce married in 1762, but about his wife we learn nothing from the *DNB*, the Bentham *Correspondence*, or her grandson's "Autobiography." The only published description of this lady is in a comment by Jeremy Bentham: "His wife was clever at all sorts of handiworks, botany, &c.: latterly she amused herself by making coverlets for beds. She made acres of them."[40] At the very least it is interesting that Bentham, the believer in the precise use of terms, should specify "botany" (rather than, say, simple "gardening") as a field in which she was "clever"; so we may infer that a daughter's interest in the science derived from both her parents. There were four children, two sons dying young (the death of one, at the age of fourteen, deeply affecting his father, according to Jeremy Bentham),[41] and two daughters, of whom Mary Sophia, born in 1765, was the elder.

There is, unfortunately, no record of the circumstances surrounding the courtship and marriage of Samuel and Mary Bentham. In October 1796 he was almost forty years of age, she thirty-one. They apparently lived at first with Jeremy at Queen Square Place, where, presumably, her love of gardening and other virtues endeared the new wife to her brother-in-law. It is certain that a strong bond of affection grew up between them, and between the uncle and the first two children, Mary Louise and Samuel, born in 1797 and 1798. As George Bentham is careful to point out, his mother "had from an early age been accustomed to take a part in her father's writings" (4) and so was well equipped to assist her husband in producing the reports and recommendations that his post of Inspector-General of Naval Works required. From the time of their marriage, shortly after his appointment, she accompanied him to the various naval establishments, on visits that often lasted several months.[42] It was during one of these that George, the third child, was born at Plymouth in September of 1800.

George Bentham, 1800–34

George Bentham's early years seem to have been remarkably happy. From the day of his birth he had the constant attention and affection of the sister and brother whose world he joined. Mary Louise, three years older than George, seems to have become specially close to him, compensating perhaps for the fact that their mother spent a great deal of her time helping their father. In young Sam, his elder by just a year and a half, George had both a playmate and schoolmate, as they soon came to share all their activities. Two younger sisters, Clara and Sarah, were added to the group at two-year intervals, and by the time of their departure from England, on Samuel Bentham's mission to Russia of 1805–7,[43] they constituted a self-sufficient, companionable young family.

During their two years' stay in Russia, Lady Bentham was able to devote herself completely to supervising their education, and she was a remarkable educator. The older Bentham children had begun to read and write very early, and once in St Petersburg they learned Russian and French from a governess, and "a great deal of German from a Finnish nurse" (5). George began Latin with his brother when he was five, and we hear of practical activities—carpentry for the boys, dressmaking for the girls, gardening for everyone. After their return to England two years later, they continued their education at home, a fact that George later believed he had much cause to regret:

We were none of us sent to school, which for my brother and myself has always appeared to me to have been a mistake. We learnt more perhaps than we should have done at school, but we did not acquire that habit of judging for ourselves when mixing with others, nor make any of those lasting friendships, which are the usual results of being made early to do battle with others of our age, and for myself it always left a kind of shyness which has often stood in my way. (8)

He recognized, however, that he had learned more from his mother and his tutors than he would have done had he in fact attended the local private school of Messrs Bidmead and Johnson, located in the High Street of Hampstead, not far from Hall Oak Farm, where they had settled on their return from Russia. Though officially shy with strangers, George made close friends with the neighbouring family of the solicitor Thomas William Carr, and that of Thomas Norton Longman, head of his family's publishing firm, both of whom, like the Benthams, could afford to raise their families in the country air of Hampstead, away from the smoky pollution of the City.

If Samuel Bentham's life was less than tranquil in the years following his enforced retreat from St Petersburg, necessitated by Napoleon's alliance with Russia in 1807, his children seem to have delighted in their various activities both at Hampstead and at Berry Lodge, near Portsmouth, a summer home purchased about 1810. They were a model family, according to the American politican, Aaron Burr, who paid a visit to Samuel Bentham in September of 1808 to acquire drawings of the Panopticon:

He happening to be occupied at the moment of my arrival, I fell in with the children, with whom I was so charmed that I paid very little attention to him. I never saw a more lovely family, nor by any approach so well brought up. I got so much in favour with them that they were all willing to come off with me to make a visit to uncle.[44]

The Benthams' move to the Continent in 1814, which proved to be crucial to the future of the children, was made, according to George's account, for Samuel Bentham's health, for financial reasons, and for the benefits that exploration of this "new world" offered to the long-isolated English. Having been retired from the Navy Board the previous year on a full pension, Samuel Bentham wanted a milder climate in which to recover from "the fatigues of his official life," and to enjoy the relative inexpensiveness of living on the Continent, in order to be able "to give his children a better education and lay by more for their future benefit than he could in England where every luxury and even every necessary of life was then so heavily taxed" to pay for the war against Napoleon. George admits that the widespread desire to visit the Continent, which produced waves of British tourists, was "a mania [that] seized our own family" (10); but the economic and educational reasons for going were certainly sound, since the hard-headed James Mill seriously entertained the same idea for his growing family at the time. Having already learned Russian during their two years at St Petersburg, the Bentham children would now be treated to French immersion and exposure to yet another society, where their father possessed impeccable credentials in both the political and the scientific communities.

The experiment initially proved successful. They spent the first winter in the Loire area near Saumur, where "the educational resources" proved excellent, the garden abundant, and the natural surroundings beautiful. George concludes that their time spent there was "always . . . reckoned by us as one of the happiest periods of our lives" (16, 17). Their plans for remaining yet another year at Saumur were, however, suddenly threatened the following spring by Napoleon's return from Elba, which sent most of the English scurrying back across the Channel; but Samuel Bentham, loath to leave their idyllic situation, was both reassured by a friend in Napoleon's new government that they had nothing to fear, and supplied with passports for Switzerland "just in case." He thus decided to stay at Saumur and await developments.

Eventually their position became too dangerous, and the family moved up to Paris in the spring of 1815, where they remained for a full year. Here they were struck by personal tragedy in the death of young Samuel, an event that completely altered the family plans. They had intended soon to return to England so that he could undertake the study of law, Jeremy Bentham's chambers at Lincoln's Inn already having been assigned to him. Though George too was destined for the bar, and presumably some sort of arrangement might have been made for the chambers to pass on to him when he reached the required age, they were given up, as George speculates, because his father wanted to put such associations behind him; "he began to think of a lengthened stay in the South, leaving it to future decision, according to circumstances, what course I should follow to make my way in the world" (29). If one may conclude that Samuel Bentham was prone to deciding on a course of action without fully weighing the repercussions in the lives of others (and there will be more evidence of that anon), one can forgive this particular decision, made in dreadful circumstances; and one can only admire the way George's parents ultimately dealt with their grief and helped their remaining son to deal with his (29, 33).

In the summer of 1816 they moved south once more, spending that winter at Angoulême and the following one in Toulouse, during which time George was allowed to set aside his formal studies. He continued to work at geography, however, which he had begun at Paris, with the encouragement of Alexander von Humboldt, explaining that it was his own "natural taste for method and arrangement, stimulated probably by [his] uncle's example and the perusal of some of his works" that made him enjoy "tabulating the geographical and statistical information . . . as to physical geography, mountain elevations, river courses and their basins, etc." Persevering with this hobby, he amused himself as well with "mathematics, music (the piano . . .), miscellaneous reading, . . . and mixed more in society" (30, 34). In the early summer of 1818, when he was ready to take on serious work again, the family moved to Montauban, where George enrolled in courses at its excellent Protestant College.

George had early demonstrated "a great fancy for languages" and a great facility in their acquisition (6). At Montauban he began the study of Hebrew, whose "peculiar construction and notation" was of particular interest to him as he had already "gone a good deal into the comparison of the grammars and alphabets of the various languages [he] had . . . learned." He also studied "the higher branches of French and Latin litterature," mathematics, and natural philosophy ("Physics, as they were then understood") (51). At home, he and his sisters had lessons every weekday in music, drawing and Spanish, George also eagerly pursuing the last with a Spanish refugee gentleman, with whom he exchanged instruction in French and English.

It was during this busy time that he also began in earnest to study botany, which was a great interest of both his uncle and his mother, though they had never tried to force-feed it to the children. She had, however, while they were at Angoulême, acquired A.P. de Candolle's edition of Lamarck's *Flore française*, a purchase that would have a significant effect upon her son:

I regarded [botany] as a mere amusement which did not take my fancy, but when the book arrived, opening it as a novelty, I was struck by the analytical tables for the determination of plants, which fell in with the methodical and tabulating ideas I had derived from the study of some of my uncle's works and from what I had attempted in geography and statistics. I immediately went out into the backyard, picked up the first weed I met with and set about finding out its name. (36)

The analytical method, developed by Lamarck in the first edition of the *Flore* and used by de Candolle to obtain the correct name for a plant, appealed to Bentham's cast of mind, and first awakened his interest in botany; but it would be about a year before that interest began to mature, influenced again by de Candolle's works, and by his studies at Montauban:

At Toulouse I had gone on occasionally finding out the names of a few plants from the adjoining hills but had almost given it up; but coming over here in May, and lodging almost in the country, my interest was revived, and the gathering and naming plants as yet new to me added wonderfully to the charm of the numerous excursions we made along the very pretty banks of the Tarn, and the rich wooded valley of the Aveyron. At my mother's suggestion, I first began to dry specimens for preservation on the 22d August, carelessly perhaps at first, but before the season was over, I had collected between one and two hundred species. And as in the course of the winter M. Benedict Prevost's lectures [in "natural philosophy"] and the arrival of successive livraisons of 3 vols of a *Dictionnaire d'Histoire Naturelle*, then in course of publication, began to open out my ideas on the wonderful variety and combinations of natural objects, I entered diligently into their study; and from the early spring of 1819, the formation and encrease of my herbarium became one great object of my pursuits. . . . [F]or a short time [I] was disposed to restrict my collections to the plants of the country; but the publication of the first volume of De Candolle's *Regnum Vegetabile* much enlarged my views, and failing at present all other sources, I procured what exotic plants I could from my mother's garden and set seriously to studying De Candolle's general works on the structure and classification of the vegetable kingdom. (53)

When the lease on the Montauban house was up, in May of 1819, the Benthams moved to the château de Pompignan, about half way along the road to Toulouse, where their lives would again be significantly altered, in this case by the wedding of Mary Louise to Adolphe de Chesnel, Colonel of a regiment stationed at Toulouse, whose family lived in the area, and whose worldly means at first seemed to the bride's parents adequate. Trying to be as cautious as possible in the matter of her dowry, Samuel Bentham decided that he would purchase an estate in the region, of which a part would be designated as her marriage portion. It presumably would produce regular income, as the family were going to develop the property and improve its productivity by introducing the latest English farming techniques.

A suitable estate had to be found, preferably in the Mediterranean region, which had been described to them by their French friends in glowing terms. George travelled with his parents in search of a *château en Languedoc*, if not *en Espagne*, in October and November of 1819, but they saw only one estate that particularly interested them, and decided against that because of the lack of social amenities. On their return to Toulouse, Adolphe de Chesnel requested the loan of a considerable sum of money, provoking suspicion that the statements of income he had shown them before the marriage had been borrowed for the purpose. The effect of this contretemps was to convince Samuel Bentham that it was essential to invest his daughter's dowry in land. The following spring, therefore, a second trip was undertaken, George and Sarah accompanying their father, Lady Bentham remaining behind with Mary Louise, who was expecting a child and who had taken refuge with her family when her husband had "gone off into Béarn" (63).

The three travellers took a different route, but through the same general area to the east and south of Toulouse, again seeing much of interest in the countryside, and consulting comte Louis de Villeneuve, "the then great agriculturist and improver of this part of France" (64) at his estate near Castres. George Bentham copied his full journal entry of this visit, with Villeneuve's comments, into his "Autobiography," presumably because it read in retrospect like an omen of the situation in which the Benthams ultimately found themselves:

As elsewhere his greatest difficulties have been from the backwardness of the peasantry in taking to anything out of the usual routine, as well as in their great poverty. He had vastly encreased the produce of his land, and saved from last winter's frosts many crops which had perished on neighbouring estates less judiciously cultivated. But with these and other great sources of encrease of revenue he complains of the little profit he derives on the whole in comparison to what he might expect, for "my villagers," he says, "are poor; they can only live on what they earn with me so that I am obliged to be continually using all my endeavours to find work for them, and my crops, sold amongst them, do not bring in so much as if they were taken to market. To be sure I have the satisfaction of being loved and respected by them, but this satisfaction will not give my daughters *dot* enough to please any sons-in-law that might present themselves." (64–5)

Villeneuve's message fell on deaf ears. Samuel Bentham found an estate, Restinclières, near Montpellier that pleased him, and invested all his capital of 280,000 francs (£11,200) in the venture. By so doing, he certainly secured Mary Louise's dowry, but he effectively deprived his other three children of the means of making acceptable marriages in the area, or elsewhere.

The purchase was completed in early November 1820, but the family spent the winter in Montpellier. Provided with the finest letters of introduction, they were immediately welcomed into the Catholic, Protestant and academic society of the town, and settled happily into a round of social activity until the following spring when they could move out to Restinclières, where George was put in charge of operations:

> I had had no voice in the determination to settle here, but now that we had it in possession, the chief management of detail was placed in my hands, my father having only planned out and determined what repairs and alterations were to be made to the house, and generally what parts of the estate were to be brought into cultivation, etc. Unfortunately, he was more of a contriver than a practical manager, and several of his plans proved failures; but such were the capabilities of the property that when it was sold years after, the improvements had counterbalanced, or perhaps overbalanced the losses, so as to repay the whole or nearly the whole of our outlay. (72)

There is a faint note of resentment here in having had "no voice," but George appears resolutely to have set about being a good "manager," taking pride in his relations with his workers, whose patois he soon learned. He became "almost as one of them, acquired the confidence of many of them and was much consulted about all their little private difficulties or projects" (75). If his father was the inventive "contriver," George was the one who was able to cope with the practical running of the estate, though not without difficulty. Samuel Bentham clearly entertained exaggerated expectations of what might be achieved and the income to be made. Ultimately he incurred the hostility of the local landowners by allegedly threatening the water supply, as he dug into underground springs to irrigate newly acquired bits of land. The Prefect, whom he had earlier alienated at Angoulême by devising an efficient, honest scheme for distributing bread during a winter of famine, issued injunctions against the digging, a move that seems to have been a major factor in discouraging even the "ever sanguine" Samuel (31, 34, 234). This row with the landowners (a scenario worthy of Pagnol), as well as the failure of a plan to establish a school for the education of poor children, was, in George's view, the result of "local prejudices insufficiently attended to" (203).

The Restinclières enterprise was also undermined from within. The

Bentham parents, at age sixty-three and fifty-five respectively, and Mary
Louise with her baby were content to settle into a quiet country life; but
George and daughters Clara and Sarah developed other agendas that
came to demand attention, and an extended trip to England for them
was planned at the end of 1822. The explanation George gives below
makes the girls' wishes the prime motive, a "taste of brilliant society in
Paris" having made "chateau life rather irksome" for them (97). It
appears, however, from George's later letters to his father,[45] that there
were some quite specific reasons for believing that his sisters would be
the better for a journey. Sarah had apparently been giving trouble about
a certain "M. de P.," and Clara was interested in "Tonin" Partouneaux,
the younger son of friends from Toulouse days who were now living in
Paris, where General Partouneaux had been appointed Governor of the
École Militaire. George, too, had been romantically involved, with the
beautiful Emma Dax, daughter of the aristocratic, Catholic mayor of
Montpellier, but at this point he had evidently no hope of being able to
marry her and had decided to try to reestablish himself in England.

To that end, he laboured on the French translation of the Appendix to
his uncle's *Chrestomathia* on the classification of the arts and sciences,
begun several years earlier (61), which he completed and had printed
during their six weeks in Paris. It was not merely a gesture to please his
uncle, but evidence of his ability, which could result in his being offered
a position by some one of his family's influential connections. Like Mr
Micawber, George was apparently hoping that something substantial
might "turn up." The trip would also give him the opportunity to make
friends among British botanists, and discover for his father the best agricultural methods and equipment then in use for application at Restinclières.

George's experiences during his five-month stay in Britain, mid-
March to mid-August of 1823, are well documented in chapters 4 and 5
of the "Autobiography." By the end of his stay, he had pretty well
accomplished two of his objectives, broadening his scientific acquaintance and studying the latest farming techniques; but the hoped-for
position and/or social opportunity had failed to materialize, though
there is no mention of this fact. Nor is there any mention of how the
journey had helped his sisters. It had, indeed, apparently succeeded in
curing Sarah of her infatuation, and given Clara cause to hope that a
marriage with "Tonin" might be arranged. These beneficial effects were
not to last long, however. By the turn of the year 1824, Clara and Sarah
once again "began to feel the contrast between the quiet country life and

the social enjoyments they had had amongst their English friends, and showed a restless disposition, occasioning some anxiety" (208) to their parents; so it was decided that the girls should accept an invitation to spend a couple of months in Paris with their Russian friends, the Gagarins, and that George should accompany them.

Anxiety was further aroused when the Bentham parents learned that the three had come down with smallpox in a hotel in Avignon, and they wrote to urge their return home; but the travellers had mild cases and persisted on their journey, George's letters to his father helping to explain their determination. It seems that the likelihood of Clara's marriage was being threatened by opposition from the General and that they were hoping to resolve the situation during their stay in the capital. George had apparently experienced another rejection by the Dax family and a row with his mother on the very eve of their departure, and had absolutely no intention of immediately returning to that painful scene. Indeed the arrangement was that his father should soon join him in Paris and that they should go to England together to further George's campaign to reestablish himself there; but Samuel Bentham almost immediately changed his mind about a journey that season, causing disappointment and frustration in his son. George wrote to his father:

Of all the plans I have formed concerning myself I only regret one, and that is my too precipitate return from England [the previous August] where nothing can be done of what I undertook to do, by one who is there for the first time, in less than a twelvemonth, but as I was situated I could not stay any longer. . . . If you had been able to come to Paris about the time of the [Gagarins'] departure, I should have been able in the mean time to have quite put an end to the uncertainties about Tonin one way or another . . . and by going then with you to England should have been in time for this year in London which you know is the object of the journey. It is not for the sake of throwing myself into company and dissipation that I wanted to go to Paris . . . ; my object is to marry, and at Paris there would be the same objections as at Montpellier. . . . [M]y dear Papa, how I long to be with you in England![46]

There were good financial as well as social reasons for Samuel Bentham's returning to London at this time, as George urged:

With regard to our pecuniary interest, I know the journey is expensive, and though 4 years ago we could have supported it so much better, yet I should think we still could do so now . . .; how essential it is for you to endeavour to prevent the different sums that ought to have come to us or to come to us at some future period, from being turned away to other purposes![47]

Samuel Bentham's share of the money his brother had received from the Treasury as indemnification for the Panopticon scheme had been invested with Jeremy's in an unsuccessful stone quarry venture and in Robert Owen's New Lanark cotton mills (184fn). The first number of the radical *Westminster Review* had appeared in January of 1824, financially supported by Jeremy Bentham, edited by the unpopular John Bowring, who, since 1820, had been the old philosopher's chief confidant. Small wonder his nephew was concerned about the family finances and how they might be further depleted![48] At this point, however, Samuel Bentham chose not to pursue either this matter or his son's plans, and George perforce had to return to Montpellier after two months in Paris—months made both pleasant and interesting, however, by the company of the Gagarins and his father's friends in the scientific community (209–10).

George resumed his duties as estate manager, but also began to devote more and more time to botany. The year 1825 became "thoroughly botanical." His herbarium received "large additions, . . . chiefly through the liberality of Dr. [W.J.] Hooker" (213), his friend Requien of Avignon, and his own efforts during an extended summer trip to the Pyrenees with his Scottish friend George Arnott. Building on the collection he had begun five years earlier, Bentham gathered enough material for a *Catalogue des plantes indigènes des Pyrénées et du Bas Languedoc, avec des notes et des observations sur les espèces nouvelles ou peu connues . . .* , which he wrote during the winter and published the following year. It was the work that would establish his reputation as a serious botanist.

By the summer of 1826 he again had personal and family reasons for undertaking yet another trip to England, as well as publication arrangements to make in Paris. He had become involved for a second time with Emma Dax, and this time the religious differences that had ultimately broken off their earlier plans for marriage were resolved; it only remained to establish some independent income for him. The problems with the local landowners and the necessity of providing financially for his son combined to motivate Samuel Bentham to pursue the matter of his share in the family estate. He hoped, indeed, during a long-overdue visit home, to persuade his brother to provide some support for George.

It was not long after their arrival in London during the first week of August that this hope was dashed by Jeremy's refusal to settle any property upon him. George's plans for life as a French *propriétaire* were thus brought to a swift conclusion (238). What was now to be done? Soldier stoically on and find some career that would provide the income necessary for marriage at a later date. Lord Colchester, Samuel's half-brother and counsellor in all things, urged that the family winter in England, thereby initiating the return to London of Lady Bentham and Clara in September. Colchester also suggested that George might try commercial banking, but George did not think he would like the responsibility involved in that. The law seemed more appealing, and besides, it might be the way to Uncle Jeremy's heart.[49]

George therefore enrolled in Lincoln's Inn and became one of his uncle's assistants, working and dining with him on a regular basis at Queen Square Place, dutifully helping with the various codes in preparation for the benefit of mankind, and trying to protect the family interests for his own benefit. His uncle encouraged him to undertake the editing of his writings on logic, an obvious extension of his work on the Appendix to *Chrestomathia* and his interest in classification as a science. Jeremy Bentham must have had some twinges of conscience for refusing to help his nephew financially, and apparently saw this project as a way of compensating him. George reported to his sister that

[M]y Uncle has imagined that he makes my fortune in giving me his logical papers to make a book of; . . . if I succeed in putting it into intelligible French, Bossange [the publisher] may give me something for it—but as for a fortune, if I get any from my Uncle it must be in a more direct way than through the medium of his manuscripts. Besides that he wishes me to do it in English. . . .[50]

George was also told—the word perhaps put out by his uncle as incentive—that James Mill and his son had studied these papers and were thinking of editing them. In any case, George had a genuine interest in the subject, if perhaps too much of a young man's eagerness to criticize the experts. By March of the following year he had completed his *Outline of a New System of Logic, with a Critical Examination of Dr. Whately's 'Elements of Logic'*, for which his uncle assumed the printing costs.

Having deferred concentrating on the law until he completed this project, which he came to think of as his own, since he had considerably expanded upon his uncle's ideas, George was keenly disappointed by its reception (though Jeremy Bentham was enthusiastic):

Mr Carr pointed out to me that the tone of my observations on Whately's book and the absolute way in which I brought forward my own views were not quite becoming in so young a writer. I acknowledged the correctness of these observations, and began to feel ashamed of the importance I had in my mind attached to several of the principles I had brought forward, especially to that which has since been termed the quantification of the predicate, and which was entirely my own, not having been worked out in my Uncle's MSS. The work, however, was very little noticed; only about 60 copies had been sold when the publishers became bankrupts. I had notice that the stock had been seized by their creditors, but I was too much disgusted to take any steps to redeem it, and the whole was sold for waste paper. I thenceforth dismissed the subject from my mind. (270–1)

This setback, even recollected in the tranquillity of fifty years on, causes Bentham to pause in the telling to reflect ruefully on his own shortcomings. Though pleased and amused by the little controversy about him in the pages of the *Athenaeum* in 1851, as the originator, before Sir William Hamilton, of the logical doctrine of "the quantification of the predicate," Bentham sums up:

This, of course, led to nothing, but I have little doubt that if I had, in 1827, gone on with the subject, I might have done something of value in Logic—but here, as in other instances, my success has been baulked by a want of perseverance, when checked by a slight contretemps (271).

The notion that George Bentham was wanting in perseverance seems ludicrous to those who know what he undertook and completed in botanical studies, but they may agree that he was probably too sensitive, too prone to retreat in the face of even the slightest criticism, particularly in areas where he was, in fact, trying to satisfy other people's ambitions for him. In the law, as well, he would experience some disappointments. His observations on the bills before Parliament, which his uncle asked him to compose, and which he sent to Sir Robert Peel in November of 1826 in the hope of obtaining employment, also led to nothing (257–9). After his call to the bar in 1831, his maiden speech in court, marred by excessive nervousness, was described by the opposing counsel as "preposterous" (383), and he subsequently sat for many hours in his wig and gown, waiting for briefs that came very irregularly. If his "constitutional inability to speak well" made him unlikely to succeed as a barrister, he nevertheless became "much interested in the unravelling of intricate complications in cases of successions, or of knotty legal questions, the draughts of bills, etc, and legal opinions," and might ultimately have made a good living as an equity draftsman and conveyancer; but in the end he believed that he "never could have risen to distinction" (425–6), and his heart lay elsewhere.

From the time of his return to England in 1826 he had continued to devote as much time as possible to botany. He gave generously of his time in assisting other botanists, for example in the distribution of Nathaniel Wallich's vast collections of Indian plants, and he wrote articles for botanical magazines. He became a fellow of four scientific societies, being particularly active as a member of Council at both the Linnean and the Horticultural Societies. Indeed he played a major role in rescuing the latter from serious difficulties in 1830.

Bentham's account of his efforts during that stormy period in the history of the Horticultural Society reveals, if in part inadvertently, some of the qualities he believed he possessed and in which he took pride. He was invited into the Council to provide help in a crisis of debt, created through the negligence of the Honorary Secretary, Joseph Sabine, and the peculation of an assistant. There was, moreover, a bitter feud between Sabine and another Assistant Secretary, John Lindley, both of whom were friendly towards Bentham and urged his undertaking the post that Sabine was perforce vacating. Bentham, though cautious, accepted the challenge and, once launched, gave his full attention and talents to the enterprise. He was able to devise an effective practical measure, in the form of a bond issue backed by the individual members of Council, which ultimately reestablished the Fellows' confidence in management; and he supported the "difficult" Lindley for the position of Administrative Secretary, because he knew that Lindley's assistance was essential for the Society's survival and he personally had no fear of working with him (329–30). It proved to be a most productive collaboration, resulting, among other benefits, in the inauguration of the Society's first flower shows. The Society's bylaws had also become a subject of controversy; so Bentham drafted a new set, and manoeuvred their passing through some opposition, in an episode that he clearly enjoys retelling:

These byelaws were discussed at two separate meetings. It appeared that there were two who were disposed to object to everything. I therefore first brought forward a few verbal points of no importance to be hotly discussed by the objectors, and on which, after long talk, I finally gave way, at which they were satisfied and allowed all the important parts to pass unchallenged. By these and other measures, perfect harmony was restored, and the Regent Street meetings became more and more frequented, their popularity much encreased by the new lady-Fellows, amongst whom Mrs Marriott and Mrs Lawrence—besides Lady Antrobus, as wife of a Fellow, contributed largely. (331)

Though he takes no personal credit for the introduction of the ladies, he is obviously pleased that a successful solution to the injustice of their exclusion from the Society's dinners was found in the introduction of the garden fêtes.

His contributions to the deliberations of the Linnean and the Zoological Societies also demonstrated his practical good sense. In the Council of the Linnean, he "succeeded in getting measures adopted for diminishing the large amount of overdue arrears of subscription entered on the books" (361). At the Zoological Society, where factions raged about the construction or purchase of a special building in which to display donated collections, Bentham bravely pointed out the folly of both proposed plans, which involved vast sums, with the simple truth that "no one would care to pay for seeing a collection of stuffed animals when one which would always be far superior could always be seen for nothing at the British Museum" (430), and effectively killed the scheme.

Avoiding or resolving conflict was much more his style than participating in it, however, and his skills as negotiator and peacemaker were apparently often in demand at home during these years. The return to London did not guarantee his sisters' happiness, and it seems that there was a good deal of domestic friction, one suspects particularly between Lady Bentham and her youngest daughter. After Clara's tragic death from a brain tumour in 1829, Sarah virtually moved in with her friend Countess Ludolf, the young wife of the Ambassador from the Kingdom of the Two Sicilies, and enjoyed the social life of the diplomatic circle. In 1831, Sarah became engaged to Simon Klustine, younger son of a Russian family the Benthams had befriended at Montpellier; and Samuel Bentham was delighted, just before his death, to make over to her his share of the estate in Russia as a dowry. On Simon's return to his mother in Switzerland, however, the engagement was, perhaps unfortunately, broken off.

George's own romantic involvements and marriage aspirations fared no better for several years after his return from France. He and his sisters once again enjoyed the society of the Carr family, and he promptly fell in love with Laura, the youngest daughter. Without the necessary income, however, there was no use in pressing his suit, and he was forced to give it up. It was only after his uncle's death in 1832 that he was able to marry, and he shortly found a most congenial partner in Sarah Brydges, daughter of a former diplomat, well connected among the landed gentry. They were married in April of 1833. When it became obvious that they would have no children and that his wife was content with the comfortable, if not luxurious, circumstances that his inherited wealth could provide, Bentham felt free to choose a life that suited him better than that of a lawyer.

He already had made a name for himself among the botanical community, both in England and on the Continent. It was, in fact, his second trip to a meeting of the international scientific society, the Deutscher Naturforscher und Ärtzte, at Vienna in September of 1832, that had made him think seriously about changing careers (382). His account of his reception by fellow scientists, as well as by the great Metternich himself, is glowing. There is no suggestion that shyness held him back either in the meetings or at the brilliant dinner parties that he attended, nor does he comment on what was probably one of the reasons for the cordiality of his confrères, his ability to function perfectly in other peoples' languages. In a sense Bentham found his métier here as an unofficial scientific ambassador, and over the years his country would be well served. On his return, with his wife, from yet another productive Continental trip in 1833,

communications with foreign correspondents, the number of botanical works and specimens which I found waiting for me on my reaching home, finally decided the question, and I immediately gave up my chambers, refused a couple of briefs which were offered me, sold my technical law books, gave away my wig and gown, and determined on adopting botany as the great business of my future life, a determination which I never, during the long period of my subsequent career, had on any occasion any reason to repent of. (426)

At last he was able to devote his extraordinary energy and abilities to what he most enjoyed. He was tireless in assisting other collectors, many of whom became his close friends and admirers. He believed absolutely that in science exclusivity and mean-spiritedness had no place, were indeed counter-productive, and he was sharply critical of those individuals and institutions where he found them (425, 345). He praised W.J. Hooker as the model of scientific liberality, which had, in fact, resulted in his having the finest herbarium in the country. If there is a moral to Bentham's story it is that a generous, cooperative spirit is essential to the development of any science.

Both by temperament and by training George Bentham was admirably suited to achieve distinction as a botanist. The particular genius he displayed in taxonomy cannot be done justice here, but he was certainly extraordinary in the scope of his labours, continuing the tradition of his father and his uncle. A Bentham could undertake to reform the Navy, codify laws for the world, or classify the genera of its plants; and this Bentham managed to complete what he began, to the everlasting wonder and admiration of succeeding generations of botanists.

The Composition of the "Autobiography"

It was not until 1867 that Bentham began to compile the story of his life, probably inspired by reading the *Memoir* of the popular writer Maria Edgeworth,[51] who had been a great friend of his great friends, the Carrs, and whom he had met during the 1820s (161). His diary for 17 November 1867 notes that he found "much interest in the memoirs of Maria Edgeworth lent by Mr. Edgeworth for us to read."[52] Bentham and his wife apparently enjoyed the volume together over a period of some weeks, finishing it during the Christmas holidays. The entry for 29 December indicates that they were "much interested . . . from the number of persons mentioned whom I knew in former days—besides the kindly cheerful spirit of all her letters."[53] The *Memoir* was indeed no more than a brief narrative loosely woven around Edgeworth's letters, but it charmed the Benthams, and must have suggested the possibility of producing something similar from the considerable store of correspondence and diaries that Bentham had preserved over the years.

Bentham's wife, Sarah, probably encouraged him to document his unusual experience as a child and young man in foreign scenes, and he responded partly because she agreed to participate in the venture. Beginning in the early 1850s, Sarah Bentham suffered from what appears to have been debilitating depression, and her husband was only too glad to initiate a project in which she could collaborate and take an interest. Hooker was no doubt right in saying that Bentham began the "Autobiography" "to please his wife,"[54] his primary audience in an undertaking that he hoped would have some therapeutic value.

Bentham does not mention his wife, however, in the paragraph that he inserted at the head of the text (3), possibly in early 1880, when he put aside this work so that he might devote himself entirely to the last section of the *Genera plantarum*. The reason for the omission may be inferred from the comment written at the moment he resumed writing the "Autobiography" in 1883, after Sarah's death, and after the completion of the *Genera*. His "wife's failing health [had] rendered it very unlikely she would take any interest in these notes, which at first amused her" (416–17). There was no need to mention that fact during her lifetime, however, in a brief preface (which she might possibly read) composed primarily for those who would have to deal with the document after his death.

The preface is indeed a melancholy testament to lonely old age. The "friends and connections much younger" than himself, who he thought might enjoy his "reminiscences'" after his death, had "for the most part gradually gone off before" him. The only use he can imagine for the "Autobiography" now is that of "supplying a few dates for the obituary notice which may have to be written of me for some of the scientific Societies to which I belong" (3). Bentham was indeed sorely grieved in the last years of his life by the loss of friends, whom he dearly cherished, but most of them were not "much" younger than himself. He probably had in mind the only son of Isabella Carr, whose family had played so large a part in his life,[55] and he was perhaps especially thinking of William Munro (1818–80), who had been a close friend since 1848. Munro had combined a most successful military career in the colonies with valuable botanical studies; he had worked with Bentham during his home leaves, and they visited regularly after his retirement in 1878. At the time of his death, on 29 January 1880, he was preparing a significant monograph on grasses. It was possibly this example of important work left unfinished that prompted Bentham to turn all his energy to the completion of the *Genera plantarum* before it was too late, adding the prefatory paragraph as he put away the "Autobiography," perhaps for good.

He survived, however, not only to complete his *magnum opus*, but to continue his life story, as Hooker said, "to please himself"; but the author had always been part of the audience, as in all autobiography. Bentham speaks of the pleasure he found in "recurring to scenes of [his] early life" (3), of "living over again, as it were, in recollection, the happy times of fifty years back" (417). When he began the project in 1867, he was the last living member of his immediate family. His mother had died in 1858, his younger sister Sarah in 1864, and his beloved elder sister, "Mashinka" (Mary Louise), the following year. There was then perhaps just enough distance to create "pleasure" in being with them all once again in memory.

Bentham correctly said that he had checked his reminiscences with "fragments of journals," since the early record is, quite naturally, far from complete. The material covering the first twenty-five years of his life in the Kew Archives is as follows, all numbered 33806:

1. "Diary MSS, 1807–11." A small red leather notebook, the gift of Alexandra Necludoff (5), dated 14 August 1807. Index on the last page lists "Journey in Russia" [in Russian]; D° from Berry Lodge to London [October 1810]; D° from Hall Oak Farm to Queenborough [February 1811]; Drawings, nos. 1–10. The second and third accounts are written on the left-hand page, for translation into Russian on the right, only a little of which has been completed.

2. "Diary MSS, 1812–17." Bentham began on 1 January 1812 to keep entries in a diary that was a New Year's gift from his parents. Daily entries become shorter over time, concluding on 24 June 1814 with a visit to Portsmouth (8–9 and n16). A journal, begun 14 July 1815, describes a trip from Le Mans to Paris, and experiences in the capital, concluding 5 September (23–5); some pages are out of order. Another journal, begun 21 August 1816, briefly gives events of a trip from Arcueil to Orléans (31–2). Three pages, dated in pencil 1817, trace a journey from Toulouse to Carcassonne.

3. "Diary MSS, 1818–19." Diary kept at Montauban, 24 June – 31 August and 13–20 December 1818. A journal, begun 8 October 1819, of a trip from Toulouse as far east as Aix, breaks off in Montpellier on 17 November (55–60).

4. "Diary MSS, 1820–25." Journal of trip begun 10 February 1820 concludes 28 April, in Montpellier. Two other notebooks contain a diary kept 1 June to 12 November 1820. A third diary, presumably intended to be a record of the activity on the newly purchased estate of Restinclières, begins 3 November 1820 and continues to 18 July 1821. Twelve pages, out of order, are from a journal recording travel from Perpignan to Barcelona during a botanizing trip, 31 May to 6 June 1825.

When one tries to relate this material to the narrative in the "Autobiography," it immediately becomes obvious that there are enormous gaps in the accounts in the diaries about events that Bentham presents in great detail below. There is nothing at all, for instance, about the family's first experience in France, from August 1814 to the end of Napoleon's "Hundred Days" the following June, all richly described in chapter 2 (15–23); and, curiously, Bentham scarcely used his journal, kept 15 July – 5 September 1815, of their move away from the unrest at Tours to Le Mans and then on to Paris. The account of their early visit to the Louvre (23–4) and of their return from Versailles (26) are certainly drawn from it, but there is no journal source for the experiences in the capital over the subsequent twelve months, nor the following winters of 1816 and 1817 at Angoulême and Toulouse, which occupy the rest of chapter 2 (33–51). Though Bentham's memory of these events was doubtless vivid, it seems not unlikely that he had at hand some other sources, perhaps the journals of his siblings.

Chapter 3, which covers the period from the spring of 1818 through to the end of 1822, is based upon the diaries of those dates described in nos. 3 and 4 above, and another document preserved in "Benthamiana" at Kew, the account of a journey to the famous fair at Beaucaire (77–91), which he copied virtually *verbatim* into the "Autobiography." This was presumably to have been the third article in the series he prepared for the *London Magazine*, only two of which were published, owing to the difficulties experienced by the periodical (251).

The major source of material for the following five chapters (4–8), covering the period from January 1823 to July 1828, are the journal-letters for the period, written to his family during his travels in England and Scotland in 1823 and to Paris in 1824, and those directed to his sister in Montpellier after his return to England in 1826. The narrative of the important botanizing trip of 1825, when he was preparing his *Catalogue des plantes indigènes des Pyrénées et du Bas Languedoc*, derives primarily from letters at the Linnean Society and the fragments at Kew (no. 4 above), but the collection is evidently incomplete. When he came to write his life story, Bentham appears to have segregated his journal-letters, together with other correspondence that related most directly to himself, culled from the family papers, in a box now in the collection of the Linnean Society of London.[56] The letters are quoted extensively in these chapters, the present tense often confirming the pleasure that he was taking in "reliving" time past, even to the extent of speaking directly to his sister Mary Louise, yet again, when copying a passage boasting about his success in drafting a good legal opinion: "With you, dear, I need not be squeamish" (280).

There is an eighteen-month gap in the record of his life, because another series to Mary Louise, written in 1829, was not preserved, as a result of her domestic difficulties. In January 1830, however, Bentham began systematically to keep a diary, and pursued the habit almost to the end of his life. The volumes for the years 1830 to 1834 (at Kew), supplemented by some further letters from abroad to his parents during this time (at the Linnean Society), along with an incomplete account of the Vienna meeting of scientists that he attended in 1832 (at Kew in "Benthamiana"), provide the source material for chapters 9 to 12, where the narrative simply breaks off after his return from one of his many trips abroad.

There are very few clues in the text as to when Bentham actually wrote the sections of the story after making a beginning in 1867. Towards the end of chapter 4, a comment that much of what he was shown by the Strutt family at Belper in June of 1823 may be gone "after half a century" (143), suggests that he was writing in or after 1873. In chapter 6 (222), describing his 1825 trip to the Pyrenees, he notes that "at fifty years' interval," i.e., in 1875, he can recall it all vividly. When he describes the Duke of York's funeral of January 1827 in chapter 7 (263), he comments that "After more than fifty years" the bottom of St James's Street crowded with mourners is still clearly present in his memory, presumably post-January 1877. A more specific indication is in chapter 12 (417), mentioned above, as he stopped writing the "Autobiography" at that point to devote himself to the last part of the *Genera plantarum*, and resumed the narrative after April 1883 when it was completed; and, finally, Bentham notes (429n) that his pen broke "after more than 28 years' constant and exclusive use (Nov. 1883)." Thereafter, with another, obviously less satisfactory pen, he added just twenty-one more pages; but by that time he had included his wife in the narrative, and relived some of the happy times with her in 1833 and 1834.

The pleasure of reminiscence and of bearing witness to "what it was like" in England and on the Continent fifty years earlier seems certainly to have been the prime motive in the writing of this "Autobiography," rather than a compelling need to find direction in the unfolding of his life or to set a record straight. But all autobiographical activity involves a kind of instinctive search for order in the life that has led up to the present moment of writing, for some comfort in the reassurance that despite a multiplicity of disappointments the self has come through to tell the tale, and perhaps for an answer to the question whether that self has become all it might have liked to be. The story of Bentham's life reveals that in the writing he was, indeed, not only taking pleasure in, but getting perspective on, the past, his family, and his own personal achievements, and even indulging, however gently, in the settling of a few old scores.

The Text

The "Autobiography" is a document of more than 660 pages, with no formal divisions indicated by its author. Bentham did, however, often begin the narrative of a new phase in his life, or a new year, on a fresh page. Chapters 2, 6, 7 and 9 to 12 have been created at these points. Two shorter segments were combined to form chapter 1, the long narrative of his travels in 1823 was divided into chapters 4 and 5, and the years 1827 and 1828 were given their own section, chapter 8. Bentham's numbering of the pages has been retained throughout.

That the text was virtually unrevised after its composition is indicated by the gaps left for information to be added, by words omitted, and by many uncorrected slips of the pen. The first are represented by a space enclosed in square brackets, and brackets also enclose words editorially supplied for sense. Appendix A contains a list of those minor errors that have been corrected without notice in the text.

Bentham's spelling, which frequently illustrates his early immersion in French, has been faithfully reproduced. His casual use of punctuation reflects the practice of his day, particularly in a document composed for the amusement of relatives and friends. As there is evidence, however, in the manuscript copy of "The Fair of Beaucaire" (Royal Botanic Gardens, Kew), intended for submission to a periodical, that Bentham punctuated in quite traditional fashion when he thought his composition might find a public audience, the following alterations in punctuation have been made.

Full stops have been added where lacking. Commas have been inserted where, as was his custom, Bentham used a larger than usual space to indicate a pause; at ends of lines when necessary; around interlined and appositive words or phrases; and to separate words in a series. Occasionally Bentham's commas between principal clauses have been raised to semicolons in very long passages. Particularly towards the end of the manuscript, Bentham tended to link clauses merely with dashes. These cases have been regularized into sentence form. Apostrophes have also been regularized and ampersands altered to "and". Missing quotation marks have been supplied by comparison with the source letter or diary entry. When a passage appeared to be more summary than quotation, however, no marks were inserted. Titles of published works have been italicized. The only other editorial intrusion on the page is the § symbol, indicating that a variant reading, involving a difference in meaning, or a textual comment, keyed by page and line number, appears in appendix B.

Bentham's notes to the text are indicated by the standard *, † symbols, enclosed in square brackets whenever he failed to specify their placement. They appear at the foot of the page.

Appendix C, prepared by Desmond Meikle, provides a list of plants referred to by Bentham.

Appendix D contains a list of persons and works mentioned in the text. Birth and death dates for each individual and a source of further biographical information are given whenever possible.

Acknowledgments

This manuscript is published with the permission of the Trustees of the Royal Botanic Gardens, Kew. I am grateful to Gren Lucas, former Keeper of the Herbarium, Sylvia FitzGerald, Chief Librarian and Archivist, and Cheryl Piggott, Assistant Archivist, for their invaluable help with this project, as well as to Gina Douglas, Librarian, and Margot Walker of the Linnean Society of London. Fred Rosen and Stephen Conway of the Bentham Project, University of London, also kindly provided assistance; and Suzanne Rancourt, Barbara Porter and Judith Williams of the University of Toronto Press have been indispensable. Librarians at the British Library, the Royal Horticul-tural Society, the University of Toronto, and the following people have been most helpful: K. and Martin Brunt, Oleg Chistoff, Ian R. Christie, Alan Dainard, the late Robert Fenn, Anna Goruveyn, Susan Hainsworth, Eric Katz, Tanya Lorkovic, Elizabeth and Wallace McLeod, Ann Robson, David Smith, and Peter Stevens. I have three special debts to acknowledge: to the late John M. Robson, a long-time friend, whose edition of *The Collected Works of John Stuart Mill* provided the impetus and the instruction necessary for this project, and who helped with it in innumerable ways; to Desmond Meikle, a long-time admirer of Bentham, who kindly volunteered to preserve me from idiocies in botanical matters and to prepare the index of plant names; and to William Filipiuk, my long-time husband, who, like George Bentham, believes in the beneficial effects of a spirit of liberality, and enjoys travelling with a purpose.

Notes

1 George Bentham and Joseph Dalton Hooker, *Genera plantarum ad exemplaria imprimis in herbariis Kewensibus servata definita*, 3 vols. (London: Reeve, Williams and Norgate, 1862–83), which provided a revised definition of every genus of the plants in the Kew herbarium and gardens, with a view of their extent, geographical distribution and synonymy.

2 Letter of 26 May 1885, in *Life and Letters of Sir Joseph Dalton Hooker*, ed. Leonard Huxley, 2 vols. (London: Murray, 1918), II, 261.

3 For the circumstances of this sale, see Peter Jones, "The Museum Is Welcome to Them—If Not Let Them Be Burnt," *Bentham Newsletter*, 7 (1983), 41–3.

4 The collection was formally gifted to Kew in 1907. Benjamin Daydon Jackson used these materials for a biography, *George Bentham*, in the English Men of Science Series (London: Dent, 1906; repr., New York: AMS Press, 1976).

5 See note 2 above.

6 References to the "Autobiography" will appear in parentheses in the text.

7 See J.H. Burns, "Notes on the History of the Bentham Family," *Correspondence of Jeremy Bentham* [*CJB*], I, ed. T.L.S. Sprigge (London: Athlone Press, 1968), xxxv–xxxix; in *The Collected Works of Jeremy Bentham* [*CW*], gen. eds. J.H. Burns (1961–79), J.R. Dinwiddy (1977–83) and F. Rosen (1983–).

8 John Bowring, "Memoirs of Bentham; Including Autobiographical Conversations and Correspondence," in *The Works of Jeremy Bentham* [*Works*], 11 vols. (Edinburgh: Tait; London: Simpkin, Marshall; Dublin: Cumming, 1843; repr., New York: Russell and Russell, 1962), X, 1–2, 21. Bowring is careful to point out that "the profession of a pawnbroker was far more elevated then than now" (1).

9 Of the five other children born between Jeremy and Samuel, two (and possibly three) died in their first year, a brother, William (b. 1753), died shortly after Samuel's birth, and a sister, Anne (b. 1755), died after their mother in 1760.

10 Bowring, "Memoirs of Bentham," 4.

11 Ibid., 54.

12 See his letter to Étienne Dumont of 14 May 1802, in *CJB*, VII, ed. J.R. Dinwiddy (Oxford: Clarendon Press, 1988), 27. Linnaeus (Carl von Linné, 1707–78), a Swedish botanist, was the first to frame principles for defining the genera and species of organisms and to create a uniform system for naming them. François Boissier de Sauvages (1706–67), a Montpellier botanist and physician, and William Cullen (1710–90), a Scottish physician, were both classifiers of diseases, the latter according to genera and species. Bentham described his own work as being "a Nosology of the body politic" (ibid.). The following discussion of method owes much to John Dinwiddy, *Bentham* (Oxford and New York: Oxford University Press, 1989), 38–53. On method and language, see also H.L.A. Hart's essay in *An Introduction to the Principles of Morals and Legislation*, ed. J.H. Burns and Hart (Oxford: Clarendon Press, 1996), lxxxiii–lxxxvi.

13 When he later undertook to improve upon the work of Bacon and d'Alembert, classifying the various branches of human knowledge in his *Chrestomathia* (1816) (*CW*, ed. M.J. Smith and W.H. Burston [Oxford: Clarendon

Press, 1983]), he coined a great number of new words, from Greek roots, which more accurately represented their subject. "Natural history," for example, he found a particularly misleading name; for it he substituted "physiurgic somatology." Here Bentham ultimately lost the rest of us, but not his nephew George, who translated an appendix to it as *Essai sur la nomenclature et les principales branches d'art-et-science* (Paris: Bossange, 1823), for a French audience; see 61, 99–100 below.

14 *A Fragment on Government*, in *A Comment on the Commentaries and A Fragment on Government*, CW, ed. J.H. Burns and H.L.A. Hart (London: Athlone Press, 1977), 391–551; *A View of the Hard Labour Bill*, in *Works*, IV, 1–35; for the *Introduction to a System of Morals and Legislation*, see note 12 above.

15 See Bowring, "Memoirs of Bentham," *Works*, X, 82, 88, and *CJB*, I, xxvi–xxviii. The Empress Catherine had demonstrated her interest in reform by convening a commission in 1767 to draft a new constitution and a code of laws, but nothing practical had resulted from it.

16 Mary Sophia, Lady Bentham, *The Life of Brigadier-General Sir Samuel Bentham, K.S.G.* [*Life*] (London: Longman, et al., 1862), 2.

17 Ibid., 3–4.

18 Ibid., 8.

19 For a scholarly analysis of both Jeremy's and Samuel's aspirations and activities during this period, see Ian R. Christie, *The Benthams in Russia, 1780–1791* (Oxford; Providence: Berg, 1993).

20 Fascinating details of his early adventures are given by Lady Bentham, from letters to his father and brother, *Life*, chapters 2–4; those to Jeremy are in *CJB*, II, ed. T.L.S. Sprigge (London: Athlone Press, 1968), III, ed. I.R. Christie (ibid., 1971) and IV, ed. A. Taylor Milne (ibid., 1981). See also Christie, *The Benthams in Russia*, chapters 3 and 4.

21 Christie, 173.

22 Ibid., 141. Foreign gardeners had already made their mark in Russia, a notable example being John Busch (fl. 1730s–90s). Born in Hanover, he was a nurseryman at Hackney until 1771, when he became gardener to the Empress Catherine, laying out the gardens at Tsarskoe Selo the following year. He and his successor at Hackney, Conrad Loddiges, were tenants of Jeremiah Bentham; see the latter's letter to Samuel of 31 December 1779, *CJB*, III, 349–50, and 108 below. Jeremy Bentham pursued his interest in the international exchange of ornamental and useful plants during his visit to his brother; a "List of Seeds gathered in 1787, near Crichoff, in the government of Moghilev, in the province of White Russia, N. Lat. 54. and communicated to Dr Anderson, Dr Trail, Dr Pitcairn, Dr Fordyce, Mr Aiton and Mr Lee" is in *Works*, X, 178–9.

23 One of these barges was constructed for the Empress Catherine's official progress, in 1787, through her new provinces. It was to have conveyed her down the lower Dnieper, but was "still not sufficiently fitted out" for her use when she arrived. It joined the imperial galleys, however, for part of the later journey and made a favourable impression (Christie, 186–7). According to Lady Bentham, Samuel "received on board not only the English and the French ambassadors, Mr. Fitzherbert [later Baron St Helens], and the Count de Ségur, but also the Emperor Joseph II" (*Life*, 83). Cf. 20, 26–7, 209, 251, and 255 below.

24 See Christie, chapter 10. Some of the seaman under Bentham's command were English, one of whom, Richard Upsal, remained in his service; see M.S. Bentham, *Life*, 89, 93, and 5n8 below.

25 Details of the estate are given in a letter of 20 September 1818, from Samuel and Mary to Jeremy Bentham, in *CJB*, IX, ed. S. Conway (Oxford: Clarendon Press, 1989), 270–1; see also 365 below.

26 M.S. Bentham, *Life*, 95. See also K.A. Papmehl, "The Regimental School Established in Siberia by Samuel Bentham," *Canadian Slavonic Papers*, 8 (1966), 153–68.

27 See Ian R. Christie, "Samuel Bentham's Library in Russia," *Slavonic and East European Review*, 65 (1987), 26–37.

28 M.S. Bentham, *Life*, 96.

29 See Jeremy Bentham's letter to William Pitt, probably of late April 1787, *CJB*, III, 534–6. In January 1791 Bentham published three pamphlets outlining the scheme, *Panopticon, or the Inspection-House* and *Panopticon Postscript*, parts I and II (in *Works*, IV, 37–172).

30 His manuscripts on these and other subjects would be edited and published first in French by his Swiss friend Étienne Dumont, as *Traités de législation civile et pénale*, 3 vols. (Paris: Bossange, et al., 1802), and *Théorie des peines et des récompenses*, 2 vols. (London: Dulau, 1811). These works established his reputation on the Continent.

31 For a full treatment of the history and significance of the Panopticon scheme, see Janet Semple, *Bentham's Prison* (Oxford: Clarendon Press, 1993).

32 See M.S. Bentham, *Life*, 97–101.

33 The management of the naval dockyards is described in Jonathan G. Coad, *The Royal Dockyards, 1690–1850: Architecture and Engineering Works of the Sailing Navy* (Aldershot: Scholar Press, 1989), 23–40.

34 Most of Lady Bentham's *Life* of her husband (posthumously published by her daughter Sarah) is devoted to a detailed desciption of his accomplishments in this post. Two years before her death in 1858, Lady Bentham had published and distributed copies of "Memoir of the late Brigadier-General

Sir Samuel Bentham, with an Account of His Inventions"; in *Papers and Practical Illustrations of Public Works of Recent Construction, Both British and American* (London: Weale, 1856), 40–79.

35 Roger Morriss, *The Royal Dockyards during the Revolutionary Wars* (Leicester: Leicester University Press, 1983), 7.

36 See Coad, 19, 31, 230–3, Morriss, 46–52, 60, 211–15, 221, and especially Carolyn C. Cooper, "The Portsmouth System of Manufacture," *Technology and Culture*, 25 (April 1984), 182–225, in which the system and arrangement of the machines is hailed as the first successful production line. Lady Bentham's "Memoir" loyally explains that her husband withdrew his own machines (designed in 1793) in favour of Brunel's "apparatus for shaping blocks, to which [his] machines were solely confined . . . conceiving that a pleasing arrangement of engines for the confection of a single article would be the most likely means of conciliating public opinion in favour of machinery. . . . It will thus be seen how the notion originated that Brunel was the inventor of all the wood-working engines at Portsmouth" (54–5); see also her *Life*, 224–5. Samuel Bentham's experiences as Inspector-General, following his son George's birth in 1800, will be seen in the text and in notes, below.

37 *Life*, 121.

38 That comment by Asa Gray is quoted in the notice of Lady Bentham in R. Desmond, *Dictionary of British and Irish Botanists and Horticulturists* (London: Taylor and Francis, 1977). For Mill's assessment, see 63n27 below.

39 Bowring, "Memoirs of Bentham," *Works*, X, 133. Jeremy Bentham depicts his friend Fordyce as a man shy and ill at ease in company, describing him as "a queer creature, without conversation, . . . in the habit of bringing people together, giving no one any account of the others, so that they were constantly in awkward plights, . . . on the whole, the coldest of the cold Scotch." Yet Bentham valued him: "I worshipped Fordyce on account of his chemical knowledge. He knew everything that was then known." (Ibid., 133, 184, 571.)

40 Ibid., 184.

41 Ibid. A brief account of her family, by Lady Bentham, in British Library Add MSS 33,553, ff. 66–8, provides the following information. Her maternal grandfather, James Stewart, held the post of Lord Conservator of the Scottish Privileges at Veere, in Zeeland (the port of entry for raw wool from Scotland, which was then trans-shipped to Bruges to be manufactured into fine cloth). Her mother, Jane Sophia, was born at Veere, and was sent to London and Edinburgh "at different times" for her education. She returned to her family in Zeeland, and there met George Fordyce, who was pursuing post-graduate studies at Leyden, and elsewhere in Holland. Lady Bentham relates that her mother was utterly devastated by the death of the boy (b. 1767) who, one

Sunday evening before returning to school, while supper was being prepared, went out in a boat on the Thames near their Chelsea home and drowned. Mrs Fordyce could no longer bear to live by the river, and moved to the country. She died, ca. 1806, "shortly after [the Benthams] left for Russia." Lady Bentham's younger sister, Margaret (d. 1814), is mentioned at 4 below.

42 It appears that her activity was one of the reasons Samuel Bentham was criticized by some superiors in the Admiralty; see Jeremy Bentham's letter to his brother of 24 July 1806, *CJB*, VII, 354–5.

43 For details of this unsuccessful mission, during which Samuel Bentham hoped to be able to build ships for the British Navy, see 5–6 and notes below.

44 Letter to Jeremy Bentham of 7 September 1808, describing the visit, *CJB*, VII, 546. Burr's enthusiasm was apparently perfectly genuine, Jeremy reporting again to Samuel on 23 September that "He is continually trumpeting about the brats" (ibid., 551).

45 Letters of 23 August 1823, 28 February and 31 March 1824; MSS at the Linnean Society of London.

46 Letter of 28 February 1824.

47 Letter of 31 March 1824.

48 Jeremy Bentham's family subscribed to the general view that John Bowring unscrupulously manipulated him for his own ends. A more sympathetic treatment of Bowring is presented in F. Rosen, *Bentham, Byron and Greece* (Oxford: Clarendon Press, 1992), 104–11, 268–76, 282–8, and "John Bowring and the World of Jeremy Bentham," in *Sir John Bowring, 1792–1872: Aspects of His Life and Career*, ed. Joyce Youings (Exeter: Devonshire Association, 1993), 13–28.

49 The evidence for this account is in Bentham's journal-letters to his sister Mary Louise, 6 August to 15 October 1826; MSS at the Linnean Society of London.

50 Journal entry for 1 October 1826.

51 *A Memoir of Maria Edgeworth*, three volumes privately printed in 1867, had been prepared after her death by her stepmother, Frances Anne Edgeworth (1769–1865) and her two half-sisters, Harriet Butler (1801–89) and Lucy Robinson (1805–97).

52 Maria's youngest half-brother, Michael Pakenham Edgeworth (1812–81), combined botanical pursuits with a distinguished career in the Civil Service in India, 1831–59. George Bentham had known him since his home leave of 1842 and had provided help with his collections.

53 The selection made from Maria's correspondence had apparently led to some distortion, as nothing was included that might hurt the feelings of the living.

Though her sisters were well aware of how Maria could "tomahawk," the cutting edge was nowhere to be felt in this "attractive account" of her relationships (Christina Colvin, ed., Maria Edgeworth, *Letters from England 1813–1844* [Oxford: Clarendon Press, 1971], Introduction, xxx–xxxi).

54 See page x above.

55 Sir Eardley Gideon Culling, 4th Baronet Eardley (1838–75). Pakenham Edgeworth was probably another who Bentham expected would read his reminiscences with interest.

56 These letters were still in J.D. Hooker's possession when B.D. Jackson wrote Bentham's biography, mentioned in note 4 above; see Jackson's Preface, i. Though there is no formal record of how they came to the Linnean Society, it is likely that they were presented as a memento by Hooker. I am very grateful to Mrs Margot Walker for her invaluable work in cataloguing them and summarizing their contents.

GEORGE BENTHAM

AUTOBIOGRAPHY
1800–1834

[A1]§ *These reminiscences, checked by various memoranda, fragments of jour-nals, and letters, written in my early days, were commenced in 1867 when I had still friends and connections much younger than myself whom I thought they might interest after my death. They have since however for the most part gradually gone off before me, but a certain pleasure in recurring to scenes of my early life has induced me every now and then to resume the narrative, although with no prospect of further use than the supplying a few dates for the obituary notice which may have to be written of me for some of the scientific Societies to which I belong.*

George Bentham

1

Childhood;
St Petersburg, Hampstead, Gosport

[1] The earliest record I have obtained of my paternal ancestors shows them to have been from father to son Scriveners in the Minories from the commencement of the seventeenth century.[1] After the middle of the following§ century my grandfather, Jeremiah Bentham, then an Attor-ney or Solicitor of extensive practice, migrated to the West End having purchased some §property in Queen Square Place and Petty France (now York Street) on the south side of the Bird Cage Walk—partly free-hold partly leasehold§—under the Dean and Chapter of Westminster.[2] Here (No 2 Queen Square Place) he resided the remainder of his life, and was succeeded in it by his eldest son, Jeremy Bentham, the well known writer on Jurisprudence and Ethics, who occupied it till his death in 1832§ when the property came into my hands. My father, Sam-uel Bentham, the only other child of Jeremiah who grew to man's age, was nine years younger than Jeremy. Having very early devoted him-self with great zeal to Naval Architecture, he at the age of 22 undertook a journey into Northern Europe chiefly with a view to visiting the prin-cipal Arsenals on the Baltic, but extended his travels far into Siberia, and having become intimate with Prince Potemkin was induced to enter into the service of the Empress Catherine (at first in a civil, afterwards in a

military capacity)—was promoted and received the cross of St George
and other honours for the [2] distinguished part he took in a naval
action against the Turks on the Black Sea—obtained at his urgent
request the command of a regiment quartered far in Eastern Siberia,
which enabled him to penetrate as far as the frontiers of China, and after
ten years' absence return[§] to his own country to see his father in 1790.[3]
Shortly afterwards his promotion to the rank of General being followed
by the death of Catherine, and the accession of Paul, and on the other
hand his friend Earl Spencer, then first Lord of the Admiralty, being
anxious to avail himself of his experience and ingenuity for the
improvement of the Civil branch of our Naval System, my father was
induced to give up the Russian service and two or three years later to
accept the post of Inspector General of our Naval Works. In 1796 he
married the eldest daughter of Dr George Fordyce, a physician then in
extensive practice and well known for his lectures and published works
on fever and other subjects.[4] Dr Fordyce had no son surviving and only
one other daughter who subsequently died unmarried.

My mother (who untill long past the age of 80 wrote a most beautiful[§],
clear and particularly legible hand) had from an early age been accustomed to[§] take a part in her father's writings and devoted herself with
still greater perseverance to assist her husband in the drawing up and
writing out the voluminous reports he had to remit to the Admiralty.
She generally accompanied him on his visits of inspection to the principal Dockyards [   ] [3] especially to Sheerness, Portsmouth and Plymouth, where these visits were often of two or three months duration. It
was during one of these visits to Plymouth that I was born, at Stoke
(now a part of Plymouth) on the 22d Sept. 1800. I had an elder sister
Mary born in 1797, and a brother born in 1798, and subsequently two
younger sisters, Clara born in 1802 and Sarah in 1804. As to other relations, I never knew or heard of any on my father's side except an old
gentleman of 96 whom I once saw when a little boy, and my mother had
only very distant Scotch cousins, very few of whom I ever knew.

I cannot boast of any such vivid recollections of my early childhood as
my uncle Jeremy Bentham used to delight in relating of his.[5] We were all
taught to read and write[§] when very young—reading especially was an
early amusement; we learned[§] to read words before letters, and were
never wearied with the unmeaning syllables of ordinary spelling books.
Two of my sisters at four years old had made the clothes they wore on
that birthday and written out a list of them,[6] and by the summer of 1805
my brother and myself (who thenceforward always followed our les-

sons together) could not only write copies, and enjoy Miss Edgeworth's Early Lessons, but were just entering upon "Hic haec hoc," under one of my father's Clerks, Mr Rogers, a good scholar who wrote the most beautiful hand I ever met with, when our further progress was for the time interrupted by our Russian Expedition. My father was entrusted with a mission to St Petersburgh, relating to a project for building ships in Russia for the English Navy,[7] which was likely to be of some duration, and he determined on [4] taking his wife and family with him. The [   ] Isabella was placed at his disposal, and the three weeks' voyage de St Petersburgh left only agreable impressions on the minds of us children, who were made much of not only by a governess whom we liked and two young men who went as Secretary and draughtsman to my father, but also by the crew of the vessel.[8]

We remained two years in St Petersburgh. I had nearly completed my fifth year when we arrived there, and was within a few days of seven when we left. Our first residence was near the Admiralty, then in the Sergievski Ulitza, and after the first winter was over, my father took a house on the Veboryskai Storona opposite the Smolnoi Monastery—to our great delight as we had a large garden to run about in in summer and build snow huts in winter, besides plenty of room in the capacious building and conservatory for exercise in bad weather.[9] Shortly after our arrival our English governess left us to return to England with one of the Clerks and we children were placed under the care of a Russian lady, Alexandra Mikhailovna Necludoff, to whom we all got very much attached and who I always understood was an amiable and accomplished person who took the greatest pains with us.[10] She did not speak English but we all soon learned to chatter away in Russian and French, and picked up a great deal of German from a Finnish nurse. My [5] brother and myself resumed our Latin under a Russian priest, whom we never knew by any other name than Pope (the Priest). Our grammars and dictionaries were Russian and Latin so that we learned both languages at once. This I well recollect interested us much and we were rather vain of our progress, although I believe it was but slow. In the summer of 1806 my eldest sister began to take regular music lessons and I was asked whether I should like to do so also. I at first positively declined but some time after, being much taken by the pleasing manners of the music mistress Akulina Borisovna (I never knew her surname) and by the little airs for the piano which she wrote out expressly for my sister and brother, besides that I had already got into the habit of sharing all my brother's lessons and endeavouring to keep up with him,

and did not much like that he should learn anything that I did not, I
announced a change in my mind. I was then six years old, and having
eagerly and rapidly learned my notes, some simple exercises and "Ah
vous dirai-je maman," I soon enjoyed the inexpressible delight of a
Cosaque written out expressly for myself, one which I cannot now play
without recalling vividly this my first musical enjoyment.

In 1807 war broke out between England and Russia and my father
was recalled; he obtained however at the Emperor's request a couple of
months leave to finish some arrangements he had undertaken at Ochta
but finally left Petersburgh early in September [6] of that Year.[11] My
mother had suffered so much from the previous sea voyage that it was
determined to perform as much of the return as possible by land. We
went first through Narva to Revel and a very rude journey it was in
those days—the roads left pretty well to nature, and when we did stop
to sleep the accomodation most scanty, a single room, with a hard
horsehair couch, a table and a few chairs—without bedding or linen was
where my father and mother and we five children had to pass the
night—very much to my mother's annoyance and to our amusement.
From Revel a Russian frigate, the *Edinarog* (Unicorn) had been commissioned to take us across to Stockholm and the second day we were in
sight of the entrance, but the wind changed, the vessel was a bad sailer,
scarcely any of the crew had been to sea before, and we were driven
backwards and forwards without venturing to enter among the rocky
islands that border the Swedish coast, till at last on the 13th day we were
very glad to land at Carlscrona.[12]

Here we were to remain several days at least, and as our stay in Sweden would probably extend beyond a month we three elder children set
to learning the language with great zeal, myself especially, as I had
always a great fancy for languages. We could then speak Russian,
French and English with great facility and knew a good deal of German,
all which gave us a wonderful readiness for acquiring Swedish in addition, and before we left the country we contrived to make ourselves
understood by any Swedish attendants we came across, as well [7] as to
read with tolerable fluency Swedish storybooks.

My father engaged a carriage to take us from Carlscrona to Gottenburgh by easy days' journeys through South Sweden. Near Engelholm
some essential part of the vehicle gave way and required some days to
repair. Fortunately we were close to Engellofta, the seat of Major
Schernsward, who received us most hospitably into his house.[13] It was
the warm limestone?[§] district of Sweden, and his grounds were so well

sheltered that amongst other Southern productions, a hardy variety of the Olive flourished without protection in the winter; and I long afterwards often heard my father and mother speak of the beauty of the place and of the delightful three or four days we spent there. Arrived at Gottenburgh we found that the last regular packet for the season was only waiting for a fair wind to start, the westerly winds being just then continuous and stormy. We engaged our passage and were ready to go on board at any time at a moment's notice, when one morning we heard that the wind had changed in the night and the packet had sailed without calling us. We found out however that there was still a vessel formerly in the packet service whose captain had died at Gottenburg and which was about to be taken home by the mate, and indifferent as was the accomodation on board, after§ a long and almost hopeless detention we were glad enough to embark in her as our last resource, sailing with a not very favourable but yet not very bad wind; we had scarcely however left the [8] coast when a violent SW wind again sprung up, and for 13 November days we were beating about in the North Sea in a scarcely interrupted storm. My mother lay prostrate the whole time; we children amused ourselves tolerably, but generally in the dark for the hatches were battened down and the seas we shipped rolled over our heads. Provisions moreover run short, and when at length on the fourteenth night we entered the harbour of Harwich and the crew hastened on shore leaving us passengers on board till towards midday, we were glad enough to pick up any broken rejected bits of biscuit we could find. The happiness of being at last comfortably seated to a good dinner by a brisk fire, in one of the warm carpeted rooms of a Harwich inn, has left a lasting impression on my mind—even my mother revived wonderfully from her protracted sufferings.

We lost no time in settling ourselves at Hampstead, where my father had just bought the lease of a house before the §Russian mission was determined on. It had been let during our absence but was now prepared for our reception. Hall Oak Farm which was thus our home for near seven years from Decr 1807 till the summer§ of 1814 was one of a small number of houses which went by the name of Frognall to the W of the church at the top of the lane leading to West End.[14] With the additions made to it by my father from the old farm buildings it gave us ample accomodation; the garden was large, and from a terrace walk, which wound round the hill, under a grove and bordering our meadows we had a beautifull view including Harrow spire. My father went almost daily to his Office first at the Admiralty, afterwards at Somerset

House,[15] and our education was [9] steadily followed up. We were none
of us sent to school, which for my brother and myself has always
appeared to me to have been a mistake. We learnt more perhaps than
we should have done at school, but we did not acquire that habit of
judging for ourselves when mixing with others, nor make any of those
lasting friendships, which are the usual results of being made early to
do battle with others of our age, and for myself it always left a kind of
shyness which has often stood in my way. My father whose thoughts
were absorbed in his business, and my mother who was chiefly engaged
in writing for him, had little time to attend to the details of our education, which was entrusted to masters, and to a governess for my sisters
who was supposed also in some measure to look after us boys, an interference in our view, of which we contrived pretty well to save her the
trouble. Mr Spowers, a teacher in the large Hampstead school of Messrs
Bidmead and Johnson, usually gave us daily one hour and at one time I
believe two hours for Latin, Greek and Mathematics. He succeeded in
interesting us so much in these pursuits that after the first year or two
we became attached to him and really zealous in our endeavours to
make progress. We had also drawing and dancing masters and kept up
our languages in various ways. Russian we found very convenient to
chatter away in amongst ourselves knowing that no one understood us,
translating into Russ the names of the habitués of the house, my father's
Assistants, draughtsmen, etc—besides we had brought with us a considerable Russian library. French we continued [10] regularly to study
with masters or Governesses; we had also for a time a German Governess with whom we revived that language, but our Swedish was soon
forgotten. These lessons suffered scarcely any[§] interruptions during the
first years[§]. Once my brother and myself accompanied my father and
mother to Portsmouth during one of his 2 or 3 weeks inspections; once
we some of us were taken by them a delightful tour with our own carriage round the coast of Kent, Sussex and Hampshire, and once we all
spent two or three weeks at Queenborough during one of my father's
inspections of Sheerness. In 1811?[§] however my father bought Berry
Lodge,[16] a small house[*][§] with a large garden and a few fields, between

---

[*] The front of the house was covered with myrtles two of which were 22 ft high, flowering abundantly every year and never covered in winter. They were however subsequently cut down by a severe frost whilst we were abroad.

Gosport and Alverstoke, and there we usually spent two or three months every summer to our great delight—for here we had more liberty than at Hampstead. We kept up our lessons indeed, for we had masters from Portsmouth and my brother and myself worked up for Mr Spowers on our return to town; but we had more time for exercise, my mother was more with us, we could, especially my brother and myself, roam more of the country. Stokes Bay Beech, where Angles en ville now stands, but then without a house, was within an easy walk and we could often go and bathe there, but above all our great enjoyment was Portsmouth Dockyard of which we had the run—making great friends with the masters of the different establishments introduced there by my father,[17] especially with Mr Burr, the master of the woodmills—with the warder of the Yard, who gave us free access at all times—and generally crossing over in my father's Official Dockyard boat. [11] Once also to our great delight Mr Spowers was induced to come down to us for his vacation and during his visit took us, my brother and myself, a pedestrian tour of three days round the Isle of Wight—roughing it at meal times and at night at the little country inns, which were all the accomodation then to be found where the large hotels of Shanklin Ventnor, etc, are now so crowded. My father also occasionally took either my brother or myself over to Ryde to see Lady Spencer, who had a very pretty villa there, and on one occasion Lady Spencer took me to the play at Ryde, the first theatrical representation I ever saw. On another occasion John Stuart Mill, then a boy of six years old in a scarlet jacket with nankeen trowsers buttoned over it, was staying with us and spent a morning with my father and myself at Lady Spencer's.[18] He was then in some respects a prodigy. He had a wonderfully precocious mind; his father, a cold Scotchman with more ability than principle, whilst neglecting his wife and younger children, took the greatest pains in developping John's mind without caring for his manners. At this time at the age of six he was a Greek and Latin scholar, a historian, and a logician, and fond of showing off his proficiency without the slightest reserve. Lady Spencer, accustomed as she was to the greatest deference from the numerous literati whom she patronised, was highly amused by the bold familiarity of the boy as well as by the ability in which he entered into an argument with her as to the comparative merits of Wellington and Marlborough,[19] she taking the part of her ancestor whilst John argued for Wellington. This extraordinary precocity of mind with neglect of social education was generally thought to forebode early exhaustion and a barren carreer, but that he has proved an [12] exception to a general rule and has falsified predictions must be owing a great deal to his own good sense. It must be added also in proof of the excellence of his mind that notwithstanding the bad example before him his behaviour to his mother, brothers and sisters was admirable; whatever indeed of education the younger children received was chiefly owing to the exertions of their brother John.

[13]The early months of the year 1814 were a period of great excitement in all classes, in which we children, young as we were, could not fail to partake. Our connection with Russia and knowledge of its language induced us already to take great interest in the events of the Campaign of Moscow.[20] My eldest sister, my brother and myself had translated for a Magazine, then publishing but which had but a short duration, a number of anecdotes connected with the war from the *Syn Otetchestva* (Son of the Fatherland)[21] and now that there appeared a prospect of a retaliation on the French of the miseries they had inflicted on the Germans and Russians, we began looking eagerly forward to[§] their ultimate humiliation. We carefully traced on our maps the alternate advances and repulses of the two great corps of Alexander and Schwarzenberg, and great was our rejoicing when news arrived at last of the triumphant entry of the allied armies into Paris and the abdication of Napoleon.[22] This sudden and complete pacification of the Continent opened as it were a new world to the explorations of tourists and pleasure seekers, as much as of those whose object was the acquiring information and enlarging older ideas somewhat cramped by long isolation, and on all sides friends and acquaintance were hurrying to Paris or preparing for longer journeys to the south. The mania soon seized our own family. My father's Office had been abolished the preceding year, his full salary being continued to him for life as a pension, with a promise of further remuneration for past services. This promise was indeed never [14] fulfilled, and he and his brother had even much difficulty in obtaining, after long delays, repayment of large sums which they had expended in the public service;[23] yet a very fair income was now insured to him for life, and he thought that a couple of years spent in a milder climate would recruit him after the fatigues of his official life, and at the same time with the cheapness of continental living he might be enabled to give his children a better education and lay by more for their future benefit than he could in England where every luxury and even every necessary of life was then so heavily taxed. He therefore immediately began preparing for a lengthened absence, and on the arrival of the foreign Sovereigns,[24] as it was known that they would visit

Portsmouth, he felt anxious himself to§ assist in doing the honours of the Dockyard. Having accordingly packed up everything for letting the Hampstead House, we went down to Berry Lodge two days before the Sovereigns' announced visit to Portsmouth. We had taken the whole inside, and the outside front seats of one of the coaches, but the remainder was crowded to excess; besides packing the roof as full as men could stow, we had one on the step on each side and one hanging on behind. The whole road was most unusually animated and at Portsmouth, Gosport, etc, every bed was taken. We however had our comfortable Berry Lodge which we all enjoyed so much and to which this was to be our last visit. When the Sovereigns came down, the scene was a very busy one, the weather was fine, and I can never forget the curious scene when the Emperor of Russia and the Duchess of Oldenburg, his sister, went on board a man of war at [14]§ Spithead, the immense crowd of boats all around, the bustle and screams, the loud hurras and cries of "Emperor a-head, Emperor a-stern," "Duchess a-head," etc, as the spectators at one or the other end hoped to get a glimpse of them. Their visit to the Dock Yard was a strictly private one, and very stringent regulations prevented the admission of any but their own party on that day. My father however who, though no longer in Office, was privileged as being the chief author of the most important establishments in the Yard, and was officially present among those who attended upon the Sovereigns, had taken my brother, myself and Philip Abbot in the day before—we spent the night in the Office of the Master of the Wood Mills,^{25} and awaited in those Mills the Imperial and Royal Party. Alexander, on learning who we were, said some very civil things to us to our great gratification.

The few following months were very happy ones; the bustle of preparation for scenes entirely new is always delightful to children. My sisters with my father and mother went to pay a two days' farewel visit to my Uncle Jeremy Bentham at Ford Abbey near Chard which he hired for a few years during the summer, and my brother and I with my father went up to London for a week, where we witnessed from the roof of Spencer House the splendid peace fête,^{26} when St James's and Green Park were illuminated and grand fire works displayed in the Green Park (the tickets of admission at two guineas) [15] the finest illumination an extemporary one. A temporary bridge had been erected over the then straight canal in St James's Park and a tall pagoda on the centre was lit up from bottom to top, but unfortunately caught fire and two men lost their lives. This however we did not know at the time, thought it all part of the programme, and enjoyed the magnificent blaze. In the morning there was rather an absurd "Naval Combat" on the Serpentine. Half a dozen boats, large enough to hold a crew of half a dozen men each, were rigged out as models of three-masters and manoeuvred like children's playthings—the men out of all proportion to the vessels. The fêtes went off as such things usually do, large crowds and many people enjoying themselves, with a great deal of grumbling encreased by the unpopularity of the Prince Regent.[27]

Among my father's old friends, to see whom had been one of his chief objects in this visit, was Admiral Tchitchagoff, with whom he had formed a great intimacy in Russia, besides Official intercourse the Admiral having then been Minister of the Marine. The Admiral had always a great admiration for England and a tender recollection of his wife, an English lady whose loss he never ceased to mourn. He had now become rather soured by the results of some intrigues, and was very indignant at Russian Official corruption.[28] He already seemed desirous of settling in England or France, the balance being determined ultimately in favour of the [16] latter by the indignation he felt at the annoying formalities of the English Alien Act.[29] However he was now enjoying himself and I well recollect his delight at reading out the following ballad then attributed to Canning[30] and which my father had had reprinted from the *Courier*—the ministerial evening paper of the day. He could not help reading "end in itch" as "had the itch," and was specially amused at the way his own name was alluded to.[31]

The March to Moscow

The following droll Ballad, written by one of the most distinguished Poets of the age, appeared in the *Courier*, Evening Paper, of the 23d of June, 1814.

> Buonaparte, he would set out
> For a summer excursion to Moscow;
> The fields were green, and the sky was blue,
> Morbleu! Parbleu!
> What a pleasant excursion to Moscow!
>
> Four hundred thousand men and more,
> Hey ho, for Moscow!
> There were Marshals by the dozen and Dukes by the score,
> Princes a few and Kings one or two,
> While the fields are so green and the sky so blue,

Morbleu! Parbleu!
What a pleasant excursion to Moscow!

There was Junot and Augereau,
Hey ho, for Moscow!
Dombrowsky and Poniatowsky,
General Rapp and the Emperor Nap,
Nothing would do,
While the fields were so green, and the sky so blue,
Morbleu! Parbleu!
But they must be marching to Moscow.

But then the Russians they turn'd to,
All on the road to Moscow,
Nap had to fight his way all thro'
They could fight but they could not *parlez-vous*,
But the fields were green, and the sky was blue,
Morbleu! Parbleu!
And so he got to Moscow.

They made the place too hot for him,
For they set fire to Moscow;
To get there had cost him much ado,
And then no better course he knew,
While the fields were green, and the sky was blue,
Morbleu! Parbleu!
Than to march back again from Moscow.

The Russians, they stuck close to him,
All on the road from Moscow:
There was Tormazow and Jermolow,
And all the others that end in *ow*;
Rajefsky and Nevereffsky,
And all the others that end in *efsky*;
Schamscheff, Souchosaneff, and Schepeleff,
And all the others that end in *eff*;
Wisilchikoff, Kostomaroff, and Tchoglokoff,
And all the others that end in *off*;
Milaradovitch, and Jaladovitch, and Karatchkowitch,
And all the others that end in *itch*;
Ojaroffsky, and Rostoffsky, and Kasatchkoffsky,

And all the others that end in *offsky*;
And last of all an Admiral came,
A terrible man with a terrible name,
A name which you all must know very well,
Nobody can speak, and nobody can spell;
And Platoff he played them off,
And Markoff he mark'd them off,
And Tutchkoff he touch'd them off,
And Kutousoff he cut them off,
And Woronzoff he worried them off,
And Doctoroff he doctor'd them off,
And Rodinoff he flogg'd them off.
They stuck close to them with all their might,
They were on the left and on the right,
Behind and before, and by day and by night;
Nap would rather *parlez-vous* than fight;
But *parlez-vous* no more do,
Morbleu! Parbleu!
For they remembered Moscow!

And then came on the frost and snow,
All on the road from Moscow!
The Emperor Nap found as he went,
That he was not quite Omnipotent;
And worse and worse the weather grew,
When the fields were so white and the sky so blue,
Cacrebleu! Ventrebleu!
What a terrible journey from Moscow!

§The Devil take the hindmost,
All on the road from Moscow!
Quoth Nap, who thought it small delight,
To fight all day, and to freeze all night;
And so not knowing what else to do,
When the fields were so white, and the sky so blue,
Morbleu! Parbleu!
He stole away, I tell you true,
All on the road from Moscow.

'Twas as much too cold upon the road,

As it was too hot at Moscow:
But there is a place which he must go to,
Where the fire is red and the brimstone blue,
Morbleu! Parbleu!
He'll find it hotter than Moscow.

2

France;
Saumur to Toulouse, 1814–18

[17]We sailed from Portsmouth in the afternoon of the 23d Augt 1814, arriving at Le Havre the following morning. The place was full and busy. The restoration of peace, the opening of the port, the revival of trade and influx of foreigners put the inhabitants and officials into excellent humor. We were well received as English, the landing and custom house formalities were readily gone through and early in the afternoon we found ourselves established amidst scenes persons and things so totally different from anything we had been accustomed to as to excite in us children more wonder than interest. The "Hotel d'Angleterre" was full in anticipation of a ball and other festivities to take place on the following day for the first celebration of the Saint-Louis[1] and we had to put up at the "Auberge de la Vierge," a picturesque corner house with a figure of the Virgin and Child protruding as a sign, in which the rooms, out of square or level, the second or third rate somewhat quaint furniture, the coarse but abundant and clean table and bed linen, the little crazy fontaîne, with its slowly trickling cock destined to serve all purposes of ablution, were to us a perfect[§] contrast to the little cosy rooms at the inns we had been accustomed to sleep in on our journeys between London and Portsmouth—and our astonishment was accompanied by no little mortification[§] when, priding ourselves on our supposed proficiency in the language we began to show it off, but whether from pronunciation or idiom or both we could not make ourselves understood.

[18]At Le Havre we remained a couple of days to see the town en fête and to wear down in some measure the sensation of strangeness in

everything we saw and experienced. The third day we crossed over to Honfleur for a night and there engaged a voiturin to convey us to Tours. This journey of six days through Lisieux, Gacé, Sees, Alençon and Le Mans was a source of great enjoyment to us. Beautiful weather, an entirely new, though not very picturesque country, our lumbering vehicle drawn by three well-fed but rather gawky horses, who seemed almost to carry on a conversation with their driver, for he guided and controlled their movements almost entirely by word of mouth, addressing them always individually by their names which they seemed well to know. The leader, a bay mare, was especially intelligent, and the word of command, "En route la Baie," "Gup," or "Io" (to the left or to the right) was always followed by immediate obedience, whilst they all seemed sensible to words of endearment or reproof or even longer speeches addressed to them. The driver was also very communicative to us children, and by the time we arrived at the Hotel des Trois Barbeaux at Tours we had become quite familiarised§ with France and Frenchmen.

We staid but a few days at Tours and a single one at Blois where my father had projected spending the winter, but the accounts he heard of the climate and the appearance of the country were not what he had reckoned upon and we descended the Loire in a boat, first to Tours and then to Saumur. This place immediately took his fancy—a beautiful country, very cheap living [19] and most promising educational resources, and he was not long in suiting himself in the hire for the winter of a country house at the head of a most lovely little retired valley, beyond the village of St Hilaire, within a short walk of the Loire and about [   ] from the town. Le Puy Giraud was indeed a beautiful place independently of youthful associations, for I was equally pleased with it when again visiting it [   ] years later;[2] a large orchard and kitchen garden supplied us abundantly with the fruit and vegetables we had been used to, my mother had quite sufficient flower garden for her amusement and the surrounding broken country gave endless variety to our walks and rides.

Here my father's first care was to secure to my brother and myself the means of resuming our studies especially in Latin Greek and mathematics, and of setting us all in the right way as to French litterature and pronunciation. In all these branches he was fortunate in securing the services of Monsieur Chiron, one of the professors at the college of Saumur, who was at once a good mathematician§, and Latin and to some extent Greek scholar and thoroughly versed in French litterature, with gentlemanly, agreable manners and an excellent method of teaching which took my fancy even more than my brother's. He gave us a couple of hours nearly every day, and we had, I believe, music and other masters, but it is M. Chiron's lessons that have remained impressed on my memory. I had considered myself as being pretty well advanced in mathematics, having gone through Euclid and plane trigonometry, and simple and quadratic equations in Algebra, and commenced with Mr Spowers in spherical trigonometry, conic sections and fluxions, [20] but with M. Chiron I felt rather pleasure than hesitation in beginning all de novo, and going through even plain Arithmetic by proving every one of the rules which we had hitherto only learned by rote. In the rule of three, we had learned that the 2d and 3d terms must be multiplied and the product divided by the 1st, and the correctness of our calculations depended on the exactness of our unassisted memory; but the moment the reasons of every step of the formula were explained in clear language, an interest was given to the operation and reason could always be called out as a check upon memory. We thus in the course of the winter went through Laplace's Arithmetic and Algebra and Legendre's Geometry, and entered into some of the higher branches of Mathematics, read some of the more difficult Latin classics, and with our sisters followed a course of French litterature, learning much by heart both in prose and poetry as dictated to us by M. Chiron, who also took great pains with our composition and pronunciation, and in this we were much assisted by the very fair French spoken by the country people as well as in the town. This autumn and summer have always been reckoned by us as one of the happiest periods of our lives—constant occupation and plenty of exercise. We often went in to Saumur shopping for the household. At first the street gamins used sometimes to follow us about with cries of "Anglishmarn, Anglishmarn," but they were soon familiarized with our appearance and we made friends with several of the trades-people. There was particularly a grocer of the name of Pinot-Tisson, who was both communicative and inquisitive. We were the first English they had seen in the town, and great was their surprise [21] to find that, barring a few peculiarities in dress and manner, we were not so very unlike other people as they had been led to believe. The idea most firmly impressed on their minds was that of the great riches of the English—but in that respect their notions were not very consistent. They firmly believed that in England it was the custom to shoe their horses with silver, whilst it was currently reported that my father was very rich, having 1000 francs (£40) to spend every month and some-

thing to lay by. In the country we also made friends; there was especially a peasant-farmer at the top of the hill of the name of Mechain, a
very worthy and tolerably well informed man, who became a great ally
of my brother and myself. He let us into all the mysteries of his agricultural operations and with him we made two grand expeditions. The
first was to the great fair of Doué, a small town about [   ] miles
distant, much resorted to by the peasantry, cattle dealers and mule
breeders of the Vendée and Poitou. It was here only that I saw those
great *bardeaux*, as they were there called, asses of enormous size with
exceedingly long hoofs and hair near six inches long, of a very vicious
disposition, but of great value (as stallions) for breeding the finest
mules for the southern market. At this fair we bought for my brother an
excellent pony of 5 years old, to whom we got afterwards much
attached, and who served some of us during the next twenty years, and
a very pretty donkey for myself, which however I was glad soon after
to make over to my sisters, on obtaining for myself a pony to match my
brother's.

[22]The other great expedition which my brother and myself made on
our ponies with our friend Méchain was to a grand wedding at a rich
peasant proprietor's some 8 or 10 miles off. We arrived there in the
morning before the procession to church, in time to make our selection
of bridal presents. According to custom, dealers had provided themselves with a stock of articles required to mount the young household,
after previous consultation with the bride and bridegroom, and displayed them in the vicinity of the church, whilst the "trousseau" or
stock of personal and household linen, etc, which the bride had provided, and the "corbeille" or ornamental dress and finery presented by
the bridegroom, were exhibited in an appartment at the bride's parents.
The party was at the Mairie when we arrived; we went in with them to
the church ceremony, in issuing from which the presents were given—
almost all useful articles of household and kitchen furniture—pots and
pans and all kinds of crockery, with a few articles of mere ornament. My
brother and myself went in for it with the others and each gave a dozen
of plates. The bride in return gave to every donor a kiss and a staylace—
what the latter was emblematical of, our friend could not well explain,
only that it was an ancient custom. Returning to the bride's residence,
we sat down not very long after to the wedding feast. The table was laid
for between 50 and 60 in a large barn and was I believe quite full, and
the repast if not very refined was abundant and good; there was especially a great profusion of game[s]. Towards the end of the meal the wed-

ding cake circulated. [23] It was a large flat circular kind of rich galette, above two feet in diameter, which was first rolled round the table on the knees of the guests, and then cut up into as many portions as guests and distributed. There were also healths drunk and glasses *trinqués*, but no speechifying. The dinner over, the barn was cleared for dancing which was still going on when we were obliged to leave on the evening dusk coming on.

Besides these friends of ours my father and mother made several agreable acquaintance amongst the Saumur gentry, and the quiet, with the healthy occupations, seemed to be of so much benefit that my father was already contemplating the staying over a second year, when all his plans were disturbed by political events. The establishment of the military school of cavalry at Saumur had brought there a number of Imperialist Officers and had given a Bonapartist tone to many of the townspeople, whilst the country people, the resident gentry and small propriétaires were strong Bourbonists, or at any rate much excited at the contemplation of the miseries induced by the last two years of the Empire. This brought on much discussion and a prevailing feeling that serious events were impending. It was observed that the Emperor's friends were becoming bolder in language and demonstrations. At a carnival ball at the Sous-prefecture where the Officers mustered in numbers, the rooms were decorated with Imperial bees, it was remarked that manoeuvres were going on to place the partisans of Napoleon in positions of influence, that an important command for instance at La Flèche was given to his favorite General, Lefevre-Desnouettes, and when [24] early in March came the news of the landing of the Emperor at Fréjus,[3] it was at once exclaimed that it was a preconcerted plan to which numbers were privy all over the country, and all was excitement or anxiety, according to the part taken. News however then travelled slowly; the papers announced that Napoleon had advanced with a small band towards Grenoble but had been joined by so few that he had taken refuge in the mountains; then came expression of the utmost confidence in the means taken to capture him, and prominent amongst all was Marshall Ney's celebrated expressions on taking leave of the King to assume the command of the army,[4] which almost every one believed he had been organising and distributing so as best to facilitate the Emperor's plans. We could hear however but little more, till the astounding news came at once of the King's flight to Ghent and the Emperor's triumphant entry into Paris.[5] The tricolor was immediately waving in the win-

dows of the enthusiastic Saumurois, whilst all was alarm and confusion in the neighbourhood[§]. The[§] English in France, already numerous
in Paris, Tours and a few other towns, with the fear of Verdun before
their eyes,[6] were rapidly taking flight, notwithstanding the assurances
of safety and attempts at conciliation made on the part of the
Emperor's government, and my father received various letters recommending him to follow their example. Seeing however that an intimate friend of his, Count Ségur, was appointed to an important post
about the Imperial Court,[7] and being very unwilling to interrupt the
tranquil course we were following, he wrote at once to consult the
Count. The reply contained the assurance that the [25] Emperor was
not only determined not to molest any English residents in France, but
that he was exceedingly anxious to conciliate our nation and that we
had nothing to fear, but in case local circumstances should oblige us to
quit, Count Ségur forwarded to us passports for Switzerland, accompanied by strong recommendations to officials on our road. Upon that,
my father determined to remain and wait the course of events. In the
beginning of May however the neighbourhood became very unquiet.
Our farmer friends reported that the Chouans were collecting about
Doué,[8] determined to resist the government by force of arms, whilst
the garrison of Saumur was strengthened and preparations made for
resistance. Already some firing had been heard in the distance, the
roads about Saumur were ordered to be cut—and although it all was
ultimately without result, my father, having reason to fear we might
be envelopped in the conflict, thought it time to depart. The threats of
the violent party were so loud that he was afraid of any ostentation in
our mode of travelling and we started in a modest one-horse charaban
and on our own rough ponies and donkey—some of us usually on
foot. On the road to Tours we were stopped for the first half of the
way by the garde nationale of every village—our passports strictly
scrutinised and we were often only suffered to proceed with very disagreable comments and gestures. Nearer Tours all was more friendly,
and stopping there for a day or two to receive our luggage and determine on further proceedings, my father finding there some [§]acquain-
tance, and hearing very reassuring accounts of the state of feeling,
resolved upon waiting here till all should be over, and engaged a [26]
house by the month in the fauxbourg St Symphorien on the north side
of the river.

We were here a little more in the way of hearing what was going on.
A very few of the English who had crowded at Tours still remained

there, amongst others Walter Savage Landor and his family, of whom we saw a good deal. The townspeople rich and poor with the exception of a few "autorités" and timeservers were unanimous in their anti-imperial feelings and in the belief that the present purely military government would not last long. Even here however news came very slowly and with very meagre details. It was many days after the occurrences that flaming accounts arrived of a great battle at Mont St Jean on the 16th June in which Napoleon had gained a complete victory over the allied forces—and then nothing more for many anxious days. Suddenly all were startled by the announcement of his appearance in the Corps Legislatif to state that all was lost—the army demoralised and dispersed and the materiel destroyed.[9] The Emperor then disappeared from the scene for a fortnight. Nobody knew where he was. Some announced that he had left the country, others asserted that he had been seen in the Rue Neuve des Petits-Champs, when one morning all Tours was alive that he had passed through the town in the night on his way to La Roch-elle. He had called up the Prefet and after an hour's conversation with him had proceeded on his way without having been recognised. Landor indeed in[§] a letter sent in his old age to one of our journals, boasted that this was owing to his forbearance. He says that he happened to be at the Poste aux chevaux when [27] Napoleon[§] changed horses, and knew him at once, and that if he, Landor, had but said a word the populace would have at once stopped their Emperor and massacred him on the spot.[10] There is little doubt but there were many sufficiently excited against him to commit any violence had they had the opportunity—but the inhabitants were in their beds, and neither they nor Walter Savage Landor himself heard of his passage till the next morning. Mr Landor's story was one of those afterthoughts he was so apt to indulge in for his own glorification.

Newspapers gave us full reports of the debates in the Corps Legislatif on a proposed new Constitution, suddenly interrupted by the entrance of the Allies into Paris,[11] and all Tours was preparing eagerly for the expected change—but still the Imperial Prefet and the tricolor flag remained. Then we heard that the remnants of the [§]dispersed forces were gathering on the Loire into a new Army which intended resistance to the last, and all was gloom. At length, about a fortnight after the occupation of Paris, the order was given for hoisting the white flag, which immediately as if by magic appeared at almost every window of the town. The inhabitants crowded the streets in their holiday clothes, a grand Te Deum was solemnized at the Cathedral, Landor wrote and distributed to his friends some latin verses on the return of the King,* and publicly and privately all was extacy. After having been with Mr Landor in the morning to the Te Deum and other ceremonies, my father with my brother and myself went in to the town again at dusk to see the illuminations which were making a great show for a provincial town, when [29] suddenly a commotion took place, the lights were extinguished, the white flags drawn in, crowds collected, intermingled with soldiers and accompanied by loud shouts and beating of drums. We

---

* Our copy of these verses is lost but I believe they were not those which he wrote on Louis XVIII's second exile, of which a copy is annexed.[12] [28] Lines written by Walter Savage Landor at Tours in March 1815 on Louis XVIII's forced exile at the return of Napoleon from Elba.

Ad regem iterum exulem

Non tibi dum reducem celebravit Gallia regem,
　　O Lodvix, Pindi florida certa tuli.
Pectore nempe meo mea solus gaudia pressi.
　　Sat reputare mihi quanta fuere tuo.
Haec dedit exilium, dixi, quae propera numquam
　　Sors daret. En populo saepe vocatus adest!
En redit eversa pulsaque tyrannide regno!
　　En redit una suis finitimisque salus!
Proh Superi! Gallis quo tempore pura cruoris
　　Libertas potuit paxve placere dice?
Proh Superi! Gallis quo tempore pura cruoris
　　Libertas potuit paxve placere dice?
Dicere gens audet fieri sua crimina paucis.
　　Stulte! quid hoc ipso crimine majus erit?
Hinc modo tercenis capitum tot millia cultris
　　Territa considici jussa secuta ducis.
Hinc patris cineres calcavit pallidus exul.
　　(Vana loquor. Patriam proditor ecquis habet?)
Clamavit celeri conspiciendus equo.
　　Tu quavis alia caperes tellure quietem,
Nec staret meritis unica culpa fides.
　　Arma senescentem stiparent civica regem
Et procerum virtus et popularis amor.
　　Sed redeas utinam, redeas victore Britanno;
Gensque sit exemplo tota reficta tuo.

From a copy taken at the time of the original given to my father by Landor in the end of March 1815.

hastened home, and early in the morning my father went in again to the town to learn what was taking place. Two regiments of the Armée de la Loire had entered the town in the evening, replaced the Imperial authorities and tricolor flag; some of the rabble had joined them in attacking some bankers and other houses where money or arms were supposed to be kept, and though pillage had been stopped, all was alarm and confusion. Going to Mr Landor's, my father found the apartment shut and no one answered the bell, but a neighbour informed him that the Landors had left in the night—although we afterwards learned that they had been unable to find means of leaving, but fearful of the consequences of having taken a rather prominent part in the previous day's rejoicings, they had shut themselves up and got the neighbour to announce their departure to all who should enquire after them. From others my father heard that more troops were immediately expected, that it was determined to defend Tours, to break up the roads and blow up the bridge, and he therefore lost no time in preparing for departure; having succeeded in engaging a voiturin we all left the same afternoon, arriving the following day at Le Mans.[13]

Here all was quiet, the Bourbon government restored, and the Armée de la Loire too far off to give uneasiness, and we therefore remained at a hotel for a week or ten days, to give my father time to learn precisely the state of Paris, whither he had determined to proceed for the winter if [30] circumstances admitted. Two days before we left, a body of Prussians entered—these next to the "Cosaques" were generally the most dreaded of the invading troops—all was however peace and civility. Whilst waiting in the principal Place for their billets de logement, crowds collected to stare at them and many offered them wine and pipes, and during our stay we heard no complaints of them, although we were afterwards told that some days later, being dissatisfied with the arrangements of the authorities, they put Baron Pasquier the Prefet in prison.[14]

At Paris my father engaged the greater part of a house with a small garden at the back on the upper side of the principal street of Passy and here we remained for three months. Saumur having become much disorganised after the restoration, M. Chiron was induced to join us and to devote himself entirely to the prosecution of the studies we had commenced with him. He also accompanied my eldest sister, my brother and myself in our daily visits to the sights of Paris. Amongst these, the great Gallery of the Louvre was our principal resort. The first day we were there it was still perfect—they were just commencing to unhang

the first pictures to pack them up for their return to the countries
whence Napoleon had brought them. The best Raphaels, Corregios,
Rubenses, etc,[15] were still in their places, as well as the Belvedere
Apollo, the Venus of Medicis, the Laocoon, etc, but the gallery soon
assumed the appearance of a wreck—half the spaces void, and all dirt
and confusion. It was closed to the general public and only foreigners
and a few artists and others admitted, and when the packing was ended
it was entirely closed for rearrangement. Paris itself was however a
wonderful sight, [31] as different from what it now is as from the then
state of any town we had seen. Picturesque, busy and lively beyond
measure, with a very few handsome buildings, and many fine views
afforded by its situation, but its narrow, crowded, dirty streets as inconvenient for the passenger as unwholesome for the resident, reminding
one continually of Boileau's "Embarras de Paris."[16] No trottoirs except
the Rue de la Paix, no gaz, no water but what was brought in carts and
carried into the house in buckets—the drainage abominable, the pavement of the street sloping to a gutter along the centre, which with a
heavy shower became a rivulet, over which, when broad, little gamins
were ready with planks for pedestrians to cross; one at the top of the
Rue du Bac was frequently a river occupying more than half its breadth.
For lighting, reverbères were slung over the centre of the street from
pullies attached to a rope stretched across it, and the cords for letting
them down for trimming or lighting had their ends in a little lock-up
hole in the adjoining house wall—an arrangement found very convenient by the mob in the great revolution for hanging up their victims "a
la lanterne." The Pont de la Concorde, or Pont Louis XVI as it was then
called, existed, and afforded one the same fine prospect it does now but
more picturesque if not so grand. The long line of the Tuileries and Louvre was there, but the quays were not so level, and[§] were much broken
beyond the Pont Neuf, the bridges were fewer and some of them very
steep; the Pont Neuf had its shops and its stalls and its shoeblacks and
boys with their placards: so-and-so "tond les chiens et les chats et va-t-
en ville."[17] The quays had no trees but more book and other stalls [32]
than now and long lines of cabriolets de place, holding one or two persons, with the driver sitting inside by your side, whilst lower down the
quay towards the barrière de Passy was a long line of two wheeled vehicles, holding from 4 to 10 or 12 persons, commonly called Coucous and
Pots de chambre which, as soon as they had got their complement,
started for Passy, Sèvres and other villages of the neighbourhood. For
Versailles and other more distant places on that line, places had to be

regularly secured in the lumbering diligences which started chiefly from
the small crowded streets then intervening between the Tuileries and
the Louvre. In other parts of Paris the Boulevards, if less grand than
they have been since, were more characteristic and perhaps more level.
The [§]trees cut down in 1830 were in full vigour, and under them was a
continuous line of booths, giving the whole the aspect of a constant fair.
The lines of houses which bordered them were very irregular, many of
them old, and the diversified aspect was encreased by the steep descents
of the road where crossed by the great thoroughfares of Montmartre, St
Denis, St Martin, etc. The Madeleine, the Bourse, the Arc de Neuilly, etc,
were only half built, and it was a standing joke for years after that only
one workman was employed upon each. The Rue Castiglione was only
begun. Of the new Rue de Rivoli one house, the Hotel de Rivoli, and the
Galerie Delorme were built, and arcades, but nothing more where the
Ministry of Finance is now, and in front of one or two other houses, and
the whole street ended just beyond the entrance to the Carousel. In the
Carousel the Venetian horses were still on the triumphal Arch when we
arrived but were soon taken down,[18] the car and the conducting figures
with the bridles in their hands remaining at least during the twelvemonth we were at Paris. [33] On the left hand of the river the lower colonnade of what was afterwards the palais de la Legion d'honneur and
du Conseil d'Etat and commencements of other large buildings showed
as elsewhere grand designs, with failure of means of execution.

But the most remarkable feature in Paris at that time was the unusual
aspect given to it by the presence of the army of occupation and the
crowds of foreigners brought by the late events, and the extraordinary
bustle and animation in the streets, in the shops and in all places of public resort. Among the inhabitants some no doubt felt annoyance and
humiliation at the presence of their victors, at the long lines of tents
under the trees of the Champs Elysées (not then laid out into streets)
occupied chiefly by British regiments—at the devastation of the Bois de
Boulogne for the huts for the German troops—at the foreign soldiers of
all nations which crowded their own barracks—at such ceremonies as
the celebration of the anniversary of the battle of Leipzig on the 18th
October[19] by a grand review on the Champ de Mars which they
explained as an ordinary parade—yet the general feeling was certainly
that of a great relief from the miseries and anxieties of the past years, a
confidence in the future, such as has rarely been since felt, a determination to enjoy and profit by the present activity and a reawakening of
speculation and individual enterprise. Judging from the gay looks of the

idle crowds of well dressed people in the Tuileries gardens and on the boulevards, from the brilliant displays at night in the shops of the Palais Royal, a favorite evening resort of foreigners, amused amongst other things at the shamefacedness with which dressed out females were allowed to exhibit themselves from dusk till ten, no one could have imagined that the country was [34] but just freed from a long period of strife, devastation and ruin. The theatres never were so full, and on Sundays and public fêtes when the weather permitted it seemed as if every inhabitant of Paris man, woman or child had turned out to enjoy it. The great day of a special display of the grandes eaux of Versailles for the distinguished foreigners is constantly present to my mind. The return at night was the most extraordinary, and how we all got safe home I never understood. The vehicles of all sorts, galloping along, racing and passing each other envelopped in clouds of dust, and amidst the wild cries of drivers of all nations, filled the broad road untill we approached Sevres where there was a deadlock. An arch of the bridge had been blown§ up in preparing for the defense of Paris and replaced by a temporary one which only admitted of one carriage passing at once—a very slow operation, rendered still worse by a deficiency in the usual police organisation. The road was kept chiefly by Austrian cavalry, whose white uniforms were usefully conspicuous in the dark but whose unintelligible language left them no means of conveying their directions but by signs and blows; the Russian postillions with their "Padi! Pashol!"[20] and other wild cries, would suffer no check to their galloping propensities, and when the Sevres blockage was reached there was nothing but a physical struggle as to who should cross first. Our French coachman got into a regular fight with an English gentleman whose carriage got entangled in ours. I and my brother were on horseback, and not understanding or not seeing the signs of an Austrian patrol I got a good blow on the back from the flat of his sabre. However we all got safe home in the course of the night without any real [35] mishap to cloud the recollections of the splendid scene we had witnessed.

My father was now enjoying himself much, and especially in the society of many of his old friends. Count Woronzoff, who commanded the Russian Army of Occupation, was the son of one with whom my father had long been on the most intimate terms. The Duc de Richelieu, the Comte Langeron and the Comte de Damas[21] had been my father's guests thirty years before on the borders of the Black Sea and, especially the Duke, were now very friendly. Count Segur, who at the same time had been French Ambassador to the Court of the Empress Catherine, was particularly empressé; and though from his attachment to the fallen Emperor he was now no longer of the dominant party, yet from his literary reputation,[22] his amiable manners and easy position, his life, his house was the centre of gathering of all that was most enlightened among the liberal society, with several of whom, such as Count Chaptal the chemist, Jean Baptiste Say the political economist, etc [my father was intimate]. Admiral Tchitchagoff, with whom my father had contracted a great intimacy during his last visit to Russia, was from this time an almost constant resident at Paris, since England had affronted him with its Alien-act arrangements. The most agreable family however that we saw much of was that of Made d'Andelau and her daughter, Made D'Orglande, in whose hotel in the fauxbourg St Honoré old Made D'Andelau lived. She was the daughter of Helvetius and my father had been much with them in his younger days before the Revolution, and I have still a locket with a miniature of Helvetius "donné par sa fille" [36] to my father. Made D'Orglande's house was now the centre of a good deal of the best society of the dominant party—neither the extreme liberal nor the "ultra-royaliste." Her sister, Made de Rozambeau (whose daughter either then or shortly after married Chateaubriand) was also frequently there, and to us they were all kind and friendly.[23]

Political events now went their course with little of sufficient moment to call the attention of us young ones. At the theatres there was a good deal of display of anti-Imperial feeling. On one occasion, on the first re-appearance of Mlle Mars after the cent jours during which she had exhibited Imperial enthusiasm, she was now called upon to make a kind of amende honorable on the stage.[24] When opportunities occurred there was much more shouting of "Vive le Roi!" than I ever heard subsequently under Louis Philippe, or Napoleon III, and the air of "Vive Henri Quatre!" was very generally played and sung with spirit, although in that respect nothing like the "Marseillaise" of turbulent times. One event which created an immense sensation was the escape of Lavalette.[25] My father and myself had been dining that day at Jean Baptiste Say's, and driving back to Passy at night the carriage was stopped at the barrière de Neuilly; my father alighting to find out the cause was told that orders were just come to close all the barriers and let no individual in or out on any pretext whatsoever, and they were in the act of receiving the order when we drove up. My father, in the pourparler with the officials who were shutting the gates, had got just outside them whilst I remained in the carriage inside—fresh and more stringent orders arrived and nothing would induce them either to let [37] my father in again or to let me out; so after a conference through the rails there was nothing for me to do but to return to Mr Say's and beg a night's lodging. It was only the next day that we could learn the cause, and it was a matter of no small wonder that, notwithstanding the extraordinary vigilance of the police, Lavalette could remain so long secreted in Paris and finally succeed in escaping for the frontier. A good deal of discontent began also to show itself on the part of the liberals at the execution of Labedoyère and Ney,[26] and on that of the ultras at the remissness in further contributions, but the great vent to the feeling was given in pamphlets and squibs. A very curious one was a *Dictionnaire des Girouettes*, a goodly sized 8vo volume, with short notices of all men who had figured in any degree in the events of the last 25 years, with as many weathercocks prefixed to their names as had been the governments under which they had served. Talleyrand stood out preeminently with a dozen such.[27]

In our private concerns, a sad event now brought on a complete change in my father's prospects and plans. He had originally intended that my brother should follow his own engineering career, and I was destined for the bar; but just before we left England my uncle, Jeremy Bentham, had expressed a wish to transfer his chambers in Lincoln's Inn to whichever of us should follow the law, as by the tenure under which he had them he could do so, to a nephew already a member of the Inn, but could neither sell nor bequeath them. I was then too young to be entered at Lincoln's Inn, and this motive, and some dissatisfaction at his (my father's) services [38] in Engineering not having been sufficiently recognised, induced him with our sanction to bring us both up for the bar, and my brother was duly entered and the chambers assigned to him; and now my father's intention was that we should remain another twelvemonth at Paris, under Mr Chiron's tutorship, and then return to England to enter my brother at least at College. The first check however was the breaking off with Mr Chiron; he got bit with animal magnetism,[28] devoted himself to M. Puysegur and, owing partly to the great discordance of these ideas with those of my father and partly to some affair with my sisters' governess, he left our house. About the same time, my brother fell from a swing in our garden at Passy, and though he did not seem hurt at the time he complained a day or two after of a pain and lump in his chest. As he had grown very rapidly my mother thought it might be weakness and inflammation of the lungs but nothing she could do had any effect—he gradually weakened and lost his appetite. After a few weeks we moved into Paris where medical assistance was more at hand, and took appartments in the Hotel de Rivoli, the only house then finished in the street, and where it was hoped that the airy healthy situation, and cheerful look out might be of service, but all was of no avail; after two or three more months of gradual sinking he died, in the latter end of March 1816, a few days after having completed his 17th year,[29] and a postmortem examination showed the cause to have been the breaking a bloodvessel in the fall from the swing and the consequent obstruction from a mass of clotted blood. My father felt the blow most severely, and entirely altered his future plans, giving up all thoughts of a speedy return to England. [39] The loss of the Lincoln's Inn Chambers, although of much minor importance, may also have had some influence on his mind, for they were so strongly associated in it with his brother's, and even his own early career, and he began to think of a lengthened stay in the South leaving it to future decision, according to circumstances, what course I should follow to make my way in the world. In the mean time we removed to Arcueil where he engaged an appartment in the house of M. Berthollet, the chemist, whose acquaintance my father had made at Ct Chaptal's. M. and Mde Berthollet, both advanced in age, were most friendly and made our stay of three or four months in their house very agreable, Made Berthollet amongst other things kindly undertaking to instruct my younger sisters in the harp, and generally taking much interest in all we did.

During this period I cannot say that I made much progress. When a boy, I was very short and chubby, and now in my sixteenth year I began to grow very rapidly which weakened me considerably. I had also for many years done almost everything conjointly with my brother; until his illness, I had always slept in the same room, taken all my lessons with him, gone through the same exercises with the same books, and although during the early part of his illness, not being at all aware of its serious nature I did not distress myself much about it, yet now that all was over, I could not muster courage enough to resume without him all that I had been used to do with him, and whatever I took to that had any connection with former habits, his image which haunted me day and night, and for many [40] a long year after, was ever present in my dreams, deprived me of all energy in the prosecution of classical or mathematical studies; and my father and mother, alarmed at the apparently weak state of my health, did nothing to press me, and rather encouraged me in turning my thoughts to other subjects. I had always been very fond of reading, which had been the only thing I did without my brother. History had been a favorite subject. When a very little boy,

my uncle had given me a copy of Rapin's *History of England* in two large
folio volumes which he had himself begun reading at the age of four.
Proud of poring over such bulky volumes, I eagerly studied them, and
acquiring a great taste for similar subjects I had before I left England
read through not only these, but also Hume's *History of England*, Henry
and Andrews' of England, Hooke's of Rome, Robertson's of Scotland,
and of Charles V, Levesque's French *History of Russia*, a bulky Russian
one of Peter the Great, besides various minor compilations of French,
Greek, and general history. Now at Paris and Arcueil, although I idled
away much time, I took to Velly, Vivaret and Garnier's interminable
History of France, Rollin's general history, and some others; but what
especially caught my fancy was the study of geography, and with some
natural taste for method and arrangement, stimulated probably by my
uncle's example and the perusal of some of his works, I set to tabulating
the geographical and statistical information I collected from books and
other sources. In this I was much encouraged by Alexander v. Humboldt, whose acquaintance my father had made very soon after our
arrival at Paris, and who with that liberal affability [41] which ever
prompted him to bring forward young men who showed any disposition to the pursuit of physical or natural science, offered me any assistance in the prosecution of my designs. I was collecting and arranging
data as to physical geography, mountain elevations, river courses, and
their basins, etc, and for that Humboldt communicated numerous notes
made in the Andes of Mexico and New Grenada which he had not then
yet published.[30] M. Chevalier also, the §librarian of Ste Geneviève, a
kind, excellent and remarkably well informed old man, gave me much
encouragement, and Humboldt before he left Paris kindly expressed his
hopes that he should hear of my progress, giving me at the same time an
introduction to one of the principal librarians of the Bibliothèque du Roi
of the Rue Richelieu, who would give me every assistance in the consultation of the books there. In this however I was disappointed; the gentleman in question, though very civil, said so much to me of the futility of
following up so inconstant and changeable a pursuit as geography [that
he] succeeded in disgusting me thoroughly with what I had commenced, and soon after our removal from the neighbourhood of Paris
turned my thoughts into other channels.

My father having determined to spend some years in a southern climate, and wishing us to see as much of the country as possible, conceived a singular plan for avoiding the dirt and discomforts of French
inns, which were then, and remained for many a long year afterwards,

rather disgusting for English tastes. He thought that if we had carriages we could sleep in, we might be quite independent, encamping in farmhouse yards, or even on roadsides, and sanguine as he ever was, he never thought of the drawbacks we were doomed to experience. [42] Much time was spent in the contriving and constructing the carriages, and the wretched weather—the summer of 1816 was one of the wettest on record—long delayed our departure.

At length, in the morning of the 21st August we got under way.[31] We had a coach with two horses which was to be arranged at night as my bed, and two long, kind of spring vans on two wheels each drawn by one horse; in one, were my father and mother's beds, and a piano, books, etc; the other was fitted for the accomodation of my three sisters and their governess. We had a half-English coachman, a peninsular cavalry soldier who had been early taken prisoner by the French and had remained in France after the peace, and proved for many years to be a most useful servant, and two French drivers for the vans. The weather seemed at length to have cleared up, and the first morning seemed propitious, but our troubles soon began. Before the day was over the springs of one of the vans gave way under the weight, and the other one fared little better the next morning. It was no easy matter to find places for encampment, §free from the annoyance of the curious inhabitants who naturally took us for travelling mountebanks or showmen. Near§ Etampes we had to make a halt for repairs and to get rid of the piano. Here however we were most hospitably invited by a very amiable family residing in the neighbourhood and spent a very agreable day in their beautiful grounds. After a fresh start we arrived towards dusk before Orleans, on the day of their great national fête, the St Louis; my father and I went on to find some good halting place, which as may naturally be supposed was not easy in a [43] large town. After some vain enquiries, my father sought out the Prefet,[32] to whom as to all other Prefets on our route he had strong letters of recommendation from the Duc de Richelieu, then prime minister. The Prefet was just gone to a grand official dinner, but came out to speak to my father, and gave orders that we should be admitted to encamp in the inner court of the Prefecture. We accordingly returned to our carriages; it was now late, the streets were illuminated and crowded with holiday folk, who eagerly followed our singular cavalcade expecting some grand "spectacle"—but when we were seen to enter under the illuminated arch of the Prefecture we were at once set down as belonging to the Royal family and greeted with a cry of "Vive le Roi!"

Here we made ourselves comfortable. We young ones had mixed too little in general society to feel anything of the ridicule that might be cast on the excentricity of our proceedings, and my father and mother did not care for it. The Prefet, Baron de Talleyrand, a nephew of *the* Talleyrand, and his wife were very attentive; they paid us a formal visit in the morning in our vans, and invited us to dinner, after which was one of the gayest evening parties I recollect. Madame de Talleyrand was an excellent musician, and after some preliminary displays the Prefet, the Premier President (Chief Judge of the Cour Royal) and three or four other gentlemen and ladies joined in some of those indefinite popular songs which give much scope for wit and humour, one of them, in turns, giving a verse in solo, and the others joining in chorus. After every variety of tone and inflection had been given to the varied phases of "Malbrouk s'en va-t-en guerre" in its fullest extent, and some others of the kind, "Cadet Roussel" was taken up, with impromptu verses [44] applied alternately to occurrences of the day or to persons present. The Prefet for instance in his turn came out with:

> Cadet Roussel eut mal aux dents
> Oui, Oui, Oui, vraiment
> Cadet Roussel eut mal aux dents
> C'est qu'il était Premier President

duly repeated in full chorus with irresistible effect, but immediately taken up by the Premier President in a deep, grave tone, with:

> Cadet Roussel eut un cheval
> Oui, Oui, Oui, vraiment
> Cadet Roussel eut un cheval
> C'est qu'il était Officier Municipal

followed by roars of laughter such as in our country would not, at that time at least, have been tolerated in a grave society composed of the elite of the aristocracy of the place.

From Orleans our next halt of two or three days was at Les Arpentilles the country house of the Count Chaptal, a short distance from Amboise on part of the estate of Chanteloup which he had bought as national property. He and his whole family were most amiable in their hospitality, and the sterling solidity of his mind and abilities was far more highly appreciated by my father than the gay frivolity we had left at Orleans. We had seen a good deal of him at Paris. The elder Napoleon, with a much higher appreciation than his nephew could ever be induced to entertain of the important services rendered to the nation by its men of science, had taken Chaptal under his special patronage, and Chaptal in return devoted much time to endeavours to replace from internal resources those colonial products of which France was at present deprived by the "Continental System" and English blockade.[33] His repeated efforts to crystallise [45] grape sugar had constantly failed, but in beetroot he was more successful, and he showed us over his promising establishment, the origin of those beetroot sugar manufactories, which in after years were enabled to compete with colonial sugars at equalised duties. Chaptal had already, when we were at Paris, taken us over a large wood-vinegar manufactory which, although I believe not his own, was one he had taken a great part in and was now very successful, as supplying acetic acid of any strength to give pungency, of which the ordinary wine vinegar had not enough for French tastes. Whilst at Les Arpentilles we drove over to Chanteloup, one of those splendid chateaux of the old French nobility, now §quite deserted and unfurnished but in its rich gildings and enormous fixed mirrors still remaining a melancholy memorial of past grandeur to be soon for ever effaced, for but few years later Chanteloup,[34] like many others, was sold to the "Bande noire," a name given to a company who bought up from the owners of national property old useless chateaux, to pull them down for the value of the materials.

On our way further south we stopped at Tours, to take up our two ponies and donkey whom we had left the previous year in charge of a friend, made a short halt at Les Ormes for my father to see his friend M. d'Argenson at his fine place, to which the Duc de Broglie succeeded,[35] and proceeded to Angouleme where my father, pleased with the country, determined to make a longer stay. Having presented his letters and met with great attention from two or three of the principal families who were asked to meet him at the Prefecture, and heard good accounts of the resources of the place, he engaged for the winter a country house about half a mile from the town off the Bordeaux road. "Le petit Girac" was comfortable and decently furnished, had a very [46] fair garden, and the surrounding country was pleasing and well wooded, but nothing in our minds by the side of the Puy Girault.

The time we here spent was not of any great advantage to me. I followed no regular courses and read very little in Greek or Latin, which I had been allowed to set aside since my brother's death. I pursued with some eagerness the statistical studies I had commenced at Paris, and amused myself with mathematics, music (the piano, for which a master regularly came out to us) and miscellaneous reading. We mixed also rather more in society, especially my elder sister and myself, my younger sisters going for some time regularly to a pension for lessons. The Prefet, M. Creuzé de Lessert, was a thorough Frenchman with ancien régime manners and ideas, a wit and a poet, having written volumes of chevaleresque poems on the §Table Ronde and similar subjects, very agreable and apparently cordial in his hospitality to us, but rather hollow and evidently incapable of any such sincere and steady friendship as we afterwards experienced under trying circumstances from French families with whom we became acquainted. Some coolness also—without any interruption of social intercourse—took place between him and my father, when in the winter considerable distress overtook the poorer population of the town. The extraordinarily wet summer had destroyed the harvest in many parts of the country, and bread, the chief article of food of the lower orders, was at famine price. Amongst various alleviating measures proposed, my father suggested that subscriptions should be entered into, not to give relief in money, but to supply the poor in distress with bread tickets by which they could obtain bread at ordinary [47] prices, the subscriptions furnishing the bakers with the means of obtaining the necessary supplies without loss or extravagant profit. This plan was eagerly taken up by the principal people of the town, and the Prefet found himself obliged to put himself at the head, but felt annoyed at not having originated that or any other measure as might have been expected from him, and in his heart did not thank my father for his interference. Many other acquaintance however made the time pass very agreably, the prime Minister's letters having at once proved the best introduction. We became particularly intimate with M. and Mde de la Molère. He belonging to an old French family, was Commander of the Gendarmerie of the department, and his wife was of a good Nantes family, both of them staunch Bourbonists and rather "Ultra," as were then styled those who thought the Government too lenient to the Bonapartists and Republicans—who were "plus Royalistes que le Roi"; from his position however M. de la Molère was necessarily ministerial and did not openly at least join in the Royalist saying that

> Quatre fléaux affligent ma patrie
> Decazes, Richelieu, la clémence et la pluie.[36]

They were often with us at le petit Girac and some of us were almost daily with them in the town. We were also at several little musical or dancing parties—always very merry ones—and gave two or three at home—and had frequent visitors. Col Darbaud-Jouques commanding the regiment in garrison at Angouleme, very fond of music, and taking great pains with his band—besides paying his addresses to Mlle de Mortegon whom he afterwards married. M. de Moutardier, a batchelor propriétaire, very fond of singing sentimental songs, accompanying himself on a [48] guitar slung round his neck by a blue ribbon—or of pathetically relating his dreadful sufferings during the one great event of his life—a voyage to the United States: "Feefty days—feefty days—alvèse seek—alvèse seek." M. and Mde de Gadbois, stiff in their petite noblesse, very cordial at first, till at one of our parties they saw come in a couple of my sisters' pension acquaintance who were not of the grade of society Madame associated with, and they left in a huff. Madame de St Avet, a rich young widow from the French West Indies, very pretty, with a lazy interesting laisser-aller and great enjoyment of society—but nothing more—and a number of those more or less agreable nobodies who, whatever they may be at home in the morning when no one sees them, render—or at least then rendered—the little social winter gatherings in French provincial towns so cheerful and pleasant. And although there was always some card playing—Boston or a bouillote for the gentlemen—that rage for écarté which a few years later overwhelmed all society had not yet come on.

The carnival over, these parties ceased, but there were several ceremonies which collected people together; one occasioned considerable excitement—the taking the veil by a lady not yet thirty who had been the life and soul of many a merry party and who had always seemed to enjoy the society of her friends as much as they did hers—the last person who could be supposed to devote herself voluntarily to a lifelong seclusion. Although therefore she gave out that the step was quite spontaneous and maturely considered, it could not but be rumoured that undue influence had been used. [49] She had money—she had a brother whose evidently covetous disposition, cold heart and want of principle made him rather generally disliked, and it was said that every effort had been used to persuade her that with her plain face she had little chance of a good marriage, and a dreary prospect of a comfortless home. However that may really have been, although the pomp of circumstance and grandeur of the ceremony made her go through it with apparent enthusiasm—yet her numerous friends who attended it could not but entertain sad misgivings as to the result—and when we saw her fine black hair mercilessly shorn off we could not but consider it as the immolation of a victim—whether these forebodings were realised or not could never be known—she was thenceforth dead to the world. The Easter ceremonies closed the "season," the fasting as much as the feasting, for the Jeudi saint which was as great a day for it as Good Friday, no one was to eat a morsel before 12, masses were attended at the different churches, alms were distributed to the poor who exposed their crippled limbs or their sores at the church doors—all was mortification and charity—till one o'clock when we sat down to a déjeuner at the La Molères, where the *maigre* was so disguised by the culinary art in such a variety of dishes that it might rival some of the best of the carnival suppers.

As the spring advanced we began to make excursions to explore such beauties of scenery or curiosities of nature as the neighbouring country afforded, and a new interest was now given to them by the purchase my mother made of De Candolle's great *Flore Française*.[37] She had [50] ever taken a great interest in plants. In London she had made friends with Aiton of Kew, with Forsyth of Kensington[38] and others, and wherever we settled, whether for months or for years, one of her first cares was to set up a flower garden. Here at Angouleme she had been particularly successful; her flowers came out with a luxuriance she had as yet had no experience of, and the sight of so many wild flowers new to her induced her to order De Candolle's work which was already recognised as the best Flora that had yet appeared. We had none of us been taught any botany. It did not lie at all in my father's line of pursuits, notwithstanding that both my uncle and my mother cultivated it in the light of a recreation of great interest. I regarded it perhaps as a mere amusement which did not take my fancy, but when the book arrived, opening it as a novelty, I was struck by the analytical tables for the determination of plants, which fell in with the methodical and tabulating ideas I had derived from the study of some of my uncle's works and from what I had attempted in geography and statistics. I immediately went out into the backyard, picked up the first weed I met with and set about finding out its name. It was the Salvia pratensis—not the easiest for a beginner—on account of the abnormal structure of the stamens—and I had not the slightest idea of what was meant by a calyx, a corolla or any of the most common botanical terms. All these I had to work out from the Introduction, and I spent the whole morning over the Salvia which seemed to me to have four instead of two stamens. By dint of perseverance I succeeded without any extraneous assistance, and thenceforth during the remainder of our stay at Le Petit Girac, one of my chief amusements [51] was to find out the names of the wild plants I picked up, but I went no further in botany, and did not yet commence collecting or drying plants.

In the summer we broke up our quarters to proceed farther south, taking again to our travelling vans, now getting much out of favor, especially with my sisters. My father however persisted in them as far as Bordeaux, but the inconvenience of these nocturnal encampments seemed to encrease so much that he there finally gave them up. He sent them on to Toulouse, to which place after a few days stay at Bordeaux we proceeded in our coach, which with our two riding ponies carried us all, my sisters not having at that moment any governess. The broad high roads, though many of them made originally at great expence, were then in a very different state to what they have since been brought to. Without the fatiguing but durable pavés of the north, their chief repairs consisted in the occasional laying down—at years of interval—a thick layer of half-broken stones, which in time ground into a choking dust in summer and deep mud in winter. There were two stages between Angouleme and Bordeaux, where in wet weather the ruts got so deep that post masters were authorised to yoke oxen in front of travelling carriages, and the two great rivers, the Dordogne at Cubzac and the Garonne§ at Bordeaux, had to be ferried over, the splendid bridges which now cross them being then unfinished. The weather however proved fine and we enjoyed the journey, but were not at all sorry to be once more at rest in comfortable rooms at the Hotel d'Astory at Toulouse.

Here my father met with a cordial reception from various persons to whom he had letters—including the "Autorités," propitiated by those from the Duc de Richelieu [52] who was still in power. He engaged for the winter a place of M. de Cambon's, called Caousou, with garden and grounds on the hill across the canal to the north, on the spot where the battle of Toulouse ended,[39] the last cannon shot that were fired having been picked up in the Caousou gardens, a residence which proved most comfortable as well as agreable, although out of the town, yet within a short walk of the best quarters; and although the Canal suburb, inhabited chiefly by boatmen and others depending on the port, had some drawbacks, it was very small compared to what it afterwards became. Toulouse was indeed very different then from the busy commercial town of recent times. Although hemmed in by its brick walls with quaint old gateways without any architectural pretensions, there were yet large districts within those walls where one scarcely met any one in the grass-grown streets—all life being centred in the two great squares of the Capitol and Bourbon, in the narrow crowded rue de Rome which connects them, in the Rue de la Pomme where were some of the most elegant shops, and in the commercial street parallel to the river, the aristocracy residing chiefly in the better streets at the east between the busy quarter and the promenades outside the walls. But picturesque as it was with its narrow irregular winding streets and horrible pavement of round pebbles, Toulouse was neither very clean nor sweet, and the water supply was only from carts and a few private wells. A rich friend of the city had indeed some years back bequeathed to it a considerable some of money on condition that within a fixed number of years after his death a public fontaine should be flowing in the Place Rouaix, but nothing had as yet been done. The municipality [53] indeed hesitated to the last moment, and the legacy was about to lapse when at length they determined on working it out on a large scale and spent two or three times the amount in carrying a derivation from the Garonne through a large filtering channel, raising the water by machines and distributing it into public fontaines in most of the principal open places.

This winter of 1817–18, though not the most profitable, was perhaps the most agreable of my life, devoted as it was to mere amusement, without a thought or care for the future. We almost immediately on our arrival got upon terms of more or less intimacy with the best of the French families of the various political and social creeds and castes here assembled who, however little cordiality they might show amongst themselves, were all full of prevenances to their English visitors—even to some who threw themselves forward without introductions, and who afterwards proved unworthy of the confidence reposed in them. The Duke of Wellington's campaign from Bayonne to Toulouse had created a great impression in our favor, owing chiefly to the discipline so rigidly enforced in the British and so shamefully relaxed in the French army, even in their own country—so that the hostile troops came to be regarded almost as deliverers from pillage, extortion and disorders of all kinds. The last battle, when it was dying out within sight of the walls, was watched we were told with the deepest interest from the gate towers and other commanding spots by many of the principal inhabitants, in the hopes of bringing about some termination to the calamities which oppressed them—for they were perfectly in the dark as to what was going on in the north. And when the next morning the cessation of hostilities, the Emperor's abdication [54] and the entry of the Allies into

Paris was publicly announced, great, indeed universal, was the rejoicing, and the acclamations which accompanied the entry into the town of
the British troops were most cordial and hearty. The feeling was
encreased by the generally believed, if not finally authenticated report,
that before the last battle Marshal Soult had received the despatches,
officially confirming the intelligence of which he had had unauthenti-
cated reports, but of which the English were totally ignorant, and commanding the cessation of hostilities; but that knowing that the[§] Duke's
army was considerably weakened by the fatigues of the campaign and
much encumbered with their wounded (it was believed that they[§] had
determined to retreat after the battle[§] but were stopped by the news of
the armistice) and confident in his own means of success, he would not
lose the opportunity of a final triumph, and would not open the despatches till the battle was over and he found that he would at any rate
have to abandon Toulouse.

We had soon established ourselves at Caousou, which we all liked so
much that my father entertained thoughts of purchasing it, had not
some difficulties occurred as to the title. My sisters' governess returned
to us from England, and masters for music and dancing attended them
from the town. I continued the life I led at Angouleme, taking few lessons besides music, reading much, but rather desultorily, and mixing
more in society. By Christmas we had become acquainted with most of
the principal French resident families as well as with the *Autorités*, and
with a few English, who like ourselves had come to spend the winter,
and our exchange of cards on New Years Day was very extensive. The
custom then was that on that day every one should call personally on all
those whose [55] acquaintance they wished to keep up—leaving cards
from which every one kept lists of their acquaintance, nobody of course
being at home to receive, except four or five of the principal Autorités—
the Prefet of the department, the Mayor of the town, the General commanding the division, the Receveur-General and the Bishop, and their
receptions were on the previous evening when every one who had pretensions to be included in their future parties made the round of the
five. Some years later personal visits were in many places dispensed
with (except to the Autorités) by sending round cards and still later in
some southern towns as in some Italian ones, by advertising subscriptions to the hospitals in lieu of New Years visits.

The Carnival of 1818 at Toulouse was a long and a most brilliant one
as far as dinners, balls and other social amusements were concerned. No
apparent traces remained of the wars of 1814 or of the famine of 1816, all

classes seemed prosperous and to devote themselves to amusement alone during the two months it lasted from the Jour des Rois (twelfth night) to the Mardi gras, which was this year on the 3d of March. During that time, I danced thirty-four nights—commencing usually about 9, and §the greater balls lasting till from 2 to 8 in the morning, and entering heartily into the spirit of the time I enjoyed them all most thoroughly. Every Monday was the official ball at the Prefecture. The Prefet, M. de Saint-Chamans, was an amiable, good-natured single man, a perfect gentleman, who received his guests with courtesy, and went through the routine of his business satisfactorily—but nothing more, and in the then quiet times nothing more was required—but his sister, Made de Lambertye who did the honours for him, [56] played her part admirably, and the Prefecture Monday receptions—balls during the carnival— were crowded. And there were then few or none of those party bickerings which later induced the vanquished political party in country towns to keep aloof from the *autorités*. The rooms were large, handsome and well lighted, the music and refreshments good, though without regular suppers, and every one appeared as much at ease as in a private party, not being ashamed to show that they amused themselves. The necessary official invitations however occasioned a great comparative preponderance of young men, and as each dancing lady entered the room, she was set upon by a crowd, who like myself did not care to miss a dance, and engaged at once for the whole evening. One evening it was announced that an important addition was coming from an Irish family just arrived, and all was eager expectation; but when the door opened for their entry there was a sudden retreat before Mrs and the five Miss Shannons. Four of them, great gaunt girls, with plain faces not set off by any of those little elegancies of toilette and manner to which French ladies had accustomed one, were enough to repel the most venturesome; the fifth however was very pretty and was immediately pounced upon, but few asked her a second time. The poor girl had an unfortunate impediment in her speech which precluded all talk, as she could bring out no replies but in harsh, discordant, unintelligible monosyllables—so that the Shannons were thenceforth voted a dead weight at all parties to which they succeeded in procuring invitations.

Thursday was the reception day at the Premier President's, M. Hocquart, a fine gentlemanly man, considered to be an excellent Judge, and most highly esteemed in his private character, with an amiable daughter. There was no dancing at his house, but he gave occasional dinners, and his evening parties were well attended. Every [57] Wednesday we had a medium ball and supper at our own house of Caousou, which seemed to be enjoyed by the young folks, and at which we had some amusement, in contriving to balk the manoeuvres of a few who tried to intrude, for the sole object of feasting on pâté de foie gras and other delicacies. Tuesdays and Fridays were often taken for the grand balls and suppers of those who only gave one or two in the season, and Sunday evenings were perhaps the most pleasant of the whole, small parties with a pianoforte dance amongst intimate friends at the D'Aiguesvives'. He, one of the judges of the Cour Royale—Madame a very amiable person, with a very pretty, lively daughter, then about to be married to an excellent young man, but who was not much to her liking, and the result was unfortunate—one of those cases where *mariages de convenance*, having led to bad results, induce us to declaim against them generally; but so far as our experience goes in the French provincial towns such cases are very few compared to those where mariages brought about by parents and mutual friends without any special previous attachment on the part of the young people have turned out to their real happiness, but which on that very account are but little noticed by the scandal-loving world.

§For the close of the Carnival we danced thirteen consecutive nights, and the grand Mardi gras ball, commencing at 9, was not over till past nine on the following morning; and this we were assured was nothing to what had occurred the previous year when, [58] by relays of musicians and occasional rest, first of one party then of another, they had kept it up till the small hours of the following night, shutting out Lent during the whole of Ash Wednesday. Now however all dancing ceased, except one ball always permitted at mid-Lent, and social gatherings were limited to evening receptions and a few dinners, Toulouse then standing very high in the gastronomic world. The poultry market in the Place Bourbon on the Lundi and Mardi gras was the finest display I ever saw of turkeys, capons, poulardes, pigeons of a large race unknown in the north, with the flesh almost as white as that of a chicken, ducks, etc. Game had been abundant through the winter; the truffle season had been good. There were many houses also where money was not grudged to secure good materials, animal and vegetable, and skilful artists to work upon them, so that although in the great run of Toulouse cookery garlick and greese may have been too prevalent for northern tastes, yet in well cooked repasts the admixture was so refined that I observed English who professed the greatest horror of the slightest contamination of the noxious bulb thoroughly enjoy various dishes in which they did not detect the *soupçon* of garlick to which the cook's success was chiefly due. The culinary art was indeed that year at least so highly prized that a society of gentlemen—one of them a magistrate, M. Combettes de Caumont, with whom my father got on terms of intimacy as a man of superior intellectual acquirements—met every fortnight at dinner at each other's house in turns, on which occasion the host had to produce a new dish, and at the end of the season a previously [59] fixed prize was carried off by the one whose invention had met with the most general approval.

Besides the large general acquaintance made by these social gatherings, we became intimate with a few who proved in the sequel staunch and valuable friends, and none more so than the family of General Partouneaux. He was an old soldier who in the turbulent times of the early wars of the Revolution had risen from the ranks, but had had a good education and proved an excellent officer. He became in great favour with the Emperor, and when in the disastrous retreat from Moscow he and the troops under his command were surrounded and captured by the Russians, Made Partouneaux, deeply hurt by the reproaches cast on him in the [   ] bulletin,[40] and knowing them to be both unmerited and insincere, wrote immediately to the Emperor. Napoleon did not, as he never would, retreat publicly from what he had said, right or wrong, but in order to show that his regard for the General was not really diminished, sent her a flattering letter, with two bourses (scholarships) at the University of Turin for her two eldest boys. After the Restoration, General Partouneaux returning from his Russian captivity, reentered the service under the new Government to which he remained a devoted adherent, and was now General commanding the Toulouse military division. His wife, of a good Piedmontese family, was a charming person, not brilliant or showy, rather quiet and unobtrusive, but with that pleasing and lady like manner, sound sense, well stored mind and kind disposition which imparted a peculiar charm to her society and conversation. Their family consisted of three sons: the eldest, a cavalry officer, was absent with his regiment and I never saw [60] much of him. The second, "Tonin," destined for a civil career,[41] was precisely of my own age and we soon became very great friends. He was lively and full of esprit, entered heartily into the amusements of his age and position, but without any frivolity; he was thoroughly well principled, and the cares bestowed on his education had given him a taste for literature and other healthy pursuits. The younger son, Bathilde, still at college, turned out one of those men not uncommon in the south, whose qualities and conduct are unexceptionable, but who with little or no ambition make no show and are content to pass their lives quietly in the position in which circumstances have placed them, with sufficient prudence to prevent them from falling below it, but with no temptation to make any efforts to rise above it.

In another division of the Toulouse Society, the Protestant, chiefly commercial branch, the Courtois family, the principal bankers of the place, were distinguished for the services they were always ready to render and on many trying occasions did render to foreigners, and especially to English. Most scrupulous as well as liberal in their dealings, all of them closely attending to their business with sound heads and clear minds, they stood high in general estimation and carried on a very thriving business. At the time of our arrival the head of the family was a little old gentleman in a pigtail, whose principal occupation appeared to be banking and eating, indulging perhaps too much in the latter, for it was after the first of their great dinners to which I was invited, at which he was supposed to have partaken too freely of the good things before him, that he was taken ill and died in a few days. He left four sons, all partners, the [61] eldest and chief manager, in a pigtail and long morning coat like his father, but tall and imposing looking, was a steady quiet père de famille—rarely leaving home, seeing very little of the world, but [to] those who attended at his country house or his dinner table, always courteous and obliging, apparently well informed but never brilliant. His wife was still less to be seen in society, an English lady in delicate health, strictly religious and devoted to her children, three boys then very young, but all destined one day to join or to replace their father and uncles in carrying on the "house." These three batchelor uncles, still young, only resembled their elder brother in their excessive courtesy and obligingness and in their steady devotion to their business in the morning; their evenings were spent in society. Fond of dancing and small talk, theatres and concerts, eschewing the card table and never heard of in connection with discreditable amusements, they were all three heartily welcomed at all parties although usually all three together. Auguste the elder, "le plus courtois des Courtois," tall and gaunt-looking, was soon to lose his position as a young man; Henri the next, was the one we took to the most, as with all the good qualities of the others he had the most general information, knowledge of the world and mental abilities. Felix the youngest, was scarcely below Henri in these respects, and had acted as Caissier to the bank since he was nine years old. On our visit to Toulouse in [   ][42] he alone was the sur-

vivor and with his nephews carried on the business, which is still continued by I believe a younger generation with the same general character, although the strictness of the religious ideas they have inherited
from their grandmother keeps them out of general society. During our
first stay at Toulouse, as [62] well as on every subsequent occasion when
we have had intercourse with southwestern France, this house of Courtois has proved one upon whom we could always rely implicitly for
kind attention, sound advice and assistance to ourselves or our friends.

Among the English who like ourselves had come to spend the winter
at Toulouse, or those who might be considered as settled there, we
made some agreable acquaintance, and contracted a friendship which in
after days proved most valuable with Dr Russell, an Irish physician of
great ability in his profession, which however having independent
means he was not then carrying on. He had married a French lady during the peace of Amiens and was now settled at Toulouse, bringing up
with great care a young family already numerous, and much enjoying
his hospitable reception, chiefly among the most intellectual portion of
the Toulouse society. He was a man who from his superior mind and
agreable conversation was always sure to make his company acceptable
and more than any one[§] I ever knew had the peculiar knack of extracting something worth knowing from any person he came in contact
with—whether an old acquaintance or a stranger casually met with in a
diligence or other public place, where most of our countrymen would
have maintained a dignified silence. He never left Toulouse except for
short visits, chiefly in later life to a married daughter. When some years
after our first visit his Irish property became unproductive he resumed
practice at Toulouse, with great success and in hearty concurrence with
the principal medical men of the place, with whom he contrived to keep
on terms of intimate friendship, much to their as well [63] as to his own
credit; and in his medical capacity, as well as from his sound sense in
general matters, he was in later times of great use to us all, especially to
my mother and elder sister in her misfortunes. He lived happy and universally respected to some years beyond 80. Three of his sons went into
the E. India Company service; the fourth, entering into the church,[43] has
long been settled in a living in Buckinghamshire; one daughter married
at Bordeaux, another to an eminent English physician; and of all his children only one died before him. Among the other English who contributed to make our winter society agreable were Mr Archdall and his
niece,[44] Major and Miss Spottiswoodes, General and Mrs Whittingham,
and a few others, whom however we subsequently lost sight of.

Before Lent was over, the attention of the Toulousains as well as of a great part of the country became absorbed in one of those Causes celèbres to which French procedure, however well calculated to elicit the truth in ordinary cases, gives so theatrical a turn when special circumstances have given to them any general interest, and on this occasion the whole town was kept in a state of eager excitement for above a month.[45] About a twelvemonth previously, a murder of unparallelled atrocity had been committed in the little town of Rodez, under circumstances unusually complicated. Six or seven men and one or two women had acted as direct participators in the crime, two women were either unwilling witnesses or indirect participators present, from two to five persons had more remotely contributed [65]§ to the deed with more or less of guilty knowledge, and a child had been a concealed but innocent and terrified witness to the whole. The murdered man and the two principal murderers[46] were men of education and§ believed to be intimate friends; belonging to the gentry of the place, they were connected moreover by family ties [and] almost daily intercourse; some of the accomplices were of the most degraded in social position,[47] and the various motives which appeared to have brought them all into combination were pecuniary gain, personal hatred, political revenge, or mere hire. At first whatever sensation the crime may have produced [was felt] in the town where it occurred, but little was heard of it at Toulouse; the worst details only came out in the course of a long investigation, and the little town of Rodez, capital of the ancient Rouergue, now Departement de l'Aveyron, lay in the heart of the mountains within the range of the Cour Royale of Montpellier and but very little in connection with Toulouse. Owing to the high state of local feeling however which gradually arose, it had been endeavoured to remove the trial of those on whom suspicion had fallen to some other place; but the Court of Montpellier, after having once acceded to the application, finally referred it to the tribunal of Rodez, where some of the parties were found guilty. On appeal to the Cour de Cassation, it was shown that the evidence had been improperly dealt with; and under some influence probably exercised by the knowledge that further investigation had given a very different colour to some of the facts disclosed, that Court, although it could only take cognisance of defects in form, took advantage of some inadvertencies in the procedure to quash the trial and direct a new [64]§ one, which was now ordered to take place at Alby, within the rule of the Cour Royale of Toulouse. A fresh preliminary investigation took place, within earshot as it were of the Toulousains; new and unexpected complications of detail were gradually disclosed. It became known that the most celebrated advocates of the Toulouse bar were engaged on behalf of the accused, those among the judges who were reputed the most able were appointed to hold the trial, the public prosecutor, Procureur du Roi, as well as the advocate for the partie civile (the murdered man's son) were equally eminent, and their whole powers were expected to be called out. Although the witnesses to be examined could be reckoned by hundreds, yet the direct evidence as yet obtained had been scanty, or vague and contradictory. One of the accused who had announced intentions of confessing and as we express it, "turning King's evidence," was the next morning found dead in his cell, apparently from the effects of poison,[48] and the greater part of the horrible details were repeated, exaggerated, disputed or contradicted on the authority of public rumour, which it was well known would be allowed full play during the proceedings. And herein lay the great difference between the French and the English procedure. Both admit the fallacies and frequent injustice of public rumour and its baneful effect on the minds of judges and especially of juries, even though it may [be] founded on facts. To obviate these evils, our system tells the juries not to listen to it and dismiss from their minds what they have already heard; the French endeavour to sift it to the bottom. They therefore admit almost unlimited hearsay evidence, which we so strictly proscribe, and often court expressions of opinion on the part of witnesses from which our judges would recoil with horror.

[66] The trial commenced on the 25th March[§49] and with the exception of Sundays and the necessary Easter interruption occupied thirty-five consecutive days to the 5th May. Numbers of persons went to Albi to follow the course of Proceedings, and each day the report of the day's sitting was printed in an 8vo sheet or half sheet of close type and distributed in Toulouse the following morning at 10 or 11 o'clock, when groups collected in every street, reading and discussing the details; the reports were in every one's hands, and little else was talked of with unflagging interest till the verdict was delivered. The facts elicited were these. The victim, M. Fualdès, was a retired magistrate, stated to have been much respected but who certainly had led a rather irregular life, and during the Cent Jours had made himself enemies by political leanings in his administrative capacity. Since then he had led a more quiet life with his wife, a devout lady who saw little of the world, his only son being married and living out of the town (of Rodez). He (the father) had contracted debts to the amount of about 48,000 francs, but had recently sold an estate for 68,000 fr. with a view to paying them off and had

received the purchase money chiefly in bills. Of these he had disposed of some, and had negotiated one for 2000 fr. on the day of the murder with the assistance of Bastide, a connection or relative of his, whom he strongly patronised, who, living at a short distance from Rodez, came into the town daily, always put up at M. Fualdès and appeared to have been in his intimate confidence in matters of business. Jausion, another friend and relative, was also closely connected with Fualdès in business and family concerns, and Made Jausion and her sister Mde Galtier, closely related to Bastide, were Made Fualdès' most intimate friends. On [67] the fatal 19th March, Bastide had been heard to say, in conversation with Fualdès, not to forget that evening when they would settle accounts, and at 8 o'clock Fualdès left his wife with two friends, telling them that he was going out on business. In a little frequented street, Rue des Hebdomadaires, he was set upon by a number of men who thrust a handkerchief in his mouth and carried him into a house of ill fame in the neighbourhood kept by a man and woman of the name of Bancal. Here they first made him sign several papers, then stretched him on the kitchen table and cut his throat. Jausion struck the first blow but was nervous and was unsuccessful. Bastide, more determined, struck deep. Bancal and a man named Colard, who appeared to have a personal feud with Fualdès, held his legs, whilst the woman Bancal caught the blood in a pail which she then gave to her pigs; a man named Bach, one of the contrivers of the scheme, a porter named Bousquier[§] and a half witted man named Messonier, one or both casually hired to assist, looked on, as well as a young woman, Colard's mistress, and perhaps the Bancal's eldest daughter. Two hurdy-gurdy players had been engaged to ply their instruments in the street, at the end of which were posted sentinels to give warning of any danger. They then wrapped the body in a rug, tied it to two poles placed on the shoulders of Bancal, Bach, Bousquier[§] and Colard, who carried it to the banks of the Aveyron, Bastide heading the convoy with a double barrel gun, and Jausion and another following, one with a gun, the other unarmed; reaching the river without opposition, they threw the body in, expecting it to be carried off by the rapid current, and trusting to some of Fualdès supposed irregularities to account for his absence. The body however floated and was found the next morning just below the town, caught by a mill dam. The wound was such as to preclude all suspicion of suicide. The police was instantly set to work. Fualdès' cane, found in the Rue [68] des Hebdomadaires and probably dropped in the scuffle, and his handkerchief near Bancal's door gave indications of the locality of the crime. It became soon known also that early in the morning after the murder, Jausion had come to Fualdès' house, with his wife and Made Galtier, and whilst they were with Mde Fualdès, he had gone in to Fualdès' cabinet, opened his bureau, and abstracted from it papers and money and some reports about Bastide's suspicious conduct; induced perquisitions in the abodes of Bastide and Jausion as well as at Bancal's [were] followed by the arrest of the two gentlemen as well as of all who were ascertained to have been that evening at Bancal's; the ladies Jausion and Galtier were also arrested but subsequently released, it having become evident that they were perfectly ignorant of what had been going on.

It was a long while before any positive implicating evidence could be obtained, but where so many not yet in custody were concerned as principals, or§ had a direct knowledge of the deed, they could not all abstain from indirect hints or unguarded expressions, and after a time Bousquier, the hired porter, made a declaration detailing with more or less of accuracy the principal circumstances. The Bancals' youngest daughter, a little girl of 8 or 9, being ill at the hospital, stated that on that night she had been sent up stairs, but hearing a great noise of men she was frightened, slunk down into the kitchen, and unperceived by her mother got into a bed under the stairs, separated by a curtain only from the scene, of which she gave an account, as observed through a hole in the curtain, but evidently tainted by the feelings of terror. Bancal, the father, then showed some intention of confessing, but died suddenly in prison with symptoms which gave a suspicion of poison. But what [69] gave the most intensity to the dramatic excitement of the public, was the conduct of a Madame Manson, whose partial revelations, assertions and contradictions showed her to have been either an unwilling witness or an indirect agent in the case. She was well connected, but had been some time separated from her husband, and had led an irregular life. She was in the Bancals' kitchen on the fatal evening, and on the approach of the men bringing in their victim, the woman Bancal thrust her into an adjoining cabinet from whence she heard all that passed. As soon as the deed was done, some noise she made was heard by Bastide, who dragged her out and would have sacrificed her on the spot, but on the remonstrance of Jausion that they had enough of one corpse to dispose of, they contented themselves with making her swear secrecy on the dead body. When her presence at the time became known, it was surmised that she had been employed to make an appointment there with Fualdès, and she was placed on her trial with the others, but though this was never cleared up, it appeared more probable that it was some other rendezvous that had brought her there at an hour which fortuitously only clashed with that of the murder.

The first trial had established to the satisfaction of all the criminality of Bastide, Colard and the Bancals, the participation of Bach and Bousquier, and the presence of the halfwitted Messonier and some others, but many believed that Jausion had not been sufficiently identified, and the hints dropped by Made Manson, and others at unguarded moments, that all the guilty were not in custody gave rise to the impression that the plot had much wider ramifications, and had been intended to have had much more awful [70] results than had been hitherto shown. As the second trial proceeded, much was disproved, many conjectures fell to the ground, but the enormous mass of idle gossip, gravely detailed and daily squabbled over between the witnesses, the accused, the advocates and the judges, the gradual and evidently partial revelations of Bach and Bousquier, and above all the reticences, explanations, and contradictions, the boldness and the faintings of Made Manson [continued], till at last at an advanced stage of the proceedings, provoked by the taunts of Bastide, she came out with a full statement of what she had seen, the terrible nature of which and of the threats hanging over her seemed partly to account for her future conduct. All tended to keep up public attention through the whole six weeks, the last days of which were taken up by the impassioned appeals of the eminent lawyers concerned. The principals were all found guilty. Bastide, Jausion and Colard were executed,[50] protesting their innocence to the last; the others were sent to the galleys. The woman Bancal was respited in the vain hope that she might assist in the new trial of suspected persons—one who was believed to have been the "Monsieur" who followed the corpse with Jausion, a Commissaire de Police who was believed to have assisted in keeping the coast clear during the time of the deed, and a third, suspected to have taken a subordinate part. This third trial took place in the following winter at Albi, but the great interest in the drama was gone, and some said for want of sufficient proof, others that because it was thought enough blood had been shed, the jury acquitted all three.

Before[§] the summer of 1818 had come on my father gave up all idea of settling at Toulouse, and thought that a twelvemonth[§] at Montauban, where the Protestant College or University Faculté de Theologie Protestante gave excellent opportunities for instruction might be advantageous to us all, but we [71] long kept up a connection with our Toulouse friends, and during the following year I frequently rode over for a day or two to see them, putting up usually at our friends the Partouneaux. It was on one of these occasions that I found the "Société" of the place much excited with one of those unfortunate occurrences which gave so great a check to the friendly hospitality shown by the French to our countrymen the first years of the reestablishment of peace. A Col and Mrs Coehorn, with their family consisting of a daughter just grown up, three boys and one or two little children, had established themselves in a very good house on the Promenade, and at first were little seen or heard of, they being apparently occupied with the education of the children. But on observing, as we were told, the readiness with which English families were received in the French Society, they got formally introduced to some of the Autorités through their banking connections, paid a round of visits, gave some dinner parties in imitation of ours, and when we left Toulouse had succeeded in establishing themselves on a footing of intimacy with several of our French friends. Some time after, a young Englishman, Mr Bramley, of a very good Yorkshire family and as we heard heir to a considerable property, travelling through Toulouse became acquainted with the Coehorns, formed an attachment to the daughter and a match was arranged. The wedding day was fixed, grand preparations were made and invitations to it accepted by several of the principal personages of the place, Mr Ellison, an English clergyman who had come to the South for the benefit of his health, having at the earnest sollicitation of the bridegroom [72] agreed to perform the religious part of the ceremony, a proceeding the irregularity of which had not then yet been established. A few days however before the one fixed for the wedding, Mr Bramley[§] received a letter from England which induced him to[§] request Col Coehorn to defer the wedding for a week. This[§] was positively refused, and Thursday next or never insisted upon. Mr Ellison, however, learning that intelligence had been received which required explanations, declined the responsibility of celebrating the wedding without them. Mr Bramley a few days later received a further letter, which[§] he showed to Col Coehorn, and proposed that it should be submitted to two of their friends and acquaintances at Toulouse (Gen Sir S. Whittingham and Mr Archdall) and if upon reading they thought the marriage ought to be proceeded with, he said he was quite ready to conclude it. Col Coehorn however refused to allow the letter to be shown, and had therefore, on the evening before the appointed day, to countermand everything and go round to his French friends to announce the postponement, laying all the blame on the unjustifiable conduct of the clergyman. All were warm in the sympathy they showed, and indignant against Mr Ellison, who bore it all with great patience, untill one day, Col Coehorn meeting him on the public promenade, insulted him in so public a manner that he thought it his duty to have the matter settled in the only way open to him. The Tribunal de Police Correctionelle took charge of it, and before a large audience, comprising some of the élite of the French Society, it was proved that Col C. had a previous wife living, that Mrs C. at the time of her marriage had had a previous husband living, that Col C's quasi-military career in the West Indies had been anything but honourable, and that the family could not be well received by their countrymen. His Toulouse acquaintance, after this exposure, hurt at having been so imposed upon by plausible statements and agreable manners, felt it as a lesson to avoid for the future any advances to English who should not be provided with very good recomendations.

3

Montauban to Montpellier, 1818–22

Moving to Montauban early in the summer,[1] [73] we settled ourselves in the Maison Collet, agreably situated in a large garden above the high bank of the Tarn at the end of the public Promenade, and here I led a very different life from that of Toulouse. We made acquaintances, went to a few balls and parties in the winter and gave one or two at home, but these were no longer occupations. I entered as a student at the Faculté, followed closely various courses[§]—the higher branches of French and Latin litterature—the latter under Prof. Encontre, an excellent scholar but a Gascon, whose principles were (it was said by his pupils) que toutés lés lettrés sont faités pour être prononcéés, ringing upon the final s's and t's—Natural Philosophy under Benedict Prevost, belonging to the Geneva Prevost family, a worthy and charming old man, well versed in Physics, as they were then understood,[2] with a remarkably clear, methodical head and gentlemanly manners. Very fond of coffee, he admitted like Fontenelle that it might indeed be a poison, but a very slow one, for with its constant use for above 70 years it had not yet killed him.[3] During the reign of the Continental System the scarcity of the berry had induced him, like many others, to try a number of substitutes, and [he] found none equal in point of flavour to the seed of the yellow flag, Iris pseudacorus, but this was of little use for, abundant as the plant is in the country, it was very rare that any appreciable quantity of the seed could be saved from the ravages of insects. I also followed a course of Mathematics, and of Hebrew, in which I went through the greater part of the book of Genesis so as to familiarize myself with the peculiar construction and notation of the language, a subject of great interest to me, as I had gone [74] a good deal into the comparison of the grammars and alphabets of the various languages I had more or less learned. I experienced great kindness also from the worthy and excellent Dean of the Faculty, Mr Frossard, a fine, venerable looking man, much respected by all who knew him, and father of the Pasteur Frossard, subsequently so well known to English and other Protestants in the South West of France, and who at this time was one of my fellow pupils.[4]

At home I devoted a good deal of time to languages, especially Span-ish, to Music, and to drawing, in all of which we had lessons daily, or at least 5 times a week. Several of the superior orders of Spanish refugees were settled at Montauban, and we saw a good deal of some of them. M. Cambronero, who had been one of King Joseph's ministers—of the interior I believe—was a man of very general information, agreable gentlemanly manners and well-cultivated mind;[5] his wife, like the ladies of several§ Spanish men of science and intelligence I have known, almost a non-entity—Mlle Cambronero their daughter a roundfaced, jolly, goodhumoured girl who would chatter and dance away till "ma chemise est trempée comme une soupe," caring for little but the amusement of the moment. M. Buron [was] a single, middle aged man, a Member of the Madrid Academy, well versed in Spanish litterature, and a good scholar in many respects besides taking interest in Natural History and other sciences; and being now in straightened circumstances, he readily undertook to instruct me in the Spanish language for a very moderate remuneration, upon my giving him some assistance in difficult points of French and a little insight into English. Of this I eagerly availed myself, and it was not long before I could get on by myself, in *Don Quixote* after having rapidly got through *Gil Blas;*[6] and before we left [75] Montauban, I managed to keep up conversation in Spanish with him and the Cambroneros and with one or two other Spaniards who had not succeeded in learning French. Some idiosyncracies of language in these Spaniards amused me much. With all his learning and experience, even M. Buron could not distinguish between the b and the v. In writing he would lengthen the first stroke of the v, so as to bring it almost to the b, and in speaking he would say "vain" or "bain," "vache" or "bache," with the most perfect indifference; and among most Spaniards I have found this confusion of the b and the v as general as that of the b and the p among Germans.

I got very fond of music. I had practised a great deal on the piano at Toulouse, as well as in earlier times, and I had there learnt the violin from our dancing master, a fussy Italian and a very good musician, M. Lamarra, or as we used to call him, M. l'Embarras. Here at Montauban I took much to this instrument and during the winter once or twice a week in the evenings, joining two MM. Debia and another, took the second violin or the alto in Haydn's concertos. We attended a few concerts in the town, and had occasionally musical parties at home, though generally we led a much quieter life than at Toulouse.

It was here at Montauban also that I first took at all steadily to botany. At Toulouse I had gone on occasionally finding out the names of a few plants from the adjoining hills but had almost given it up; but coming over here in May§, and lodging almost in the country, [76] my interest was revived, and the gathering and naming§ plants as yet new to me added wonderfully to the charm of the numerous excursions we made along the very pretty banks of the Tarn, and the rich wooded valley of the Aveyron. At my mother's suggestion, I first began to dry specimens for preservation on the 22d August, carelessly perhaps at first, but before the season was over, I had collected between one and two hundred species. And as in the course of the winter M. Benedict Prevost's lectures and the arrival of successive livraisons of 3 vols of a *Dictionnaire d'Histoire Naturelle*, then in course of publication,[7] began to open out my ideas on the wonderful variety and combinations of natural objects, I entered diligently into their study; and from the early spring of 1819, the formation and encrease of my herbarium became one great object of my pursuits, and for many a long year after I never let a single month pass without making more or less considerable additions to it. In selecting the scenes of my botanising excursions, I was a good deal guided by an old Flora of Montauban by Gatereau, and for a short time was disposed to restrict my collections to the plants of the country; but the publication of the first volume of De Candolle's *Regnum Vegetabile* much enlarged my views,[8] and failing at present all other sources, I procured what exotic plants I could from my mother's garden and set seriously to studying De Candolle's general works on the structure and classification of the vegetable kingdom.

[77]When our term was out at the Maison Collet, my father again moved, engaging for a twelvemonth the chateau de Pompignan, on the high ground overlooking the village of the same name near the little town of Grisolles, about halfway from Montauban to Toulouse. The estate had by some means or other remained through the revolution in the family of the original owners; the present Marquis de Pompignan, the representative of the one who was the butt of so much satire on the part of Voltaire,[9] was an elderly man of somewhat excentric habits who had much impoverished his estate, and had an only son with whom he was not on very good terms, and they were very glad to live separately in a small way whilst the chateau was producing rent. We saw very little of either of them when they occasionally came into the neighbourhood to see how matters were going on. The chateau was a large building with several suites of unfurnished apartments; the one we occupied was very fairly comfortable, and the [78] Marquis's own bedroom and cabinet, which though open to us remained at his disposal, were particularly snug. Adjoining was a considerable library of which we had the use, chiefly the litterature of the days of Louis XIV and Louis XV, with a few modern works—and which to me was a great resource. The chateau also comprised a theatre, and reception rooms now abandoned. Outside were terraces and something of gardens, with wooded grounds extending over the broken country behind, whilst in front the view extended beyond the village over the wide plain of the Garonne, bounded in the far distance by faint ranges of hills, over which on clear days towered the picturesque and often snowy outline of the Pyrenees. The plain itself was uninteresting—a dead flat, covered with interminable cornfields, over which the road to Toulouse, a distance of about ten miles, was traced in long, perfectly straight lines, in one instance a reach of five miles without a turn or an angle or any break in the scenery to relieve its monotony. In the more varied ground between us and the Tarn, there were however pleasant walks in fine weather, and even in the plain, the forest of Montech was an agreable terminus to a six or seven mile drive.

It was not long after we were established at Pompignan that[§] family occurrences took place seemingly of much promise, but which much influenced our future lives in a way far from satisfactory. It was chiefly through our friends the de la Molère's that the marriage of my eldest sister was arranged with the Colonel of a regiment then in garrison at Toulouse. M. de Chesnel, or as he [79] styled himself on authority which afterwards proved to be doubtful, the Marquis de Chesnel, was a man of agreable manners, much information, fond of science, especially of botany, and entomology, in which he had made collections, of good social position, apparently popular with his brother officers and general acquaintance, and able fully to satisfy my father as to the sufficiency of his worldly means. My sister, of a most excellent disposition, clear common sense, highly cultivated mind and the sweetest temper, but very quiet and unassuming, was much pleased with his attentions and the marriage was settled. The civil and the protestant religious ceremonies were performed at Toulouse,[10] and repeated before a catholic priest at Pompignan, where we had a large wedding party after the French fashion, and a few days later my sister and her husband went to settle in an apartment at Toulouse. With regard to the pecuniary settlements, the French laws, although they give to the wife much more independent controul over her property, especially as to the ultimate disposal of the capital, than ours do, yet they do not recognise our system of trustees, which affords so much security against its loss from the husband's extravagance or the wife's weakness,[11] and the best substitute consists in the securing it by hypothèque upon landed property. This it was, probably, that first suggested to my father the idea of purchasing an estate in France, and with that view he determined on making a tour in the more southern Mediterranean region, which many of our French friends had described to us in such glowing terms. The Chesnels having invited my younger sisters to spend the time of our absence [80] with them at Toulouse, my father, my mother and myself took our coach with the pair of our old Paris horses which we had kept, and as a leader a white mare we had bought from M. de la Molère when he left Montauban, an excellent creature, full of intelligence, then about nine years old, and who remained in our service still doing very fair work for seventeen more years.

Remaining a day at Toulouse, where we deposited my sisters we started on the 8th of October travelling by easy stages,[12] with a good servant to look after the horses, and generally finding pretty fair inns for the night at moderate charges, much better than we met with even years later on some of the high roads of the north—the usual charge for supper and beds being then 3 fr 10 sols per head in the smaller places, 5 or 6 francs in the good hotels of the larger towns. Our first three days through Carcassone to Narbonne [were] not very interesting. The open cultivated corn region of Toulouse, usually bare looking in autumn, when there is so much of stubble, was rendered more so by the unusually dry summer of 1819, the forerunner of a remarkably severe winter. Beyond Carcassone, the change to the Mediterranean district—to the

Region des Oliviers—showed itself in the bare, rocky but not picturesque hills and the greyer aspect of the vegetation. The garrigues, as
these rocky wastes are called, notwithstanding the lavender, rosemary
and other sweet herbs that abound, and the abundant and varied Flora
they show to the botanist in spring, are particularly ugly at the end of a
hot summer; and although, now being possessed of a herbarium which I
had encreased by the contributions of my new brother-in-law, [81] I was
now on the look out for every opportunity of adding to it and was well
provided with drying apparatus, I could at this time of year find but
very little. One thing I learnt in vegetable physiology—the intense
degree to which acridity could be carried. When we came upon the first
olives between Carcassone and Narbonne, I could not resist gathering a
fine damson-looking, dark purple berry and putting it into my mouth—
and it was days before I quite got rid of the astringent sensation it
caused.

From Narbonne to Montpellier, we halted—but not for more than a
part of a day at each place—at Beziers, Pezenas, Agde and Cette; my
notes made at the time contain many expressions of disgust at the
untidy and filthy state of these little towns,[13] with their narrow, irregular, close streets, and that notwithstanding the beauty of some parts of
the country, especially near Beziers and Pezenas, the roads and other
means of communication at that time [were] sadly neglected—and the
bookseller of Beziers gave but a poor account of the litterary demands of
the gentry, being chiefly confined to school books and missals. At
Beziers we came in for an execution. Arriving in the afternoon we had
scarcely settled ourselves in the principal hotel on the Place, when
observing the large crowds that soon filled the place, we found that the
guillotine had been erected, and soon the procession appeared of the
officials, some guards, three men condemned to death for robbery and
attempted murder, and several penitents. This was the principal part of
the show, for the execution itself was so rapidly gone through, the guillotine descended and the heads and bodies fell out of sight so suddenly
and with so little[§] signs of blood or suffering seen at a distance, that it is
not surprising that the mob should regard it as a spectacle without any
feeling of horror [82] or disgust.

At Montpellier we made a stay of three days. My father made
acquaintance with Messrs Berard, friends of Chaptal's and proprietors
of chymical works, and other men of science and intelligence, who first
gave him an inclination to settle in the neighbourhood, and I procured
from the Botanic Garden some interesting specimens for drying.[§] The

botanical garden was now under the temporary directorship of Dunal, De Candolle's pupil and friend, and as it was hoped his destined successor, but political considerations subsequently prevailed and induced the appointment of Delile to supersede him. Though not kept up with the prestige it had attained under De Candolle, the Garden was in good order, and contained many very valuable plants, amongst them numerous types of De Candolle's species, the collection in the plant houses amounting to about 5000 species.

From Montpellier we went on to Nîmes where we stopped to visit the antiquities; thence to Tarascon to inspect Audibert's nursery, the largest in the South of France, prettily situated on the banks of the Rhone with a rich alluvial soil. The collection of trees very large and the prices kept high for the time. From Tarascon to Aix [83] we deviated a little from the road to visit the Roman arch of St Remy. From Aix to Marseilles the road traffic was then the busiest I had yet seen and was in aftertimes only recalled to my mind by that over the Monte Spaccato on the Trieste Road, or the approach to Odessa at a moment of corn-exportation excitement.[14] The constant succession of heavy roulage—immense long two-wheeled carts, with teams of four to six horses, the shaft horse necessarily one of great power, and requiring very careful balancing and attention on the part of the driver in changes from up to down hill—all tending to cut up the roads, with very soft material to repair them with—all now superseded by the railroad. At Marseilles we staid a few days for there was much to see; an old friend of my fathers, Baron Damas, was in military command—and in M. Lajard we found an intelligent naturalist with an amiable wife and a beautiful collection of minerals, with some shells and a well preserved herbarium—he had however abandoned botany and never looked at his plants for fourteen years.

From Marseilles to Toulon, through Aubagne and Cassis, the road lay over a country in some places barren, but in others exceedingly beautiful. The little towns in which we had to stop for the midday rest for the horses, or for the night, miserable, black dirty holes, with generally a dungheap before the door, on which we often saw the inmates sitting of an evening—but the valley of the Huveaunce, for instance, rich and green. Here we paid a passing visit to M. Albertas of Gemenos, whose chateau is in a beautifull park, an old gentleman of 82, a fine instance of energy and cheerful exertion retained after having spent the best years of his life in combating a long succession of misfortunes and anxieties. His father had been one of the first victims of the great revolution, assas-

sinated [84] at Gemenos in the midst of a fête he was giving to his peasantry.[15] His chateau was afterwards laid in ruins, and everything in the
grounds destroyed which man could lay his hands upon. At length the
son had succeeded in recovering the property, and with more peaceable
times, when verging upon 80, he set to the task of restoration. When we
now saw it, the chateau had been rebuilt, the park replanted and the
cheerfull old gentleman, bareheaded and in his dressing gown, showed
great delight in showing us all that he had done, the waterworks (really
good) which he had restored, and descanting upon all that still
remained for him to do. Nearer to Toulon, the drive from Le Beaufort to
Ollioules, down the pass and valley of Ollioules was in the end of October one of the most beautifull I have seen. Winding down through bold
rocks which at first closely hemmed in the road, and lower down
opened out leaving a rich valley of gardens or orange grounds whilst
the rocks themselves were decked out with a profusion of shrubs
amongst which the rich colours of the Erica vagans were now conspicuous; the whole was lighted up by one of those brilliant suns which are
characteristic of the South of France under the regular afternoon
seabreeze.

At Toulon my father had obtained special orders for visiting the
Naval Arsenal, in which however he was disappointed in finding anything of interest. At the very small botanic Garden, I was much more
pleased. The hot climate and abundance of water, with skilful management, compensated for very limited space and means. Here I first saw
the Palma Christi as a tree of 15 to 20 feet (3 years' growth), several Pel-
argonia which stand the winter itself, and (in the beginning of November) procured from the open air beds specimens in flower of 140 good
plants for [85] my herbarium. From Toulon we also made an excursion
to Hyères, spending a whole day there amidst the orange gardens.
These were now in full vigour. A severe frost in 1788-9 had obliged most
of them to be cut down to the ground; they had again suffered in the an
3 and in 1813–14, but had now completely recovered—to be again
checked by a severe frost two months after our visit.—M. Filke, at
whose house we lodged, had 17,000 trees, and had already sold this
year's crop, not ready for gathering till Christmas, for 36,000 francs, the
previous sale of flowers for 3000 francs having paid the year's expence
of cultivation. The whole of the Hyères orange plantations was calculated to have that year produced about 500,000 francs. The space where
they can be cultivated is very limited by the extent of the shelter
afforded by the mountain to the north and by the water available, the lit-

tle stream by which they are irrigated being regularly divided in a weekly routine among the different growers. For propagation they are generally grafted on cutting, but when raised from seed the trees (called pépins) are more hardy and the majority give better fruit.

Returning by Marseilles to Aix we staid a day there,[*]§ having met with an English acquaintance, and visited the plaister quarries already celebrated for their fossile impressions, and on to Avignon, where we put up at the Hotel du Palais Royal, now suffering from the violence of political feeling amongst this hotheaded race. It was here that Marshall Brune on his way to join Napoleon at Elba had put up and was assassinated by the mob[16]—comprising men of education who ought to have known better—and because the host as in duty bound had endeavoured to protect his guest, everything had since been [86] done to endeavour to discredit his house. The hotel proved however very comfortable. We spent a day with some English acquaintance we met with in visiting Vaucluse, fortunately under a beautiful sky and calm weather, for the two previous days we had a taste of the mistral which sometimes blows so hard at Avignon as to make the bridge over the Rhone unsafe for a carriage to pass, and the day following our Vaucluse visit we were detained by deluges of rain. We found however agreable society at our friends the Archdalls', and on the 13th Nov. resumed our journey, spending a morning in the wild scenery surrounding that magnificent Roman bridge-aqueduct the Pont-du-Gard—a day at Nîmes and a morning in the Muscat vineyards of Lunel, and made a second halt of a few days at Montpellier. In consequence of the enquiries about estates to be sold made for us by our friends there, my father was induced also to stay a day at Pezenas, to see one called le Parc near there.[17] It was in a very pretty situation, and altogether the country about Béziers and Pézenas seemed in many respects very attractive; the small estate in question had also many advantages and was to be had cheap, but Pézenas affords no social advantages. The inhabitants said to be better than at Béziers, where to the saying (in allusion to the beauty of the country)

---

[*] It was during this, our second stay at Aix that George IV's Queen Caroline (then Princess of Wales) and suite were in the same hotel (des Princes) and excited commentary by their behaviour, Bergami being considered as secretly her husband. One morning she went out on foot with an attendant, when presently Bergami came out evidently in a passion and scolding her in the public street, gave her his arm and brought her back to the hotel—and similar scenes were said to take place daily.

"Si Deus habitet in terris habiteret in Biterrois," it has been added "ut iterum crucifigitur,"[18] but yet at Pézenas there would be no one to exchange an idea with in litterature, science and art.

We now hurried back to Toulouse in consequence of a first intimation of those difficulties on the part of [87] M. de Chesnel, which afterwards so much influenced our proceedings and which embittered so many years of my sister's life. An urgent request of an immediate loan of a considerable sum of money took my father by surprise, and although on arriving at Toulouse, M. de C. succeeded in prevailing on him to accede to it,[*]§ and §in still turning aside any suspicion that the inscriptions de

---

[*] The current money in France at this time and for a long while after was almost entirely silver. Gold was at a premium, such that it was little used except by foreigners, especially English. Besides the Napoleons, there were still louis d'or's in circulation, of the nominal value of 24 francs, but which "lost" several sous, passing usually, except in the western departments, for 23fr. 11 sous. Paper money existed in 500 and 1000 franc notes but the recollection of the assignats was so fresh in people's minds that it was taken very unwillingly and it was difficult to get change for a note without a loss of 3 or 4 francs. The bulk of money transactions was in silver five-franc pieces, which were now spreading generally over the country—and replacing the old ecus de six livres and the petits ecus (3 livres), now gradually called in. These ecus "lost" four sols, and the petits ecus five sols, passing for 5fr. 16s. and 2fr. 15s. respectively, except in the western departments, where they passed for their nominal value. The consequence was that at Saumur [88n] in 1815 we scarcely ever saw a five-franc piece. Now they were general—in bags of 500 or 1000 francs, which in travelling one generally carried loose in the carriage on account of the weight, and when on this occasion I had to pay 20,000 fr. (£800) I had to hire a porter to carry it in a hotte on his back from the bankers' to M. de C's. The smaller coins were very various, copper and bronze abundant; our millers near Montpellier (some years later) would pay 80 to 100 francs of their rent in copper—old sou and two-sous pieces of Louis XV and Louis XVI—the shining sous made from the melting of church bells during the last years of Louis XVI—the cap of liberty decimes and cinq centimes of the following years, a few small base metal 10 centimes pieces of Napoleon—none had appeared yet of the Restoration—some of the old base metal six liard pieces like little bits of thin dirty tin, with all impressions worn off—in silver, a few of the old 1 livre pieces now almost worn blank, a large number of the 15 and 30 sous pieces of very impure silver coined in the early years of the Revolution, and the new 1 and 2 franc pieces slowly spreading into circulation. No accounts were yet kept on the decimal system—centimes never heard of—nor the new decimal weights or measures adopted, except in such official accounts and acts as would be otherwise illegal. The names given to small sums were a singular mixture. Under the sou were the *liards*; a sol and a half always *six liards*; 2½ *sols*, six blancs; 1 franc was usually *vingt sols*; 1½ fr., *trente sols*; 2 fr., *quarante sols*; 2½ fr., *cinquante sols*; 3 fr., *un petit ecu* or *trois francs*; 3½ fr. *trois livres dix*—and so on: *quatre francs, quatre livres dix, cent sols, cinq livres dix, six francs, six livres dix*, etc. 1000 francs was usually called *cent pistoles*.

rentes he had shown at the time of his marriage were not his but only lent for the purpose, yet it made my father all the more anxious to purchase land on which he could secure my sister's dot, and he already planned a second visit to the south in the spring for that purpose.

In the mean time, affairs having been smoothed over for the present, we returned to Pompignan for the winter with my younger sisters, leaving the de Chesnels [88] at Toulouse. The winter proved a very severe one.[19] From ten days to a fortnight's frost in January made great havoc amongst the oranges of Provence and the olives of the Mediterranean region generally. The great corn plain we overlooked from Pompignan was a vast expanse of white—and as one effect, larks were caught in enormous numbers and went in cartloads to the Toulouse markets; and as the snow disappeared it was found that not only the early crops, flax, beans, pease, etc, had been killed, but that a large proportion of the oats and rye and some wheat was destroyed, the thermometer having been for five nights down to –12° [89] Réaumur, and the whole plain which a fortnight before had been of a bright green was now a dirty brown. We however enjoyed ourselves much. I took to reading a great deal: Royou's *Roman History* and other historical works in the Pompignan Library, Destutt-Tracy's *Idéologie* and other philosophical and logical works. I commenced also the translation into French of portions of my Uncle's *Chrestomathia*, and as a relaxation eagerly followed up the pursuit of Natural History. Besides the abovementioned *Dictionnaire*, we took in the *Revue Encyclopédique*, which just then gave excellent resumés of what was going on in the way of science, the *Annales de Chimie* and some other periodicals; and though at this season little was to be done in the way of botany, I took to shooting birds and assisting one of my sisters in stuffing, mounting and naming them—forming by the end of our stay a very fair collection of the ornithology of the district—to be afterwards abandoned and suffered to decay. From the first burst of early spring however I zealously resumed the search for plants to encrease my herbarium.

Political events produced considerable excitement this winter. In England the death of George III and accession of George IV[20] was the subject of much comment even in this part of France, till it was quite superseded by the assassination of the Duke of Berry,[21] which inflamed all the angry passions of the excitable South—followed by the fall of Decazes who had for some time past been almost the Dictator of the country.[22] At the same time, the Spanish revolution—or I should now say a Spanish revolution—caused great commotion at Montauban, opening a way for the return of our friends the "Josephinos," exiles, and many other Spanish refugees of various parties[23]—amongst others of the poor simple bonhomme, the curé of Pompignan—a zealous believer in the Catholic faith who did his duty conscientiously, but could not make [90] much of a sermon beyond explaining the rules of diet in fast-time, who would explain the mysterious Trinity in Unity to the enquiring peasant by making three folds in the sheet of his soutane and then opening them out to show that though three they were but one—and who going out in the evening with us to shoot a rook for stuffing, fired at a barn door fowl—but ignorant as he was, and poor, and not over clean, he was a good man, and I believe a happy one—overjoyed at last at the prospect of returning to his native country.

Either alone or with my father, I paid several visits this winter to Montauban and to Toulouse, generally for a night only. Amongst others, on the Lundi gras to a grand ball at the Toulouse Préfecture, returning the next day for the country Carnival festivities—chiefly dancing (the assassination of the Duc de Berri on the 13th was not known at Toulouse till the 18th, two days after the Carnival was over, the Estafette having thus taken 5 days from Paris to Toulouse), and on Ash Wednesday they performed the ceremony of executing the Carnival. After receiving the blessed ashes at Church in the morning, the peasantry of Pompignan dressed up a straw effigy in some old clothes, giving it the name of Carnival. After parading him all over the place on a donkey, they cut his head off, carried the body about weeping over it whilst others poured wine down his throat saying, "There you may now drink as much as you please," and after much mourning made a bonfire of him. It was usual in this and other villages before his execution to try him in form for debauching young people, making them drink and riot, and then condemn him to death, but this year the Pompignan peasants could not [91] muster quite funds enough and curtailed this part of the ceremony. Another party of peasantry went round the village in the morning with drum and fife collecting eggs and bacon for their supper, of which 60 or 70 partook in the great salon in the chateau, bringing with them above 200 eggs. After supper that party danced and made a great noise till between 9 and 10, when they were followed by a second party who kept it up till 12 at night—and although this was a stretch beyond the nominally legitimate period of dancing, they had another edition of the dancing the following (Thursday) evening.

As an instance of the primitive state of some matters at this period, I may mention that in the country, insurance against fire was almost unknown. A company recently established at Paris sent about this time circulars to local authorities all over the country, and with the sanction of Government to the country clergy, urging them to point out the advantages of insurance in their discourses from the pulpit.[24] Our curé, after two or three fruitless endeavours, gave it up; the peasantry could not understand it and only laughed at the idea.

During this winter we had with us for a few months a lad whom my Uncle Jeremy Bentham had engaged as an amanuensis, and was desirous that he should acquire some knowledge of the French language. The visit was most agreable to us. Richard Doane was an excellent and most amiable youth; he remained a long while with my Uncle, became his confidential manager and, as it were, secretary, in succession to Mr Koe, and after long service, only left him when his business at the bar came to occupy the whole of his time. His life however was too soon[§] cut off for him to acquire a name.[25] He left us in the [92] end of February and was succeeded, after our return from our second journey to the south, by John Mill (or John Stuart Mill), already mentioned above (11). Although he had not the winning ways of Richard Doane, and had a somewhat ungainly manner which only left him late in life, he struck us much by the quickness of his perceptions and the powers of his mind, which showed none of that falling off which had been predicted from his great precocity as a child. I find among my notes made at the time memoranda of his rapid progress[§] in French, of his readiness at difficult algebraic problems which had rather puzzled me, etc.[26] His visit was also on many accounts a pleasant one to us, and we had every reason to be satisfied with his conduct, disposition and principles during the seven or eight months he remained with us.[27]

In April of this year (1820) my father made arrangements for a second excursion to the South for the same purpose of acquiring some estate there, where he could settle, and on which he could secure my eldest sister's dot. This time, I and my second sister accompanied him, whilst my mother remained at Pompignan with my eldest sister (who had taken refuge with us, her husband having gone off into Béarn), my youngest sister and John Mill.[28] Just however as we were starting, an incident occurred which delayed us a few days, giving us some insight into the character and superstitions of the peasantry about us. I had then for some time had the charge of the family money and the daily payments, etc, and now in the hurry of the last moment I had laid down the money bag for a moment, and getting into the carriage missed it. I went immediately back to where I had left it, but it was no longer there. As less than a quarter of an hour [93] had elapsed, it was evident that some of the household had taken it up. We had reason to believe our servants honest, and we could not imagine their being so stupid as to seize what would be immediately missed, but we could hear of no strangers being about the house. Unwilling to incur the scandal and delays of calling in the police and instituting an official enquiry, we assembled our servants, with one or two occasional helps, and left it to them to find out amongst themselves, telling them that if the guilty were not detected or the money replaced where it had been left, the following morning we should proceed to a judicial investigation. They suspected a peasant girl who did the work of the Curé's house and used to help in ours; we thought rather of Pierrotot, an apparently harmless fellow whom we all liked for the readiness with which he did all our hard work, and for his constant good humour, but who was not over-witted. We however charged no one, promising only that, if the guilty one would restore the money and confess, we should forgive him on the ground of the temptation my carelessness had held out, and we left the rest to them. They sent for the wise man of the village, who we heard collected them all and proceeded to incantations, which worked upon them in such a manner as completely to clear poor Bello (the servant girl) and to strike Pierrotot almost dumb with terror; and on rising the next morning and going at once to the place, there was the moneybag intact on the shelf where I had left it.

Having hired a caleche and pair at Toulouse, we started from thence on the 21st of April taking a different and much more pleasant route than that we followed last year. Going by Albi, Castres and St Pons to Beziers, we crossed a great deal of very pretty, rich and interesting country, visited the masses of granite heaped up [94] in wild confusion in the valley of Fontes near Lavaur, spent a morning with the Comte Louis de Villeneuve near Castres, the then great agriculturist and improver of this part of France. As elsewhere his greatest difficulties have been from the backwardness of the peasantry in taking to anything out of the usual routine, as well as in their great poverty. He had vastly encreased the produce of his land, and saved from last winter's frosts many crops which had perished on neighbouring estates less judiciously cultivated. But "with these and other great sources of encrease of revenue he complains of the little profit he derives on the whole in comparison to what he might expect, for 'my villagers,' he says, 'are poor; they can only live on what they earn with me so that I am obliged to be continually using all my endeavours to find work for them, and my crops, sold amongst them, do not bring in so much as if they were taken to market. To be sure I have the satisfaction of being loved and respected by them, but this satisfaction will not give my daughters *dot* enough to please any sons-in-law that might present themselves.'"[29]

Between Castres and St Pons the road crosses the division of the watershed of the Ocean and Mediterranean, with a more rapid change of aspect than on the Narbonne road. Here we are already amongst the Cevennes, the southern declivity of which is every where broken and rocky, the ravines sometimes bold, narrow and barren, sometimes opening out into richly watered valleys, all now in their spring beauty, whilst the villages and little towns encrease in their miserable filth. We made however no further halt till Beziers, which after crossing so pretty a country as we had done did not appear in a light [95] even as favorable as last autumn. At Pezenas we again visited the estate of Le Parc, only to be still more decided against it and pushed on to Montpellier, the present terminus of our excursion.[30]

Our stay here was from the 29th April to the 10th May, chiefly occupied with the main object of our expedition, the search for an estate to purchase, and especially the visiting and procuring information about that of Restinclières, about 8 miles from the town and which my father subsequently obtained.[31] We visited also some others, especially Chateaubon, near La Vérune, made several acquaintance amongst the best informed residents, made an excursion to the island of Maguelonne, in the midst of a lagoon, said to be the original site of the town, or rather of the mother-town of Montpellier, but now showing nothing but the ruin of the ancient residence of the Bishops, and altogether spent our time so satisfactorily as to give my father a pleasing anticipation of a residence in the country. In the botanical garden, M. Delile was now established as professor, received me very politely and gave me a number of specimens for drying from the garden. M. Berard also took me to M. Gouan, the once celebrated botanist and correspondent of Linnaeus, long Professor at Montpellier, author of several works chiefly on the Flora, and who had made numerous attempts to enrich it by the sowing and planting of exotic species in places where they would be most likely to flourish and propagate—all however failed, and I could never in my later herborisations discover any remains of them in such of the stations indicated by him as I had been able to visit. M. Gouan was now 88 and almost totally blind, but he still liked to be led about his garden and indicate his favorite plants, especially to feel his Gingko biloba (Salisburia) [96] which he had introduced.[32] The day after our visit the Prefet

and other "Autorités" of the place went officially to his house to present
him the decoration of the legion of honor, which had been awarded to
him some 24 years back, but which by carelessness, red tapeism and
other mishaps had been withheld till now.

We returned from Montpellier by a most interesting though little frequented road across the Cevennes. Leaving the town by a northern
road, which after a few miles of cultivation, crosses the stony, rather
dreary wastes of St Gely and St Martin etc, we descended into the valley
of the Herault, at first wild and rocky with eagles hovering over our
heads, and little of habitation, except here and there a shabby, dirty,
compact village, with the street too narrow for two carriages to pass—
then opening rather wider between the rocky hills or mountains and
showing the greatest industry and rich cultivation, chiefly mulberries
and silk; the whole country indeed from Ganges to Le Vigan is amongst
the most beautiful and interesting that we had seen in the south of
France, especially at this time of year when all was clothed with the rich
spring verdure, and the main crop of the country was at the most critical
period—the silkworms had already passed successfully their third
change of skin. At Sumène, between Ganges and Le Vigan, we stopped
to see an estate (La Salle) which was said to be on sale, a beautiful spot
in the midst of rocky, wooded mountains, but an hour and a quarter's
walk from the nearest road practicable for a carriage. A Sumène lawyer,
an old gentleman of 75, accompanied us to it, and on our return, Gen.
Boussegnolles,[33] brother in law of the owner, met us and prevailed on us
to accept his hospitality for the night instead of going on to an inn (we
had slept the night before at Ganges). This was a very pleasant episode,
entailing a delightful evening, and a morning ascent of the Montagne
[97] de la Faye, overlooking Sumène, from whence the view is magnificent, including a vast expanse of sea with the intervening country we
had crossed the day before, Montpellier itself appearing between the
two perpendicular rocks of St Loup—to the north the higher mountains
of the Esperou and the Lozère—the latter some 50 miles distant, and in
the greater distance of perhaps 100 miles, the Eastern Pyrenees to the
SW, and the lower Alps to the East.

A day was soon spent at Le Vigan in visiting the silk breeding establishments, etc, besides the interest given to the town by its position, and
by the richness of the mineral products in the neighbourhood, especially
as to coal and iron, then still but little worked, and for many a long year
afterwards uninvaded by machinery and great chimneys. Leaving it on
the 14th, we still found reasons for congratulating ourselves on not hav-

ing suffered ourselves to be deterred from taking this road, the interesting and varied country we passed more than counter-balancing the rough accomodation and occasional badness of roads we had been threatened with. I had added much to my herbarium from the rocky banks of the Herault, particularly gay at this time of year with large tufts of Saponaria ocymoides and other flowering plants. About Sumène we had admired the large Chestnut woods—cultivated not so much as large trees for the fruit, as cut as coppice for the wood itself, for barrel staves and hoops; and now "from Le Vigan to Alzon, along the beautiful valley of the Arre, high mountains and deep valleys present scenery continually changing and each more beautiful than the last—sometimes bold rocks quite bare, more often covered up to the very tops with fine thick chestnut woods, or with mulberries, olives, walnuts and vines planted in terraces made to keep up the soil—in the bottom of the valley the little river Arre winding down among rocks embellishes the landscape, the colours much heightened by a bright sun and beautifully clear sky. A few villages lie scattered about, some buried in the depth of the valley, [98] others perched on the tops of the mountains," this southern mountain scenery terminating in a "petite côte" as the peasantry termed it, up which the road led us for above an hour, winding up 22 "rampes" or terraces, with a short descent to Alzon. We had now left the high cultivation of the southern part of the Cevennes but were no less pleased by passing over the mountains from Alzon to Sauclières, covered with rocks of all shapes, with box growing in their chinks, besides a considerable variety of plants for my vasculum. After Sauclières we came upon the Larzac—a bare, cold, dismal, elevated table land which covers a wide extent of South Central France, intersected only by the deep valleys of the rivers. Here everything still wore a more wintery aspect than the country about Pompignan when we left it a week previously—a few thin fields of corn just beginning to come up—no meadows, none of the fine chestnuts, none of the apples and pears nor even of the wild gooseberries and currants so plentiful before Sauclières, only here and there a few stunted oaks still retaining the brown leaves of the previous year, and even these soon disappeared, with little to be seen but a stone desert without habitation or living beings, except some thinly scattered flocks of sheep picking up the scanty herbage, and more large eagles than I ever had a near view of, rising up sometimes almost close to us. In the midst of this desert, where it is crossed by the high road from Rhodez, we had to put up at the Hotel des Associés, at Lhospitalet, one of the most wretched in point of dirt and bad accomodation,

and noted in my memory with Cujès, Anduze, Toledo, [   ], Calati-
fime, [   ], and [   ].

A descent of about an hour brought us down from this scene of desolation to St Rome du Cernon, whence we walked up a narrow valley or
gorge to see the famous caves of Roquefort, which give the name and
peculiarities to the Roquefort cheeses. [99] These cheeses are all made of
sheep's milk from the large flocks which pasture over the rocky wastes
not only in the neighbourhood but at distances of fifty to a hundred
miles; the lambs (born usually in winter in the lowlands before the
sheep are brought up to the mountains) are killed young, the milk collected for four or five months and made into cheeses, bought up by the
Roquefort proprietors, and deposited with a little salt in these caves
where, either from the excessive cold and damp or from the fact of the
peculiar germs there bred, they acquire in the course of a month or six
weeks the well known variegated moulds and peculiar flavour. At the
time of our visit the manufacturing season was just commencing, very
few cheeses had as yet been brought in, and none were ready. Few
indeed are sent out before the end of August.

From St Affrique to Alby we had again a wellwooded, hilly, almost
mountainous country, often very beautifull, and after a couple of days
stay at Alby to see some of the natural curiosities of the neighbourhood
with our friend de la Molère, who was now stationed there, and crossing an interesting country between Alby and Toulouse, rejoined my
mother and sisters at Pompignan on the 21st May.

My father appeared now quite to have made up his mind to settle in
the south of France, purchasing if possible the estate of Restinclières—
the doubt arising in the chance of the owner M. de Murles being able to
reestablish his affairs without selling it. In the mean time it appeared
that M. de Chesnel had quite deserted my sister, leaving her entirely to
our care. The time of her confinement was approaching, and for that it
was thought advisable to move for a time into the town of Toulouse; my
father wished also to visit the Pyrenees before leaving this part of
France. The remaining month therefore that we spent at Pompignan was
chiefly occupied in preparations for moving—in excursions to [100]
Montauban, to take leave of our Spanish friends about to return home—
and to Toulouse to establish ourselves there temporarily.[34] The six or
seven weeks we spent there were very agreable. Quiet lodgings in the
Rue St Anne, behind the Cathedral, disturbed only by the Cathedral
bells and chimes, to tunes often somewhat profane—the "bon Roi
Dagobert" amongst others—frequent intercourse with our friends the

Russells, the Partouneaux, and others. Hot summer weather made me doubly enjoy my morning baths with the young Russells, in the broad and rapid Garonne, which I soon learnt to swim across backwards and forwards, and steady reading in doors. John Mill had been with us since the first June, and eagerly pursued his French studies with my assistance. I also took to several philosophical works we had lately purchased: Dugald Stewart, D'Alembert,[35] amongst others Lamarck's *Systeme analytique des connaissances positives de l'homme*, which "I happened to open at the passage, 'Dieu créa d'abord la matière,' followed by the statement that nature was the second thing created and that this produced every thing else—and discouraged by this galimathias gave up the book."[36] I also advanced considerably my translation of my Uncle's *Chrestomathia*, without neglecting opportunities afforded by excursions in the neighbourhood to add to my herbarium and to acquire some knowledge of entomology, tabulating insects as I had acquired the habit of doing to most subjects I took up, whether geography, natural history or philosophy.

My eldest sister having sufficiently recovered from her confinement, we left Toulouse for the Pyrenees on the 10th August, travelling in our "family coach" with three horses, and I and generally one of my sisters on our two ponies, purchased at Saumur in 1814. [101] We followed the Bigorre road through Lisle en Jourdain, Auch and Tarbes, stopping at Auch to see the cathedral, one of the finest in the south, and crossing an undulating or hilly, often very pretty country, from whence we descended to Rabastens, on the northern limits of the plain of Tarbes, on the evening of the 13th. Our ride and drive the following day from Rabastens through Tarbes and to Bagnères de Bigorre was most striking. I had never seen high mountain ranges, except from Toulouse and Montauban, where the Pyrenees look almost like a ridge of clouds on the horizon, and as we neared them the previous day, clouds had hid them from our sight, but this morning, with a beautifull clear sky, they burst upon us like a huge rampart abruptly rising from the broad plain before us and bounding its southern extremity as far as the eye could reach to the right and to the left, rising more and more stupendous as we crossed the rich plain, straight through the town of Tarbes and nine large villages between that and Bagnères, Bagnères itself close at the very foot of the range at the entrance of the valley of Campan, the high steep mountains rising from the streets of the town.

We remained a month at Bagnères de Bigorre,[37] from whence I made numerous botanical excursions—short ones with John Mill or my sisters, longer ones with our manservant, ascended the Lhéris, and other celebrated botanical stations near at hand, and went on a five days' expedition over the Tourmalet to Barèges, St Sauveur, up to Gavarnie whence I ascended to the Brèche de Roland—ascended the Pic du Midi with my younger sisters, and the latter half of our month with my father, mother and younger sisters to Pau, Oléron, Navarreins and Peyrorhade to Bayonne, where we remained a couple of days, going down one day to the mouth of the river. I watched there the great eclipse of the 7th Sept.—and also I took a quiet bathe in the sea, the [102] since celebrated bathing establishment of Biarritz being then but a small fishing village—one of the objects of the excursions en cacolets of the bourgeoisie of Bayonne—the cacolet being a pair of small arm chairs, one on each side of a pack horse, like a pair of panniers. In returning to Bagnères we diverged from our former road, first to Orthès, and after Pau to Lourdes, and altogether enjoyed much this Béarn trip, during which, besides the beauty of the country, my father had come across several intelligent Spaniards, both at Pau and Oleron, waiting for the ratification of the amnesty to return to their country.

On the 17th September we left Bagnères de Bigorre for Bagnères de Luchon to which the only carriage road then existing was up the valley, first of the Garonne, which we reached through Montmedy and Lannemezan, and then up the narrower valley of Luchon. Ten days spent in this delightful watering place established it at once in my mind as the richest botanical centre and the finest place for exploring mountain beauties in the whole of the central Pyrenees, a view fully confirmed by three subsequent visits at long intervals.[38] On this occasion I made acquaintance with Paul Boileau, the veteran botanist of the higher Pyrenees; we also made several of the ordinary excursions but the weather was often unfavorable, the fresh snow covering the mountains one day down to no great distance from the town, and winter appeared to be fairly setting in when we finally left Luchon and the Pyrenees, returning to Toulouse by the direct road through St Martory. Disagreeable circumstances connected with family matters induced my father to establish our party at Muret for a fortnight, whilst J. Mill and I and sometimes my father were chiefly at Toulouse, now the scene of official rejoicings for the birth of the Duke of Bordeaux[39]—well seconded by a portion of the public [103] including the côté droit of the pit of the theatre, little heeded by the côté gauche and apparently by the majority of the population. We finally left Toulouse on the 8th October, and taking the route by Castres and St Pons to Beziers, arrived at Montpellier on the 15th.

We here settled ourselves temporarily at the Hotel du Palais Royal, engaged an unfurnished appartement on the Cours for the winter and set about estate hunting and visiting some of the most interesting spots in the neighbourhood. Amongst other estates on sale, we saw the small one of the Mas de Limaçon near the town on the Beziers road, remarkable for a very fine Cupressus patula (the spreading variety of C. sempervirens) which goes here by the name of Arbre de Montpellier, and this individual aged tree is believed in the country to be the only one remaining of a cypress forest, which tradition reports to have once covered the site of the town of Montpellier. We were also several times at Restinclières, which my father had a great hankering for, but the owner could not make up his mind about parting with it. At length on the first of November, M. de Murles sent his agent to our friends the Berards to treat with us. After a long discussion, the price was fixed the same evening at 280,000 francs, the notary received his instructions the following morning, 2d, the "contrat" or deed of sale was executed on the 3d and we drove out to take formal possession on the 4th in pouring rain.

This estate of Restinclières consisted of rather more than 2000 English acres all contiguous (except one or two small detached portions) and with a nearly circular outline, with the Chateau in the centre in a commanding position looking down the valley of the Lez. The greater [104] portion consists of waste land called *garrigues*, partly rocky, but with large parts also well capable of cultivation—these garrigues covered with low brushwood of which Pistacia lentiscus (*Restincle* in the patois of the country, whence the name of the estate is derived). Quercus coccifera, Genista scorpius, Rosemary, Thyme and Lavender form the great mass, but interspersed with a great variety of Helianthema, Lina, and numerous other low shrubs undershrubs or herbs, the whole yielding in its present state only pasture for between 2 and 3 sheep per acre during 8 months of the year—and small brushwood, "petit bois pointu," used for heating limekilns, bread-ovens, etc. A small wood of evergreen oaks lay to the north of the chateau. Within the property the river Lez issues from under a perpendicular rock in a circular bow, like that of Vaucluse, and immediately turns a flour-mill, not then belonging to the estate, but which we afterwards purchased. The river then winds through a broad flat valley of great fertility amidst watermeadows, vines and arable land, and turns another set of millstones just before it leaves the estate near the village of Prades. Some strips of the meadow-land were also at the time in other hands, but land so frequently changes owners when belonging to the peasantry that we were enabled gradually to buy up nearly the whole of them. We had thus a compact property situated in seven communes or parishes, the villages of which lay around us at a distance of from one to four miles of the chateau, and divided into two large farms by the river. The only buildings on the property being the two sets of farm buildings (one close behind the chateau) and the two flour-mills abovementioned. The produce consisted of grain, hay, wine and sheep, and in a small degree [105] of silk-mulberry leaves, olives, a few fruits (quinces, straw-berries, etc) and roseleaves for distilling, all farmed in the most primitive manner. The Chateau was a considerable one, with farm buildings behind, and in front a long broad terrace over-looking the garden, first in terraces, and below them the kitchen garden, intersected by a horsechestnut avenue opposite the centre of the cha-teau, the avenue itself in grass between the trees, and down the centre a zigzag walk dignified by the name of Jardin Anglais. Below the garden a walk down the valley, with the wild brushwood bank bordering it on the left, and on the right the fields and meadows separating it from the river. About ¾ mile from the house, the little river Lirou—almost dry in summer, a furious torrent after autumn storms, bounds the property as it falls into the Lez, and ¼ mile farther is the village of Prades. The view from the Chateau overlooks all this and the second farm, "La Grange du Pin," on a small eminence on the other side of the Lez, and beyond to the south the view bounded by the wooded hills of Montferrier, the bright green of the Pinus halepensis, contrasted with the sombre grey tint of the evergreen oaks, relieving also the monotonous grey of the rocky wastes. Through life I have had present to me many a delightful evening spent on our terrace, especially in spring and early summer and again in autumn, contemplating this pleasing landscape.

Our main object was now to be the managing and improving our pur-chase, from which my father anticipated great things. I had had no voice in the determination to settle here, but now that we had it in possession, the chief management of detail was placed in my hands, my father hav-ing only planned out and determined what repairs and alterations were to be made to the house, [106] and generally what parts of the estate were to be brought into cultivation, etc. Unfortunately, he was more of a contriver than a practical manager, and several of his plans proved fail-ures; but such were the capabilities of the property that when it was sold years after, the improvements had counterbalanced, or perhaps over-balanced the losses, so as to repay the whole or nearly the whole of our outlay.

The first steps taken by my father were to prepare the chateau for our residence as a permanent home, to commence upon those operations for the improvement of the estate as would take the greatest time to effect, and to provide for the introduction of modern instruments as yet entirely unknown to the primitive cultivators of the soil. As he never intended that we should renounce society, he engaged an "Apartment" in the Cours des Casernes for our winter residence, and as a pied-à-terre in summer, and thanks to the introductions he had brought, we were immediately admitted into the best of the society of the two factions which prevailed in the town—the Catholic, and perhaps more aristocratic, which included most of the "Autorités" and some old families—and the Protestant and generally more enlightened, and perhaps more wealthy. Although however they formed thus two factions, political as well as religious, with no great cordiality between the two, there was by no means that hostility which prevailed in many other Southern towns, they interchanged visits as well as invitations to their larger parties, they met without outward show of disagreement at the Prefecture and other neutral grounds, their differences interfered in no way with their business [107] intercourse, and they were both equally well disposed towards foreigners who came to them sufficiently recommended. We formed intimacies with several members of both parties, who proved in after times real friends, who rendered to some of us most valuable services. During the first winter, we went a great deal into society. My younger sisters made great friends with the family of M. Dax, then Mayor of Montpellier. Made Dax (née Saint-Priest), was sister of Made de Calvière,[40] whom they had already known at Paris, and was connected with several of the old families of France; and of the two daughters one was just married to the son of a very rich Montpellier banker, the other was of my sisters' age, and these formed the centre of the Catholic society. My father became more intimate with the Levats, a most excellent family, M. Levat a banker and merchant, the Lichtensteins, M.L. (brother of Lichtenstein the Prussian Zoologist and explorer of South Africa)[41] the head of the wealthiest mercantile house in Montpellier, and the Paulin Farels, owner of a fine property half-way between Montpellier and Restinclières, and cloth merchant in town—all these belonging to the Protestant society and the principal houses where they met socially. We were thus not only regularly invited to all the balls and parties given in both societies, but many were also the more limited and friendly and therefore the more agreable gatherings in

which we spent our evenings,[*]§ and when strangers of literary or scientific eminence were entertained as they passed through the town,
my father and myself were generally asked to meet them. Amongst
others, it was, I believe, this first winter that we were much pleased at
spending an evening with Augustin Thierry, the historian, at the Lichtensteins. In a weak state of health, his mind was not the less active,
and the matter as well as the tone of his conversation gave a special
intellectual character to the dinner, notwithstanding the material excellence imparted to it by the cook.

[108]Our chateau was soon sufficiently furnished for a partial occupation; my eldest sister, entirely occupied with her baby, gave up society
and established herself at Restinclières, which I now also made my chief
home, going into town for the night only for social purposes. I devoted
myself indeed almost wholly to the practical carrying out of my father's
plans for the improvement of the estate—extensive planting of trees on
certain parts of the garrigues or waste lands, breaking up others to convert them into arable land or vineyard, rendering the "chemins de service" which crossed the estate in every direction passable for our carts—
rendering available the great resources for irrigation afforded by several
springs entirely our own—repairing the farm buildings, etc, all of
which, if they had been properly followed out in future years, would
soon have doubled the value of the property. In the farm buildings, the
expenditure was perhaps not so great in proportion to other expences as
it would have been with us—there was no refinement—the farmservants were used to sleeping on straw in the stables—there was but little
luxury in the shape of glass windows and internal fittings. The great
expenditure was labour, which, though paid at rates which would now
be considered ridiculously low, was very much higher than in Upper
Languedoc and other corngrowing parts of France. Our permanent staff
consisted of a *payre*, and his family, at each of our two farms—that is a
kind of bailiff or head man who not only directed but fed the farmservants, we giving him certain quantities of "mixture" (half wheat, half
rye), wine, salt and oil per man per annum, with a small allowance in

---

[*] I also gave up a good deal of time to music. Col Darbaud-Jouques, whose acquaintance we had made at Angouleme, was here with his regiment, and passionately fond
of music had paid much attention to his band, and we had many musical soirées, in
which I played Steibell's, Dussek's, and other Concertos, accompanied by the Col and
his band.

money for each man. Each payre had under him a carter, and four or five permanent men. We had also on the estate four shepherds for our flock of about 1200 sheep (before the annual sale) and a garde-champêtre. All the remaining work was done by day labourers. For some years [109] we absorbed nearly the whole available labour of the five communes in which the estate was placed, paying them 30 sous a day in winter, and 40 sous in spring and early summer—about 10 sous a day less than what was paid in the great wine districts on the other side of Montpellier, and we had 3½ hours more work out of them. Our day was from six to six in winter, five to five in summer, with three and a half hours' deductions, that is Tue-ver[42] half an hour, Breakfast half an hour, Dinner one hour, Sleep one hour, and Buvette half an hour (besides occasional five minutes for drinking). At Gramont and other wine districts, the working time during vine digging time in spring was from five till two, with four hours eating, drinking, and sleeping deductions. They certainly however worked very hard whilst at it and got through a great deal in the course of the day. We had generally a gang varying from 15 to 30 or even 40, with one head man paid rather more than the others—a worthy, stout, hardworking labourer from our principal village (Prades) named Pagés, with whom I soon got on very friendly terms. He served us faithfully and zealously during the whole of our stay at Restinclières and showed great attachment to us. We had indeed every reason to be pleased with our labourers and the peasantry generally. I soon learned their patois, which took off all awkwardness on their part, and being a great part of the day with them, checking their work and accounts, and often assisting with my own hands, I became for a time almost as one of them, acquired the confidence of many of them and was much consulted about all their little private difficulties or projects. They were most of them very well off. Notwithstanding the poor look of the villages, they, with their few requirements, were very comfortable; a large proportion had their little patches of land on which they grew corn or wine or both, enough for their own consumption, besides occasional Olives, Mulberries, Almonds or other accessary crops. Their pride in these bits of possession was great—the necessary work was done at odd [110] times after their return from their day's labour or by staying at home an occasional day or two in the week (for their hire was always by the day and they gave no previous notice when they did not come), and being thus always cultivated by zealous hand labour, these bits of land were generally very productive. With all the incentives to industry however, they were also the cause of many heart burnings and disputes. As the young women saved up from their day's earnings with a view to their future trousseau, so the young men saved up with a view to the purchase of a bit of land, and if once they had accumulated 500 franks, they would buy a patch for 800 or 1000 franks, borrowing the remainder on hypothèque. The lender, generally some lawyer or homme d'affaires from the town, would sometimes allow the interest to accumulate till the debt got beyond the peasant's means, and he had to submit to a judicial sale and begin again. Then again, when a peasant died, it was very seldom that the children could agree about the division of his land. If he left half a dozen patches, there were no means of judicially distributing them, giving to one the house, to another the vineyard or a meadow, to a third a cornfield, etc, but as each one had a legal right to his share of each description of property, and as in many cases the patches had already reached the limits of profitable division— and as, like the peasants of all countries, every one would stand to his rights—there was often no course left but to sell and divide the money. Thus it was that the bits of land were continually changing owners. In a large extent of meadow land bordering the river, the greater part of which belonged to our estate, there were enclosed some eighteen or twenty narrow strips belonging to as many different people, and for the due irrigation it was very important that the whole should be incorporated in the estate. During the five years we were there, no less than nine of these strips came successively on the market and I was able to secure them at prices not much beyond their productive value—and two more could have been had, but for the [111] difficulty of making a good title, owing to the complications of the law of forced distribution amongst children. A peasant had, during the troublous times succeeding the revolution, gradually saved up so as to buy patches of land to the amount of some 25,000 francs (including some of the strips of meadow in question). He had three children. A son married and settled in the world, and his father made over to him a third of his property, reserving sufficient to meet the legal claims of his other children in case of his death. He lived long afterwards, met with various fortunes, good and ill. When at last he died, it was found that his estate had become very much reduced, that the married son had received more than the quotité disponible,[43] one of[§] the other children was far away, and the third was trying to make his brother refund, as the law requires, what he had received from his father, in order that the whole might be redistributed by a legal process, which under the circumstances would be dragged on to an indefinite number of years. In the mean time, the settled son, who had received the bit of meadow as part of his share, came to offer it for sale; but upon enquiry, I found I could not safely pay for it without the consent of the two other children, one of whom was inaccessible, and the other refused to give it unless his brother settled his claims on his own terms. The peasantry all complained of the law as interfering with the advantageous settlement of a parent's property, and as a great source of family quarrels—yet any attempt at altering it was always met with irresistible sentimental opposition. And this opposition was much intensified by the injudicious proposal under Villèle's administration to reestablish the principle of primogeniture, by enacting that the quotité disponible, if left undisposed of by the parent should go to the eldest son,[44] leaving the really objectionable part of the law, the taking from the parent the right of distribution of his property amongst his children untouched.

[112]The extensive repairs which my father contemplated in the farm buildings and mills and various other works required a supply of timber, planks and other materials not supplied by the country and usually purchased at the great fair held annually in summer at Beaucaire in Provence. Oak timber for water mills [was] brought down the Saone and Rhone from Burgundy, Norway, deals, etc, up the Rhone from the Mediterranean, and I was induced by the advice of our friend Paulin Farel and others to go to Beaucaire myself this year (1821) to lay in the required stock. I wrote an account of this visit as No. 3 of "Sketches of Manners in the South of France" for the *London Magazine* in the beginning of 1827 which however, owing to the stoppage of the periodical, was never published,[45] and I therefore here transcribe it.

"By the middle of July the tradesmen of Montpellier had settled their annual accounts, debts were called in, creditors had been dunned, and the huissiers actively employed in conveying protests and notices of suits—and now all were thronging to Beaucaire to lay in their next year's stock. The roads were literally crowded with diligences, voituriers, horses, donkeys or foot passengers, the canals covered with passage boats, all eagerly tending to the fair. Year after year nearly the whole of the mercantile population of the south of France from Toulouse to Lyons is either present at Beaucaire, or represented by envoys. Wherever a mass of persons is seen to move periodically towards a particular point, the unconcerned looker-on is desirous of following, and if otherwise unoccupied, he cannot resist the current. Such was my case. I had seen Beaucaire empty, I had wandered in winter and spring* through its abandoned streets when half the houses are [113] shut up and I longed to witness the contrast exhibited by the same Beaucaire in fair time. But determined to see the fair itself, and not the exterior only, I associated business with pleasure, assimilated myself to its frequenters, procured a grey linen suit of clothes and a broad-brimmed straw hat, and styling myself M. B. . . de Montpellier, commissioned a friend to procure me a room for a week and thus went to make my purchases at Beaucaire.

"But how should I go?[†] Here were diligences by the dozen, into which I might be crammed with five or six stout tradesmen, with all their appurtenances of great coats, night caps, tobacco pipes, children and pug dogs, and thus jog on during eighteen or twenty hours. There were post horses, 'bidets de poste,' poor lean and jaded creatures, who by working night and day with the thermometer at 80 to 90 in the shade (and where was that shade to be found?) had actually lost all but skin and bone, and almost their very power of locomotion—or here was the poste-aux-ânes by which I might make my way from stage to stage through clouds of dust raised by the long-eared, halfwalking, halftrotting *montures*, sidling away at every blow inflicted by their merciless pedestrian drivers—or I might trust to my own means, certain of finding every house of accomodation filled from the cellar to the garrett, from the stable to the cartshed. The taking my carriage was therefore out of the question—my legs I might have, and I had before undertaken much longer journies on foot for pleasure, but then it was not on the 22d July on an open flat road, the sun beating down in a vertical direction, the roads ankle deep in dust, which the afternoon's breeze raised in clouds to obstruct the view, uninteresting as it was at the best. So I repaired to the office of Bimar et Glaize, universal entrepreneurs for the conveyance of passengers or goods from Montpellier to Beaucaire [114] 'and to all parts of the world.' 'Will you go by land or by water?' was the answer to my application for assistance.—'By land or by water? Which is the most pleasant, or rather which is attended with the least inconvenience?'—'By land you may have the dust in the day time, by water the

---

* Besides my visit with my father and mother in 1819 I had been there in the winter and spring of this year 1821, to my friend Audibert, the great nurseryman of the country, in connection with the trees for our plantations.

† Steam boats had not yet reached the South, and railroads of course were not dreamt of.[46]

mosquitos at night, but the weather is calm, and "le vent est droit"
(N.W.) so you may chance to escape either evil.'—'Well what kind of
places can you give me?'—'By land you may have the grande diligence,
at morning, noon or night, which will take you in eighteen hours for
nine francs, but' (on turning to his books) 'all the corners are taken for
some days to come—or any of the extra carriages we send, which do not
take so many passengers nor go so quick but are cheaper, or, if you like,
the passage boat; you will have bonne et nombreuse compagnie, and it
will cost you but cent sous.' So thinking that the more the merrier, I paid
down my four shillings and was booked for the following morning, to
be taken up at the Office in Montpellier at 10 a.m. and landed at
Beaucaire the morning after at 9, with the privilege of carrying my dinner in my pocket or going without.

   "At the appointed hour I was at my post, where I found three long,
four-wheeled vehicles like covered carts, and men, women and children
scrambling into them by the score. Such were the means provided for
transporting the passengers to Perols, the place of embarcation, distant
between five and six miles; but as I saw that these vehicles had each
nearly made up their complement of thirty, and as their form was not
such as to give any idea of a comfortable ride, I preferred making one of
the pedestrians, and actually arrived at Perols as soon as the caravans.
After half an hour spent in the bustle of embarking two or three hundred persons—of those who can never greet a friend without noise
enough to make a stranger think they are quarrelling—after half an hour
of this vociferation, I found myself at length fairly embarked on the lake
of Perols in the midst of a motley crowd of Languedociens, [115] Roussillonais and Catalonians, seamen, merchants, tradespeople or propriétaires, with a proportionate number of women and children, who,
under pretext of helping their lords in transacting their affairs, help
them to spend their money by figuring away on the 'beau Dimanche.'

   "We had sailed across the lake, and were now entering the fine canal,
but lately finished, which connects the Rhone with the Canal des Etangs.
During the three hours of our voyage which had already elapsed, the
turmoil of contending voices had given way to another operation,
equally important even to a Frenchman. As each man's dinner hour
approached, he had drawn from his leather bag or his basket the meal
which he had provided for himself. Here was a rich ironmonger and his
family collected round a cold fowl, a filet de boeuf and a sallad—there
the poorer tradesman, his legs hanging over the edge of the boat, displayed his saucisson, dried sardines, or whatever strong and piquant

food the season afforded—here the Languedocien peasant was devouring his mutton chops or cheese preserved in rancid oil—there the Pyrenean or Catalonian mountaineer was feasting on rye bread and garlick. The deck was a perfect labyrinth of eatables and eaters, and as for the cabin, I attempted to take a survey of it but was quickly repulsed by the mixture of perfumes with which I was assailed—perfumes of which the prevailing were garlick, salt fish, tobacco and rancid oil, independently of the effluvia to be expected from *such* a meeting, in *such* a cabin, at *such* a season.

"The sun set beautifully as we glided along in the midst of the universal calm. Not a ripple could be seen on the surface of the long broad canal, not a blade of the surrounding reeds was disturbed, not a sound could be heard, save the croaking of the frogs or the occasional clack of our driver's whip, for our noisy companions were digesting their suppers in silence. The country [116] around was open and desolate, extensive marshes without habitation or culture. The tall thick flags and reeds, the long rows of pollarded willows, denoted that materials for cask hoops and a coarse kind of winter fodder for cattle were the only produce that could be extracted from these unhealthy swamps, except the feed they furnish for the wild horses and bullocks that inhabit them. We occasionally caught a glimpse of some herds of these *chevaux de la Camargue*, as they are called, a race of small, coarsely built, thick bodied horses which are suffered to breed in these plains and to live as they can for nine months in the year. Towards the end of June, each proprietor sends to catch from his herd the number requisite for threshing (or rather treading out) his corn, and when that is done, they are sent back to the marshes, there to remain till the next season, undisturbed but by the occasional visit of a herdsman who comes to count the new born and examine into their general state. The wild bulls and cows are less numerous, particularly in the part we crossed; they are considered the property of the land holders upon whose extensive domains they roam at pleasure, till their turn arrives to figure in the bull baitings at Nimes, Beaucaire, Arles or Aiguesmortes.*

"But to return to my fellow passengers. I had met with a friend, a

---

* All this is now I believe much changed. The greater part of the Camargue was submerged by the extraordinary inundation of 183[ ],[47] and since then companies have, I am told, been undertaking the bringing portions of it into cultivation. The custom of treading out the corn is also, I am told, not near so universal as it was at that time.

young countryman of mine, and according to a most laudable English custom, we were pacing up and down the deck, enjoying the serenity of the atmosphere, and congratulating ourselves on our escape from the mosquitos with which we had been threatened. By degrees the limits of our walk were straightened by the extended bodies of our companions, who were snoring away the [117] fatigues of the day, dreaming no doubt of the fortunes they were going to make at the fair. At last we were literally reduced to a standstill, the moon had clouded over, all was darkness and we could not stir a step without stumbling over a leg or an arm. We seated ourselves on what we took to be a bale of goods, but a loud squall from underneath convinced us of our mistake and of the necessity of shifting our quarters; at last we established ourselves near one of the cabin entrances, and, little disposed to follow the example of the slumberers who covered the deck, we amused ourselves by listening to the voices that proceeded from below. Two Catalonian females, apparently somewhat superior to the rest of the party, and whose crowded situation had prevented their indulging their drowsiness, were killing time by joining some of their Montpellier friends in patois glees and choruses. The southern Europeans are born for music; with little or no instruction they sing in parts with the most perfect ensemble, and always in tune.

"Towards midnight however these beautiful songs had gradually died away, the voices had dropped off one by one as their owners had at length fallen asleep, all was now quiet and, indifferent as was my seat, I myself was beginning to nod, when a sudden tumult around me roused all my faculties. The clouds, which had been for some time gathering, were sprinkling a few drops upon the slumberers, a sudden cry was raised of *plöou, plöou*, (it rains, it rains), and that of fire could scarcely have created more confusion and uproar. All sprang upon their legs, and gathering their cloaks around them rushed into the cabin, already to all appearance as full as it could hold. Obliged thus to stand up and crowd upon one another to the very door, they remained there for half an hour, scarcely able to draw their breath in the dense atmosphere, without room to turn or to stretch a limb, and all for a few drops of water which did not cover the deck whilst it lasted. So much is rain feared by those who have none for months together.

[118]"My friend and I had now the deck to ourselves, and, stopping soon after opposite Aiguesmortes, we landed and took a hasty walk round the walls of the town, once the famous seaport where Saint Louis embarked for the Holy Land,[48] as is proved by the still remaining rings

to which his galleys were moored—now wretched and lonely in the midst of these marshy plains, where the dreadful effects of the ague are imprinted on every face. The distance at which it lies from the sea is adduced as one of the strongest proofs of the gradual retreat of the Mediterranean, and our companions, in showing us the marks left by the cables of Saint Louis' fleet, did not fail to comment on the accumulation of miles of land in the space of only five and a half centuries. All this is very curious, but unfortunately for the able theorists, historians have of late taken it into their heads to prove that Saint Louis never moored his fleet to the walls of Aiguesmortes, and that in order to embark his troops he had almost if not quite as far to march over dry land as he would have had at the present day.

"At day break the scene had considerably changed, the sky had completely cleared, the sun rising majestically from behind the distant mountains of Provence gilded the beautifull vine-clad hills of Villeneuve under which we were now proceeding. The regular uniformity of the canal, broad enough for eight or ten barges abreast, perfectly straight for miles and planted on each side with a treble line of pollarded willows, contrasted with that variety and boldness of contour which [is] so characteristic of the hills in the neighbourhood of the Rhone. On our right the plain extended as far as the eye could reach, and in its centre we could discern the steeples and ancient ruins of Arles. The scenery was delightful, hours passed away like moments, and it was not without feelings of regret that we found ourselves towards nine o'clock moored to the quay of [119] Beaucaire in the midst of the noise and turmoil of a crowded fair.

"The passage boat was soon cleared; the police would have too much labour in inspecting the passports of the multitude who flocked to Beaucaire and therefore very wisely did not ask for any.* We had fortunately not been without the line of customs, and in a passage boat there was nothing liable to *octroi*. My first care therefore was to find out the friend (M. Paulin Farel) who had invited me to his table, and to take possession of the lodging he had provided for me. It was a small room, up two pair of stairs, with a bed, a table and a chair and whatever other furniture was *strictly* necessary in a bedroom. There were no superflu-

---

* At that time on ordinary occasions, even for the shortest journeys, it was frequently necessary to exhibit one's passport on securing one's seat in a public vehicle, on starting and on arriving at one's destination.

ous luxuries, for my application came too late to secure the best rooms, but all was clean, so that I was well pleased to pay my guinea (26 francs, a large sum at that time in France) for the week or whatever time I might like to stay.

"Having thus established myself in my quarters I accompanied my friend, who was to initiate me into the mysteries of the fair. Just without the walls of the town, on the banks of the Rhone and at the foot of the steep and lofty hills· upon which the antique castle of Beaucaire is built, is a triangular plain called the *Pré* or meadow. Upon this are marked out two broad *allées* placed at right angles to each other, planted on each side with a double row of *Abeles* (a species of white poplar). The longest of these avenues was covered with booths for the retail sale of goods of all descriptions. On the other avenue, beyond a shorter row of booths, was the carriage fair. The triangle in the centre, enclosed by the two avenues and the river, was occupied by immense piles of Burgundy boards and timber. On the surface of the Rhone and of the canal [120] were floating innumerable barges, rafts and Mediterranean barks, loaded with goods, either not yet landed, or which it was most convenient to dispose of on board. In the interior of the town, the ground floor of every building was converted into a wholesale or retail warehouse.

"As we were returning to the top, I was surprised to find many of the shops and counting houses shutting up as if for the night. On enquiring into the cause of this proceeding, my friend said, 'It is now near one o'clock, which is the universal dinner hour. As time is here so precious, all parties, purchasers as well as sellers, find it most convenient to dine at the same hour, during which all business ceases. Let us therefore return home where our own meal probably awaits us, and on our way we may pass through some of the public dining rooms.' We accordingly entered an immense shed, erected outside the town, in which were some hundreds of the lower class of tradesmen, arranged along the sides of three or four long tables, each one or each party with his own meal before him, such as he had ordered it. Further on was a better sort of building, decorated with the title of *Restaurat*, in which the *commis voyageurs* were seated two or three together at each table. In each of these eating houses, means are provided for furnishing dinner with order, regularity and expedition to two or three hundred persons at a time, but when the fair business is at its height, and every one dines at the same hour, twice as many persons as it can well hold seek to enter each house, all screaming after the Garçons who in the hurry and bustle cannot even get through the business they might have been legitimately called upon to do.

"As for myself, I was most hospitably entertained. My friend was a rich manufacturer of linen and cotton goods from the neighbourhood of Montpellier, a partner also in similar manufactures in Béarn, Anjou and Normandy, and articles from these several establishments were exposed for sale in a large house he owned in the town. His party at table consisted of two partners, and five or six foremen and head clerks. The table was laid out with [121] all the profusion of Provençal and Languedocien dainties. There were fish, flesh and fowl, stewed down with every variety of sauce that could be created by the combination of oil, eggs, garlic and bacon, from the mawkish *boulliabaïss* of the Provençaux (boiled fish of various kinds served up with all the liquor and seasoned with oil) to the high flavoured *ragoûts*, the fruit of the ingenuity of gastronomic societies, with a profusion of Hermitage, Cote-rotie, a due proportion of Champaign and Bordeaux, and an occasional bottle of Malaga, or other Spanish wines, enough to impair the faculties of all the guests were they left time to enjoy them. But scarcely has the dessert appeared and the numerous dishes of fruit gone round, when business is resumed, the shops reopened and the streets are again choked with the motley groups of purchasers, again they ring with the energetic language and loud vociferations of the *marchandeurs*.

"I returned to the timber fair, where my principal purchases were to be made, but the time was not come. It was not all landed, besides that it is difficult to strike a bargain at the commencement of the fair. So I spent the afternoon in wandering about the town. I stopped some time on the quay, watching the various arrivals and listening to the jargon of languages issuing from the barks collected from Genoa, Catalonia, Greece and other Mediterranean countries. Towards evening, I strolled along the Rhone, and at length seated myself on its banks at a short distance above the town to await in quiet the hour that should summon me to supper. The sky was clear and bright, the air was still, the sun as it approached the horizon was already communicating something of a golden hue to the surrounding hills. The universal silence was interrupted only by the distant buzz of the fair, by the song of the peasant as he returned from his daily labour, or by an occasional plash in the noble stream at my feet as it rolled [122] along tumultuously in innumerable and ever changing eddies. Few situations induce the mind to give way to a melancholy, though pleasurable, train of thought, [more] than this evening calm in the pure atmosphere of the Mediterranean climate, and on the present occasion the picturesque scenery contributed not a little to enhance such sensations. Before me, on the opposite bank of the river, was the dungeon-like castle of Tarascon,[49] and it was impossible not to call to mind the memories of those who had there in former days wasted their lives in solitary confinement, or not to think of the more acute sufferings of the revolutionary victims who had so lately been starved to death immured in those horrid cells. I had not many hours before listened to the dreadful tale of the lofty tower of Avignon,[50] into which the unfortunate aristocrats had been precipitated from the roof, and if they survived the effects of the fall, there left to perish from hunger, sometimes after days spent in the midst of the mouldering corpses of their fellow-sufferers. I had heard that similar atrocities had been perpetrated at Tarascon, and I could almost fancy that the groans of the dying still issued from the grated holes in the castle wall.

"But my attention was now caught by a lively and interesting scene. Two large barges loaded with passengers were shooting down the stream together, as if striving which should first reach the town. The awnings had been taken down, and their numerous inmates, dressed in all the colours of the rainbow, were crowded on deck, eagerly watching for the first glimpse of the fair and loudly and merrily expressing their hopes of profit. The first impression which is imparted to their minds is of more importance than one would imagine, for accordingly as it is favourable or not, their spirits and thence their powers of talking rise or sink; and the striking a bargain is with them but an assault of words. He who has the greatest [123] flow overreaches his antagonist and goes off with a prize, and if the vendor were to cut the argument short by fixing a price and sticking to it peremptorily, he would sell nothing.

"A propos of this haggling, I was much amused by an instance of it which occurred in the shop of my friend, the dealer in cotton goods. I had one day, for the purpose of dispelling ennui, spent a morning with him behind the counter. After having listened to a long debate with a customer for a dozen of handkerchiefs, for which he had demanded twenty francs and which he had finally given for eighteen, I asked him whether it would not at once have saved time and trouble if [he] had from the first asked but eighteen, or at least had come down to that price as soon as he saw that his customer was determined to give no more. 'It would indeed be more agreable to the seller,' answered my friend, 'if the purchasers were equally pleased, but their vanity being gratified in proportion to the difficulty they have had and their final success in inducing us to abate, they would not buy anything at our first price however low we might fix it, and would even, from the fear of having been outwitted, contrive to evade the bargain if we were at once to accept their own offer. Of this I shall presently convince you.' And turning to two young Provençales who had come in and were waiting for one of his shopmen to be disengaged, he enquired what they wished for. It happened to be handkerchiefs of the same description as those he had just sold for eighteen francs (the lowest rate he had fixed for their sale). After descanting as usual on the beautiful quality of the article, he asked only ten francs a dozen for them. The young women raised a laugh with a loud exclamation of the exorbitance of the demand, examined the goods with great attention, held them to the light, commented upon their real or supposed defects, entered into a conversation upon the weather, the prosperity of the fair, etc, and one of them finally settled her offer at eight francs. 'Eh mon Dieu, Mademoiselle, c'est impossible; tout est ici à prix fixe. Nous faisons tant d'affaires que je me suis fait une loi de ne jamais marchander. Regardez seulement la beauté de ces mouchoirs. Voyez-les au jour. D'ailleurs avec les connaissances qu'indique un si aimable [124] extérieur, vous devez vous être apperçu que je vous les donne à moitié prix.' She admitted that their quality was good but said she could give no more than eight francs. The altercation went on for near half an hour, during which she offered successively eight and a half and nine, and finally nine and a half francs. This not being accepted she left the shop but soon returned to add five sols to her offer. The dealer would not abate a liard, and the offended fair one crossed the street to a rival *magazin*, where she probably paid double the price, but had at least the satisfaction of having talked the vendor out of a part of his original demand. Another purchaser, being asked 20 francs, fixed the value at 15. 'Eh bien Monsieur pour vous faire plaisir, ce n'est pas qu'ils ne m'en coûtent davantage, mais c'est la première fois que j'ai l'honneur de vous servir; tenez, pour avoir votre pratique, tenez, les voilà.' The poor man, surprized at so sudden an agreement, sneaked out of his bargain by finding some flaw in the texture or colour, satisfying his conscience by the consideration that he had not offered fifteen francs, but had only said the goods were worth that sum.

"But to return to the Avignon passage boats, I hastened to the quay to witness their arrival, and at the same time stopped to see the landing of a cargo of carriages from Lyons. Most of the visitors from the north come down the Rhone, but as the up navigation is very tedious and difficult, the boats are usually broken up after the voyage and the passengers return by land. Thence a large sale of carriages, and great was the variety, at least, of the new and old ones which the Lyons speculator was now unloading from his barge.

"Supper was served at our table at eight with the same profusion as the dinner, differing from it only in the preponderance of cold over hot dishes. At desert, I produced my *bec-jaune*, a set-out of ices and cakes [to] which every new comer on his first visit to Beaucaire treats the rest of his party the first night of his arrival. I had ordered a provision for a party of ten; it cost me but six and twenty francs and we had each of us as many ices as we could swallow. [125] There is an immense consumption of this article at Beaucaire. The vicinity of the Mont Ventoux renders it plentiful, and the excessive heat and dust of the fair obliges every one to stop at a café for refreshment more than once in the course of the morning. The profit of the cafetiers is of course considerable; the principal one pays for the hire of his saloon during the fair five thousand francs, an enormous sum in that country, two or three times as much as the whole house would have let for in other towns of the neighbourhood.

"Next morning the town crier, attended by a band of trumpets and drums, publicly proclaimed the opening of the fair, which strictly speaking commences the 23d July, although many sales had long been effected, and some part of the business, that of hides and leather for instance, was already nearly terminated. The principal manufacturers who purpose attending the fair, those in particular who own warehouses in Beaucaire, send a foreman to open them by the first of July. The first fortnight is chiefly spent by the various tradesmen in erecting booths to lay out their stocks, by the owners of more bulky articles in piling them up in the portions of the pré or quays allotted to them, by the mariners in landing such goods as they do not purpose to sell on board. Towards the middle of the month, a number of bargains are commenced, but few of any importance are completed before the legal opening. As the beau dimanche approaches, the arrivals encrease, that being the great day for the idle and curious; it is on that and the preceding day that the retail sellers dispose of their goods to the greatest advantage, and in the three or four following ones (unless the beau Dimanche be near the end of the fair) the greatest number of large sales are effected.

"The beau Dimanche is always the first Sunday after the opening of the fair, and this year it was the second day after my arrival. Every house at Beaucaire was now full and, even at Tarascon on the opposite bank of the Rhone, lodgings were scarce and dear. The day was *beau* in

every sense of the word. The weather was uncommonly fine, [126] not
only fine from the clearness of the sky and the brightness of the sun, for
never is a summer's day without the one and the other in the Mediterranean region, but fine for Beaucaire, without any of those hurricanes
which often raise the dust so as almost to blind any one who might venture on the pré, without the no less to be dreaded *marin*, that sultry
damp wind which weakens the constitution and enervates the facultés
so as to deprive one almost of all power of thinking or moving, without
any distant storms hovering over the mountains and consequent swell
in the river threatening inundation and ruin. The morning having been
generally spent in making small purchases, in attending mass and in the
necessary preparations for the display of the evening, the belles and
beaux began to collect on the pré as the heat declined. At five o'clock the
great avenue was so crowded that it was scarcely possible to circulate in
the throng. Here were promeneurs of all ranks, visitors from all nations,
all in their holiday dresses, all come to see and be seen, and none more
so than the beautiful Tarasconaises, beautiful from their costume, for
certainly till then I had not perceived that their features were so. Swar-
thy complexions and coarseness of feature can seldom please in a
working dress, but on the beau Dimanche, when the whole female population of Tarascon display the result of their year's study, they succeed
in producing an agreable illusion. This is the day when they must support the critical eye of thousands gathered together with no other view;
here it is that they must keep up in the eyes of all France their farfamed
reputation of elegance and beauty; here it is that they represent the
whole body of Provençales, and they must be excused if some time and
art had been spent for the honour of their country. They must be for-
given the days bestowed on the contriving the proportions of the several
colours that enter into their gaudy headdresses, as well as the hours
which it may have taken to [give to] a bow or a curl its proper tournure,
and we strangers above all must not complain of the efforts taken to
please our eyes when [127] they are thus crowned with success. It certainly was a fine sight. The diminutive crown of a cap appearing behind
a broad band of yellow, orange and scarlet silk, tied in a magnificent
bow on the top of the head, leaving their fine, high foreheads quite bare,
seemed to add lustre to their large black eyes, to encrease the energy of
their countenances and the vivacity of their features. The short waists of
their jackets, the gaudy handkerchiefs on their necks, their petticoats
collected in a huge bunch between their shoulders, a light step and
coquettish demeanour entirely turned the attention from any want of

placid sweetness or of regular beauty, which a closer inspection might have discovered.

"The Tarasconaises are however not the only female ornaments of the pré on the beau Dimanche. It often happens that ladies from Nîmes, Avignon, Montpellier or Marseille come to spend two or three days at the fair; of these days the Sunday is always one, and that Sunday cannot pass without following the crowd to the promenade till dinner or supper time. In the evening, if sufficiently numerous, they generally assemble at a ball, and perhaps spend another day in a walk to Tarascon or to the castle, then return home or complete their tour by Arles or Avignon, as convenience, business or pleasure may chance to direct them. Few of those who merely visit Beaucaire stay more than three days, and even those three can scarcely pass without giving a taste of ennui to whoever has no business to attend to. The majority of the temporary population consists of shopmen and commis voyageurs, a useful race of men no doubt, and who believe themselves to be endowed with as much of amiability, elegance and even instruction as may be desirable in any young man, but who in their grey jackets or redingottes, cut and made up as if in caricature of the fashion, with their enormous curls over each ear, their would-be fashionable, but coarse and dirty linen and hair, their pedantic language which they take for refined or scientific, betray that vulgarity in mind and in person which would only be excusable if they did not pretend to refinement. Their time is indeed fully taken up with commercial business and this may be the reason why none of those allurements to vice and dissipation, [128] which usually swarm in all places where a large number of young men are collected for any purpose, are never to be met with at Beaucaire. Disorderly females, it is said, are expelled by the police, gaming-houses would not repay the speculatory outlay, bull-baitings, common at other seasons of the year, are not held during the fair, because they can only take place by daylight, that is during business hours, and the plays acted at the theatre of Tarascon are no more than what the town itself can support in winter.

"But for the amusement of the peasantry, there is no want of mountebanks and quacks, who reap a plentiful harvest from the pockets of their wondering and delighted *cultivateurs*. Here the most celebrated of French Quacks (whose name I have not noted) never fails to attend in a handsome calèche and pair, with a lively coachman and footman, and attended by a band of eight musicians on horseback. He first gathers around him a large assembly, to the sound of no indifferent music; then the venerable old man, in a short but well-worded speech, enumerates his various services during the fifty years he had devoted to the welfare of man, laments his growing infirmities which may so soon deprive him of the happiness he enjoys in imparting the treasures of his science to the public, and lastly cheers his audience with the consoling prospect he has of living a second life in the person of his son, to whom he must now resign the pleasure of explaining the virtues of his panacea. At the close of his speech he quits the calèche, and is succeeded by a tall, stout young man with a would-be martial face buried in whiskers and his clothes in embroidery. This promising quack, with a powerful voice, descants so successfully on his specifics that ere half an hour has elapsed hundreds of hands are eagerly stretched out for fear the last bottle should be gone, and in this manner for some years was the son gradually initiated into the mysteries of the art of gulling. The old man has now retired from business, but his son is still to be met with periodically in every town from Lyons to Bordeaux, and notwithstanding the expenses attending on the travelling in this style with ten horses and as many attendants, he [129] clears some 25,000 francs a year, his country customers wisely considering that the inefficiency of a remedy on one occasion is no reason for its being so on another.

"The glorious Sunday had now gone by, and with it everything that had the appearance of amusement. Business was actively resumed, as all were in haste to return home. Bargains which had been discussing for days were now concluded in a moment, generally with an encrease or decrease of price of from five to ten percent according to the preponderance of buyers or sellers. The booths, the stalls, the warehouses, the piles of bulky goods, were gradually cleared away, and the roads once more crowded with travellers priding themselves on having out-talked and out-witted their adversaries, each seller pleased with the high price he had obtained considering the low prices of the fair, the buyer with the bargains he had struck at a time when goods were scarce; such at least were the excuses they were preparing for their wives or employers. Towards the end of the month, the whole population seemed transformed into carters, boatmen, measurers, packers, etc, or into bankers and bailiffs, for the 28th is pay day, when many an unfortunate speculator may be seen hurrying from creditor to creditor in hopes of obtaining a respite or a farther loan, whilst the moneylenders are eagerly hunting down their prey, backed by a host of huissiers armed with protests and summons. As for myself I had finished my own business in the beginning of the week, and whilst waiting for my host, with whom I was to return *en poste*, I loitered about, a prey to ennui, and to the first attacks of an ague brought on by the climate. The only amusement I could still enjoy was the watching the progressive clearing of the booths. Among these I was struck with the observing some twenty or thirty filled with child's drums of all sizes almost to the last, wondering why so many should be brought to be carried back again, when on the last day, strolling round the pré, my ears were assailed by a din resembling that of a numerous and boisterous school. Every domestic peasant as he goes home carries a drum for his child and a paper fan for his wife, and now there were hundreds trying the sound of the drums they were purchasing. The stock was almost [130] entirely cleared off before night.

"I had had quite enough of Beaucaire, and was not a little rejoiced on the 30th of the month to hear the crack of the postillion's whip, and no less to arrive the same night at Montpellier. Oppressed as I was by dust, little interested in crossing the bare and monotonous plains I had seen so often, my ague prevented my enjoying even the bustle of the road. This malady is very prevalent§ in summer all along the Mediterranean; foreigners are particularly liable to it* at least once during their stay. For my part, I was confined three weeks to my bed, and as many months to the house. Beaucaire however is not in general reckoned unhealthy; the substantial suppers immediately before bedtime and the bad quality of the Rhone water may have contributed to my disorder, yet I should not advise anyone who has not business at Beaucaire to spend more than three days there if he wants to avoid les fièvres et l'ennui."

It was late in the autumn before I could take to my usual outdoor occupations, and when at last I was able to leave the house, one of my first duties was to lay a ghost. A servant girl from the farm, going one evening down a hollow path way to fetch water from a brook running between high banks covered with tall brushwood, returned in a great fright, saying that she had seen a ghost on the opposite side of the water, warning her away. This was much talked of the next day, and nothing would induce any of the farm people to go down for water after dark, especially when two days after it was hinted that the ghost had again appeared. This induced some of the farmservants with our own, partly to show their unbelief, partly from curiosity, to form a party to go down to the spot, relying on the safety of numbers; and sure enough, after waiting for a time, a great white object appeared to them suddenly on

---

* Quinine was then only about to be discovered.[51]

the opposite bank. The affair now got noised about in the neighbourhood, strangers were attracted to the exhibition, which was repeated
almost nightly, exciting the more implicit belief, as on [131] going round
by the bridge to the spot, no trace of the ghost could be discovered. The
excitement reached our house. I was still afraid of going out at night, but
directed our garde champêtre to go with the others, take his gun, and
fire at the ghost. This he did in fear and trembling, and fired without
effect. The ghost remained immoveable. I now thought the matter
becoming serious and went myself attended by a large party. After
waiting a little, a tall white object appeared from behind the bushes. I
raised my gun, and had scarcely taken aim when before I let off, the
ghost collapsed, and immediately crossing the brook, there we found
the sheet of one of the farm servants and a long pole. It proved on
enquiry that the first ghost was an old grey-haired donkey, solacing its
thirst at the brook, who raised its head when disturbed by the girl,
which was easily interpreted as a warning gesture, and that seeing the
effect produced on the household by her exaggerated narrative, a young
man among the servants, aware of the real fact, determined to play her a
trick, which he persevered in when he saw the effects he produced.
When the garde champêtre fired, he observed that in his fright he aimed
far wide of the mark, and it was only when he saw a gun more steadily
pointed at him that he thought it high time to give in. But though the
deception was thus fully proved by the young man's confession, it was
very long before the majority of the servants would admit that the first
apparition was not a real ghost.

The following winter was one of great activity to me, in superintending the *defrichements*, enclosures, roadmaking, planting, and other works
going on at Restinclières, and frequent evenings spent in society in
town. I was however chiefly in the country with my eldest sister, who
never left it, and in the evenings, amongst other things, took a good deal
to the study of my Uncle's and other works on logical and allied subjects. As spring came on, botany became the chief amusement of my leisure hours. Already in February, the fallows and stubbles attracted my
attention, from the great variety of Phascums, Gymnostomums and
other minute mosses, which gave the ground a rich [132] brown tint
from their closely packed fruits. At the end of that month and in March
our garrigues were already coloured by Narcissi and other bulbous
plants, Aphyllanthes, etc, followed by innumerable Helianthema,
Linums, Genisteae and others, Papilionaceae, and the young cornfields
invaded by a variety of weeds, of which we have no idea in northern

countries. A very favorite botanical excursion was that to the Pic St Loup, a conical rock of some 500 or 600 ft, about 7 or 8 miles to the north of our place and very conspicuous from Montpellier. The northern side of this rock is almost perpendicular and can be ascended with the greatest difficulty by the aid of narrow ledges and clefts, amongst which are many rare plants in small quantities, whilst large masses of Linum suffruticosum and many generally rare species luxuriate in the garrigues and wastes behind the peak. The front of the Pic, though steep, is more accessible, and from this side is the ordinary ascent, especially on the day of the pilgrimage, when the peasantry from the surrounding villages to a distance of seven or eight miles assemble for their devotions, followed by a jollification, every one carrying their dinner or purchasing it from the caterers who flock together on the occasion. Each village sends its body of *pelerins*, *blancs*, *bleus*, or *gris*, according to the colour of their vestments, most of them white—bodies answering in some measure to our Odd Fellows.[52] These ascend in procession to hear mass in a chapel on the summit, after which, and after refreshing themselves among the rocks about, they descend in procession, winding down to a small level about two thirds the height of the mountain, where there is a cross, at which the priest delivers a sermon. This scene is very picturesque and is the subject of a painting now in our drawing room by Captn LeBlanc,[53] a very faithful representation. In an almost inaccessible cave about half way up the northern perpendicular side, are to be found remains of box shrubs (which abound on these rocks) which according to popular belief are chips left by St Joseph who used to work there! and are invaluable as tooth picks—but very [133] few indeed are those who, as far as I could learn, have ever ventured to go there in search of them; and young and strong as I was, with a head never affected by a precipice, I had the greatest difficulty in reaching the cave, and still greater returning safely from it. At the east end of the rock on a lower cone, are the ruins of the chateau de Montferrand which, like many others in these rocky regions, excite one's surprise how the materials for building could have been collected with the scanty mechanical contrivances in use in the middle ages, and why a castle was built so far from habitations or cultivation. On the northern base of the Pic St Loup are now extensive thickets of box, Arbutus, and other shrubs or low trees, and but very little cultivation or water for miles.

A very interesting botanical excursion was one I made in the month of March with M. Delile, then Professor of Botany and Director of the Botanic Garden of Montpellier, to Les Arcs and Les Capouladoux, wild

ravines in a rocky, thinly wooded, scantily inhabited and little frequented district above St Guilhen on the banks of the Herault. These
ravines, botanically rich, had been explored by Magnol two hundred
years earlier, and the localities of the plants are very accurately noted in
his *Botanicon Monspeliense*; they had however been very rarely visited by
botanists since his time, and the *Cyclamen hederrefolium*, for instance,
unknown as a Languedoc plant to modern botanists, we found in great
abundance in the precise locality indicated by Magnol. On a subsequent
visit to Les Arcs, I found the Althaea rosea in its wild state, a showy plant
in the chinks of the rocks, though very different from our hollyhocks. I
made several other excursions with M. Delile, who with all his peculiarities was full of anecdote and esprit, very liberal and obliging and an
agreable companion. One burning hot day in the end of June, we had
been wandering for a couple of hours amongst the scorching white rocks
of the Pic St Loup, bathing in perspiration, whilst eagerly gathering
plants and chatting away, till finding ourselves in the shade of a tall rock
on the northern side we [134] stopped to rest, when Delile, looking back
and surprised to find the Pic behind him, exclaimed, "Tiens, nous avons
traversé le Pic St Loup sans nous en appercevoir," a feat which but few
even of the natives would care to perform in midday at Midsummer.

In the spring of 1822 my father was induced to take my two younger
sisters on a couple of months' visit to Paris, chiefly to meet his old
friends the Gagarins of Moscow, who had been spending the winter
there. Princess Gagarin was the daughter of the Count and Countess
Pushkin, whose acquaintance my father had made at Tobolsk, where the
family was then residing as exiles[54]—and the intimacy then formed was
kept up through the subsequent generation, though generally at a distance geographically. Prince Serge Ivanovitch Gagarin, the husband,
was one of the upper Moscow nobility, and more enlightened than the
generality of them. At Paris he kept up an intimate intercourse with men
of note in science and litterature as well as politically, and was making
large collections of articles of taste, and of notes, information, and specimens, which he thought might further his industrial projects on his
return home. With them was Lise Gordon, who before we went to Russia in 1805 had been brought up as one of us. She was about two years
older than my eldest sister, went with us to Russia, and when we
returned home was left in the Gagarins' family as a demoiselle de
compagnie, and ultimately took charge of their youngest daughter as a
kind of governess, in which capacity she was now with them in France,
the eldest daughter having a Russian governess of inferior capacity, and

the son a French tutor, M. Marin, a very well informed and able young man. Lise Gordon was a very superior person in intellect and mental capacity and had taken every advantage of her education, commenced by my mother and very judiciously continued by the Gagarins. She believed herself to be a natural daughter of my father's, though he declined to acknowledge it to her; but when this same year, on their passing through [135] Montpellier, I took much to her, whom I remembered as a favorite in our family when children, she confided to me her suspicions, entreating me to verify them, which I had subsequently the means of doing, beyond all doubt and very much to her satisfaction. This discovery led to an active correspondence, from which I benefitted greatly, from the sound advice she always gave me, and the high moral principle which pervaded in her thoughts, conversation and letters.[55]

This same summer of 1822, I made a botanical tour in the Cevennes and Lozère, commencing with spending a couple of days at the Dax's country house at St Felix, at the foot of the Cevennes. We, and especially my sisters, had contracted a great intimacy with this family, one of the principal ones in the aristocratic, catholic and royalist society of Montpellier. Monsieur Dax, d'Axat, had considerable properties in Roussillon and had now been for some years Mayor of Montpellier. He had now remained in town, but Madame Dax (a sister of the Saint-Priests and of Madame de Calvière, whom my sisters had known at Paris) was there with two handsome daughters, Made Felix Durand, lately married to the son of a millionaire, royalist banker and Mademoiselle Emma and two lively girls, their cousins—not a man in the house besides myself and a single manservant. The house, with its stone floors, as is almost universal in lower Languedoc, and simple accomodations, was certainly not what we should expect in the country residence of a family not stinted as to means, but it was comfortable according to their views, and Madame Dax showed me in detail all the improvements she had made, priding herself upon what they were pleased to term "Lieux à l'Anglaise," though certainly still very far from our WCs. The weather (July) was intensely hot, and under the thick shade of some trees in the yard or in the cool rooms with watered floors, playing at battledore and shuttlecock or other games with the young ladies, all of us in a loose negligé, I was almost [136] forgetting the object of my excursion. I had indeed already become very intimate with Emma Dax, and l'Anglais de Restinclières et la fille du Maire had been already talked of in the town. She was an excellent girl, a great favorite of my sisters, and on two subsequent occasions a marriage between us was all but concluded—but at the last moment difficulties of detail as to religious arrangements obliged us finally to renounce it. She afterwards made a very good match with a Monsieur Lajard, proved an excellent wife and mother of two nice children, when last I saw her after my own marriage,[56] but died still young.

I broke away however from Saint Felix the second day, and the next morning sent back the horses with my servant (I had till then been on horseback), and hiring a guide to carry my small valise, I took my vasculum and cartable on my own shoulders and proceeded across the mountains on foot, intending to sleep that night at a roadside inn recommended to me, not very far from a small watering place called Bagnols. Arriving there however at a little after 6 p.m., I found I could have no accomodation there, all their beds had been sent to Bagnols, which was unusually full. I had started at 3 in the morning and had already gone over full 35 miles, but there was no help for it, so after a hearty though very simple meal, I started at 7, and walked the remaining 15 miles down to Mende by 10 o'clock. I now felt really tired, and whilst my supper was preparing, fell half asleep in my chair, when I was startled by the appearance of the Commissaire de Police, demanding my passport.—I had none, not deeming it necessary at so short a distance from where I was so well known. I explained who I was, and the object of my tour—he seemed but half satisfied.—I appealed to the people of the house, who found that the daughter of the Entrepreneur des Diligences of Montpellier was there, who knew all about me and vouched for my identity. The Commissaire retired and I thought all [137] was over, when presently he returned with two Gendarmes in full uniform and told me I was under arrest because I had no "papiers en règle." I then took out my pocket book and showed I had letters—amongst others to the director of the Post Office, M. Prost, a well known botanist, and said that if he only took that letter to its address, he should be fully satisfied. "No," he said, "unless M. Prost will come and answer for you I must leave you in charge of the gendarme." In short, nothing would do but send a gendarme for M. Prost, who, when called out of bed, came in some alarm. I handed him the letters; the moment he saw the address, before he opened it, he exclaimed, "Ah, c'est de M. Delile; c'est un botaniste, je vous en repond." The Commissaire gave way. M. Prost, profuse in his civilities notwithstanding the rude interruption I had been the cause of, pressed me to spend the next day with him, and promised to set all right with the police. In the morning I had scarcely got to my breakfast when in came the Commissaire, humbly begging me to intercede for him with the Prefet, who threatened to dismiss him for his last night's stretch of authority, saying that they had particular instructions to look out for the aide de camp of General Delon (who had been attempting an insurrection at Saumur) who was known to be hiding in those mountains, and whose signalement agreed generally with my person.[57] I saw the Prefet and settled that business, spent a few very pleasant hours with M. Prost amongst his dried plants, and started on my return home by the Espérou, walking thirty miles that day and twenty more the following one.

With the exception of the above short tour, I was the whole of this year 1822 fully occupied at home. My father and mother quite fixed themselves in the chateau, we gave up the large appartment in the Cours des Casernes, taking a small one at the other end of the town, near some of our friends, as a pied a terre, when after parties we wished, some of us, to sleep in town. My father availing himself [138] of a permission he had obtained to import our personal effects and machinery and implements for our own use free of duty, not only had sent over from England ploughs, thrashing and other machines, which had never yet been heard of in Languedoc, but had also imported his library of considerable extent, a great ressource in the winter evenings—and I varied the occupation which my encreasing herbarium was giving me with much of my favorite historical reading, and resumed the study of various works connected with logic and mental philosophy, working §as the season advanced at the French edition of my Uncle's "Essay on Nomenclature and Classification" I had begun some years previously and which I now thought of completing, under the prospect of a visit to England. I felt well§ satisfied with my position, without looking forward much to the future; but my two younger sisters, having had a couple of months' taste of brilliant society in Paris, began to feel the chateau life rather irksome, some of our English friends expressed a wish that they might come over on a visit to them, and my Uncle invited me to his house. My father and mother felt unwilling to leave home, so it was determined that I should go with my sisters over to England for a few months, renew our connection with my father's friends, and that I should collect information serviceable for promoting our plans for the improvement of our estate, from which my father expected so much. In November my Uncle wrote to me direct, to offer me a bed and express a wish I should bring with me my translation of *Chrestomathia*, in answer to which I wrote on the 27th Nov—after accepting his offer, "As to my translation of *Chrestomathia*, I am afraid that either R. Doane or J. Mill have given you too high an idea of my undertaking. About three years ago when I first read this work, I had just followed a course of lectures, in which an attempt was made at classing the principal branches of Art and Science, which in some few points seemed to approach towards the classification given in the Appendix No V. to your *Chrestomathia*. This gave me the idea of studying the subject [139] more particularly, and as the best means of doing so, I set about translating that number of the Appendix. I was the more disposed to do so, as nobody else, in this country (France) at least, seemed to be occupied on the same subject, and having thus the less rivality to fear, I hoped to be able to suit it to the taste of the French public. Before our journey here I had got through a great part of it, but since our acquisition of Restinclières, the many agricultural pursuits I have been engaged in have obliged me to lay it aside. I have now taken it up again, and still hope to compleat it before my departure for England, that is to say, inasmuch as concerns the classification of art and science. As to the principal object of the work, the system of education, I do not feel myself at present competent to the undertaking a subject on which I should have to encounter, in this country at least, so much opposition and rivality from the many whose attention is now turned towards it. If ever I should attempt it, it will require a great deal more study not only of the subject itself, but also of what others have written in it, than I can find time for at present."[58]

4

A Visit to England, 1823

We left Montpellier, my sisters Clara, Sarah and myself, by the malle poste of the 25th Jany, and I immediately commenced a diary, in the form of letters I regularly despatched to my elder sister during the whole of our absence, and from which chiefly the following is compiled or extracted. This was our first experience of the then lately improved and accelerated mail carriages, holding three inside and one outside by the Conducteurs. It was "easy and comfortable, and it is such a comfort not to have all sorts of strangers clean or dirty nodding and falling asleep on our shoulders. We staid two hours at Nîmes, where we were shown into the *salon* of the Hotel du Gard where the courrier stops, in which were two gentlemen, the one genteel and goodlooking from Montpellier, the other—from Marseille. Our conducteur who had become merry from the pains he had taken to dispel the damp [140] from his stomach, came and took his bouillon in the same room, entertaining us with his ill humour for the delay of the horses, and his stories of wine having been given to horses to drink—used to make mortar, etc, instead of water, during the drought of last summer, and other similar tales of what took place, or were at least invented, in his native country on the banks of the Garonne. We were however surprised there should be so many delays in the service of the mail where celerity is so important—we were waiting of horses at Nîmes nearly an hour after the packets were ready. The roads are also so bad that we did not arrive at Avignon till 6 in the morning instead of 12 at night. The weather, which had been very wet and gloomy, cleared up soon after we left Nîmes, the moon came out bright, and its effect on the picturesque rocks after Remoulins and on the stupendous arches of the Pont du Gard was magnificent. We were luckily obliged to pass along these noble remains of Roman grandeur owing to the height of the river Gardon, which prevents the passage of the ferry on the direct road."[1] The impression caused by the sight of the bright moon on the picturesque structure, decorated with wild shrubs and plants which had established themselves between the stones, remains still vividly impressed on my memory.

We were detained a day at Avignon and two at Lyons, waiting for places in the mail, although we had written several days back to secure them; the journey from Avignon to Lyons occupied 36 hours, and from Lyons to Paris three nights and two days, arriving at Paris early in the morning of the 2d February. At Avignon we found an English friend, and at Lyons we were shown the few things worth seeing by a friend of Paulin Farel's. I went there to the play also to see Leontine Fay, the wonder of the day, as an actress of 12 or 13 years of age, but spent a good deal of my time in working up my *Essai sur la Nomenclature et Classification des Arts et Sciences*, or as my sisters nicknamed it, my "Scopies," which I had brought with me, still in an unfinished state. The rapid mail journey afforded but little more means of observation on the road than we now [141] obtain in railroads, as no stoppages were allowed beyond what was absolutely necessary for meals; and the letters I wrote at the time contain but little relating to the country passed through, except that I was struck with the great *localisation* of a variety of customs, the changes from province to province almost as great as from nation to nation, a distinction which modern improved communications have tended so much to eliminate. The ornamentation of country villas and cottages, for instance, was totally different at Montpellier, at Lyons, and at Moulins, peculiar colours and patterns, the special fashion of each district, and the national coiffures of the peasant women, still more strongly illustrative of local fashions. About Tarascon, caps with broad bands, large bows and flat crowns, surmounted by little black flat hats the shape of soup plates—about Tarare and Roanne, begin singular straw bonnets lined with pink, with black bands, basin-like crowns, and broad borders turned up at both ends boat-like—as we proceed northward, the hinder end rises, and the front lowers, till they are transformed into helmets, and all these not here and there, only put on in full dress, but universally worn by all the peasantry we met. Similar localisation was observable in the trappings of horses and a number of other petty matters, showing how little progress modern centralisation had then made.

[142]It had been arranged that we should remain at Paris the time requisite for revising and printing the *Essai*, and my sisters, having procured through the kindness of Admiral Tchitchagoff a temporary home, in a pension in the faubourg Montmartre where his youngest daughter had been for some time, I established myself in the Hotel Vauban, and immediately took measures for getting the work accomplished with as little delay as possible. Our friends the Partouneaux were now comfortably settled in the Ecole Militaire, of which the General was now Governor, and my own particular friend Tonin agreed to look over my manuscript with me. To this work he devoted an hour or two every morning that he was not otherwise engaged, either at the Ecole, where I sometimes went to breakfast, or he came over to my hotel. Bossanges frères, the publisher of the French (Dumont) editions of my Uncle's works,[2] engaged to get the *Essai* printed in 8 or 10 days from the time that the whole copy was placed in his hands, and answered for the receipts covering the expences with more or less of a balance over, and I generally sat up late at night finishing the rough copy of the manuscript, which my sister Sarah copied out fair for me. I placed the first portion in the printer's hands on the 14th and the remainder on the 23d and 27th, and notwithstanding repeated failures on his part in fulfilling his promises, I was enabled to correct the whole of the proofs in the first week[§] of March.

During the whole of this six weeks' stay in Paris, although the finishing up this work was my chief occupation, I was enabled also to enjoy the society of some of our friends and to visit some of the theatres. I dined with Admiral Tchitchagoff the day of our arrival, notwithstanding our three nights travelling. He had quite made up his mind never to return to Russia, and though he was always abusing the French, yet he had just bought a place near Sceaux, on which he was laying out a good deal of money—for the Alien Act prevented his thinking of settling in England.[3] I spent several evenings at his house near the Boulevard des Italiens, where one was sure to meet some [143] of the enlightened members of Parisian or foreign Society. I had also most agreable, as well as excellent, dinners at Count Chaptal's, the chymist, in the faubourg St Germain. His Society was chiefly scientific, and his dinners very recherché, he being a great connoisseur and always dressing the salad himself, the lady members of the family all very agreable; but I was most with our former friends the De la Molères, M. de la Molère being established in the Gendarmerie here, and especially with the Partouneaux, with whom I often dined or breakfasted. It was also with the Partouneaux and the De la Molères that I had the first enjoyment of theatres, "the grand Opera for the eyes, the Italiens for the ears, the Français for the mind"; but above all I was carried away by the Italiens, which was then exceedingly good, Mlle Cinti and Zucchelli at their best, Rossini's operas with all the charm of novelty, and the orchestra perfect. The *Gazza Ladra* and the *Cenerentola* had an effect upon me that I was long in getting over, and [S]was scarcely exceeded by that produced a few evenings later on, first hearing and seeing Pasta in *Tancredi*. At the Français, Mlle Mars was creating a great sensation by her wonderful acting in *Vulérie*, her recognition of her lover by taking his hand before he has said a word, and above all her bursting into the room and throwing herself on her knees on recovering her eyesight had an extraordinary electrical effect on the whole audience. At the Opera, the *spectacle* in *Aladdin* was glorious, and several evenings at the Opera comique amused me as much as any.—I also visited at Mde d'Orglandes, one of whose daughters was married to Chateaubriant,[4] the Calvières and a few others, but only in the evenings, my days being taken up with my work and a few necessary courses. Among botanists, I only made acquaintance with old Prof. Thouin at the Jardin des Plantes, and with M. Bosc at the Luxembourg.

[144]Paris was at the time in a state of great political excitement. The Duke of Angoulême's expedition to reestablish Ferdinand in Spain was determined upon.[5] The prospect of war was raising the spirits of the army and all who had any, or hoped to have any, connection with it,

whilst the liberals were taking advantage of it to raise an outcry against the Government, and many joined in furious attacks on the English, who, it was thought, would interfere in Spain, the military boasting that, if the redcoats did appear, it would be a war of extermination. Great crowds assembled at the departure of the Garde Royale; but the part taken by the mob in the proceedings of the Chambers soon superseded everything and seemed to threaten serious disturbances. The scenes in the Chamber of Deputies were of the utmost violence. The expulsion of Manuel was carried in a noisy tumult, which can only be witnessed at Paris; the next day he appeared in his place, the President ordered him out, he would not go till the gendarmes seized him by the collar and dragged him out. He became of course the idol of the mob, who completely covered the Place Louis XVI and the Boulevarts to a great distance. Manuel was borne in triumph home,[6] and it seemed from the noise and uproar as if a revolution was at hand, but a body of two or three hundred Gendarmes à cheval, with a little determination and arresting a few of the foremost, turned the tide; the rest thought it wisest to go home, and the next day all seemed forgotten and the town resumed its usual aspect.

We left Paris on the 8th March, by the malle poste which started at 4 in the afternoon and arrived in Calais at 12 at night the next day, the weather bitterly cold and snowy. We crossed the next day with a tolerably quiet sea—our first experience of a steam boat, for none had yet made their way to the Mediterranean. It was a small one, very safe but slow, as we were 4½ hours crossing and had to land in boats, and submit to all sorts of vexations, impediments and extortions, from boatmen, laddermen, porters, commissioners, customhouse, [145] etc, all now things of the past. We could not get our luggage landed and examined till the next morning, too late for the day coaches, and to add to the discomforts there was a steady cold rain. We were however much amused; everything was so new to us. A nine years' residence in France had made us see everything with foreign eyes, and the contrast between Dover and Calais, which is striking even now, was then very much stronger. The beefsteak and oyster sauce, and cheese afterwards, instead of half a dozen little dishes for dinner—the people, the houses, the streets and roads, the hedges, ditches, posts and railings, the very stones on the roadsides, the language, the gestures, the dress, everything so unfamiliar.

It was 11 o'clock before we could leave Dover in a post chaise, expecting to get that night to Hampstead, as we had announced by letter, it having been arranged that my sisters should spend a few weeks with the Miss Baillies[7]—whilst I went to my Uncle's. The weather had cleared up and we were in capital spirits, enjoying everything we saw.—I wrote at the time "What would a Frenchman say" (and we were pretty nearly in the position of French) "if after having gone a stage in a French chaise de poste covered with mud, drawn by two shaggy horses with rope harness and a pigtail driver in jack boots, he were all at once transported into an English post chaise, with English drivers on English roads. Neat chariots, washed at every stage, perfectly clean inside, well hung, with large, well cleaned glasses, handsome, sleek and active horses, well blackened harness, with their brass work new and bright, a driver dressed like a gentleman, excellent roads without ruts or holes, rather narrow it is true, but winding gracefully over hill and dale through a beautiful country covered with parks and villas, all this must appear in the eyes of a foreigner more like a drive in one's own carriage through a nobleman's grounds than like common posting on a high road. Then the great number of passengers we meet every minute give the whole a gay and bustling [146] appearance we scarcely ever observe, even on the most frequented of French roads. Between Dover and London we met no less than 32 stage coaches coming from London, all loaded with travellers inside and out, each drawn by four beautiful horses, and all in excellent order, besides numbers of post chaises and private carriages, horsemen, carts, waggons, etc," all in contrast to the heavy, lumbering, often shabby and always dirty diligences, pataches, chaises de poste, charabancs, carts, etc, of the French. We had however miscalculated the time the journey would take, the posting on that road being exceptionally slow; it was dark when we drove through London—giving us however the then striking spectacle of streets lighted with gas, the first we had seen—and it was 11 o'clock before we got up to Hampstead—every body in bed; we could not get in to the Baillies, and no beds to be had for my sisters at the inns, or rather public houses—and it was near 2 when we accepted the kind offer of a widow lady, who heard of our distress, to give my sisters a bed, whilst I got an indifferent one at the "Red Lion."

In the morning, I saw my sisters safely installed with those charming and excellent old friends, Joanna Baillie and her sister, and I drove down to Jeremy Bentham's in Queen Square Place, where I found my room all ready, but that I was not to see my uncle till dinner. Accordingly as I then wrote: "A quarter of an hour before dinner, that is to say about 8 o'clock in the evening, my Uncle called me up stairs and received me with great kindness and affection, though he says he never should have known me (I was much altered from a short fat boy, nicknamed 'Devonshire dumpling,' to a thin young man of 5 ft. 11½ in.) and took me to the light to see whether my white lock still remained that he might be sure I was no impostor. After dinner he sent down the two 'reprobates,'[8] and kept me till 11, to talk to me about my sisters, about his own occupations, and many other things. I do not know how he will be persuaded to see my sisters, which he now [147] says he is determined not to do. He says that either he will like them or he will not. If for argument sake he should not, then there would be only harm done by their meeting. If he should like them, and should see them once or twice, there would come the pain of parting, but this would be, I should think, just as good a reason for not seeing me or any one else. I hope however that in time he may alter his determination. He is now entirely occupied with his writings, and cannot bear the least thing that will either affect him or disturb his thoughts. Constitutional codes are now the subject he is at work upon. He gets up at 10 or 11, breakfasts at 3 or 4, whilst Mr Colls reads the paper to him, and dines at ½ past 7 or 8 in his room. About six weeks ago he caught a cold and cough, which are now quite gone, but since then he has never been out of his room, even to take his morning walks; he intends now to begin them again, but says that habit has made him lazy and that he regrets the time his walks take him. He looks very well and brisk, and scarcely older than when I saw him last. R. Doane is living in the house; the other young man is a Mr Colls, who writes for him and dines here but does not sleep or breakfast. This Mr Colls seems a mere machine; he can scarcely speak two words, but copies and reads well. He sees Mr Mill once a week after dinner, his dinner hour being too late for Mr M. to dine with him. He also sees now and then the Tripolitan Ambassador, Mr Bowring,[9] and a few others." And two or three days later, "M. Lavigne, a Frenchman going to Egypt with a view of establishing Lancasterian schools there,[10] dined and spent the evening with my Uncle, so I saw the two 'reprobates,' as he calls the two young men, had our dinner brought to us down stairs, which is the case whenever Uncle has any one with him on any particular business. I believe, though, he is disappointed in this M. Lavigne, whom he then saw for the first time." Whoever thus visited him, at or after dinner, would generally remain till 11 or a little after, when Doane would go up to warn Mr Bentham that it was time to go to bed.

[148]The remainder of the month of March was spent chiefly in renewing acquaintance with our old friends in town or at Hampstead,

besides matters of business which obliged me to go frequently to Lincoln's Inn and to the City. My father's friends all received me most kindly; Lord and Lady Colchester were not in town, but he sent me several very useful letters, and Lady C. introduced me to her friend Lady Calthorpe, mother of Lord Calthorpe, so that one way or another, I was soon overwhelmed with dinner invitations, often two or three for the same day, and even obliged to engage myself beforehand if I wished to dine at home with my Uncle. I went frequently up to Hampstead, where my sisters were most cordially received, but even those we had been most intimate with—even our excellent old master Mr Spowers—said they never should have recognised me, so great had been the change in nine years from a short, round, fat boy of 13 to a tall slender young man of 22; and as for myself, wherever I went, the details of life, then in greater contrast to those of France than now, were all new and strange to me. The first dinner party I went to was with my sisters to the Longmans of Hampstead.[11] They had left their old house next door to us at Frognall and had an excellent one, in very pretty grounds, on Red Lion hill. "When we got there, it was still just light enough to enable us to admire two beautifull cedar trees in front of the house and a most elegant and neat garden, with clean and smooth lawns, tidy clumps, and everything wearing an appearance of neatness, which still strikes me in all English houses and gardens as something unusual and extraordinary. We were shown into a most elegant drawing room, built by Mr Longman, one end of which is occupied by a magnificent organ; the other terminates in a handsome bow, with three windows looking on to the garden. On a table were pots of hyacinths, amongst others one of a beautiful vinous pink colour, very double, which is said to be very scarce, and [149] is certainly a very handsome variety. There were also bouquets of lilacs and other flowers that at this season can only be forced. Mr and Mrs Longman appeared but little altered; I should have known them both immediately from their voice and manner, as well as from their appearance." The sons and daughters, the elder ones now grown up, were not so easily recollected after nine years. The party consisted chiefly of Hampstead people, several of them old friends. "We were in all eighteen at table; the dinner was magnificent, not perhaps so much in the profusion of dishes, but rather in the manner of serving. The most brilliant mahogany table, beautifully fine mangled table linen, and above all the extraordinary brightness of the knives and plate seemed quite magnificent after the French deal boards covered with comparatively coarse linen and pewter-like plate. According to English

custom, the cloth was removed for desert, and after the ladies had partaken of it, they retired and left us poor gentlemen to sit over our wine.
After a good hour's conversation, for very little wine was drunk, we
returned to the drawing room and found Miss L. playing psalms and
partitions on the organ, the sound of which is grander than anything I
remember hearing, though perhaps it is not the kind of music I like the
best. After this music was over, Miss F. played us a couple of quadrilles
on the piano, and between them, the two young ladies sang. After the
second quadrille the party broke up, at 11 o'clock, and I returned to
Queen Square Place."

The novelty however of these dinner arrangements soon wore off,
especially after having been present at several of very various styles, the
small, quiet, most friendly and charming parties at the Miss Baillies, and
at their brother's, Dr Baillie, the truly English dinners at Mr Koe's, Mr
Ainslie's, and others, and the more refined ones at Lady Calthorpe's,
Lord Maynard's, Count Woronzow's.

[150]In the then state of London, much time was taken up by the
actual moving from place to place, or at least so it appeared to those
who visited it with Parisian habits. Both towns were then very different
from what they are now, Paris more altered than London. Paris life was
concentrated in a limited district of a town which was altogether a dense
mass of narrow tortuous streets, among which even the quays and boulevards were nothing like the handsome, open ventilators they have
now become, although on the other hand, the contrast of the atmo-
spheres of the two towns was more to the disadvantage of London than
it is now. In the end of March I wrote:

"The walking from one end of London to another is much more than
the little short walks I was used to at Paris, though much less fatiguing,
on account of the flag foot pavements. There are no cabriolets de place
here" (no omnibus's, and stage coaches were not allowed to take up or
set down in the town, except at their Office) "and I see and hear so much
of the inconvenience of hackney coaches and the insolence of hackney
coachmen that I have not yet had the courage to make a trial of them,
putting out of question the high price of their fares"; then "we have had
very uncomfortable weather, a continued fog since we arrived. Yesterday was perhaps the first day that I could see this town that I have been
crossing in all directions for these three weeks past, and even then,
whether from smoke or fog, I know not, the houses could only be seen
through a yellowish mist which some think picturesque, but which to
me appears, to the last degree, dull and disagreable." On the occasion of

going to spend the afternoon and evening with a barrister and his young family in Upper Woburn Street,[12] [I saw] a new part of the town, built [151] since we had left England. "This is certainly a great improvement; the streets are broad, the houses very neat, and a number of fine large squares with gay gardens are every where to be found. There is only one thing which I think does not look so well in the modern English houses, which is that there are no visible roofs, so that they look as if unfinished, while at Paris, the form of the roof is one of the beauties of the new streets of Rivoli and Castiglione. With the exception of these two streets, the Rue de la Paix, the Place Vendome, the Rue Royale and the principal public monuments at Paris, London is certainly much the finer town of the two, though it can never be seen to as much advantage, on account of the smoke which causes a continual haze in the streets and is so frequently thickened by fogs. As to the extent, there is certainly no comparison between the two towns; this is owing partly to the difference in the population, partly to the great breadth of the London streets, the extent of the squares and the comparative lowness of the houses. The bustle in the streets is very much greater than in Paris, though perhaps it be not quite in proportion to the space occupied by the town. . . .

"There is here a great deal more luxury in the household and equipages of the great people. In all the great houses where I have been, there has almost always been one servant to open the door, a second either to help him or to conduct me to the bottom of the stairs, or to give auspices, for I really cannot make out his distinct duty, and a third to show the visitor up stairs. The liveries, the carriages, and particularly the horses and harness, are much finer than at Paris, sometimes perhaps less showy, but always ornamented with more taste, and kept in better order. At Paris there is more *recherche* in the linings, which I have often observed to be of the richest silk and the finest casimir. One thing in the servants who attend the carriages here appears to me both odd and inconvenient, which is the canes they carry [152] with them as *bâtons* of office and which are ornamented with silver tops and ends. The furniture of the rooms of those of the middling classes in particular pleases me much more here than at Paris. It is less gaudy in general, but the brightness of the tables, the neatness of the chairs, the carpets, etc, gives the whole a great appearance of comfort. I did not expect to like the coal fires, but now I find them very pleasant; the only inconvenience from them is the smoke they throw out in the streets, and the consequent dark and gloomy appearance of the houses, though in doors we never feel any inconvenience from it, as I have not yet seen a smoky chimney" (then so very frequent in France, especially in the south). "I have not yet dined in many places, but where I have, I do not think the dinners in general either as good or as comfortable as the French ones. In the first place, many people give no napkins, which is a great source of discomfort; then I do not think the manner of helping so pleasant, and with the exception of some puddings, the cookery is certainly far inferior. On the other hand it is certainly true that we have the advantage of being sure that everything we eat out of is clean. The plate and knives are so very bright that those we use in France seem like pewter. In cookery, in the soups particularly, there is generally a great want of salt and rather a superfluity of pepper. Not much variety, few dishes dressed with sauce (made dishes), large joints, boiled greens, mealy potatoes, and two puddings with cheese and desert generally form the dinner, always with a great appendage of sauceboats. The bread that I expected to find so good I think much inferior to the French; the crust is not hard but exceedingly tough, and there is so much crumb that has too strong a taste of yeast and alum." The want of napkins and some points of etiquette, such as the drinking wine always with some one else at dinner, the gentlemen sitting for half an hour or an hour after [153] the ladies, the formal taking leave and shaking hands when the party broke up in the evening, etc, were topics to which I recurred more than once as being anti-French customs.

During this month I had little time to think of my already favorite pursuit of botany. I had brought with me some South of France specimens, but had as yet no opportunity of making botanical acquaintance. I availed myself however of an offer to see Loddiges' establishment, then at its height, of which I gave the following account.

30th March. "Yesterday morning I rose early and went with J. Mill (John Stuart Mill) and R. Doane to breakfast at Mr Bowring's (Sir John Bowring) who was to take us to Loddiges' hothouses and gardens. These are at the end of Hackney, and surprised me by their extent and the rarity and number of the plants they contain (I am now speaking of the hot and green-houses); the principal one, where we were first taken, contains chiefly palms. It appears to be about 40 feet high, is of an arched form, made of very narrow bars of iron, and all glass.* It may be about 40 ft. broad and 80 long. We went first up some steps inside from

---

* This antedates Paxton's crystal palaces.[13]

whence the view over the beautiful plants was quite enchanting. After enjoying this for some time, we proceeded to examine them with a little more detail. The first thing that struck me was a noble banana, whose immense leaves, in the most healthy and vigorous state, seemed, notwithstanding the height of the building, still to be rather stopped in their growth by the roof, whilst from their axillae hung a rich cluster of fruits terminated by a long stalk, at the end of which was the bunch of flowers, many of which remained still to open. There is a Banana in the Montpellier garden, but it is quite a dwarf to this one. Next to this was the Doryanthes excelsa, whose straight, single stem, 30 feet high, is terminated by a large head of flowers of the deepest crimson. There was also another [154] kind of Banana, the Musa rosacea, which, though much less than the sapientum, is remarkable from the pretty pink-coloured flowers issuing straight up from the middle of the leaves. There were also several beautiful liliaceous plants, Cannas, etc, showing their noble flowers amidst a forest of palms. These majestic plants, of which Loddiges has near 100 species, have all of them the most beautiful appearance, from the variety and gracefulness of the form of their leaves, some expanding in broad fans at the top of long petioles, others formed by innumerable long folioles, arranged symmetrically along the middle stalk, some perfectly smooth and shining, others thick set with long thorns. One of them, I forget its name, was loaded with clusters of flowers. From the sides and top of the hothouse hung the elegant pink clusters of the Passiflora racemosa.

"Descending amongst the plants, we were first struck with a large collection of ferns and particularly of tropical Orchideous plants, principally parasitical; Epidendrums growing on pieces of wood buried in the pots and covered with moss. Amongst those in flower I observed particularly the cochleatum, remarkable for the shape of the flower something like the bee-Orchis, and the elongatum, whose delicate pink flowers are at the end of long stalks. Amongst the palms, were also other plants, particularly a Pandanus, remarkable for the thick round-ended roots that shoot from the lower part of the stem, and for the spiral disposition of the leaves, resembling those of a Yucca, but much longer and larger.

"With this hothouse are connected greenhouses containing large collections of liliaceous and fleshy plants, of Geraniums, Proteas, Acacias, Oxalis, etc, and a collection of about 400 Cape Heaths, of which some few were in flower. There were also amongst the palms in the hothouse three or four beautiful little tropical birds, particularly a small kind of scarlet and green parrot.

"From thence we went to another very large greenhouse, like the others glass all over, full of Camellias now at the height of their [155] beauty, with one Araucaria or New-Holland Pine, the most elegant of evergreens, rising in the middle. Amongst the Camellias, the pomponea, paeoniflora, myrtifolia, atrorubens and anemoniflora seemed to me to be distinguished by their superior beauty. Young plants of a foot and a half high cost from half a guinea to a guinea, according to the rarity of the variety."

Early in April, I made a short tour in Norfolk for the purpose of seeing the then celebrated agricultural system introduced by Mr Coke at Holkham,[14] and having accepted an invitation from Lord Calthorpe to spend a few days on my way at his seat, Ampton Hall, near Bury St Edmonds, I went thither on the 5th, on the top of the stage, starting at 8 in the morning and arriving at Bury at ½ past 5. The contrast between this English and the then French coach travelling was very striking to me. I wrote: "Imagine an elegant coach, not hung, but supported on horizontal steel springs, neatly painted, in excellent repair, and clean washed every journey, wafted like lightening over the smoothest of roads by four handsome horses, with leather harness (not cord) adorned with bright brass buckles, rings, etc (instead of rusty iron), a jolly coachman, generally fat by nature, and always by art, his neck being buried in cravats and his body in coats. Ours had besides two cravats, a thick cotton coloured kerchief round his neck, and over his coat two great coats, and a third when it rained on his body. He is continually exerting his whip and his voice to encourage the poor animals he drives, but he does it in so regular, quiet and composed a manner that the horses seem to go on entirely of their own accord. How different is this from a French postillion in his uniform jacket, long pigtail and jackboots, exerting all his faculties in the smack of his whip, the keeping his seat, and the cry of 'Gee-up!' all of which, from the anticks he plays, would seem to the spectator to be a matter of [as] much importance as difficulty!

"But to return to the vehicle on which I was carried, or rather by means of which I flew, from London to Bury. I own that at the first set-out I did not feel quite at my ease, though little used to fear [156] anything in carriages. However I soon got used to it, more particularly so as I happened to be seated between two lusty fellows who would have served as cushions to break my fall if our luck had been to overturn. Then I considered the smoothness of the roads, which is one great cause of the general absence of similar accidents. What would it be on a French road—from Paris to Lyons for instance. If not overturned within

the first stages, the coach would, I am sure, fall to pieces before the end
of the journey. Hills they do not mind. Many have we passed, down
which a French postillion would have to be dragged, or which he would
have ascended procession pace, then stopped at the summit to give
breath to his horses. Yet from London here, except when we stopped to
change horses, etc, I do not think that we once ceased either galloping or
quick trotting."

I arrived at Ampton Park on the Saturday to dinner, and staid till the
Monday afternoon. Lord Calthorpe was very prévenant and obliging,
the party was a bachelor one, his brother Frederick (who afterwards
succeeded to the title), two Scotchmen and an Irishman with very
national names, two local clergymen and two or three others. They were
all very civil to me and I much enjoyed the visit, although the greater
part of the Sunday was occupied by a kind of grave domestic devotion I
was little used to: besides two long church services, long prayers to the
servants in the morning, and again with a third sermon in the evening,
altogether five or six hours I found rather too much. On the Monday
morning, Lord Calthorpe sent his steward to show me over the farm, he
himself having to go to a meeting, and in the afternoon, Mr F. Calthorpe
and the Irish Mr O'Brien went with me to Bury to show me the lions,
amongst which the gaol and the then new treadmill system particularly
interested me.[15] Lord Calthorpe was then very much engaged in plans
for checking the alarming encrease of crime amongst the rural population, of which he recognised one great cause in the stringent enactments
and ill advised administration of the game laws,[16] and [157] although
strongly opposed in general politics to the radicals of the day, he was
joining them in their efforts to obtain a total reform, if not the abolition
of the game laws, so as to treat game as other private property—poaching being almost always the first step to all rural crimes.

The weather being far too bad for any more farm-explorations, I took
the afternoon coach to Norwich, where I slept at the Angel, and the next
morning, directly after breakfast, called on Sir James E. Smith. I found
him very poorly, with one of his usual headaches, and overwhelmed
with proof of his *English Flora*, then nearly ready, but he devoted a couple of hours to me with great civility, showing me Linnaeus's herbarium, library,[17] etc, and taking notes of my desiderata of British plants,
most of which he afterwards sent me. I had a glimpse also of Lady
Smith, then about 50, and though very handsome, appearing to me as
elderly.—I little thought that she had not yet attained the half of her destined age. In the afternoon, a young lawyer, a friend of John Mill's,

showed me over the town, which struck me as dirty and ill-paved—the fine, square castle disfigured by the county gaol, and the cathedral, with its elegant tower, overweighted by the immense plain, pryamidal spire—and the difficulties and delays in seeing the inside were an unpleasant contrast to the liberal manner in which catholic cathedrals on the Continent are always open. We found all locked, till we came to a side door with a bunch of keys hanging to the lock.—We went boldly in, but soon a little girl came up to us with, "'Please, Sir, there's a gentleman always shows the gentlemen that wants to see the church,' but this gentleman lived too far off for us to have him fetched. The little girl durst not show us about herself, and it was not allowable for gentlemen to show themselves about," but we contrived to see all we wanted during the pourparler.

Wednesday, 10th§ April, was spent with Mr and Mrs Southwell at Wroxham Hall, about 6 miles N.E. of Norwich. Mrs S. was a correspondent of my Uncle's in the way of seeds, etc (with diametrically opposed political ideas), and Mr S. does a good deal of amateur farming. My uncle was anxious I should see them, which produced me a very agreable and, with my then views, a somewhat useful day. I walked [158] out there immediately after breakfast, with a cold but fine and exhilarating atmosphere, met with kind hospitality and returned in the evening to Norwich.

From Norwich, I spent a day with Lord Calthorpe at Blakeney, where he had considerable property but no house; we eat with the Rector, and I slept at a farmer's—a fat and ponderous John Bull, but clever and intelligent, in an elegantly furnished house, with everything in excellent style, and a large family being brought up as ladies and gentlemen. After a long morning spent in being indoctrinated in Norfolk farming by Lord Calthorpe's steward, I went on to Holkham, armed with a letter from Lord Spencer to Mr Coke's steward. He however was absent, and meeting Mr Coke with a party on his way to a Bible meeting at Wells, I gave him the letter—he sent me on to Holkham, with instructions to his household and an invitation for dinner and the night. I spent the afternoon in riding over the farm with the bailiff, "as fat and as grave and nearly (but not quite) as intelligent as any Norfolk farmer," and having in due course been shown the pictures of the house by the housekeeper, at a charge of 5'/, I dressed for dinner. "The party consisted of about 18—first Mr Coke himself, a tall, strong, vigorous, gay and agreable man, though his white hair and bald forehead made him look more like the father of the whole company than a young bridegroom—his second§

daughter, Lady Anson, looking at least as old as himself—next her daughter, who has been some time married, then Miss Coke, Mr Coke's third daughter, rather younger than his granddaughter, and lastly his wife, younger than any of them. Lady Ann is very pretty, very amiable, agreable and engaging in her manner. She and Mr Coke appear exceedingly fond of each other, and the whole family seems very happy together. After dinner appeared Mr Coke's great granddaughter, a little girl of about two years and a half and his own son and heir, a little boy of three months old. It is not usual to have a great uncle so much younger than one's self."[18]

[159]The rest of the company were all men—a gay young Quaker, one of the Gurneys, who notwithstanding his "thous" and his "thees" and his drab coat, struck me as cockscombical and affected, a couple of ponderous farmers, a clergyman and others. Mr Coke was very civil to me, but my awkward shyness, which I always attributed to the want of school roughing, stood in my way on this as on many other occasions. I happened before dinner to overhear a young man who is learning farming here, and who had been with me in the afternoon, give Mr Coke a very disparaging account of my proficiency in the art, and to Mr Coke's question whether I was any connection of Jeremy Bentham's, reply that he understood I was of quite another family—and I never could summon courage to make it known to Mr C. that I was Jeremy's nephew, which would have at once insured me a much more cordial reception.

Having been pretty well imbued with Norfolk farming, a full account of which I sent in my long letters, I returned to town, spending the Sunday at Cambridge, where I was shown the lions by Mr O'Brien, the young Irishman I had met at Lord Calthorpes. The whole collegiate system and manners were a matter of some astonishment to me, so totally different from anything I had been used to in France—the college buildings in their lawns and grounds—the college gowns and caps of the men—their wining party—their apparent levity, evident even when in their gowns or surplices attending the services, which, from the manner in which they were performed, appeared to me a mere mockery after the earnest soberness of the South of France Protestants.

I spent the next six weeks in town, then in full season, which gave me the opportunity of seeing much and making many useful acquaintances. On Thursday, 15th[§] April, through a friend of Lord Colchester's, I got a seat under the gallery of the [160] House of Commons to hear a Catholic question debate,[19] of which I gave at the time the following account. "It was a little after four, the regular petition receiving business was going forward, the House was beginning to fill, so there was a great crowd in the doorway. The public gallery had been full for some hours. Each member who has a petition to present is called on by the Speaker; he comes and gives it to the Clerk, who reads the first lines and throws it *under* the table; then the Speaker mutters something about ayes and noes in a drawling tone, speaking out 'that it do lie on the table,' and after a little more drawling calls on another. After half an hour or more of this tedious business, Mr Coke was called on for one from the clergy of Norfolk and the Bishop of Norwich in favor of the Catholics. This one was read through, and gave an opportunity to Sir F. Burdett to rise to speak against this annual farce and mockery, brought every year into the House to encourage the poor catholics in their hope, by an apparent certainty of success only to disappoint them more cruelly—that Ministers must know that if it passed the lower House, it certainly would not the Upper, under present circumstances, so that he should think it his duty, however much he may wish well to the catholic cause, to abstain from the debate, and would quit the House with several of his honorable friends as soon as Mr Plunkett should rise to make his motion. His speaking seemed to me very good, though I do not agree with many of his reasonings. He was much cheered, particularly when in the end he quoted a passage of a former speech of Mr Plunkett's, somewhat at variance with the opinions Mr P. now professes.[20] Lord Nugent, an indifferent speaker, then rose and expressed his concurrence with Sir F. Burdett's opinions with the exception of the secession, for, whatever might be the hopeless state of the question, he should always think it his duty to be there to support it to his utmost, etc.[21] Whilst he was speaking, Mr Canning entered and, being told by some of his companions that Sir F. Burdett had [161] spoken very freely of his conduct when about to enter office, and seeing the Baronet about to quit the House, he interrupted the member speaking to say that he could not help interrupting the proceedings to give a flat denial to what Sir Francis had been saying of his conduct before the honorable baronet left the House, and as soon as Lord Nugent had done his speech he rose to explain his conduct. By this time, the House had become full, as the interest of the debate encreased; and when Mr Canning rose, a general silence prevailed, which is said always to be the case as long as he is on his legs. There seemed now to be about 400 members present; afterwards there were, I believe, between 450 and 500. Mr Canning contradicted the report that he had given up his own principles in order to come into office, said that he always would vote as he always had done in favour of the question, but that now it appeared to him to have much less chance of success than at any preceding session,[22] and that he would have thought it better if his honble friend (Mr Plunkett) would withdraw his motion, etc, etc. Mr C. Wynn, who had also been accused of truckling by Sir F. Burdett, spoke to the same effect, in his squeaking voice, which had procured him the nickname of Squeaker Wynn.* Mr Peel professed his constant adherence to the opposite principles, and his intention of never ceasing to use his efforts to resist the catholic claims. Mr Tierney made a speech full of *esprit* which several times made the House laugh out. Lord Archibald Hamilton and several others made speeches more or less long.[23] Mr Brougham rose, a plain man, speaking with great vehemence of voice and action still more than of language, which was violent enough, against Mr Canning in particular. He even spoke of Mr Canning's having given up his opinions to come [162] into office, and having 'used more truckling than had ever been known in the history of political tergiversation.' On hearing this, Mr Canning rose suddenly and said in a violent tone: 'I rise to say that that is *false*.'[24] Mr Brougham immediately took up his hat, and was going, when the Speaker rose, and after expressing his sensation of the painful situation in which he was placed, by the Secretary of State's having used an expression so contrary to the order of the House, endeavoured to persuade him to recall it; but Mr Canning persisting, the Speaker appealed to the House for advice and assistance in this difficulty, and particularly to Mr Peel, who made a poor sort of speech, and said that Mr Brougham ought first to explain the expressions that gave rise to the interruption. This Mr B. refused to do,[25] and some of his friends said for him,[26] I think with reason, that as what Mr Brougham said was not, when uttered, considered unparliamentary, it was necessary that the interruption, being recognised as quite contrary to the rules of the House, should first be disposed of, and that afterwards, when Mr Canning had made his submission to the House, he (Mr Brougham) would be ready to give any explanations the House might require. The Speaker again appealed to Mr Canning, who again repeated that after mature deliberation he saw no reason for not persisting in the sentiments he had given or for recalling any expres-

---

* Mr Wynn had prepared himself with a thorough study of House of Commons' practice in the hopes of being one day Speaker, in which however he was always disappointed, so it was said that as he could not be Speaker Wynn, he consoled himself as Squeaker Wynn.

sion he might have uttered. Mr Bankes moved that the two members be taken into custody; Mr Sergt Onslow seconded, but Mr C. Wynn observed that they could not be taken into custody till it was settled in what light the expressions were to be considered; but that the House had a right to require them both to give their word of honour that this affair should go no further out of the House, and to prevent their quitting the House till they had so pledged themselves.[27] Two or three more members spoke on the subject, and at last Mr Canning said that if Mr Brougham's expressions alluded to his (Mr C.'s) *official* conduct, he retracted what [163] he had said, but if, as he thought most likely, to his personal character—he persisted most strenuously in the sentiments and words he had uttered. After some other speeches, this retractation was considered sufficient, and the House proceeded to the catholic question.[28]

"The House* struck me as I entered it as exceedingly small, and the galleries over the lower part must be productive of some inconvenience, as but very few members can see the whole House. I think the arrangement at Paris much better suited for the debates; the members here, speaking generally from their places near the bottom of the House, are not nearly so well heard as they would be from a tribune. They also look as little like gentlemen as gentlemen can be, all in morning dress, and sitting with their hats on. In other respects the speaking and parliamentary decorum are incomparably superior to what we see and hear in Paris. I was surprised at the readiness with which they delivered their speeches impromptu without the least hesitation or mistake. Sir F. Burdett and Mr Canning in particular, if they had written their speeches before hand, would certainly not have worded them better. Mr Tierney was very amusing, and he seems very ready at repartee. Mr Brougham and Mr Peel appeared both to me to have too much violence of action, which is I think the fault of most of them."

The debate lasted till ½ past one, but I left early to go to a ball at Hampstead at the Rector's, Dr White—for in those days, the clergy had not yet generally arrived at denouncing dancing as sinful. I was again in the House on the 5th May, at a very different scene. After a long and tedious debate on a petition from Edinburgh for parliamentary reform,[30] in which one could hear little but £5 and £10 electors, 150,000

---

* The old House, since burnt down.[29]

inhabitants and 7000 signatures repeated over and over again with all manner [164] of versions and comments, at last came on the "Irish business" (some enquiry into the conduct of a Sheriff Thorpe).[31] "The first witness was a Mr Ricky,[32] an attorney of Dublin, a close and cunning fellow, always evading the questions that were put to him directly, giving ambiguous answers, and often lying through thick and thin, which brought him into two or three scrapes—as, for instance, denying being at all acquainted with a certain Mr Moore, and afterwards admitting that but two days before, on meeting him, he went up to him, shook hands and asked news of his family, etc, which circumstances he soon after again said he did not recollect. Then came Terence O'Reily, who was asked where he lived in London. 'At a hotel.'—'What hotel?'—'I forget the name.'—'In what street?'—'I do not recollect.'—'What way do you go there?'—'I can't tell exactly.'—'Then where shall you go when you leave the House tonight?'—'To the Salopian coffeehouse.'—'I thought you said you lived at a hotel.'—'No, I only go there sometimes in the day time.' Mr Macnamara, an attorney who had been in prison some years for stealing cattle out of a pound, was asked where he lived. 'At the Salopian coffeehouse now.'—'Then where did you go when you first came to town?'—'To bed Sir.' He was made also to tell a story of a client of his who, some time ago, directed him to offer a bribe to a Mr Marsden, one of the heads of the law in Dublin, to pack a jury, but that Mr Marsden answered that he would not do it, for that was the business of the Crown. Another witness,[33] relating the story of Sheriff Thorpe's having said, 'I have an Orange jury in my pocket,' persisted at first that he did not know what Sheriff it was, but only knew he was a Sheriff because he had heard him thus addressed by another person. Soon after, he said it was Sheriff Thorpe, and when asked why he now said so, when a little before he had affirmed he did not know his name, he answered, 'Why, I believe there's only two Sheriffs in Dublin, [165] and I was shown the other, and saw it was not him, so it must be this one.'[34] Another witness, when called, was not to be found, and on enquiry being made, the answer came that he had fallen off a stage coach on arriving in London and that he was so much hurt that he could not attend, but a member having said that he had been seen in the street in perfect health, he was immediately summoned and made his appearance as sound as ever.[35] This will give you some idea of the nature of the evidence they are able to draw from such witnesses, and the degree of credit that is to be given to them. What use the examination is to be of, or what result can be expected from it, nobody can tell—indeed most people consider it a mere waste of time. Those members who seem to take the greatest part in it are Mr Brownlow and Col Barry—Mr Brownlow, a young man who appears very clever at cross questioning and puzzling the witnesses, Col Barry, a violent Orangeman, who has taken it much to heart that this examination should turn out favorable to Sheriff Thorpe and his party—but it must be said to his credit that in order the better to be enabled to proceed with the affair in full freedom and liberty, he gave up a lucrative place he had in the Treasury. Many other members appear also to pay much attention to this odd sort of enquiry, where no witnesses are on oath, and most of them in direct contradiction to one another, or even to themselves, and where the members may ask any questions the furthest from the question, because they may turn out to have some connection with it. Col Barry, for instance, asked a witness 'How many dinners does your guild give in a year?' In this case the house got a bull (a laugh) at the answer, being 'Three quarterly dinners.'[36] These bulls are said to be the principal object the members aim at, and the enquiry is therefore called the bull-fight. It was to have been brought on only twice a week, but they now have it every day, and will [166] continue it, it is supposed, at least another week, till the members are tired of the bulls, and they will then put a stop to it without coming to any decision."

The next morning,[37] I went with Lord Calthorpe to a very different kind of meeting. Bible Societies were then at the height of fashion and prosperity, and this was the annual meeting of the parent society in the great room of the Freemason's tavern, fitted up with platform, galleries, etc. "On this occasion, it was completely full, between 1200 and 1500 people, as near as I could count, all men, for ladies are not admitted at these anniversaries. After a short speech from the chairman, Lord Teignmouth, the report was read, by which it appeared that the Society is extending its relations in all parts of the world to a surprising degree. I really cannot conceive that such immense sums should be given for this purpose, that there should be so many who imagine that giving bibles alone will instill religious principles into those who receive them. Three millions of copies have been already distributed, and have been printed in numberless languages. I remember particularly 33 as the number in which it is printed in London, in above 20 Indian languages in Calcutta, and I do not know how many more in the many parts of the world where auxiliary societies are established. Lord Harrowby rose amidst loud applause and, after a few commonplace expressions, spoke of the state of society in Ireland, said he would wish the exertions of the Bible society to be greater and more active in that country, as he was well convinced that the spreading of the bible was the only way of allaying the disorders in that distracted country. His language was in general florid; one phrase was particularly applauded, when he compared the President of the Bible society to Sir Christopher Wren, who having laid the first stone of the temple of God, had the rare felicity of seeing its towering dome ascend to the clouds and crowned by the cross of Christ. Lord Bexley spoke of the [167] beneficial effects and the great comforts the spreading of the bible had produced on the inhabitants of Ireland. The Bishop of Gloucester,[38] dangling as usual from side to side, spoke of the effects the bible would have in Ireland. Lord Teignmouth made another short speech. A Russian Vicepresident of the Russian auxiliary society made a speech in broken English, in which he mentioned 160,000 copies as having been printed last year, and 100,000 more about to be printed this year in St Petersburgh. Lord Calthorpe made a long speech, less applauded than the others on account of his stammering, which however he did less than usual. They say he takes great pains to cure himself of this trick and has in a great measure succeeded, as he does it much less than he used to do. Sir Charles Grant, a tall, stout young man, made a long and very animated speech, using much florid language and great vehemence of action. He was close by me and I heard him very well, yet when he had done I was at a loss to make out what he had been saying, which seems often to be the case with English orators, who possess to a high degree the art of speaking without saying any thing. One of the speakers mentioned the number of bibles distributed at Aleppo shortly before the earthquake,[39] and expatiated much on the comfort these sacred volumes must have produced on the inhabitants during the dreadful catastrophe. When Sir C. Grant sat down, the exit of two or three people at last enabled me to do the same, after having been closely penned up in this crowded room for nearly five hours without being able to go out, and that on the hottest and most sultry day we have yet had."

My evenings were now generally spent in Society—to meet my sisters, at dinners, evening parties, concerts in the Hanover Square rooms, etc, and two or three times to some of the principal theatres; but one great result of these last six weeks [168] in London was the establishing definite relations with some of the principal botanists, and becoming acquainted with the few botanical and horticultural establishments of the day. Sir Humphrey Davy was then President of the Royal Society, my father had known him well, and on several visits to us at Hampstead he had been very kind to us children. I had never seen Lady Davy, but as soon as I heard they were come to town, I called at their house, found Lady Davy, who was exceedingly civil, made very friendly offers of assistance, tickets, etc, for my sisters, which she afterwards carried into effect, spoke of her own ill health (of which there was no appearance), entered fully into her grievances against Sir Humphrey, who monopolized the carriage, etc, at the same time taking care to impress me with an adequate idea of the high social position he occupied, and in his name invited me to his Saturday parties, begging me to excuse his calling on me, his time being so fully occupied.

I accordingly went to Sir Humphrey's party on the 26th April—at first rather embarrassing, for the visitors were not announced and there was nothing to indicate which was the host; however upon my finding him out and making myself known to him, he received me very cordially, made many friendly offers, and introduced me to Mr Lambert, as a means of becoming acquainted with the botanical world. I also met here Dr Baillie, Dr Wollaston, and other scientific friends or acquaintances of my father and mother's. "Seeing a gentleman of foreign appearance a little embarrassed from want of speaking English, I entered into conversation with him. I was surprised to hear him talk of the *Physiologie du cerveau que le vulgaire appelle Craniologie* as the object of his *recherches*, and on enquiring who he was, I found he was the celebrated Dr Gall, who has made so much noise at Paris by his pretensions of discovering people's characters by the inspection of the form of the head. He is just come over with the intention of giving lectures here, but it is much [169] doubted whether he will contrive to get any audience. He spoke to me of Admiral Tchitchagoff, with whom he is acquainted, and who is a zealous disciple of his and Spurzheim's mad ideas."[40]

Breakfasts at Lambert's were the natural result of so good an introduction, besides that David Don, then keeper of his herbarium as well as librarian of the Linnean Society, had heard of me from Sir James Smith, and my reception was all the more favorable as I carried with me duplicates of Montpellier plants, to which he attached much more importance than Sir James Smith had done. Philip Barker Webb received them also very thankfully. I met him at Lambert's, and breakfasted and spent a morning with him, the commencement of a friendship I had frequent opportunities of cultivating in after years at Paris, and always experienced the greatest liberality on his part, in the shape of full sets of his collections, and copies of his valuable works. Lambert was very profuse in his offers, and occasionally I had a few specimens from him, but he had a peculiar way, when he found that what he offered was highly appreciated, of contriving to back out, thinking he ought not to part with what was so valuable. However his countenance and civilities were of great use to me in promoting my connection with other botanists.

My next botanical introduction was to Robert Brown, who was living, as he did to the end of his long life, in Sir Joseph Banks's house in Dean Street, going through to Soho Square, the Square side being tenanted and occupied by the Linnean Society. Mr Brown received me very kindly; he seemed to know all about me and mine, our estate in France and John Mill's visit to us, etc, "though," I wrote, "I am sure I cannot guess how he can have got all this information, as I do not know of any one who is acquainted with him and with us." He had however an extraordinary faculty of acquiring information of all kinds and storing it up in his mind so as always to be ready [170] for use at a moment's notice. He, at this first visit, paid great attention to me, showing me his own and Sir Joseph Banks's herbaria, the latter being then still in his possession. It was left to him for his life, and although he already contemplated transferring it at once to the British Museum, the arrangements for that purpose were not yet determined upon.[41] Another morning he showed me in more detail some of his own New Holland collections, amongst which the wonderful series of Droseras especially struck me.

On Tuesday, May 6, I attended for the first time a meeting of the Linnean Society. I had previously been over their library and museum—then consisting chiefly of Genl Hardwicke's and some other birds,[42] with Mr Don, and this evening I chiefly enjoyed the introduction to botanists. The business itself was not much. Sir James Smith was not yet come to town and Lambert was in the chair. There was the formal proposal, reception and ballotting for members, and during the process, a paper was read, "containing the critical examination of some plants mentioned by ancient authors."[43] All this was soon over, but amongst my new introductions, I took very specially to Joseph Sabine and Archibald Menzies. Sabine was then Secretary of the Horticultural Society, which he had brought into a high state of fashion and prosperity. I spent a morning with him at the Society's rooms in Regent Street, when he made me liberal promises of seeds and plants, asked me to become a corresponding Member, and offered various civilities, which promises and offers he afterwards fully carried out. He was then most successful in his endeavours to work the Society in a liberal spirit, and was met on all sides with correspondingly liberal contributions to the garden, contrasting strongly in many persons minds with the management of Kew. "Mr Sabine," I wrote, "complains much of the illiberal spirit in which the Royal Gardens at Kew are managed. [171] Parmentier[44] he says is the only one who can obtain plants from Aiton, so that the British nation pays a great deal of money to enrich foreign gardens."

With Mr Menzies I spent a very pleasant morning. He had well known my grandfather Fordyce, and before he started on his voyage round the world with Vancouver,[45] Dr F., he told me "gave him a great deal of good advice, among the rest never to bring more than half a dozen of any rare shell that he might find, as that number would always bring him more than any greater quantity"—a piece of advice characteristic of the exclusive spirit too general among collectors of that day in all branches of natural science, but more especially in regard to shells and insects. Menzies had presented all his plants to Sir Joseph Banks, with the exception of grasses and cryptogams, which he was particularly devoted to, and of which he was endeavouring to encrease his collection.[46] It was mounted on paper of a very small size, and closely packed in small cases.

During the last week of my stay in London, I was again with Sabine in town, §and spent a morning at the Horticultural garden, where I first met Mr Lindley, then Garden Secretary§. In my account of this visit, I dwelt much on the apparently flourishing state and brilliant prospects of the Society, adding, "If well-managed, this may become the most useful and extensive of all scientific Societies; they must only remember what their brother Societies are apt to forget, I mean the old proverb of *out of debt out of danger*, but they are not come to that yet." Unfortunately they were not long clear of it. I had also in the earlier part of the month visited the other principal gardens about London. Lee and Kennedy's nursery at Hammersmith, which before we left England had been *the* great one of the country, though still very extensive, was yielding the palm to Loddiges. The Apothecaries' Company's Garden at Chelsea was then very interesting,[47] under the management of a well known character [   ] Anderson, or "Old Charatrastic," as we used to call him at my Uncle's, who in his latter [172] years made this garden several times the terminus of his "antejentacular"[48] walks and delighted much in Anderson's quaint explanations of the "charatrasticks" of plants. At this time however they had not met, and I went there one morning without introduction. "This garden was once under Miller's direction, and is now in a most flourishing state in the hands of an exceedingly clever and intelligent Scotchman of the name of Anderson. I applied to him in the name of Mr Lambert for leave to see the garden, upon which he left his work, accompanying me over the garden and greenhouses and mak-

ing a number of useful and interesting remarks both botanical and horticultural, and after spending two or three hours with me would not
accept of anything for his trouble. His information seems extensive and
varied—that is with respect to his particular pursuits, for on other subjects he seems rather out of his sphere. In Archeology, for instance, he
explains the origin of the names of Chelsea and Battersea by saying that
they were two celebrated fords, to which the Romans gave the names of
Shallow sea and Better sea, and thence they were called by corruption
Chelsea and Battersea. Such may have been the origin of the names but I
doubt much whether they were given by the Romans.[49] The garden is
nearly square, surrounded by walls and situated on the banks of the
Thames, from which it is separated at low water by a narrow beach; at
high water the river washes the foot of the wall. On the beach are
planted several aquatic and semiaquatic plants, particularly the Acorus,
the American rice or Zizania, some Carexes and other plants. The garden is rather small, the side opposite the river is nearly all occupied with
the greenhouses, looking rather to the eastward of the south, which was
the aspect preferred in former days. The middle body of the houses is
built in a style now becoming rather antiquated in England but very
common in France, a great deal of wall and a very little glass, [173]
which etiolates the plants and gives them an appearance less healthy
than any I have seen in the country. Over this part is the habitation. This
greenhouse is very old and said to be the first where glass was used.
Before that, oil paper supplied the place. On each side are more modern
hothouses covered with glass and heated in the usual way, not however
by steam. A little way in front, nearer the middle of the garden, are
some other lower greenhouses, almost entirely glass and very prettily
arranged. In front of them, a basin for water plants, *baches* (or frames) for
raising young plants, and piles of stones and mortar for those that prefer
dry rocky situations. Under the north wall (i.e. exposed to the North) is
a shady bed for Saxifragas, Primulas, etc. There is also a bed reserved for
a pharmaceutical collection of plants, and another for Umbelliferae,
which is the only Natural family separated from the general collection
arranged according to the Linnean system. Among these Umbelliferae
are above thirty Heraclea, all handsome in their leaf and *port* (habit),
and, all according to Mr Anderson, good for cattle. There is also, by the
greenhouses, a large collection of alpine plants in pots, many of them
rare and curious from the mountains of Germany and the south of Russia.

"The hothouse plants are handsome, though nothing comparable to

Loddiges' palmhouse. There are some fine Acacias, Proteas and a few palms, some healthy Caoutchouc plants, Nutmeg, Tamarind, and other officinal plants, but scarcely any Heaths (these by the bye belong to the greenhouses, as well as the Proteas). In general this collection of tropical plants is small when compared to that of the hardier ones. The greenhouse contains many fine specimens, but they have in general, as I have already observed, rather an etiolated look. Mr Anderson gave me two or three heads of Proteas which we [174] happened to meet with ripe. One corner of the garden is occupied by a collection of near 1200 annuals, another by a few trees, and the rest by the botanical collection of hardy herbaceous, or subligneous plants, arranged according to the Linnean system and all in high order. A piece of wood is placed in front of each plant, the first of each genus has the name of the genus, the following ones have the numbers 2, 3, 4, etc, which refer to the catalogue. This is a much better way, I think, than the one most common in France, of putting nothing but numbers, of which there is but one series throughout the garden, creating a confusion when new plants are to be inserted, which is much lessened when the numbers begin again at each genus. Amongst the standard trees, I observed particularly two ancient Cedars, which by Anderson's account are 200 years old, and about 15 feet circumference at five or six feet from the ground. Their lower branches have all been clipped or torn off by the winds, so that they now present their tall stems crowned by a broad umbrella of a dark, gloomy green. They are venerable and beautiful trees but remind one too much of the destructive effects of old father time. A Quercus sempervirens, or American evergreen oak, tall, healthy and vigorous, the leaf much like our Q. ilex but the tree much taller, more regular and far more beautiful; in short, I think I have scarcely seen a tree which has pleased me more. Another smaller Quercus sempervirens, but of another variety, the leaf much broader, and rather shorter. A very fine Sophora japonica, three planes, planted by Miller, P. occidentalis, orientalis and americana. A Quercus Ilex, two Quercus Suber, fine trees but rather sickly and stunted and scarcely any cork upon them, and several smaller trees, amongst which an ash, remarkable from the manner in which the branches weep, touching the ground.* On this occasion, Mr A. remarked that when we observe the fasciculi of little branches, you may have seen on some [175]

---

* The weeping ash was then unknown or nearly so in France, and rare in England.

forest trees and that proceed apparently from some insect or other disease, if we take grafts from one of the branches thus shortened and collected in bunches, and plant them pretty high up on a vigorous tree, we are sure to have a variety with very pendulous branches. This he has not only seen practised, but has made the experiment himself, and it is a way frequently resorted to by nurserymen for obtaining weeping varieties, and he says always successfully. Along the wall are several trees rather more tender, some Phillyreas of different kinds—an Olive of some feet high, but so poor and miserable that I scarcely knew it—several Corchoruses—a Broussonetia, scarcely able to bear the frosts, whilst with us it is so common and so hardy—two or three New Holland shrubs—an Aucuba Japonica in full flower, the first I had seen in this state, but being only a female they can obtain no seed, which is also the case with the finest Pistacia terebinthus I ever saw. With us this tree (for so I now find it must be called) is very common, but never have I seen it above five or six feet here; here it grows to the top of the wall, which is about 12 feet, and would evidently have been much higher, were it not for frequent amputations made to keep it within bounds. A little beyond this tree is a Jessamine, on which Mr Anderson is making experiments on variegation. It is an old stem of the common species, which has frequently been cut down, and has shot up several branches. On one of these he grafted, at about a foot from the ground, three years ago, a bud of the variegated Jessamine. The following year the whole branch above the spot where the bud had been inserted produced variegated leaves, and last year the whole tree was variegated, with the exception of one branch of which he made a layer, and is now waiting to see what it will produce. From this might be deduced several interesting conclusions about the circulation of the sap. It proves also that variegation is a [176] disease. The same experiment may be repeated on Privet. Exotic Jessamines grafted on J. fruticosum are much more hardy than those grafted on J. officinale.—Against the same wall is an old Styrax that has also been frequently subjected to the axe, having outgrown its situation. This tree, remarkable from its size and healthiness, is peculiarly interesting from the attachment Sir Joseph Banks had for it, according to Mr Anderson's account. Sir Joseph planted it when very young: 'it was then no bigger than a quill and not yet ramnified,' and the object of his peculiar care and attention. A few years ago, being in the garden, he recognised his old friend, and observed that the poor fellow was going very fast; 'however,' he added, 'I believe I shall go down first.' Poor Mr Anderson seemed affected in speaking thus of Sir Joseph Banks."

Availing myself of Mr Anderson's liberal offers, I returned to Chelsea a few days afterwards to take specimens for my herbarium. He "put the Catalogue in my hand 'that I might know the names,' and told me to go over and take what I pleased, whilst he went on with his work, and after I had looked over the beds in which the plants were numbered and named, he himself went over the greenhouses and separate beds, giving me whatever was in flower, often when there was but one, apparently quite pleased, as he said he was, to spend the time with one 'who rode the same hobby horse as himself,' often giving me whole plants, 'because pieces would not have enough of the radical business about them,' or 'were not ramnified enough,' and making at the same time a number of critical or practical observations on the different plants, so that you may well conceive that I carried home a good harvest; at the same time he asked me with great earnestness to come again when I returned from Portsmouth, and when [177] I should arrive from Scotland, as he said by that time the garden would have time to transmogrify, the old set would be put down, and a new one started out of it. In short, he could not possibly have been better disposed. I should have provided myself with cuttings if I had thought there would be any chance of my preserving them till my arrival at Restinclières."

"From Chelsea," on the 3d May, "I continued my walk to see the Longleys.* I went along what is called the King's private road, bordered with kitchen and nursery gardens nearly the whole way on both sides. The weather was beautifull, the trees and hedges just covering themselves with bright green leaves or with their white blossoms, the meadows beginning to grow, the gardens full of neat beds of fruit and vegetables, everything tended to render the walk delightful, and the more so from the great contrast with the dingy, smoky streets of London." ... "In returning to London I could not resist the temptation a waterman held out to me, and suffered myself to be rowed down the Thames. I had heard much of the beauties of the banks of this river and was by no means disappointed. The rich gardens, the elegant paths and country seats, the number of trees that there are everywhere about, certainly render the prospect very varied and pleasing; the only thing that is against it is the too close succession of villages and towns and the too visible effects of the clouds of smoke that issue from the chimneys of London

----

* Old Hampstead friends, parents of the late Archbishop.[50]

and of the number of distilleries and other fabrics that there are about.
Passed under the wooden bridges of Putney and Battersea; the new
Vauxhall bridge, with stone piers and cast iron arches, is elegant and
light and upon the whole looks very well, but I [178] do not like it near so
well as Waterloo Bridge.[51] This last is perfectly flat, the piers are much
thinner, and the whole is much more light and elegant than Vauxhall
Bridge. These bridges will be, I dare to say, very useful in time, but at
present I see but few people going over them, perhaps on account of the
tolls they have to pay." The same evening, I went again to Sir Humphrey
Davy's reception, "where I was introduced to Mr Knight, the famous
horticulturist and president of the Horticultural Society. He is a tall,
rather odd-looking, gardener-like man, seems very clever in gardening,
but confesses himself quite ignorant on all other subjects, though I
believe he really has much general information."

"On Thursday morning (8th May) I went into Picadilly, and mounted
on the top of a Brentford coach, which took me in an hour to Kew
Bridge, nearly all the way through an uninterrupted street, crossing
Knightsbridge, Kensington, Hammersmith and Turnham Green, which
all form now part of London, and but three quarters of a mile further is
the beginning of Brentford. The road is bordered all the way with lamps,
and near Brentford with gas lights. I then went to Aiton's,[52] and at his
door met two French gentlemen, who had come in the same coach for
the same purpose of seeing Mr Aiton, and in a few minutes we were
joined by three Germans who had also come with us for the same purpose, so that we were a coach full of foreigners going to Aiton's without
knowing it as we came along, being all in different parts of the coach.
The Frenchmen were the famous Parmentier, and a friend of his who
were come over to bring plants and take others away. Parmentier has
the finest collection of exotics in France, or rather in the Netherlands, for
it is at Enghien that he lives. He has written, as I suppose you know, a
good deal on potatoes [179] and other subjects.[53] The three Germans
were on a visit to England, and though not much of botanists, came to
Kew to see the gardens as a curiosity. The name of one of them is
Schmidt, which by the bye is as good as no name at all. I do not know
who the others were. I gave Mr Aiton my mother's letter, which he
seemed very glad, or at least said he was very glad, to receive; he spoke
much of his old acquaintance with her and was exceedingly civil to me,
though he was much occupied with Parmentier. We went over the
grounds together. I had expected to find a very large garden, with one
side occupied by greenhouses, but I do not know why [I] felt very much

surprised at seeing it all divided into a number of small gardens, walled round so as not to be able to see from one to another, with one or two greenhouses in every one. This has certainly the advantage of having a great extent of wall for fruit trees, but does not improve the appearance, as it makes it look very *mesquin* for a Royal Garden. The collection of green and hot house plants is very extensive, and in one of the houses are many of the most beautiful Banksias I have ever seen. There were also a number of handsome Proteas, Acacias, Palms, Pandani, Zamias, and many other rare and valuable ones, chiefly tropical and transtropical. This is by far the most extensive I have seen, but not near so handsome as Loddiges', which must still bear the palm in the green and hothouse way. There are at Kew but few heaths and geraniums, comparatively speaking, but a large collection of succulent plants. There are many forcing houses, chiefly for cherries, grapes, figs and strawberries, of which fruits George the third was particularly fond. One of the houses is heated by steam, the rest by flues. They are in general low, and of simple construction, not as light as many that I have seen. The collection in the garden I do not think kept in the order that they ought to be in a public botanic garden, [180] where so many plants are cultivated that have no beauty, but merely to facilitate comparison. Among the outdoor plants, the most striking is the Araucaria imbricata or Sir J. Banks's pine, a tree which in its native country is said to grow to the height of three or four hundred feet. This plant is but twenty years old and about twelve feet high. It certainly is a very beautiful tree and must be most magnificent in its native country. There is also in the garden a fine red Magnolia (on a wall), a large collection of trees and of grasses, but not many herbaceous plants of other kinds. The walls are covered with fruit-trees. In the forcing-houses, cherries and strawberries have been ripe for some time, but scarcely show their flowers in the open ground. Mr Aiton showed us everything, but was much occupied with M. Parmentier, who was noting down what he wished for in exchange for what he brought." Mr Aiton was also very liberal to me in the offers of seeds, etc, to take home to my mother on my return from Scotland, "which I am very glad of, although I know that *promettre c'est un, tenir est un autre,* and though he is said to be very ungenerous to every one except Parmentier. Indeed I am told, but I do not know with what degree of truth, that he absolutely refuses to exchange with any English collectors, and that the only way they have of obtaining any of his plants is by buying them of Parmentier, who often, just before he leaves England, sells what Aiton has given him; but all this may be much exaggerated."

"From Kew Gardens I went with the three Germans to Richmond, where my poor companions met with a curious adventure. In the middle of the town was a crowd of men, with one of them dressed up. We were quietly making our way [181] through, when they seized hold of the hindermost of us. We thought it must be some drunken men who wanted to do him some mischief or other, and turned round to help him out, when the whole crowd turned to us, and seized another; the third and myself escaped by taking to our heels, and from a little distance contemplated the fate of the others, at first with some uneasiness; but we soon saw it was a joke, the object of which was to seize all gentlemen who should pass and give them three hearty bounces against the one who was dressed up, and then set them down and send them about their business,* §which they say is the custom to do every seven years on this (Ascension) day. The poor Germans who could not speak a word of English were terribly frightened at first but as soon as it was over laughed most heartily."

My uncle Jeremy Bentham, who had at first so positively declined to see my sisters, had now relented and this was "the day he had at last fixed upon for seeing them at dinner. A little before dinner, he came down to them, kissed them with great affection and spoke to them the whole evening with the greatest kindness. He seemed much pleased with them and quite happy in their company, but I do not think he will see them again, so firmly is the idea rooted in his mind that the time he spends with them is so much lost to no purpose."

One morning, Sir Humphrey Davy showed my sisters and myself over the British Museum—together with Madame Thénard, a very pretty young Frenchwoman, wife of the chemist. The Museum was then in a very different state from what it now is,[55] and struck me as poor after the Paris ones. "The Library is nothing like the Parisian Bibliothèque [182] du Roi for extent or conveniency of arrangement, which is all I could judge of in so cursory a view. It is dispersed in a number of small rooms, in which the books are heaped and crowded as if about to be sent abroad. There are two small rooms, but I believe it is not every body who is allowed to read. There seems to be a considerable collection of minerals, a gallery of antiques of different nations, another of antique bronzes and other ornaments, but all very much inferior to those of the

---

* There was then no police but nights' watchmen. This bouncing we afterwards learnt was beating the Parish boundaries.[54]

same kind at Paris. The Portland vase is certainly a very handsome thing.[56] There is an Egyptian tomb, reckoned very curious, but only worth looking at because it is curious. The best of the museum is a very extensive and well arranged collection of fossils, amongst others a great part of a human skeleton encrusted in a sort of stone, large pieces of the Ichthyosaurus, Ornythorynchus, etc. In another room, a considerable collection of British mineralogy, and in another, of British Zoology, chiefly birds but badly stuffed, as are all the birds in the Museum. In this British zoology room is an immense tortoise. On the staircase a musc ox, well stuffed and brought by Capt Parry,[57] two Cameleopards (they were not yet called Giraffes) male and female, a zebra, etc, and I think this is pretty well all that is worth mentioning. Great projects are on the tapis for building three immense galleries round the garden, one for zoology, one for paintings, and the other for statues." Nothing in the way of botany or vegetable products was then shown or spoken of as part of the Museum.

"May 17th. Here I am again, after having spent two days in revisiting the places connected with some of the pleasantest days of our childhood, and though it be not yet so long since we [183] were there as to have obliterated in the least the little daily occurrences, my ideas were then so very different that at the sight of Berry Lodge, I could not help looking back to the time we lived there as to ages past, with a pleasure mixed with some regret. When we think of our early days, we are always apt to say 'how happy children are,' but to which must be added 'if they did but know their happiness,' for their little wants are to them as great as any other ones to full grown people.

"On Wednesday morning, I took my sisters with me as far as Dorking, where they were to spend a few days with Mrs Mill (J.S. Mill's mother). We set off about nine o'clock, crossing Westminster bridge and travelling many miles before we got into the country, as Kennington, Clapham, Balham, and several other little places are now completely connected with London, and indeed it was not till we had passed Tooting, two miles further, that we were in what could be strictly called the country. The scenery was now more and more beautifull every step we took, the ground became more broken and tastefully laid out in paths and woods, and this beauty is now much heightened by the brilliancy of the spring verdure, the weather also, though cold, was fine and clear. We passed very near Lord Spencer's Wimbledon Park and several other fine seats, among which Norbury Park struck me as particularly beautiful, in the manner in which the planters have profited of the hills and valleys and other accidents of Nature, which are all improved by art. The environs of Dorking are celebrated here for their beauty, and though I had heard much of it, I was not disappointed. We arrived at 12. Mr Mill has [184] taken a pretty little house for the summer with a fine large garden. I walked about with John Mill till dinner, and immediately after set out for Guilford in a gig, there being no stage on this little bit of crossroad, hurrying on in hopes of being there in time for some of the day coaches, but on my arrival found them all gone, so I had to wait till 12 at night for the mail.

"On the way from Dorking to Guilford the road crosses the Merrow Downs, from whence is one of the most extensive views I have yet seen in England. These downs are all covered with sheep pasture and waste land—here perhaps the soil is not rich enough to make it worth while breaking it up, but what surprises me much is that there should be so many heaths and wastes in the rich soil of this neighbourhood of London. From London to Dorking we crossed many of these pieces. There seems in England so little corn land in comparison with the parks and ornamental grounds that we cannot conceive where such an immense overgrown population can find nourishment, and yet complaints of the superfluity of corn are here louder than in France,[58] where half the country appears to be corn. This must be owing to the greater proportion of meat and less bread eaten by the English, and perhaps also to the better state of agriculture in this country. I was rather surprised, in reading Simond, to see that he observed the quantity and beauty of the wild flowers,[59] but now I find he was correct in the observation, for I really think there are as many showy flowers on the banks here as on our garrigues—not so much variety but several very pretty ones—those now in flower and everywhere plentiful are the furze, the deadnettle (Lamium album), Scilla nutans, [185] violets, primroses, cowslips, grounding (Glechoma hederacea) and a few others; the Scilla nutans, not common in the south of France, is particularly pretty and plentiful. I shall endeavour to bring over some roots.

"I left Guildford at 12 at night, and the country being chiefly an immense waste, I did not regret much the passing it in the dark. Daylight began some time before we reached Petersfield, and as we stopped here to change horses I got outside. We had already stopped at Monsall to drink tea, where was also the mail that was going up, in which was a Dutch lady, just arrived from the Cape of Good Hope, bringing with her a Boa constrictor, a parrot and two sons, all of which seemed equally to divide her cares and attention. From Petersfield to Portsdown hill the country, you may remember, is bleak and unpleasant. Here and there only a pretty vale, with a few groups of trees, broke a little its sameness. From the top of Portsdown hill, I once more enjoyed the magnificent view I had when young seen so often, and always with encreased pleasure. This is the part of the road that I remembered the most, and indeed was so much associated in my mind with the idea of some of my early journeys that I could scarcely persuade myself of the many changes we have since undergone, and the number of eventful years that divide us from those days when I last contemplated the view from Portsdown hill. Portsmouth and Langton harbours, the islands of Portsea and Hayling between the two promontories of the mainland, the towns and villages of Portsmouth, Portsea, Gosport, Fareham, Porchester, etc, that surround the principal harbour, the beautifully varied hills of the Isle of Wight in front, with the town of Ryde rising from the sea [186] directly opposite to us, the sea itself bounding the prospect round half the horizon, every thing seemed just the same as it was ten years ago. The only feature that seemed changed was the shipping. Spithead is almost clear of vessels, and the harbour is full of the ships in ordinary, without masts or rigging—the appearance of the Dock Yard is also changed by the immense roofs of the Docks and slips."

I alighted at Mr Goodrich's, who was living with his daughter, a young widow, in a small house at Mile End, a kind of suburb of Portsea. Mr Goodrich had been my father's chief clerk (when Inspector General of Naval Works) and his locum tenens when absent, always an intimate and confidential friend, and had now the superintendance of the engineering, mechanical and other works going on in Portsmouth Dock Yard. With him I spent a couple of days, going over all my old haunts in the Dock Yard, hunting out our old friends, carefully enquiring into the progress of all my father's innovations in the Yard, upon all which subjects my letters home contain long details. I also went over to see our dear Berry Lodge, and our fields at Alverstoke, the letting of which was managed by Mr Goodrich, and returned to town for a few busy days previous to my great journey to the north, §dining out almost every day—at Lord Calthorpe's—at Mr Bentham's of Gower Street—at the Baillies'—at the Koes', etc, visiting also the Opera, Drury Lane theatre, and Vauxhall Gardens, then in their state of prosperity and well attended from 10 till after the fireworks at 12—and open till 3 or 4 in the morning.[60]

[187]Saturday, 24th May. After spending the morning first at a breakfast at Lord Calthorpe's, then at the Exhibition of Sir Joshua Reynold's

and other pictures in Pall Mall—to the Cosmorama in Regent Street,[61] and some calls, collecting letters for my northern tour—dressed and "to the Linnean Anniversary dinner[62] in the Freemason's Tavern, Great Queen Street. Here I met Sir James Smith, the President, who was just come up from Norwich for the purpose, though still very unwell. He was very civil to me. There were also of my acquaintance Mr Lambert, Mr Sabine, Mr Phillip Barker Webb, Mr Macleay the secretary, Mr Menzies, Mr Lindley, Mr Don, Mr Ed. Forster the treasurer, and my old friend *Charastrastic* in his Sunday gardener's dress. There were about sixty present, at a horse shoe table, at the top of which sat Sir J. Smith with the Bishop of Carlisle, vice president,[63] on his right and Lambert, the other vice president, on his left, then all the others promiscuously. I was at the upper end at the corner, between Mr Forster and Mr Sabine, and next but one to Mr Lambert and Mr Webb, so that I was very well off. This is the only one of these great dinners that I have seen. The food was very good and abundant, soup, boiled and broiled fish, roast and boiled joints and poultry, boiled vegetables, and sauces by the dozen (no made dishes), also pigeon pies, gooseberry tarts and puddings, then cheese and deserts. After dinner toasts were given, but not as I expected, no standing up and holding up of glasses, and often not half the gentlemen drank or even touched their glasses. The president merely delivered the toasts, and, if it was particularly approved of, a clatter [188] ensued just as if all the glasses and decanters were coming down together—if not cheered, the different private conversations were not interrupted. This clatter was made by all the gentlemen knocking the table with their fists or the handles of their knives (the cloth having been removed). The toasts given by the President or others were 'the King,' 'the Royal Family,' 'Success to the Linnean Society,' 'Prosperity to the Royal Society,' 'The President,' 'The Vice Presidents,' 'The Treasurer,' 'Mr R. Brown,' 'Mr Sabine,' and 'the absent members.' On some of these occasions short speeches were made by Sir J. Smith, the Bishop of Carlisle, Mr Lambert, Mr Macleay, and Mr Sabine—another health was drank, but I forget whose. At half past eight the president rose, some of the company returned to the drawingroom to tea, some staid to drink—perhaps all night—and some went away. I went with Sabine to the Horticultural rooms, where he gave me a letter to Hooker of Glasgow and then to the Opera."

I left London early on Monday morning, 28th May, on an Oxford coach. It was a lovely day, the sun was shining bright and warm, after a sufficiently rainy season to give life and vigour to the vegetation. After we had passed what even then appeared a long and tedious string of suburbs, through Knightsbridge, Kensington, Hammersmith, Turnham Green, Brentford, Isleworth and Hounslow, and passing a somewhat uninteresting country to Maidenhead, [we] came into a more diversified and hilly region; and I shall never forget the delightful impressions I received from the fresh green studded with flowers [189] I saw every where around me, as we trotted or galloped along the beautifully smooth roads. The stage from Maidenhead to Henley struck me with the greatest delight. A long hill gave the opportunity of a walk and botanising by the way, and I arrived at Oxford in the highest spirits and well disposed to admire a town so different from what I had been used to, notwithstanding what struck me as rather monastic and dull in its aspect. "It has the appearance of an assemblage of convents, the colleges much resembling monastic establishments, which is not the case at Cambridge, where many of them look like shabby hospitals. They are here all built of stone instead of brick, but the stone being a bad limestone scales off in the course of time, so that the buildings have all an antiquated appearance, but not so shabby as one would suppose this would make them. Some of the pillars that support a sort of dome over Queen's College gate are almost eaten through."

I remained the Tuesday at Oxford, lionised chiefly by an undergraduate, a friend of the Baillies, Mr Mylne (afterwards a Commissioner of Lunacy). At the botanic garden I was well received by the gardener, who gave me a few specimens to dry for my herbarium. "It is very poor, the hothouse very small, as also the greenhouses, which are moreover very dark, so that there is nothing of any value there. There is a pretty good collection of British plants, but this part of the garden suffers much from the inundations of the Isis, which frequently lays it all under water. Sibthorp, the author of the *Flora Graecea*, was long the professor here, but could never muster fourteen scholars, the number he had said would induce him to read his lectures. The present professor is a Dr Williams, but he cannot get a single pupil. The Oxonians attend to nothing but classics, and a very little of divinity. A professor of Medicine set up some years ago, but could never get more than one pupil, so he left off."

[189A]§I visited in due form the principal halls and colleges etc, not forgetting Queen's college, to see the room on the ground floor once my Uncle's, duly impressed with the degree in which division of labour was carried out by the showmen, with a corresponding multiplication of shillings exacted; and in the afternoon I enjoyed more than anything a stroll in the rich college meadows, teeming with spring flowers. On the Wednesday morning I breakfasted with Mr Urquhart, an undergraduate of St John's—for a short time afterwards an utilitarian hanger-on of my Uncle's through "the Tripolitan Ambassador," and afterwards went out to fight for the Greeks, with a commission which he did not [190] quite particularise, but which we of QSP assisted him in qualifying as Deputy last lieutenant. With him at breakfast was a Welsh amateur of botany, an undergraduate of the same college, these two having then the reputation as the only two of the college who had any claims to sobriety. "There are sorts of club-meetings amongst many of the young men in the University, of which debauch is the object, and in which the haut ton is to put learning into ridicule. Mr Urquhart and three or four others have formed, in opposition to these meetings, a literary society which meets every week to talk on literary subjects. Just now, it being near the end of term, all the men are obliged to be more or less at their studies on account of the approaching examinations, yet even now a great deal of drinking, etc, is evidently going forward. The contagion of so much bad example is enough to corrupt the most sedate."

I went on the same morning to Woodstock, "approaching the town along the walls of Blenheim Park, of which the injured state warns one of the noble proprietor's broken finances."[64] After a hearty luncheon, I had time for a walk over Blenheim Park before the hour came for seeing the house; and coming from France, I was particularly struck with the noble trees, "allowed to spread on all sides their immense branches, which is the distinguishing feature of English trees." The house and grounds reminded me of Holkham, though it seemed to be magna parvis comparere, the whole being on so much grander a scale than at Holkham. "When the hour came, I proceeded to go over the house and gardens with the several cicerones under the shape of porters, house keepers, etc, stationed for the purpose, and here I had another admirable instance of the advantages of a great division [192]§ of labour, for what one man might easily have shown for half a crown cost me here seven shillings, divided amongst as many persons, and I only got off for so little because there happened to be several other Lions and Lionesses at the same time, so that the showmen had not to go about for me alone." In the pleasure grounds, I much admired several trees, especially the finest cedar I had yet seen, and a bushy portugal laurel, spreading to a circumference of ninety yards. "The poor Duke, poor in the literal sense of the word, lives here on the slender pittance which the trustees of the estate allow him for his daily use. He has four sons and two daughters, but none of them with him. He is alone at Blenheim and amuses himself with gardening, having enclosed a fine piece of ground along the river, from the house to the cascade, which is the only part where the public is not admitted. The house, estate and grounds are kept up by the money attached to the estate for that purpose, and under the superintendence of the trustees. The house is open to the public every day from two till four, during which time the Duke generally takes a ride."

The next morning I left Woodstock by a cross country coach, starting at 7 in the morning and arriving at Warwick by about 3 in the afternoon. "I breakfasted at Banbury, where was held this morning a cattle fair, the first English one I have seen. The quantity of cattle exposed for sale was not very great, consisting of sheep, horses and black cattle. The sheep, some of them close shorn and presenting their bare skin quite clean and swelled out with fat, some with their long shaggy wool still dragging almost on the ground, this race appearing far below the South Down at least as to the *quality* of their wool, the horses remarkable to my eyes, at least from having all a certain degree of elegance in their appearance, none of those clumsy big-bellied *rosses* that crowd the French fairs. But [191]§ what struck me the most was the quiet and calm that prevailed over the scene, none of that loud vociferation, none of the energetic ges- ticulation, none of those hearty claps on the hand, none of that bustling crowd, the never failing accompaniments of a French fair, can here be observed; all is cool and quiet, every thing is uttered in a low and soft (I mean not loud) tone, even their jokes and their continual oaths. So also there is nothing like the gaiety and show of dress displayed in French fairs.

"The agriculture seems in general indifferent, though I passed many fields where the crops appeared pretty clean and good, but they are mostly backward, irregular and choked with weeds, notwithstanding the powerful instruments they use. Five horses to a plough, three to a harrow, four to a harrow with a little roller before, and six to the scari- fier have I often seen, and have not observed a single instrument with only two, always one before the other. What a loss of force there must be when there are six harnessed in this way to such work as requires fre- quent stopping and setting off again.

"The first part of the journey was over a flat country, beautiful only from the brightness of the verdure and the fineness of the weather . . . but from Southam to Warwick it is really fine. The road lies through Leamington, now celebrated as a watering place and situated on the

Avon, two miles from Warwick. It is a small town, containing little besides lodging houses, which make it look elegant and fashionable. It is lit with gaz, but as their gaz is not so good as that of Warwick, they are now laying pipes all along the road to convey it there. What would a Frenchman think of laying a league of cast iron pipes for the sake of procuring a more agreable light to a small watering place scarcely inhabited but in the four *summer* months? There are not many people as [193] yet at Leamington as the season is but just commencing. It lasts till October.

"The approach to Warwick from Leamington is at first along the south bank of the Avon, which we afterwards cross over a handsome stone bridge. The view is then peculiarly gratifying. Before you a little to the right is the town of Warwick on the side of a hill, half buried amongst fine trees, and crowned by two or three handsome steeples. Straight in front the antique, but neat and clean looking, towers of the castle rise majestically from the banks of the Avon, which seems to bury itself in the midst of an extensive and well wooded park. We passed under the wall of the gardens and entered a clean, well built and generally elegant town, full of hotels, coach offices, and other accomodations for travellers. I stopped at an inn at the top of the town, ordered my dinner and sallied forth to see the Castle. The entrance is by a winding road, hewn for some way out of the rock, which, rising on both sides from 2 to 20 feet from the ground, is covered with ivy and crowned by trees and flowering shrubs. It then opens to a handsome lawn, with clumps of American shrubs, and after crossing a drawbridge, we enter the precincts of this castle, the exact representation, as to exterior, of what we may imagine them to have been at the times when the lord and master was obliged to be in constant readiness to resist an attack or prepare for an expedition.—I am wrong perhaps in saying an exact representation, for the ditch is dry, and the walls rather encumbered by trees, but what I mean is that the walls are in excellent repair and, not being ruinous, do not look as useless and abandoned as we might expect. The interior of the castle is not equal to that of Blenheim. The collection of paintings is not so good, the rooms are not so splendid nor so [194] extensive, but there was one thing I admired much, a full size portrait of King Charles on horseback,[65] at the bottom of a long passage into which the light is thrown in a very advantageous manner. An old gardener who appeared to be near 80 conducted me over the garden. He seemed much attached to the place, where he has been above forty years, but vexed that his Lordship[66] does not allow him men enough to keep everything in good order. Some of the beds were quite overgrown with weeds. There are eight gardeners—at Blenheim there are near forty. The pleasuregrounds here, not so extensive as those of Blenheim, pleased me more. The views are not so grand, but the look-outs over the river, castle and neighbouring scenery much more romantic. The walk winds among some of the finest trees I have yet seen, down to the banks of the Avon—continues along its banks, crossing sometimes a neat lawn or clumps of Azaleas and Rhododendrons, sometimes taking you under the shade of wide-spreading trees collected from distant regions, and terminates at the foot of the broad and lofty castellated mass. Here after ascending two or three stories, I was brought out on an elevated shelf of the rock and conducted along a winding path to the *Keep*, an artificial mound raised to the level of the top of the castle, and on which stands the ancient lookout. There is here a small flat, once open to leave free scope for the sentinel's observations, now surrounded by sycomores, horse-chestnuts, oaks, hollies, etc, in the midst of which stands a Scotch pine, towering over not only its immediate neighbours, but also over the whole surrounding country. Through the breaks of these trees, the scene opens all around to the extent of many miles. Leamington, in particular, appears to great advantage. . . . Returning to the entrance gate the porter asked me whether I would see 'Guy's porridge pot,' 'the rib of the dun cow,' and a [195] number of other curiosities, which I consented to, the fee being due at any rate, and was shown into a small room containing old swords and pieces of armour, with an immense bell metal soup-pot and a number of similar rarities, all according to my Cicerone connected in some way or another with the famous Guy, Earl of Warwick[67]. . . . On the whole, I got off cheap at the Castle, five shillings amongst four persons enabled me to see everything. In the town there is a handsome Church, and it seems quite a genteel place. There are a number of Leamington cars about—a sort of light, one-horse, four-wheeled carriage, like a small open coach turned side-ways, and carrying four people. Some ply like hackney coaches, others go at stated hours from Leamington to Warwick and back."

Friday, 30th. "Left Warwick by the eight o'clock (or rather half-past-eight o'clock) coach and arrived at Birmingham, a distance of twenty miles, by a little after half past ten, a very pleasant drive through a country which I dare to say is pretty, but the horizon was so hazy I could not see very far round. The road was in some places bordered by trees, and all the way crossed a well-wooded country. Some miles before entering the town, the little cottages spread about indicated the approach to a populous and manufacturing place, and two miles at least out of the town the fog smelt strong of the coal smoke which thickened it. The town is a large, dirty, confused mass of red-brown brick buildings, intermixed with towering chimneys, from whence there issue continual volleys of black smoke that wraps the whole in a thick grey cloud. At least so it has been almost constantly during my stay here, on account, I suppose, of the foggy weather [196] that prevails at present. The streets are paved with the sharpest pointed pebbles I ever met with—that is, they compose the footpaths, for the middle of the streets are somewhat better. After crossing the town the first time, my feet were really so sore I could scarcely stand. Flag pavements are introducing into some few streets, but the Birmingham people, or *Brummichers*, are, like all others, attached to the old routine and complain that the sun shining on the flag pavements fatigues the eye—a reason almost as good as that our peasants give for not *spoiling the garrigues*.* I stopped at the Royal Hotel, but going immediately to see Mr Harris (Lord Calthorpe's Steward above mentioned) I was offered and accepted a bed in his house. It is the one occupied by Lord C. when he comes, the only spare one in this, the only house reserved by Lord C. for his and his steward's use, amidst his large street property here. Mr Harris, whom I have already described as a remarkably clever and intelligent man, received me very well, took immediate measures for procuring me admission into the principal manufactories, and sent his clerk Mr Cooke to accompany me over them. . . . To the Eagle Foundery, where was nothing remarkable. . . . To Thomason's showrooms. Thomason is a man who does not manufacture much himself but has in his warehouse a brilliant display of the produce of most of the Birmingham manufactories, alias Brummichem ware. In speaking of Warwick Castle, I forgot to mention an immense antique vase, placed in a greenhouse erected for the purpose of sheltering it from the inclemencies of the weather. This vase was found in the Tibur [197] near Tivoli, and purchased and brought over by the late Earl.[68] It is of marble, in a good state, but little touched by modern hands, of handsome proportions, and well ornamented and said to contain 163 gallons. Thomason cast in bronze a facsimile of it of natural size and has placed it in his showrooms. I think this imitation looks better still than the orig-

---

* When unprofitable waste lands, not bringing in above 2'/ an acre, were proposed to be brought into cultivation so as to produce at least 30'/ an acre annually, the Restinclières peasantry objected that it would spoil these garrigues or waste lands by interfering with the sheep walks.

inal, on account, I suppose, of the difference of the material. There was a great deal of imitation of china, made of painted iron, very well done—a quantity of plated copper and steel, the latter apparently advantageous from its hardness and exact resemblance to real silver—a great variety of little articles of metal furniture and gim cracks, many of them with curious contrivances for saving danger or inconvenience to idle and careless people. But these contrivances did not please me so much as those of the French in variety and ingenuity, and on the whole, I did not think the display so brilliant as I have often seen in France."

After Mr Harris's half past two dinner, "I went with Mr Cooke to Hazlewood school to see Mr Hill, where I found several of the family, and spent about an hour till Mr Harris's teatime . . . after which I went with him to the play. The house is small, but very light and elegant, the theatre itself (the audience) is semicircular, the best form for enabling the whole audience to see well, the ornaments are nice and fresh, and it is lit with gaz, but this must be very badly managed, for the smell of it was at times intolerable. The play acted was Sheridan's *Trip to Bath*, in which was some very good acting, but of which I cannot say I quite approved the story, or rather the stories, for there were at least three distinct intrigues carrying on. After this a young Frenchman of the name of Longuemare performed surprising feats on [198] the tight rope. Besides common dancing both with and without the pole, he made summersets, played on the tambourine, etc, and what seemed to me most difficult, he played with little balls like the Indian jugglers, kneeling all the while on the rope. I cannot think how he kept his balance whilst his attention was taken up with the balls. After him came a musical farce called *Brother and Sister*, a poor thing poorly acted, and so full of broad hints and jokes that I cannot think how the audience can suffer it to pass. Though the inside of the house was well lit, there were no lamps outside, and I should have been much at a loss to find my way out without Mr Harris's arm."

The next morning under Mr Cooke's guidance, I made a tour in the manufactories—Mr Phipson's rolling mills, where the engineer, Mr Hill, one of the Hazlewood school brothers, showed me every thing in the best manner possible, and of various of whose operations my letters contain full details. To the gun-barrel proof-house.—To Small's Japan manufactory (tea-trays, etc) which much interested me. To the pin-manufactory, "not that there was anything new enough to make it worth while entering into details; I merely went because every body goes there and because it is a pretty thing to see." The whip manufac-

tory however pleased me much, from the neat contrivances for winding
the threads round the centre, etc. The button manufactory, where Mr
Eaton's machine for making the shanks is used, was the only one which
no interest could open to view.

The afternoon was most agreably and usefully spent in going over
Lord Calthorpe's Edgbarton Hall Estate with Mr Harris, whose intelligent and instructive conversation, whilst detailing the improvements
going on, deeply interested me, and [199] on our return to his home, Mr
Rowland Hill joining us at dinner, our conversation was carried on till
late at night. The next day, Sunday, little could be done. Early in the
afternoon, I strolled out again over the estate with Mr Harris. The day
was very hot and we had a delightful lounge under some fine beeches in
Edgbarton Park before going to Mr Hill's family dinner at ½ past 3 at
Hazlewood school, in which my Uncle took great interest and which he
particularly wished me to see in detail.[69] "The building is a very handsome one, on Lord Calthorpe's estate about half a mile out of the town,
surrounded by houses and gardens. In front is a little front-garden. The
part of the house occupied by the boys is separated from the servants'
rooms by the appartments belonging to the family. The interior arrangements appear good. The school is getting into great repute and has
already 101 boys. Behind it are two extensive playgrounds and a large
kitchen garden, and at some distance, in a retired and concealed spot in
the valley, is a very nice bathing pond, through which runs a little rivulet, and in which the boys bathe every night. . . . All the members of the
Hill family seem remarkably clever and clear-headed. The head of the
family, Mr Hill the father, is now an elderly man, and is of course the
one who has the general authority, but the chief management rests with
Mr Rowland Hill* or Mrs Hill par excellence. His three brothers assist as
teachers, his sister and cousin and Mrs Hill in managing the household
concerns, and there are three other teachers. . . . I do not stop now to
give you the interesting details of the daily proceedings of the school
boys, as they are all, I believe, printed in Mr Hill's work on Public Education. I shall only mention [200] that religion is not at all interfered
with—that is counteracted; on the contrary, the boys are all conducted
to their respective churches, chapels or meeting houses according to
their several religions, grace is regularly said before and after dinner,

---

* Of Post Office celebrity.[70]

and Sunday is kept as gloomy as any where else, and all this would not have been shown off to me [if I had not been] coming from my Uncle's. Mr Hill says that the parents would take it amiss if the boys were allowed even to bathe on Sundays—indeed. I have not yet seen this day so strictly kept as in Birmingham, where even cakes and fruit are not allowed to be sold. This want of gay amusements must in some manner contribute to the grave, cool manner of the English peasantry—unless the latter be the cause of the former."

Monday, June 2d. "Left Birmingham in the morning on the 'Amity, new light and elegant post coach going in eight hours from Birmingham to Sheffield,' as their advertisements say. Two other coaches, equally puffed in their advertisements and with names just as fine, left at the same time for the same place, and we continued close behind each other all the way to Litchfield, galloping at the rate of ten miles an hour, notwithstanding the length of the stage (fifteen miles). The road was pretty, especially from Sutton Coldfield to Litchfield. Near Sutton is a very fine view over the town and plain of Litchfield. At this town we stopped twenty minutes for a cross coach, which gave me an opportunity of admiring the magnificent cathedral, on the outside at least, for I had not time to send for the man who keeps the keys. The highly ornamented, Gothicy front has lately been renovated, if there be such a word for *rafraichi* as we should say in French.

[201]"From Litchfield, the long plain, through which runs the Trent, and the distant hills with the straight road, reminded me something of some parts of France. We changed horses at Burton-on-Trent, famous for Burton ale, and from thence to Derby crossed a range of hills, from the top of which was a beautiful and very extensive view, on the one side over the Litchfield plain, on the other over the town and more varied neighbourhood of Derby."

I spent three or four days at Derby, where I was most kindly and hospitably entertained by the Strutts.[71] They were then three brothers, partners in the great cotton mills of Belper, and some silk mills in Derby. Mr William Strutt, my father's old friend, the father of the present Lord Belper, was the inventing, contriving and as it were scientific, partner. He was living at St Helens, in an excellent house at the end of the town, on the Belper road, but standing in very pretty grounds or park of about fifty acres, extending quite into the country. He received me into his house. He was a widower, his son, afterwards Lord Derby, was at college, but his three daughters—the eldest a great invalid—were at home, and rendered the evenings most agreable, whilst Mr Strutt, in the most friendly manner, contrived that my mornings should be spent most profitably. The morning I arrived he was out for the day, but his brother, Mr Joseph Strutt, well represented him in cordiality and attention. He was the financial partner, and lived in the town of Derby, where he had collected a very good gallery of pictures.[72] He spent the afternoon with me in the infirmary and silk mills, and kept me to dinner. He also was a widower with two daughters; the eldest had been lately married to Mr Howard Galton, but the second, Caroline, afterwards [202] Mrs Edward Hurt, was at home, and a most charming, accomplished person, painted beautifully, and an excellent musician, whose acquaintance was in after years a great enjoyment. After a pleasant dinner party, we adjourned to Mr William Strutt's, who induced me to take up my abode with him during my stay. He spent one long day with me in the cotton mills at Belper, and there introduced me to his brother George, residing with his family at Bridge Hill, in a fine house and park in a beautiful situation close to Belper, and being the practically superintending partner in the daily business of the mills. Another day, although pouring rain kept me in the morning at home with the young ladies, Mr Strutt took me over various institutions in the town in the afternoon, and my letters from hence are full of long details of all I saw—all of the greatest interest to me, and much that was then entirely new, not only to me but to the world in general, although now after half a century much may be superannuated. The gasworks were entirely new to me. Before we left England, gas-lighting was unknown, and it had not yet found its way—or was scarcely being introduced—into France. The Derby Infirmary was a model one, full of Mr Strutt's and Mr Sylvester's contrivances for the comfort and aid to the patients, especially in the heating, ventilation and internal arrangements,[73] then so grossly neglected or ill managed in most local hospitals and infirmaries—but above all it was on the cotton mills themselves, and on all the arrangements made by the Strutts for the comfort and well-being of the 2500 hands employed, that I expatiated the most. The father of the three Strutts had been the original partner with Arkwright in the cotton spinning patents, and the present generation, the rivals but friends of the Arkwrights, seemed almost to outdo [203] them in the important part of the business—due consideration for the workpeople themselves—so shamefully neglected in most mills set up after their example. "I drove with Mr Strutt in his carriage to Belper. My father and mother may remember the road there, though it must be still prettier now from the number of neat cottages spread about having so much augmented. As we passed a field where were a number of cows grazing, Mr Strutt observed to me, 'Those are all for working my manufactory,' and as I did not seem to understand him, he added, 'You know we carry on here a great manufactory of children for, as we want a great number, and they are continually becoming men and women, we are obliged to keep up a constant supply.' As to the means he employs, he says he builds cottages, puts a young married couple into each, gives them plenty of work, and the manufacture goes on in the best manner possible—and the cows are kept exclusively for the little children." The happy results of constant attention to the great working family were the more forcibly impressed on my mind when I afterwards came to compare them with what I saw in some other mills and manufactories.

Friday, 6th June. "I left Derby on the Leeds mail at about one. The road was at first very indifferent. Till Atherton it was far inferior to those I had hitherto met with. It lay along a little valley for a great way, alongside of a railroad. We passed several trains of ten waggons of 23 cwt coals, each drawn by 4 horses. We ascended almost all the way to Atherton. Here the country grew much better. The approach to Chesterfield is very pretty. The town in situated in a valley, or rather small plain, and on the side of the slope. In the middle is a most remarkable spire to the Church. From some accident or other it has got bent in the middle as if it [204] were made of pewter and some giant had given it a blow. Beyond Chesterfield, the country is very pretty, and appears to be still more so some way to the left. It is well wooded and covered in some places with little *wimseys*, or small steam engines, working coal mines. Sheffield is a large black town, prettily situated in the bottom of a valley. From the hill just out of the town is a fine view back over it. Barnsley, the next place, is another manufactoring town, chiefly I believe in wool, and has a great many little cottages, something like Mr Strutts at Belper, but not near so neat and clean, and the people do not look half so healthy, though their town be in a more airy situation. Wakefield is a large black manufactoring town, on a broad canal full of vessels, with a very fine bridge, on which is a most ancient chapel. Some way beyond was a fine view over a sheet of water. The whole country from Chesterfield, or at least from Sheffield, is very hilly and perhaps the prettiest I have seen. A good deal of wood, but the most shocking farming, particularly about Atherton, where the weeds are more prominent than the crops. Many stories were told me of some of the principal farmers there having lost carts without finding it out, etc. As we approached Leeds, it began growing dark, which is perhaps the best time, on account of the curious appearance the neighbourhood has from the number of fires issuing from the chimneys scattered over the country. The smoke of the place is smelt from a great distance."

The following morning I took a walk to Middleton colliery to see what was then quite novel to me, a locomotive engine carrying trains of coal-waggons along the railroad; it was on [205] the old cogwheel plan, carrying the trains on a level at the rate of about five miles an hour. I was much struck with it and gave in my letter full details, adding, "I expect we shall soon have railroads and steamengines for mail and stage coaches."[74] A few days later I saw several such coaltrains with locomotives at Newcastle and some already that acted without the cogwheel, merely by the friction of the driving wheels on the rails.

"Middleton colliery being elevated, I had on my way a view over the town of Leeds, that is over as much of it as the smoke would permit me to see. It is in a small plain, which is almost covered with its immense ugly manufacturing buildings, wrapped in a cloud of smoke. Its ramifications extend quite to the neighbouring hills, and as far as we can see, large black buildings, with immense chimneys pouring forth volleys of smoke, are dispersed over the country. What makes the town much more smoky than Birmingham is that the steamengines do not burn their own smoke.

"I left Leeds in the afternoon by the 'Wellington' coach, being obliged to take the inside on account of the bad weather. Though heavily laden, we got to York in 3½ hours (35 miles) over a flat, uninteresting country, apparently in good cultivation. York is an old-looking town, with less new building about than any other. It is walled round and is situated on a little river, over which is a new broad and handsome bridge. The streets are narrow and winding and many of the houses have a very curious appearance, from a sort of metallic resplendency that bricks made in the north have. The Minster is a large building, reckoned one of the handsomest cathedrals in England. The outside appearance is not so well proportioned as that of some others, the building is generally low, but the front is handsome and well ornamented and the interior is really beautiful, the proportions of the columns and gothic roof particularly so. There [206] [is] some very handsome, finely carved stonework, but not so fine as that at Auch—numerous painted windows and an octagon chapterhouse [   ] feet [in] diameter, without any central support to the roof. I was much amused with the stories of the man who showed it to me. Speaking of the painted glass, he pointed out the figures: 'This is old father Abraham, the patriarch of Israel. This is Moses, whom you

may have read of in Scripture; the sculpture is very fine, etc.' At a cupboard where a number of relics such as bishops' crosiers, etc, are shown,
he said, holding up two little brass coronets, 'Here are two coronets that
were carried before King James I, in token of the happy union of the two
crowns by his accession to the throne of England.'[75] Then, putting them
down, a little interruption ensued by some question of mine about
something else. This put him out, and taking up a chalice and saucer, he
began again, 'Here are two coronets that were carried before King James
I, in token—Oh dear no, it's not that; I have said that already,' and it
required some thought and cogitation before he could go on with, 'This
is the chalice and saucer which,' etc. He was very amusing also in pointing out the beauties and merits of the several monuments, [$]but he
would have been of just as much use to me if he had repeated 'This is
the house that Jack built,' etc.

   "The weather having the appearance of settled rain, and the country
from York to Durham being reported to me as flat, tiresome and uninteresting, I thought that as, at any rate, I must go inside, I had better get
on, so I took the night coach and arrived at Durham by eight o'clock on
Sunday morning. As long as I travelled in daylight, the country
appeared to answer [207] the description I had heard of it. As we
approached Durham, it grew more hilly but without much beauty.
Durham itself is remarkable for its curiously picturesque situation. It is
chiefly upon a hill almost surrounded by the Wear, which runs at the
bottom of a deep valley. The town extends also a great way along the
ridge which connects this promontory with the adjoining high ground,
and across the valley, up the hills along the York and Newcastle roads.
The Cathedral and Palace on the highest part of the promontory, the
steep gardens along the banks of the river and the ancient houses every
where, in steps one above the other, give the whole a romantic appearance. From an elevated field by the Newcastle road there is a fine view
over the whole scenery, giving a very good idea of the general disposition of the place, which otherwise it would be difficult to understand.
The town itself is by no means handsome. The streets steep, narrow and
winding, the houses old and shabby. The two bridges have nothing
remarkable, but the green banks of the Wear, particularly as they appear
from the Newcastle road bridge, are very pretty. The Cathedral is a fine
structure, but I did not like it so well as the York Minster. The Bishop's
Palace is a heterogeneous mass, being the modernised ruins of the old
castle. On the market place is a curious statue of Neptune, in the form of
a slim young man with a golden trident and crown. From his being

there, I suppose that a fountain ought to issue from under his feet, but I saw no water—perhaps because it was Sunday.

"I dined at Durham, and left at ½ past five by the 'High Flyer' coach, the weather having improved and enabled me to go outside. I was particularly fortunate this time in meeting with a very clever Officer, with whom I conversed agreably the whole time. Several times, indeed, I have met with pleasant and well-informed people in or on the different coaches. From Derby to Leeds [208] in particular, two gentlemen, the one a Col Jebb, the other an inhabitant of Wakefield, made the journey very pleasant, but sometimes we meet with people who will not open their mouths if the journey be a hundred miles or more.

"I saw nothing remarkable between Durham and Newcastle, when once we had lost sight of the former, till the numbers of smoking chimneys indicated the neighbourhood of Newcastle, and soon afterwards, we got to the edge of the elevated hill, from whence that town appears in all its black, vaporous majesty, with an extensive prospect on one side up two beautiful vales, on the other down the Tyne, with its banks crowded with manufactories and collieries, and its bed with vessels of all descriptions. From the hill, the eye can trace its windings quite to Shields, where it joins with the vast extent of sea that borders the horizon on that side. Clouds of smoke indicate the spots where are North and South Shields, Sunderland and Wearmouth. Before you is seen nearly the whole of the comparatively flat country of Northumberland, bounded at a distance by the Cheviot Hills. Notwithstanding the haziness of the weather, this view was, if not the finest, at least the most interesting I have yet seen in this country—but all vanished from our sight as we descended into the smoky abyss at our feet. It was Sunday night, and as might be expected, the people were out before their doors in their Sunday attire and finery, but such people and such finery as never I saw. Their hollow, distorted features, sallow countenances, as well as could be distinguished under the dark coating of dirt that covered their ragged, dirty, shabby dresses, notwithstanding the partial attempts at finery. Everything, in short, about their persons tending to excite disgust and give the idea of misery, which effect was certainly much heightened by the appearance of the town, which never can be agreable, and was now particularly dark and gloomy, from the heavy weather which confined the smoke. The houses are [209] very old, the upper stories projecting over the lower, and especially in the lower part of the town covered with a thick coating of soot. The streets are very irregular, some of them apparently almost perpendicular. This town might indeed very well represent the Cyclops' Cave,[76] inhabited by fifty thousand of those gentry. Leeds is perhaps, however, nearly as bad, with eighty thousand of them. Stopped at the Turf hotel, in one of the best streets of the town, with a long row of coaches in front of the door, which all disappeared the next morning. Ten is, I believe, the number that arrive at this inn every evening and leave every morning. Went to the Revd Mr Turner's, a dissenting minister to whom I had a letter, found him in a nice house, in the upper part of the town, a good deal out of the soot but not out of the smoke, commanding a very fine view over the valleys that open to the Tyne, the shot tower at the entrance of the valley being a great addition to the ornament of the scene."

"Monday morning (9th), breakfasted at Mr Turner's and went with him, first to a nurseryman at Gateshead, just about Newcastle, of the name of Falla, walked over a part of his grounds and descended through a number of little mining and manufacturing villages to the Tyne, which we ferried over almost opposite to Mrs Ibbetson's at St Anthony's. The banks of the Tyne would all the way be beautifull, if they were not so covered with manufactories, and the air not so thickened by smoke, and everything blackened by coals and soot. The banks are rather elevated and the river makes many very pretty turns. It is full of small vessels, keels and boats, which give the whole an air of bustle and flourishing commerce—here, small collier vessels receiving their load directly from the spouts—there, others discharging their ballast on to the artificial mounds thus formed—keels going up and down the river to carry coals [210] to those vessels that are too large to come up the river themselves, and every now and then, steam packets going slap dash and splashing along, agitating the river to the very brink, sometimes loaded with passengers going to or from Newcastle or Shields, sometimes towing vessels in or out of the river. On the hills, at the same time, are to be seen horses drawing coalwaggons in every direction along the railroads. Here we may see the proverbial expression of the cart before the horse actually realised, for when the road descends a slope, they take the horse out and tie him behind, so that from a distance it really looks as if the cart were drawing the horse. There are steam carriage railroads in the neighbourhood, but I did not see any. This busy scene looked the better from the weather, which had at last become a little clearer though still very cloudy. The ballast hills I just mentioned are considerable elevations, formed on the banks of the river by the gravel brought in ballast by the coal-vessels, chiefly those trading to London, whence the return goods are out of all proportion to the coals sent. The crane for lifting it out of the vessels is worked by a steamengine, which also draws the carriages into which the ballast is emptied up the hill where it is to be discharged. .... These ballast hills, originating sometimes from distant countries, are frequently covered with exotic plants and shells. I remarked particularly a quantity of fine fennel, a plant not usually wild in England. The coal spouts above mentioned are elevated jetties, at the end of the railroads, by means of which the coals are shot at once from the waggons to the vessels placed in the river under the spouts."

Mrs Ibbetson, the lady to whom this visit was paid, was an old friend connected with a family with whom we had been intimate since childhood;[77] she was living here at present alone, with her mother, Mrs Morton, now 92, and who was soon after [211] one of five generations living at the same time: Mrs Morton, her daughter Mrs Ibbetson, her grand daughter Mrs Ellison, and her great grand daughter, Lady Vernon, who had children before the death of Mrs Morton. "Mrs Ibbetson's place, St Anthony's, is on the banks of the Tyne, just by a beautifull turn it takes about three miles below Newcastle bridge. It is a handsome house, with a pretty garden, amidst half a dozen or more smoking manufactories, in a position which would otherwise be beautifull, but it is not only on human senses that this smoke, imbued with all sorts of smells, has a disagreable effect, but the very plants look sickly and smoke dried— though perhaps they suffer more from the vapours of the ammoniac and other manufactories. Mrs I. has a little greenhouse and in front of her house myrtles, which are covered with glass in winter only. We dined with her, and in the evening returned to the town along the river side, that is through coal yards, rope yards, glasshouse yards, pottery yards, etc. We passed along the quay, which is perhaps the oldest part of the town, the streets or lanes that come down to it are most of them three or four feet broad at most, the houses being three or four stories high and looking like pigstyes. These little black lanes are called in the country *chairs*. On that, Mr Turner told me he was once present when a judge, holding the assizes at Newcastle was going to have a man taken up as insane who swore he saw three men coming out of the foot of a chair."

Tuesday, 10th. "To Mrs I. to breakfast; she showed me some of her curious collection of dried plants. You know how she made it, gathering what came in her way, drying them and sewing them into a book, according to the order of time, with the date and place where gathered, an interesting collection to her perhaps, but not very gratifying to a bot-

anist, who cannot but be rather scandalised [212] to see the leaf of a
Lathyrus with the flower of a Lotus, the stem of a Blue-bell with the root
of a Biscutella, and feel rather indignant at the barbarous manner in
which the botanical names are distorted and misapplied. The specimens
are neatly sewn in, the threads passing through every leaf and over
every stalk. There are three volumes in a handsome morocco binding,
and interleaved with silver paper. . . . Went to Mr Falla's, where [I]
dined and spent the rest of the day. He is a very clever man, and has
attended much to different kinds of cultivation, particularly to the raising of trees. His nursery is perhaps the most extensive in England for
seedlings. He has nearly a hundred acres in trees, which he always sells
off under four years old, excepting fruit trees, of which his collection is
but small. Besides the immense number which he sells from the seed
beds, he transplants or rather pricks out every year about four millions
of trees. In this number, about 800,000 larches, 800,000 oaks, and 400,000
Scotch firs. The rest chiefly beech, birch, ash, elm, silver fir, alder, chestnut, maple, sycomore, nut and holly; he has also immense beds of thorn
and sloe for hedges. He carries everything to so great an extent that he
finds great advantage in a bruising mill, turned by a horse, solely
adapted to the bruising larch-cones in order to get out the seed. He has
also stoves for extracting the seed from pine and fir cones, which cannot
be done with the larch. He sowed this year the seed of 2,000 bushels of
larch cones, some hundred bushels of acorns, etc. Sometimes a seedbed
remains on his hands; he has not room to transplant them, and is
obliged to root them up—two such beds of uprooted Scotch firs were
lying on the ground when I was there, in each bed some forty or fifty
thousand. He sends seedlings to all parts of England, water carriage
being so easy from Newcastle, and I really think it might be worth our
while to have some from him for Restinclières. . . . He sells oak, Wey-
mouth pine, [213] Cluster pine, Silver fir, Mountain ash at 5'/, Beech
and Sycomore at 3'/, Norway Spruce and Alder at 2'/6, Larch 2'/, Ash
and Thorn 1'/6d and Scotch fir at only 6d per thousand. He has also a
great quantity of grass-seed, which he finds more profitable to raise
than corn. He has been making experiments on the comparative advantage of hand-digging and ploughing, and finds that, though in price one
hand digging is equal to three ploughings, that one does the ground
more good than all three ploughings. The principal defect he finds in the
ploughing is that which I had suggested, as you may remember some
time since, which is the pressing the subsoil into a hard and compact
mass through which the roots can with difficulty penetrate. This is not

the case with the hand digging as it is done at Restinclières with the bigot, still less so with the spade. Mr Falla has paid a great deal of attention to this, and cultivated land in both ways side by side, with a view to substituting cattle to human labour at the time work was here so very dear, and even then he found considerable advantage in spade culture. Wages here are rather cheaper than with us, 1'/6d a day in ordinary times, more during the busy months. The women 1'/ to 1'/6d, according to the work they do. Weeding is done by the piece—so much per acre for keeping the ground clean from May to October, paid only at the end of the season, when it can be shown that they have earned it. He employs from one to two hundred men and women according to the season, more women than men and, clerks included, pays about £50 per week in wages. Some women were employed in a curious operation, pricking out seedling Rhododendrons just come up, to save them from the kind of moss which attacks them, the plants being so small as not to be seen without looking quite close. Workmen all [214] about here and at Berwick work about ten to ten and a half hours a day, meals excluded, which is rather more than ours do, but I think they are much less constant when at it than ours."

Wednesday, 11. "Left Newcastle in the morning, outside the 'Union' coach for Berwick-upon-Tweed, but bad weather soon obliged me to get inside, and remain in nearly all the way. The country is comparatively flat, pretty about Felton, where we changed horses the first time. We passed through the little town of Morpeth, and stopped to breakfast at Alnwick (pronounced Annick), where is the ancient seat of the Percy family or Dukes of Northumberland. The castle is quite a castellated building of a curious shape, and looks very remarkable and somewhat ridiculous from the number of grotesque figures stuck upon the battlements. The grounds are extensive, well wooded, and seem beautifully arranged. They are crossed by a river, canal or lake, I do not know which, every piece of water in England being more or less artificial. Over this is a fine bridge on our road. Different obelisks and monuments are placed on different parts of the grounds, one to commemorate the spot where the first Duke is supposed to have killed King James IV of Scotland.[78] From Belford, half-way from Alnwick to Berwick, the road, not interesting in its immediate neighbourhood, is very pleasant, from the view on one side over the ocean, and on the other over a large tract of country intersected by valleys and terminated by the Cheviot hills, still bearing a few patches of snow. The descent to Berwick must be very pretty in fine weather, from the extensive view over the town and the river Tweed. We arrived there at about two, and I employed the rest of the day in writing [215] and strolling about the town and pier. The town is small and insignificant, black, though without manufactories. It is surrounded by ramparts, and is situated on a promontory between the Tweed and the sea; a stone pier projects into the sea to form the harbour, and over the river is a heavy, clumsy, irregular bridge, which the roadbooks call *very elegant*. I walked a good deal along the seashore and the meadows between the ramparts and the sea, but could not find any plants worth picking up. I was better rewarded for my walk round the walls. From one point I had a very extensive view up the valley and along the sea coast. The Cheviot hills still in sight, the weather had also become a little clearer so as to enable me to enjoy it. Near the town are what are called interesting ruins of the Castle, but I thought they resembled very much the ruins of the two old towers at the corners of our *menagérie* (farm buildings). In the town is an example of the fashion the reformers adopted of doing everything exactly contrary to what the papists did. The church is built without any steeple and, as bells are useful in the town, there is a steeple to the town hall, so that at first I took the church for a town hall and the hall for a church. I am now quite amongst Scotch, and cannot help remarking the great tendency to Methodism amongst the Scotch Presbyterians. The booksellers' and print shops are full of methodistical works, and they talk a great deal about religion. The very strict observance of the Sunday must be particularly gloomy. No kind of amusement whatever, and travelling on that day most strictly forbidden."

Thursday, 12th. "I hired a horse this morning, and took a ride before breakfast to the chain bridge over the Tweed about six miles from this. It was built about three years ago, and is remarkable for its lightness and simplicity. . . . The [216] span is about 300 feet, and what surprised me was the straightness of the bridge, notwithstanding its thinness and great span, for it would seem difficult to stretch the chain sufficiently tight. Nothing can be more elegant, nor, as it is said, cheaper. . . . The banks of the river are here very pretty. There is a fine seat and park, belonging to the Mr ——, so famous in the Portsmouth case, which is still much talked of. He had Lord and Lady Portsmouth down here for a long time.[79] I went on one side of the river and returned on the other. The country is varied as to hills, and in high cultivation, but destitute of trees; the fields are also very large, this being a great country for farming. I had occasion to see some turnip-sewing . . . but I reserve further details on North Country farming till I have an opportunity of seeing it properly. Here at last are tolerable carts, much like our *tombereaux*, but broader, shorter and shallower, all with one horse and very light, a system which all intelligent people allow to be far better, but is not adopted in any part of the south or centre of England. Acts of Parliament are indeed just made against conical wheels,[80] but their effect seems very slow, for I have scarcely seen in England any but conical wheels to the carts. Rain obliged me to hurry home to my writing. . . . The weather is here continually cold and hazy after rain, which they do not seem to think anything unusual for the season."

5

A Tour in Scotland and the Lake District

The weather cleared up in the afternoon and allowed me to leave Berwick outside the mail at ½ past two, arriving at Edinburgh at nine in the evening. "The journey was very pleasant from the variety of the scenery. The road lay mostly along the seacoast, and at first was only pretty from the exceeding calmness of the surface of the water, which is here, I believe, a very unusual circumstance. The [217] country is in general bare of trees, and consists chiefly of immense fields of arable land, many of them now being sown in turnips, in straight lines of interminable length. . . . We changed horses, the first time at Renton Inn, in a beautiful glen, along which the road runs for some miles, having quitted the coast to cross a headland projecting some way into the sea. From thence to Edinburgh the road is, if possible, harder and smoother than any I have yet seen. I should think it must be nearly equal to a railroad. The horses galloped along apparently without fatigue although the coach was full. This is owing to the entire adoption of the McAdam system.[1] The country now became flatter. We passed through the towns of Dunbar and Haddington. In the first, is a fine house belonging to the Earl of Lauderdale, ridiculously placed at the top of the street. We passed many beautiful seats belonging to the Scotch nobility, and when we had passed Haddington, we began to see the hills that surround Edinburgh, and particularly Arthur's Seat, compared by the Scotch to a lion crouching. At first the horizon was so hazy that we could not distinguish much, but soon the sun shone out; it was near the horizon, and reflected on the scenery in a most remarkable way, the haze contributing to give everything a beautiful golden colour. The country immediately around us, adorned with numerous parks and well built villages, the bold scenery round the metropolis a short distance before us, and on the right an immense sheet of water as smooth as glass, made the whole the finest sight I have seen for a long time. As we approach Edinburgh, the towns follow close upon each other: Tranent, Musselburgh, Portobello and Leith, most of them bathing places, and all built of stone, Portobello in particular, where is a very fine street called Brighton Place."[2]

Friday, June 13. Edinburgh. "I have now been here a whole [218] day—walking about without having seen anybody or any thing—that is to say, any sight other than the town itself, which to be sure is the finest of all possible sights. I presented most of my letters, but did not find any body at home—but I have had a note from Dr Thomson's son, who called at the inn whilst I was out to ask me to breakfast tomorrow.—I have not found Edinburgh as I expected; the town is very different from any other one, and the inhabitants, who I supposed would have appeared different, are exactly as in London or any other large English town in dress and manners and everything except accent. They may appear also rather gayer and more elegant, but perhaps this is only from the contrast with the shabby, dirty, smoky Cyclops I have been amongst of late in the manufacturing towns. I somehow figured to myself that Edinburgh would be full of Scotch dresses, or at least would have something Scotch about them, but I have now been walking all day, and with the exception of a couple of little boys just out of petticoats, and perhaps two or three boys' caps, I have not met with the least vestige of plaid about man, woman or child. The town itself is very grand and remarkable and, as has been often repeated, consists of two quite distinct towns in position as well as in appearance, the old and the new. The former stands on a long hill terminated on the west by a bold rock, on the top of which is the castle, and descending gradually to the eastward, till it is lost in a valley between two hills, the one steep and elevated, more like St Loup than any other that I know, and known by the name of Arthur's Seat, the other lower and crowned by two buildings, a rather shabby observatory and a very handsome and high monument erected [219] to the memory of Lord Nelson. Here also it is contemplated to erect another building, to be called National monument—on what occasion I know not.[3] The new town runs parallel to the old, from which it is separated by a deep ravine called the North Loch. Over this is a handsome bridge of three or four arches, from whence the view over the houses below is very curious. The new town consists chiefly of a large parallelogram, formed of three principal parallel streets in one direction, with several cross ones in the other, and two handsome squares, St Andrew's at the east end with a fine monument dedicated to Lord Melville, and Charlotte square at the west end. This perhaps with a few houses east of St Andrew's Square is as much of the new town as existed at the time of my mother's stay in Edinburgh, or perhaps much of that was only then commencing, but now below it and north of the parallelogram is an extensive tract of streets, still finer than the others, particularly Heriot Row, Abercrombie Place, etc, and a beautiful Circus quite at the northwest. To the North East the new buildings have extended quite to Leith Walk, and near Calton Hill a beautiful opening has been made opposite Princes' Street, which now, by a handsome bridge over the cross street below, comes by a very gradual ascent straight to about half way up Calton Hill. This has much reduced the apparent height of the hill, which will soon be surrounded with houses, an extensive and magnificent plan being laid out for building round it. These details may perhaps be uninteresting to you, but my mother will understand how much this town is daily encreasing in size and beauty. The houses are all of stone and built with much taste, and regularly reminding me more of the new part of Marseille [220] than of any other town, but are handsomer. The old town, as you may suppose, is very different; the very high houses and narrow streets resemble the long close streets of some parts of Paris. This part of the town spreads over the central hill and the adjoining valley on the south, and consists chiefly of two streets, High Street on the ridge, and Cowgate in the valley, between which are a number of little passages called lanes or closes, just like the chairs of Newcastle. To the south of the old town, buildings have considerably extended over a third hill, but they are not so handsome as the new town to the north. Opposite the North Bridge, a fine broad street crosses the old town at right angles to High Street with a bridge over the Cowgate, all these streets crossing over each other having a very curious appearance. There are many handsome public buildings, although the inhabitants complain that there are none. The Royal College, as yet unfinished, promises to be a very fine one, the interior something like the Louvre in miniature, but three sides only are yet built. In Parliament Square, the parliament house contains the libraries of the writers to the signet and of the advocates (corresponding to English solicitors and barristers). The Advocates' library is very extensive, being one of those to which a copy of every work published is obliged to be sent.* It is chiefly kept in a number of half underground rooms, some of them quite dark, at the back of the house, others pretty good but not in general in good order; a portion however is upstairs in a large handsome room, very elegantly furnished. In the same building is a small but, I believe, good library, collected by the writers to the signet. In the courts of law there was I [221] believe but little doing, and that amidst so much noise and bustle that I could not hear a word. The outer room is large, and contained several hundred men walking up and down, besides two or three small circles, in the middle of each of which sat a judge, as I was told, for a first hearing. In two other rooms were five judges in each, in wigs and scarlet robes, most of them having remarkable faces, all old, and two completely deaf. Amongst the other buildings are the Register office and some of the hospitals, of elegant construction, as well as several of the chapels, [a] particular one in London Street something like King's College Chapel in Cambridge. There is also a small theatre, very shabby on the outside, but said to be pretty good inside. I shall not see it, for the Scotch are so little dramatic that this town can only support a play in winter. How different from Marseille, for instance—a town resembling Edinburgh in extent, appearance and population, though surpassing it in commerce, and consequently in bustle and business." Closed the day by a family dinner at Dr Thomson's.

Sunday, June 15. "Breakfasted at Mrs Fletcher's, where I found her with her son, a young man of two or three and twenty, a daughter of about that age, reckoned very handsome, and a married daughter of the name of Taylor.[5] After leaving them, joined W. Thomson, and with him on horseback on a country excursion, he being one of the very few here who are not strictly regular in their attendance at church. We went in the direction of the new Carlisle road, now making, to a farm at the foot of the Pentland hills, four or five miles from the town, and kept by a Mr Cleghorn, who communicated to me what intelligence he could [222] about the farming here. This is much the same as the Haddingtonshire or East Lothian farming, reckoned the best. Mr Cleghorn's is on a comparatively smaller scale, but from him I have obtained information about the work, perhaps as correct as any I should get from the greater ones, which I shall also see." (Then follow long details about the person-

---

* At that time eleven copies of every work published had to be sent to different libraries.[4]

nel of the farm, the working arrangements as to men and horses, the mode of proceeding as to various crops etc—day labourers' pay, ten hours' work meals excluded 1'/6d to 2'/ a day, women about half as much.) Returning in the afternoon, rode through the town to Newhaven, to see the then new chain pier, and dined at Dr Thomson's.

Monday, June 16. "To the botanical garden to see Mr McNab, who is now very much occupied in changing the garden. The old one is on the Leith Walk, and was a great deal too small to hold a tolerable collection, besides which the green and hothouses were of a bad construction. It is now near two years that a new garden of nine or ten acres was bought, in an excellent situation on the Newhaven road. They have since been building green and hothouses on an elegant and extensive plan, a large circular one in the middle, higher ones on each side, and lower ones beyond to a great length. It will altogether be very large when finished, but there is as yet only part of one side ready; the centre and the other side are little more than begun. In those that are finished there seems to be a very good collection of plants, and the groundwork of an extensive one. There are now some very showy plants in flower, particularly some new Calceolarias, a fine Cypripedium and others, and some of the palms are already large. The roof is of iron, the rafters elegant, all of one piece, the top and front, as in all [223] British greenhouses, entirely covered with glass. The garden shows from far by means of an immense chimney belonging to the steam boilers, for all the houses are heated by steam, and there is besides a small steam engine for pumping water into a cistern, from whence pipes lead to all parts of the garden. The plants in the new garden are better arranged than usual in England, but might, I think, be still better. Besides those spread about in different parts for ornament, there is a large *quartier* in which herbaceous perennials are arranged according to Linnaeus's system. British plants are excluded from hence, and are collected in a separate bed, which at one end contains those peculiar to Scotland; another bed is set apart for medicinal plants, or at least those reputed medicinal, and a large part of the garden, is or will be (for it is not yet finished), laid out in a very good way for an arrangement according to the natural orders. Instead of straight rows, each family is contained in a bed of appropriate size, and of an irregular shape, in order that the number of different sized beds might not hurt the eye. These beds are separated by turf and look exceedingly ornamental. If ever the time comes when we can afford a botanical garden, it would be in this way that I should like to lay it out, but here annuals are excluded, which I do not quite approve of. The object of a botanical arrangement is to bring similar plants together for the purpose of comparison, and this should therefore be persevered in as much as possible according to one system, whether natural or artificial (as they are called). But if some are subtracted because they do not live so long as the others, others because some quack or other has made use of them in his medicines, and others again because they grow in a particular country, the collection of those that [224] remain cannot afford half as much scope for comparison as they would otherwise. It may indeed be useful to have extra collections of such as are applicable to particular purposes—as collections of textile or tinctorial plants—such as afford food or forage for man or cattle; it may even be interesting to have a separate collection of those that grow naturally in the surrounding country—but if so, all these plants should be repeated in the general arrangement.

"The aquarium in this garden is of a very pretty form. It is a large crescent shaped basin, divided round the edge into compartments for the different species of aquatic plants. In the hothouses there are also basins for the tender ones. They are particularly rich in Nymphaeas, of which they have eight or ten species. But the most remarkable thing in the garden is the size of the transplanted trees. They carried from the old garden to the new, besides many trees of 20 to 30 ft high, a Fraxinus ornus of 40 feet, and a cut-leaved Alder of 45 feet, all doing very well. There is particularly a weeping Birch in a very flourishing condition that was brought the winter before last, being 35 feet high. Mr Macnab superintends the works going on, and is, I believe, a clever botanist, though he does not at first prepossess much in his favor from his cold manner, and almost extinct voice. He was, however, very civil to me, and after I had been with him long enough to get accustomed to his manner, I got much pleased with him. I have not yet seen Dr Graham, the botanical professor here.

"In returning from the botanical garden, I called on Mr Neill (Patrick Neill) to whom I had also a letter from Mr Don. He lives at Canon Mills, a village adjoining Edinburgh on the same Newhaven road. I found him in a little place looking on [225] a small garden that he cultivates with his own hands in his leisure hours, that is before breakfast and after dinner. Spending the whole of the intermediate time in his business (the law I believe), he returns here to rest himself in the midst of his plants and his birds, which to him supply the place of a family, and afford him perpetual amusement in watching their growth and movements. This garden is small, but thick set with plants, forming very pretty variegated groups arranged in different ways. In one part a thick shrubbery, in another an artificial rock, with a small basin of water plants. In the midst of them, I was surprised to see so many tame birds of various descriptions. Here stalks a heron, drawing itself up as if to be admired when it sees a stranger—there the Soland Goose agitates its beak as if in a passion, and the greedy Cormorant runs up to you in the hopes of receiving a slice of fish, which, when you give it, it swallows up with amazing voracity. Seagulls of various descriptions keep at a little distance, uttering their piercing cries, and amongst the fowls you may perceive several musk-ducks and a fine tame wild-goose. These birds are in perfect liberty, the garden opens upon a large pond where they bathe, and yet no one attempts to escape. The Soland Goose has been there for four years, which is longer than they can usually be kept. The birds were all taken young and are perfectly tame. The plants consist either of rare or showy ones, the collection being small but good. There was a double Sagina procumbens, the smallest double flower I have ever seen, being only 1/10 inch in diameter at most.

"Dined at Professor Pillans's, and met there Mr Napier, the editor of the *Supplement to the Encyclopedia Britannica*,[6] and two young men, the one I believe Russian from his name, Prince Czartoriski (as they usually spell it), the other a Lord Somebody or other, a younger brother of some noble family. [226] I had much agreable conversation with Mr Pillans and Mr Napier, both very learned men, and after dinner went with them and Prince Czartoriski to the Royal Society. This was the last meeting of the season, and was pretty well attended, but I was disappointed in not seeing Sir Walter Scott, who is President, but seldom attends. I shall contrive however to get a sight of him before I leave Edinburgh in some of the courts of law. The meeting was not very interesting—a paper on the deviation of the magnetic needle, explaining some experiments recently made—an account of a new substance called Hopeite—a paper on the visionary power of the eye, and another on the correct tenses of Greek verbs were read,[7] but could only be interesting to those who are well versed in the sciences to which they relate; besides that mere abstracts were given, and those ill read. There was to have been a further account of Perkins's famous engine,[8] but Mr Hall, who was to have read it, was not present, and something was said about Perkins's wish to have no more divulged till his patent was taken out, but I believe the real truth to be that he is now beginning to doubt himself of the reality of his invention, now reckoned by most men of science a mere humbug. The chair was occupied by Dr Hope, Vice president. There were present Sir John Sinclair, President of the Board of Agriculture, but who for some reason or other is considered a very tiresome and plaguing personage, Dr Brewster, secretary of the Royal Society, Dr Coventry, professor of Agriculture etc; Dr. Pillans, with whom I went, is professor of Humanity. Coming out of the Society, we took a walk round Calton hill. This was a particularly favorable time of day for the picturesque view of the town from this hill, the best point for seeing it to advantage.

[227]"The contrast between the old town and the new is very striking, and some buildings lately constructed for a gaol, and especially the governor's house, harmonise well with this romantic situation. The governor's house is in a castellated style just at the edge of a perpendicular rock projecting from Calton hill. These buildings were planned and constructed by Elliott, a famous architect, who has just now, within these three days, unfortunately died from an improper bleeding and subsequent imprudent treatment; he is reckoned a great loss. It was he who planned the Regent bridge which joins Princes's Street to Calton hill, and the magnificent buildings along the connecting street. Another striking view presented itself to us coming out of St Andrew's Square and looking along St David's street. The view of the old town rising before us by confused and irregular gradations crowned by St Giles's elegant steeple was exceedingly picturesque, and the effect was much heightened by the red haze given by the setting sun.—This St David's street, by the bye, is named after David Hume, and was originally called David Street. I fancy this author, generally reckoned as an atheist, would have been a little surprised to learn that he was to be thus sanctified after his death. His tomb is in the burying ground by Calton Hill, a plain cylindrical tower, just on the limits of the ground. It has remained untouched, though part of the burying ground was cut through for the new street.

"A very curious circumstance shown me this evening is the number of books disposed of in Edinburgh every night by auction. During the winter there are some ten or twelve of these auctions going on every evening, each selling on an average about 120 volumes, so that, during six months at least of the year, above 1200 volumes are sold every night by [228] auction, chiefly to the lower classes. Every facility is here afforded for purchasing books of all sorts, but there is no public library like the French ones[9]—and, indeed, judging from the general disposition of the Scotch, still more than the English public, it would be impossible to preserve any collection open to them.* I never saw such a

---

* This was at that time the prevalent opinion among those who observed the habits of the people, and appeared to be very well founded, although now that collections in England at least are so generally open, the public has shown that they may be well trusted.

mischievous race as the common people, nor can conceive the pleasure they find in destroying things. Milestones, direction-posts, benches on the public walks, nothing escapes their fury—if of wood, one might imagine they steal it for fuel, but when they tear up a stone bench or deface a milestone or break a lamp, one is at a loss to guess their object. Sawny Scot, as well as John Bull, likes to show off the liberty he enjoys.

"After walking about for half an hour or an hour, I left Dr Pillans for Mrs Fletcher's, where there was a party to meet Miss Edgeworth.[10] She was there with two sisters—you may remember her at Mrs Carr's, ten or eleven years ago. She is a very little woman, and as you may suppose, very ready in conversation. . . . There were several people there, enough to fill the room, but without any one doing anything more than in the London parties. This one was indeed a little more lively, on account of the Edgeworths. There was also a bust to admire, the first essay of Mr A. Fletcher, and really very well done. I got into conversation with the French Consul, who is married to a Scotch lady, and also with Mr Craig, a friend of the Baillies. Mr Jeffrey, the editor of the *Edinburgh Review*, was there—a little man, apparently between forty [229] and fifty. It seems very odd to hear so much broad Scotch spoken in company, or at least English with a Scotch accent. It is not very unpleasant, but only sometimes rather provoking to hear the strange use they make of the auxiliary verbs. *Would* and *could* often supply the place of all others. *Would you go* may mean *did you go, have you been, were you at, are you going, must you go*, or even *will* or *shall you go*; although *could you go* means more particularly *will* or *shall you go*, the auxiliaries *will, shall, have, did, must*, etc, being scarcely ever used. The common people also aspirate their words like the Germans, *recht* and *lecht*, for *right* and *left*."

Tuesday, June 17th. "As soon as I had breakfasted I took my carton under my arm and sallied forth on a botanical excursion. Passing along Calton Hill and before Holyrood House, I went up to Arthur's seat. Passing first under the picturesque ruins of St Anthony's chapel, I got into a wild, sequestered valley, so completely silent and solitary that I might have fancied myself in the midst of the Cevennes or Pyrenees, many leagues from the habitation of man, instead of being within half a mile of so flourishing a city as Edinburgh. By the time I got to the top, I found the country overspread with a thick haze so as to prevent my seeing the view, so I descended on the opposite side, gathering by the way a number of specimens of a pretty little purple, leguminous flower (*Astragalus hypoglottis*), also *Cistus helianthemum, Rosa spinosissima* and many other showy flowers in abundance. The object of my walk was

Duddingstone loch, at the bottom of the hill, where are found, amongst other rare aquatic plants, the large-flowered *Ranunculus* [230] *Lingua* and the *Stratiotes alooides*, but neither were quite out. I gathered various others and returned by another path under some fine basaltic rocks. I climbed up again to Arthur's Seat, from whence I now enjoyed a fine view, and returned home by Salisbury Crags, loaded with plants, good, bad and indifferent. . . .

"To dinner at Mr Mackenzie's. Here the family consisted of the 'Man of Feeling' himself,[11] an agreable *spirituel* old man of about eighty, his wife, apparently not much younger, his son, a grave, steady, Scotch, clever and gentlemanly man between thirty and forty, with his sister, an old maid of much the same age. There were, besides, at dinner two gentlemen and a lady and Dr Coventry, the professor of Agriculture, very savant in that branch, but exceedingly absent. He only came in when we had half done dinner, is said to forget frequently to give his lectures, and the day that he was married he was taking a walk to Queensferry long after his bride was waiting for him. I had much conversation with him, and learnt from him many interesting facts connected with his pursuits."

Wednesday, June 18. "This morning, I went out to breakfast to Millburn tower, Sir Robert Liston's seat about six miles from the town near the Glasgow road. Forty years ago when Sir Robert first had possession, it was a little cottage in the midst of a considerable tract of waste land, with a small stream, on which was a mill dam, which gave the cottage the name of Mill Brook. Sir Robert has since then planted it all over, fitted up the cottage with the addition of a tower, laid out several gardens, etc, and given the whole the name of Millburn tower. He has lately added a considerable corps de logis, now fitting up as a drawing, dining and best bedrooms. The whole is of an [231] irregular, castellated form, not in my opinion built in an elegant or particularly pleasing taste, though some views of it be very good. Near the house was a barn, now converted into a library and opening into a conservatory built about twenty years since. This conservatory is the most interesting object about the place; it is not very large, but a very good size for a private house, and contains in the middle several fine trees, particularly two Metrosideros, the first I have ever seen, and said to be the finest that exist out of Botany Bay. There had been some very fine *Acacia decurrens* and others, but they outgrew the building and are now cut down. There are besides Palms, Clethras, Volkamerias, Goodenias, Sparrmannias and a number of others which I now forget. Some fine Passifloras, Bignonias, Jasminums, Dolichos, Clematis, and other creepers, tastefully arranged in arbours along each side and up the pillars and along the rafters of the roof, also a number of African Geraniums, Begonias, Liliums, Pandanus, Heaths, etc, and in the little hothouse adjoining, amongst other rare plants, was a little *Dionaea muscipula*, the first I ever saw. This you know (or do not know) is a little American plant which has at the ends of its leaves a curious appendage, which, when touched, doubles together immediately untill all irritation has subsided, and then shuts up any fly that may rest there till it dies.

"From the conservatory, Lady Liston took me to the American garden where she had collected a number of American trees, shrubs and plants, chiefly what they brought themselves.[12] A number of Oaks, deciduous and evergreen, Itea, Clethra, Jasminum, Snowdrop-tree, Mespilus, etc, several Rhododendra, such as *punctatum, sericeum, azalifolium*, etc, Azaleas and many others. In the West and South gardens are flowers, trees and shrubs, mixed with fruits and vegetables. Here are Rhododendron [232] caucasicum, etc, and a young plant of the arboreum, which appears to be spreading over the gardens, but has not yet flowered in Britain, the largest not being yet above 15 inches high. In another quarter is a long, winding, shady walk, with a little nursery for trees, and what Lady Liston calls a Flora Britannica, that is a number of wild plants promiscuously cultivated without much ornament or use, for the Listons are no botanists, and the plants are all nameless and without order, and mostly without any pretension to beauty. Near the Flora Britannica is a large basin of water and 'a beautifull waterfall dried up by the sun,'* for, it being now some days since it has rained, there is no water running over the dam, which in rainy weather is *very fine*, according to Lady Liston's account. I spent the whole morning till past one walking about with Lady L., who is a notable, active personage, though droll in her manner. She seems particularly to manage her household in a curious way, not apparently very agreeably to her servants, who get sent half a dozen ways at a time, or half a dozen on the same errand. But otherwise she is a very good-humoured and obliging lady, very fond of her gardens, and of showing off her conservatory and American plants. Sir Robert is a very gentlemanly, agreable man, of most polished manners and apparently extensive information. He quite enjoys this place of his

---

* From a favorite song of ours in those days descriptive of an Irish garden.

own creation and to which he is continually adding. They both, indeed, seem to take very great pleasure in it, but Lady Liston has still a [233] great love of locomotion, and lays plans of travelling in Holland and France, and coming to see us at Montpellier. They asked me to stay to dinner, but I was engaged at Mr Craig's. . . . I met there a very pleasant party. We sat down to dinner at a quarter past six (the Edinburgh hour is earlier than the London, generally from five to six), the cloth was removed at 20 min. past 7, the ladies sat till as much past 8, and the gentlemen till near 10, which was a pretty good séance over the bottle. However the company was pleasant and I was not ennuyé."

Thursday, 19th. "Breakfasted at Mr Mackenzie's in order to go with him to Dr Coventry's. We went first through some of the old lanes and closes in the old town, to see in what kind of places our forefathers lived. The only entrance from the west was by the Western Bow, a narrow street so exceedingly steep that I cannot conceive how carriages ever went up and down. Near the Parliament stairs, I had the pleasure of counting thirteen stories, garrets and basement included; these are the highest houses in Edinburgh and really look as if intended to reach up to the skies. Dr Coventry lives in Argyll Square, a small semi-modern square to the south of the very old part of the town. We remained some hours with him, conversing on various subjects; he is exceedingly well informed and has much talent and readiness in conversation. He has given me letters for East Lothian, and directions for making the most of my visit there." One great object of my enquiries here was to endeavour to meet with some one who should correspond to my father's anxious wish for a good Scotch bailiff and gardener, but all resulted in failure. The [234] salaries "required by Scotch bailiffs and stewards would be quite out of proportion to anything else at Montpellier as well as to our means. . . . The Scotch make, it is true, excellent gardeners, and in general seem fond of emigrating for that purpose, but then they carry with them so great a sense of their superiority that they will always have their own way, and adhere obstinately to their own opinions, and that, you know, would not do for us or for any one who wishes to attend much to their own concerns. . . .

"After leaving Dr Coventry, we went into the Courts of law for the sake of seeing Sir Walter Scott. The Courts had just done, but fortunately Sir Walter was still there. He is Clerk to the High Court. He is not at all the man I expected to see, stout, heavy and rather coarse in his general appearance, his hair is gray, thin and combed straight down; he is rather tall, but walks exceedingly lame with the help of a stick, one of his feet being quite turned and deformed. . . . To dinner at Mr Neill's. Here I met with three scientific gentlemen, Mr Stevenson, Mr Bate and Mr Arnott; the last is one of the most active of the Scotch botanists and will probably be of much use to me in that way. Mr Jameson was invited to meet me, but had been long engaged. I have not yet been able to see him, though he has twice called on me. Mr Neill was very pleasant; though in some respects a rather curious kind of man, he is quite learned in natural sciences. To the catalogue of his inmates which I gave you in a former letter, I must add two kinds of wild duck, an ichneumon, a parrot of an uncommon kind, and two cats, all living in perfect harmony, and all extraordinarily tame."

[235]Friday, June 20th. Haddington. "This morning I came here by the 'Union' coach to an early breakfast, and then walked over to Mr Bird's farm about three miles off. I had a letter from Dr Coventry to Mr Bird, who took me all over his estate, explaining every thing I wished. He is a specimen of one of the famous East Lothian farmers, of whom I shall see two or three more before I leave Edinburgh. He has a farm of 381 Scotch, or 457 English, acres arable land.[13] On this he has six pairs of horses, and one odd one in case of accident, six ploughmen and two other men by the year, called servants, and paid partly in money, but chiefly in oats, barley and pease, in quantities larger than they consume, enabling them to sell a portion—in leave to keep a cow at the farmer's expense, to work at their own gardens out of work hours—to grow a certain length of potatoes on the farm—straw for litter for their pig—and full feed in harvest time—besides a cottage to live in, they being all married men—high and complicated wages (as compared to ours at Montpellier), and not well managed. The cottages are built in rows of a uniform size, with gardens behind them, and are clean and neat outside, but *inside* many of them are as filthy as you can suppose Scotchmen to put up with— besides they are always dark, and from their small size and being so full of the furniture necessary for the host of children that inhabit them, they certainly have not at all the appearance of comfort I expected to find from their outward aspect. Besides these servants, day labourers are employed to the extent of about 300 days' work in the year." My letter then proceeds to give long details of crops, cultivation, etc, as in the case of other farms I visited. After leaving Mr Bird's, I went on to Dunbar to see Sir James Hall's farms at Dunglass.

[236]Sunday, June 22d. Edinburgh. "Here I am again at Edinburgh, after a delightful visit to Dunglass. I do not think I have yet spent my time so agreably since I have been in England. The grounds themselves

are so much varied and so beautifully romantic that weeks or months could be spent in solitary retirement, and when a kind reception is added, from so agreable and well educated a family, it makes one feel quite sad to have left it. The family was not all there, so that I found the house empty of visitors, of which they have usually many. I went there early yesterday morning, and found Sir James Hall, a very well informed elderly man, very fond of his estate, his family, geology and shooting—out-walking his sons when on a shooting party, but rather deaf, which is a little drawback to his conversation, otherwise so sensible and well informed. Captain Basil Hall, the second son, is the one who was to have read the paper on Perkins at the Royal Society the other evening. He is a captain in the Navy, has been twice round the world, has lately returned from a three years stay on the South American coast, was at Rio Janeiro with Mr Lawrence, from whom he has a letter to my Uncle,[14] whom he admires much and has a great desire of seeing.* He has also performed the European tour, has studied a good deal of mechanics and astronomy, besides general science and litterature. All this, of course, has given him much and valuable information, but the consciousness of that has in some measure given him a positiveness in argument, and a number of *knock-down* phrases in speaking, and a general disposition to pronounce hasty judgements on men and nations [237] which seems at first a great bar to agreable conversation. This, however, disappeared in a great measure when I became a little more used to his manner. Miss Fanny Hall is, I believe, the youngest daughter, and is one of the most pleasing young women in person, manner and conversation that I have yet met with. There was also another personage, not the least amusing, whom I must not forget. This is a little girl of sixteen months that reminded me so much of Adèle that she caught my attention immediately, and we were soon the best friends in the world. She is grand daughter to Sir James Hall. Her mother was married very young to Sir W. Delancey, who, eleven days after his marriage, was dangerously wounded at Waterloo. His wife went over and found him in a small cottage, where she watched him till his death a week after, and then returned to Dunglass. Some years after she made acquaintance with a Mr Harvey, a friend of Captain Hall's, married him, and had three children when she died about a twelvemonth ago.[15] Mr

---

* This was afterwards gratified.

Harvey is in England with the two eldest, and the baby remained at Dunglass, the universal pet but spoiled by no one. After breakfast I went on horseback with Captain Hall to Mr Bell's, the best of their farmers, where the Captain left me in his charge and that of Mr McEwen, the bailiff, with whom I went over that and some other farms and returned to dinner, where I found an accession to the family just arrived from Edinburgh, James, the third or fourth son, quite a young man, studying, I believe, the law at Edinburgh, and Miss Catherine Hall, second daughter, just arrived from a tour to the south and west of England and Scotland, and full of news and gaiety. Young James Hall made, a couple of years ago, a tour on the Continent, [238] going down the west coast of France and the Bayonne road to Madrid, returning thence to the Haute Pyrenées, and along the Mediterranean to Switzerland, and back by Lyons and Paris. Miss Fanny has also made her tour, through France, Switzerland and Italy. Lady Helen, their mother, is at present on a visit with one or two more sons or daughters. After dinner, Sir James and Mr J. Hall went out shooting, Captn Hall took a book, and I remained with the young ladies, who gave us some music, etc. This morning after breakfast Sir James took me over the ornamental part of his grounds and surprised me much by his activity. We walked without stopping from 11 till 3, hurrying over an ever varying scene, which would take weeks to admire in detail. The park lies chiefly along a deep glen, closely shut up by its elevated banks clothed with very vigorous beeches, firs and oaks, sometimes rising thick and straight to a very great height, sometimes spreading their hooked and shattered branches in most picturesque directions. Sometimes bold rocks, rising perpendicularly, seem to hang over your head; higher up, the glen widens into a little circular plain, with the hills gently sloping down to it, and in the middle a neat water mill. A little below the house, the glen opens to the seashore, which is always beautifull, but now particularly so, as the waves were dashing with great fury against the coast, throwing up to an immense height its foam, as if in a rage at the effectual resistance opposed to its progress by the rocks. Returning from the sea, we ascended another glen, not so wild, nor presenting scenes so grand and picturesque, but beauties of a mild and peaceable nature, such as we might imagine the ancient Arcadia, where shepherds [239] used to spend the day, piping and singing under the shade of a tree. Scenes of many other descriptions presented themselves in the course of this walk, here a neat drive through a well-kept park, there a wild path beneath the shade of a thick and ancient wood, every here and there fine views breaking out over the sea or in the surrounding country. The house, too, of an elegant though irregular form, comes in remarkably well in many places. Any one coming from the Pyrenees or Alps would laugh at me for this description, and I am almost disposed to do so myself, thinking it exaggerated and foolish, but I have only been telling you the feeling I experienced."

(Here follow long farming details.)

"Having finished our walk, we returned to the house where I had an early dinner with Captn Hall who was also going to Edinburgh. We went down to the road in hopes of getting in or on the mail, but it was full, no other coach being allowed in Scotland on a Sunday. We therefore rode on to Dunbar and, meeting with another gentleman likewise disappointed in a place in the mail, we took a chaise amongst us and arrived in Edinburgh after a pleasant journey just at the same time as the mail."

Monday, June 23d. "This morning I went to Mr Arnott's, the botanist whom I had met at Mr Neill's, to breakfast, and spent the whole morning in looking over his duplicates of mosses. He has a particularly large collection and gave me a considerable number. Lady Helen Hall was to have been in town today, and I was to have seen her, but Captn Hall called to say that she will most likely not be here till tomorrow, when I am engaged to some East Lothian farmers, and I may perhaps go again to Dunglass on Thursday or Friday."

[240]Wednesday, June 25th, Haddington. "I have been yesterday and today with so many farmers that I am now heartily sick of them and their manners, clever and intelligent as they are, and am now going to repose myself tomorrow and Friday with the excellent family I made acquaintance with at Dunglass. Sir James is a great mineralogico-geologico-chemist and is one of the principal supporters of the Huttonian or, as it is by some called, the Plutonian system.[16] The controversy between this and the Newtonian, alias Vulcanic or Neptunian system, has ever been a very important one among the scientific gentlemen of Edinburgh. Captain Hall pleases me much better than he did at first; he is the author of the *Voyage to the Loo Choo Islands*, and is really a man of great knowledge, talent and experience; his manner that I spoke to you of is only that of a sailor in a small degree.

"I came here yesterday morning by the 'Union' coach from Edinburgh, arriving at 5, and then took a horse to go to Mr Gilberton's at Gifford. Dr Coventry had written to ask him to shew me some farms there, and I had settled to breakfast with him yesterday. He is factor to the Marquess of Tweedale (pronounced *Twiddle* by the farmers) and lives in a neat and elegant house near the village of Gifford and about half a mile from the Marquess's house. He is a single man, so I had a tête à tête breakfast with him, and then went out, first to the Marquess's park, but here the rain came on so hard that we were obliged to stand up, and only go on between whiles. . . . The house, grounds and gardens showed nothing remarkable. . . . The stables for the hunters, riding and carriage horses are fitted up with peculiar elegance. I thought I was going into a drawing room; the oaken doors with brass locks and hinges were, I am sure, as elegant as those Sir Robert Liston is putting into his handsome new appartments; close glazed windows, rubbed as clear as crystal, [241] neat stone floors as fine as those of any Montpellier sitting rooms,* the racks, mangers and stall-partitions all of the same handsome kind of Oak called, I believe, Dutch oak. . . . From thence we went to the farm buildings . . . and mounted our horses to go over the land, and saw in the course of four or five hours a great deal of good, bad and indifferent land, in good, bad and indifferent state of cultivation. Some of it is lately come or coming into the Marquess's hands after long leases at low rents, such as used to be given in good old days, such as 'for three nineteens, two fifteens, and the life of the last occupant.' I do not know whether you understand the phrases, but it amounts to 102 years,[17] besides the remainder of the life of the one who has it at the expiration of the 102 years, and this generally at the rent of 1'/ or 1'/6d per Scotch acre. The farmer, not having any powerful motive for making the most of his land, lays out no capital and returns it in a state of the most compleat degradation I ever saw—worse even than we found Restinclière, which is saying a great deal. . . . (There follow long details of the Marquess's improvements—of the planting, draining, farming, etc, the Marquess being a great sheep-farmer.) After riding about till near three, we returned to Mr Gilberton's to change our clothes, which had got a good soaking, and to dinner—when we had a Mr Macnab, a little, short, fat, rosy-faced, little-eyed writer to the signet, very jovial and gay, and apparently intimate with every farmer in the country. After dinner, that is at 8 or 9 o'clock, we walked a little in the garden before tea and bed."

Thursday, June 26th. "Yesterday morning we were all three, Mr Gilberton, Mr McNab and myself, seated on our horses by 7 [242] o'clock, and proceeded sauntering over the country in a zigzag line to a farm a

---

* The drawing rooms at Montpellier, as well as all others, were then floored with flag pavement like our kitchens.

mile or two on the other side of Haddington, where we breakfasted with a Mr Carr, the farmer, a youngish man, more of a bean and not so powerfull in body as most of the farmers, but just as red-faced. After breakfast he joined us, and after a few hours' more ride, and occasional stopping to see farmers or their fields or their implements or their machinery or something of theirs, we got to a Mr Howden's, who is as stout and weighty a farmer as any of them. He joined us, and shortly after we met General Dalrymple (whom they call De Rumpole), in his working dress, looking over his fields. He, knowing Mr Howden, set about showing off his fields, and soon took his horse and joined us in perambulating the country, which we did till 4 o'clock. Genl Dalrymple then left us, and the rest of our troop, five in number, adjourned to Mr Howden's to dinner, after having been on horseback since 7 in the morning, with the exception of three quarters of an hour at Mr Carr's. The dinner lasted with its accompaniments till 9, when we again mounted our horses, and bending our course homewards, dispersed gradually. I went to the inn at Haddington in order to be ready for the coach this morning. I there found a very obliging note from Captn Hall, asking me to stay the night and next day, and went to bed in the full prospective enjoyment of the pleasure I expected at Dunglass. This morning however brought a sad disappointment. Just as I was going to set off for Dunglass, Captn Hall's servant brought me a note to say that Sir James was suddenly taken very ill, and I had to turn the other way and take the stage to Edinburgh. . . .

"Of the company I was with these two days, Genl Dalrymple was the most remarkable. He is brother and heir presumptive to Sir Hugh Dalrymple, the father of Miss Hamilton Dalrymple, who [243] married the Duc de Coigny last year. He had a family living with him in the village of North Berwick. He was particularly agreable, being much pleased at showing off his crops and kept in good humour by flattery, but he seems a brutal kind of man, and is generally disliked. He was a long time in the army, and is now retired here, and I believe farms for his brother. He took us over all his fields, through the little town of North Berwick, and to his park of North Berwick house. This, if inhabited and taken care of, might become a very fine place, but is now much neglected. The land about here is remarkably rich, the climate mild, though quite exposed to the north, manure abundantly furnished by the sea, and the ground kept in excellent culture; the crops are in consequence finer than any I have seen, excepting perhaps in some of the rich fields near the Mediterranean. . . .

"I cannot say I should much like living with the farmers here. Two days have sufficed to make me heartily tired, of their dinners at least. They generally rise early, and transact all their business in the morning and forenoon. They breakfast at 8 or 9 o'clock on tea, bread or oatcake and butter, a fresh egg and often cold meat and cold boiled haddock. The women and children often eat only porridge and milk for this first meal. They are then occupied in their farm business till 4, the general dinner hour, when they have frequent parties of three of four together. The dinner is much as in England; they drink a glass or two of wine with one another during the course of the dinner. This method of drinking wine, universal in Britain,* is very curious and inconvenient. One person asks another to take a glass of wine with him; they fill their glasses and nod at each other previous to drinking. It is highly ill-bred and uncivil in any company to take a glass of wine during dinner without asking another to do so with you, and when [244] you are asked, you must fill up your glass and make believe at least to drink under pain of affronting the one who has asked you. The master of the house, or the mistress, must drink a glass with every one of their guests, and each guest is supposed to do the same with his two neighbours and with every one with whom he is acquainted. This certainly is all very illiberal in a free nation. The Scotch farmers, after they have done their meat, drink a glass of whiskey, which they sometimes denominate their *vin ordinaire*; the same glass generally serves for all the company. With their cheese they drink beer, all out of the same silver tankard. When the cloth is removed the wine bottle goes round once or twice, every body drinking the first glass to the health of every body present, naming them all one after the other, always with the prefix of *Your health, Mr so-and-so*, and, as all cannot speak at once, this ceremony, most ridiculous in appearance, may, when the company is numerous, last a considerable time. This is not only the custom amongst Scotch farmers, but I believe used to be general among the English gentry, and is still preserved by those of rather an inferior class. I met with it at Mr Goodrich's, at Birmingham, at Newcastle, etc. After this general health-drinking operation, the one at the head of the table (I am speaking of Scotch farmers), almost every time the bottle goes round, gives a *toast*, generally to some person connected with those present. He also, in the course of the

---

* Fortunately gradually brought into disuse since about 1830.

evening, asks each guest to give the health of some gentleman, but after the first glass or two it is no longer wine that the Scotch farmer drinks, but his favorite whiskey toddy. This is made by mixing whiskey with an equal quantity of hot water and a good deal of sugar. In this manner they will sit for hours over their whiskey toddy, giving every now and then a toast, amongst which *Success to the* [245] *Spaniards* is never forgotten. At Mr Howden's they drank two bottles of whiskey amongst four, at Mr Gilbertson's, he and Mr Macnab alone almost finished the two, which, strong as it is, only had the effect of making them much pleased with their own wit and emitting it with more gaiety and noise than they generally show. But they tell me that they sometimes sit up in this way till one or two in the morning, and then find great difficulty in keeping on their horses, whose instinct, I suppose, prevents them and their masters from losing their way. In their persons, these farmers are generally thick and square-shouldered, their faces broad and red, and their dress and manner that of a would-be gentleman, showy but vulgar. Like all classes of Scotch, they are immoderately fond of politics. They all contrive to get a sight of a newspaper, though perhaps sometimes rather out of date. It is really a most remarkable thing to hear the poorest farmer, nay even the labourers and herdsmen, reasoning on the probability of a favourable or unfavourable issue of the Spanish cause.* On what is favourable there is no disagreement. Never did I see a nation so loudly and unanimously supporting the same side of a question. From the highest nobleman to the poorest laborer, from the high-church-and-tory to the most violent radical, there is not one but that wishes the Spaniards to succeed in driving off the French. Scarcely have I seen any one who does not wish that every Frenchman belonging to the army may perish in Spain. It is this feeling that excites them to make subscriptions for the Spaniards and, were it not that many are reasonable enough to perceive the folly and inutility of attempting to help people who seem not to make the least attempt or even [246] to desire, to be able to help themselves; were it not for this, I dare to say immense sums would be collected in a very short time. The common labourers, in this part of the country at least, would willingly give up a part of their pay to

---

* This was at the time of the Duke of Angoulême's Expedition to restore Ferdinand to absolute power. It was to me particularly striking to observe the much greater interest exhibited by the Scotch farmers than by the French countryfolk, whom it so much more nearly concerned.

promote what they are taught to consider[§] the good cause.—Of political news I give none, for I suppose you still keep up *Galignani*,[18] and have had an opportunity of observing the tendency of the British Cabinet to favour trade, and to take off rather than add to the restrictions on various branches of Commerce. I now more than ever hope that we may live to see something like a free, or at least a freer trade established between France and England"—a hope subsequently realized, as we all know, beyond the most sanguine expectations.[19]

"Leaving Haddington after my disappointment, I took my place in the Edinburgh coach, but as it was not to set out for nearly an hour, and as I was not much disposed for the slow driving and inferior company to be met with in these short-stage coaches, I walked on, intending to be taken up when the coach should come up. But the weather, though sunny not being very hot, I went on at a good pace, and reached the 14th milestone before the coach overtook me, so I did not take it at all and walked the remaining two miles, doing the whole 16 in 3 hours 33 minutes, generally 12 or 13 minutes from milestone to milestone."

I spent three more days in Edinburgh, chiefly with the Mackenzies or with private friends. Saturday morning, 28th, I breakfasted and spent the morning with Mr Arnott and his mosses, meeting there with Dr Greville, and on Sunday morning, 29th June, "I breakfasted at Mr Greville's. He is the principal Edinburgh botanist, and next in Scotland to Hooker. He is a young married [247] man of very pleasant manners, and author of the *British Cryptogamic Flora*, a sort of continuation of the *English Botany*, representing the fungi not there figured. He has also published many memoirs, alone or in conjunction with Arnott, and has almost ready for publication his *Flora Edinensis*. He has a large collection of cryptogamic plants; his fungi are better preserved than I should have thought such substances could be. He draws beautifully the originals of all his plates. I gave him some of my French plants, of which I have now but few remaining, and received from him a number of Scotch and American ones. I have also written to a Dr Torrey, his correspondent at New York, to propose to him to enter into correspondence with me at Montpellier. I remained with Mr Greville till late in the afternoon, and dined and spent the evening at Dr Thomson's."

Monday, 30th June. "I left Edinburgh at 9 in the morning, on the coach, arriving at Glasgow at about half past 2, crossing an uninteresting country, at first in good cultivation, but afterwards little besides extensive moors and bogs the picture of desolation. From Airdrie to Glasgow it is well peopled, and covered with great chimneys and smoking steam engines. I was struck with the great numbers of children about, ragged, shabby, dirty, lighthaired, bareheaded and barefoot; their sole occupation seemed to be to play about the road and run after the carriages."

Dr Hooker (afterwards Sir William), to whom my letters were addressed, being only to return from a week's Highland excursion with his pupils the following day, I had a day to myself to explore the town in its then state: "a large, populous town, quite the reverse of Edinburgh in every [248] respect. Edinburgh is full of genteel people. Young ladies go about there alone at any time of day, and every thing is clean and nice. Glasgow is a great, black, smoky, dirty town, full of shabby, ill-looking fellows, girls of all ages going about bareheaded and barefoot. There were even several, pretty well dressed in other respects, without shoes or stockings, and a great many with shoes only and no stockings. The town is large and built of stone, extends along the Clyde chiefly on the north bank, and consists of one long, broad, exceedingly bustling street parallel to the river, running under different names from one end to the other. This street is crossed at right angles, or nearly so, by the High Street and several others leading either on the one side to the river, or on the other up the hill. Over the river are two stone bridges, and a very light, airy-looking iron one for foot passengers only. Up the river is an immense public green called Glasgow Green, and to the West of the old part of the town above the river is a large tract of ground that was marked out for building all at once; and, notwithstanding the great demand for houses, is not near covered yet—but every here and there is a bit of a street—half a row of fine houses or solitary habitations, separated by enclosed fields in which cattle are feeding. When all these loose houses get joined, the streets will be fine, but in the mean time it is all the picture of disorder. On the other side of the Clyde are some good streets, particularly a row overlooking the river called Carlton Place. There are two or three good public buildings, but the High Church, formerly the Cathedral, does not deserve its reputation, for I think it [249] cannot be compared to any of the fine English or French Cathedrals. The principal character of the town lies in the great crowds that are circulating in the great streets. Coaches are arriving and setting off continually, and every corner of the streets and every bare wall is covered with boards announcing the hours of sailing of the different steamboats, of which, on some days, as many as fourteen ply down the Clyde, without counting the Liverpool, Belfast, Staffa and other distant ones.

"In the evening I took a walk in the neighbourhood, but without receiving any great pleasure. The roads about are so strewed with coal cinders that they are thickly embedded with a fine black dust that covers you all over as soon as you attempt to walk. I had, from the top of the hill, as good a view of the town as the smoke would allow. What struck me most was the groups of vessels in a little hollow, near the top of one of the hills. I thought it was an illusion, but when I went to Dr Hooker's, I had to ascend a great deal, and still I saw the same vessels a great way above me. They were at Port Dundas, the end of the Caledonian canal[20] which admits of large vessels close up to Glasgow."

Dr Hooker having sent to ask me to breakfast the next morning, I spent the whole of the Wednesday and Thursday, 2d and 3d July with him, Dr Arnott arriving also on the Thursday; and this was the commencement of that long intimacy with the Hooker family,[21] which has been through life the source of the greatest personal pleasure to me as well as of the greatest advantage in the pursuit of my favorite science. Dr Hooker had his father and mother living[§] with him—Mr Hooker without his son's talent, but an excellent and obliging old gentleman, of quiet disposition, a [250] great favorite of his grand children, and an excellent walker, who readily undertook the lionising of all non-botanical strangers recommended to Dr H. Mrs Hooker and one of her sisters, a girl of 16, daughters of Mr Dawson Turner, the Yarmouth botanist, both of them lively, merry and clever, made me feel at once at home. Of the four little children, I scarcely saw anything on this occasion, for they were just recovering from the measles. Dr Hooker himself was all kindness to me, a perfect stranger and a very beginner in botany, armed as I was only with a letter from Joseph Sabine, and he only a new acquaintance. "Dr H.," I wrote, "is the one who pleases me the most of all my botanical acquaintance; he is ranked among the very first of all the British Botanists and yet has no *pretensions*. He has been most generous to me." He gave me up his whole time, spending the morning in giving me specimens from his already vast stores of exotic plants—and in the afternoon in the botanic garden. I was the more struck with the unpretending liberality I here met with as with some of my Continental friends, as it contrasted with the petty closeness and exclusiveness of some London collectors, a liberality which was one of the chief means by which Sir William was enabled to accumulate in so comparatively short a time the finest herbarium in the country.

I had agreed with Dr Arnott to make a short botanical tour with him in the Highlands, and for that purpose he had come to Glasgow on the Thursday. In rambling about the town on the Friday, I had seen a board announcing that the Inverary steamer would leave the Broomilaw at 7 on Friday morning; relying upon this, I had made no further enquiries, and would not believe the Hooker ladies, who insisted that it only went on Saturday. But when on the morning (of Friday [251] 4th July), Arnott and myself, after some trouble at the hotel, got down to the quay by 7, "to our great surprise we found that we had taken all the trouble for nothing, for the Inverary steamer went that day only as far as Rothesay, and not to Inverary as on all other days. However, unwilling to go back to Dr Hooker's after our bravado of the previous evening, we determined to go so far at least on our way, and embarking on board, the 'Towered Castle' soon began puffing and splashing away at a great rate down the Clyde. This river is at first narrow and runs through a plain; its banks have lately been repaired by throwing large stones all along on both sides. This was rendered necessary by the damage done by the steamboats that are continually plying up or down. There are near forty steamvessels lying or travelling on this river, and every day no less than from twelve to twenty start from Glasgow, either going merely down the Clyde to Greenock, or going on to different ports on the western coast and islands up the different Highland gulfs, to Liverpool or to Ireland. These vessels* have a very curious appearance, certainly not elegant. Looking on the side, one would think they were dismasted vessels, with the stump of the mainmast pouring forth clouds of smoke. The front view may be compared to a hen sitting, very broad, with two wings as it were sticking out from the sides; behind they leave a long train of waves, diverging from the stern till they reach the shore, which, of course, when the channel is narrow, they break into a good deal. Their puffing smoke and steam and the giant splashing noise they make give them a blustering air of importance, [252] whence the familiar name of *puffers* we gave them appeared to us very appropriate. The one we were in was a 50 horse power, but there are some here of 100 or 120 horse power. We went at the rate of eight miles an hour, no wind either with or against us. They say that the first of these steamboats that appeared off Portsmouth excited great alarm, it being thought to be a dismasted vessel on fire, and numbers of boats were out to give succour, when to their great surprise, the vessel stopped to see what they wanted. But to return to ours. We had a beautiful—sail I cannot call it—

---

* At that time entirely unknown in the Mediterranean region.

but steaming down the Clyde; the weather was fine for Scotland—that is to say we could see through the mist to the distance of two or three miles. The Clyde soon breadthened into a Firth and the banks became higher and more picturesque. Dumbarton castle on a projecting rock is a fine object. It is to this town that steamboats bring passengers for Loch Lomond. Coaches wait there to carry them across to the bottom of the Loch, a steamboat takes them up on the arrival of the coaches, puffs up to the top of the Loch and returns in the afternoon, when coaches again carry them to Dumbarton, and a steamboat to Glasgow. Thus a tour in the Highlands can be made in a single day. We passed Port Glasgow, Greenock and Gourock and then crossed straight to Rothesay. Greenock is at the mouth of the Firth of Clyde. It is a considerable town, the seaport of Glasgow for vessels of too heavy a tonnage to go up the river. The road from thence to Glasgow used, a few years ago, to be constantly covered with coaches, chaises, etc; now scarcely a carriage is ever to be seen; the travellers all prefer the puffing as the easier, cheaper and speedier mode of conveyance. Even the mail coach has been obliged to stop. In the steamboat we got an excellent breakfast [253] very cheap, and arrived at Rothesay at half past 12. Rothesay is now a neat-looking town, on a pretty bay on the Bute coast. Nine years ago it was a miserable fishing village, consisting of a few shabby huts grouped round the ruins of the castle. Now, thanks to the puffers, it is a fashionable bathing place (I mean fashionable for Glasgow) with two good inns and a number of neat and comparatively elegant houses. The position seems warm and sheltered, but must be much exposed to the western rains. Four steamboats come here every day loaded with passengers, and four others stop on their way to different parts of Argyleshire, depositing a number of people here three times in the week.

"As for us, being thus deposited in this island against our intentions, we determined to make the best of it, so we took a walk to the highest hill in the island, and gathered a few plants in the bogs, though nothing remarkable, for the island is by no means so elevated as the land about it. However we considered ourselves not so very ill off, as we got a good dinner and good beds, and laid out a plan for another excursion in the morning along the sea coast.

"But when morning came, it was then that we had reason to be *impatientés* at being shut up in that island, for the rain poured down in torrents, and we had nothing to do but sit looking at each other. We spun out our breakfast as long as we could, then wrote what we had to write, and then—it was pretty near the time (½ past 11) when we expected to be liberated—we looked out of window to watch for the puffer. The air was so thick that we could not see far, so we had the pleasure of sitting for four hours, straining our eyes and 'attendre sans voir venir' (one of the 'trois choses à faire mourir').[22] At last at half past [254] three, a streamer of smoke began to appear through the mist at a distance, and by four o'clock we were on board and had left Rothesay, and never did I quit a place with more pleasure than I felt on leaving this abominable island of Bute. The wind had been very high all the morning straight in front of the vessel, and this had been partly the cause of the delay, the principal reason of which was that she could not start till two hours after her time. The ladies were all so sick that half of them got out at Rothesay. But the weather now cleared up and [we] were at liberty to admire the Chyles of Bute. These are a narrow strait between the island and the main land, and it really was a very fine thing, winding between two ranges of mountains, at the same time the Belfast steamer puffing before us, and two or three other smoky streamers at a distance behind added to the beauty of the scenery. Coming out of the Chyles of Bute, the sea became a little rougher, which to me was a great pleasure, though the ladies on board were beginning to make an hospital of the cabin, and dropping off one by one from deck, soon left us there almost alone. But this did not last long. We entered Loch Fine, a long gulf projecting into Argyleshire; the water became quite smooth, and the wind being favorable, we set up some sail and went on at the rate of ten or twelve miles an hour. We called at West Tarbet, a very pretty village in a little bay on the loch, and again at Loch Gilphead, another little village at the mouth of the Caledonian canal. Here we took up passengers from other steamboats, and proceeding up Loch Fine, arrived at Inverary at half past twelve at night, having gone a little more than seventy miles in eight hours and a half, which was pretty well, considering that we stopped at least a dozen times to take up [255] and set down passengers from different parts of the coast. We got tolerable beds by our activity in being the first out of the boat, and having fed well on board for little money, we slept heartily the rest of the night.—I have forgotten to mention the manner in which these steamboats are fitted up. Besides a small cabin for the steerage passengers at the fore-end of the vessel, there is at the stern end a handsomely fitted up cabin, with seats all round and mahogany tables, etc, and another where fifteen to twenty people can dine at once, and which accomodates all the passengers by their dining in succession, one party when they have done going away to make room for others. In the main cabin is a small library, perhaps fifty or sixty volumes, for the accomodation of the passengers. Among these books I observed the *Spectator, Rambler, Tatler,* and *Adventurer,* different books of literary extracts, Sermons and theological tracts, Itinerary Guides and Pictures of Scotland, *Rob Roy, Lady of the Lake,* etc. The food was good, though the dinner consisted of cold meat. The steamboats for longer distances are fitted up in a much grander style, with a number of private cabins."

Sunday, 6th July. "The morning proved again rainy; however, as it cleared up a little after breakfast, we went out into the Duke of Argyle's park, up one of the valleys that opens into Loch Fine. The Duke's house is a neat castellated building, very near the banks of the loch and surrounded by a fine park. From the top of a projecting hill, the end of the high ground that separates the two valleys, there is a fine view down the loch and over the little town of Inverary. Like Rothesay, this place has sprung up only since the institution of the puffers. We strolled about the park for several hours, picking mosses and lichens from the trees, found some rare and [256] beautifull ones, also some good phaenogamous plants, and returned to the inn to dinner. We could not go into the Duke's house on account of its being Sunday. On all other days it is open to the inspection of the public, as the Duke is very seldom there.

"Left Inverary on Monday morning, taking a boat across and a little way further up the loch to Cairndow, a solitary inn on the banks of the Loch. Here we got a good breakfast. The people of the house were also at theirs and the look of it was certainly not very tempting. Oatcake and oatmeal porridge form their food, water or milk their beverage, with continual recourse to the whiskey bottle. At Cairndow we took a boy to carry part of our things, having a great deal of paper with us, and set off for Tarbet, up a glen, through which is a very good road made some years ago. When we had got four or five miles up, we sent the boy on by the road and turned up another glen, leading to Ben Voirlich. After wading for three or four miles through the eternal bogs that cover mountains and valleys, we came to a little hut, at the point where two or three glens meet. Here we went in and drank a bowl of milk. This Highland hut was certainly, like most of them, the picture of wretchedness. Built of rough stones and covered with peat, there is a hole in the middle of the roof to let out the smoke from a few lumps of turf burning slowly on the floor. In one corner is what is called a bed, in another a sort of cupboard, which, with a dresser and a few half broken chairs, form the whole of the furniture. One opening serves for both door and window. From thence we went up the side of the hill and got nearly to the top above Loch Sloy. This hill (Ben Voirlich) is very rugged and stony, and lies at the upper end of Loch Lomond. We spent some time in gathering plants on it, and then descended to [257] the banks of Loch Lomond, after wading through bogs for three or four more miles. We thus continued along the road to Tarbet, a little village on the banks of the loch, of a dozen houses. We there found an excellent inn, arriving there at eight o'clock to a good dinner."

Tuesday morning, 8th July. "Took a walk before breakfast, a couple of miles down the Loch, in search of a couple of rare mosses, of which we found good specimens, and having despatched our breakfast by half past eight, took a boat across the lake—rowing ourselves to relieve the maiden in charge of the boat—and ascended the famous Ben Lomond, one of the highest of the Scotch mountains, and visited by almost all those who make the 'tour of the Lakes' on account of the view from the top. We scrambled about for hours amongst the rocks and bogs, found some good plants, and got to the top in the afternoon. The weather was clearer than it had been for some days, and we enjoyed a fine view over the Highlands to the north, and Lowlands to the south, with the sea at a distance, appearing among the western islands; but we neither saw the Edinburgh hills nor the Irish coast, which are said to be distinctly visible on a clear day—but that does not happen here perhaps more than once a year. We descended by a very steep way straight to the Loch, walked along its banks to the ferry, and crossed over to Tarbet, where we arrived by nine o'clock to dinner, which we were not sorry to partake of, having been twelve hours on our legs without food, having omitted to carry any luncheon with us."

Wednesday, 9th July. "Occupied till three in the afternoon spreading our plants, which we sent by the carrier to Glasgow, and taking our knapsacks on our backs, crossed Loch Lomond in a boat to a little house called the Mill; thence walked through a glen by Loch Arkit to Loch Cathrine, passing two or three shabby [258] half-ruined hovels, one of which is dignified with the name of Inversnaid Fort. At Loch Cathrine, we took one of Stewart's boats down the Loch. Stewart is the name of the innkeeper at Ardkenechrocan, in the Trossachs at the foot of the lake, and every morning sends up two or three boats for any one that may chance to come by the Loch Lomond steamboats, and for that purpose the men cross to the Mill and there wait to serve as guides, but as the road is so easily found we thought it unnecessary to pay a guide and conducted ourselves.

"We were about two hours rowing down Loch Cathrine, the scene of the *Lady of the Lake*, a distance of about ten miles, our two boatmen conversing in Gaelic, the language of the country, and the most uncouth one you can conceive. All the *c*'s and *k*'s and *ch*'s are pronounced like the German *ch*, and, as these letters occur two or three times in three fourths of the words, it seems as if they were continually speaking from the bottom of their throats. The weather was fine, the surface of the lake perfectly smooth and, as we approached the Trossachs, the scene was really beautifull; the rocks projecting into the lake are covered with wood, the lake is here very narrow, and the high mountains at the upper end appear to great advantage. It is the lower end of the lake that is so accurately described in Walter Scott's poem, but it is hard to conceive what made him fix up on so small an island for Ellen's habitation.[23] It does not appear to contain above an acre of land, and consists of a rock projecting out of the lake covered with underwood. We landed at a very romantic spot at the bottom of the lake and walked through the narrow and picturesque pass called the Trossachs to Stewart's inn at Ardkenenocan (or Ardkenechrocan as they appear to pronounce it), [259] a distance of about a mile and a half; we found, however, the inn full, and after getting a tolerable dinner, we were obliged to set out again for Callander; we had scarcely gone two or three miles, when a return gig took us up and brought us in to Callander by half past ten."

Thursday, 10th. "We spent in an excursion to Ben Ledi. This is a mountain that rises from Loch Lubnaig a few miles from Callander, the road passing through the pass of Lennie, reckoned another of the beauties of the Highlands, but not equal to the Trossachs. There is some wood here also, and the banks of Loch Lubnaig appear to be pretty. We left it below us, and ascended the mountain to gather a couple of rare plants, which we found after a little search. We remained some time botanising, and returned to Callander to an early dinner, heartily tired of driving the flies off our faces. I scarcely think I ever was so much annoyed with them as that morning going up the mountain. Buzzing about and settling on our clothes, which were quite brown with them. If we took off our hats for a moment to drive them off, our hair was immediately so full of them that we could scarcely drive them out. In the afternoon, however, rain came on, and dispersed them in some measure, and we got to Callander in tolerable quiet. Callander is a pretty little town, just at the foot of the Highlands, and appeared particularly well to us, who for so many days had scarcely seen anything but Highland hovels. It was a *fast* day, as it is called, that is a day on which the people prepare for the sacrament to be administered, I believe, on the next Sunday. These fast days are like Sundays, no work is done, and the day is spent mostly at church. It gave me an opportunity of seeing a real highland dress, which is little worn on weekdays, but [260] many appear in it on Sundays at church. I had very frequently seen people dressed partially in it, indeed most of the Highlanders have something tartan about them, but this was the first complete dress I had seen, and it certainly looked very well.

"After dinner we walked on to Kilmardock manse, to Dr Murray's, a friend of Mr Arnott's. A manse in Scotland is the same as a parsonage in England, the habitation of the minister. Dr Murray is minister of the parish of Doune, and his manse is about two miles from this town, six from Callander. There was once also a kirk at Kilmardock, but it is now in ruins. Dr Murray is a facetious and witty old man, has two farming sons, and a daughter who never opened her lips the whole time. We spent a very pleasant evening there, though they sat terribly long over their whiskey toddy after supper, and did not get to bed till 12. The rain prevented our walking out in the evening, as we had intended. Next morning, however, it was pretty fair, and after breakfast I parted with Mr Arnott, who is going into the northern mountains, and walked on to Sterling, passing through a beautifull park belonging to a Mr, or Sir something Blair Drummond. Doune Castle, on the opposite side of the river, is a picturesque ruin—the river, or rather torrent, comes from Loch Lubnaig and Loch Cathrine, passes through Lochs Achray and Venacher above Callander, and afterwards runs into the Forth. Sterling, ten miles from Kilmardock, is on the side of a steep hill, rising in some parts almost perpendicularly from the plain. The castle on the top is a picturesque object, and the view from the Esplanade in front is fine and extensive, the forth below winding in a remarkable manner. Steamboat communication is very active between that town and Edinburgh. The town is old and has [261] nothing remarkable. I got there by 11, had some luncheon, went up to the castle, and at 12 got into the Glasgow mail, which took me there by three o'clock. I spent the rest of the day at Dr Hooker's, receiving from him more plants, etc.

"Thus I have seen the celebrated beauties of the Highlands, but I must own that I was in a great measure disappointed. They are very well characterised by four lines, which may be applied also to all the western lowlands. These lines are in everybody's mouth with several *variantes*, but this is the most accredited version:

Bare are thy hills, O Caledonia,
  And barren are thy plains.
Barefoot are thy nymphs so fair,
  And barebreeched are thy swains.

"For nothing can have more the appearance of sterility and desolation than the generality of the Highlands. With the exception of the Duke's path at Inverary, the passes of Lernie and the Trossachs, and some parts of the banks of Loch Lomond, all is either rock or bog—not a fine, rich matting of grass as in the Lozère, for instance, but bogs covered with heath and rushes, amongst which a few sheep contrive to find here and there a little indifferent grass. There are but few picturesque rocks, and, with the exceptions I have made, no trees, no cultivation, but few habitations, and those few are miserable, black huts, built of loose stones and covered with peat. The women all go barefoot; even the servants at Dr Murray's waited at table barefoot."

Saturday, 12th July. I returned to Edinburgh and spent Sunday with my friends there, breakfasting at Dr Thomson's and dining at the Mackenzie's, the venerable "Man of Feeling" now having his whole family about him, and on [262] Monday, 14th July, "I left Edinburgh for good and all, and this time I made no mistake, but got into the Lanark coach at eight in the morning. The road was at first pretty. It passes by a fine house and park belonging to Sir William Forbes, the banker. Near there we crossed the Union Canal—not by a bridge over it—that is now common and vulgar, but we drove under it in proper style. Close to that place the canal is carried over a seven arched bridge, and under it are other roads, a river, etc. It looks very curious to see vessels sailing over your head. After this, we came to bare, barren and bleak moorlands, of which we had at least twelve miles to cross, as they extend very near to Lanark itself. This town has not at all the appearance I expected; I had imagined a pretty little town in a pleasant valley on the banks of the Clyde; instead of that it is a shabby, dirty, straggling town and appears at first in an open and bleak country. I knew that the cotton mills and falls were at a very short distance, and looked all about for them as I drove in, but could not discover anything like a river. I enquired, however, and being told it was but three quarters of a mile to New Lanark, I left my things at an inn and walked out on the road that leads to it, without discovering anything till I got half a mile out of the town, when coming to the edge of a deep valley, the village appeared suddenly to view, some hundreds of feet below me, on the banks of the Clyde. This river, swollen by the late rains, was rushing along with great violence amongst the woods and rocks. I descended first to Brackfield House, the habitation of the Owen family, but was disappointed in not finding any one at home. The father, I knew, was in London, but I had expected to see [263] the sons;[24] but I learnt that they had been for some days past at Leith, and were not to return still for two or three days. I then went on to the establishment, and enquiring for some of the resident managers, found them to be all absent different ways, excepting one, a Mr Alexander, who, on hearing my name and relationship to my Uncle,* showed me every civility in his power, stayed with me the whole day and, instead of sending a man to show the place as they usually do, went himself with me to the falls and all over the establishment, gave me a dinner, etc, and went in the evening with me to Cartland Craigs. He pressed me much to stay till next day, as he thought Mr Owen junr might possibly be back, offering to desire a bed to be got for me at Brackfield House, etc. But as I saw as much as I wished that day, I was glad to get on my way, so I slept at the inn in order to be ready for the Glasgow coach in the morning.

"The village of New Lanark, belonging entirely to the Company,[27] has a very remarkable appearance. Built entirely of [264] stone, and covered with slate, that alone gives the houses a neatness and elegance that is more striking in a country where all is rubble, stone and thatch or peat. The mills are three in number, on the edge of the river, and look handsome with their immense number of neat glazed windows in regular rows; there are, besides, seven or eight long rows of houses for the workpeople, regularly built two or three stories high, also thickly covered with windows. The rest of the village consists of the house and garden inhabited by the secretary or chief manager, the school, a large and handsome building, another neat edifice as yet unoccupied but destined

---

* When Government, after annulling the contract they had entered into with Jeremy Bentham for a Panopticon prison for the reception of convicts, agreed with some difficulty to return to him the bare capital he had expended towards the execution of that contract, and accordingly handed him £20,000, my Uncle, who was no man of business himself, and rather too easily led by those who could bring forward plausible philanthropic views, was induced to invest £10,000 in a concern which failed in a very short time,[25] and the other £10,000 in the Lanark Cotton Mills, which he hoped to see a means of regeneration through Owen's socialistic plans—and thus he had become owner of a sixth share. The other partners were Friend Allen the Quaker, the Owen family and I believe one other.[26]

for a publick kitchen and dining room according to Mr Owen's plans, a small Millwright's shop and foundery, and a long, low building in which some branches of the works are carried on. The neatness and cleanliness of the whole village, both inside and outside of the houses, is a perfect contrast to the shabby, dirty, black hovels that are generally seen in this part of Scotland. The Company's land consists of about a hundred acres. What lies above the village is laid out in a public kitchen garden, and in plantations for the workpeople to *promène* in. It also contains a farm, let out to the gardener, I forget to what extent. A little above the mills are the falls of the Clyde. The principal one, called Corra Linn, is really beautifull. The water, confined by the rocks on both sides, rushes down a height of 80 feet, in a length of about 40 or 50. The river, swollen by the late rains, made it appear to great advantage. The colour was such as I had seldom seen, a deep reddish brown, owing, I suppose, to the soil it comes from. The other fall, called Burrington Linn, or some such name, is not so high but is also fine, the principal beauty of the scene, however, consisting in the wooded and rocky banks.

[265]"As to the cotton mills themselves, though far superior to the general run of similar establishments, they are equally inferior to Mr Strutt's at Belper. Sixteen hundred is the number of workpeople employed, 130,000 the number of hanks spun in a day, all unbleached, for there is no bleaching establishment and no bleached cotton spun. There are eight waterwheels, 24 feet in diameter, making a total breadth of about eighty feet, which they value at about 140 or 150 horse power. They are bucket wheels, the axles and framework of iron, the rest of wood; the machinery of iron, steel and wood, but no polished steel as at Belper. The principle the same as at Belper, but carried to a less extent, more handwork and less machinery. Contrivances for airing, ventilating, and carrying away dust, like all the rest, superior to the generality, but far inferior to Mr Strutt's. Some of the operations, the pulling and teasing, for instance, are attended with a good deal of dust. The machinery is not kept so clean-rubbed as at Belper, though certainly it is by no means dirty. The rooms are kept constantly whitewashed. This operation is performed, I believe, once a week; it tends much to health and cleanliness, though it be the source of some dust. Contrivances for taking goods up and down from one floor to another are very far inferior to Mr Strutt's—for carrying them along horizontally there is no apparatus. There are checks established on the conduct of the workpeople; a list is kept in which they are numbered 1, 2, 3 and 4, according to their good or bad behaviour, but this appears to be attended with little or no advan-

tage, as there are perhaps never any marks but no. 1. The different operations of packing, weighing, etc, as well as all others, appeared to me on
a small scale when compared to what I had seen elsewhere. In the
smith's shop, there are a *few* turning lathes, but *none* of the other
machinery I mentioned to you having seen at Belper. They cast nearly
all of their iron works in the foundery here. In dry [266] weather they
are sometimes stinted for water, only half of the river belonging to them,
as they have land on one side only. The waterchannel from the dam-
head to the mills is carried for a length of 170 yards through a tunnel cut
in the solid rock. This was done by Mr Dale, and must have been very
expensive. A few years ago one of the mills was burnt down and has not
been rebuilt; they are all liable to fire on account of the quantity of wood
in the roofs, floors, stairs, etc,—no fireproof buildings as at Mr Strutt's.
The great thing here is the school; the building, in the first place, is large,
commodious and handsome, but it is especially the number of things
taught. All the children are, in the first place, taught reading, writing
and arithmetic before they are old enough to enter the manufactory.
They all wear a kind of blouse made of unbleached cotton and bound,
for the boys with red, for the girls with blue; this dress comes down to
their knees, for the girls perhaps a little lower, and leaves their arms and
necks bare; they always go about, too, bareheaded and barefoot, so that
no dress is seen but this cotton one, which gives them a very odd half
naked look, particularly when we see above a hundred of these little
brats running about all in the same uniform. I missed the school hours,
so that I cannot say anything of the method of teaching, but went over
the rooms. The schoolroom is nicely fitted up with two sets of benches,
one for the boys, the other for the girls. There is a large room hung
round with representations of various objects of natural history, mathematical and astronomical drawings and tables, geographical maps, etc.
This is the lecture room, in which the children are taught zoology, botany, geology, mineralogy, mathematics, astronomy, geography, chemistry, etc, and every evening after working hours these lectures are
attended by many of the working people. I forget [267] whether this or
another room is the one where they are taught music and dancing. So
that you see nothing is wanting to give them the most finished education, and to teach them all and every accomplishment that a gentleman
may wish to learn, but which, in my opinion, are one, and all at the best
useless for working people. Dancing I like to see among the lower
orders, but with them dancing *lessons* are superfluous, as the mere
jumping about, without making any fine steps, is quite enough for

them. The Lanark workpeople have three balls in the year, which is all very well, provided they are not induced too much to imitate and vie with the balls of the superior classes. There are, I believe, eleven male teachers, and almost as many female. Religion, notwithstanding the recent exertions of Mr Brougham and others,[28] is certainly very little attended here—only just enough to prevent popular outcry in a country [such] as Scotland. Every one is suffered to do as he pleases, without any religious instruction, and the bible is said to be prohibited in the village. This has been denied. I could not learn the truth, but believe that the introduction of it amongst them is, at the least, discouraged. The teachers are of different sects, so that the workpeople are composed of presbyterians, unitarians and a number of other sects whose names I cannot remember.

"You have heard, I suppose, of Mr Owen's plans for the improvement of human society. I believe they are described in a pamphlet we have, entitled *A New View of Society*. My father, at least, will know it all, though I never heard of it till I came here. He proposes that all mankind should live in villages, built in a parallelogrammic form,[29] with a common garden in the interior, common fields on the exterior, one kitchen and one dining room for the whole village, in short everything to be in common, no distinction of rank, no difference [268] in extent of property, and everything to be on the footing of the most perfect equality. Mr Owen—whom every body allows to be very clever and intelligent and the most sensible, reasonable man on every subject but this one, at the same time that his disposition is the most benevolent—Mr Owen, I say, not only thinks his projects feasible, but verily believes and uses all his eloquence to persuade others that his plans really will be followed at a period not far distant. But notwithstanding his agreable manners and persuasive language, there are but few who have allowed themselves to be convinced by his reasons and arguments. Amongst those few is a Mr Hamilton, who has a village and large estate at [   ] between Lanark and Glasgow. Mr Owen is collecting subscriptions for building his first village, on the ground furnished by Mr Hamilton and, as soon as £60,000 are collected, the building is to commence, and I hear there is not much wanting to complete the sum.[30] Mr Owen has long had in view the introducing something similar at New Lanark, and for that purpose had already built the public dining room and kitchen I spoke to you of. But his partners and coproprietors, not so sanguine as he is as to the benefit the public is to derive from putting his projects into execution, and unwilling to sacrifice so large a sum of money, when there is an almost certainty of their receiving at least no pecuniary return, opposed the continuance of the work, and the building remains in the state in which I saw it. This it was that gave rise to the report that Mr Owen was excluded from the concern—far from it, he is still the principal partner. The company still goes under the name of Owen and Co, and he still possesses the most [269] extensive share; the only difference is that he has not now so great a share in the management as he formerly had, and cannot misapply the company's funds. He is the only resident proprietor having a house and estate there of his own. I have not met with him or any of his family, but from all accounts he is the most agreable and gentlemanly man—when he does not fatigue you by explaining his views.

"These details on New Lanark are perhaps rather long, but I wished to give you my opinion on so celebrated an establishment, and I have told you many things which I should be afraid to say to some people, particularly to Scotchmen, who are so proud of New Lanark, which they consider superior to anything of the kind anywhere else. I found it far inferior to Mr Strutt's, but New Lanark is quite a show place; being so close to the falls of the Clyde and celebrated for the school and for Mr Owen's mad plans, it is daily visited at this time of year by from ten to twenty persons. Mr Strutt, on the contrary, uses his endeavours to make his place anything but a show one, and thus its superior excellence is very little known.

"I mentioned Mr Alexander's having taken me in the evening to Cartland Craigs. This is a deep gulley or glen, about two miles from Lanark, and in the bottom of which runs the little stream called the Mouse. The sides of the glen are steep, rocky and well wooded, and consequently romantic and picturesque, but the thing to see is a handsome new stone bridge that carries the new Glasgow road across this glen. It consists of three arches, and is [270] remarkable for the great perpendicular height of the piers, the central arch being 126 feet above the bed of the stream, and it certainly is altogether a beautifull thing—an excellent subject for painting.

"Having taken leave of my conductors and got to the inn, I found that the next day was not one on which the morning coach went to Glasgow, which to me was a disappointment, as I had expected to be at Dr Hooker's to breakfast and thus gain a day. As it was, I slept a little later, got my breakfast and, preferring to wait at Hamilton, where there is something to be seen,[31] to remaining any longer at Lanark, and the morning being tolerably fair, I set off on foot for Hamilton, a most beautifull fifteen mile walk down the banks of the Clyde. On leaving Lanark, the road descends into the vale by a long and steep descent, crosses the bridge, and passes through the little village of [   ]. This is, I believe, the most beautifull spot in the whole road—the river swollen by the late rains foaming through the rocks, the steep banks varied with wood, parks and cornfields, the Cartland Craig bridge, directly opposite, made the whole a beautifull landscape; even the black hovels called cottages, being rather more regular than usual, did not disfigure the scene. The first miles of my walk I enjoyed exceedingly, but before I had got half-way, the rain came on and kept encreasing the whole day. When I got into Hamilton, it poured so hard that I felt little desire to go out to see the palace. This weather lasted the whole day. I had forgotten to bring with me the letter I had begun to you,* so that I had no occupation [271] the whole afternoon but watching the clouds, as at Rothesay in Bute. I had left my things to be brought on by one of the evening coaches, which generally pass at Hamilton at 7, but this being Glasgow fair time, the heavy loads made them later than usual, and when they did come, they passed one after the other, all full and without my trunk. At last, the very last coach, the mail, deposited a traveller at Hamilton, and I took his place, but without anything but what I had on, writing to have my trunk, etc, sent on to Glasgow.

"Wednesday 16th and Thursday 17th I spent at Glasgow, as I only got my things late on Wednesday night. I was all Wednesday at Dr Hooker's, and, this time, I met a larger party there: Mr Trevelyan, a young naturalist, heir to a baronetcy and to a large estate, who has spent much of his time in the north, and is a very genteel and sensible young man, though he certainly has no personal advantages; also an Irish and two English tourists, who all go to see Dr Hooker, and certainly no one can receive strangers better than Dr Hooker does all those who bring letters from his friends. I spent the whole day with him and his plants; those that I have got from him will be a great addition to my collection.

Thursday, 18th.§ "I was again all the morning with Dr Hooker, who went with me in the afternoon to a banker's, and thence to the Hunte-

---

* These letters, to save postage, were written on blank post paper, large folio size, folded into 16 pages; the paper was thin, to diminish the French postage, and limited to a single sheet (irrespective of size) to save double English postage, and yet each letter cost on the French side three francs, and on the English 1'/2d if from London, 2'/2½d from Edinburgh or Glasgow.

rian Museum.[32] This collection I dare to say my mother knows as much about as I can tell you, for there has been no addition to it since Hunter's death, or at most a very few objects have been presented to it, and no other means are used for encreasing it, no one taking a sufficient interest in it. As far as it goes, it is a very good collection, and must have been a very valuable one at [272] the time it was made, though it be now out of proportion to the present state of science. Minerals, shells, birds, insects, medals, books, paintings, etc, etc, it contains a little of every thing, very neatly arranged in an elegant building of two or three stories. It is the best collection in Scotland, and is consequently daily visited by numbers of strangers. The curator or keeper (I am ignorant of his precise title) keeps it neat, clean and in good order; he also occupies himself in stuffing birds, and has, within a few days, set up a beautifull East Indian Antelope that died here a short time ago; it is not for the Museum, but for a private gentleman.—I dined and spent a very pleasant evening with the Hookers, taking leave of them not without regret."

Friday, 19th[§] July. "Left Glasgow at 6 in the morning by the 'Robert Burns' coach, following as far as Lanark the same road I had gone before, but this time the weather was fair enough for us to enjoy the beautiful drive along the Clyde from Hamilton to Lanark. I was not, it is true, quite so favorably placed. I had taken an inside place on account of the bad weather, and could not get outside at all, the coach being loaded the whole day—indeed it carried more than its number, both out and in, which did not render my seat very comfortable. It is a four-inside coach. On one seat were a gentleman and a woman, neither of them very small; by my side, was one of the fattest women I have ever seen; and three children, the biggest about 12 to 14, were crammed in into the bargain. Later in the day, however, the children got out, thinner passengers took the places of the stout ones and, as the afternoon proved rainy, I [273] was not sorry to be inside. We breakfasted at Lanark, and proceeded up the Clyde, but through a very different country from what we had seen in the morning. Trees soon disappeared, and cultivated ground was not to be seen long. A few miles out of Lanark, we came to barren, bleak, monotonous hills and moorlands, which continued all the way to Moffat—rather improving perhaps as we went on, that is the pasturage appeared better for the sheep, and, at one time, when two or three loaded coaches were in sight, the view for a moment was not unpleasant. Moffat, just as we came out of this mountainous moorland, is a very pretty little village with a fine park adjoining, making altogether a striking contrast to the lands about. After leaving Moffat, we had a little more barren country, till we came into the comparatively rich and well cultivated plain of Dumfries.

"Dumfries is a very pretty little town, situated near an arm of the sea, which entitled it to the denomination of a seaport. It is neatly built, and the country about it looks pleasant and rich, particularly when compared to that which we had crossed in the morning. It has been proposed to remove the St Andrews University here and, at any rate, it is believed there will be one established.[33]—We got a very good dinner, and started immediately after. The fine environs of Dumfries were soon passed, and we continued along a poor, uninteresting plain, the sea frequently at a small distance on our right. The crops seemed generally thin and backward, and we often met with miles of barren moor or peat called *moss* in the country. These immense boggy wastes, cut up in many places for fuel, have a very desolate and dreary appearance. We passed through the town of Annan, and some time after by Gretna Green. This place, so famous for [274] runaway marriages,[34] consists of a few houses about a mile on the Scotch side of the boundaries and at a short distance from the road. The inhabitants of these houses are ready at any time to join in matrimony the fugitive couples that still arrive occasionally from England, and such marriages by Scotch law can never be dissolved, though the unqualified officiator be liable to punishment. But this does not appear to be ever inflicted, which appears to me rather surprising in a country where they are so very strict in religion and morals. The passage from Scotland to England is soon perceived by the innkeepers' signs: 'Dealer in foreign spirituous liquors,' instead of 'Dealer in foreign and *British* spirits,' the *British Spirits* generally meaning whiskey, which is not allowed in England. Another difference between the two countries, which I had not before observed, now struck me very forcibly. In the first village where we changed horses, the hostlers mixed with their conversation every now and then one of those tremendous volleys of oaths so continually uttered by the lower orders in England, and it was only the novelty of the sound to my ears that made me recollect that I had scarcely heard a single oath since I had been in Scotland. Carlisle is a pretty, good looking old town, surrounded by walls and retaining its old castle. It looks as if it was rather improved of late, but even now I see nothing to entitle it to its denomination of *merry Carlisle*. We merely changed horses there and, continuing in the same flat country, got to Penrith in Cumberland by one o'clock in the morning, when I was glad enough to go to bed after a squeeze of 133 miles.

Saturday, 19th July. "Rose rather late and after breakfast [275] took a

gig to Patterdale. Penrith is a small town just where the ground begins
to rise at the end of the extensive flat we had crossed. There is nothing
very pretty about it nor in the road to Patterdale, till we get to the side of
Ulswater reckoned one of the most beautifull of the lakes and, of this
also, the end I first came to is very tame, the hills low and not picturesque. There are however some well ornamented estates about, and as
we go up the lake this scene improves at every step. The road is all along
very near the lake, and in general through woods—private property,
which put us to the trouble of stopping every five or ten minutes to
open a gate. But as I approached Patterdale, I began to admire the scene
very much—remember I am comparing to what I had generally seen in
the country. The lake is narrow, and takes a turn amongst high and rugged hills, often of a picturesque appearance, as well as I could judge
from what I saw in the intervals of fine weather. Patterdale is in a pretty
situation at the top of the lake, and near the foot of Helvellyn, a mountain of 3000 ft above the level of the sea. The place itself is a small scattered village, with a good inn, where I got a dinner and took a walk in
the woods. I should have gone on to Keswick that night, but as next day
was Sunday, I should have found no coach at Kendal, so I determined to
sleep at Patterdale, which would give me the opportunity of botanising
next morning on Helvelyn.

"Accordingly on Sunday morning (20th July) after breakfast, I set out
armed with my plant-portfolio and my umbrella, an indispensable uten-
sil in all walks in this part of the world. The top of Helvellyn is but four
miles from Patterdale, and at first I went on very well, though disappointed in finding [276] no plants of value. But as I approached the summit, the storm was so violent that at last I was obliged to desist within a
quarter of a mile of the top, and make the best of my way to the inn,
drenched to the skin. I there changed my clothes, spread the few plants I
had picked up, got some luncheon in the hopes of fairer weather, but
was obliged, after all, to take it as it was, and proceeded in my gig to
Kendal, sheltering myself as well as I could with my great coat and
umbrella. The road lay at first down part of Ullswater, which appeared
occasionally beautifull from the rays of sun darting here and there
through the mist and rain. About four miles from Patterdale we left
Ullswater, and ascending the hill came into the valley of Matterdale.
There is a road to Keswick nine miles shorter, but as it crossed some
high *fells* or downs, the driver dared not venture there in the storm; we
accordingly proceeded along the dreary valley of Matterdale, till we got
into the great road from Penrith to Keswick, which we followed, driving

up and down hill through long and dreary wastes, a country—with the exception of one or two pretty spots—always desolate and in every way uninteresting, and rendered now still more so by the clouds and mist that wrapped up the hills, and by the rain which fell almost constantly around us. The road was pretty good, but those who made it seemed to have had for their object how many and how steep hills they could carry it over. At last from one of them, we got a good view of Keswick and the surrounding country. Keswick and Bassenthwaite lakes in the midst of hills are pretty enough, though we could not see to the tops of the hills [277] on account of the mist and clouds. We descended into the town, where I dismissed the gig, stopping at an excellent inn, all in high style. It was too late in the day for me to go out, or do any thing but get my dinner and write a little. The town is in considerable bustle for so small a place, from the number of strangers arriving and departing. Keswick is the head quarters of the lake tourists, who seem to be very numerous. The town, of course, is full of people ready to wait on them: Guide Mineralogist, *Mineralist*, Botanist, etc, are here as common as Baker or Butcher. One of the name of Hutton has a *museum*,[35] and is the head-guide, said to be a most determined[§] talker, a great story-teller, and fond of draining your purse, but an active man and well acquainted with the country. He of course is continually employed in conducting strangers up Skiddaw[§], a mountain a little higher, but of a good deal easier ascent than our La Grange hill—or round Keswick lake or any other such excursion where you might be afraid of losing yourself—in the high road.

"Monday morning (21st July) proved still rainy; however I was determined if possible to reap some benefit from my visit to Cumberland, and knowing that three aquatic plants which I had never gathered were common in the lakes, I took a walk to the nearest one to endeavour to get some specimens, but to my great disappointment all was in a flood. The late rains had raised the surface of the lake six or seven feet above its usual height and no aquatic plants were to be got at. So I was obliged to return to the inn and wait there till the Kendal coach passed, at two o'clock. The weather had now cleared up and I was enabled to ride outside and see the country, though the tops of the mountains [278] were still occasionally wrapt in mist. Behind us was the famous Skiddaw, ascended by all tourists, chiefly on account of its vicinity to Keswick and facility of ascent. We left the valley and lake of Keswick, and proceeding along a very hilly road came into a very pretty vale, and soon after to the banks of a long narrow lake, almost divided into two in the middle where there is a bridge. This is called Leatherwater, and has some pretty seats around it, as indeed we met with all over the lakes. Quitting Leatherwater, the road ascends a little, and just where the waters divide, between this and another valley, is also the division between Cumberland and Westmoreland. There happens to be a rough stone wall between two properties just upon the boundary; there is also a heap of stones called Dunmail-raise, stones said, in the tourists' guide books, to have been raised by Dunmail, king of Cumberland, in commemoration of a victory he gained over king Edmund.[36] This may be very probable, but it was so much like the heaps we are raising continually by bringing a few cartloads towards the erection of a rough-stone wall or other building that I could not bring myself to attach any idea of importance to this Cumberland heap. But a little further on I was really pleased by the sight of Grasmere and Rydal water, two small but pretty lakes. The first, Grasmere, has a small island, celebrated as the place where Wordsworth wrote several of his pieces of poetry. What these pieces are, I know not, for I have never seen or read them, but [279] I believe he is a celebrated poet. His seat is close by, and a little further on is a very fine one called Rydal Hall. We changed horses near there, at the pretty little town of Ambleside, situated near Winander—or Winder-mere, and remarkable for the magnificent inn it possesses.

"From Ambleside, the road lies at first near the banks of Windermere, the largest of the lakes, and really fine as seen from several points of view. But we now soon lost sight of it, and crossed a much less interesting country, with a good deal of moss, to Kendal, a considerable manufacturing town in Westmoreland, full of inns and public houses. Here I slept, and next morning (Tuesday 22d) set off for Liverpool in the 'Telegraph' coach. I have but little to say on this road, which is in general bare and uninteresting, though as we get farther south the moss gradually disappears, and we get into a more flourishing, and better cultivated district than what I have seen of late. We breakfasted at Lancaster, a considerable town with a large castle, and afterwards passed through the manufacturing towns of Preston and Ormskirk, the first a large and populous place, the other famous for gingerbread. We arrived at Liverpool at a little after five, but by the time I had got my dinner, been to the post, etc, it was too late to go out anywhere; besides, I was rather tired, and not much disposed to walk much about[§] in the rain. I had had a good day's journey, though the distance was only eighty miles, but the roads about Liverpool being roughly paved made it very jolting, besides that the bad weather obliging me to go inside, I was terribly cramped all the way, not having been so fortunate as I sometimes am in my fellow-travellers. This is as yet the only part [280] of England where I have observed paved roads, and now that the new road-making system begins to be duly appreciated, they are by degrees taking up the pavement and *macadamising* the road, for the name has been quite made a verb of. The superiority of his plans are so generally recognised, that they are now thinking of macadamising several of the broad streets of the metropolis. I see that a little bit of Tottenham Court Road has been unpaved, and they are talking of trying the same experiment in St James's Square, and if it should succeed to extend the system to many of the principal streets.

"I spent the whole of Wednesday (23d July) at Liverpool, walking about the town, the docks and the botanic garden, all day in the midst of a pelting rain which, combining with the solid dirt always lying in a sea-port town, filled every street with a mud as bad or worse than that of the worst streets of London. Liverpool is a large and ill-built town, at least so it appeared to me, after the fine town houses I had of late been accustomed to. Yet they have stone in plenty, but I believe it is not easily worked. The streets are straighter, and better looking, in general, than those of Birmingham or Manchester, but often narrow, and all very dirty, particularly about the docks. The basins containing the ships, here called *docks*, are very fine, especially the new one finished but a few years ago and called Prince's Dock. It is a large rectangular basin, surrounded by a quay enclosed in a high wall. It was to all appearance full of ships, though they tell me there are sometimes double the number. The quay is an exceedingly busy scene, the number of vessels loading and unloading, carts going about in every direction, and every body going about at a [281] quick pace, and with an air of business, much more the case in a commercial than in a manufacturing town. The season when there is most activity is not come yet, as the American vessels are only now beginning to arrive; the shipping also being spread in a number of docks or basins does not show to so much advantage as when collected together in a single harbour, but there seemed to me to be about double the number of vessels there were in the port of Marseilles when I was last there. I was struck with the elegance of many of the ships. I did not go into any, but I have been told that several of the American packets are as handsomely fitted up in the interior as any drawing room. There are five or six docks, and they are now making a new one, or rather enlarging an old one. The stones they use are from a neighbouring quarry and some of them are four or five feet in their smallest dimensions. The buildings and warehouses about the docks are very shabby, built in brick in a very plain manner, and of a smoke-dried colour. They are large and numerous—but there does not seem to be much machinery, as I saw no great chimneys. I could not even learn of there being any block machinery here, which I am much surprised at, for the consumption must be very great[§]. The finest thing is the view of the harbour formed by the river Mersey. It is of great breadth as far as you can see up to the south, and to the north it terminates in the Ocean. From its mouth to the town, it is covered with vessels of every size and description going in and out, with some few riding at anchor. I always admired the sight of a vessel in full sail, and here I was so much pleased with seeing so many that I [282] could not help staying a considerable time to watch them, notwithstanding the rain. Amongst them, the steamboats form a considerable part, strutting along with their long streamers of smoke. Two are continually crossing and re-crossing the harbour to a village opposite, and several others are occasionally to be seen going up the harbour, starting for Ireland, Scotland, etc, or towing vessels up or down against wind or[§] tide. Some of the new Irish packets are beautiful vessels, that is as beautiful as such awkward things can be made. Liverpool has but few handsome buildings; indeed the Exchange is perhaps the only one worth mentioning. The customhouse is admired by some, but looks to me like an ugly brick warehouse.

"From different accounts, I had formed a very high idea of the Botanic garden, but though in some respects it went even beyond my expectations, I found myself more generally a little disappointed. It is in the hands of an active and clever curator, Mr Shepherd, to whom I had a letter from Mr Sabine. His assistant is also very zealous and well qualified to bring on the garden. What they want is a hothouse room and even garden room, although it be nine acres in extent. It was made and is kept up by a company of proprietors, and is quite a fashionable walk; some time ago they had, and I believe they still have occasionally, music there in the evening once a week, so that it is then very crowded. This is either the reason or the consequence of a considerable part of it being laid out as a pleasure garden, so that, with the exception of American bog plants, the collection of hardy plants is not so extensive as some others that I have seen. The hothouses have nothing extraordinary in [283] their outward appearance, though there be nothing amiss in them. As a general collection, too, there are some others that I have seen much more numerous, but there is one most beautiful class, of which no such collection exists any where; I mean the Scitamineae of Jussieu, Monandria of

Linnaeus.[37] Some of the Hedychiums in flower were the grandest things I had ever seen, the Alpinias, Zingibers, Globbas, Roscoeas, etc, were all remarkably fine, particularly Alpinia nutans, which, if I mistake not, is the same as one of my mother's drawing copied from the Chinese. Amongst the other plants, the most curious are the Dionaea, the Nepenthes, and the Ferns. The first Dionaea muscipula is a North American plant allied to the Droseras, and remarkable for its leaf, bordered with spines and jointed in the middle. When a fly or anything rests on it, the two lobes close and keep the insect in prison till it dies, and consequently ceases to make the least motion. Mr Shepherd has known a woodlouse, an animal difficult to kill, kept for a month imprisoned before the leaf reopened. This plant is difficult to cultivate and, though I have seen it in other houses, it is nowhere so fine as at Liverpool, from whence indeed most of those in other houses were sent. That is also the case with the other plant I mentioned, the Nepenthes distillatoria. The leaf of this plant has a cup at the end of it, which is generally almost shut. A liquor like water distils from the interior of the cup and fills it about half full, that is about a desert-spoon full. The ferns are very fine, and the collection extensive, and would be much more so if there were hothouse room to contain them. This is the first place where they sowed ferns, and now propagate them in this way [284] with the greatest facility. The brown dust at the back of the leaf is, you know, the seed. They have raised some from seed that had been fifty years lying in Forster's herbarium. I asked about the mode of culture, but he said it was too long to explain then, and referred me to the Linnean Transactions.[38] Mr Shepherd gave me a copy of the garden catalogue, and took my direction, promising to send me various things in the winter.

"I slept at Liverpool and Thursday morning (24th July) left it in one of the Manchester coaches, at first inside, but soon the weather allowed my getting outside. The road is interesting only for the great population of the country, and even that does not show so much as I had expected, for the people are closely collected in the towns. The country in general is in good cultivation, but still in many places the moss shows itself at no great distance from the road. Here and there they are taking it up for fuel, which leaves a good soil underneath, but the expence is scarcely repaid by the profit, as it must generally be cut away to the depth of three or four feet. The road is very busy. A number of half-starved Irishmen are at this season coming from Liverpool and spreading over the country in search of work. Their clothes hang about them in rags, they carry their all upon their backs, but this is never any great burden to them, so that they really look wretched, and their misery cannot be much alleviated by the insults they receive as they go along, from the English they meet on the road. Yet there is frequently something in their look so disagreable that one can scarcely pity them. Of other travellers there are plenty. I met nineteen coaches in the space of thirty seven miles, all loaded with passengers and driving at the rate of from twelve to fifteen miles an hour. [285] The stage coach opposition on this road is so great that they will take you sometimes the distance of thirty seven miles for three shillings in less than two and a half hours, that is fifteen miles an hour, stoppages included. Two opposition coaches starting at once drive on full gallop the whole way, *ventre à terre* as is the French somewhat vulgar phrase. When they arrive at the place where they change horses, a crowd gathers round each coach, encouraging the hostlers to be quick, huzzaing '"Lord Nelson" for ever!' or '"Telegraph" for ever!' etc, and seeming as anxious for the success of each of the coaches so named as the coachmen themselves. The change of horses is thus sometimes performed in twenty seconds, and the whole four changes together in two and a half minutes. When they get to a broad part of the road, they set to racing, the horses of each one striving with all their might to get first and seeming themselves much animated with the contest. It is surprising, with all this, that accidents should be so very rare, and really the coachmen must have the credit of managing their horses better than those of any other nation. I have known them, on anything happening to one of the leaders, stop the coach suddenly when going quick downhill, as happened to myself several times. Often, also, they have contests with unruly young horses, in which they always get the better, and I have not heard of any accidents from this or any other cause, except when the coachman was drunk.

"I did not get to Manchester till twelve, and was obliged to stay there till ½ past 2. This was owing to the mis-statements of the bookkeepers at Liverpool, who mind no lies, so that they get people to their own coach. I wanted to get to Derby that night, and was told that the coach by which I came to Manchester was the earliest and would be in time enough for one that went from Manchester to Derby by Buxton and Matlock, but when [286] I got to Manchester I found it was no such thing; half a dozen coaches at least had arrived there before me, and I found I could only reach Buxton that night, which vexed me much, as it took off another day from the time I had to spend at Derby. I dined at Manchester, took a walk about the town, and then got upon the Buxton coach. We first crossed a well cultivated country through Stockport and

other large manufacturing towns, passing innumerable canals that inter-
sect in every direction the rich manufacturing districts of Lancashire
and Yorkshire. A few miles beyond Stockport, we quitted the plain and,
following an excellent road, crossed into Derbyshire, and ascended the
hills by a gradual ascent winding for miles up the valleys to within a
couple of miles of Buxton, to which place we then descended. After tea I
took a little walk round the town, which is soon seen. It consists of a
Crescent worthy of the handsomest cities, and a few other houses,
chiefly inns, with a few trees and a public garden close about them, all
together planted in the midst of as barren, bare and bleak a country as
you can conceive. Yet the waters of Buxton are much frequented in the
season, and the place is much patronised by the Duke of Devonshire,
whose beautiful seat, Chatsworth Hall, lies between this and Matlock.

"Leaving Buxton on Friday morning (25th July) by the 'Lord Nelson'
coach, we soon entered a beautifully romantic valley, with high, steep,
rocky and wooded banks, and narrow at the bottom, frequently just
broad enough for the road and the Derwent, here a little stream, but
encreasing at every step. The road lies chiefly along its banks, frequently
crossing and recrossing it, and occasionally leaving it altogether for a
mile or two. It is all the way excellent, and more level than usual in the
hilly parts of England; indeed all the roads, and there are several, which
cross this part of Derbyshire, seem well laid out and excellently kept.
[287] Passed through Bakewell and a little farther on by Haddon Hall,
an antiquated building, but large and admirably suited to the country in
which it is placed. About Bakewell, the valley of the Derwent becomes
broad and richly cultivated, but as we approach Matlock it closes again
and forms the celebrated valley of Matlock, which is really fine. That little town is still, and was much more, romantically situated in a narrow
part of the valley, where bold projecting rocks, half concealed by the
trees, have a very fine effect. But this is in some measure spoilt by the
regular and handsome houses lately added to the town. There seemed
to be a good deal of company here, though Buxton be as yet very empty.
Below Matlock we soon came to Belper, the scene of Mr Strutt's ingenious and benevolent contrivances and establishments. Having now so
lately seen Lanark, I had a better opportunity of comparing the general
external appearance, which may perhaps be in favour of New Lanark.
That place, belonging entirely to the Company, has been more regularly
built and can be kept neater than Belper, where half the houses, belonging to others, are not at all under Mr Strutt's controul. The many public
houses, necessary on the high road, tend to make the place less orderly,

but in every other respect Mr Strutt's is far beyond New Lanark and excels, I believe, all other mills in the Kingdom.

"I got to Mr Strutt's at about two, and found that I was on the last day of a week of gaiety for Derby. The Assizes, the Races, the Bowmeeting, etc, had been very gay and numerously attended. The ladies were this day just setting out for a bowmeeting at Lord Scars[dale's] fields. The ladies forming this Society shoot at a target for prizes, and the whole ends in a dinner and ball. I spent the afternoon very pleasantly with Mr Strutt and a friend of his from Manchester. Mr Strutt is so [288] very agreable and ingenious a man that we never get tired of his company, and may always learn something from him, though his language and costume may not be so refined as those of his brother Joseph. The weather this day has been tolerably fine, though there fell during the greater part of it a small drizzling rain.

"On Saturday morning (26th July) after breakfast we walked round Mr Strutt's grounds; his wall has made great progress, but what surprised me was to see that, during my absence, three or four houses had already sprung up towards a street Mr Strutt had told me was in contemplation. It is the same all round Derby; building is the order of the day. In a manufacturing town we can easily conceive a rapid encrease; at Liverpool the flourishing state of commerce has the same effect; at Edinburgh the emigration from flats to entire houses; but at Derby no reason can be assigned for so rapid an encrease as there seems to be at present. Visited also Mr Strutt's household arrangements; he has in his own house a steam engine for washing, cleaning knives, blackening shoes, etc, but the last-mentioned operation is given up, as it did not succeed very well.—I took leave of this excellent man at three in the afternoon; he expressed great friendship for my father and mother, and wishes that he may see them at Derby. Notwithstanding his great aversion to moving, he says he would go two hundred miles to see them, but that eight hundred is rather too far for him.

"Leaving Derby in the London mail, and following for some time the course of the Derwent across a flat country, I soon got into the rich Leicester plains, celebrated for their cattle and for their cheese, known under the name of Stilton cheese, and the best perhaps of all English ones. We passed through many [289] villages and small towns, stopped to tea at Leicester, thence across a flat country through Northamptonshire and Hertfordshire, and lastly by the Highgate tunnel, which is now no more than a hollow with a bridge over it. We entered London by Islington, where I left the mailcoach, and taking a hackney coach, reached Queen Square Place by about eight in the morning" (of Sunday 27th July).

The rest of my last letter from London is occupied by details of my endeavours to execute commissions from my father, most of them failures, especially as to engaging an agricultural manager, and the transmission of agricultural instruments.—Drawings and descriptions of the best threshing machines and other important agricultural instruments that I had promised to bring for Prince Gagarin,[39] as well as for my father, I could not procure, "for no such thing exists," and generally I was surprised at the almost total want of works on arts and manufactures. In botany and horticulture I was more successful. "The Scotch botanists have been very liberal to me in dried plants, and I hope from Glasgow, Liverpool, Kew, Chelsea, and particularly from the Horticultural Society, to get gratis many very valuable plants and seeds. . . . I have got several seeds from the Hort. Soc., and am promised many things for the winter; I am now a corresponding member, and can be of use to them, as well as they to me, and correspondence with them will be attended with less expence than with any other Botanical correspondence I shall carry on with Mill, Hooker, Arnott, Greville, Menzies and Webb, very profitably to myself." I found subscriptions to English botanical periodicals, which my mother had suggested, too expensive, but from this time I commenced taking in regularly the Ratisbon *Flora oder Botanische Zeitung*,[40] which I continued till I handed over my library to Kew in 1854.

[290]Two days before I left I had a very interesting dinner at Friend Allen's, the Quaker—well known at the time for his influence with all those concerned in social reforms. "I found him at Stoke Newington, in a very nice house, about three or four miles from Shoreditch churchyard and yet in town, for town extends in that direction all the way to Ware; and as I went along through Hoxton, Kingsland, etc, I was obliged to ask continually where I was, for otherwise I could not tell where one village ended and another began. Mistaking the distance, I arrived a few minutes after the hour fixed, and they were all seated at dinner. After making profuse apologies, I took my place in the chair left vacant for me, when to my surprise and horror there was perfect silence and stillness all round the table for five minutes, which I afterwards learnt was to leave me time to say a proper grace. However I soon got over all awkwardness. The party consisted of 1. Mr Allen, whose sensible and agreable conversation are well known, and in whom the quaker formalities are not so unpleasant as in some others; 2. his brother (or brother-in-

law) as polite and prevenant a man as quaker habits will allow; 3. his sister, as stiff a quaker as any, who could talk of nothing but human nature and divine bounty; 4. another sister or sister-in-law, who did not say a word the whole evening; 5. a daughter of some one of the family, a young girl who seemed to have quaker manners but not enough of quaker disposition; 6. a young french quaker girl from Congenies, between Sommières and Nîmes. When Mr Allen was there some years ago, his daughter (now dead) took a fancy to the girl and brought her over. She is indeed exceedingly clever and intelligent, and the manner in which she has learnt English is a proof of it. She has been altogether about two and a half years in England, did not know a word when first she came, and now speaks so well and with so good a pronunciation that when she mentioned having been near Nîmes, I asked her [291] whether she had learnt the patois, little thinking it was her native language; 7. a Mr—I forget his name, but believe it was Graves, a man who was the source of much ennui as well as much amusement to me in the course of the evening. He could join with the old lady in any abstract considerations on the sublimity of nature, and this formed the subject of conversation for some time after dinner—so far it was only ennui—but then he insisted on supporting some of the most extraordinary paradoxes I ever heard. One that he strove the hardest to prove against Mr Allen and me was that no book could give any knowledge, and this he thought he proved to us by the most inconceivable chain of reasoning, entirely founded on words, for, as we observed, he would have been quite of our opinion if he would but condescend to give to the word *knowledge* its usual meaning. What was unpleasant was his bringing on these paradoxes at every moment. He is said to be a very clever, as well as a very benevolent man, but he cannot bear not to be one of the principal actors in conversation. When Mlle Majolies, for instance, happened to observe that everything had a beginning and an end, he added, 'and every thing has two ends,' and then proceeded to prove that the beginning is the first end. I told him he might as well call the end the last beginning, and each side a middle end, for these are but relative words and each point of the limits of a body may be the end or the beginning according to the direction in which we examine it. This is another example of the absurdity of disputing on any subject without first assuring one's self that both parties attach the same meaning to the names of the objects they are discussing.—But enough of all this nonsense. I have only now to add that I was much pleased with Friend Allen himself, though there is at all times a something in the affected simplicity of

Quakers, which has the same effect upon me as the puritanical cant of [292] Cromwell's time. I believe Quakers are, in general, a very moral sect, but their outward forms are certainly very affected. The female dress, for instance, must cost them nearly as much trouble as that of the finest *élégante*.

"Mr Allen, besides his house, has, at a little distance from it, in the same village of Stoke Newington, a little garden where we drank tea in a pretty little summerhouse he has built there. The garden is small but, according to Mr Allen's benevolent views, he is trying experiments of different vegetables, to see what will give the most food for the poor in the smallest space of ground. Setting out from the same basis as Mr Owen—the necessity of providing for the poor the means of earning their living, instead of giving it for nothing—but with different views as to the mode of attaining this end, he has also in view the building of villages for their accomodation and alloting to each family ground enough to furnish their food. But he has sense enough to perceive that, if the produce as well as the labour is to be common to all, the consequence will be that every one will endeavour to reap the benefit himself and throw the labour on his neighbours. Of schools in general for the education of poor children, Mr Allen is continually the advocate and zealous supporter, as well as the projector and patron of many in particular. He has built in his garden a small house, containing his stables, his coachman's lodgings, a school (not yet set going) and two or three rooms over for any home inhabitants. Besides his experiments on man's food, he is making similar ones on cow's food, to the extent the narrow limits of his bit of ground will allow. He has two cows that furnish him with milk for his family, and serve him to make his experiments upon.—He has been in great affliction from the loss of his daughter, to whom he appears to have been particularly attached."[41]

[293]We left London on our return home on the 6th Augt. My sisters took with them three little girls, children of our old nurse, to form part of an establishment for the education of poor children my father was setting up at Restinclières (an establishment that commenced well but soon came to grief owing to difficulties encountered from local prejudices insufficiently attended to). As we were thus six altogether, we took the steamboat direct from London to Calais, where we arrived the same evening, but were detained the next day at Calais by custom-house troubles. We left it, however, on the evening of Thursday 7th, in the Diligence, of which we engaged the whole *intérieur*, arriving at Paris in the morning of Saturday 9th. Here my first care was to square matters with

the custom house. Our friend M. de la Molère had procured from M. de Saint-Cricq, the Directeur Général des Douanes, an order to have our packages *plombés* at Calais, and sent on for examination at Paris—a rather unusual favor at that time. When at Calais, I ascertained that the order had been duly received and registered in the order-book—but the Officiers were§ in a state of angry excitement by the attempt of a print-seller to enter a set of engravings worth £100 as of the value only of 100 francs, and the Inspecteur, in a flood of words, in which, notwithstanding some habit, I could not match him, absolutely refused to comply with the order, which he pretended was not clear. Immediately, however, on arriving at Paris, I went with M. de la Molère to M. de St Cricq's Office, where red-tape delays were dispensed with, and by that day's post a peremptory order was dispatched, desiring the packages to be immediately sent up to Paris, with a strong reprimand for disobedience of the former order.

Another traveller's nuisance, now fortunately pretty well at an end, was the passport, which took me *four hours* of the [294] second day at Paris. The passport I had brought over from England was taken at Calais, to send direct to Paris, and a passe provisoire given me; in order to be en règle to leave Paris, I had to go to the Prefecture de Police at the other end of the town, to wait, *faisant queue* at the passport office there for above an hour, before I obtained the English one, already loaded with several visas, then to the British Embassy two or three miles off to get it signed there, for which I had to wait half an hour, then back to the Prefecture de Police for another definitive visa, for which I had again an hour to wait—the Official in the passport Office there being one whom I, for many a year after, well knew as a most priggish little man, without a notion of civility, who would insist on talking almost unintelligible English, when I was at least as ready in French as in English.

A few days after arriving in Paris, I went down by diligence to Dieppe to spend a day with the Gagarins but, with that exception, we remained in Paris till the end of the month, partly to see our friends the De la Molères, Partouneaux's, Calvières and others, partly to execute some commissions and other business for my father. I was two or three times at the Jardin des Plantes, where I was kindly received by old Jussieu, Bosc, Thouin, Desfontaines and others, and made acquaintance with Adolphe Brongniart, then young in the science in which he so soon distinguished himself. Of my letters during this period, one only is preserved,[42] from which the following extracts are connected with some previous observations on the then contrast between France and England, or with the then state of affairs in Paris.

"Calais is a sort of amphibious, or ambiguous town, half French, half English. The inns in particular are carpeted, furnished and kept a good deal in the English style, though with some French modifications. English is a good deal spoken. Shop-signs are many [295] of them in English; in some places also, there are attempts at English shop-windows and English trottoirs, but the general character of the town is French, the streets irregular, with the gutter in the middle instead of underground drains, and no attempt, at least no successful attempt, at neatness. The common people, en revanche, have already that gay and agreable look, which forms a striking contrast with the shabby finery of the English mob. The women have not indeed the regular features, the fair skin, the tall and well-proportioned body of the English, but their superior skill in the art of dressing, and their fresh and merry countenances, their vif and expressive eyes, are really much more pleasing. Their dress is also much better suited to their rank. In England, no woman thinks she can appear in the streets without a bonnet, a spencer *à pointes,* with the waist stiffly laced up (which must much impede her work) and the texture of her whole dress rather flimsy than fine. These articles, being dear, cannot be often renewed, and you may imagine the state in which they usually are—add to this a threadbare shawl, and a dirty face, and you will have an idea of the pleasure it gives to see once more the peasantry dressed more suitably to their station. Neat and clean caps instead of the old shabby bonnets, their handkerchiefs, jackets and petticoats strong and coarse, but new and clean, and the whole dress in each instance becoming the wearer. Remember it is only of outward appearance that I now speak, though perhaps in their character, the sober and industrious, tho' crafty French peasant is at least equal to the plain and ingenious, but idle and drunken English mechanic. The difference of dress in the men is analogous to that of the women, shabby finery in the English, coarse but neat and clean in the French."

The two nights diligence from Calais to Paris made us [296] "heartily tired with this long and dreary journey, so different from the rapid and agreable travelling I had been used to for the last five months. A great, heavy, awkward vehicle, rough, coarse and clumsily made horses, their long hair hanging in disorder from their manes, tails and hoofs, like Poitou *bardous,* trotting almost à l'aventure like wild animals, without any controul but slender packthread reins and the gruff voice of the postilion, who, sitting on the near wheel-horse in his muddy jack boots, his long pigtail and threadbare uniform, smacks his whip and calls to his horses as if he were driving a herd of swine. The rope harness, rotten with the mud in which it is always embedded, and such as the poorest English carter would be ashamed of, is continually breaking in some part or other with the weight of the cumbersome machine to which it is attached, whilst the remainder of the tackle makes a clatter, announcing far and wide the approach of the vehicle. Continual stoppages occur also from other causes—for the horses to take breath after ascending a hill—to fasten on or take off the dragchain at every slope—to have our passports examined, or for the octroi people to search the *impériale*, and a thousand other such reasons. Such is the effect this mode of travelling has on those who are used to the elegant coaches that swarm on the English roads. Leather harness with brass, or plated ornaments as bright as that of the finest Parisian équipages, fine spirited horses, well trimmed and in the best order, trotting or galloping over hill and dale without other stoppage but changing horses every stage, and that often done in less than a minute—no passports—no octroi—turnpikes paid and mailbags exchanged without the horses' slackening their pace in the least degree, and on the few occasions when the drag is necessary,* it is taken off or put on with a scarcely perceptible stoppage. [297] How is it that for these nine years past the continued intercourse between the two nations, the immense concourse of English on the Continent and the universal sense entertained of the advantages of English coaches, how is it that the French have scarcely even improved upon their own, much less adopted the English mode of travelling? The malles poste are indeed very much better than they were, but still they are but little above the diligences."

"We went yesterday, Sunday 17th, with M. and Mde La Molère, to St Cloud where we got admission to the Duke of Bordeaux's private mass, a permission very difficult to obtain. The day being fine, the mass was in the open air. In the centre of a ring of tall elms was erected a little pavilion, under which were seats for Made Gontaut, the Royal children,[44] and two or three others, also the altar. On each side were seats for the few persons admitted, I suppose about fifty. The circle of trees and the alley leading up to it were lined with a company of the Garde Royale; behind the pavillion was the band of one of the regiments of the Garde,

---

* Mecaniques[43] were then unknown on the Continent as in England.

who played all the time most beautifull pieces of music, which in those circumstances in the open air had a particularly grand effect. In returning as well as in coming, Made de Gontaut led the two little children, and as they went up the steps of the chateau, they stopped to see the guards march by. The little Duke (not quite three years old) took off his hat, and as they went by said, 'Voilà mes lanciers, mes gendarmes.'

"As the children were to go off almost immediately to Paris, we waited for another opportunity of seeing them in M. Laforet's rooms, overlooking the Park and the beautifull banks of the Seine, with Paris in the background. . . . At one o'clock we [298] went again into the hall to see the Duke and Mademoiselle. There were two or three people only besides our party and, as the children came to the foot of the stairs, Madame Gontaut, who is always exceedingly complaisante to those who come to see the Duke, stopped and told him to take off his cap to the ladies, but the poor little child, tired with the ceremonies and etiquette of the day, was a little cross, and held his cap tight on with both hands saying 'Non non non.' He cannot be said to be a remarkably fine child, but is much improved by his stay at St Cloud. Mademoiselle is a fine girl."

My letters contained also accounts of festivities in the Champ de Mars, and a grand review in honor of the Duke of Cumberland[45]— details of the visit to Dieppe, where I went by diligence, three of these enormous carriages in opposition to each other, each with about twenty passengers, starting at ½ past 6 in the evening, and arriving at Rouen at 7 in the morning, etc; and the first days of September we definitively left Paris on our return home to Restinclières—by diligence to Lyons, and thence in an open boat down the Rhone to Pont l'Esprit. This was a very pleasant trip of 24 hours—no wind—a beautiful moonlight, without which boats did not venture on that rapid river with its constantly shifting shallows—the boat, one of those little barges built upon some of the affluents of the river in Burgundy, where wood is comparatively cheap, and usually broken up for sale on the lower Rhone, where wood is dear, the very strong current rendering it a very tedious and expensive business to carry goods up the river. Arriving at Pont l'Esprit, where we were told we should readily meet with[§] conveyances on, we found that there were none but the through diligences from Lyons, in which it was hopeless to find places [299] for our party of six, and the only vehicle we could rout out for hire was a one-horse patache, which engaged to take us to Nimes during the night. This was a kind of covered cart upon 2 wheels, without springs, with boards slung across inside for seats, which did not much ease the jolts of the illkept roads. We had a strong, vigorous-looking horse and a young driver, and calculated at any rate on getting over the ground rapidly, but before long, continual stoppages showed an over-somnolent disposition both of man and beast.—This, however, the driver positively denied every time I woke him up, till at last, "Tenez, Monsieur, à vous dire franchement, je n'en peux plus," and he handed me the reins (cords) and dropped into a heavy sleep. After a weary night, we arrived at Nîmes, with bones half broken, early in the morning. There, however, we met my eldest sister, and with her returned in the course of the next day to Montpellier and Restinclières, to resume the quiet life of the previous winters.

6

France Again; Botanizing in the Pyrenees, 1823–25

[300] The autumn and winter of 1823–4 was spent at Restinclières, like the previous winters in the direction of the improvements, etc, going on on the estate—occasional social parties in Montpellier, etc, amusing myself with my usual course of reading on philosophical subjects, and now taking with encreased zeal to botany, having the large accumulations made chiefly during my visit to England and Scotland to arrange in my herbarium. My two younger sisters, however, began to feel the contrast between the quiet country life and the social enjoyments they had had amongst their English friends, and showed a restless disposition, occasioning some anxiety to my father and mother. At the same time, the Gagarins, who were spending the winter at Paris, wrote very urgently to request them to come again for a couple of months to Paris, and it was at length agreed that I should accompany them.[1] We accordingly started in the middle of February, although for the last few days I felt feverish and uncomfortable. This was attributed to other causes, but we had only got as far as Avignon, when both my sisters felt so unwell that we were obliged to send for a medical man, who pronounced it to be the smallpox, then very prevalent, and which the next day declared itself in me also. We all had it in a mild form, having all been vaccinated

as children,[2] but it occasioned a fortnight's detention in the Hotel du
Palais Royal, and, after a stoppage of a couple of nights at Lyons it was
only on the 7th March that we arrived at Paris. Our friends the Gagarins,
with their friends, Countess Ostermann Tolstoy and her niece and suite,
including a Doctor, Governess and a Manager (besides the Gagarins'
two Governesses and Tutor), occupied the whole of the available
appartments in the Hotel Choiseul, Rue St Honoré, but we settled ourselves in the adjoining Hotel Vauban, it being settled that we should
generally have our dinners at least with our friends, who [301] had all a
common table. Here we sat according to the then Russian fashion, the
ladies on one side, the gentlemen on the other. The Prince, Princess and
Countess at the head, then on the ladies' side, my sisters, Olga and her
governess and the two little Gagarin girls and their governesses,[3] and on
our side, myself, the young Prince and his tutor, the Doctor, the manager, and a young man, I forget in what capacity attached to the Countess's suite.

We spent two months in this way very pleasantly—not much in the
way of science, though I did go now and then amongst the botanists at
the Jardin des Plantes, or Jardin du Roi, as it was then called. Of my letters at that time very few remain, and those chiefly on family matters,
with short mention of some of the parties we were at. We saw a good
deal of our friends the Partouneaux, at the Ecole Militaire, and also of
the Collots (he was then Master of the Mint), went to a few balls and
evening parties, but the most agreable dinners I had were at Count
Chaptal's and Count Segur's. Chaptal, the chymist, then retired from
political life (although Pair de France), and almost from scientific pursuits, was living very comfortably with his family in the Fauxbourg St
Germain, where he gave excellent dinners, the party chiefly consisting
of men of science, or more or less distinguished otherwise, of a Bonapartist tendency, he being warmly attached to the ideas of his great patron,
the first Napoleon, and as such, a zealous opponent of free-trade principles. These were now attracting some attention in France, and some of
the influential daily papers were speaking favorably of the system of
commercial liberty then being initiated in England by Canning and
Huskisson,[4] and to which many then thought Villèle was being converted in France. At Count Segur's (the historian, whom I have previously mentioned as my father's old friend) we met the elite, and
perhaps more than the elite of the then [302] liberal party—at a small
dinner party were Lafayette, then still in full health and vigour, and the
Miss Wrights—very warm in their Owenite, communiste, antimatrimo-

nial etc, ideas,[5] which they soon after went out to America to put into practice, in an Owenite establishment, which soon failed as well as their ideas, for one at least of the two soon took to a husband.

It was during this stay at Paris that I was enabled to procure for Dr (Sir William) Hooker, at moderate prices, a few valuable French botanical works which he had been looking out for, and to complete others which had come out in parts irregularly. There was in the Quartier Latin a bookseller of the name of Meilhac, one of those dealers then more numerous in Paris than they are now, "who are constantly on the lookout for sales and other opportunities for getting books cheap, and who, living like pigs and avoiding all ornament to their shops or stalls, can afford to sell them with very little profit. He buys chiefly botanical and medical books," of which he had a large stock in very good order, notwithstanding the apparent dirt in which they were stowed. Since his death the trade in valuable second-hand Natural History and Medical works has passed into greater houses, such as that of Baillière, who know how to keep up their prices.

We returned in May to Restinclières, where I found abundant occupation in the affairs of our estate, which left me little time for botany, besides that the drought which had set in in November still continued. With the exception of a shower or two in February, no rain fell from November 1823 till September 1824, although farther north, at Lyons at least, they had had too much of it. The [303] corn in many places was cut with the straw under a foot high; in others, however, where the soil was loose, and especially in a few limited instances where it had been sown in rows and howed between, the heavy dews had given it a better growth. I contrived, however, to make a few herborisations, a successful one along the lagoons and salt marshes between Montpellier and the sea, and in the autumn I was enabled to spend a few days with my friend Requien, in his herbarium at Avignon. It was also during this autumn that I negotiated for Dr (Sir William) Hooker the purchase of Gouan's herbarium and botanical correspondance.[6] His representatives required at first 2000 fr. for the herbarium, and 600 fr. for the correspondence, which containing, amongst others, many of Linnaeus's letters would without doubt sooner or later [have] reached fully that price, but they were soon persuaded to reduce very much their demands for the herbarium; and I find that ultimately £50 covered the whole expence of the purchase, packing and transmission of the herbarium to Bordeaux for shipment to Glasgow[§], and the carriage of the correspondence to Paris. No sooner also was the bargain concluded, than an order came from Avignon to purchase the whole for a larger sum than I had given.

After the Michaelmas storms and subsequent rains, vegetation revived, and already in November I had gathered many more mosses than I thought could have vegetated under this climate. The stubbles and ploughed fields in many cases turned of a rich brown, with the closely crowded capsules of Phascums, Gymnostomums, etc, [304] and my having been so much with Arnott during my visit to Scotland had induced me to take particular interest in the study of that class, so generally neglected by Mediterranean botanists. In this winter, also, of 1824–5, I saw a good deal of M. Delile, the director of the Botanic Garden, of whom I wrote: "though he is far from equalling his predecessor De Candolle, and is generally placed much below Dunal (who was to have had the place), yet his unremitting zeal and attention to the garden has brought it into a much more flourishing state than it has ever been yet, though the scantiness of the funds allotted to this, the second garden in France, place it so much below similar ones in England. Amongst the remarkable plants, there is now a fine tree of Convolvulus arboreus (Ipomoea murucoides, R. et S.).[7] The hothouse furnishes his Majesty yearly with a fine dish of bananas, Solandra grandiflora lines a whole hothouse, also fine specimens of Cheirostemon, Strelitzia, etc, and in the open ground Lagerstroemia indica, Solanum auriculatum, the latter in full flower 4th Jany, Mespilus japonica, Sterculia platanifolia."

It was during this winter, also, that we made the acquaintance of the Klustine family, with whom we became so intimate. One bitter cold January morning, a message was brought to me, with letters from our Moscow friends, recommending a Russian family who would be glad to see me at their hotel. I immediately went over and found Madame de Klustine, an elderly remarkably quiet widow, her daughter, Anastasie, a bright, lively, intelligent girl in her sixteenth year, but apparently delicate, Antoine, a year younger, a rattling lad of most [305] agreable manners, showing like his sister the pains taken with their education, but in excellent health, and Simon, a couple of years younger, more quiet and partaking more of his mother's character. They had been recommended to come to Montpellier that Anastasie, who was threatened with consumption, might benefit by the warm climate and the advice of its celebrated physicians. The reputation of the physicians was perhaps well deserved. Dr Chretien, a rather stately Doctor of the old school with a gold-headed cane, had great experience and good sense, M. Delpech and other surgeons were among the best in Europe, but the climate had a false reputation, resulting in so many consumptive patients coming there from a great distance to die, and the Klustine prospects did not seem promising. They had come direct from Moscow, posting through every alternate night as well as all day, stopping only a whole day at Dresden to rest, and had left there their furs, thinking they should have no further need of them. They had been recommended to an hotel at Montpellier, which had once been the principal one, but for years had been superseded by the Hotel du Midi, one of the best in the South of France; they had arrived there late the night before, with a man and a maid who could not speak a word of anything but Russian, and a kind of managing German, half tutor, half homme d'affaires, and there I found them, shivering and helpless in a large room—paved as are, at least were, all the Montpellier rooms, with flagstones like our kitchens, no carpets, the large windows allowing the cold wind to blow across the room, a large open [306] smoky fireplace, and for fuel half-dry wood, which went on fizzing and smoking long before it gave out any heat. Poor Madame de Klustine, drawing her cloaks close round her, after the first exchange of communications, could not help exclaiming, "Can this be Montpellier and its delicious climate?" However we soon got them into a comfortable appartment, their helpless Russian servants who could not bear the French mode of living were sent home, the services of the German dispensed with; Dr Chretien, by his snail prescriptions and really sensible advice, restored confidence in Anastasie's health. Young Antoine, ever joyous and happy, went rattling on in spite of his mother's sententious "Tishe, tishe, my drug, tishe" (quieter, quieter, my friend, quieter); from his intimacy with the Fischers and others in Moscow, he had acquired a great taste for botany, which he could indulge in as the season advanced, and with his sister became exceedingly popular in the Montpellier society. We became most intimate with them, they remained at Montpellier the winter and spring, I met them in the summer in the Pyrenees; they were afterwards again a short time at Montpellier, then left for Paris, travelled in Italy and Switzerland. The young men subsequently returned to Russia, Antoine entered into the military service, and was killed in the campaign in Turkey in 1828. His brother Simon returned to France and Switzerland, and was in England at the time of my father's death in 1830,[8] when he had engaged himself to my younger sister—the marriage was, however, necessarily put off, and for reasons not very clear finally broken off, and Simon returned to his estates, married a Moscow family, had two or three daughters, and died early. [307] Madame de Klustine and her daughter Anastasie, after visiting Italy, settled for many years at Geneva, where Anastasie became intimate with, and almost the soul of, the society of the principal literary and scientific celebrities of the place—the Sismondis, De Candolles,[9] Delarives, Prevosts, Bonstetten, etc. She finally married M. de Circourt and, settling at Paris, her appartment in the Rue des Saussaies, or her country house, "Les Bruyeres" at Bougival near St Germain, became a rendezvous of literary persons. I often corresponded with her till she married, and afterwards spent many an agreable hour with her and her husband, both great talkers, each one taking up the discourse the moment the other made a pause, but both of them possessing such a fund of information and applying it so well that they were very popular.

1825 became with me a thoroughly botanical year. My herbarium received early in the year large additions, chiefly through the liberality of Dr Hooker. I went over to Requien at Avignon early in the winter, and again in the beginning of April to meet my friend Arnott. It was on one of these occasions that I saw the Pont du Gard to the greatest advantage. Violent rains had swollen the Gardon so that the ferry on the main road about a mile below the bridge could not ply, and the diligence had to go round by the bridge, along the lower arches of the aqueduct. It was in the night, the diligence was full, but my friend the conducteur allowed me to settle myself as I best could amongst the luggage on the top. After a shower of rain, the moon burst out [308] bright just as we approached the aqueduct, and gave to these splendid ruins and the picturesque scenery in which it is placed a brilliancy I have never seen before or after. I spent some days with Arnott at Requien's, in his herbarium. Arnott had come over to France with a view to spending the summer in a botanical tour in Switzerland. He remained some time at Paris absorbed in muscology, and I persuaded him before going to Switzerland to pay me a visit at Restinclières, where he would find so rich a botanical field, not without a hope that we might go together to the Pyrenees instead of the Alps. At Requien's we had as usual a most cordial reception. He had very good sitting rooms on the first floor, his herbarium in two large ones, opening on the one side to his bedroom, on the other to a terrace looking south, where he could heat his paper in the sun and rapidly dry the enormous masses of plants he collected; a perron and steps led down to the kitchen, where he had his meals, and where his old mother lived, and managed and cooked, and half took her meals with him, the said kitchen opening by glass doors on to the tannery. Tanning indeed was Requien's business, but he was rich, and entirely devoted to botany and to municipal affairs, and would have given up the tannery but for his mother who had spent her life in it, and could not bear the idea of parting with it. On Sundays, Requien had generally a few friends to his twelve or one o'clock dinner, but then they dined in the herbarium, and his mother did not appear. There was always supper at seven or half-past.

[309]Of our 4 or 5 days at Avignon we spent one with Requien in an excursion to Vaucluse, where Arnott revelled in the Hypnum Vallis-Clausae, which he identified with H. filicinum, and the rest of our time availing ourselves largely of Requien's well-known botanical liberality. Leaving him, we spent a morning botanising about the Pont du Gard and thence straight home to Restinclières, where with the aid of my sisters I soon overcame Arnott's scruples about giving up predetermined plans, and our Pyrenean journey was settled for the next month. The intermediate time was given up almost exclusively to botany. The vegetation of the neighbourhood was at its best season for botanists—the great mass of it new to Arnott. He was anxious to carry home good stores for his botanical friends. I was also desirous of a stock of duplicates for exchanges with the encreasing number of my correspondents, and in one month we put up between us above twelve thousand specimens of phaenogamous plants, besides a few thousand cryptogams; and already before starting, we sent off a box to Hooker, with some of our own gatherings, a large parcel from Requien and Salzmann's Tangiers plants which I had bought for him.

On the 17th of May, we joined Requien and Audibert at Montpellier and took the diligence to Narbonne,[10] and the next morning began our work by a short excursion to the neighbouring Pech de la Nivelle, gathering a few interesting plants, but most of them already dried up, besides that we had with us some Montpellier botanical students who had come over for a day's change. The following day, the 19th May, was our first serious herborisation. Starting at day break, [310] we crossed La Clape, a dry, bare, limestone mountain, offering a few interesting plants in the chinks of the rocks, and on the dry downs on the summit a quantity of the Medicago leiocarpa, which I published as new[11] but proved afterwards to be only a glabrous, fruited variety of M. suffruticosa. Winding down to the seacoast for the Viola arborescens, which had already shed its seed, we wandered for three or four hours along the broad, sandy seacoast, without a trace of vegetation, and nothing to amuse us but the long lines of fishermen and fisherwomen hauling in their nets. The short dumpy women, with their woollen petticoats tied up between the legs so as to look like Dutchmen's breeches, leaving the lower half of their thighs bare; and when the long net was hauled in, the

sorting the produce, the haggling with the dealers—chiefly women—
was a lively, noisy scene, contrasting with the stillness of all around,
under a burning sun.

Arriving at length at the island of Sainte Lucie, we came suddenly
into the midst of a rich and varied maritime vegetation. A number of
Statices and others, which never reach the coasts of Lower Languedoc,
filled our boxes and portfolios, and following the banks of the canal, we
got in rather late to La Nouvelle and put up for the night, after our long
fatiguing day. Whilst supper was preparing, we laid out our plants. I
happened to have gathered some fine specimens of Euphorbia paralias
and, whilst laying them out, I touched one of my eyes, which began
immediately to smart. I took out my handkerchief to wipe them, but had
previously wiped my hands so that it was imbued with the Euphorbia
juice, and both my eyes became inflamed, with such violent pain that I
could not go on with [311] my occupation, nor eat any supper, and it
was only after two or three hours' fruitless endeavours by bathing, etc,
to alleviate the pain that I could at length get to bed and close my eyes.

Quite recovered the next morning, we returned to Narbonne and
spent the two following days, 22d and 23d May, in an excursion to the
lower Corbières, where the woods of Fontfroide proved very productive
of interesting plants. The Cistuses were in great beauty. Besides the
common C. salvifolius and Monspeliensis, miles of C. crispus, and C.
longifolius, or C. populifolius, covering the ground in the early morning
with a sheet of pink or white of the greatest beauty, §apparently to the
exclusion of everything else.—At eleven the petals began to fall and by
noon all was gone, nothing remaining but the grey foliage. Arriving in
the evening at Séjean, we took the 10 o'clock diligence to Perpigan.

This place was our headquarters for a few days. The brother of our
friend Mde de Partouneaux, M. de Bréa, was here as one of the principal
financial autorités and made the stay pleasant to me, in as far as I could
afford relaxation, but I did not let it interfere with our botanical pursuits. We collected most of the good plants of the valley of the Testa, and
made a three days excursion to Collioure, Bagnols and Port-Vendres
near the Spanish frontier. The low chain of the Albères where the
Pyrenees reach the Mediterranean is like the Alpes maritimes near Nice
and Mentone, one of the richest (botanically) points of the whole coast.
The majority of plants were in the best condition, and we made an abundant harvest.

Returning to Perpignan, learning that Catalonia was, owing to the
French occupation, perfectly secure, we determined on a trip to Barce-

lona, for which however we could only [312] afford a week—not sufficient to include in it the Mont Serrat, for even at Montpellier the
accounts of the brigandage and unsettled state of Catalonia were so
exaggerated that we were unwilling to let our families know that we
were going to affront them till our return. Accordingly on the 31st we
took the diligence and, sleeping at Gerona, arrived at Barcelona on the
1st June. After crossing the ridge, the first day's journey and part of the
second was over an almost desert-looking, impoverished country, and
the arrival at Gerona in the evening was anything but cheering, passing
through long streets of unroofed, ruined houses, the effects of the late
war, the scanty population of the suburbs and of the villages we had
passed through in a low state of degradation and disgustingly filthy. In
Gerona itself were the headquarters of the Spanish authorities of the
province and of what remained of its troops (the French being in garrison at Barcelona), giving it some appearance of temporary activity.
Coming down the second morning to Pinède on the sea coast, the whole
character of the country had completely changed. "Between this and
Barcelona (as I wrote at the time), a distance of forty miles, fourteen
large villages or towns with clean and neatly plaistered houses, a
numerous, clean and healthy looking population, rich culture and
numerous fishing barks along the coast, give an air of richness and comfort that I was very far from expecting in Spain. The road winds under
the rocks close to the sea beech, between hedges of aloes (Agaves) shooting up every here and there, flower stalks, which in their present young
state look like gigantic Asparagus stalks. In the fields the Caroubier
(Ceratonia), cultivated for horses, under the [313] name of Garrojos, the
Orange and the Lemon and the Olive denote the beauty of the climate,
though they are rather too closely mixed with the vine and the different
kinds of grain to indicate very learned agriculturists." Arrived at Barcelona just in time to call on M. Paulin Durand, a connection of our Montpellier friends, and go with him to a very good Italian Opera. These two
diligence days had not been unproductive in botany. We four (Requien,
Audibert, Arnott and myself) had the inside to ourselves, and, whenever owing to a hill or bad roads we went at a foot's pace, we jumped
out two on one side two on the other—or when the dilatory changing of
horses or mules gave us time, we hastened on before, and snatched up a
number of very interesting specimens.

   We were four whole days at Barcelona, made a few botanical excursions close around the town, but had much besides to see that was new
to us, amongst other things the procession of the Fête Dieu, which hap-

pened during our stay, and was so very different from the religious processions in the south of France under the Restoration. "Two regiments
of the French garrison formed a double line all along the streets it was to
pass through, behind them crowds of people to witness the scene. The
balconies lined with well-dressed females and covered with silk hang-
ings in scarlet, blue, crimson and other rich colours, the noisy gaiety and
eager expectation of the crowd, gave them the appearance of being prepared rather to witness a masquerade scene than to perform an act of
devotion. After an hour and a half's tedious expectation amidst the
crowd in the street, the procession at length appeared, but much were
we surprised to see, instead of the bigotted devotion the Spaniards are
celebrated for, the most indecent conduct I ever saw in a religious ceremony.—The approach [314] of the procession was hailed by loud accla-
mation and roars of laughter from the multitude of children assembled,
and well might they laugh, for at the head appear the *Giant and Giantess*,
two figures of about 16 feet high, dressed up, one in a sort of Turkish
dress with a mace on his shoulder, the other in an elegant modern ball
dress with her fan and rédicule—which dress, by the bye, we were told,
sets the fashion for the year among the Barcelona ladies. These figures
are well proportioned, the lady very handsome, and are borne each by a
man concealed under the dress, so that they appear to walk. Every now
and then they stop, and dance one opposite the other to the sound of
fifes and a couple of drums, beaten by two whimsically dressed creatures on large asses. These giants are supposed to represent pagan dei-
ties driven away by the true cross. Next followed two or three
companies of the garrison, with the band at their head—the banners of
the different parishes—the crosses of the parishes—about 600 monks
and abbés of various orders—a number of priests, the choristers, playing on violins and base viols—the dais—the municipal authorities,
drums and music—a company of soldiers closing the procession. Of all
these, the monks alone had some appearance of decency in their conduct, the rest talking and laughing as if it were really the masquerade it
appeared to be."

On our way to the botanical garden, called at the principal and almost
the only bookseller, "in search of Spanish botanical works, but not one
to be had in this—one of the first towns in Spain. Scarcely any but religious books, [315] and not one music seller in the whole town, which
proves how accomplished must be the female part of its 200,000 inhabitants." At the botanic garden we found Dr Bahi, the Professor and Director, "one of the best of the very few botanists now in Spain, but who

knows not even the names of half the miserable collection in his garden," and who was very thankful to us for spending an hour or two in
naming them for him. "To what a state is the science reduced in a country which could so lately boast of some of the first botanists, and which
no political calamities can ever deprive of the valuable gifts nature has
bestowed upon it." Dr Bahi was, however, an amiable man, an excellent
companion, and a very able physician; he was, at that time, scarcely
reestablished at Barcelona, after three years of persecution from the different governments which had succeeded each other in Spain.[12] Having
been the first to pronounce that the epidemic of 1822 was the yellow
fever, he brought himself the enmity of the commercial classes, whose
interests were affected by the sanitary measures. Accused of servilism
under the constitutional regime, of liberalism under the absolute government, he was obliged for two or three years to remain concealed in
the mountains of the interior, and it was only very recently that, having
at length obtained his "purification," he had been able to return and
resume his profession in Barcelona. The garden, which had never, like
that of Valentea, had the advantage of a zealous botanist,[13] had been
almost destroyed during the recent troubles, the gardeners' wages even
not having been paid during two or three years. But the health and
vigour of tender trees such as Schinus molle, Varronia alnifolia, Caesal-
pinia Sappan, Acacia [316] longifolia, A. horrida, Physalis aristata, etc,
showed what might be done in this most favored of climates. Coming
the next day from Sarria, where we had been to see the very irregular
garden of the Capuchin convent, we observed some remarkably fine
Caroubiers (Ceratonia siliqua), and measured one whose dense, dark
foliage covered a space 220 feet in circumference, with a trunk 6 feet in
diameter.

We left Barcelona on the 6th June, arriving at Gerona in the evening
just in time to witness another of the fete Dieu processions, "which,
though more decent than the Barcelona ones, still appeared extraordinary. The giant and giantess, who I hear precede these processions all
over Spain, were far less elegant than at Barcelona, the procession less
numerous, but in it were Cordeliers and Dominicans, two orders of
monks, of which there were I believe none at Barcelona, although there
were there monks of six orders. The Spanish military amused me
much—there were above a hundred officers, most probably on half pay,
though, poor fellows, it is long since they have seen a maravedi, even of
that—of so many different arms and corps that it seemed as if some collector had taken a fancy to collecting uniforms, and sent a specimen of

each to the procession. The band was very good and the two companies manoeuvred with tolerable precision, but they cut a curious figure with their threadbare coats and their caps slung behind their backs (not to be in the procession with covered heads). When the dais stopped, a band of priests sung and played on violins, and various wind and stringed instruments, music that would be good if they had but been able to keep in time and tune, the airs rather animate and profane for so devout an occasion."

[317]Returning to Perpignan, it took us two days to dry, pack up and send off for Montpellier the six or seven thousand specimens Arnott and myself had collected, and on the 10th June we started for our strictly Pyrenean exploration, taking the *tartane* up the valley to Arles (now Amélie-les-bains). This tartane, which was then the only public conveyance, was our first experience of this Spanish kind of vehicle which we found still in general use thirty years later in Valentêa and Catalonêa[14]—a covered cart on two wheels, without springs, open at both ends, with a bench along each side, holding eight or ten persons, or a few more when on four wheels and then called a *galère*. From Arles, during the remainder of our tour in the mountains, we travelled usually on foot, seldom finding carriageable roads, with one or two mules to carry our paper and provisions, and personal luggage limited to a small sac-de-nuit each. Starting at daybreak on the 11th, we soon found so much that was new to us to gather as we went along, that notwithstanding the heat and glare of a scorching sun, it was 1 p.m. when we arrived to breakfast at Prats-de-Mollo. In this pretty little town we staid two whole days, availing ourselves of the good offices of the excellent juge de paix, M. Xatard, a most intelligent and amiable man, thoroughly acquainted with the botany of the department, and who had supplied Lapeyrouse with the plants cited in his *Histoire abrégée* as from Collioure, Bagnols, and Prats de Mollo. We went through his collections, made a rich harvest of interesting plants in the mountains close around the town, and one of the days, notwithstanding a pouring rain, we dispersed in different directions in search of rarities. We sent a man to Saint-Andiol to fetch a stock of Lithospermum [318] oleaefolium, and my part was a long and arduous expedition on a mountain pony to the Bac del Fau on the Spanish side for the Anthyllis erinacea, a veritable hedge-hog a couple of feet [in] diameter, opposing its thickset formidable spines in every direction, and of which, late in the evening, I brought back a good provision.

From Prats de Mollo we sent our luggage round to Prades, and took a direct path over the Canigou, starting in the evening, in pouring rain, to sleep at the foot of the mountain in the hermitage of St Guilhen—a wretched-looking cabin, with two cavern-looking chambers on the ground floor and two small garrets above, in one of them two coarse but fairly clean beds for us four, in the other the hermit's pallet—little more than boards and straw. This little, dark, stubby man with his coarse brown attire, without any linen, [with] his long black beard and piercing eyes, had a most ferocious aspect and spoke nothing but Catalonian, but our guide being owner of the hermitage and surrounding mountains, the hermit was most attentive to us, and proud to show off his chapel and the bell, showing still the impression of Saint Guillen's hands when he took the metal hot out of the furnace and moulded it into the bell.

On the 15th, starting rather late when the rain cleared off, we crossed the mountain, which had still too much snow near the summit for the alpine plants to be in a good state, and slept at the foot of the principal summit on the North side at Cady, a shepherd's hut, where we fortunately found some straw to lie upon and plenty of wood about to keep up a fire all night outside and in. The whole of the following day was taken up by a long and rich herborisation down to Prades, [319] which was to be our headquarters for a few days. Here we met with the same cordial reception from M. Coder, which M. Xatard had given us at Prats de Mollo. M. Coder was the principal *Pharmacien* of the place, a zealous botanist who had been in active correspondence with M. de Lapeyrouse, and who gave us the means of again verifying the original specimens of many species of the *Histoire Abregée*, and by his assistance, or company in our excursions, enabled us to make the most of the richest botanical stations of the environs. At the end of four days, however, we had to part with our excellent friends and companions, Requien and Audibert, who were obliged to return home, and who had hitherto added so much to the pleasure of our expedition. Arnott and myself, after having dispatched to Montpellier the collections we had hitherto prepared, and replenished our stock of paper with some twenty reams of "papier Joseph" at 2 francs the ream, started up the valley for the higher Pyrenees, taking[§] Mont Louis as our first headquarters. Here we found our friends M. and Mde de Perrin in command of the fort, but to avoid the inconvenience of the shutting the gates at night, we established ourselves in the little village or suburb of La Cabanasse at the foot of the hill—arriving there in the middle of one of those violent thunderstorms which reverberate so grandly in the narrow valleys of the Eastern Pyrenees.

Our first grand herborisation was a three days' excursion to the Valley d'Eynes and Nouri, with a guide and a mule-load of paper. Starting very early on the 24th, "we spent the whole [320] morning in this beautiful valley, justly celebrated as one of the richest in plants of the Eastern Pyrenees, and in the afternoon crossed the high ridge of mountains which form the Spanish frontier, and descended into the picturesque and rocky vale of Nouri. This place is a large building with a church, built partly for a religious congregation, partly for the accomodation of travellers. At present it is inhabited[§] in summer only by the Curé of Queraus, and on the day of the fête of the place, hundreds of French and Spaniards flock there for diversion under the name of devotion. It was formerly rich and well stocked with all sorts of accomodation, but Mina (the guerilla general) in the last war spent there one of the coldest nights that had been known for some time. The country about was all buried in snow, no wood could be collected for fuel, and glad enough were his famished soldiers to crowd round a fire made of doors, windows, bedsteads and whatever combustible could be found in the place. Since then it has not recovered from this devastation, and we unfortunately arrived the day before the Curé, who, we had been told, was already there. Four shepherds were the only inmates, and these had amongst them for all furniture a saucepan, a frying pan, a dish, two plates, a wooden spoon, a blanket and their cloaks. We supped, however, pretty well on our own provisions, collected wood, made a good fire, wrapped ourselves in our woollen cloaks, slept on the benches fixed round one of the rooms in which the fire was in the middle, and with the exception of a little friction our bones underwent from the bare boards, slept tolerably well. The next morning we partook of the shepherds' soup, i.e., a large kettle of hot water, with a bit of lard (rancid bacon) as big as a nut, and a pinch of salt poured on bread—however our bread was white, [321] and we added a little cheese we had with us, which really made us an excellent breakfast. We then went herborising a short way down the valley, and soon met the Curé's vanguard, consisting of first a man with a gun, and two others with axes and other woodcutting utensils to open the march. If to serve as a guard, they were well chosen, for as we descended, dressed in grey, both of us in spectacles, with our canes in one hand and our dagger-knives drawn for plant gathering in the other, they were seized with such a fit of trembling, that they were nailed to the spot till they had seen us shut up our knives and pass them quietly; but not even then were they recovered, for as they told us afterwards, they trembled for an hour after they lost sight of us, though we were not two hundred

yards from Nouri. Next followed four men with pickaxes to arrange the
road for M. le Curé, for fear his horse should stumble. A quarter or half
a mile after, came the main body, consisting of the Senor Rector himself
in that delightful shabbiness and dirt of clothing which characterises the
Spanish lower clergy, with five sumpter mules, his head servant, and
three maids; last of all the rearguard consisted of four or five more
mules, with three or four men, and all this in the constant pay of a paltry
village curate."

The above is from a letter written at the time, but now at fifty years'
interval, I have the most lively recollection of the singular scenes
afforded by the two nights and intervening day at Nouri. After our
night with the shepherds, early in the morning, having to make up the
fire, and sitting round it waiting for daylight, it was curious to see these
poor wild men at their simple culinary preparations, and listen to their
[322] excited narrative of Mina's adventures and escapes in these mountains, how after repeated repulses in his attempts to break through the
French troops, having exhausted his supplies, he determined on dis-
banding his men, so as to enable them to escape individually, whilst he
himself, with a considerable body who still stuck to him, passed boldly
under the towns of Puycerda, where Baron d'Eroles, with a corps of
Royalist Spaniards, let him pass without interference, out of jealousy of
the French.[15]

After a successful botanical day, we returned at night to Nouri, and
mustering our stock of provender, we found that our three days supply
was nearly exhausted. The mountain air, the botanical excitement, the
splendid weather and scenery, had over-sharpened our appetites, and
besides our guide we had with us his dog, a splendid specimen of the
gigantic Pyrenean breed. We had expressly stipulated that he should be
left at home but the dog himself thought that he had a right to agree in
the matter and followed us in spite of his master. We would not give
him our meat, but having picked a leg of mutton bare, we threw him the
bone, which he crunched as an ordinary dog would a chicken bone, and
at last we were obliged to have some compassion on him. We therefore
"asked our Curé whether he could not supply us with a supper, and
knowing that it was in the neighbouring province of Roussillon a frequent custom for curés to treat travellers to a meal where there are no
inns, it was with some fear of giving offence that I added that we should
pay for what we took. But we were soon reassured. 'To be sure,' he
exclaimed in Catalonian, 'you will of course pay'; and of this we were
well convinced the next morning when he made us up the [323] follow-

ing bill. A pound and a half of (black) bread, one piécète (about a shilling); half a pound of rostes (dry and very salt ham fried in rancid oil), one piécète; Sopas for three (Sopas a l'aigo, like that of the shepherds but with the addition of garlic poured on our own[§], or the separately charged bread) one piécète; three bottles of Rancio (a peculiar wine of Roussillon and Catalonea, which though at first black and heavy, acquires at the end of two or three years in mountain cellars or eight or ten years in the plain, a peculiar flavour called rance, and is then a much esteemed light coloured wine) at one piécète each, three piécètes, total six piécètes; and then he added, 'You will give something to the girl for your bed.' An innkeeper would have thought himself well paid with a piécète for the whole, but we had to submit. The Curé's only answer to our objections being, 'You were very lucky to find any supper at all in these wild regions.'" The scene over the supper is another of those strongly impressed on my memory. Sitting with the Curé's attendants, male and female, round the blazing fire in the middle of the room, the talk was most animated, chiefly on local topics, the morning adventures, the fright we occasioned, etc; the three maids were all young and good-looking—one a very handsome, lively, nut brown girl, with bright black hair and large dark eyes, mingled freely in the conversation and laughter—and there was neither shyness nor unseemly boldness in any of the party. We returned to La Cabanasse by the evening of the 28th, loaded with a rich and varied Flora in more than five thousand specimens.

A week was now spent in the quiet enjoyment of the society of our friends the Perrins, in preparing the rich harvests we had made, and in short excursions on the neighbouring mountains; and early on the 3d July we started on an expedition [324] to La Seu d'Urgel and Andorra, "on foot with a man and two mules to carry our paper and baggage. Soon crossed the Col de la Perche, a low ridge which separates the two watersheds, though here the southern one is still in France, stopped at the Curé's at Saliagouse, whom we had met at Mde de Perrin's, and crossing the rich plain of Cerdagne, arrived at Bourg Madame (formerly La Guinguette) at the extreme frontier just in time to avoid a tremendous storm. As we had to cross and recross the frontiers and to encounter customhouse officers without end, we had procured a letter for the director here which we presented, but found as surly a being as could be who told us, 1st, that we must pay a duty to the French customs going out; 2d, that the Spanish douaniers would seize it all and make us pay a very heavy penalty because the entry into Spain was prohibited; and lastly we must pay duty for our plants in coming in. This alarmed us a little, but fortunately a little after appeared our good friend M. Paulet, on his return to La Seu. This M. Paulet is a French military surgeon attached to the garrison of La Seu, whom we met at table d'hote at Prades, and who offered us all assistance at La Seu, where he was now returning from a visit to Perpignan. He told us he would go with us, so that we had nothing to fear, and on the whole, now that we are returned to France, I may say that we could not have got rid of all duty more cleverly. We avoided the export duty by starting before the bureau was open in the morning. We did not see the face of a Spanish douanier till we got to the gate of La Seu, and they dared not speak on seeing the French uniform. Coming out of La Seu, they asked what we carried, to which our man replied, 'Ce sont des medecins Français et cela ne vous regarde pas,' upon which they bowed and took their leave, and coming into France, the weather was not very good and though [325] we have passed through six 'postes de douane,' nobody has put us a single question.

"Bourg Madame is just under the Spanish town of Puycerda, a large but sad looking place at the edge of an eminence, from whence is a beautiful view over French and Spanish Cerdagne. This town of Puycerda is furnished with water by a channel derived from the French river of Carol which is rather awkward for the inhabitants, to depend on a foreign nation for water, and gets them sometimes into scrapes, as for instance the other day, on the occasion of the fête, they got into a quarrel with those of Carrol who had come to the dancing, and who, after some exchange of blows, escaped with difficulty out of the town. In revenge they turned off the water, and it is only now that the affair is pretty well made up and their water restored to them.

"Monday, 4th. A long and tedious walk over a stony road, down the hot valley of the Segre, brought us to La Seu d'Urgel, a distance of near 40 miles or perhaps more. At first we crossed the Spanish Cerdagne, a broad and rich plain inclining to the south and encircled with mountains, which renders it burning in summer but exposed to storms and cold in winter. Here we recognised many of our southern plants with others new to us, particularly after we entered the closer part of the valley, a little above Bellver. From hence to Le Martinet where we got a good breakfast, through St Vincent, where are hot springs and baths, and to a couple of miles above La Seu, the road winds up and down along the bottom of a wild romantic valley, the steep, rocky sides often crowned with wood, the torrent gushing down the bottom, which is scarcely ever wide enough to admit of a few fields and meadows.

Nearer La Seu the hills get clothed with vineyards, and [326] still lower the hills open into a little plain covered with fields and orchards, rich by nature, but sadly neglected by man. At one extremity of this plain at the foot of the hills is the famous town of La Seu d'Urgel, and a little further on, at the mouth of the river of the Vallée d'Andorre, is Castelciutat, at the foot of the forts of La Seu which sustained the different sieges. The town of La Seu cannot be held for a moment; the inhabitants always fled to the forts or to Andorra and left their town to be ransacked by the besiegers, so that its houses are many of them in a sad state. It has walls and gates, which are shut every night pro formâ, but I am sure I could knock them down with my fist. The forts are stronger, but much beneath their reputation; they are commanded by the surrounding hills as the Spaniards found to their cost in the last war. The French, with great expense and trouble it is true, brought cannon over the mountains out of sight of the forts to the hills just above, and raised their batteries with so much secrecy that the Spaniards never dreamt of the possibility of such a thing, till one morning they were saluted with a shower of bombs, and on looking up, to their horror and surprise saw a well-dressed battery just above them, which of course caused the immediate surrender of the whole set of forts. There is now in this town a battalion of French infantry and the inhabitants are perfectly quiet and amicable to them, but whether from good will or from terror is more doubtful here than at Barcelona. We stopped in an inn, if it may be dignified with that name, kept by a Frenchman come for the purpose, and eat with the Officers who have their *pension* there. Our food you may suppose was coarse, and beds—or rather bed, for one of us slept on the floor, indifferent, yet with all that they charged us pretty high, and on the whole I see little to tempt travellers to go to La Seu d'Urgel."

[327]We staid four days at La Seu, making several excursions, though much inconvenienced by the daily storms. One very long and arduous one to the summit of Mount Cady, from whence is said to be a splendid view over the plains of Catalonêa, but unfortunately we became envelopped in clouds and could see nothing, and had to make the best of our way back with a violent thunderstorm following us. "During our stay we found two of our *commensaux*, M. Paulet and M. Fougeray, head military surgeon, very civil and obliging. We had also an opportunity of judging of Spanish music. Opposite our inn was the cathedral, where singing with the organ was going forward every day from about 7 to 9 in the morning, and from 2 to 7 in the afternoon§. Next door is the Spanish town hall, on the ground floor of which is the prison. The gendarmes

to guard the prisoners had leave to sleep above; they wear no arms nor uniform, and were almost all day at the balconies so constant to all Spanish windows, in their singular Catalonian dresses, playing on the guitar or tambourine and singing, sometimes solos sometimes in chorus, the same air over and over again, and apparently the same note, which might I think be noted thus: [musical notation] and nothing more, only varying in the degree of intonation from loud to very loud. Both these kinds of music, well enough for a minute or two, got at last so tiresome that they seem to be still ringing in my ears. The dress at La Seu is Catalonian as well as the language, but neither of them so elegant as on the east coast. Women wear generally the handkerchief and capuchon, but often without the fine rêt[16] worn in Cerdaigne. The men [wear] the red cap, short jacket, red or tartan sash, short breeches, stockings with the feet cut out, only a strap passing under the middle of the sole, spadilles, a sort of sandal made of pack thread, and a cloak. The real Catalonian one is a piece of tartan or carpeting, very much like [328] coarse Scotch scarfs, perhaps a little longer and broader. This they sometimes throw over one shoulder and under the other and round the waist, sometimes folded over one shoulder, and when it rains, over their heads to protect their red caps. There are also other cloaks of so many sizes, shapes and dimensions that it would be difficult to describe them.

"Friday, 8th July. Leaving La Seu, the Spaniards at the gate asked for our passports, but they could not read them, so they returned them with a bow. Soon after appeared the customhouse people, whom we sent about their business, and a little after we entered the valley of Andorra—happy land in as much as it is plagued with no such nuisances as customs and excise—happy land of liberty as some would say, but I fear its happiness extends not much farther. Wild and unproductive by nature, it is but little improved by Art, and if it still enjoys its liberty it is because it is beneath the notice of its neighbours. If it pays no customs or other duties it is because it cannot afford it; indeed it is only by the commercial privileges the inhabitants enjoy that they can earn their livelihood, and with that benefit even, they are all, as I am told, miserably poor. And from their appearance I believe it! The first entrance into the valley is by a narrow passage between impassable rocks; in one place, indeed, one of these projects so far over the torrent that the narrow road has been cut through it. There at least (the *easiest* pass into the valley) a handful of men might easily repel all invading armies who may be tempted to intrude. After winding some time through these savage passes, a Virgin-Mary stuck up every here and there to protect travellers and to receive their adoration in return, the valley broadens and divides, and the village of St Julin, the most civilised of the valley, appears in all its grim and black splendour, for even the hovels of some of the Newcastle suburbs are white in comparison; the outside of the houses from the colour of the stone, a black schist like the surrounding rocks, the inside from the [329] eternal smoke of the fires they use as candles. Here we began our Andorra fare, *rost* (fried ham) and eggs, eggs and rost. Fortunately we had stocked ourselves at La Seu with white bread. The nine loaves we bought from thence, a loaf we found at St Julin, half a loaf at Canillo and one at La Massane, all there was in the valley, lasted our six days, till we got once more into France. From St Julin, another wild pass brought us into another little plain in which are the several villages of St Colomb, Andorra, St Andrea, Las Caldas, etc, all in a semicircle, with houses towering one above the other, all black as pitch, with high rocky mountains rising above them, and vieing with them in blackness. We stopped at Andorra, the capital, asked for an inn, were directed to the best, but there was no bed—at the other one we found one consisting of a paillasse, which seemed stuffed with iron, with a pair of sheets woven with packthread, and a blanket that could scarcely be distinguished from them in texture or colour. However the sheets were washed, and as a farther precaution we kept on the greater part of our clothes, and though the first nights we were sadly cut by the coarse sheets, we at last slept very soundly. Habit reconciles one almost to anything."

Food was another difficulty. The only butcher of the place was just returned from a smuggling expedition, most of the men of the place were absent on similar "voyages," and the butcher did not care to kill meat which he could not hope to sell off whilst it remained sweet. However he agreed to kill a kid for us, on condition that we took the whole, and with this we had to be satisfied during our stay. We had with us a fine saucisson d'Arles, which we had kept as a resource when reduced to such straits. We laid it out on the table [330] for our first Andorra dinner, when suddenly a great tom cat jumps up, seizes upon it, and carries it in a moment far out of our reach.

"On arriving at Andorra we enquired for the curé Doria, a relative of Cardinal Doria, to whom the curé of Saliagouse had given us a letter, but found that he had mistaken his friend's place of residence. We had passed him at St Julin, and it was not worth returning, so we had only to prepare for a mountain excursion the next day.

"Saturday, 9th July. At 5 a.m. started for the Pic de Casemaigne, a high mountain projecting in the centre of the valley. From Andorra, turned up another wild and narrow pass of about four miles, winding along a narrow road with high rocks clothed with underwood towering above us, a precipice below with a torrent gushing along the bottom, the dark colour of the rocks and the short time the sun appears in the depth of these gorges adding to their savage wildness. A little higher the valley opens, and disclosing to our sight the encircling mountains, induced us to alter our course and direct our steps to Port Nègre, as the Casemaigne did not look so promising. We accordingly stopped to breakfast at Massane, where an old man, in a little black hovel called an inn, furnished us with a few eggs fried in rancid oil and a bottle of sour wine; but as we had a good luncheon on our backs we contented ourselves with a poor breakfast, ascended the mountain, spent the day in the alpine regions about Coumallemps, gathered a good many plants, though we found nothing new, and descended in the evening to Andorra, after a walk like those of some other days of between 40 and 50 miles.

"Sunday, 10th, was spent at Andorra, arranging the day before's plants amidst a crowd of mowers and reapers looking on in wonder [331] and now and then with rather troublesome curiosity. The crops in Andorra do not appear too extensive for the inhabitants to reap them themselves, but either they are too lazy, or prefer the smuggling trade, for almost all is reaped by men who come for the purpose from the more populous districts of the Arriège. This being Sunday, they had nothing to do but to idle away their time at the inn over a bottle of wine, and finally spread themselves on the floor and snored away in chorus, eighteen or twenty of them together.

"Monday, 11th. Bid adieu to Andorra, and ascending the eastern branch of the valley, passed through a less romantic but richer and more populous district to Canillo, where we breakfasted, and thence to Saldeu, which we had fixed upon as a sleeping place, on the faith of the assurances of our guide who told us we should find there, so near the French frontier, anything we pleased. The first thing we asked for on arriving at the poor, miserable hamlet was beds, and it was only at the last house that we found one; the poor woman of the house professed to keep an inn, and with some difficulty procured us an old cock which she stewed, and a bottle of milk. This, with three quarters of our last loaf, made us a tolerable supper for three, and our bed was really better than at Andorra, but our bill amounted to no less than six piécétes (shillings). This was our last day in this 'land of liberty and ease,' which I longed to see and which I am very glad to have crossed, though our botanical harvest is less abundant than we expected, and than it might have been, had we been able to profit of the experience of predecessors. But we seem to have been preceded by one botanist only, who has left in the country a recollection which will not be easily effaced. [332] Like us, he spent a few days at Andorra and a night at Saldeu, but it seems he visited more mountains and perhaps gathered more plants. Any future visitors might do more by establishing their headquarters at Canillo, which is at the foot of Casemaigne, and contrarily to our first opinion should explore this mountain and the Pics of Astagnon, Serrerre and others above it and, securing a better stock of provisions, one might live I think at Canillo with much less inconvenience than we experienced at Andorra.

"The account I read at home, in the *Annales des Voyages* of the Vallée d'Andorre, is, as far as I recollect, pompous and exaggerated.[17] The inhabitants are *free*, and as a sign of it have in each village, as high and straight a mast as they have been able to find, with a branching top crowned by a red cap or pompon. They pay neither customs nor taxes, and consequently their valley serves as the entrepôt of the various goods smuggling continually between France and Spain, but all this renders them but little more at their ease and but little more civilised than their Spanish neighbours. They are very devout and superstitiously attached to the minutious parts of the Catholic ceremonies, at least a great proportion of the inhabitants are so, and this spirit is kept up as strictly as can be by their sovereign lords and masters the Curés, who are here everything. It is they who profit by the only contributions paid by their parishioners, it is they who decide without appeal any quarrel which may arise amongst the inhabitants of their village. There are mayors at St Julin and Andorra, but I could not well learn what are their functions; they themselves seem to be governed by the Curés, and these in their turn depend solely on the Bishop of Seu d'Urgel, who is consequently the real [333] sovereign of the valley. The valley has the privilege of securing from the hand of justice all those who can escape into it, be their crimes civil or political, but of neither class do there appear to be many at present; the former can live with more profit in the heart of Spain, and also with more security in the midst of the organised Spanish police than in the neighbourhood of the French Gendarmerie, the latter are scarcely even here really out of the reach of the revengeful avidity of the Spanish Government and clergy.

"Leaving Saldeu on the morning of Tuesday 12th July, we ascended to

the head of the valley and over the port of Francseuil, stopped to breakfast at a little cabin near one of the sources of the Ariège, and inhabited
by a man who has the superintendence of a neighbouring iron mine. He
furnished us with ham, eggs and French wine, on which we made a good
breakfast, though we were obliged to put up with black bread after
gnawing the dry crust we still had of our own. We had intended to visit
here some high rocks which looked good, but mist[§] came on and, though
we had a good guide, we were afraid of venturing amongst them and
started at a good round pace for Bourg Madame, crossed the Port de
Puymorent and descended to the French Vallée de Carrol, passed by
Porté, stopped at Porta, where we made a good luncheon, on new white
bread, and descending the valley through a number of rich villages,
inhabited by few besides smugglers and custom-house officers, with
storms raging all round us but treating us only with their outskirts,
arrived at 6 at Bourg Madame, after another walk of above forty miles.
During the last ten or fifteen miles we passed through six brigades of
douaniers, and not one of them asked what our mules carried. It is true
our packets [334] of paper showed pretty well that we were botanists,
but then we might have had something contraband also, as was really
the case, for as a remembrance of Spain we brought a red cap a piece, and
a pair of *spardilles* from Andorra. This chaussure is very comfortable for
a long walk; I wore mine a whole day, and found much benefit from
them, but was obliged to discontinue them, because in the evening when
I took them off, I found that the soles of my socks had entirely disappeared. We had also a few pounds of chocolate, which I had bought at La
Seu. These three are the chief articles smuggled through this route from
Spain into France. The Roussillonais attach great importance to wearing
red caps of true Spanish manufacture, and rags [are] the chief article
exported in return, as well as the one of which the export is the most
strictly prohibited. Paper and rags for making it are very scarce in Spain,
and in France, I suppose, they are afraid of their becoming so there also,
from the importance they attach to them. Smuggling is here very much
favored by the manner in which the frontiers are marked out. Livia
belongs to Spain and is surrounded by French territory, which obliges a
free road to be left betwixt it and Puycerda. This is said to have been a
contrivance of some rich ecclesiastic here in the time of Louis XIV, for the
express purpose of favoring smugglers."

From another letter written at the time describing our night at Saldeu,
of which I have still the most vivid recollection, I find that on arriving
there we learnt that there was no inn, and the Curé had no bed to spare,

and it was with some difficulty that we found out the old woman who sometimes gave lodging to smugglers, and supplied us with the above-mentioned supper—but when showed our bed we found it to be precisely [335] that in common use by the Andorra peasantry, a great sack made of dried, untanned sheepskins with the wool inside, into which the Andorrains insinuate themselves undressed. This we could not do, but luckily our hostess had a large sheet in which we could enclose the sack and lie down in our clothes outside. I learnt also on further enquiry that, although the trumpery articles abovementioned were the principal ones smuggled through the Valley of Andorra, there pass here also, as over other passes in the Pyrenees, leeches, cork, a little tobacco, and occasionally a few piastres, in exchange for mules, and a few articles of luxury, besides the rags supplied to Spain by France.

On the 13th we were back at Montlouis, where I found letters which induced me to leave Arnott to fulfil our engagements with the Perrins, and I went down to Perpignan to spend a day with the Bréas, to meet the whole family of our friends the Partouneaux. We were a large party at dinner, the cookery very refined, but a dish very much relished by the ladies as well as the men, which I tried in vain to enjoy, was a large bowl of snails, served after the roast, and which they picked out of the shells with Gleditshia thorns.

Leaving Montlouis definitively on the 19th July for the higher Pyrenees, and sleeping at the little village of Le Pla, we made a good herborisation the next day in crossing the Port de Paillères, adjoining the chain of the Llaureati, well known to Pyrenean botanists. Detained three days at Ax we took the first diligence down to Foix, after our first tussle with douaniers. They wanted to stop our paper, and could not or would not understand that it was paper bought in France and for botanical [336] purposes. They seemed even disposed to pay little attention to my threat of appealing to the Prefet of Foix, and, if necessary, to the Directeur Général at Paris, till one of the employés, who had been at Montpellier when our English articles were passed by a special order from Paris, recognised me, and the Official got frightened, and released us and our paper with humble apologies. From Foix we went up on the 25th to Saint Girons, and early the next morning up to breakfast at Castillon, to prepare for crossing the Crabère. In this rich and populous valley we expected to find every facility for exploring the mountains to advantage, but we had a number of petty obstacles to get over. In the first place it was market day and every one was too busy to attend to us; then the gendarmes, always suspecting some secret object, were scarcely prevailed on to consent to our crossing the mountains instead of taking the high road to St Béat; then about our provisions, we got a fine leg of mutton, which we had put on the spit, but the cook insisted on inserting a couple of slips of garlick, which my friend Arnott could not bear, and though she yielded at last, yet we found that she had secretly slipped in a small piece—otherwise she afterwards said we could not possibly have eaten it. But the great difficulty of all was a mule to carry our paper and effects, and a guide, and we were about to give it all up when our landlord agreed to let us have his own mule, notwithstanding the lamentations of his family, who thought their dear animal would come to grief among the rocks and embraced it most tenderly in bidding it the last adieus. The muleteer to whom it was entrusted did not know the mountains we had to cross, but at Sentem, higher up the valley, procured us a guide who assured us he well knew the paths over to Melles, and that they [337] were frequently travelled on mules. We planned our day, therefore, so as to sleep in a large cabane, built on the crest of Chichoy, or Sissoy, as a post of observation during the last war. But after the first ascent, we found how much we had been deceived as to the case of the paths; they ascended so rapidly among the rocks and woods that we had frequently to unload the mule, carry the packages on our shoulders, and help the mule by the head and tail over the mauvais pas. These portages occasioned so much delay, that on issuing from the woods night overtook[§] us, near a little abandoned hut called *Rougé*, about five feet square, built without mortar and nothing inside but large stones to lie upon. Here however, making a large fire outside, we had a few hours sound sleep, and started again at 3 in the morning; and after a few small portages found the path much improved, had the men and the mule wait for us at Chichoy, and spent the day in a very satisfactory herborisation among the rocky peaks of Crabère. At 4 p.m. we rejoined our guides and started for Melles, but soon the portages recommenced and, arriving at 5 at the top of the pass of Bassiouhé, our guide declared we had come to the end of his commune and he knew nothing of the way further on, and a shepherd told us that from there to Melles it was impracticable for mules and very difficult for pedestrians. The mule was nearly knocked up, and the muleteer quietly unloaded him and returned to Chichoy, leaving us with our luggage on this alpine pass, where we could hardly pass the night without any hut, fire or supper. Some shepherds about there declined at any price to carry our packages down to [338] Melles, some fifteen miles distant, so we had nothing to do but to deposit our paper at the entrance of the woods and to hoist the rest on our shoulders. Arnott took charge of the knapsack, the tin boxes and plant *cartables*. I had for my share carpet bags, which I ascertained afterwards to weigh sixty pounds, and our guide, the cause of all our difficulties, could be scarcely prevailed on to take half that weight. The precipitous paths were rendered most formidable by the ravages of a violent storm a few days before, and it was only at half past eight that we at length landed at Melles. From hence, a young woman agreed to fetch our paper for the sum of two francs, would not accept of any assistance, and after six or seven hours returned with a weight of nearly a hundred and fifty pounds on her head.

From Melles we went to Saint Béat, where we spent three days going through the herbarium of M. Marchand, a Pharmacien, who had supplied M. de Lapeyrouse with a considerable number of the plants described in the *Histoire Abrégée*, and were enabled to verify a number of supposed species which we should otherwise have been at a loss to guess at; amongst others, Potamogeton bifolium, for instance, had been a great puzzle to us. M. Marchand showed us the typical specimen, which he had found floating on a pond, and therefore presumed to be a Potamogeton, and sent it as such to M. Lapeyrouse, who published it as a new species without seeing any flowers;[18] a close investigation proved it to be a young bean plant which had been accidentally thrown into the pond with kitchen garden weeds.

We spent the first ten days of August at Bagnères de Luchon, and two more at Bagnères de Bigorre—much in the society of friends [339] and acquaintance we met at these watering places—not abstaining from evening dances, but we also made two very good botanical excursions, one of three days over the port de Benasque round the foot of the Maladetta to the town of Benasque and back, another of two days to the Esquierry, where we slept in a shepherd's hut, and over the Port d'Oo and by the lakes back to Luchon. At Bagnères de Bigorre our leavetaking of the Pyrenees was a picnic party to the cascades de Grip with the Klustine family, whose society and champagne detained us to the last moment, when we galloped down to Bigorre just in time for the Toulouse diligence. Two days at Toulouse gave us time to look through much of Lapeyrouse's herbarium, which the son showed us with pride as "les pièces justificatives de l'ouvrage de Papa"—making us rather ashamed of detecting Papa's blunders. Nothing, however, could make M. Isidore, as a dutiful son, believe in the possibility of his father's ever having been mistaken. In his lectures, if he came to a disputed point in botany, he would say, "Jussieu was of such an opinion, De Candolle thought so and so, Papa however believed the fact to be so and so; *moi, je suis de l'avis de Papa"*—and certainly we could not have found it in our hearts to disabuse him.

On the 19th August we were back at Montpellier. Arnott left us very soon after, and about the middle of September I paid another short visit with my father to our friends at Toulouse. The remainder of the autumn and winter was spent, like the preceding ones, chiefly on our estate at Restinclières, partly in society at Montpellier, and in botany, in working up our Pyrenean collections, and preparing my *Catalogue des Plantes des Pyrenees et du Bas Languedoc*.

7

Return to England, 1826–27

[340] In the course of the spring of 1826 various domestic complications arose. My eldest sister was induced to return to her husband, who she vainly hoped had reformed his ways, and was living quietly with his mother at Pompignan, my two younger sisters were getting restless and longing for a more genial life at Paris or in England. We had seen a great deal of our friends the Dax's in Montpellier and I had again become entangled with my attachment to Emma Dax, and negociations for our marriage were far advanced; a compromise was entered into as to our separate religions; there were still only some little difficulties about settlements, which however might easily have been got over. But at the same time some disagreables arose relating to our property. Some of the little neighbouring proprietors showed signs of jealousy at my father's success in some of the measures he had taken to improve its value, and raised an outcry that by digging for springs he would drain off, or at any rate diminish, the supply of water in the Source de St Clement (two or three miles from our estate), which supplied the town of Montpellier. The Prefet, M. Creusé de Lessert (who never forgot his old grudge against my father for being too forward in organising aid to the poor of Angouleme during the famine of 1816) was very ready to take action, and fulminated an edict or *Arrêté* at my father, forbidding him to search for springs on his estate.[1] My father's only remedy was an appeal to the minister at Paris. He began also to have a longing to

see once more his old friends in England, and it was thought that arrangements might easily be there made for my settlements. It was accordingly [341] determined that, although I was formally accepted as Mlle Dax's futur, no final arrangements should be made till after our visit to England, but that on our return in the autumn I should natura- lise myself as a Frenchman, which would, it was hoped, do away with the prejudices against us foreigners, and settle permanently as one of the propriétaires of the country. We started in the beginning of July, my father and my youngest sister Sarah and myself, travelling en poste, stopping a day at Lyons, where I went to see Seringe at the botanic gar- den, and a few days at Paris, where my father readily obtained the reversal of M. Creusé de Lessert's arrêté. From Paris, travelling all night, we were 36 hours posting to Calais and, crossing to Dover the next morning, arrived in London on 3d August, stopping temporarily at a hotel in Covent Garden.

Our first object was to see how matters stood with my Uncle, with whom my father, besides the renewal of the strongest attachment, had some family matters to arrange, relating to my future prospects. We had understood he was at Harrogate, and had been disappointed at not hearing from him at Paris (his letter had been written but forgotten to be posted till too late), so while my father went to seek out old friends, I went down to Queen Square Place for letters and, to my surprise, found my Uncle there; "he immediately came down to see me, embraced me very affectionately, and at a quick pace walked with me for half an hour round the garden, notwithstanding the rain, for which he took no umbrella, saying he was not made of salt. I found him exceedingly friendly and, after saying much of the value of his time and how it was wholly taken up even after dinner with his writings, he said that he would [342] nevertheless devote a whole afternoon to us, that we must come on Sunday and dine there, when he would take a turn round the garden alone with his brother and then spend the evening with us three."[2] I spent the next morning with the young men at my Uncle's; "R. Doane does now little for him except attendance to some of his personal wants, copies for him no longer but occasionally writes letters for him, and, for himself, has been for some time studying the law. My uncle has also with him Jack Colls, the same foolish, silly lad that ever he was, but who serves the purpose of a mechanical copyist perfectly well—and a very intelligent, clever American from New England, or Yankee, as he calls himself out of pride, and others call him in derision. The Yankees are, properly speaking, inhabitants of the six New England States who

are generally supposed, or suppose themselves, to be more gifted in the
way of intelligence, learning, litterature and civilisation in general than
their countrymen from the remainder of the United States. In England
the term Yankee is used in the same manner as one would those of
North American savage or Wild Irishman. This particular Yankee,
whose name is John Neal, certainly gives a favorable idea of his nation.
A great flow of words and a sort of restless activity in his manner might,
indeed, justify to a certain degree the attribution of wildness to his
nation, but it certainly is only in his exterior, for his mind is well furnished. When in America, he wrote several novels, a good deal read
there, but rather low in the scale here, but he has lately written one
(*Brother Jonathan*), reckoned a very good picture of Yankee manners. His
articles are also much prized by the editors of various Magazines.[3] At
my Uncle's, he is at work at the Penal [343] Code, and it is this that they
do together in the evenings after dinner.

"Mill, Place, etc, still keep up regular, though not frequent, intercourse with my Uncle, and Bowring, to the regret of all his other friends,
still retains the same command over the whole of my Uncle's actions,
and which power he has the art to preserve by the grossest flattery and
the most egregious nonsense and stories that he makes my Uncle swallow. This man has succeeded in getting a hand in a number of undertakings (chiefly by my Uncle's means) and has the knack of spoiling
whatever he puts his finger into. The Greek Committee is doing nothing
because Bowring is Secretary. The *Westminster Review* is going to the
dogs—because Bowring is Editor,[4] and so it is of every thing, whilst the
said Bowring is securing to himself a comfortable fortune, and my Uncle
is spending his to keep up Bowring's undertakings."

John Neal, the American above alluded to, remained with my Uncle
till the following spring when, various arrangements having been broken off in consequence of disagreements with Bowring,[5] he returned
home, and on the day of his departure I wrote as follows: "I am very sad
today from Neal's departure, so you must not be surprised if what I
write is a little tainted with my sadness. Ever since I began writing regularly at Queen Square Place, I had always sat in the room with Neal and
found him such an excellent, good-hearted, friendly, affectionate fellow
that I had become exceedingly intimate, and it is with no little pain that I
have separated from him, never to meet again. He has been fifteen
months with my Uncle, at first on a scheme for managing a Panopticon
in America, then at work for my Uncle on his Penal Code,[6] etc, undertakings which he entered into in the belief that my Uncle and Bowring

were very rich and could [344] afford to be liberal—but my Uncle's were mere schemes, which Bowring encouraged for flattery sake only, and for which he made arrangements with Neal as if from Jeremy Bentham. Neal, after having devoted his whole time to my Uncle for seven or eight months, perceived that my Uncle was unable to carry such projects into execution, so he immediately applied himself to writing a novel to get some money. This he lately finished, but has not succeeded in selling. He has been disappointed, too, in a translation he had been led by Bowring (as from Jeremy Bentham) into engaging to do, and from which agreement Bentham and Bowring are now off, so that in fact poor Neal has been dreadfully ill used, and is now going off to spend three weeks in Paris and then return to America, with scarcely a farthing in his pocket. He had been induced to borrow £25 of my Uncle through Bowring, but as this was made to appear as Bowring's lending, and as that was very humiliating to Neal after the ill usage he had met with from Bowring, I have induced my father to lend him the £25, and he has repaid Bowring. . . . This morning, as I have already mentioned, Doane and I accompanied Neal to the Custom house stairs and saw him off on the steamboat for Calais. He was exceedingly affected at leaving England and parting with his friends, as he felt he should not return, and that notwithstanding his eagerness to return home."[7]

John Neal returned to his native town, Portland in Maine, and there soon got into profitable business as a lawyer and newspaper editor.[8] When I handed him over the £25, I had little expectation of repayment and, like all loans to friends, I set it down as a gift; but $not many months had elapsed, when I received from him a bill sufficient to repay not only that £25 but various little debts amounting [345] in the aggregate to above twice as much, to the no small surprise of the various creditors who had marked off as hopeless debts due from an absent Yankee. Neal afterwards published in America an edition of a part of Jeremy Bentham's Legislative works,[9] translated or abstracted from Dumont's editions, with an excellent pen-and-ink portrait, taken by an American who sat opposite to him one day at dinner. Of this work Neal sent me a copy, which I afterwards lent to a friend, who unfortunately forgot to return it, and died whilst I was abroad. Neal acquired, in several respects, considerable reputation in his own country, judging from a short obituary notice I met with after his death in 1876. I had personally not heard from him for the last forty years.

Sunday, Aug. 6th. The afternoon at my Uncle's came off very satisfactorily. The meeting of the two brothers after twelve years "was very affecting, both of them laughing with pleasure, yet with tears in their eyes, which does not happen often to Jeremy Bentham. They took a turn together round the garden, we then dined all together *down stairs*, and after dinner my father and my uncle were for hours together in the garden, talking over old stories."

A few days were now spent in renewing old acquaintances; we went also, all three, for a couple of nights to Kidbrooke, Lord Colchester's place in Surrey. The family was alone, Lord and Lady C. and their two sons; we had a very pleasant day driving, amongst other things, to see the ruins of Brambletye House, then very interesting on account of the recently published novel of H. Smith's,[10] then very popular, and my father had long consultations [346] about future plans and prospects with Lord C. then, as he always had been, his most intimate, confidential friend and most usefull adviser, and on our return to town my father had another day at his brother's. The result was, to me, a long and serious discussion with my father, ending in a total subversion of all my own plans and chateaux en Espagne. I do not know whether my father, although he agreed willingly to my intended marriage, had not planned this journey to England in the hopes of something occurring to break it off, but he certainly now, fortified by the result of his interviews with his brother and with Lord Colchester, who had always been a brother to him, put forward very strong arguments derived from pecuniary circumstances, which would prevent the settlements which Made Dax had agreed should be a condition upon which the completion of the affair should depend—and from the previously urged considerations of difference of religion, country, etc. I was most grievously disappointed, for I believed Miss D. was the person to make my future life happy, and the other objections were but the necessary consequences of the investment of our whole property in the French estate—but my father put it all in a light which forced me to yield and, after a day or two's painful hesitation, I determined to give up France and a French wife, and remain permanently in England. The necessary letter to Made Dax was very difficult to write, for I felt I was greatly in the wrong, both towards mother and daughter, in going so far and then backing out, and a reproachful answer from the mother greatly encreased my distress at the time. Mlle Dax, however, though I heard she was much affected, behaved very well, continued her friendly correspondence with my sisters, and the following spring [347] was induced to marry a countryman, a gentleman admirably suited to her in person, as well as in position. Some four years later,[11] I saw her with two fine little children, much happier than she ever would have been with me; and, as for myself, much as I was cast down by the disappointment, as also by the reflection that all our labour at Restinclières and money spent for the last five years was thrown away, yet I afterwards saw that my future in the south of France, with all the social and political disturbances which supervened, would have debarred me from much of the happiness I have enjoyed in after life.

When all the arrangements connected with this painful affair were concluded, we left my sister with her friends at Hampstead, and my father and myself went down to Derby to his old friend Mr Strutt; his son (the present Lord Belper) and his three daughters were there. The eldest, however, owing to a nervous illness never appeared, and Mr and Mrs Howard Galton with their three boys being at her father's, Mr Joseph Strutt's, a good deal of dinner and archery parties, etc, was going on. After three or four very pleasant days, I left my father there and returned to town, taking lodgings in Warwick Street, Pall Mall, to be near my Uncle's. I expected to have to go shortly over to Paris, and I took advantage of the interval to collect some notes on Medicagos and Cistus's still wanting for my *Catalogue* of Pyrenean plants, the manuscript of which I had brought with me from France. I spent a couple of mornings with Robert Brown and Joseph Sabine, but London then afforded no resources for botanical researches. Lambert being in the country, his herbarium was closed, the British Museum had no public herbarium, and the Linnean Library was very scanty. I was more fortunate at the Horticultural garden, where I spent a day with Dr (then [348] Mr) Lindley, with whom I then contracted that intimacy which lasted till his death. I also collected some information at Chelsea Garden, where old Anderson cultivated a considerable herbaceous collection. I spent the evening either with my sisters' friends at Hampstead—chiefly the Carrs—or sometimes at the theatres, specially amused with the original *Paul Pry*, then in full vogue.[12]

The moment our remaining in England was decided upon, my father wrote to my mother relating to the arrangements to be made for leaving Restinclières, and we were now waiting her reply before fixing the time for my going over to Paris to meet her, when on the 21st Augt I received a letter from her, to say that immediately on receiving the intelligence, she determined to come over at once with my sister Clara, and was now actually as far as Toulouse on her way here. I wrote directly to ask my father to come to town to settle matters before I left for Paris and, in the mean time, made another effort to see the Cistineae, etc, of Lambert's

Herbarium, and this time with better success, for David Don had just returned.[13] I found in the herbarium many interesting and scarce Cistineae, but of Medicagos, whilst I had some half a hundred species, Lambert had barely half a dozen.

Early on the 23d my father returned from his most enjoyable visit to the Strutts, and I prepared to start that evening, leaving my father and sister Sarah in lodgings at Hampstead, but in those days passports required various signatures; "mine was promised me for this morning, but red-tapeism interfered and notwithstanding all my exertions, I was put off 'till tomorrow' for no reason given." I had to submit, and it was only the following evening that I could leave [349] by the Dover coach, which then took about twelve hours. It was "a sort of lame imitation of French diligences, that is they had clapped on a coupé in front but, mistaking them in other respects, they had hung the body on six points instead of four, so that the two middle springs were either of no use, or tended to break the carriage asunder. It is astonishing what strange blunders are still made in a country where all mechanical science is carried to so high a degree of perfection. It is the same with Lord Cochrane's steamboats. The Greek Committee confided the building them to a stupid engineer, so that there are now six or seven lying in the Thames that have cost immense sums of money and of which the machinery is so bad that it won't work."[14]

I had a beautiful passage on the 25th August just twelve years since we had first crossed the channel, and going on by the malleposte, arrived in Paris early on the Sunday morning, finding my mother and sister at the Hotel Vauban, where they had arrived a few days previously. Here we remained a week; already on the day of my arrival I had communicated with Made Huzard (the principal Agricultural bookseller and publisher, and wife of M. Huzard, a then well-known scientific Veterinary surgeon) and the following "Monday morning, I gave my *Catalogue* to her printers. I had all the proofs of the text by the Saturday night, and without anything like the number of faults I might have expected. I wrote, during this week's stay at Paris, the Preface and account of the journey[15] (except a few pages finished and sent from Calais), which I assure you was hard work, considering that I had a great deal of going about the town for commissions, besides the time I spent going over [350] some of the principal herbaria (chiefly M. Delessert's and the Jardin) for the genera Cistus, Helianthemum and Medicago. Among the botanists I saw this time, I was most with Guillemin, a friend of Arnott's and Conservator of M. Delessert's herbarium. He is a very obliging young man, and seems to be proof-corrector general to the principal botanists. He corrects all Decandolle's and Delessert's, and is now doing the same for Achille Richard; he set into French and corrected Arnott's paper on mosses,[16] and has undertaken to look over the revise of my work, and both proofs and revise of the Preface. In this he renders me a great service, for he saves me the trouble and expense of having them sent over to London. I saw Bosc two or three times and looked over some of the plants both in the garden (of the Luxembourg) and in its herbarium. He is going on well now. Before he was named to the garden, it was quite painful to see the poor man in an obscure lodging in the Rue des Maçons, obliged to work so hard with his pen (at scientific works,[17] the least profitable of all) to support a large family of daughters and give them anything like an education. Now he has a handsome apartment in the garden, and [is] enabled to live at comparative ease and procure masters of all kinds for his daughters.

"I called once or twice on Bossange, the printer of my *Scopées* (*Essai sur la Nomenclature et la Classification*, etc), and received some three hundred francs from what has been sold, towards paying the expences. Bossange offered to exchange the 500 copies that remain for books of his catalogue of equal value. This I caught at eagerly, glad to get anything for a mass of copies I knew not what to do with, but when I came to select from his catalogue 3500 francs worth (my book being set down at 5 francs) of books, I found it impossible without burdening myself with a quantity of works I had no occasion for, or which are already in our library; [351] so now I have left all in statu quo." On my return, however, to England, several of my friends were very glad of an opportunity of getting French books at a reasonable price, booksellers then charging generally two shillings per franc [so] that I readily realised the £100.

During these few days, I went once with my sister to the Opéra comique to see the *Dame Blanche*, which was then at the heighth of its popularity, but which did not quite come up to our expectations—and had only time to see a few friends, amongst others that "best and kindest of all friends possible, Made Partouneaux." General Partouneaux was then in command of the Ecole Militaire, and from his windows overlooking the Champ de Mars we gazed at the enormous crowds collected to see a mock fight on the occasion of the laying the first stone of the Gendarmerie barracks at Chaillot, where the king of Rome's palace was to have been. The barracks, however, did not share a better fate than the palace—neither one nor the other, nor several other projected buildings there ever came to the last stone. Amongst the visitors at

Madame Partouneaux's was "Madame de Villèle, who, though apparently exclusive in her conversation and perhaps a little reserved and sullen in her looks, certainly showed nothing of her immense power written on her person, for she it is, as is said, who governs her husband who governs those who govern the nation."

We left Paris early in the morning of Tuesday, 5th September, in the diligence, arriving at Calais the evening of the following day, but the weather had now turned so stormy that no packets crossed for two days. On the Saturday it calmed a little, but my mother was afraid to encounter the drenching rain that lasted all day. In the evening it cleared and we made arrangements for going over in a steamer that was to start at 5 in the morning, but late [352] at night we learnt "that the Marchioness of Downshire had prevailed on the captain to wait till two in the afternoon in order to be able to land at the pier. The early part of the morning was beautifully calm and fine and, as the wind rose in the course of the day, I regretted much the delay, particularly when thick clouds rising at 1 made me fear we should not go even then. However they blew off, and we actually embarked at three, without the Marchioness, who had changed her mind, and without Lady Mary Lindsay Crawford,[18] whose carriages were on board. After a rough passage of five hours and a half, the wind directly in our teeth and the spray covering the deck and wetting us through, the packet full of passengers, and all sick except my sister and myself and one or two gentlemen, my mother very ill"—arriving at Dover at ½ past 8 in the dark, a bar prevented our entering the harbour; we had to land in small boats, and no sooner had we left the steamer than the boatmen said, "Now, gentlemen, four shillings each, if you please, for landing you," and would not stir till every one had paid—then sixpence apiece for the plank-boys, landing from the boat.

After a great deal of Customhouse trouble and heavy duty to pay for bonnets, dresses, etc, we left Dover by post on the Monday afternoon, and sleeping at Sittingbourne, we joined my father and sister Sarah in town on Tuesday, 12th September, and by previous arrangement all dined together at my Uncle's, who had had the large table set out in the dining room down stairs for the first time since we had left London twelve years before.

[353]We now set to making arrangements for a permanent stay in England. After a few days in our Hampstead lodgings we took a furnished house in Welbeck Street for three months, hired a harp and piano for my sisters, who began to enjoy much their intimacy with the Carr

family, my father took to writing on engineering matters, my mother put up very well with the new life in a smoky town, and resumed the management of the house and family after having left it for years with my eldest sister—and the estate of Restinclières, upon which all my father's permanent capital had been invested, was left to take care of itself. I felt very low—the disappointment at Montpellier, the feeling that I had not acted fairly, and the effect my conduct had on the Dax family, although I did not see how I could have gone on with the engagement, the uncertainty about my future career, brought on feverish headaches, which however I fortunately shook off. On the 22d, my birthday, usually a day of festivity, I was particularly low and gloomy, thinking myself really ill. In the evening I was surprised by a special invitation to dine with my Uncle the next day, which excited me a good deal, "certain as I was that he must have invited me for some particular purpose, which might either be something of consequence regarding myself, or merely some unimportant whim of the moment. During a turn or two round the garden before dinner and the whole of dinner time, nothing came out that I could describe as a tolerably adequate reason for the invitation. The young men left the room as usual after dinner, and I remained alone with my Uncle. He continued conversing with me on a variety of subjects, connected both with his and our pursuits. I even began to think he had only invited me to ask about my botanical catalogue, of which he enquired many particulars. He also spoke of my intention to settle in England and study the law, and offered to introduce me to his legal [354] friends and acquaintance. At last, a propos of Chancery abuses, on which topic we then were, he said, after enumerating various means the Masters in chancery have of getting money for no service, 'It is the custom there for young men to give to barristers as their masters in chancery two or three hundred pounds, for the privilege, during five years, of spending the whole day in copying their unmeaning grimgribber. Now lookye here, here's my hand (laying it on the table) open to receive five hundred pound, for the privilege of doing the same to mine, which will serve as an antidote to the grimgribber you will get from the lawyers.' The strange manner in which pleasantry and seriousness were mixed up in this proposal, and which led me to believe that some offer of replacing those who copied for him and thus devoting to him nearly the whole of my time was to follow, startled me at first, and I waited some time for a more distinct enunciation, just observing (as to what I knew not to be serious) that five hundred pounds was more than I had to give. After a considerable time, he added, 'Well come, I won't be too severe upon you; you shall give the five hundred pounds to my executors, and you shall come to write with me twice a week from eight to eleven in the evening.' The result of this, and of a good deal more conversation we had, is that I shall dine with him twice a week, and after dinner write with him. Besides, he gives me a number of his manuscripts to complete and set in order for reference or publication. This will be of great advantage to me in two ways; first, in point of ability, I may much improve by it, and, next, it will ingratiate me with him, and counteract the influence of some of those about him who use it to no good." I entered forthwith into this regular attendance, and continued it whenever I was in London during the remainder of Mr Bentham's life (that is till he was incapacitated by his last illness), deriving from it all the advantage I expected.

[355]I now commenced regularly to spend the mornings at Queen Square Place, partly making marginal notes for my Uncle to some of his writings, but chiefly studying my Uncle's papers on logic, which he had put into my hands. My first idea was to edit them in French, as a sequel to the French series of his works, which had been mainly instrumental in making him so widely known on the Continent. I knew that Bossange would readily undertake the publication on his own account, and I thought that in English I should not succeed in the style of writing, besides that I learnt that James Mill had a work on Logic in contemplation, founded in a great measure on J. Bentham's papers, which both he and his son had studied. I actually began in that language, but the preliminary step was to study the general divisions of the subject. On the day fixed for me to report to my Uncle, "As soon as dinner was over and the 'reprobates' had gone down, we began talking of various subjects. Bowring had been there that morning to communicate to him a piece of intelligence that he was so full of that he would enter into no discussion till he had disburthened himself of it" (this related to some correspondence he had had with Peel relating to that minister's new Larceny bills, etc,[19] and to some eulogistic expressions Peel had been heard to use with regard to J. Bentham). "When this affair was out, we went to discussing logic. First, however, I read to him the notes I had made on his 'Statistic function' papers.[20] Then I proceeded to discuss the general division of the subject of logic, making some alterations to the method he had laid down in his papers. It is a subject that interests me so much that I had tolerably clear ideas upon it. My uncle got so elated and so pleased to find that 'I had a head of my own,' that he began to propose a number of schemes he had in view for me, and said, 'I see you will be

able to help me in the most important of all [356] things—in Codification, and if I don't live to finish it, which I certainly shall not, I may perhaps bring it to a state for you to go on with it after I am gone.'—We sat talking in this way till ½ past 11, when we separated, highly pleased with each other."

I had several others of these after-dinner discussions and consultations with my Uncle before my plans for the future were definitively settled, and I also went with my sisters to spend three or four days at Lord Colchester's at Kidbrooke, where he entered in a most friendly way into my affairs. Warmly attached as he always showed himself to my father, and always very friendly to my Uncle, the very wide political differences of opinion in politics between him and Jeremy Bentham kept them a good deal apart, and the advice I got from the two was necessarily very different, when at all connected with this ticklish subject; but I had been so long intimate with friends of my father's and my own, abroad and in the country, belonging to such very different parties, I had had opportunities of observing so much exaggeration in various directions, that I had got into the habit of disregarding, in a great measure, pure politics, listening willingly to any, even the most violent declamations, which generally afforded amusement at least, and very cautious as to expressing any opinions of my own, which might commit me to one side or the other. I had now given up all desire I may have entertained to enter into any career which might connect me with the affairs of the country, content with devoting myself chiefly to two subjects, law and science, law for my bread, science for recreation; and to these two I adhered for several years, till at length feeling myself in a position in which work was not absolutely necessary for my livelihood, I allowed science to prevail and abandoned law.

[357]I had much, however, to discuss with my Uncle before all was settled. There were two professions which he was in the habit of declaiming against, much more in his conversation than in his writings, the law and the Church, and yet every one of his amanuenses, who all, for many years, had the full benefit of his advice and instruction, all ended by entering into the law or the church and some of them very successfully, but now he could not at first bear the idea of my doing the same. He tried to persuade me that I could make my fortune by editing some of his works, only writing articles for his *Westminster Review*, of which I entertained a very indifferent opinion, and in his zeal broached a number of plans for me, all of which broke down as soon as they were attempted to be put in practice. Having however by the advice of my

father and Lord Colchester determined to take immediate steps to prepare for a profession before it was too late (I was now 26 and, not having
been to College, should have to wait till I was 31 before I could be called
to the bar), I went on Saturday, 21st October to Lincoln's Inn, where,
with Philip Abbot (Lord Colchester's younger son lately called to the
bar), "I went to the Steward's office, and there got the necessary recommendation made out and signed by him and Mr Koe. This is the first
step to entering. On Thursday I shall execute the bond and pay down
the money, and from thence will commence my five years. Spent then a
couple of hours with Koe,* consulting him about what measures I
should take to study to the best advantage. He certainly is the best to
give advice, from the manner in which he himself has arrived at the eminence he now enjoys in the profession. [358] He began young, it is true,
as compared with my age, but did little at first. Strongly imbibed with
my uncle's principles about lawyers and law, he paid little or no attention to the subject before he was called to the bar, and consequently then
got but little practice. It was only after his marriage that the necessity of
providing for a family stimulated him to application. He says he then
found law not so bad nor so complicated as he had been led to think,
made himself soon master of it, and by close study soon got plenty of
work, and consequently plenty of money. He told me that if I wished to
do anything in the law, I must fix in my head the necessity of getting
money; this stimulus is alone sufficient to ensuring application. Lawyers' business depends upon attorneys, and attorneys' object is to get
their business well done, and as there is great competition amongst lawyers, it is §those who show the greatest abilities who get the most work.
No *interest* is of much avail in this line. He said that if I applied myself
closely to business, I might make money in the conveyancing line long
before I should be called to the bar, that is as soon as I shall have made
myself well master of the business. As I am determined to the profession, I certainly should be ashamed of not being up to it, so I must even
set to studying hard."

"From Lincoln's Inn I went to Queen Square Place, where I was to
dine today. I found my Uncle waiting for me with impatience. He asked

---

* I believe I have already spoken of Koe, as for many years an amanuensis of Jeremy
  Bentham's, who afterwards entered the law, but remained to the last my uncle's confidential adviser and best friend.

me where I had been. I told him I had been entering at Lincoln's Inn. He said all was very well, though he seemed displeased that I had not brought *him* my recommendation to sign. However he was in very good humour with me after dinner, till speaking of Blackstone's *Commentaries*,[21] I observed that that book must now become the object of my study. He then [359] asked, 'What! you are not going to study the law for practice?' I answered, 'You know that in my circumstances I must earn money.'—'Well then, if you must earn money by the practice of insincerity and dishonesty, there will be an end of all communication between us. In practising the law you must learn insincerity, and where there is insincerity with me, there can be no sympathy, there is no use in coming together, so we had better separate than quarrel.' I then said, 'I have no money of my own. So long as my father lives I am comfortable, but after that I have nothing to depend upon, and though I do not wish to hoard or accumulate money, yet I must live.' Upon which, he said over and over again that he had given up everything for the public good and he did not see why I should not, that as to mere living, what should come from him would be more than enough for that, and that I should not have more than two or three years to wait. I said that I could not think of depending for my livelihood upon anything so uncertain, that I must have means of living dependent only on myself, that so long as I was in France I could have secured that out of Restinclières, that here I could not, but that if he could point out any better way of my earning my living, I should be most happy to conform to his wishes and study the law only as much as necessary to follow his pursuits. He began talking of the Logic, which he considers as being to make my fortune, etc, etc, and by degrees we made it up, but he will not hear of my studying the law in any shape. What I must do is to go on as much as I can without his knowledge and continue following his pursuits to keep him in good humour with me, but this I see will be very difficult. He will now have me to dinner twice a week and this they say is the way for him soon to get tired of me (a prediction which fortunately was not verified). Three hours tête-à-tête between dinner and tea, [360] without anything to do are very difficult to fill up by one who has so active a mind as he. He must always have something new to think of, somebody new to see. §Bowring alone has the art of keeping him constantly under his influence, and thus makes him the more easily tired of any one else. Bowring makes himself scarce, only appears once a week and then in a very great hurry—has so much business—can only bestow a very short time, and even for that sacrifices very important affairs, and then has so much city news and flattery, with foreign intelligence, real or invented, that he takes care my Uncle shall not get tired of him. When at Dover, Bowring spent three whole days with J.B., and then his influence began to flag so much that he has taken care that that shall not be the case again."

As an earnest of good will, I was obliged the very next morning (Sunday) to give up what I had anticipated much pleasure from, the spending it with our friends the Carrs at Hampstead, with whom we were forming the closest intimacy. I drove out with my sisters to an early breakfast there, and returned to town and to Queen Square Place immediately after, on foot and in pouring rain (for I missed the only coach), because "last night my uncle said he wanted me much to come today to read over his Codification papers, as he had sent for them with that view from the man by whom he is having them translated into Spanish, a job Bowring has procured for a creature of his at J.B.'s expence,[22] and he was in a hurry to return them." Spending the whole of that and the next day, "I finished reading these Codification papers, with which I hope I shall have nothing else to do, as I cannot discuss with my Uncle on a subject on which we cannot agree as to principle."

[361]I now made up my mind to defer the practical study of the law (beyond a little reading) till I had done something in Logic, to which I devoted[§] most mornings at Queen Square Place. I had, however, some other calls on my time. My father, being now settled in England again, had taken to his old pursuits, and was working hard at the preparation of his *Essays on Naval Management*,[23] in which he was anxious to have my assistance. The subject was not one in which I felt much interest never having had any object in studying it, but I could not refuse. "I have promised to lay apart for him a certain number of hours per week, which I must deduct from the time I give to my Uncle. He gives me his work, such as he leaves it, to correct and criticise. I take up his long phrases, split, clip and arrange them, so as to make, on an average, five or six out of one, and then give them back to him to have copied. He will look them over, and who knows how many of them he may not restore to their former glorious incomprehensible integrity. But as to the words, I have little to change. My father's stile is good, apt and correct, and far from unpleasant. The length of his sentences comes from his letting them grow like ideas, one out of the other. You may have observed, sometimes, that an incident excites a train of thought that leads to a subject totally disconnected with it, and which we entirely forget in our chain of reasoning. Just so the end of the sentence has sometimes nothing to do with the beginning. On the whole, however, I approve of the

work and think that my father will render it acceptable to the public—to that part of the public who care anything about the subject."

The evenings (except the two per week given to my Uncle) I generally spent with my sisters and in society. My mother, after having once dined out with us all, ceased going out in [362] the evening, and my father, who never went to parties, contented himself with quiet dinners at old Count Woronzow's and one or two other old intimates, so that the chaperoning my sisters fell upon me, and at home we had always music, which my father much enjoyed. We particularly got up Bochsa's quatuors, one of my sisters on the harp, I on the piano, William Carr on the flute, and Seymour Larpent on the violincello. We went also occasionally to the theatres, very rarely however to any but the Opera, which I very much enjoyed, now and then to a morning Concert, but it was very seldom I could make up my mind to lose a morning.

I continued also to keep up botany as an amusement. My herbarium was still in France, but I had some plants and books with me, and could study them at times after I came home at night. I had also a chat now and then with Robert Brown, or with other botanists at Lambert's. Sir W. (then Dr) Hooker came to town for a few days. I met him at Lambert's and, as he expressed a wish to make my father's acquaintance, he "came and spent the evening with us. He is as lively, as amiable and as agreable as ever; he pleased every body exceedingly, is very friendly to me and pressed much a visit to Glasgow, not only from me but from my sisters. He has undertaken the editorship of the old established *Botanical Magazine* instead of old Dr Sims, who retires. This will bring up this work, once the very first of its kind and of most extensive sale, from the degraded state in which it now lies, to the level of, or rather to a superiority over, the *Botanical Register*, edited by his friend Dr Lindley.[24]

"Monday, 9th Oct. Dr Hooker to breakfast, then with him to Lagasca's in Camden town. This poor man, the first of Spanish botanists, one who has devoted his whole life to science and has [363] acquired considerable celebrity, has now been this twelvemonth dragging on a miserable existence, almost brokenhearted by his misfortunes, and scarcely able to keep himself and his family from absolute starvation with the help of the miserable pittance afforded him by British charity which thus supports numerous victims of Ferdinand's despotism. He had collected, with much labour, an extensive herbarium and had prepared materials for a Spanish Flora, and other important scientific works. The greater part of both the one and the other were with him when he left Madrid with the Cortes at their last expulsion. At Seville a report was spread of his being a conspirator, and the mob gathered round his mules, tore open his packages, and before his eyes spread the whole collection, plants, papers and all over the streets and into the river, thus wantonly destroying in a moment the fruit of so many years' toil and study. We found his lodgings better than we expected. We asked for M. Lagasca; an English maid said he was at home, and showed us up. There we only found Madame Lagasca, sitting with her hands before her, as I suppose she does all day long. For like most Spanish ladies, she looks as if she had never learnt to read, write, work or even to wash her face and hands, which were as filthy as her dress. She then began talking Spanish, when we made out for certain that her husband was not at home."—Later in the day we met him at Hooker's lodgings, and I made an appointment to look through some Cistineae he had with him.

"Saturday, Nov. 11. For the last fortnight I have been every day at Queen Square Place from breakfast till dinner, partly in writing my Logic, which I do sometimes in French, sometimes in English first. Wherever the subject is pretty extensively treated in the MSS, and where I have not much to add, I write it first in French, in order to get rid of my Uncle's stile, and then from [364] the French, I write it out in English. Wherever the subjects are only hinted at by my Uncle, or where I make additions entirely of my own, I do it at once in English. As to which language I shall first publish it in, is another question. I must write it first and then think of that. Probably I shall not do either one or the other during my Uncle's lifetime, partly on account of the difficulty of putting it into such language as he will approve, partly on account of some inconvenience of publishing it as a joint work.

"He has employed me a good deal of late in going over some of his Codification papers, previous to sending them over to South America. I have also copied a little, as Jack Colls has been ill for the last fortnight and has not been here. And when I have time, I read a chapter of Blackstone's *Commentaries*, for I must not forget my business, and the sooner I know the law, the sooner can I earn money (I was definitively admitted at Lincoln's Inn, and instructed how to keep my terms by dinners in the Hall, on the 28th of last month). I have not begun my *eating* yet, for I have plenty of time for that, and it is not very convenient for me just now to deposit the £100 that are necessary for the purpose. These £100 are returned when the student is called to the bar, but without interest. (Yes, but as I found afterwards to be paid again at the same time as a fee on being called.)

"I have dined at the fixed times with my Uncle; the two or three hours tête-à-tête after dinner are generally spent in discussing his logical manuscripts; he is still very much pleased with me, but I begin to lose any hopes of all this being of any use to me in a worldly way. I shall go on because the subject interests me much, extends my ideas, and I do not think I could employ my time better. The review-writing project seems to have blown over for the present. In the mean time, I sent an article the [365] other day to the London§ Magazine for the December number, and shall continue probably to do so every month." This last was the result of an arrangement I had made with the Editor, whom I had met a short time before, and who promised me a guinea a page for a series of articles on the manners, etc, in the South of France.—I wrote two or three, but soon discontinued, finding it did not answer, and that moreover the magazine seemed to be in difficulties and reduced the pay by half. It ceased soon afterwards.[25]

"Friday, 3d Nov. It had been settled that my Uncle was to spend the evening with us to hear our music, and Lord St Helens, who heard of it, said he would call that evening to meet my Uncle, on his own responsibility, for we could not venture to *invite* any one to meet Jeremy Bentham. But when the evening came, it began pouring of rain so hard, that my uncle (who had taken, as he said, half an hour from codification to *adonize*[26] himself) could not venture out, and would not take a coach, because he said that would not answer the purpose of exercise. Lord St Helens came, however, and spent an hour with us. He is very pleasant, quite a courtier, full of civility and anecdote, of which he has a surprising stock from the many countries he has visited as Ambassador.[27]

"We have also had the visit of another Ambassador and his lady; they are just gone off to Naples to spend the winter there. Lady Liston, who has seen so much travelling as Ambassadress, is very anxious to know what it is to travel as a private person. He is now 82 or 84, I forget which, and the greater part of his long life has been spent in the diplomatic line. He first went out as private tutor in the Elliott family to Berlin, where my father made his acquaintance five and forty [366] years ago.[28] I believe he remained there as Chargé d'affaires and has been Ambassador ever since. His wife, as well as himself, is Scotch. Lord St Helens met him one day here in London, when he said he was in a great hurry to go off to Scotland to marry. Lord St H., asking him who it was he had fixed upon, he answered that he had forgotten her name, but he had known her thirty years before, and knew where to find her now, and that he had settled that if he found her, still single and disposed to accept him, he was determined to offer himself. He accordingly went, found her out, and married her. Now that they have retired from political life, they have settled at a beautifull little place near Edinburgh, where, you may recollect, I saw them three years ago.[29] But to stay long there quietly cannot suit their active habits and disposition. He would now, at his age, accept of any embassy of importance, and wanted very much to be sent to the congress of Panama,[30] where, however, he could not prevail on Government to send any representative. So he has taken himself into his own hands and is just gone off to Naples."

"As you take in *Galignani* you will no doubt have seen a great deal about the Greek loans,[31] but as the statements there are so contradictory and the thing altogether has made so much noise here, I shall just endeavour to give you an idea of it in a few words. When first subscriptions were raised for the Greeks, a Committee formed itself for receiving and distributing them. Of this Committee, John Bowring got himself named Secretary, and, they being all of them good friends, they managed to raise a loan for the Greek Government, pocketing each of them a handsome *commission*. Bowring's amounted to some £11,000, a pretty little sum, which enabled him to pay his debts, set up a gig, take a house at Brighton, etc, whilst all was done [367] so nicely incog. that he got the name of a disinterested patriot, exerting himself for nothing in the noble cause of the Greeks. The greater part of the first loan was, however, really remitted to Greece and no complaints were made. Some time after, when first the sending out an expedition to their aid came in question, a new loan was raised, chiefly for that purpose, by three Greek deputies,[32] who came here with that object. As it was thought that the gentlemen who had raised the first loan had had commission enough, this was entrusted to Ricardo[33] and others, who again were allowed a handsome fee. This was at a time when speculation was at its heighth, there was every probability of Greek bonds rising, and consequently the Greek *patriots* gladly accepted of subscriptions to large amounts. Joseph Hume subscribed £10,000, John Bowring £25,000, at the price at which the loan was negotiated. So far all was well. The managers, both Grecian and English, none of them responsible, allowed each other abundant fees and gratifications for services in the Greek cause. Lord Cochrane was induced to take command of the Expedition. He was dispatched to the Mediterranean with a steamboat, and seven others were appointed to meet him there. A stupid Colonel[34] was sent out to purchase frigates in America, with £150,000 to pay for what might have been had for £50,000. So by degrees the whole loan went off, and by degrees Greek bonds fell down to almost no value. The poor bondholders began then to look about them, and to ask what had been the result of the sacrifices they had made. None, or next to none, of it had been remitted to Greece. Lord Cochrane was kept at Malta waiting for the steamboats still lying in the Thames, for alas! the machinery was so bad it would not work. They then began to make enquiries, and at last called upon their Committee [368] to enter into an investigation of the accounts of the expenditure of this second loan. Now it so happened that the most active members of the Committee had either acted only a secondary part in the pillage, or were absent at the time, so that those who met thought themselves quite safe in imputing all the blame to the Greek deputies, to Sir F. Burdett, to Hobhouse, etc, and accordingly, in an elaborate article of Bowring's in the *Westminster Review*,[35] and in a report, framed by him and read by Leicester Stanhope at a meeting of Greek bondholders,[36] a detailed tissue of embezzlement and plunder was laid open to public view—a report, by the bye, for the printing of which there was not money enough remaining. Luriottis, the only one of the three Greek deputies who was still in England, in defence of himself and his comrades, wrote a long suite of accusations against Jos. Hume, E. Ellice, Bowring, Ricardo, etc. They riposted.[37] The 'rogues' had now fallen out tout de bon, and for a fortnight the papers have been full of mutual recriminations and attempts at disculpation, from which the following facts are pretty clearly proved.

"Joseph Hume (the eternal maker of motions, passing for a patriotic and honorable man, rich but excessively stingy and miserly) bought £10,000 Greek Stock. The time came when Greek Stock began to fall, Hume became alarmed and, under some pretence of necessity, although really interested in Greek affairs as bondholder, gave out that he was going to sell out, well knowing what would be the result. The deputies, afraid of the disfavour which would have been thrown on their cause by such a man as Hume's selling out so large a sum, offered to take his stock, on the part of the Greek Government, at par, though the market price was then 15% discount. Hume accepted, but the Greek deputies changed their mind, and did not think they ought to make good the whole of his loss, so they at first only [369] paid up a little more than the market price. However Hume made such a piece of work that at last they did pay up to par, thus making up to him for losses which certainly were of no others' fault than his own for thus speculating.

"John Bowring, the hero of Boulogne,[38] the correspondent of all nations, the poet, the patriot, my Uncle's factotum and editor of the *Westminster Review*, honorary secretary of the Greek Committee and meddler in all concerns where he hopes for profit or fame, has meddled here to some purpose. Not content with £11,000 commission for the first loan ('and I leave it for the Greek deputies themselves to judge whether I was overpaid for my numerous and important services')[39] must needs do what he could to help off with the second loan. Like Hume, he took stocks (£25,000), and when stock fell he required the Greeks to take his at par. After much demurring they were too much afraid of his power of doing injury to the Greek cause to refuse him. Two months later the stock rose above par. Then says Bowring, 'I never sold you my stock. I only deposited it with you as security for money you lent me; here is your money, give me back my bonds.'—'Not so indeed,' said they. 'What! are the bonds *ours* when of less value than they cost, *yours* when of more value? We paid you your loss, it is not fair that we should also make over to you our subsequent gain.' However Bowring would have it, and again poor Greece was obliged to pay for his 'services.' So much Bowring admits; much more is said of douceurs and other good things he has worked out of them and others.

"Edward Ellice is accused of mismanagement as to the money for the steamboats that are lingering in the Thames. He flatly denies what others boldly assert, and I have no means of knowing as positively about him as about the other two.

[370]"Mr Burton held £9,000 and his Secretary, Mr Lee, £4,000 Greek stock.[40] He must needs be done by as Bowring was, and, being intimate with Luriottis, persuaded him into it. Since then, they have been collaring and scuffling and what not.—Their case is coming on before the law courts, so we shall have it all out.

"Ricardo, the banker, was no otherwise in fault than by taking an enormous commission on the second loan. The exact sum is not known, but it appears to be near £30,000.

"Col (I forget his name) who knew nothing about frigates, was sent to America to buy a couple, and bargained to pay three times their value for two, which would not have been half so useful as what might have been had in Europe. Galloway, the contractor for the steamvessels, is a stupid, ignorant fellow who does not know how to build them.[41] The Greek deputies, and all others who had anything to do with the business, have turned aside what they could, more or less according to their means. And how came all this to be allowed? Why, because there was no one to prevent it. No one is responsible. All managers and all embezzlers each allowed the other to do what the other did not molest him in doing. Hobhouse and Burdett were supposed to be managing, but one is in Russia and the other in the South of France. Meanwhile, poor Greece, what you have suffered! and what infamy is cast on England by these men who have pocketed such enormous sums offered you by British charity!"

The remainder of the year 1826 was spent in a regular routine. We moved from the gloomy house we had temporarily taken in Welbeck Street to a more cheerful one in Manchester Street. I went thence every morning, after an early breakfast, down to Queen Square Place, where I staid writing till late in the afternoon, when I went either to fetch one of my sisters from [371] Bloomsbury Square,[42] or did any other business I may have had in town. Wednesdays and Saturdays I staid all day at Queen Square Place to dine with my Uncle, and generally did not get away till about 12 at night, and now and then I devoted a part of the day to correcting for my father. The evenings, when I was not at my Uncle's or otherwise engaged to dinner, were generally spent in music with my sisters, either at home or with the Carrs, with whom we had become very intimate. Among my father's old friends he saw the most of, were the Bedfords (of the Admiralty), Lord St Helens, and old Count Woronzow, with whom he frequently dined, and I occasionally with him. The Count, now 84, had been 40 years in England since he first came as Ambassador from St Petersburgh, and had never learned to speak in English, and scarcely to read it. French was always spoken at his table, at the foot of which sat Mr Smirnove, who had been Russian chaplain here nearly as long, a fine, venerable looking man of very general information, and universally esteemed and respected. The Count was always most friendly and in every respect a thorough gentleman of the old school, but very refined, and there were sure to be always persons of note or interest at his table.

My *Catalogue des Plantes des Pyrenées et du Bas-Languedoc* was published in November, and the following month I was much pleased with a passage in a letter from Guillemin in which he says, "Je pense néanmoins que vous n'aurez aucun regret d'avoir produit cet ouvrage botanique, il est agréable et instructif dans son introduction et fort bien travaillé dans la partie vraiment scientifique. C'est l'avis de tout le monde, c'est-à-dire de tous ceux qui l'ont lu avec soin. Parmi les [372] personnes qui m'ont témoigné leur satisfaction, je vous citerai MM. Adrien de Jussieu, Achille Richard et Bory de St Vincent. Celui-ci s'est chargé de l'annoncer dans la *Revue Encyclopédique*. Pour moi, j'en ferai l'analyse dans le *Bulletin* de M. de Ferussac. Quoique vous ne m'eussiez donné aucun ordre à ce sujet, j'ai fait hommage d'un exemplaire à l'Académie des Sciences, et j'ai accompagné l'envoi d'une lettre que j'ai signé seulement de ces mots, *Un ami de l'auteur*, et dans laquelle j'ai sollicité un rapport. L'ouvrage a été renvoyé à M. Ramond. J'espère que vous ne désapprouverez pas cette démarche, elle n'a rien, ce me semble, que de très convenable, car j'ai parlé de votre intention de publier un jour une flore des Pyrenées pour laquelle les conseils des savants de l'Institut pourraient vous être utiles. D'ailleurs il vous est absolument nécéssaire qu'on sache que vous avez publié un travail sur les plantes des Pyrenées, et c'est en en parlant dans les sociétés savantes qu'on en répand le mieux la nouvelle."[43] I was also pleased with the terms in which Robert Brown and two or three other botanical friends in this country spoke of the work.

Dec 9. "Last night at the Smirnoves' met Mrs Cochrane, the Kamtchadale, widow of Captain Cochrane, the pedestrian. She is very young, scarcely more than 20, pretty and interesting looking and speaks English very well. She brought her husband a good fortune (in furs) but is said to have been sadly neglected by him. He left her here when he went to British Columbia, where, you know, he died last year from excess at table."[44] Decr 21. "Last night at the Smirnoves'; amongst others was Prince Gortchakoff (pronounced Kortchakoff)"*[§]

The following is characteristic of the cheerful vein in which Jeremy Bentham would so frequently take up trifles in the midst of his serious works. Some two or three years back he [373] was in Paris, at one of the great hotels in the Place Vendome,[45] and in consequence of some gross overcharges was leaving it, when the landlady came to him, imploring him to look over it, as it would be such a disgrace to her for so celebrated a *poet* to have left the house in dudgeon, since which he had frequently indulged in a joke about his poetical reputation, so contrary to his real nature, and Wednesday 15th Dec.,[§] one of my dining days, he was in high spirits, "and amused us much with his poetry. He had now and then rimed a couple of words in conversation as a joke, but now he said he had had an inspiration, from the joy he felt at Jack Coll's return to copy from him (J.C., his automaton amanuensis,

---

* A young Russian attached to the Embassy (long afterwards Chancellor of the Empire) whom I had met at Count Woronzow's and who rather surprised me though he is a Russian with the facility with which he conversed in Russian, French, German, Italian and English, passing from the one to the other according to the person whom he addressed and all without the slightest effort or hesitation.

had been laid up for a week). So after much pompous preparation and emphasis he began:

> Behold our Jack
> In health come back

Here was a dead stop, he had forgotten the rest, but after *vibrating in his ditch* for a little while, he stopped suddenly and with a serious face came out with:

> Behold our Jack
> In health come back.
> The Lord be praised therefore.
> Let him that's meet
> My song compleat
> For I can go no more.

The last a Yankee phrase, for which he used sometimes to quiz John Neal."

My work at my Uncle's was now diversified, with some observations on Peel's bills for the consolidation of some branches of the criminal law.[46] I wrote on the 18th: "At my Uncle's all day long, dining there, and in the day time not stirring from the [374] room where I sit. This is the 'study,' where Neal and I sit the whole day, writing without speaking. At one o'clock, I go to the next room to eat some luncheon and read the paper; the rest of the time I am writing, sometimes my Logic, sometimes for my uncle. Just now I am making out some observations on the heads of consolidation bills, which Mr Peel sent to my Uncle. I shall endeavour to make up a letter to Mr Peel and send him my observations, in the hope he may be induced to employ me in some way or another. My father has urged me much to do this, and so has my uncle, who, from his intercourse with Peel, is persuaded that it will be of use to me; but I myself have very little hopes of the kind, for young men fit for the purpose are in great abundance, and few have so little recommendation as myself."

I sent in these observations towards the end of November, and some time after, received the following letter.[47]

Whitehall, Jany 17 1827

Sir

I take great blame to myself for having so long omitted to acknowledge the very sensible letter which you addressed to me on the 27th November, and to thank you for the suggestions respecting the Larceny bill by which your letter was accompanied.

I shall very shortly have an opportunity of reviewing in detail with the legal authorities whom I am in the habit of consulting—the various clauses of the con-solidated Larceny Bill—and I beg to assure you that each of the Remarks with which you have favoured me shall undergo very full consideration.

I have added to this letter Heads of the Larceny Bill and of two other Bills, relating to Offences against Property—which have been printed subsequently to those which I sent to Mr Bentham.

I have the honour to be

Sir

Your obedient servant

Robert Peel

George Bentham Esqr
Queen Square Place Westminster

[375]"This letter is entirely in his own handwriting and I think does him credit, as it shews that he personally and privately attends to the important improvements he is introducing into our system of laws, as he must have read over my letter (eighteen pages long) himself. I received it yesterday; my father and my uncle are of course very well pleased with it. Mr Peel sent with it a reprint of the Larceny bill on which I had made the observations, and copies of the two other bills which he had formerly sent to my Uncle."

Some days later, "My Uncle had the other day a letter from Mr Peel in answer to some of his,[48] in which Mr P. says, 'I have shown to more than one competent Judge the letter and observations which your nephew Mr George Bentham was good enough to address to me. Their opinion is in conformity with my own, that they are highly creditable to him. They are at this moment in the hands of one most fully capable to appre-ciate their merit—Sir J. Richardson, lately a Judge of the Court of Com-mon Pleas and employed since his retirement from the bench in suggesting reforms in the legal institutions of the island of Malta.'

"This Sir J. Richardson is, I believe, an acquaintance of the Carrs; at any rate, I am glad that my letter has been approved of by more than one, as circumstances may come to pass when their good opinion may be of use to me. On the whole this letter pleases me more than the last, as not being so much attributable to mere civility."

Again some days later, "In a former page I have given you an extract of a letter from Peel to my uncle. This, with his letter to me, are considered by the few friends to whom they have been shown (un peu malgré moi) as very good. Lord Colchester observed to my father that it was better to be begged than to beg. *What* he implied is less difficult to guess than *how much* he implied, but I see little chance of anything substantial resulting from it yet a while.—You [376] may remember I spoke to you on a former occasion of a circular, addressed by a Mr Hammond to the 'Members of the Circuit,' explaining what he was doing under Mr Peel's authority for the forming a general code of laws. A long extract from this circular appeared in the papers last week, when the next day, in the ministerial papers, appeared the following article in answer to it.[49] I copy it for you, first because, since Peel's letter everything relating to consolidation becomes very interesting to me, and next, because the letter of Peel's having been originally written nearly at the same time as the one to me, contrasts with and shows off mine to advantage.

"A statement having appeared in the papers, entitled the Consolidation of the Criminal Code, from which it would appear that a gentleman of the name of Hammond has been employed, under the authority of Mr Peel, in various projects connected with the Criminal and Civil Law of this Country, it is thought necessary to give publicity to a communication made to Mr Hammond on the 9th of January last, which explains the circumstances under which Mr Hammond received any authority whatever from Mr Peel, and the limits within which that authority is restricted.

'It seems wholly impossible to reconcile with this communication the statement above referred to entitled Consolidation of the Criminal Code.'"

Copy   Whitehall, Jany 9

Mr Peel considers that it would be for the convenience of Mr Hammond and himself, that Mr Hammond should distinctly understand the nature and extent of the authority which he has from Mr Peel to proceed in the consolidation of a certain branch of the statute law of England.

Some time after Mr Peel had undertaken, with the assistance of Mr Hobhouse and Mr Gregson, to consolidate the laws relating to the trial and punishment of criminal offences, he learnt that Mr [377] Hammond was employed, under the direction of a Committee of the House of Commons, in preparing drafts of bills, consolidating the law relating to Forgery and some other crimes.

Though Mr Peel had, previously to the appointment of this Committee, undertaken a similar work, which he proposed to carry on gradually, and with that mature deliberation which is essential to success, he was unwilling to interfere with the performance of the duty assigned by the Committee to Mr Hammond, and was ready, so far as his intentions corresponded with those of the Committee, to stand in the same relation to Mr Hammond in which the Committee stood.

Mr Peel contemplated, if time and opportunity were permitted to him, the ultimate consolidation of the whole of the statute law relating to crime.

From the first Resolution of the select Committee on criminal law, he presumes the object of the Committee to have been the same with his own. The Resolution is to the following effect, "Resolved that it is the opinion of this Committee that it is expedient that the Statutes relating to the Criminal Law should be consolidated under their several heads."[50]

Mr Peel is perfectly willing that Mr Hammond should proceed under his authority in completing what remains to be performed by him within the limits above prescribed.

Mr Peel understands these limits to be, the collection under one head of the several existing Laws in the Statute Book relating to criminal offences.

Mr Hammond has sent to Mr Peel the result of his labours, with respect to the laws relating to forgery, to coining, and to Offences against property.

[378]The only material heads that remain are the laws relating to Offences against the person, and the laws relating to the preservation and destruction of Game.

As to the latter, Mr Peel has to observe, that as the subject is to be brought before Parliament in the present Session by Lord Wharncliffe,[51] Mr Hammond's labours upon it will probably be thrown away, unless they are completed before his Lordship's motion.

Mr Peel does not feel himself enabled to give Mr Hammond any authority respecting the reduction of any part of the Common Law to writing, or as to the consolidation of any other portion of the Statute Law than that which relates to crime.

Anthony Hammond Esq
Tanfield Court Inner Temple.

"Poor Mr Hammond, his labours are strangely restricted; he is sadly thrown down from the eminence he boasted of having attained. Had I deserved such a letter, I should never dare open my mouth again for very shame. But I suppose he does not mind it. The fact is Peel knows well that Mr Hammond, though exceedingly laborious, is totally unfit for any such task as the forming a digested body of laws. The two Assistants mentioned by Peel (Hobhouse and Gregson) are, on the contrary, said to be very clever men."

As for me, the affair led to no result. I did not follow it up as I might have done. On this, as on other occasions, a certain shyness, a want of energy and perseverance, prevented my taking that advantage of opportunities which young men of more ambition would have seized for their advancement in life.

[379]The year 1827 began very pleasantly for me. My sisters were on a visit to the Carrs, at Hampstead, and I joined them on the evening of New Year's Day. "The Carrs had indeed urged me to come up to dinner, but I did not like to leave my father and mother alone, besides that since my needle adventure I, who am so little superstitious in general, do not much like the dining out on that day; so I promised to go out to Hampstead after dinner only, and accordingly took the six o'clock coach and got there by desert time. The party consisted of the whole family, including Dr and Mrs Lushington (besides Mrs Lushington there were four daughters and three sons), the two Miss Baillies (Joanna and her sister) Mr Rolfe, an old friend of Mr Carr's (afterwards Lord Cranworth), Miss Mulso, my sisters and myself, in all eighteen. This is a grand day with them, being Mr Carr's wedding day and is always kept by them with great solemnity. The young ladies were all dressed as bride's maids, in which Laura looked beautifull. Punch was made, and toasts were drank, after each of which Anna, Isabella and Laura sang most beautifull glees—some composed for the occasion, one sent by Maria Edgeworth.[52]—I never was so much delighted with singing. Anna, who generally sings but small songs, called forth her powers and they are really very great. The whole closed with 'God Save the King,' in which every one joined in chorus. The ladies then retired, but we had not been long alone before we heard a violent explosion of laughter in the drawing room, to which we were summoned. Isabella had dressed herself in the character of an old woman of the last century, and supported her character so admirably that it was some time before we found her out. We then danced an English country dance, Mr Carr with Mrs Lushington, Mrs Carr with Morton (her eldest son), even Miss Baillie and [380] Miss Mulso went down the middle once. After that we had quadrilles, waltzes, reels, etc. Mr Carr danced a minuet with Isabella, then a dance called 'the Country Bumpkin,' Mr Carr dancing and jumping as if it were his real wedding day, not the thirtieth anniversary of it. I never saw him look so well. We concluded this delightful evening

with 'petits jeux' and retired at one o'clock. In the morning I rose early, not having been very well, and walked for an hour up and down the terrace walk, enjoying a sight I had not seen for months, the rising of the sun, and a beautifull rising it was. I amused myself in tracing our ancient gardens (the terrace walk on the brow of the hill with a fine view towards Harrow, the kitchen garden, etc, had formerly been within the grounds of the house we occupied for many years, next door to Mr Carr's); mine is cut across by the paling, yours is converted into turf, but the large variegated holly remains, the magnolia is dead, the only one that remains in its former state is my poor brother's. It was a great pleasure, but a melancholy one, to recognise the large Portugal Laurel and even the Lilac, which you may remember was one of the first to flower. It is a sad thing to think how those whom I have most loved and confided in have been separated from me, my poor brother whom I had never quitted a single day till his last fatal illness—after that, Lise separated from me so far, and now I am away from you, who would have consoled me for anything, could I always have lived with you and Adèle. And if I have attempted to form other attachments you know how ill they have turned. My thoughts are now much taken up with Laura. I admire her exceedingly, but even with her I am afraid of disappointment. She is so much admired and looked up to by the family that I am afraid they look much higher than me for her, and as to herself I cannot perceive that she entertains towards me [381] any such thoughts as she did when a child" (at four years old she had vowed she never would marry anybody but me).

This was the first of three happy New Year's evenings we spent in much the same way—with nearly the same party—after which they were broken off by the death of Mr Carr and the dispersion of several members of his family, with whom, however, my sisters and myself remained on the most intimate terms for life. I began to feel much attracted to Laura, but had gradually to make up my mind to give up all thoughts of any closer connection, which never would have been sanctioned by her family. Mr Rolfe was courting her with great assiduity, and his suit was encouraged by her father, who fully appreciated his sterling merits, and by her mother, who foresaw his rise in his profession; but as a young man, his exterior was not attractive to young girls, and she positively declined him. It was only after eighteen years perseverance that he succeeded, and I believe that no one was happier in her married life than was Laura Carr, as Lady Rolfe, and afterwards as Lady Cranworth, wife of the Lord High Chancellor and mistress of Holwood Park.

Sunday, 7th Jany. "The Duke of York has died. You will have seen the account in the papers before this reaches you, and you may perhaps have seen how scandalously the *Morning Chronicle* has chosen this moment to rake up all the abuse they could collect.[53] The fact is that, though people in general are not sorry that he should not come to the throne, yet he is much regretted as Commander in chief of the army, in which all parties agree that he acted with great justice and impartiality. His sufferings had been dreadful for the last fortnight. . . . (10th) Every one is busy preparing mourning, which will be put on tomorrow for six weeks. The Duke will lie in state for two days, and will be buried [382] in a fortnight. . . . (17th) On Thursday I went to see the lying in state, that is such was my intention, but *l'homme propose, Dieu dispose*. You may have seen in the papers the accounts of the crowd that was at the door. St James's Street was full of well-dressed persons, all in black. At first I thought I should easily make my way, till I got so far into the crowd that I could no longer retreat. Here I remained above an hour, gradually borne forward towards the door, amidst the shrieks of the fainting females and even of the men who, being short, were half suffocated by the pressure, or whose heads or limbs got squeezed between the shoulders of their taller companions. The heat was so excessive, though it froze hard, that a dense steam arose from the crowd—the screams of the sufferers were at last quite dreadfull and, in one sudden press, the line of guards was broken through, and a violent rush into the park extricated some thousands and relieved them from the imminent danger in which they were. I profited by the opportunity, and was heartily glad to get home safe and sound, though losing the sight, which was said to be a fine one. It appears that very few, if any, lives were lost and not many serious accidents, considering the circumstances. The reason of this extraordinary crowd was that above 150,000 persons came to see it and not 20,000 could be admitted in the course of the day." After more than fifty years, I can never forget the bottom of St James's Street at the corner of the hotel, seeing a woman sinking under our feet closely in front of me, and only saved by another man with the same physical strength I then enjoyed, assisting me in setting our backs against the crowd and forcing out a small gap in which she could rise, whilst close by a young man was in the greatest agony, from his ankle being pressed against the scraper of the hotel door.

"I was now heartily glad to rest the remainder of the day, particularly as I had to dance at night. It was at Mr Koe's, where I went with one of my sisters to a dinner and child's ball. . . . At [383] dinner we met John

Romilly (afterwards Lord Romilly) who had been voted a dull, awkward, unmeaning kind of a personage, but who now appeared clever,
intelligent and agreable—Mr Paley, a young Oxford beau, 'studying the
law' like everybody else, something of a dandy, and certainly no *bête*,
was judged to be very pleasant—Mr Coleridge, a friend of the Carrs as
well as of the Koes, a travelled man whose *Six Months in the West Indies
in 1825* has excited some interest, though considered as somewhat sentimental. Mr Romilly the tutor, a cousin of John's, a bon vivant like all *Fellows* (who are our Chanoines), a young man with great pretensions to
esprit, a squeaking voice, and a probable prospect of a bishopric—and
his brother, a man of studied *pointes*, who speaks little, but what he does
say comes out in the form of a pun or a joke."

The next day "I strolled out to St James's Street to see what was going
forward, as the lying-in-state was to continue as the day before. The
crowd was as great as ever, but some arrangement had been made to
endeavour to protect the poor fainting females; they were so far
favoured as to be lifted over the barriers by the guards, and indeed, at
one time, the fair sex alone was admitted into the palace. I do not know
whether this was quite fair. If the ladies suffered so much, why did they
get into the crowd at all? Many, after having fainted and been brought
out, recovered, and thrust themselves again into the thickest of it. Upon
the whole, the soldiers and police behaved admirably."

Herrera, the Guatemalan patriot,[54] spent two evenings with my Uncle
on my days for dining there. The first day, Prandi and I were to act as
interpreters, but my Uncle, finding that Herrera spoke French, preferred
being en tête a tête; but on Wednesday, 10th Jany, "Herrera came in
after dinner, and sat with my Uncle and me till ½ past 11. My Uncle is
delighted with him, and says that [384] they understand one another
very well and go on well together, so I was quite surprised to find that
in fact they either do *not* understand, or *mis*understand every word that
the other says. My uncle speaks French well, but his manner of speaking, both in French and English, is such as to require a good deal of
attention to follow him. Herrera cannot catch even French very readily,
and so contents himself with assenting to whatever my Uncle says. He
told me that he was delighted that I was there, for it was very painful to
him not to be able to keep up the conversation with my Uncle. He is
active, and a very well informed man for a Guatemalian—for a native of
an outlandish country, without roads, without any of the interior or
exterior comforts of life, where ignorance and superstition bear the
same proportion to those of the Spaniards that theirs do to those of the

French peasantry, if it be possible to be, in this respect, worse than the genuine Spaniards."

"The famous number of the *Westminster Review* is out. The articles are in general poor—my Uncle's in all its pristine absurdity of style. I have not yet heard what 'sensation' it may have produced."[55]

Tuesday, 16th. "I staid late with my Uncle on Saturday. I read to him some of Del Valle's speeches,[56] and his account of himself (translating them as I read). They are well written and, partly for that reason, partly from the natural beauty of the Spanish language, appeared quite eloquent. Del Valle, Herrera's cousin, is really an extraordinary man. Without ever having been more than fifteen leagues from Guatemala, he had acquired an extraordinary proficiency in both political and physical science. His description of his departure for Mexico upon his nomination as deputy there, a journey of four hundred leagues, over a wild and mountainous country, at the rate of five leagues a day, his account of his two years' stay at Mexico, the various vicissitudes he met with, six months as a member of the Constitution [385] Commission, six months in prison, taken from thence to be Iturbide's prime minister, etc, and particularly the raptures he expresses on his return to his native province, interested me exceedingly."[57]

"I brought home the *Revue Encyclopédique* for November, in which is a short article upon my *Catalogue* which you may have seen, or at any rate which you will see. It is by Bory St Vincent,[58] one of the first rate botanists, who lives in Ste Pelagie, where he is confined for debt, but lives comfortably with his mistress, under whose name he has all his books, collections, etc. I am proud of his éloges, but should be more so if they were in a work which has not the reputation for indiscriminate praise which the *Revue* has acquired. He complains of my not having spoken of Léon Dufour.[59] The fact is, I only knew of him as a cryptogamist and entomologist, and neither of these branches of Natural History belong to my *Catalogue*. I knew he had visited the Pyrenees, and longed to enter into correspondence with him, but in my *Catalogue* I do not speak of all the men who had visited those mountains in a scientific point of view, but merely of those who had, by their works or their communications, contributed to the observations I published.

"This morning I have been here at Q.S.P. (Jeremy Bentham's) since breakfast. My uncle had had several copies of his Article on Humphreys in the *Westminster Review* printed off separately,[60] and sent a copy to Mr Humphreys himself. Last night he received a very flattering letter in return, which, with my Uncle's answer, I shall here transcribe, the first

as an instance of good sentiments on Mr H.'s part, the second as a model
of invitations to dinner, both as promising mutual pleasure in the
acquaintance between these two respected legislators, meeting on such
an occasion [386] at such a time of life, Mr H. as I understand being very
far from young.[61]

Lincoln's Inn, 15 Jany 27

Mr Humphreys presents his respects to Mr Bentham, and begs to acknowledge the favor of the separate print of Mr Bentham's review of Mr H.'s observations on the law of real property.—Mr H. was yesterday occupied in reading the
article *pen in hand*, as he deemed it too precious a study to let a single reflection
resulting from it escape him. He will be bold enough, however, even in this first
communication, to point out one signal error which pervades the whole, namely
that in speaking of the author and reviewer, *master* is miswritten for *scholar* and
the reverse. (Jeremy Bentham, in his article, often calls Mr H. his learned master.)

Mr Humphreys proposes to avail himself of the services of Mr Butler of this
Inn, whose pupil he formerly was, for enabling him to pay his respects to Mr
Bentham.

Mr H. begs Mr Bentham's acceptance of a letter which he lately addressed to
Mr Sugden, in reply to some strictures of that gentleman on the proposed measure of a Code. Mr S. has since, in a third edition, withdrawn from the discussion.[62]

Queen Square Place Westminster
16 Jany 1827

Dear Sir

Don't "avail" yourself of the "services" of any body except your own coachman,
or what would be better for health, your own shoemaker, but come and share a
Hermit's dinner at my hermitage, as above, on Thursday at 6, with Yours most
truly,

Jeremy Bentham

J. Humphreys Esq

The last half of January and commencement of February, the weather
was very severe, but did not interfere with my walks to Hampstead on
Sundays or in the evening, whilst the mornings, except [387] those days
I worked for my father, were spent at Queen Square Place over my
Logic, "always thinking I shall have done in a day or two, but still there
is more to write and rewrite."

"Thursday the 8th February was the day of days. My Uncle took my sisters and myself to the play. For some time, we had been endeavouring to persuade my Uncle to go and see the pantomime, but he made many difficulties; first he contended that he could not go so early—then he would go with Place, and Place would not go. At last, the other day, of his own accord, he sent Richard to take four places in the front row of the central box, exactly opposite the stage, and me to invite my sisters to dine with him and then go to the play, and I got Neal to take another ticket to go with us, and, accordingly, dinner was set out in the parlour down stairs. My Uncle sat between my sisters, and was affected to tears. He was exceedingly pleased and attentive to them. We went in our carriage to Drury Lane, and got there at the first scene. The play was *A New Way to Pay Old Debts*, the principal actor the far-famed Kean, he who was hissed off the stage eighteen months ago for immorality when Miss Foote was so over-applauded for the same thing,[63] who has since been receiving some compensation in the applause of the Americans, and is now returned here, attracting immense crowds of the same public who had hissed him, and earning £50 every night that he acts. I had heard much of him as a tragic actor, but was disappointed on seeing him; though he had some excellent moments, he generally ranted too much. He acted Sir Giles Overreach, an artful character whose intrigues fail, and who is carried off at the end mad or dead with vexation, so that it is what is here called a serious comedy, in France a *drame*. (I saw Kean a few days later in *Othello* and liked him much better.) [388] My Uncle attended to it, but I believe found it long; the weather, too, being dreadfully cold, the frosty wind penetrated into the theatre, and he was not very comfortable, but he amused himself much with the pantomime, which from beginning to end is a collection of the most extraordinary feats, tricks and absurdities that can be imagined. The name of the pantomime is *The Man in the Moon*, and it is reckoned one of the best of the year§ (the letter here broken off) a ridiculous piece of business from beginning to end. The scenery, however, is beautiful—a view of St Paul's, another near London Bridge—the battle of Waterloo—some lunar landscapes—Boulogne, Brighton, and above a dozen others, all producing great illusion. The caricatures of the romps of a 'finishing school for young ladies,' of the 'Royal patent Expediter from London to Brighton in half an hour,' the dialogues between the clown and the moon, to the tune of the 'Tyrolienne,' etc, were very amusing. In the last scene, representing Vauxhall Gardens, were introduced extraordinary feats of rope dancing, Indian jugglers, etc.—In coming home, my Uncle, to whom it was severe penance thus riding in a carriage, got out at Charing Cross and walked the rest of the way with Neal, notwithstanding the severity of the frost, encreased by the wind."

Friday 9th. With Clara to an evening literary party at Miss Spence's, a second or third cousin of my mother's,[64] author of some novels, etc. "We found her *au second*, in a small house in Great Quebec Street. . . . Amongst the ladies, was Miss Wheeler, daughter of my Uncle's friend Mrs Wheeler, a beautiful girl, but affected and bold looking, and lives apart from her mother, not liking her favorite radicals; . . . also Miss Landon (L.E.L.), a young lady of nineteen, already well known as a poet. Some say her poetry is excellent, others that it is exaggerated and absurd. I am no judge, but I do not like it. Ce n'est pas [389] mon genre.—But Miss Landon appears to be a lively, good-humoured, unaffected person, endowed with an extraordinary volubility of speech. The remainder of the party had all a slight tincture of blueism, which characterises Miss Spence's acquaintance."

Sunday 11th. "Called at Lady Davy's, whom I found in a very nice house in Park Street, Grosvenor Square, overlooking the Duke of Grosvenor's gardens and Hyde Park as far as Kensington Gardens. She was very gracious and civil. Sir Humphrey is just gone to Italy for his health. His gourmandise has of late become quite disgusting. He has been overeating himself so frequently, having been twice almost killed by it, that his physicians ordered him abroad, in hopes that he might not there be tempted to eat so much. He is already arrived at Turin. His wife, though brutally treated by him, attended him here with the greatest care. She must be glad of his absence."

"I finished last Monday my *Outline of a new system of Logic with a review of Dr Whately's 'Elements'*. I took it to Longman's, but he declined engaging in it, that is, taking it at his own risk, because works on Logic have no great sale in general. So my Uncle said he would be at the expense of printing it for me and, accordingly, after some days spent in making agreements with the printer, it was sent yesterday. My father, too, has commenced printing a mass of papers relating to Portsmouth Dock Yard, etc."[65]

My letters are now much filled with accounts of social amusements—dinners, balls and evening parties—reflections on hearing of the satisfactory marriage of my French flame, Emma Dax, and some political news. Friday 9th March. "Went to the Royal Institution[66] weekly evening meeting, a sort of Conversazione, at which the members and those friends to whom they give tickets meet a little before nine in the library, then go to the [390] lecture room to hear a half-hour's or hour's lecture, return to the library, where they are treated with excellent tea and coffee, and there remain till near eleven. This evening there were about two hundred persons present, and consequently the room was densely crowded. . . . The lecture was on Naval Architecture, a most unmeaning one, which disappointed every one. The lecturer, Mr Holdsworth, spent the whole time in saying what he should do and what he should not do, and when we thought that these preliminaries were at last over and that he would enter upon the *fonds* of his subject, he withdrew to make room for a 'more important communication'—the trial of a filtering machine!" Friday, 16th. "At the Royal Institution, much pleased with a most magnificent set of engravings of Lapland scenery, belonging to Capel Brooke's travels. . . . [67] The lecture was very good, on suspension bridges. Many very interesting theories were explained, in a clear and agreable manner, by a young man whose name I forgot to ask."

Sunday, 17th[§] March. "Called on Mr Bentham of Gower Street. The poor man has just had a great disappointment. I have formerly told you how much importance he attaches to pedigree, to armorial bearings and such things.—Well, about twenty years ago, he found, in searching for ancestors, that his family had always lived in the same part of Yorkshire as Thomas Bentham, the first Bishop of Litchfield and Coventry, in the beginning of Queen Elizabeth's reign, and from various other circumstances he concluded that he was descended from the said Bishop; he had also had left to him a grant of a handsome coat of arms, which had been made to that Bishop by Queen Elizabeth. He had, in consequence, adopted the arms, had them pasted into his books, and painted on a variety of places in magnificent style. Now, two or three days ago, accident made [391] him meet with quite a different coat, granted to his grandfather,[68] and which of course are his. He is sadly vexed at being obliged to lay aside those he has borne for the last twenty years and for which he has spent so much money. He showed me the original grant of Queen Elizabeth to the Bishop, a handsomely illuminated deed, in high preservation. He has a great passion for investigating the affairs of the Bentham families and in tracing their descents. He is intimate with those of Canterbury (a General, with two sons and three daughters like ourselves), one of whom, a young man of 32, bears my name, and is a Post Captain. Mr B. of Gower Street is to ask this Captain and myself to dine together with him some day, and then he will 'introduce the two Georges to each other.'"[69]

Wednesday, 21st. After an account of some H.B.![70] "A propos of caricatures, Friend Allen, the head of the Quakers, the benevolent, charitable and indefatigable Allen, has just married, at the age of 65, a rich Quakeress of 70.[71] Of course, every one calls out that it is a marriage for money, and innumerable caricatures are out. He was so angry that he would have broken off the marriage if the bride had consented, and so foolish as to buy up the first that appeared; the consequence was that the publishers next day came out with a double stock. Friend Allen's friends did what they could to dissuade him from the marriage, but he persisted, and considering his family misfortunes, perhaps he was right."

Thursday, 22d. . . . "Met at dinner at the Koe's, amongst others, Mr Coleridge, a young man who has published a work called *Six Months in the West Indies*, which has been a good deal read. He is [392] a clever and agreable young man when he lays aside conceit and sentimentality."

Saturday, 17th. "My *Logic* will be out next week.[72] I have just now corrected the last proofs. It is a volume of 287 pages. . . . I am very anxious to know what will be thought of it, for the last two or three days I have been very fidgetty about it. This my offspring, that has cost me some months' labour is now coming forth to be judged by the world, and its parent may be allowed to be a little feverish on the occasion.— Patience—son sort se saura avec le temps." Saturday, 24th. "My work is out. I received it on Wednesday night. My uncle has read it, but I have not yet his opinion of it." Monday, 26th. "My uncle is much pleased with my work; he says that *in Logic, I have already gone beyond him.* Mr Carr has begun reading it; he objects to the hard words, but though there may be one or two, which I may still give up, I cannot but think that I have, in general, suppressed all but those which are indispensable for the expression of the ideas." April 7th. "Lord Colchester called on my father yesterday; he has read my work and expresses himself much pleased with it. I am much pleased to have heard it highly spoken of, both by Lord Colchester and Mr Carr, and do not care for the fault John Bowring finds in it. He observed to my uncle that it was full of gallicisms, but *that he liked it better the second time he looked into it than he did the first,* and probably when he said so he had not read it at all." May 12th. "My *Logic* is mentioned in the *New Monthly Magazine,* without anything of a review of its contents."[73] After this, I find no mention of the book. My friend Mr Carr pointed out to me that the tone of my observations on Whately's book and the absolute way in which I brought forward my own [393] views were not quite becoming in so young a writer.[74] I acknowledged the correctness of these observations, and began to feel ashamed of the importance I had in my mind attached to several of the principles I had brought forward, especially to that which has since been termed the quantification of the predicate, and which was entirely my own, not having been worked out in my Uncle's MSS. The work, however, was very little noticed; only about 60^s copies had been sold when the publishers became bankrupts.[75] I had notice that the stock had been seized by their creditors, but I was too much disgusted to take any steps to redeem it, and the whole was sold for waste paper. I thenceforth dismissed the subject from my mind. I do not think I ever saw Sir W. Hamilton's notice of it in the *Edinburgh Review*,[76] and it was only seventeen years later that, when in the country at Pontrilas, I was much amused by a little controversy regarding it, raised by Mr Warlow in the *Athenaeum*, at the end of 1850.[77] I took no notice of this, and heard no more of it for above twenty years, when I one day received a note from Profr Jevons of Owen's College, Manchester (with whom I was previously unacquainted), asking me whether I was connected with, and could give him any account of the author of, the Logic in question.[78] This led to some correspondence. Mr Herbert Spencer took it up, in an article in the *Contemporary Review*, which was answered by Professor Baynes, and led to the subjoined article of Profr Jevons.[79] This, of course, led to nothing, but I have little doubt that if I had, in 1827, gone on with the subject, I might have done something of value in Logic—but here, as in other instances, my success has been baulked by a want of perseverance, when checked by a slight contretemps.

[394]Saturday, March 31. "Went yesterday with some friends to see the wild beasts at Exeter Change. I had never been there, and was surprised to see so many rare and fine animals crowded together in this miserable place. There are three rooms, one on the first floor, the two others on the second, or rather in the garretts, for they are immediately under the roof. The animals are all confined in small cages piled one over the other, with scarcely room to turn, and though kept pretty clean, the stench and closeness are quite suffocating, besides that this menagerie is immediately over a sort of bazar, and the whole is constructed of wood and other very combustible materials, half rotten with age, so that if a fire should break out, it would be almost impossible to stop it; and what would thus be the consequence of the escape of all these lions and tigers, enraged by the heat of the flames, and rushing into the midst of one of the most crowded and populous parts of the metropolis! However, there is now some chance of their removal. In consequence of the projected widening of the narrow parts of the Strand, Exeter Change will come down entirely, and I see they are already commencing opera-

tions at St Martin's and at the Strand. The animals, it seems, will be removed to the Regent's Park, where a piece of ground has been allotted to the Zoological Society, who, it is probable, will purchase the Exeter Change animals."[80]

Monday, April 2d. "I dined on Saturday at my Uncle's, as usual, and in the evening spoke to him upon my affairs and prospects. I had, for some time, thought it necessary, but delayed it for fear of bringing on a quarrell; but now, several circumstances made it very urgent to do so. You know that when I first entered at Lincoln's Inn, on my telling my Uncle of it, he required that I should not study Law for the *practice*, and that if I did, there must be an end of all communication between us; and as to money, he had said that I should always have plenty from him. I did not think it necessary to press anything more then, as I saw I should not lose time by studying logic for a short time, besides that I could still be reading Blackstone. But now [395] my *Logic* is out, and for the purpose of becoming a practical lawyer, it is absolutely necessary that I should devote my whole time to the study of it—that I should go a pupil either to a conveyancer, a special pleader, or a chancery barrister, and it is the more important that I should depend upon my own means only, as my Uncle's fortune is daily diminishing. Bowring has had the audacity to demand £1000 for the *Westminster Review* for this year, and my Uncle borrows it, without perceiving that such a demand can only be the result of downright knavery. With all this in my mind, ashamed of idling away my time as I am, and further excited by the thought that I could not entertain any idea of marrying till I should be getting money or in a money getting way, I determined to encounter all risks of displeasing my Uncle, and to give him the alternative of allowing me to prosecute my legal studies or of providing for me in some other way. As you may suppose, I was not a little nervous all dinner time, but when the *reprobates* were gone down, and I entered upon the subject, what was my surprise when I found him agree with me entirely, and notwithstanding his having but a day or two ago absolutely forbidden my thinking of practising law, he now completely entered into my views, told me what practical books he had that might be of use to me and, in short, entirely precluded the need of my proposing the alternative, or of saying any thing about his money. The fact is—at least so I suppose it to be—that he dreaded something of the kind. His finances are in so disorderly a state, he is so ready at ordering, and finds it so difficult to *pay* (besides that he feels he has not done justice to my father in this respect), that he cannot bear to have a word said about money, and it is astonishing how cunning he is at finding out when a discourse may turn to that subject and at warding off the blow. It is evident he does not *like* my becoming a lawyer, [396] a class of persons against whom he certainly has a most inveterate hatred—for in the evening he said, a propos of something else, *I would rather see you a tailor, a butcher or a Jack Ketch than an indiscriminate defender of right and wrong.*[81]—However, immediately after, as I thought it necessary to resume the subject, when I told him of the necessity of my earning a livelihood myself, and of there being no other profession besides that of the law which I could adopt, he again agreed with me, so that now I shall act accordingly, and shall be able to do so without the least diminution of the good understanding between us. His opinion of me is the most extraordinarily extravagant you can conceive; he even says *I go beyond himself*, which certainly is the most *he* can possibly say. He sent my book to Peel the other day.[82] Speaking of this, he said to me, 'My only fear is that Peel's mind will not be up to it; you see, they are all poor-minded—all these men whom he has for the consolidation business—amongst all of them, there is not one—I am well persuaded there is not another man in the world who has such another mind as yours and mine.' Then his projects and chateaux en Espagne are really singular. If Peel says in the House that he intends to proceed with the reform of the law of real property, J.B. imagines that Peel will come and codify with him at Q.S.P. If the next day Peel talks of instituting a commission for the purpose,[83] then Peel is weak-minded, hampered by the lawyers, and nothing good will come of it; however, J.B. will threaten him with injuring his reputation abroad, and Peel will be obliged to come to! This is the effect of Bowring's gross flattery upon a mind which, though still very powerful as to its reasoning faculties, is every day more accessible to adulation. In his memory too, I am sorry to say, symptoms of a decrease of strength have lately shown themselves. In other respects, his health of body and mind still continues, and I have every reason to hope may long continue, to be excellent."

[397]I now took regularly to the study of the law, as a pupil to Mr Koe, in whose chambers at Lincoln's Inn I spent the greater part of the morning, devoting every now and then an hour or two to my father, assisting him with his papers, or two or three hours to my Uncle at Queen Square Place, dining there regularly twice a week. My letters at this time contain chiefly accounts of evening parties and other amusements—regrets at the final departure of my friend J. Neale—speculations as to my future prospects under the diminishing course of my Uncle's means, and details on the politics of the day and the ministerial

crisis consequent on Lord Liverpool's disability and the difficulties in forming the Canning administration.[84]

Saturday, April 21. "Dined with my Uncle as usual. He has been writing a letter to the *Globe* evening paper, which has been copied into other papers as a curiosity. Couched in the very perfection of the Benthamian style (or Babylonish, as the *John Bull* calls it),[85] it is no very easy task to catch the drift of it—one person understood it to mean than he predicted Canning's elevation thirty-six years ago, another that there should be no Cabinet at all. His real object seems to be to show that he was intimate with the first Lord Lansdowne, and that he thinks that in the Cabinet, which then consisted of nine, there were eight too many, and that if the ministry were reduced to one, it would save the time and trouble of deliberation, as well as the indigestions and gouts arising from Cabinet dinners. The letter ends: *Allegation of facts requires attestation, attestation requires signature, so here follows that of Jeremy Bentham*, a perfect model for concluding a letter."

"Thursday morning (April 26) to the famous tunnel under the Thames.[86] My father went with Count Woronzow (the younger, afterwards Prince Woronzow), Baron Humboldt and Count Bulow, the Prussian Minister, and as they filled the carriage, I went to meet them there on foot, but having mistaken the side of the river on which it began, [398] I took a boat at the Tower and had a sixpenny row down to Rotherhithe. There I met Mr Brunel, and soon after the gentlemen came. (Then follows a description of the tunnel and the contrivances for excavating and building.) There are now near 500 ft. done—wanting still about 100 ft. of being halfway. The view of the tunnel lighted up with portable gaz is really fine, and, when finished, it will be a most magnificent work, but will it pay?—to the engineer, yes, for his pay is certain and fixed—to the proprietors, no, for, after all, it will be by many preferred to go round by London Bridge, with no toll to pay, than to pay their tolls to travel in this way, underground and under water, though it may be a little shorter journey for them. For the present, however, they have adopted a plan which brings them in a little money. A great number of visitors solicited admittance, and having gained it, annoyed the workmen so much that at last Brunel absolutely refused every one, when at last it came into their heads to smarten up as much as they could what was finished of one of the tunnels, leaving the other for the workmen, and admitting any one who chose to pay a shilling. This plan has perfectly succeeded, and they get near £100 a week, and will probably soon get more. On Good Friday they had above 500 visitors, and would have more than as many every Sunday, if it were open on that day.

"After having gone all over the works, examined the drawings, etc, my father returned with Counts Woronzow and Bulow. Baron Humboldt and I remained some time longer, for the Baron, in the course of his voyages and travels, had never met with a diving bell, and as Mr Brunel happened to have had occasion to go down to the bottom of the Thames, and had borrowed the bell belonging to the East India Company,[87] Baron Humboldt asked to go down in it, and I, as you may suppose, begged to be of the party. We got five into the bell, and were lowered down to the bottom of the river, a depth of about [399] 30 feet, as it was nearly high water. Air is changed by pumping it in at the top, whereby it is driven out at the bottom. The air under this pressure gets very much compressed, which is generally supposed to give very painful sensations, but the only effect we felt was a slight pain in the ears, which, however, soon went off. It was quite dark down there, as you may suppose, but we were provided with candles. Humboldt wrote a few lines for young Brunel, who was with us. We remained down in the river about half an hour.

"In returning to town with Mr Brunel, we stopped (Baron Humboldt and I) at Barclay and Perkins' brewery in Southwark, a most magnificent establishment. The ready made beer is contained in 99 vats (or foudres), containing each from five hundred to eleven hundred *muids*, and of which the staves and hoops are scarcely thicker or stronger looking than our 20 muid foudres. The immense square vats in which the beer is cooled, fermented, etc, piled up one above the other, the enormous stocks of malt and hops, the oceans of yeast which are seen rising from the beer, the compact manner in which all is stowed in these elevated premises covering eleven acres of ground, would make one think that Messrs Barclay and Perkins were providing means for supplying the place of the Thames in the case of an earthquake swallowing it up, rather than that theirs was one only (though perhaps the most considerable) of the numerous breweries necessary for quenching John Bull's thirst."

"Monday afternoon (30th Apl) went to the laying the first stone of the University of London. Seeing that the Universities of Oxford and Cambridge are so exclusive, that learning is so difficult to be got there and, when obtained, so confined to Latin, Greek and mathematics, a number of the Whig nobility and gentry, together with a knot of [400] radicals, laid a plan for erecting an University in London, for giving lectures on the sciences, and which should be carried on in a liberal way, like some

of the Scotch and Continental Universities.[88] Of course this University
will not be on a level with, nor interfere with, Oxford and Cambridge,
for it can have none of the privileges for degrees in law and church,
which induce so many young men to go to the other two. It is not, either,
to have any resident students, but only lectures for those who choose to
attend. The project was entered into, and the subscription commenced,
in 1825—the year of projects[89]—the explosion of the bubbles delayed in
a great measure the completion of the subscription. However, in the
mean time, nine acres of land were purchased near Russell Square, and
last summer or autumn the subscription being at last filled up, the foundations were commenced. These foundations have now been brought
up to the level of the ground, and on this Monday the Duke of Sussex
laid what is called the first stone. A platform was erected all over the
foundations for the purpose of accomodating the spectators admitted by
means of tickets, and a portion was railed off for the Council, who
attended the Duke at the ceremony. There were about a thousand persons present, and many ladies. We were all standing there for an hour
and a half, under a most scorching—almost a Montpellier sun, waiting
for the Duke. The band of the Coldstream guards played some beautiful
pieces of music. The Duke came in the midst of the Council of the University, and proceeded with the usual ceremonies to lay—or make
believe to lay—the stone, into which was put a fine Latin inscription and
some coins of the present reign and year. After the stone was laid, the
Chaplain read prayers; then Dr Lushington made a very good speech
and the Duke answered, also very well. He is an immense man, and his
face certainly looks rather vulgar, particularly with the enormous whiskers he now wears, but he went through the ceremony very well; he
[401] was dressed in a plain suit of black. At six o'clock, they had a
grand dinner at the Freemason's Tavern, where there was, I am told, a
dreadful squeeze, and where all was crammed as close as could be at
table. Brougham, the Marquis of Lansdowne, and others made
speeches. I was not there. I had intended to go, but thought it not worth
the twenty shillings. The university has been terribly attacked, chiefly
with the arm of ridicule, by the Tories,[90] who are scandalised at the pre-
sumption of attempting, by calling it an University, to set it up in competition with Oxford and Cambridge, and perhaps this is their great
fault, for it will be nothing like those Universities. It has also been
laughed at for being built on a dunghill, and for many other equally
foolish reasons, but now that it begins to appear above ground, the
laughers are not so loud."

"Monday evening I dined with my Uncle.—To show you what bright ideas come into his head, I must tell you of one, which he imagined and executed forthwith on Sunday afternoon. He had lately sent a copy of one of his works to Courtenay, the clerk of the House of Lords, and had had in return a civil letter of thanks.[91] Now as Courtenay is a friend of Canning's, or at least my Uncle supposed him so to be, it came into his (J.B.'s) head to write to Canning to ask to have his Codes printed at the expense of Government by the King's printer, but not to ask it as a favour, but rather to offer it as an advantage to Government, and to enclose this brilliant offer, couched in the most extraordinary style, to Courtenay to give to Canning. As I had been lugged into this letter without my participation (for my Uncle sent it off [402] without waiting to show it even to Bowring), I got Koe to explain to Courtenay. I hear, however, that Courtenay did not take it ill, but only laughed at it. The letter, of course, was not transmitted to Canning, but I have not heard whether it be returned to my Uncle."

Tuesday, 1st May. "After spending the morning as usual, went with Mr. W. Bentham to dine at the Westmoreland Society anniversary dinner. This is a charitable society, a sort of county charitable club. I went because Mr Bentham gave me a ticket and I did not like to be uncivil in refusing it, but it was a stupid affair. Above two hundred persons were there, and none whom I know or wish to know. The dinner itself was not grand, and the music of the city band very bad. However, after dinner between the toasts, there was some very tolerable singing, and some even very good, by professional singers, hired for the occasion."

After details of the formation of the Canning administration, "The Commons met on Tuesday night, with a very full house, and an extraordinary sight it is said to have been. So complete a revolution in the Ministry, so strange a medley of parties in the new Cabinet, that it was very awkward for members to know where to sit. Burdett, the champion of the radicals, he who was persuaded that none of the evils, none of the distresses of the country, could ever be remedied without a complete radical reform of Parliament, goes and sits side by side with Canning, the most violent enemy to Parliamentary reform. Brougham also, the constant antagonist to Canning, Hobhouse, the enemy to all ministers, and the Whigs, who 'never could accept office unless Catholic emancipation were [403] to be made a Cabinet question,' all are now on the ministerial benches, when the Cabinet is formed under the express understanding that it is to be neutral on that question. The old Ministerials are on the neutral, and even some on the opposition, benches. Hume,

who can never quit an old seat any more than an old idea, or go on in
any way except in the usual way of attracting every thing that sounds
like pounds, shillings and pence, retains the seat where he has always
sat on the Opposition benches. Calcraft, a Whig, when he came in, stood
for a moment in the middle of the House, looked round to the right and
left, and seeing his friends so strangely placed, exclaimed aloud, 'And
where the devil am I to sit?' Peel's speech is a good one, and makes out a
good vindication of his own conduct, but he has failed, I think, in making out a case for his colleagues. Canning's answer was good, but
beneath his usual excellence; Dawson's (Peel's brother in law's) speech
was a most violent and injudicious diatribe. Burdett failed in excusing
himself for joining ministers against his declared principles,[92] and the
other speeches were very indifferent. The interest excited by this sitting
has been very great, the House was crammed in every corner, and what
had scarcely ever been seen, many bishops attended."

"The Lords met on Wednesday, when Eldon, Wellington, Melville,
etc, made their respective explanatory speeches.[93] Eldon got sentimental, Wellington spoke like a soldier, Melville like a Canning-hater, which
he is, but they failed, I think, in disproving a certain degree of precon-
cert, and at least what is the only thing I find objectionable in their conduct, the not intimating to Canning that they would resign in such and
such cases before they actually did, a dishonorable conduct I think, and
which Peel was not guilty of, for *he* gave Canning previous notice.
Melville is the least excusable, for he cannot put forward the Catholic
question as an excuse, for he always votes for the Catholics.

[404]"But great as has been the excitation of the public feeling on this
head, it has suddenly given way to the interest excited by what is going
on in Paris. The first news of the review and disbandment of the
National Guard[94] has, of course, been accompanied with a number of
alarming reports, which time only can clear up. . . . "

"We are going on comfortably. My father has been much better since
the return of the warm weather, and frequently dines out.—I am always
in perfect health, and very glad to be busy with the law. I shall keep the
present term, that is, visit the necessary five dinners, which I must do four
times a year for three years." It was only necessary to attend at the dining
hall in Lincoln's Inn, enter your name, put on a robe, and wait till grace
was said, when you might leave, being considered to have eaten your
dinner. At the Temple it was necessary to stay until dinner was over.

Tuesday, 8th May. After accounts of an agreable dinner party with the
Denmans and Crofts at Mrs. Baillie's,[95] and of the enjoyment of hearing

Pasta at the Opera, etc, "Now for my discussions with my Uncle. I know not whether the general triumph of the liberal part of the ministry, or what other cause, appears to have agitated him a good deal for some time past, and even excited his ambition and a desire and expectation of getting a place under Government, and also made him very hot upon his codes, etc. For some time, I have been no longer a regular attendant at Queen Square Place and, with his consent and approval, had been studying the law at Lincoln's Inn. This he did not much like, though whenever I spoke to him, he approved of it. For two or three times past that I had dined with him, he had been rather pettish, yet I thought that nothing more was coming. However on Saturday night he suddenly announced that I must give up every thing and come [405] every morning and work at the Procedure Code.[96] Unprepared as I was for any such request, and feeling the importance of persisting in the course of legal studies I had commenced, I at once objected to this, whereupon he told me that if I preferred to do so, he must immediately come to a complete rupture with the whole of our family. Discussion continued, in the course of which he got exceedingly irritated, raked up all manner of imaginary complaints against my father and mother, reproached me with breaking my engagements with him (I never made any but what I have told you), threatened me with altering his will; in short, there is nothing harsh or disagreeable which he did not say, particularly as I was obliged to answer him rather positively in some things. In short, after discussing during the whole two hours that he was undressing, we separated, with a complete quarrel if I did not give a satisfactory answer to his proposition, for which I had a day or two to consider.

"I returned home at the usual hour, between one and two in the morning, in no very gay humour, and the next morning talked it over with my father, but could not determine on what course to pursue. I then went to Mr Koe's to consult him, and talked it over for a long time with him, but still without coming to any decision; so much mis-application of a time which should be devoted to the study of my profession did I see in yielding to his fancies, and so little certainty of any permanent harmony, and, on the other hand, so great are the inconveniences and mischiefs which would result from a breech with him. Monday morning I came to enquire of Doane what had been the result with my Uncle, but my Uncle had not said a word, and was as gay as ever. At last, after much further consultation [406], I determined on yielding, and wrote to my Uncle that I acquiesced in his proposal, and would give him up my morning after this week, telling him at the same time that if I heard nothing from him, I should be at dinner today (Wednesday) as usual. I called here yesterday, and to my great alarm learnt that a letter had been despatched for me, but which, owing to a wrong direction, had not even now come to hand. However, I now know that it contained no further refusal or dismissal, and that I am to dine here as usual. I shall be perhaps a little embarassed at first, but he will soon forget what passed the other night, and I shall again be a regular attendant here in the morning, giving up the law for whatever my Uncle may give me to do. It is possible that I may derive considerable benefit from this, but dependence to such a degree is a hard pill to swallow."

Saturday, May 12th. "All went on well with my Uncle on Wednesday night. He was remarkably friendly and full of *petites attentions*, and did not allude to our quarrel—so far so good—but now I am in for it, and must spend my time in occupations which will be of little, if any, use to me, but every body says that I have done quite right to yield to him. . . . In the little time that I have been studying with Mr Koe, I believe he was tolerably pleased with me, and as a proof of my *bonnes dispositions*, he told me the other day that an opinion he had given to me to make out upon a case that had been submitted to him had needed scarcely any alteration on his part, but that he had given it to his clerk to copy, and it had served him almost in statu quo.—Never mind if I repeat to you any approbation I hear of myself. With you, dear, I need not be squeamish."

"From the *New Monthly Magazine*, I learn that on the 13th Jany [407] I was admitted a Member of the Edinburgh Wernerian Natural History Society.[97] This is my friend Arnott's doing, but I have received no diploma nor application for guineas, nor heard of it even from Arnott, though I have had letters from him since the 13th Jany. It must be his doing, because he is an influential man in that Society, but I suppose he forgot to tell me—and, after all, it is no very grand Society, nor a very distinguished honor to belong to it."

8

London Society; Further Travel, 1827–28

My sisters had expressed a great wish to see a ball in Almack's rooms,[1] and Lady Colchester applied to the Marchioness of Stafford for tickets for them to the Caledonian fancy ball, on the 14th. Lady Stafford recalled having known my father at Paris forty years previously,[2] and expressed a wish to see him again, my father much enjoying the visit, recalling to him old times. We had made acquaintance with Sir Murray Maxwell (who commanded the Alceste that took Lord Amherst to China,[3] and afterwards had the severe contest for Westminster with Sir Francis Burdett),[4] and Lady Maxwell offered to chaperone my sisters. This ball was to my sisters a great event and a great delight, as they both, particularly Clara, looked exceedingly well in full dress, and I sent the following account to my sister at Montpellier.[5] "In the evening, Joanna Baillie and the Longleys came in to see my sisters dressed for the ball, and at a little after nine we set out, calling at Mrs Denman's and at the Magens's,[6] where Lady Colchester was dining, to shew the dresses, then to the Maxwells, where the party whom Lady Maxwell was to chaperone had assembled. Our party consisted of fourteen: Lady and two Miss Maxwells, two other young ladies, Sir Murray, his son and four other gentlemen, one of them a naval officer, who has been for many years engaged to [408] Miss Maxwell, but is waiting till his rank is high enough to enable him to marry her. The ball was at Willis's rooms[7] and was certainly one of the most splendid sights I have yet seen. The principal room is magnificent, illuminated with above five hundred wax candles and contained near nine hundred and fifty persons, without being so overcrowded as many private balls are. The ladies were all resplendent with jewels and finery, the gentlemen in every variety of costume, not one being admitted in ordinary dress. There were a great many in highland dress, which admits of so great a variety in colour—a great many also, too many indeed, in uniform, which gave rather too great a preponderance of scarlet. My sisters both wore Russian dresses. Clara had one like what she wore at Montpellier. Sarah's was made from the drawing of a Russian peasant, which the Klustines gave her for her album; they both looked very well, even amongst the forty and fifty guinea dresses which many ladies displayed, and by the side of the diamonds, of which there was a great profusion. Lady Colchester had lent a beautifull topaze parure, and the Carrs, Mrs Lushington and the Baillies had also lent them some very valuable jewels. I had a highland dress. The company was of the first order. The Duke and Duchess of Clarence came in with the Lady patronesses at about eleven, and remained till two. The Duke of Sussex was also there, in a highland dress which became him very well, the drapery in some measure concealing his corpulence. The Duke of Clarence wore a naval uniform. He was in the highest spirits, going about talking to all whom he knew, particularly to naval officers. He conversed for a long time with the Maxwells, with whom we were. The Duchess sat at the head of the room with the lady patronesses. She is an exceedingly ladylike, elegant-looking person; she was dressed in black with white plumes; she had all the [409] appearance of being what she is said to be, mild, amiable, and possessing all the good qualities necessary for subduing her husband's sailor-like roughness. The two together will probably make no bad king and queen."[8]

"Dancing began soon after they entered, but at first the room was rather crowded for the purpose. Quadrilles and reels were alternated during the night, with now and then a waltz. The reels were danced with great spirit, there being so many Scotch present. At about twelve o'clock, the boys of the Caledonian Asylum,[9] in highland costume, marched round the room with bagpipes at their head, and several of the company who happened to be in highland dresses, I amongst the rest. At the head of the room, they stopped to make their obeisance to the Duchess of Clarence, and then marched out again. Towards two o'clock, the members of the Royal family left the room, and the company gradually thinned. We remained till five in the morning, when we drove off in broad daylight, leaving above a hundred persons waiting for their carriages to be able to draw up. The music was Colinet's full band, the refreshments, cakes, lemonade, etc, in an adjoining room, the whole exceedingly well conducted. My sisters were much pleased with their evening; they danced a good deal, and though at first it was excessively crowded for the purpose, yet towards the end it was very pleasant. As for myself, I admired much the beauty of the scene, the brilliancy of the costumes and the great display of beauty, which may always be seen in an assemblage of the English nobility and upper classes of gentry, but I soon got tired and ennuyé. I only like balls where I get agreable partners whom I know, and I am rather spoilt in that way since I have danced so much with the Carrs. . . ."

Tuesday 15th. "After spending the morning at Queen Square Place and dining at home, went to the Opera to hear Pasta in *Semiramède*. This is one of her best parts, and though I always think whenever [410] I hear her that it would be impossible to hear anything better, yet she certainly surpasses herself, as the French say, in this opera, of which the music itself is so very beautifull. Galli, whom I had never yet heard, has a magnificent base voice, and Curioni's tenor is also fine, but the rest of the singers were but indifferent. The orchestra is not nearly so good as that at Paris, and the chorus scarcely so good as at Toulouse. Arsace, a very important part in the piece, was acted by a young and pretty actress, Brambilla, but her beauty was all that could recommend her. Not always in tune, a disagreable expression in singing, and a total want of gracefulness, could not be compensated by a voice not bad in itself, especially by the side of Pasta, whose graceful action is as surprising as her extraordinary voice and méthode. So much did Brambilla spoil it, that the duet of 'Giorno d'orrore' between her and Pasta, one of the finest of Rossini's duetts, was, notwithstanding Pasta, upon the whole inferior to what it is when sung by Isabella and Laura. They sing it so perfectly together, and both with so much expression and feeling, as to have the most powerful effect upon you—which an awkward gesture or a note out of tune of Brambilla would quite destroy. After the opera, we had one of those divertissements, which at the English opera are the most disgraceful and stupid things that can be conceived. You know how stupid are the ballets at the French opera. Here it is ten times worse, the music very bad and the dancing still worse."

Wednesday 16th. "After spending the morning at my uncle's, went to Lincoln's Inn to commence term-keeping, but finding that it was not necessary actually to eat, but merely to go into the dining hall at the hour and have your name set down, I did so and went to Morton's chambers, where he had asked two or three friends to dine upon the occasion of his being called to the bar. He himself, however, dined in Hall (at Gray's Inn, of which he is) [411] where we joined him after dinner to *drink him in*, together with the others who were called at the same time. They were four who, with their friends and ourselves, made a party of about thirty. We had dessert and wine, and sat there till past ten—some of them remained till twelve, drinking, speechifying and singing, as at club dinners. Some years ago at a calling to the bar, those called had to find dessert and claret for the whole hall, two or three hundred persons, at an expence of from sixty to a hundred pounds, but now this has been in a great measure stopped, and at Lincoln's Inn and the Temple they had frequently no drinking in at all. Gray's Inn is much frequented by Irish students, and is therefore ranked perhaps rather below the others."

I was now in daily attendance all the morning at my Uncle's, and gave accounts in my letters of various dinners and evening parties, chiefly musical. I also "kept" the term at Lincoln's Inn, and Friday, 18th, "I actually dined in hall. At the upper end of the hall is a cross table, at which the Benchers eat a dinner of superior quality. Below this is a cross

table for the barristers, and the remainder of the hall contains a number
of tables, laid length ways for the students, but it appeared to me that
students and such barristers as dined in hall sat promiscuously. There
were between two and three hundred present. The dinner is served in
messes for four. To each mess a dish of fish, a dish of meat (in the mess
where I was today a roast leg of mutton), a dish of potatoes, and
cheese—also a bottle of port wine—bread, beer and water ad libitum—
steel forks and iron spoons. Every one must put on a gown over his coat,
which gowns are given you as you go in at the door. Such is the way in
which one is to eat one's self into a lawyer, and to make the dining in
hall as conducive as possible to the [412] students' instruction, etiquette
forbids your saying a single word to your neighbour, unless you are
previously introduced to him." All that was allowed was to ask for the
salt, and to drink your first glass of wine with your opposite neighbour,
the second with the one on your side, the third diagonally, which made
up the twelve glasses the bottle held.

My letters have also a good deal about family matters, and my hopes
and fears about an attachment which ultimately proved unsuccessfull,[10]
and I add, "Though I have frequently little causes of vexation and anxiety, I cannot say that upon the whole I am not happy. I am happy when
wrapt in my logic or law—happy when sitting at dinner with a party of
friends, happy surtout when in good spirits about *her*, though certainly I
have occasionally the irksome task of peacemaking at home to perform.
I am well in health, though some say I am rather thin, but I do not think
so. I have also the satisfaction to tell you that I think I have got over a little (though but little) of my backwardness in company—but I am slow
in making friends, and new acquaintances do not in general think much
of me."

Thursday, 24th to Saturday, 26th May. The West End much taken up
by the great bazar in Hanover Square Rooms for the benefit of the Spanish and Italian refugees, patronised by some of the ladies of the highest
rank, as well as by the Duke of Wellington and others, with some of the
greatest beauties of the day behind the counters, amongst others two
Miss Sheridans, then conspicuous not only for their beauty, but for their
fastness, not yet then in fashion, as it has since become—and their impudent sayings and offhand dealings much quoted. §My sisters there with
their friends the Carrs, one of whom was one of the shopladies, and one
of my sisters sent some drawings which sold well. The [413] produce of
the three days was £2400, clear of all expences. "Townsend, the police
officer, contributed his share by giving his attendance for the three days

gratis. (The new police was not then yet established.)[11] This veteran of the police, the attendant upon royalty wherever his majesty goes, the constable always employed in royal processions, is the most good-natured, droll, impudent old fellow that can be imagined, and is allowed a tone of familiarity with the highest personages in the Kingdom. On the first bazar day, he went up to the Duke of Wellington—'I say, Duke, there is such a d—d rush at the door they almost had me over, and there are three hundred carriages waiting to set down. Am I to let them in or not, for the room is already fuller than it can hold?'—and in this way he goes on to everyone. Everyone knows him, and everyone excuses the freedom."

The rest of this season (1827) spent the mornings usually either writing, or supposed to be writing, for my Uncle at Queen Square Place—occasionally two or three hours at home, writing for my father, who continued to entertain great expectations from his writings on Naval affairs.—Kept another term at Lincoln's Inn—and much out at balls, parties, operas or concerts in the evenings—two or three small parties at home.—The Colchesters, Murray Maxwells, Pole Carews, etc, among Tories, Edward Strutt (afterwards Lord Belper) and his sisters, John Romilly (afterwards Lord Romilly) etc, on the other side; generally music, in which Isabella and Laura Carr (afterwards Lady Eardley and Lady Cranworth) carried off all suffrages, from their splendid singing—especially a grand duo in *Semiramide*. One of our great balls at the Pole Carews. Mr Pole Carew, an old friend of my father's, with a family of thirteen, mostly daughters, the eldest married and 35, the youngest "not quite come out yet." Saw also a good deal of M. de Bruloff, a young Russian architect, [414] returning home from a some years' stay at government expence in Italy, whom we took about, and with whom we were much pleased. Went to the Somerset house Exhibition of the Royal Academy—to de Beriot, the violinist's, concert—to the grand, but stupid "Battle of Waterloo" at Vauxhall, followed by fine fireworks, and attended by eight or ten thousand spectators, etc.

Monday, 4th June. "With my father and mother and Sarah to spend the day at General Sabloukoff's, at a house they have temporarily near Woodlands, his brother-in-law, Mr Angerstein's place in Kent. Met there Lord Bexley. This you know is the quondam Chancellor of the Exchequer, Vansittart, alias 'Nicky Van,' one of the heads of the party of Saints, a member of the late Cabinet, where he held the sinecure of Chancellor of the Duchy of Lancaster. He went out with the seven, but ratted, and returned to the new Cabinet,[12] where he was readmitted more for his insignificance than for any other reason, for it was not worth making a piece of work about him. However, he seems proud of being able to say *we* in speaking of the Administration. He spoke a great deal of the Corn bill, which, you may have seen by the papers, was going through the House of Lords with considerable majorities, when the Duke of Wellington brought an amendment, which quite altered the principle of the bill, and somehow or other the outs got this amendment carried by a majority of four, to the astonishment of many, the exultation of the noble landholders, and, I think, to the shame of those ex-ministers who are thus damning their own work. For this bill is the child of Lord Liverpool's administration, and Lord Bathurst, for instance, a member of that administration, and the very one who introduced the bill to the house of Lords, is now voting against it."[13] General Sabloukoff was about to leave for St Petersburgh, and left in our charge, against his return, to make what use we liked of, a set of Russian books. Amongst them, I took to "reading a book which [414]§ interests me very much, that is Karamsin's *History of Russia*—the same one which the Klustines used always to be reading. I then never looked into it, thinking I should find it dry and not understand it, not knowing enough of the language to feel the beauties of the style; but I am surprised to find it the most agreable reading that I have had for some time, and there are but very few occasions when I have to refer to the dictionary. It is only a pity that he did not live to finish it."[14]

As time went on, I found I could gradually take more from my idle time at Queen Square Place to spend at law in Koe's chambers. In botany, I did but very little, having little time for it, except at night, on my return home from dinners or parties. I received, however, a very good set of Caucasian plants, forwarded from Paris by my friend Klustine, together with a diploma of Foreign Member of the Société Impériale des Naturalistes de Moscou, and I generally endeavoured to keep myself a little au courant of what was going on in the botanical world. "Some numbers of the *Flora oder Botanische Zeitung*, a German botanical period-ical which I have taken in for several years, which have just come to hand, contain, amongst other things, a letter to the editors (Hoppe and Hornschuch) from Gay, of Paris, from which I cannot help sending you the following extract: 'M. Bentham, jeune Anglais établi depuis quelques années à Montpellier, vient de publier un *Catalogue des plantes des Pyrenées et du Bas-Languedoc*, très-curieux à plusieurs égards. Ce *Cat-alogue* a été composé à la suite d'un voyage fait aux Pyrenées dans le cours de l'année dernière, et après un séjour à Toulouse, pendant lequel l'auteur a pu visiter une bonne partie de l'herbier de Lapeyrouse. De là, une foule de synonymes rapportés par M. Bentham, et une multitude de doubles emplois et autres [415] erreurs relevées. Désormais il faudra nécessairement consulter le *Catalogue* de M. Bentham pour connaître les plantes de Lapeyrouse, le plus ignorant, peut-être, des botanistes qui ont ecrit dans ce siècle. (*I* should never have ventured to have *said* as much, though I have often *thought* it, but I can't help if the facts I have published should make *others* say so. Fortunately this will probably never meet with the present M. de Lapeyrouse's eye.) La production de M. Bentham se recommande encore par une ébauche de la monographie des genres *Medicago, Cistus, Helianthemum* et *Cerastium*. L'auteur se propose de traiter ces genres *ex professo*, lorsqu'il aura réuni un plus grand nombre de matériaux. (Yes, if I ever again find time to meddle with the delightful, though futile, study of botany.) Il y a quelques erreurs dans ce petit ouvrage (some few I have discovered. I know not what M. Gay alludes to, but in some cases Lapeyrouse's synonyms[§] are equally applicable to a number of plants, so that what may appear to Gay to be errors may not really be so) et toutes les fautes de Lapeyrouse n'y sont pas rapportées. (This I will also admit. I do not profess to point out *all*, but only such as I knew to be mistakes. Gay has had the means of ascertaining several which I did not know of. He has known of them for years, and kept them secret with a view to publishing them himself in his French Flora, which he is so long in bringing out. He is afraid of being forestalled, and will be so in a great measure, and very deservedly, if he is so dilatory. Some of his discoveries I knew of, but did not *publish*, from motives of delicacy, anything which I knew of in an underhand way, though in scientific subjects the merit is considered as less in him who discovers a thing than in him who first publishes it) mais on ne peut s'empecher de [416] convenir qu'il rend à la botanique française un service bien important.' Ratisbon *Flora*, Jan. 14, 1827.[15] Whatever Gay says in favor of my work cannot be said to be purchased eulogium, as that in newspapers and suchlike periodicals, to which copies are sent for the purpose of being puffed. I do not even think that any copy of my *Catalogue* was sent to Gay, for he passes for a dry, uncommunicating, jealous, and not always very fair dealing botanist, and he is particularly jealous of those who write on the French and Pyrenean botany, on account of his own French Flora, which he is preparing. He and Arnott are acquainted, and it is through Arnott that I have obtained some valuable information, which I have mentioned as having abstained from publishing, although he told Arnott no more than he could not conceal.

Gay and Arnott distrusted one another and parted no very good friends.
I therefore am anything but a friend of Gay's, and his commendation is
the more valuable to me." To this, I may now add that, in after years, I
became more acquainted with Gay, and think there is no ground for
attributing to him anything like unfair dealing. Dilatory, particular, and
somewhat jealous he certainly was, but I always found him upright and
friendly, and have no reason to complain of any comment he may have
made on any of my botanical publications.§

[417]Saturday 23d June. "To the Horticultural Society's fête at their
gardens at Chiswick.[16] The occasion of this fête is the same as of the
anniversary dinner, which they usually have, like all other clubs and
societies, at which dinner there was always a great display of fruit; but
as no ladies could partake of a club dinner, and were only admitted to
walk round at desert time to see the fruit, the ladies connected with the
Society (they were not yet admitted as Fellows)[17] did not like that the
gentlemen should thus enjoy exclusively the festivities of it. So this year
it was determined to substitute a public breakfast in the gardens. Tickets
were issued for the members, two ladies' tickets were allowed for each
subscriber to the gardens, and 24 Ladies patronesses of the first nobility
were entrusted with fifty tickets each for their friends, making in the
whole about three thousand tickets which, being thus distributed at the
price of a guinea or a guinea and a half each, ensured a proper selection
of company and the exclusion of low and vulgar people. The weather,
which for the last day or two had been unsettled, became favourable,
though cloudy and rather chilly. The company began to assemble§ at
about 2. When I arrived at a quarter before three, the string of carriages
waiting to set down was about half a mile long, and they continued setting down as fast as they could till past five. Nearly two thirds of the
company were ladies, and amongst them the greatest beauties of the
day, all dressed in the height of elegance and fashion, and though white
prevailed, there was a mixture of every colour of the rainbow. Bands of
music stationed in different parts of the Garden played alternately during the whole day. The Coldstream Guards' band was particularly beautifull, also the Artillery band, the trumpets of a regiment of cavalry and,
in a retired corner, two Scotch Highlanders with their bagpipes. Over
the pond was [418] erected a stage, on which the Rainer family (four
Tyrolese brothers and their sister) sung two or three times. Their mode
of singing is very peculiar, and had a very striking and beautifull effect
in the garden, though it is said to be rather loud in a room. However
they are very much admired, and are every night engaged to sing at

some party among the nobility. They appear in their Tyrolese dresses, wear moustachios, and though one be a very handsome man, they have a sad, brigandish look. In another part of the Garden, a portion of the lawn was marked out for dancing, in front of a stage on which was Collinet, with as full a band as perhaps even he had ever commanded for quadrille playing. There was not much dancing, for in this land of stiff etiquette, it was only those who could make up a set of their own party both partners and vis-à-vis, who ventured to dance so publicly.

"The principal part of the fruit was exhibited in a large tent extended for the purpose. This desert consisted of every rarity of the kind that could be collected from all parts of the country. Notices were stuck up that it was not to be touched till six o'clock—but at six—and this was the only thing at all approaching to disorder that could be remarked during the day, those who were round the table rushed on the fruit at once, and to the astonishment and dismay of the waiters carved the pineapples with their penknives, and soon made an end of the whole desert. At the refreshment tents, which opened at five, the scene was much more rational, though they were excessively crowded, and though, from the miscalculation of the furnishers, the quantity of food turned out insufficient for so large a company, yet all was perfectly orderly. The meats were such as form the ingredients of the supper tables at balls, but it was a great error of the Society to employ Jaurin of Bond Street and not Gunter, who is the only one in town who can judge what is [419] necessary on such occasions as this. Jaurin gets 12'/ a head, for which, it is said, Gunter would not do it, but the price seems pretty fair. Other tents with tea, lemonade, etc, were open all the day, and in one called the Royal tent, a regular meal was set out for the Duke of Sussex and the heads of the nobility and lady patronesses present. Other tents again were provided for shelter in case of rain, but fortunately were not needed. All these tents were lent from the Woolwich depot, and several soldiers were ready, as well as the gardeners, in case of need (the new police was not yet in existence). But, excepting the fruit table, the company behaved remarkably well; not a flower was gathered. The company spent the day in circulating over the lawn, or seated on the numerous benches and chairs placed about the tents and bands, etc. I joined the Carrs and staid with them the whole time, meeting, however, several other acquaintances. We left the garden at about nine, the company having begun leaving at half past seven. I believe it was near ten by the time they could all get to their carriages, of which I never saw so many collected, and, amongst the number, perhaps not above a dozen hackney coaches (no cabs then). There must have been above twelve hundred gentlemen's carriages, and such rows at the doors amongst the servants, who were not nearly so orderly as their masters. As the Carrs went to Hampstead across the country, I walked home. Upon the whole I was very much pleased, and hope they will renew it another year."

My father being called down to Portsmouth, partly on some business connected with our house there, but chiefly for the pleasure of seeing again some of his old associates and subordinates there, on Friday 29th, "Left town with my father at half past seven in the Portsmouth coach—a six-inside—travelling companions three [420], well enough, two of them young women from the north on their way to Plymouth, for since the steamboats, the shortest and cheapest way from London to Plymouth is to come down to Portsmouth and from thence take the steamboat; the third companion a garrulous old lady, but not disagreable—but the fourth—a widow by her dress, whom we took up at Vauxhall. When we stopped to take her up, hearing her speak of having taken a place and a half, and seeing a boy with her, we were already preparing to complain of having him stuffed in beyond the number. The boy however got outside, but instead of him, there was thrust in an enormous cage with a parrot. At this we all remonstrated, but the widow was obstinate, and the coachman drove on. This cage, which extended over all our knees, was of course not much relished, and more than one of us testified our dislike, but the widow persisted. 'It's no use. I shan't part from my dear Parrot, poor thing; she is dearer to me than all the world, and I have a right to have her with me for I have paid for her. I've paid for my parrot and my dog (the dog, fortunately, had consented to go outside) and they shall be with me. I would not have my parrot go outside for the world; she is dearer to me than my own child, for I've put my child outside and paid for my parrot and my dog inside, and when I've paid I'll have my right against all the coachmen in the world, and there is no getting on with these people without showing spirit. Poor Poll, we won't let you be used so ill, so you shan't go outside. I'll have you with me, I've paid for you, etc.' And as her spirit began to make us laugh, and as she saw the wry faces that we were making at the effluvea, which issued more from her than from her parrot—and perhaps we were laughing at her round, fat, greasy face, her little eyes, etc, she put up her veil and, looking round as angrily as she could, she exclaimed, 'No, I won't be used in this way; my parrot and my dog [421] shan't be abused. I've paid for them, and they've a right to be here. I belong to the Navy, and won't bear it. Yes, I belong to the Navy, that is I did. If he were here that is no more, he would not suffer my parrot and my dog to be used in this way. If I had still my husband, I should never have been treated in this way, but though I'm a widow, I'll have my right. My parrot and my dog, etc.' She got quiet at last and began chattering to the parrot, till at last, by the end of the first stage, she was herself tired of holding the cage and had it put outside. We thought the smell would go with the cage, but were disappointed, and soon found the reason, when the good widow took off her bonnet and showed her widow's cap, which once had been white, but now plainly indicated that weeks if not months elapsed between her clean-linen days; and with that you may conceive what must be the effect of a fat and greasy dame in such circumstances in a six-inside coach on a summer's day. However the weather was fine enough to have the windows down, and freed from the gêne of the parrot, we got through the day tolerably well."

We remained a week at Portsmouth with my father's old friend and former Assistant, Mr Goodrich, now superintending the engineering works at the Dock-Yard. My father much enjoyed revisiting the Yard, where he was well received by the few remaining of the Officials who were there when he was Inspector-General; he had a Dock-Yard boat placed at his disposal, and every civility shown him, but he specially enjoyed a couple of mornings spent at Ryde, where he had some hours' gossip with his old friend Lady Spencer.—He also completed his private business by the sale of our house at Berry, near Gosport—considerably below the price he had given for it in the war time—and we had some regret at finally parting [422] with a place so full of pleasing recollections—but we had no prospect of ever inhabiting it again ourselves, and in other respects it was only a burthen and a trouble to us.

Returning to town, it was now the beginning of July; dinners, balls and musical evenings were becoming less frequent, and my Uncle less exigeant. I was enabled to give more time to my legal studies, in which I began to take great interest. The two days in the week that I dined at my Uncle's I could spend the morning at Mr Koe's chambers in Lincoln's Inn, going through his Equity cases and pleadings—thence to Queen Square Place, sitting with my Uncle after dinner till twelve or one o'clock. Other days, I was at Queen Square Place in the morning for a few hours only, and at Mr Koe's chambers in the afternoon, and often again in the evening for an hour or two, for at that time barristers in practice generally dined at five and were in chambers again from ½ past 6 to ½ past 8—the Rolls Court often sitting in the evening.

I could also give my father occasionally a few hours, although I found it very difficult to enter as thoroughly in his naval engineering subjects as into practical law in Lincoln's Inn, and theoretical law at Queen Square Place. My letters for these five or six weeks are full of details of these various occupations, parties, etc, frequent visits to the Baillies and the Carrs at Hampstead, visits from foreigners, etc. From these letters I give as a sample: "Monday 23d July. All day at Lincoln's Inn. In the evening Frances and Anna Carr spent a few hours with my sisters, but I was too much interested in a cause I was studying at Mr Koe's to be able to stay at home for them, as I cannot go to Lincoln's Inn tomorrow. I am particularly anxious to get on with Mr Koe whilst he remains in town, [423] and if I lose a moment that I can devote to law, it is a great loss, now that I have so much of my time necessarily taken up with my use-less visits to Queen Square Place and the writing I must do for my father." Again, Tuesday, 31st. "At Lincoln's Inn from 9 till 4 and again in the evening from ½ past 6 till ½ past 10," with many similar entries as long as Mr Koe remained in town.

Wednesday, 1st Augt. "To my Uncle's to dinner. He is in high spirits about the Cape of Good Hope. The chief Justice, Sir John Wilde, who is going out there, is something of a liberal, and an admirer of my Uncle's, but he is not a man of great abilities, and his nomination does not in general give very great satisfaction. But my Uncle is delighted, imagin-ing that Sir John will adopt his Codes. Sir John listens to all my Uncle says to him, but I suspect he will confine himself to listening, and in the mean time feeds my Uncle with admiration, which is what he likes best."

Saturday, 4th Augt. "At Lincoln's Inn all the morning, went home with Mr Koe to dinner, and was to have staid the evening at work with him, but he thought it a pity to let the season past without going to the Opera and, as this was the last night, he went there with his wife and sister in law; so I went home to dress and went also to the Opera. Though so few persons be in town, the pit was excessively full and, as I came late, I had to stand all the time. Pasta in *Didone* was, as usual, most beautifull. Her extraordinary singing is combined with such graceful-ness and nobleness in every gesture and every motion, such expession in every feature of her countenance, that from the moment that she is on the stage it is impossible to see or hear anything but her. Her sudden changes from the fierceness with which she adresses Jarbas, to the utmost tenderness in speaking to Aeneas, and then again her rage at the departure of the Trojans, [424] and indeed her very sitting upon the throne, is what no one else could do like her—and in the last scene, she really surpasses what she herself can do at other times.—Curioni was good, but I was much disappointed in Made Puzzi. Her face is pretty, but she is too tall, and now thin, and her long lanky arms and rather awkward make have neither gracefulness nor expression."

There is much now in my letters on the political excitement caused by the death of Canning, the break up of his administration, and the difficulties in forming a new one, terminating in what proved the miserably weak Cabinet of Lord Goderich,[18] though at first better expectations were entertained. "Saturday, 17th.§ The ministry is now all settled, and filled up by men chiefly belonging to Canning's administration, so that the policy followed will be his, and probably as firm, or firmer, than if he had lived. The Duke of Wellington has accepted the Commander-in-Chiefship, which will give it strength and consistence, though he takes no part in the Cabinet or Cabinet-measures. Herries takes the Chancellorship of the Exchequer, and Huskisson the Colonial office, with the lead of the House of Commons, if he is able and willing to take that arduous task upon himself, for his health is very precarious. Charles Grant, who is named for the Board of Trade, is a most indolent and absent man. He forgets even his invitations to dinner, goes on the wrong days, or recollects them just at dinner time, calls a hackney coach in a hurry, and dresses as he goes along. He is a great 'Saint.' Lord Manners, addressing him one day in an Irish Court, broke out with 'You d—d whining, sneaking, snivelling hypocrite,' which shows his character with some persons, at least. I wonder they admit such a man."

[425]London season was now over, my last attendance at Mr Koe's chambers before he left for the vacation was on the 20th August, my father and sisters were absent on a four or five weeks' visit to his old friend Mr Strutt (Lord Belper's father), and I was alone with my mother in Manchester Street. It was settled that on their return I should make a tour to the north, chiefly for the purpose of visiting my botanical friends in Glasgow and Edinburgh, and to my great delight young Klustine from Paris promised to come over, spend a few days in town, and then accompany me to the north. In the mean time, I contrived to find time after my morning's work for sightseeing, and went often to the theatres in the evening.

Saturday, 18th. "With Andrew Morton to the King's collection of pictures, exhibited in Pall Mall, which I had not yet seen, and of which this is the last day. They are to form part of the National Gallery when the National Gallery is built, but it is not yet definitively settled *where* it is to be built.[19] These pictures are all first rate. . . ."

Monday, 20th. After my last morning at Lincoln's Inn, went "after dinner with W. Carr to the Haymarket theatre. The plays were *The Way to Keep Him*, a comedy in five acts, *The Rencontre*, an opéra-comique in two, and an afterpiece, *Twixt the Cup and the Lip*. Farren in the first two is excessively good. He is one of those whose very face sets one laughing, besides that his acting is good. In *The Rencontre* he has the part of an old Baron who is a great enemy to duelling, and we see a nephew in danger of disinheritance should a duel he has fought come to the Baron's knowledge (after two which the Baron had formerly with great [426] difficulty pardoned). But soon the Baron himself is provoked into a challenge, and is surprised by his nephew just as he is on the point of firing. His own arguments against duelling are then retorted upon him. He pleads excessive provocation and a threat to kick him round his park, etc. The other answers, in the Baron's own words on a former occasion. 'Well, for a little kicking. . . .' The Baron takes this up with, 'A *little* kicking do you call it? Why my park's three miles round,' in such a manner as to set the whole house in a roar of laughter. Made Vestris, so celebrated for her impudent licentiousness, plays the coquette most admirably, and really looks quite bewitching on the stage, when far enough off to conceal the paint that covers her cheeks, lips, face, neck and arms. In the afterpiece, Reeve, in Liston's character of Simon Pengander, is good but unequal to Liston, who I think will never be equalled in comic, or rather in humorous characters.

"After sitting six hours in the theatre, for the curtain was drawn up at 7 and it only closed at 1 in the morning, returned home and found Antoine (young Klustine) already arrived. He left Paris on Saturday night, got to Calais Sunday night, stayed there thirteen hours, and landed at the Tower Stairs (by steamboat) by 8 on this Monday night, 49 hours in the whole. He is come over with Mr Evans (a former tutor), but on landing they got separated, Antoine lost himself, got misdirected, and it was only after two hours' anxiety for each other, that they at last met again at our house. Mr Evans had gone to their hotel, but Antoine, in his anxiety to see me, had sat up for me, and slept with us the first night. I find him much less altered than I expected; he is grown taller, but his countenance and manner are the same. I find he has [427] escaped, or rather resisted, the dangers I feared for him from Paris society. Left entirely to himself, he has still the same excellent principles he had, and I am confident is confirmed in them. Towards me, he is as warmhearted and affectionate as ever."

Wednesday, 23d.§ After doing duty at Queen Square Place, Klustine "joined me there, and we called together at the Horticultural Society, where we saw Lindley and Sabine, who both seemed pleased to see me. They said they were wondering what was become of me, and were every week expecting me to spring up from some quarter or another. The fact is law leaves me no time for botany, and I do not well know what to do about it. I do not like to give up botany, yet have no time to keep it up. . . . Klustine dined with us, and in the evening my mother, he and I went to a small tea party at Mrs Baillie's in Cavendish Square, to meet a Mr Lloyd, a literary man, who seems to know every thing and every body, but is rather eccentric. He translates the foreign mails for (I don't know who, by the bye), and knows all that is going on all over the world. I had a great deal of conversation with him, and one thing he told me may be worth repeating, for it shows how things are managed. You have heard, probably, of the new colony in the Gulf of Carpentaria on the north coast of New Holland. This is the history of its establishment. Captain King was employed several years ago to make a survey of the north-east coast of New Holland,[20] and brought home a very accurate one of several thousand miles of coast. When his charts were laid before the Admiralty, it appeared to them very desirable that some settlement should be made in that [428] distant part of the continent, in order to secure the possession of it to Great Britain, and to prevent any other Power from being beforehand with us. When the matter was laid before the King, His Majesty himself fixed upon the spot (no great task, if, as I believe, it was the only one where had been found a river and abundance of water), and an expedition was settled to be fitted out with all possible secrecy and dispatch. Accordingly, Captn B—n (I forget his exact name) was commissioned to go out to Sydney, and there take in the necessary stores and materials and proceed to found a colony in the gulf of Carpentaria.[21] The secrecy of the Affair was such that they did not mention it to Capt King, whom it seemed necessary they should consult, whilst the Dutch, from whom the secret was to be kept, knew all about it, as the event proved. Three days, however, before Capt B—n sailed, Capt King heard of it, and also found out that they were not sending a single sailor who knew anything at all of the coast. Upon which, Capt King thought it his duty to speak to Sir George Cockburn, one of the Lords of the Admiralty, who admitted that it would be highly desirable to send some one who had been there before, but they had not thought of it! And now where should they find one? Capt King mentioned his first mate, who had assisted him in all his surveys, knew the coast as well as himself, and was now unemployed, with his friends, a hundred miles from London. A letter was sent down that night, and the young man came up by the next day's mail and sailed the day after. On reaching the vicinity of the Cape of Good Hope, bad weather obliged Capt B—n to put in to repair some little damage to his vessel. He had scarcely cast anchor when in comes a Dutch vessel, which soon proved [429] to be going to the very same place on the very same errand on the part of the Dutch Government. It appears that Baron Falck, the Dutch ambassador here, had heard of the project and, alarmed at the English settling so near their spice islands, had induced his Government to use all possible despatch and endeavour to be beforehand with us. Capt B—n, alarmed at this, refitted with all despatch, but could not get off from the Cape till two or three days after the Dutchman. Fortunately, however, the latter had to go to Batavia for the same purpose that Capt B—n had to touch at Sydney, and having then to go farther round, gave time to Capt B—n to reach Carpentaria first. He had not been there a fortnight, when in sails the Dutchman, but too late. Possession of the whole coast was formally taken in the name of King George IV, and the Dutchman had to steer back to Batavia, to his no small mortification. Baron Falck is said to have been in a terrible rage when he heard of it."

The next few days were spent chiefly with Klustine, whom I introduced to the botanists. R. Brown showed himself very friendly, and we spent a most agreable morning with Sabine and Lindley in the Horticultural Gardens, where several of the roots and shrubs I had sent from Montpellier were flourishing, and where the garden was exuberant with the first results of Douglas' N.W. American expedition. My father and sisters returned home on the 25th, and on the Wednesday 29th, I started with Klustine on our northern excursion. "Left Manchester street at 2 p.m. in a hackney coach to the 'Peacock' at Islington, there at 3 got outside a Liverpool coach, and drove to Brickhill, about 40 miles, where arrived by 8 o'clock. Klustine, whose first journey in England this is, was much pleased [430] with the roads and astonished at their smoothness, the number of coaches, etc. The weather was beautiful, and we enjoyed much our drive and our tea after it, had good rooms and a comfortable sleep.

"Thursday, 30th. Up at half-past five and off to Salden, a walk of about six miles across country, not very interesting in itself, and rendered still less so by a thick drizzling rain, which fell all the morning. Got to Salden by a little after seven, and were received by them all in the most friendly manner. Mr Carr being for a day or two in town, we only found Mrs Carr and the four Miss Carrs, and spent with them the happiest and most delightful day I have passed for this long time. . . . Directly after breakfast we had music; Laura played on the harp with me, and afterwards sang with Isabella. In the afternoon, we walked out with all but Mrs Carr over their woods, and through Whaddon Chace adjoining, to their manor, all of it exceedingly beautiful. The weather had become rather fine, and our walk, which took four or five hours, was exceedingly pleasant. We dined at half-past two, and after dinner sat in doors, had tea at half-past six, and at seven left this enchanting place on our return to Brickhill, regretting that this day should be so soon over. They all seem so happy there, and were all so kind and friendly to me. I shall call there again on my return, and these two days are the two that I have all along looked forward to as the most essential to the pleasure of my journey. One is gone by like lightning—as to the other . . . but I will not now trouble you with my hopes and fears.[22]

"We walked to Brickhill, the six miles in an hour and a quarter; it drizzled a little at first, but before we got in it cleared enough for it not to be pitch dark. At half-past eight, we got [431] outside a Liverpool coach, and reached Litchfield by half-past six in the morning. The weather was clear and not very cold, but we did not get much sleep. Travelling outside in the night, on one of those galloping coaches, for the first time, was not a very somniferous sensation. As we were wafted down some of the steep descents, good as the roads were, the occasional rolling of the coach from side to side at the least turn of the road made us think a little of our necks—but we soon got accustomed to it and secure in the talent of the coachman, so as to consider our bones perfectly safe, and towards morning got a little sleep."

Friday, 31st. Breakfasting at Litchfield, went on to Derby, where we arrived at the Strutts' between 12 and 1 o'clock, and were received in the most friendly manner. The family were all at home. Edward Strutt (afterwards Lord Belper) was to leave for Paris only in a couple of days, and Miss F. Strutt had put off a projected absence till after our visit. It so happened, however, that Mr Strutt had this day a large dinner party of gentlemen, municipal dignitaries and other magnates of the place, "some of whom did not visit the ladies," so the Miss Strutts did not make their appearance. The dinner was, in accordance, grand, substantial and heavy, the venison *very high*, and the wines strong and abundant, to the great enjoyment of the city guests; but my poor, lively, joyous friend, accustomed to the refined luxuries and gaieties of the comparatively short and varied Parisian fashionable dinners, at which the men are never left to themselves, was quite taken by surprise and, sitting hour after hour after the cloth was removed, was quite overcome, and slunk off to his bed at half past ten.—It was only half-an-hour [432] later that the party broke up and we joined the ladies in the library.

We remained the next day at Derby, visiting Joseph Strutt's picture gallery, etc, and Edward Strutt drove us to the Belper cotton mills, and Sunday, 2d Sept, "Left Derby at eight in the morning by the 'Nelson' coach, driving through Matlock and Buxton to Manchester, the same beautiful road by which I went from Manchester to Derby in 1823. The weather, though foggy in the morning, cleared up beautifully, and it was difficult to enjoy more than we did this scenery, the finest in England, or almost the finest. Klustine enjoyed it much; he is hitherto pleased with everything he has seen here, and is a very agreable companion, though sometimes a little impatient and restless. On the top of the coach we generally speak Russ, which we are pretty sure of not being understood, and which is of advantage to me. . . . At Manchester, merely stopped to change coaches, and arrived at Liverpool at nine in the evening."

Monday, 3d. After breakfast, and walking round the docks, left Liverpool by the steamer for Glasgow, the weather beautifully calm and clear—at dusk stopped for an hour off Douglas in the Isle of Man, passed Ailsa Craig at half-past five in the morning—admired much the scenery, up the forth to the Clyde, were transferred to a smaller steamboat at Gourock—and thence, struck chiefly with the very active steamboat traffic on the river, "arrived at Glasgow at about three, cleaned ourselves and repaired to Dr Hooker's, where we are established, that is to say we eat and drink there, but sleep at an hotel. Dr Hooker having at the moment [433] but one bed to offer, I did not like to leave Klustine to sleep at the hotel alone. The inmates at Dr Hooker's are himself, his wife and five children, Mrs and Miss Ellen Turner (Mrs Hooker's mother and one of her sisters), and two young men, who came as boys two or three years ago. They are sons of some rich Scotch manufacturers, who like to place their sons for a few years in English families that they might, whilst following their studies, have also the benefit of the English language. Mrs Hooker is quite recovered, and they are all as friendly and merry as ever. There is also a Mr Wilson, a Welsh botanist, staying with them for a few days" (Mr Wilson, the bryologist).

Wednesday, 5th. "After breakfast to the Botanical Garden, which is in a very flourishing state. They have encreased their houses and have a great collection of hardy plants. There are altogether above 10,000 species. Amongst some of the most curious are the Nutmeg, the parasitical

Orchideae, the Ferns, particularly a Cyathea, the first tree-fern that has been brought alive to this country. It was brought a few months ago and is thriving and growing. Also Nepenthes distillatoria, most remarkable by its leaves having at the end a sort of cup or pitcher with a lid which opens and shuts at different times of the day, and which cup contains a particular liquid very much like water, distilled from the plant. It is very difficult to cultivate, and has only lately been brought to any tolerable state of perfection. From the garden we went to the Museum. . . . In the afternoon looked over a few plants.

Thursday, 6th. "Spent the morning looking over plants, got a good many very valuable ferns from Dr Hooker, who also gave [434] Klustine a collection of mosses and other plants which I have already. In the afternoon, with Dr Hooker and Miss E. Turner, walked out to Garbraid to call on Miss Graham, whom I had met so often at the Baillies', and who returned to Scotland about a fortnight ago. She lives about three miles from Glasgow in a very pretty country, though sadly spoilt by steam-engines, coalpits and cotton mills. Her property is considerable—the village of Garbraid, entirely hers, contains several cotton mills. Her house is something in the French style, formal, solitary and comfortless in outward appearance, by the side, not at the end, of a straight avenue, of which half the trees are dead. Near it, however, is a beautifull glen or ravine, crossed by the great canal by means of a massive bridge. Miss Graham was as talkative and as Scotch in her stories, language and accent as ever, and it is really with great difficulty that I can understand her. She made me, however, promise to come and dine with her tomorrow. Klustine was not with me; he preferred going to see the high church, the green and other lions, which fortunately for me I saw on my former visit."

Friday, 7th. "Arnott arrived early this morning. He had promised to meet me here and, as I had written to tell him the day I should arrive, we were wondering what was become of him. He had been detained by Col Graham (the county member)'s visit to Kinross. After breakfast we examined, determined and took plants and in the afternoon I went out to Miss Graham's and dined and spent the evening with three Scotch old ladies, of which two old maids and two Scotch parsons, a dinner which was more edifying than gay for me, who am not very fond of old maids, Scotch accent or Scotch sermons."

[435]Saturday, 8th. "Mr Wilson left us after breakfast. The whole of the day we spent in Dr Hooker's study at work at his plants, and only in the evening a walk to the botanic garden."

Sunday, 9th. "The greater part of the day spent in church, where every body goes morning and afternoon, each service lasting from two to two and a half hours. I was with the Hookers at an English church, of which there are two here, for I do not care for hearing Scotch presbyterian sermons. Between services, called with the Hookers at Dr Hooker's father's. Mr and Mrs Hooker came to Glasgow at the same time with their son the Doctor, and are living within a few doors from them. The happy manner in which they thus live with their son and his family is a good proof of the excellent character of the whole family."

Monday, 10th. "Rose early and despatched Klustine by the *Oscar* steamboat for Arrochar on a trip to the Lakes—with Arnott joined the Hookers at breakfast and spent the whole day (and the two following ones) in arranging, determining and taking specimens of New Orleans and Louisiana plants."

Wednesday, 12th. "Klustine returned in the evening, having had a most delightful trip down the Clyde, then up Loch Long to Loch Goil, from thence to the top of Loch Long to Arrochar, across to Tarbet on Loch Lomond, then to Inversnaid, Loch Katrine and the Trossachs, slept two nights at the inn at the Trossachs, spending the intervening day in an excursion up Ben Lomond, and in shooting at the foot of it and fishing in Loch Katrine with some friends he had made or met with; returned the next day up Loch Katrine, down Loch Lomond, across to Dumbarton and up the Clyde to Glasgow, thus in a [436] three days' excursion seeing the most beautiful part of the Highlands—all thanks to the steamboats—and with very little expence. He met with and made several friends . . . and returned in the highest spirits."

The whole of Thursday, 13th, and the morning of Friday, 14th, with Arnott at the Louisiana and some Cape plants in Hooker's herbarium, "Klustine ennuying himself perhaps a little." Arnott left in the afternoon, and Saturday, 15th, Klustine and I, "after breakfasting with the Hookers, came to Edinburgh on the top of a coach, over an uninteresting and dreary country, though more animated§ at this time by the harvest, which is now at its heighth. But how beautiful is Edinburgh after the dull, dreary, smokey town of Glasgow! Glasgow, as Robert Brown says, is the most disagreable of all towns. The climate is bad, the houses are ugly, the streets dirty and disorderly, though intended to be well laid out, the inhabitants immoral and filthy, everything unpleasant and bad, except Dr Hooker and his family, an exception of Robert Brown's in which every one concurs who knows this 'most excellent of botanists,' as Fischer terms him in a letter to Klustine. Edinburgh, on the contrary, is the finest and most picturesque of all §possible towns, in the most romantic of all possible situations—or at least so one thinks on coming from Glasgow. New streets continue to spring up with the usual rapidity. The upper classes move further and further to the north and northwest. The newer the streets, the more do fashionable shopkeepers follow in the rear. Many fields that had only a few foundations marked out when I was last here are now become fashionable streets, whilst others, then inhabited by [437] persons of fashion, are lined with shops. A handsome building has started up at the northern end of the eastern mound in Princes' Street. This edifice, containing the Royal Society and School of Arts, is built in a classical style, but for want of a *pedestal* (that is not the proper word but you will understand me), and from its low position its beauty is lost. Of the *National Monument*, which was commenced when I was here before, nothing appears as yet but the scaffolding.[23] The castle and the old town are as they were before. In the old town, the houses piled upon houses, streets crossing each other at right angles, one at a great perpendicular heighth above the other, the narrow closes and common *stairs*, well-named perpendicular streets, dark and filthy, the miserable black holes more like dungeons or dens of wild beasts than lodgings for human beings, piled one above the other to the heighth of eight to fourteen stories, and the, if possible, still more miserable looking inhabitants, all remain just as I left them, only that, if anything, the whole looks still more black and smoky and picturesque—and forms a still more striking contrast than ever with the regular beauties of the new town. The houses destroyed by the fire[24] are mostly rebuilt and, though rather better than the old ones, are, I am sorry to see, nearly as high and as close and as picturesque as before."

I remained rather more than a fortnight at my friend's, Morton Carr, and though much cast down on finding that the hopes I had entertained with regard to his sister were groundless and not likely to be realised, I determined to get the better of my feelings, and spent a good deal of my [438] [time] with botanists. My friend Klustine's departure was also much felt; he left by the mail for London early on the 19th, and I never saw him again. Soon after his return to Paris, he went back to Russia, entered the service and was killed in the Turkish war.[25] This, however, I could not foresee. Morton Carr was all day engaged in his business (Solicitor to the Excise), and I was chiefly with Arnott. Made the acquaintance with, and most hospitably entertained at breakfasts and dinners by, Dr Graham, the Professor of botany, under whose care the beautiful botanic garden was brought to a greater state of perfection than any other one then in the country.—Had breakfasts also with several of those who had received me on my former visit to Edinburgh— with the Mackenzies, old Mr Mackenzie (the "Man of Feeling") now 82 and getting much broken—his wife about the same age, but still active and strong, my friend James, who had been so active when I last saw him, much cut up by an Italian fever—with Dr Greville, now a rival candidate with Arnott for the Glasgow professorship, expected to be vacant on Dr Hooker's taking the professorship at the London University, which however he ultimately declined[26]—with Dr Thomson, whom I had some difficulty in finding—his former home and street had, in the four years, been turned into shop and shopstreet, and getting the address of Professor John Thomson in a distant part of the town, found my way there and was shown up, to a gentleman I had never seen in my life—turning to the Directory, found no less than eight Dr Thomsons in the town, of which two were Professor John's—with Mr Ellis, making acquaintance there with Professor Dunbar.

Friday, 28th. "Though gloomy as yesterday, yet as it did not [439] rain, rode out on one of Morton's horses to 'Milburn Tower,' old Sir Robert Liston's, to breakfast. Sir Robert is very well, as keen as ever in his buildings and his improvements. Lady Liston, though she has been unwell from the effects of a cold caught last winter at Naples, is as lively, active and bustling as ever, orders her servants about and gives all her directions devant le monde as before, and has not forgotten—as I had—that on my former visit[27] I had a spoiled egg, 'which she had never had before or had since seen in her house,' whereupon followed a long history of how she buttered her eggs to keep them for cooking, but always gave newlaid ones to strangers, etc. . . . Sir Robert and Lady Liston are really a very interesting old couple, excessively entertaining from the great deal they have seen of the world in the course of their several embassies to Washington, to Stockholm and several other European capitals, and especially to Constantinople. They are now, as every one else, anxiously looking to what is going forward in Turkey and to the steps the three European powers are taking. From the known boldness and decisive character of the Grand Signor,[28] Sir Robert is confident he will stick to his answer; the European potentates appear equally determined, so that a commencement, at least, of war will be inevitable. What will be the result, or how far the Sultan will remain resolute, is a problem difficult to resolve. Sir Robert gave us some interesting anecdotes of his boldness. At one time, he heard that the Janissaries held meetings, at which he was violently attacked, and of which the object was to concert measures against him. He therefore put on Janissaries' dress, for he formerly belonged to their corps, and attended the meeting. Seeing the truth of the report, he advanced amongst them slowly, [440] opened his dress and asked what complaints they had to make against the Sultan, for here he was ready to answer them in person. Not a syllable was uttered, and he remained unmolested when completely in their power. At another time, they were violently exasperated against him, and it was considered excessively dangerous for him to go as usual on the Friday to the mosque. It was publicly whispered that, if he did, he would be massacred. He chose that day for going to the most distant mosque. He rode calmly through the streets, when known to be aware of his danger. The streets were lined with Janissaries, but struck with his courage not one dared to harm him.

"After breakfast, Lady Liston took us round her garden to admire her conservatory, her hothouse, her American garden, her American oaks and a number of valuable plants of all sorts collected in her various peregrinations. We then went with Sir Robert round his tenements, the old cottage retained, with its thatched roof, but well fitted up in a little detached apartment, where they sometimes go and dine for old remembrance sake—then over the new tower and house actually inhabited, the library, the grounds, etc, all of which, like Lady Liston's plants, were showed off to us, and the beauties, comforts and excellencies pointed out—and we admired as in duty bound—but plaisanterie à part, il y avait de quoi.

"Sunday, 23d. Dined at Patrick Neal's, where met Arnott and his brother. Perhaps you may remember, on my former visit to Scotland, my describing Patrick Neal and his curiosities,[29] [441] his little cottage, garden and hothouses on the banks of the millpond of the Cannon mills, all filled with plants of all sorts, so crowded as that his acre or less contains as much beauty and variety as many a garden of acres and acres, his wall overgrown with creepers and pierced with lookouts on the mill pond, his large ash tree half blown down by the wind and supported in its fall by the wall, so as to make a natural berceau, his soland geese, wild ducks, herons, salamander, syren and ichneumon, his dogs, his venerable old cats, and his Poll nearly as old as himself, and last not least, his Peggy, an extraordinary factotum with an extraordinary face. Now, however, the two greatest curiosities, the ichneumon and Peggy, are dead, but quant au reste, sitting at dinner in the same company as in 1823 in the same room, with the same dogs and cats and Poll, it seemed but a continuation of that dinner, when I was first introduced to Arnott. But what changes have happened since then!"

Monday, 24th. "After breakfast, left town with Arnott for Arlary, walked down to Newhaven, crossed to Burntisland on the opposite side of the Forth in the steamboat—there a gig awaited us and we drove seventeen miles up the country, at first over high hills, then through a bare, barren, dreary, bleak country, through Kinross to Arlary, Arnott's estate. The house is but small and like many Scottish country houses, uncomfortably situated in the middle of an open grass lawn or court yard, the garden and what plantations there are being separated by it from the house, but the interior was *comfortable and pleasant*, to use Adèle's expression.[30] The inmates [442] consisted of Mrs Arnott, my friend's mother, an old, tall lady, excessively nervous in company, but apparently a very good kind of a person and who looks like one of those who never lent against the back of her chair.—Miss Arnott, his younger sister, too much like her brother to be pretty, but lively, unaffected, and far more agreable than I could have expected, and Miss Walker, an old maid, but not very old—a relation, perhaps an aunt, and nothing remarkable. Soon after us there arrived also, on a two or three days' visit, Mr Farr, a relation, a London merchant, come to spend two or three months to enjoy Scottish scenery and Scotch whiskey, with his wife, a little creature with a little face, pretty and pleasant enough, and with them Mr John Bayley, a relative of theirs and of Judge Bayley's, a young lawyer, tall, not unhandsome and something of a beau, and *Tom Baird*, as they call him, the son of the Principal of the Edinburgh college. He was destined for the law, but did not like it, and lives in the country, shooting and farming and visiting his neighbours—coarse and Scotch in his manner, he is a franc bon-vivant, full of plaisanteries, though perhaps a little too coarse, and serving as a sort of merrymaker for the company, withall exceedingly good-humoured and obliging, so that they like him much.—With such company, you may suppose that the evenings were spent in the true style of country Scottish landlords. Whiskey toddy circulated in abundance after dinner till teatime, when an hour or two was spent in the drawing room till supper—more a pretext for drinking than a meal. The toddy was again produced, and by bedtime some of the gentlemen began to appear puzzled how to find their way to their bedrooms.

[443]"Tuesday, 25th. This day was intended to be devoted to an early party to Lochleven Castle, but the weather, which yesterday had been so fine, looked dreadfully gloomy; however, after breakfast it cleared up,

and Mrs Farr, Miss Arnott, John Bayley, Tom Baird and myself, some of us on foot and some in the gig or on horseback, started to visit this celebrated prison of the unhappy Mary,[31] whilst Arnott and Mr Farr walked out with their guns. Lochleven is very near Arlary and close to Kinross, where we took a boat to cross over to the island. The remains of the castle occupy the greater part of this little, flat island, but they are now little more than a few ruined walls without floors or covering. A dismal place this must have been, a small island not twice the size of the castle, in the centre of a broad lake, and that surrounded by an extended moory plain, with here and there a high but barren mountain, all desolate and dreary. The spot where the signals were made to the unhappy Queen, where she embarked, and where she landed after her escape, were of course all pointed out to us, as well as a hawthorn, said to be planted by her during her captivity, and of which I cut a sprig for my herbarium. On our return, we went over Kinross House, a handsome building in a fine park, the only one in the neighbourhood on the banks of the lake. At present this property is in abeyance, that is, it is waiting for a proprietor, for by the late Mr Graham of Kinross's will,[32] it comes to the first of his grandsons who attains the age of 21 years; the eldest of them is now six, so that for fifteen more years this handsome property must lie in waiting, the house unfurnished, and the grounds ill kept. Yet it is a beautiful place, and the views of the ruins of Lochleven Castle, of the lake, of the distant hills, [443]§ in short, of everything good that the country affords, are well taken advantage of, whilst all that is barren and bare is concealed by high plantations. But I would not live there if it were given to me. Surrounded by moors and fogs, in the midst of half civilised Scots living in black hovels, and in winter often confined for days or weeks by the deeply drifted snows. Il y aurait de quoi mourir d'ennui.—The whole party met again at dinner and the evening was spent like the previous one, in all the delights of whiskey and whiskey toddy—and Wednesday, 26th, after breakfast, returned with Arnott to town, in a drizzling rain, and not without regret at not being able to stay another day, notwithstanding the fog and the bogs and the whiskey toddy."

It was now time for me to leave Edinburgh, "not without regret for I have been very comfortable here, and spent my time pleasantly with Morton and Arnott, both of whom I am very fond of. But it is now time for me to return to London to resume my studies. At my time of life, I must not remain long idle."—And Tuesday, 2d October, "After an early breakfast, took my leave of Morton and Arnott, who both came down to the coach office, and started at about seven in the morning, outside the

Carlisle and Manchester mail. The heavy, uncompromising mist, which overspread the town as I left it, continued the whole morning, but was of little consequence, as we were chiefly crossing naked and barren moors. The banks of the Tweed alone, during the few miles that we were in the valley of that river, appeared to be pretty. At noon we stopped to breakfast at Hawick, after which the weather cleared up, and at the same time the country [444] improved much. At Langholm, we got into the most beautiful valley, full of fine parks and plantations, which continued over the border till near Carlisle. The very great natural and local beauty of this tract of country is heightened by the romantic ideas attached to the names of Canonby Lee, Netherby Hall, and other places famous in the *Border Minstrelsy* and old ballads.[33] Our guard was also a capital one for pointing out what was most worth looking at as we galloped along. A stout, jovial, ruddy-faced, red-whiskered Scot, talking all the time, interrupting his, 'Now, gentlemen, this bridge is reckoned one of the most picturesque *sichts* in the three kingdoms,' with appeals to the coachman, 'Come, Willie my lad, keep 'em alive my lad, let's be toddling along or we'll be backward,' whilst the poor horses were doing their best to keep up to his unmerciful time-piece. The sun set beautifully as we entered Carlisle, famous for its castle, its strong prison, as the deathplace of Fergus McIvor in *Waverley*,[34] and now, as the last stage which anxious lovers have to count on their way to Gretna. A propos, a new road has been made from Carlisle to Glasgow, which, by crossing a new bridge over the Solway, cuts off a couple of miles. This road goes also through Gretna, and accordingly, at the branching of the new and the old roads, a board is put up, saying, 'This is the nearest road to Gretna Green,' et plus bas, Glasgow and a number of other places are enumerated, so well is it known that to those to whom the nearest road is the most interesting piece of information, Gretna Green is the important place.

"At Carlisle we had half an hour for supper, and I again started on the top of the mail as before. I had never travelled outside for so long, and had rather been afraid [445] of not accomplishing it, but fine as was the weather I never enjoyed a journey of the kind more. There really is a pleasure in the feeling of pride at the difficulties mastered by man, driving at the rate of nine or ten miles an hour, under a clear moonlight, over the smoothest roads imaginable, with such steadiness as not to feel the slightest degree of apprehension—so far from it, indeed, that I gave myself up to a quiet sleep, though I was not seated in the middle but on the edge. To one who sees a coach loaded with passengers, wafted by at a good gallop, it seems a wonder that any one contrives to stick on, but when you are up, it seems to you as impossible that you should fall, though you know that if you did fall you would have but little hope. Coaches do sometimes overturn, though not so often as in France, but I never heard of a man's falling from the roof of one.

"From Preston to Manchester, however, the road was so bad as to jolt us unmercifully. It is surprising, and at the same time disgraceful to the local trustees, that in a country where generally the roads have attained a degree of hardness and smoothness inconceivable to foreigners, that in the neighbourhood alone of one of the largest towns they should still be so bad—so utterly neglected. The two great roads, from Manchester to Preston and from Manchester to Liverpool, are, I believe, the worst in England—though bad as they are, nearly as good as many of the best in France, and travellers who elsewhere complain of the slightest asperity submit patiently to be jolted on these two unfortunate lines. There is now, however, some talk of repairs to be done. I only hope that will take place before I next go that way."

[446]Wednesday morning, 3d Oct. "[I] got to Manchester by half-past eight to breakfast, and at half-past nine started again by the London mail and, once more on a well macadamised road, galloped through a beautiful country, well broken into hills and dales, rich in verdure, in parks and plantations. Arrived at Derby by four, where stopped at the Strutts, whom I found at dinner; . . . remained there till after their dinner the next day when again took my station on the top of the London mail and, wrapped in my cloak, enjoyed another moonlight drive—enjoyed—yes, as much as I could, when obliged to drive so near Salden, where they are expecting me,[35] yet where I dare not to stop, but am sending an excuse now that I am come home.—But no more of that—I will not let such thoughts prevent my enjoying the many circumstances which ought to make me happy, and which *shall* make me happy."

On my return to London, I found I had still a little time to spare before Mr Koe's chambers would be open—but resumed my visits to Queen Square Place, and dinners and evenings twice a week with my Uncle—who had just now Bowring as an inmate for a short time.—I found his amanuensis Colls, "with parsonic projects in his head. Some relatives are to leave him some money on condition that he enters the church, so that he is studying divinity *à force*, but with such a genius, studying and learning are two different things. Poor Colls, how will ever a sermon issue from his brains! And if it does, what will be its nature? May I never be condemned to hear it." So I wrote, but after many years' curacy at

Hampstead, his parishioners presented him with a handsome testimonial, and he died at an advanced age, incumbent of a good living in Essex.[36]

[447]I spent several days of these days of expectation working for my father at his *Naval Papers*—also went the round of my friends and acquaintance—the Lincoln's Inn men, who were not to stir during the vacation, had not borne it long, and were still away—in Scotland, Denmark, Wales, etc.—I spent a very pleasant day with Lindley, and first made the acquaintance with his family—the real commencement of a long and valuable intimacy. Spent another pleasant day with my father at Mr Larpent's[37] at Putney Park, a house he has lately built, and where he has a well selected library and fine collection of engravings.

October 25th. "My uncle has been in high spirits lately in consequence of a correspondence with Brougham. My uncle wrote to him some time ago, to recommend Bowring as professor of litterature to the London University. Brougham returned a civil answer, showing himself willing to conform to anything my Uncle should propose, but evidently evincing the most utter contempt for Bowring (which, unfortunately, I believe my uncle does not understand) and speaking of some grand projects he has.[38] My uncle wrote again, asking what those projects were, which he said he supposed related to law reform. Brougham wrote again to say that such was the case, explaining his plan of moving for a commission on the present state of the law,[39] particularly of the common law, and in which he expects to be supported, not only from his position as leading counsel on the Northern circuit but by his influence in the ministry, and at the same time he writes with great deference and compliments to my Uncle—who, upon that, supposes that he will have great influence and goes to work preparing propositions, etc. Brougham [448] dined with him on Sunday, and he is in high glee about it,[40] and thinks that he will get me employed in it, etc. I should like very well—more than anything else—to get employed about law reform; but, as to this, in the first place, I can do nothing till I am at the Bar, nor then, unless my Uncle allows me to study a little more, and, in the next place, I am not so sanguine about what Brougham will do, or can do. That Brougham is a man of very great and versatile talent and that he has at present very great influence, there is no doubt, and he will almost certainly get the Commission appointed; but, in the first place, I fear he will make a job of it, as he is a great jobber, and, in the next place, his imprudence is such that his ministerial friends feel very awkward about him. At present he is a sort of half semi official man; though having no place, he is in a manner half in and half out, just enough to get the Ministry into a scrape. Ministers would very probably discard him, were it not that, if they were to set him against them, they have no one to compete with him, and in the House he might do them a great deal of mischief. He has an eye upon the Attorney Generalship, as a step to the Chancellorship! As to that, he certainly never will get it, if lawyers, and all who know what the Chancellorship is, can keep him out, for a Chancellor must be the steadiest, the calmest, the most prudent man possible. As to the Attorney Generalship, though they want to keep him out, yet he is said to be very eager, so that perhaps they may one day give it him, rather than quarrel with him. Next spring, the Session will be the time for the development of these 'intrigues.'"

Friday, 26th Oct. "Dr Hooker, who is come to town to endeavour to determine on accepting or not the professorship at the London University, breakfasted with us this morning. He has seen Brougham, the [449] manager in chief, and several others connected with the University, but can learn nothing satisfactory. A charter, it seems, even they do not hope to obtain, and without that it is no University, and consequently the professorship would be inferior to that which Dr Hooker now has.[41] As to the botanic garden, it seems very uncertain whether Dr Fellowes, who was to have given ground for it at Islington, will now give it, and they can scarcely afford to purchase land for the purpose, and the emoluments of the Professors will at first be very uncertain. Other Professors are disposed to withdraw, because it seems they cannot afford to have an hospital as was at first promised,[42] and there are some of the Professors named, also, who are not of a character to do credit to the institution. In short, it seems altogether in a bad way, chiefly from want of funds. Of 300,000 pounds they expected to collect they have as yet got but 150,000, and of that they are spending so much in building and various showy things, that they will have but little for the essential parts of the plan.[43] On the other hand, it would be very advantageous for Dr Hooker to be in London, and I wish much for my own sake that he may come, but I hardly think that I should, in his place, accept the appointment."

"After breakfast, called with Dr Hooker at Robert Brown's, whom we found in all the confusion and disorder of déménagement, that is the déménagement of the Banksian collections and library, which are now transferred to the Museum,[44] and Brown is appointed sublibrarian for the care of the botanical collections in the Museum, with an assistant under him, so that at last the valuable collections, hitherto buried in the cellars of the Museum, [450] will be rescued from danger and destruction and once more become accessible to science.[45] Robert Brown still keeps his house and his private collections at the back of the Linnean Society. From Brown's, went to Don's, at the Linnean Society, then to Dr Boott's, an American physician settled in London, an excellent young man, friend of Dr Hooker's, to whom Dr H. introduced me, for the purpose of exchanging plants with him—then left Dr Hooker, and to Queen Square Place, it being too late for both Lincoln's Inn and Queen Square Place."

Monday, 29th Oct. "Commenced today a regular course. Immediately after breakfast to Lincoln's Inn, working there till three or a little after, then to Queen Square Place till near six, then on the days when I do not dine there, home to dinner and the evening," which I continued with very little interruption through the winter, varying it only in term time by "going first to Queen Square Place for a couple of hours, then to Lincoln's Inn, staying there to dinner to keep my term, and till eleven o'clock at night."

Sunday, 11th Nov. "The news of the battle of Navarino, arrived yesterday, occupies every one today.[46] The Whigs, and in general a large proportion of the public, are much pleased, the Tories are enraged, and every body much surprised. So sudden and decisive a blow, after six years' doubt and uncertainty, would scarcely be believed, were it not so very authentic. Not a rumour, nor any surmise of the possibility of an approaching battle of such importance, preceded the official despatches. Coming on a Saturday it has been a capital thing for the Sunday papers, who had, moreover, the good fortune of a catastrophe at the Lord Mayor's feast to relate.[47] [451] The dinner was just over, the Grandees were speechifying over their dessert, when a whole set of coloured lamps, representing a crown and anchor, came tumbling down upon the heads of the principal personages, and anointed with oil from head to foot the Lady Mayoress, the Dukes of Clarence and Wellington, the Lord Chancellor, and two or three others, several of them being scratched enough to get a sight of their blood. However, I believe but little mischief was eventually done, beyond the destruction of their fine dresses."

Sunday, 17th.[§] "This battle of Navarino seems to have been a most dreadful one. All speak very highly of Captain Hugon of the *Armide*'s conduct.[48] Indeed, there seems to have been in general the most admirable cooperation of the three fleets. This is the first time since the beginning of history that the French and English fleets have fought together on the same side. They joined in Charles the second's time but did not fight,[49] and a glorious battle they have had for the first. It is true that some persons begin now to consider what *right* we had to fight at all—but c'est égal. Every one now is very anxious for news of the effect the intelligence will have had at Constantinople. It is said that there are heavy wagers pending that the three ambassadors' heads will be off by the 15th."

Tuesday, 17th[§] Decr. "If your ministry is dans l'embarras, ours is but little better. Parliament meets on the 22d January, when will be a full attendance, and an obstinate conflict of parties. Ministers will be violently attacked about the Navarino business. Lord Goderich dreads it, and wants to get out of the mess, but he is ashamed of abandoning his colleagues in the [452] moment of difficulty. But, poor man, he is of a most peaceable disposition, and has much affliction from his wife's illness and other domestic calamities, and cannot bear the badgering in the House of Peers, besides that it seems he cannot preserve very great harmony in the Cabinet."

Saturday, 22d. "At the bottom of Lord Goderich's vacillations, his going out and coming in again, etc, is his wife. Lady Goderich has formed to herself a long list of calamities likely to befall a Prime Minister, and is continually falling into hysterics, for fear some one of her catalogue should happen to her husband. If he goes to the Council, or to Windsor, or anywhere else out of her presence, she is sure to send messengers after him, in her impatience to see him again. I do not recollect whether I told you of a steam engine, erected in the park to empty the canal, and pulled down as soon as erected; this was because it affected Lady Goderich's nerves; the job cost her lord some three hundred pounds. On Guy Fawkes' day, the guns were not fired because of Lady Goderich. If Mr Herries, living in an adjoining house,[50] separated by thin walls from that of the Premier, sneezes too loud, Lady Goderich hears it and sends a message to him not to sneeze, etc, etc. With all this, it is no wonder that a man of Lord Goderich's easy temper should not very well know his own mind, particularly when his situation is rendered so much more uneasy by the mutual dislike and disagreement of the two principal ministers under him, Lord Lansdowne of the Home Department and Mr Herries, Chancellor of the Exchequer."

Wednesday, 26th Decr. "Yesterday we all dined here at Queen Square Place with my Uncle down in his parlour. We had a regular and excellent Christmas dinner and all in very good [453] spirits; my Uncle was quite delighted. After my father, mother and sisters were gone, I staid to put him to bed; he seemed quite happy with his evening, and has invited a similar meeting on every future Christmas day. This is a great deal for him, who could formerly never bear the idea of a family party."

The year 1828 began with the Carr's family party like the previous year, whilst I continued the regular routine, commenced after my return to town in October, although as the approaching meeting of Parliament brought people more generally to town, I had more dinners and evening parties to attend. My father worked very hard at his *Naval Papers*, etc, and staid much at home, excepting dining frequently with his friend, old Count Woronzow, who was much cut up by the death of his son-in-law, Lord Pembroke. My letters contain much about the ministerial changes, how Lord Goderich went whining to the King, to say that, with the quarrels between Herries and Huskisson, he could not manage the ministry, as both were determined that one or other must go out—how the King sent for Wellington,[51] who made up a new ministry with both Herries and Huskisson remaining in—how "on Tuesday the old ones went to Windsor, to give up their seals of Office, and the new ones to be sworn in, but, by some blunder, no Privy Council was summoned; consequently, no Clerk of the Council was in attendance, and the business could not be done; so that after waiting till eight o'clock, they all returned to town half-starved, to a magnificent dinner at the Duke of Wellington's, half spoiled by having been [454] kept three hours waiting,"—how, on the meeting of Parliament, "Huskisson, Herries and Lord Goderich have been explaining and explaining away, till they have enveloped the whole break up or, as some of them stiled it, blow up, of the Administration, in ten times as much mystery as ever.[52] I lay the great blame on Lord Goderich's weakness and lacrymose disposition. If his underlings quarrelled, he should have investigated the subject of dispute and turned out the party in the wrong, not vacillated and shilly-shallyd for a month, run away and come back, and having two resignations for some time in his pocket, gone whining to the King, who, of course, thought, 'Well, if you can't manage them, I'll find some one who can,' and immediately sent for the Field Marshall Duke."

"My uncle continues remarkably well in health, and in good spirits, notwithstanding the new Administration. He has had Brougham two or three times to dinner, and a visit from Lord Lansdowne, both of which pleased him, but he never has me to meet any of these people. He does not like more than one guest at once, for he likes to have such guests, as he admits, *all to himself*. He goes on writing, at the rate of ten to twenty pages a day, and is never discouraged by anything."

15th Feby. "The principal political topics this week have been Huskisson's speech at his election at Liverpool[53] . . . and, above all, Brougham's speech in the House on Law Amendment. He spoke for six hours and a half without appearing exhausted; he exposed many of the evils of our present system of administering justice, supported his story by examples taken from his own practice, bestowed great, and even extravagant, eulogiums on the individuals concerned, on Judges, etc, but laid [455] the whole blame on the system, and finally moved a Commission for examining into legal abuses,[54] particularly in regard to what we call Common Law. There was much in what he said that was good and striking, and it will be difficult, now that the abuses are admitted by all, not to accede to the Commission. Yet there did not seem to be a sufficient connectedness in his plans, and he went too much into trifling and tedious details. His known want of prudence and management will be a great impediment in the way of his doing much good, notwithstanding his extraordinary talents and abilities, if he alone has the conducting the affair. The best would be if Peel were to take it up, and if Brougham could be satisfied in acting with him, and with the glory of having originated the motion.

"My uncle is much disappointed. He had seen much of Brougham lately and conceived that Brougham would exactly follow his instructions, and that he, J.B., would get the credit of it, as it is in fact to him that all this late attention to the law is originally due. But not only Brougham did not once mention, or allude to my Uncle in his speech[55] but, in many things, proposed expedients directly opposed to some of my Uncle's favorite principles. I cannot, however, blame Brougham for this, any more than for his eulogies on the present Judges. The course he has followed is much better calculated to gain people over to his plans than if he had set them against him by indulging in that personal sarcasm to which he is apt to give way. And my Uncle's name is still too much connected with party ideas to be usefully brought forward on such an occasion."

March 1st. "Brougham's Law Amendment motion came on [456] last night, and the Commission was granted, though with very great restrictions. In the course of the debate, Mr Peel spoke of my Uncle with praise,[56] though Brougham never once mentioned his name."

My father was now very busy preparing his *Naval Essays* and *Papers on Naval Management*, etc, for press, and I was obliged every now and

then to give him a morning, taken from my otherwise constant attendance at Queen Square Place and Lincoln's Inn. Lord Althorp applied to
him, on the part of the Finance Committee, for hints and facts connected
with the management of the Naval Department and Dock-Yards, and
he, accordingly, early in March sent in a string of observations, and the
first parts of his *Naval Essays* and *Naval Papers* were published the same
month,[57] and he was always over-anxious about my revising all that
proceeded from his pen. I contrived, however, most days to have all the
morning for Lincoln's Inn, and entered heartily into various Chancery
causes Mr Koe had charge of. My evenings began to be too much taken
up with dinner parties, balls and musical parties, and often procured me
agreable acquaintances and sometimes valued friends. I only regretted
that, at my Uncle's, he did not like to have me when he had a friend or
stranger to dinner, whom he always wished to have to himself, and
liked no one to interfere between him and me the two days in the week
when I was his dinner guest. Only once I was there with Mr Parkes. "He
is an eminent solicitor of Birmingham, who has just published a *History
of the Court of Chancery*, which is being much spoken of. He is also a great
admirer of my Uncle's, and an excellent man. He was employed on the
last contested election [457] for Stafford against Col Beaumont. To give
you a specimen of our elections. When Col Beaumont went down, it was
soon seen that his opponent would not be able to compete with Col B's
enormous fortune, and after some days' contest the unsuccessfull candidate's Committee determined to give it up but, in order to save as much
loss to themselves as possible, they bargained with the Colonel and
actually sold themselves over, candidate, voters and all. Colonel Beaumont's account of the affair is, 'I was entirely unknown to every voter in
Stafford when I went down, upon general constitutional principles, to
vote with ministers when they are right and against them when wrong,
and bought the whole concern for £17,000.' Col B. had just lost a contested election for Northumberland, which had cost him two or three
times that sum. So much for contested county elections on a grand scale
for the rich. Those who are not ambitious to throw away so much
money can buy a seat for from £1,500 to £3,000, according to the degree
of dependency of voting attached to the seat."

Friday, 4th April. "Called on Dumont, who is over here for a short
time. He was very friendly and appeared pleased to see me. He has
brought over with him another volume he has just published, *De
l'Organisation Judiciaire et de la Codification*, which now makes ten volumes published by him from my Uncle's manuscripts.[58] The second edi-

tion of the *Traités de Legislation*, the third of *Peines et Recompenses*, the second of the *Tactique des Assemblées Législatives*, and the first of the *Preuves Judiciaires* (the last work) are all nearly out—indeed the *Traités de Législation* are scarcely to be had, but owing to the manoeuvres of the bookseller who has the few remaining copies on hand a new [458] edition cannot yet be printed. Of the others, new editions will shortly be commenced. Spanish translations of them all have also a very large sale. In short, my Uncle's reputation on the Continent, great as it has become, is spreading still more; and here, where it has always been much more limited, it is now gaining ground rapidly. In Dumont's new volume there is a chapter entitled 'Montesquieu et Bentham,'[59] containing a parallel of those two writers, which will probably excite no little interest amongst French jurists."

Early this same month of April, our library and other effects arrived from Montpellier, and amongst others my herbarium, which induced me now and then to steal a little time from law, but generally only before breakfast or after I returned home at night, and the whole of this "season" was spent in great activity, with very little sleep, enjoying a vigorous health and seldom really fatigued.

Tuesday, 15th April. "Went to the Opera with Andrew Morton to hear Mlle Sontag, who made her first appearance that night. Her fame had spread so far and wide, and expectation had been so much excited that the house was excessively crowded. The Opera was the *Barbiere di Seviglia* in which she appears as Rosine and, at her first entrance on the stage, sings that most beautiful air 'Una voce poco fa.' With that, and with some variations on an air of Rodes,[60] which she introduces into the Opera, and with some other parts I really was very much delighted— but I was a little disappointed in her beauty, which had been so highly extolled. She has a german face, short nose, long chin, high cheek bones, light hair and light blue eyes, and as pretty as can be with such features, a beautiful complexion, and exceedingly pretty hands [459] and feet. She is rather little but well proportioned, was very elegantly dressed, looks ladylike, but has not expression enough in her face and, though graceful, has but little action. Her voice is remarkably high and clear and distinct, and she has extraordinary execution. It is very difficult to compare her and Pasta, because their voices and style of singing are totally different, but I confess that Pasta pleases me infinitely more than Sontag. Sontag was, however, exceedingly well received and loudly and repeatedly applauded. Pasta was in a box, and all eyes were turned on her to see how she received the success of one who is come to share with her the public admiration—but Pasta is said to be exceedingly good-natured to her would-be rivals. She joined in the applause, but this she would do, of course. Of the rest of the Opera, Figaro was well sung and acted by Pellegrini. Curioni was rather cold as Count Almaviva, and Angeli, who is only fit for the most inferior parts, was most wretched as Bartholo." I gave accounts of several visits this month to concerts and the Opera, to hear Sontag, etc; and again, Thursday, 15th May, "Went to the Opera to Pasta's benefit and, after waiting an hour, fesant queue outside the door, and an hour and a half in a hot, crowded pit before the commencement, I was fully rewarded for my trouble by the finest representation that can be conceived.§ It was Rossini's *Otello*, in which were united the talents of Pasta, Sontag, Zucchelli and Curioni. Pasta as Otello was most magnificently fine, the passions her countenance expressed, joined to her inimitable acting and her extraordinary voice and method, were most admirably displayed. Sontag's voice and sweet, clear execution drew forth no less admiration, and her action as Desdemona, in which I was afraid she would have failed, was [460] really very good. Desdemona is Pasta's ordinary part and said to be her best character (I have not yet seen her in it), and Sontag had the good sense to imitate her action, so that, added to her own exquisite gracefulness, nothing could exceed the last scene, closed by Otello's stabbing Desdemona. Curioni as Rodrigo exerted himself more than I have ever seen him do, and exertion is all that he wants; and, in order to render the whole more complete, Zucchelli consented to take the inferior part of Iago. The house was crowded to excess, notwithstanding the King's juvenile ball which happened the same night. (My father and sisters, with the Maxwells, had to pay fourteen guineas for a small box on the third tier.) After the Opera was over, Pasta and Sontag, being as usual called for, appeared on the stage, and were received with loud applause that lasted many minutes."

Friday, 25th April. After a pleasant visit and dinner with my father at Mr Larpent's at Putney Park, came in to town to my work in the morning, and "in the afternoon out with Lindley to Turnham Green, and after going over the Horticultural Garden, dined with him and spent the evening looking over plants, of which he gave me many valuable ones from the West Indies, New Holland, etc, and particularly from the N. West of America. Douglas, who brought them over, was sent out as a collector to the Society.[61] He spent three years in that country, living amongst the Indians, shooting for his food, wandering sometimes quite alone with his collections on his back. At one time, he crossed the Rocky

Mountains, a journey of several days, quite alone in a country inhabited, thinly it is true, by a savage race of Indians, from whom he was obliged to run more than once for his life. When the long-continued rains prevented his using his fire arms he was frequently reduced to great distress for food. [461] Once he was obliged to devour the skins of animals he had dried to send over with his collections, and twice to eat up his horse. One of these horses was a favorite, whom he called his botanical horse, because he had taught it, in going through the woods, to stoop when passing under branches of trees, which might tear off the bundles of plants which it carried on its back. The whole expedition cost the Horticultural Society between £300 and £400, including Douglas's salary. His whole expences for food, etc, whilst amongst the Indians, three years, amounted to £66, including a wager of £5 he lost to an Indian chief. He used to pay the Indians by drafts on the Hudson's Bay Co for little articles such as a few nails, a scalpel knife, beads, etc, which makes the detailed account transmitted by the Co to the Horticultural Society a very curious document. Douglas is now living at Turnham Green, preparing for publication an account of the plants he has discovered. He came in to Lindley's for a short time this evening. He is quite a *sauvage* in his appearance and manners, and is dying to go out again upon some expedition. He wants to go farther south than he was before, between Fort Vancouver and Mexico, but the Indians are so very ferocious in that part of the country that the Society do not like to risk the sending him there. He will, however, probably be sent somewhere or other.[62] The collections he brought over are very valuable to the Society, as many of the new plants he has discovered are very beautiful, hardy enough to flourish in this country in the open air, and are now doing exceedingly well in the garden. Amongst others, some of the Lupines are very fine."

Tuesday, May 6th. "Dined at the Linnean Club, and went after dinner to the meeting of the Society. Several members [462] of the Linnean Society have formed themselves into this Club,[63] where they meet to dinner on the days when the Society meets in the evening, twice a month during the season. Sabine, Lindley, and the secretaries of the Society belong to this club, as well as most of the efficient and scientific members, whilst Lambert and several of the titled people of the Society form another club, which two clubs have got themselves the names of the Bees (Sabine's) and the Drones (Lambert's). In the Society, the Bees are completely masters, and carry every measure they please against the Drones. The new President, Lord Stanley, belongs to the Bees' club. At the meeting this evening, I had myself proposed as a member, and when my certificate shall have remained suspended in the room the time required by the Society—during three successive meetings, I shall probably be elected. As there are but two more meetings this season, my election will be in November next. It costs some money to be a member, but I think it worth while, on account of the opportunities it affords of making and cultivating botanical acquaintance."

Sunday, 11th May. "Went out to Camden Town to spend the morning with Lagasca and look over his Cistineae. This poor Spanish botanist, whose misfortunes I have before mentioned to you,[64] seems to have saved something, though it must be but very little. He has now a very small, but nice enough house in one of the back streets in Camden Town, where he has stowed such of his books and plants as he has been able to have brought over from Spain. He has two boys who go to school in Camden Town, and have learnt English enough to make themselves very well understood, but do not seem to be remarkably clever. From Camden Town, I went out to dinner at Turnham Green to Lindley's, to meet Robert [463] Brown; I had a pleasant dinner and returned to town in the evening with Mr Brown."

Wednesday, 4th June. "At my Uncle's, my usual dinner—a young man, a Paris friend of his, M. Felix Bodin, is just arrived and stays some two or three weeks with him. This M. Felix Bodin is the son of the author of *Histoire d'Anjou* and is himself a distinguished writer in the *Constitutionel*, the *Revue Encyclopédique*, etc, and is well known in the Parisian literary and liberal world. He is a very pleasant young man (that is to say above 30) and is come over chiefly with a view of searching amongst some old records in the Tower."[65]

Saturday, 7th. "Dined at QSP. Mr Lawrence, the American Minister, dined there and as all the inmates of QSP, Bowring, Felix Bodin, Colls and Doane dined at home, we were seven, and my Uncle came down to the parlour, an extraordinary event for him. He looked quite happy at the head of the table. I wish he would do it oftener. It looks so much more comfortable than to be confined in his study up stairs as he generally is. Mr Lawrence is a young man without any extraordinary brilliance in any way. He is often at my Uncle's."

Friday, 6th June. "Went out to dine and sleep at Lindley's at Turnham Green with De Candolle's son, who is come to visit England. Young De Candolle is a very gentlemanly young man, who has only lately taken to botany. He is now studying the Campanulaceae. We went over the garden both in the evening and on Saturday morning, and got a number of specimens to dry. The roses in the garden are now making a fine show, as also the Ranunculuses, Anemones, and a number of fine American plants brought from the North West coast by Douglas. The Clarkia, Collinsias, Lupins, etc, are beautiful additions to our hardy [464] ornamental plants. Amongst the plants in the garden of which I took specimens was a curious new Borragineous plant from the same country, which Lindley is about to publish as *Benthamia*; he has also dried specimens of three others of the same genus from the same country, all quite new. (The genus, however, proved to have been already published under another name.)[66] The garden is full of workmen, etc, preparing for the fête which is to be on the 21st, and for which they are taking all precautions to prevent the failure as to quantity of food which there was last year."

Thursday,[§] 10th. "Young De Candolle breakfasted with us. After breakfast he looked over and named my Campanulaceae. We then went to Westminster Hall, and spent the morning in the Courts of Law, which De Candolle wished to see, and where we heard Brougham, Scarlett and others of the principal lawyers, speaking at length, and the whole Court occupied as they are every day with £50 bills of exchange and other such paltry matters, whilst causes upon which depend whole fortunes are delayed for years, for want of time to attend to them. In the afternoon, we went together to the Chelsea botanic garden, which like Anderson, the 'caratrastic' gardener,[67] is growing old. The smoke of London and the want of funds, as well as old Anderson's want of order, and headstrong opinions, are the cause that this garden, once one of the the first in England, is now scarcely anything. The two old cedars planted by Miller still remain, to show that they were there at a time when their presence alone was enough to give great value and interest to the garden. From this garden we returned to town and, it being too late for my Lincoln's Inn dinner, we dined together at a coffee-house, and went to Drury Lane Theatre."

[465]Tuesday, 17th June. "Dined with young De Candolle at the Linnean Club, and then went to the Linnean Society, where we met most of the principal botanists. The Society will probably succeed in purchasing Sir J. Smith's (including Linnaeus's) herbarium and library.[68] This was the last meeting of the season."

Thursday, 19th. "Breakfasted with young De Candolle and then went with him and Felix Bodin to the tunnel, one arch of which is lighted up and open to the public at a shilling a piece. There are a few men still employed in clearing out the mud, but autrement the works are stopped till enough money shall be collected to go on with it. They have got an act of parliament enabling them to borrow money on debentures,[69] the new lenders to be paid first, before the old shareholders get any dividend from the tolls to be received, the ordinary way of raising money in such cases, but it is still doubtful whether they will succeed. The Duke of Wellington is said, however, to be a shareholder and therefore much interested, and exerting himself a good deal in endeavouring to find lenders. If they succeed in raising the money, there is little doubt of Brunel's being able to conquer the many obstacles he has to meet with from the nature of the soil. From the tunnel, De Candolle and I went to the Tower, which I had never seen, and were there shown through the armories, told by the *beefeaters*, as they are called, to whom this and that armour belonged, shown the heaps of piques, lances, etc, taken from the Spanish Armada, etc, etc, and lastly taken over the new armories, in which 800,000 stand of arms are said to be kept in constant readiness for service. What useless waste of labour and expense, if it were only in cleaning, without counting interest on capital,§ is incurred by keeping such a stock of arms, of which not one eighth part can possibly be counted on [in] any emergency. By [466] the time we had been over the armories, we were tired of Tower sights, and on our way back to the West End went in to St Paul's, also the first time I had ever been there— and admired the fine cupola, but did not think it worth going up to take a four-and-sixpenny view of London smoke."

Friday, 20th. "After dinner, with Doane and Felix Bodin to Vauxhall, where we had a pretty good vaudeville—such a concert as we usually get there—and the battle of Waterloo. The company there is, as you may suppose, always very much mixed, and it is an ennuyant enough amusement. The great difference between that and Tivoli (which is in itself dull enough) is that at Vauxhall there are no chairs for those who do not eat, and no ice, nor lemonade, nor other refreshments than solid provisions, wine and beer."

Saturday, 21st. "The day of the long expected Horticultural fête.[70]— We had had a week's fine weather. This morning, when I returned from Vauxhall at half past two, it was fine and clear. At half past four when I woke, it was pouring of rain, which fell unceasingly till past eleven. Then, however, it cleared up a little, so as to encourage us to think of going. I went, however, to make fresh arrangements with De Candolle and Felix Bodin, with whom I had settled to go by water. Instead of that, we took a hackney coach and, starting at half past 12, got to the garden at half past one. The weather had now become pretty fine, and carriages were beginning to arrive very quick. By two o'clock there was already a long line setting down, and in half an hour more the queue was two miles long, reaching to Kensington. By half past four, almost all had set down, the weather had become beautifully fine and the gardens presented a splendid display of rank, beauty, fashion and toilettes. I joined the Carrs, who came about three. Sarah and my father arrived soon after, about the same time with Mrs Maxwell, and we continued walking about the lawns, which got dry immediately, the whole afternoon listening [467] to Rossini's finest music played by the finest of the military bands, or to the Tyrolese singers, or following the crowd to the refreshment and fruit tents, or watching those who were dancing on the green, or sometimes seated so as to enjoy more leisurely the gaiety of the whole coup d'oeil. The display of fruit was very grand. A table, sixty or seventy yards in length under a tent or shed, lined with white and pink drapery, was completely covered by the plates of grapes, melons, peaches, apricots, nectarines, cherries, raspberries, strawberries, and other fruits in countless varieties, amongst which 60 pineapples, some of them weighing six or seven pounds each, were the most conspicuous. These fruits had been collected from all parts of the three kingdoms, a steamboat load had even been sent over from Holland, but so badly packed that scarcely any of them were available. At half past three, the fruit tent was closed whilst the fruit was cut up. At four it opened again and the crowd poured in and rushed upon the pineapples[§] with an eagerness not over decorous. These of course soon disappeared but of the other fruits there was enough to satisfy all. As they began to be cleared off, Gunter's *ladies* appeared behind the table, serving us cakes, tea, lemonade, etc, in the greatest profusion the whole evening. Next to the large tent were four others, of at least equal length, covered with more substantial provisions, and which, though crowded till seven o'clock, were even then very far from being cleared of their contents. Gunter determined not to fail as Jaurin did last year and, knowing well what suits such an assemblée, had provided everything in the greatest abundance. Besides meat-pies, hams, etc, jellies, cakes, etc, there was here also an apparently inexhaustible stock of strawberries and wines, Champagne, Moselle, Hock, etc, in profusion. The *Royal tent*, as it was called, was fitted out with great taste, and such members of the Royal family as were there, and some of the principal of the nobility, were seated to their repast. The Dukes of Sussex and of [468] Cumberland, Prince Leopold, Princess Esterhazy, the Duke and Duchess of Leinster, of St Albans, etc, were among the number. The Grenadier Guards and the Artillery band played alternately the whole evening, and the Tyrolese sang at intervals in another part of the garden. There were also three of the first quadrille bands, consisting of 25 musicians each. Not many, however, danced. English etiquette is a great bar to dancing in so public a place, but what dancing there was was kept up with great spirit till near 9 o'clock. The company began to depart at about half past six and by nine the gardens were cleared. . . .§ Upon the whole, this fête was more brilliant than last year, notwithstanding that the walks were a little muddy for the ladies' satin shoes. There were about 4000 persons present, of which 2000 were ladies. . . . De Candolle and I remained to the end, when we went across to Lindley's. Sunday, 22d. After breakfast, De Candolle and I went over with Lindley to the garden to take specimens to dry. De Candolle then returned to town, and I staid the day with Lindley, looking over plants, and got specimens received from Ledebour, who has lately returned from Asiatic Russia with a great number of new and good things."[71]

July 4th. "For some time past my mornings have not been so profitably employed as they might have been. I have been obliged gradually to give up Lincoln's Inn since last term, and to spend at Queen Square Place almost the whole of the time. I am now obliged to be going about town doing commissions, etc, and have now so many persons to see and so many little things to do before I go over to France that I have taken leave of Lincoln's Inn till next autumn, when I hope again to resume my legal studies with vigour."

[469]The remainder of this first fortnight of July I appear to have been every evening engaged in balls, parties, etc, dining out almost every day, besides the two I continued every week to dine at my Uncle's. I was also much engaged with the Collots (the family of the French Master of the Mint). Made Collot and her two eldest handsome daughters being over in London for a short time and anxious to do and see everything—also in the endeavour to promote the efforts of M. Roux, a friend of the Calvières, to obtain the Professorship of French at the new London University.[72] "Wednesday morning, 16th. Left London after breakfast by the Dover coach and having dined at Canterbury, got to Dover by 8 in the evening. The weather fine comparatively speaking, for after ten days of sultry, hot weather, we had had a week of violent storms, many showers, and even hard continued rain. Today it has cleared up, and we have had the sun nearly all day, but this afternoon it has been so cold that I was really glad outside to put on my cloak—in the sun in the middle of July!"

Thursday, 17th. "Crossed over in the *Salamander* steam packet, the weather fine but windy, the sea rough, but we were only two hours and twenty five minutes crossing. At Calais staid a few hours to get my things cleared, get my passport, etc, and left at six in the evening by the diligence, arriving at Paris at the Hotel des Etrangers, Rue Vivienne, in the morning of Saturday, 19th." Remained a few days at Paris, and started for Montpellier on the 23d. But here end my journal-letters to my sister, for although I continued them for some time after my return to London in the autumn, they were no longer preserved, or accidentally destroyed in the confusion resulting from my sister's distresses at a later period.

[470]Here my journal-letters to my sister come to an end, and, although on my return to England in the autumn I resumed them, yet owing to the distressing circumstances in which my sister was placed, some were intercepted, and those which reached her were not preserved, and for the next eighteen months I have scarcely any record to rely upon to check my recollections.

I left Paris on the 23d July, 1828, and on my way to Montpellier staid a couple of days at Tonnerre with my friend Tonin Partouneaux, who was then Sous-prefet there, taking the opportunity of visiting in detail some extensive Champagne making establishments—the fermentation carried on partly in bottles, the frequent bursting of which required curious provisions for saving as a secondary quality the wine that escapes. I also staid a day at Lyons, chiefly with Seringe, then in charge of the botanic garden there, arriving at Montpellier in the first days of August. I remained two or three weeks with my sister, settling the affairs of our estate, which we unfortunately left under the management of her husband, who at parting gave me a grand dinner at the principal restaurant of Montpellier, from which I got into the malle poste for Paris, rather overcome by his wines, the only time in my whole life that I ever felt the effects of drink. In this "accelerated" mail, I was five nights and the intervening days from Montpellier to Paris, with the exception of two or three hours one morning at Avignon, which gave me an opportunity of seeing my friend Requien, still as active in his herbarium as ever, and about six hours the next day at Lyons, arriving at Paris at six o'clock the fifth morning, and after a busy day there, spent the evening at Admiral Tchitchagoff's.

[472]§I staid some time at Paris, and was frequently at the Jardin des Plantes, but chiefly in the society of other friends. It was during this visit that I learnt the death of my poor young friend Klustine. I had not long since had a letter from him from Pultawa, where he was detained on his way to join the army in Turkey[73] by an attack of fever, from which, however, he soon recovered; but he had not been long with his regiment when, being sent with a small detachment to communicate with another

corps, he was surrounded by a body of Turks and the whole detachment killed. The news was communicated to me by M. de Circourt, from the French Foreign Office; and being then the one in Paris most intimate with the Klustines, and in correspondence with Anastasie, I was induced to undertake the communicating the news to her and her mother, then in Italy, M. de Circourt himself, who had already his eye upon Anastasie and who afterwards married her, being unwilling to be the messenger of bad news himself.

I believe it was October by the time I returned home and resumed my previous occupations, my dinners at my Uncle's twice a week—rather shortening my morning visits to Queen Square Place in order to have more time at Lincoln's Inn, where I took eagerly to my legal studies—kept my November term, etc, but began to turn also rather more to botany. I was elected into the Linnean Society at their second November meeting, joined the Linnean club on meeting days, which I now pretty regularly attended.

[471]§It was during one of these visits to Paris, probably in the autumn of 1828, but I have not the exact date, that I breakfasted one day with Count Damas (nephew of an old friend of my father's, Count Roger Damas),[74] who was then Governor of the young Duke of Bordeaux. This little prince, about 8 years old, as heir to the throne lived apart from his mother, in a kind of state. He breakfasted by himself, with two tall livery servants behind his chair, and Count Damas in the room, superintending, and it was only after he had done that, the Count retired with me to his private room to his own breakfast. The boy looked intelligent but very quiet, without any of the liveliness of his age, and indeed the kind of treatment, friendly and attentive as it appeared to be, seemed enough to cow down any spirit he might naturally have. The Count was a very strict Catholic, but much liked by his friends, and evidently much attached to his pupil.

9

Legal Studies and Botanical Pursuits, 1829–30

[473] The year 1829 was one which had considerable influence on my future life. Various circumstances tended to prevent my giving way to

social enjoyments so as to interfere with the two rival pursuits to which I devoted myself with more and more zeal, law and botany. We had begun the year like the two preceding ones, with the Carrs' family New Year's party, still a happy one, though with some signs of dissolution; and early in March, Mr Carr died from a sudden attack, brought on by overwork, which carried him off after two days suffering, and this broke up the family, with which we continued the intimacy, but under much altered conditions. The death of Lord Colchester in May was also a great blow to my father, and deprived my sisters of the social enjoyment they owed to the friendship of Lady Colchester. As the season advanced, the state of my sister Clara's health began to cause us much anxiety. The extremely violent pains in her head, which proved afterwards to have been caused by a tumour in the brain, made her utter the most piercing screams, and seriously affected her temper, and she would listen to no one of her family but myself, and fortunately her French maid, who had been many years with us and was devoted to her. She was advised to try the quiet of a seabathing place and I took her down to Southend, where I left her with her maid, and went down several times to see her. Here, however, she caught cold, and I brought her up to town in the end of October; inflammation of the lungs came on rapidly, and she died the first days of November.

Being thus detained at home the whole summer, I was enabled, during the legal vacation, to give up a good deal of time to botany. Dr Wallich's return from India, with the immense stores of Indian plants of which he was authorised to distribute the duplicates, [474] gave a great impulse to the study of Indian vegetation.[1] I met him at Lindley's very soon after his arrival, and at once contracted an intimacy with him which I was fortunate in keeping up during his life. He was very anxious to get his Indian collections published as well as distributed, and made arrangements with various botanists to work up separate families. For that purpose he hired the first and second floors of an unfurnished house in Frith Street, Soho Square, which he had fitted up with shelves and tables and induced several foreign botanists to come over successively and assist him in sorting and selecting specimens of the families they respectively undertook—amongst others, Kunth of Berlin, Meissner of Bâle, Graham of Edinburgh, and later Alphonse de Candolle of Geneva, sending over selected specimens to many others. At Lindley's suggestion, I undertook the Labiatae in the first instance, and also promised to call in Frith Street occasionally on my way to Lincoln's Inn, and give more time during the vacation, to assist him in the general sorting and distribution, the mechanical part of the business, aided by an assistant he engaged[2] (who first invented the natural order *Dubiaceae*). On the very threshold of the domain of Labiatae, I met with so much confusion in the arrangement and delimitation of the genera that I determined to undertake a revision of the whole order—commencing with the detailed examination of one or two species of each genus. To this I devoted any leisure hour I could spare, generally late in the evening or before breakfast, or in the steamboat up and down the river on my visits to my poor sister; and during the vacation I spent many a long morning in Frith Street, where the joyous Wallich, in his free, hearty way, had always [475] an oyster luncheon for his friends—untill he found that it attracted second rate botanists to encroach too much upon his time as well as his oysters—especially one constant Northumbrian proser, whom he got to designate as —— *borealis*. So the luncheons were dropped, and the work went on the more steadily. By the autumn, I had so far got through the general revision of Labiatae that I ventured to give to Lindley a sketch of the generic characters, which he inserted in the *Botanical Register* for November and December.[3] With term time, however, I resumed my legal studies, devoting the best part of the day to practical equity drawing at Mr Koe's Chambers, and began to take great interest in some of the intricate questions which came before him; and by the close of the year, we had got pretty well settled again at home, where I generally spent the evenings with my father and mother and my remaining unmarried sister, Sarah, who, however, began to be very much with her friend, Countess Ludolph.[4]

Henceforth my recollections will be checked by notes I daily made, commencing 21 Jany 1830, and continued to the present time, although of late years my daily occupations have been so uniform that I have frequently made memoranda for two or three days at once, and throughout, these notes give only dates and facts, without any expressions of feelings and thoughts, which I had previously put into my journal-letters to my eldest sister.

[476] The year 1830 proved, in some measure, the turning point which determined the future course of my life. The struggle between law and botany fairly began, and although for a time the former maintained its importance in my mind as that on which I was to rely for future support, yet the latter was gradually gaining ground, though it was still some years before it obtained complete mastery. My long journal-letters to my sister had now ceased, or the few that I wrote in the encreasing

difficulties of her position were not preserved, but very early in the year I commenced a kind of diary which I have ever since maintained—not that it commemorated my opinions and feelings like my letters, but it is a record of facts and dates, serving to check any recollections of my occupations, and of the various events by which they were influenced. Fifty years of these memoranda are contained in nineteen volumes.[5]

For the first three months of the year, I worked hard at Lincoln's Inn—the best part of every day at Koe's chambers, preparing chancery pleadings and often discussing them with him, in all of which he took the greatest pains with me, and I began to feel deep interest in the business. In the mornings early, I was often taken up with assisting my father in his writings,[6] and at my Uncle's, I contrived to satisfy him with two evenings a week, when I dined with him, and occasionally an hour or two after leaving Lincoln's Inn. [477] I had thus but little time for botany but, when at home in the evenings or before breakfast in the mornings, I contrived to work up the "Synopsis of Indian Labiatae" for Wallich's *Plantae Asiaticae Rariores*, and to describe some Medicagos for Sowerby's *Supplement to English Botany*.[7] I also attended the Linnean Society's club dinners and evening meetings, and occasionally dined out with my father and sister, so that I had little time for idling. The weather in January was very severe, the coaches stopped by the snow almost all over the country and, when the Argyll Rooms were burnt down, the ruins the next morning were most beautifully covered with enormous icicles. The English Opera house was also burnt down,[8] catching fire about half an hour after my sister had left it.

My uncle Jeremy Bentham was at this time in high spirits. Some notice had been taken of him in the House of Commons,[9] and he had had O'Connell twice, and Burdett once, to dinner. Though my uncle never liked two to dine with him, I met O'Connell there one day, who with all his eloquence in a popular assembly was not particularly brilliant in private conversation, but appeared like a rather coarse, fat, jolly bon vivant. I had also interviews with Joseph Hume who, in his anxiety to show the superiority of French judicial procedure over our own, had got me to give[§] him some statistical details as to French bills of costs, etc, but was much disappointed when I could not contradict Scarlett's statements of the enormous Judicial establishment kept up in France and the multiplicity of Judges sitting in the same Court.[10]

[478] In the month of April, circumstances occurred which turned my thoughts and occupations into an entirely new channel. I had, some months previously, been induced by Sabine, as well as by Lindley, to

join the Horticultural Society, and had attended some of the meetings, which Lindley always rendered interesting by his comments on the objects exhibited; but now they were exciting attention in a far less agreable manner, from the violent dissensions which had broken out amongst some of the Society's leaders.[11] Joseph Sabine, the Secretary, to whose zeal, energy and undoubted abilities the Society owed the high degree of prosperity and prestige it had attained, had been, from the first, its real manager and dictator, the Council doing little more than sanction and register the measures which he proposed. With all his administrative talent, however, he was not a good calculator of ways and means. Meeting with unexampled success in procuring the liberal support of the wealthy classes interested in horticulture, and in spreading far and wide that interest, he was ever oversanguine in his expectations of the degree in which that support would be continued and encreased, and conducted the expenditure of the Society with a liberality which could only be justified if those expectations were realised. As it was, however, the annual outgoings always exceeding the income, the Society soon had established a debt, which was encreased, first by the nonpayment of promised subscriptions (amongst others, £500 subscribed [479] by George IV was never paid, and could not be obtained after his death), and then by the defalcations of Turner, the Assistant Secretary, which, notwithstanding the security he had given, amounted to above £2000.[12] After that, the deficit encreased rapidly—the Council never looked into the matter, but signed the bonds required of it, till now, in the beginning of the year, it suddenly discovered that the Society was indebted for some £22,000. The intimation may have been brought under the Council's notice in a somewhat irregular form,[13] but could not any longer be concealed, and produced violent dissentions and recriminations. Sabine, at the same time, by a too rigid enforcing of regulations and a somewhat despotic redtapeism, had made some enemies in the Society. Robert Gordon, one day at the Garden, had greatly admired the great Wisterêa, then in full flower, and induced Mrs Gordon to drive out to see it; she forgot to take with her an order from her husband and was refused admission, which so irritated him that, hearing of the debt incurred and kept secret, he determined in revenge "to expose" Sabine to the Society at large, and Bellenden Ker, with his fiery temper, having had some tiff with Sabine about some plants he wanted from the garden, followed suit with the most violent accusations and invectives. Two or three stormy meetings,[14] which some of the real friends of the Society endeavoured in vain to calm down, spread among the Fellows generally that they might become personally liable for the Society's debts, and resignations came in by dozens. Sabine and four other members of Council resigned, [480] creditors became clamorous, and it really seemed as if the Society would have to be broken up.

Under these circumstances, Mr Barnard, one of the Vice Presidents, and a friend of both Sabine's and of Lindley's, called on me one morning in the end of March, to say that the real friends of the Society were anxious to replace the members of Council who had withdrawn by Fellows who had taken no part in these quarrels, and that my name, amongst others, had been suggested by Sabine, asking me therefore whether, if appointed, I would accept and act. I had some hesitation at the prospect of the interruption to my legal studies, but after consultation with Lindley and others, and the assurance that it would probably take only a few hours once a fortnight, I called in the afternoon on Barnard and accepted, and for the next two or three§ days continued my steady attendance at Koe's chambers. On the 6th April, spent the morning at the Horticultural Society, where the new members of Council were elected with little opposition—none against me—indeed, I found that there was a general wish, strongly supported by Lindley, that I should succeed Sabine as honorary Secretary. Going afterwards to the Linnean Club dinner and to the evening meeting of the Society, I had a long talk with Sabine, who strongly urged me to accept the secretaryship of the Horticultural Society. I felt much flattered by the manner in which it was proposed, but had some misgivings as to its interference with my legal studies, and declined giving a positive answer till I should see how matters proceeded in the new Council. As a fact, however, I never resumed my attendance at Lincoln's Inn till I was called to the bar in the end of the following year.

[481]Although I continued my attendances on my Uncle, as well as the assistance I gave my father, in preparing for, and passing through the press various papers he was printing, I devoted a great deal of time to the study of the financial condition and prospects of the Horticultural Society, and of the circumstances attending the bitter feuds between Sabine and Lindley. The new Council met on the 19th, when Sabine's friends brought forward a proposal to convert the Assistant Secretaryship to what it was before Turner's defalcation—a Garden§ Secretary, and a kind of head clerk in town, each at a low salary, a plan solely contrived for the purpose of turning out Lindley, who could not have accepted of either. The proposal was unforeseen, and I was not prepared to meet it, though I felt that, if it were carried, I could not under-

take the Secretaryship, Lindley's assistance being indispensable to carry the Society through its difficulties. I procured, however, the postponement of the decision till the next Council. In the mean time, I called on those members of Council who were not distinctly pledged to support Sabine's plan, to discuss the question with them, and prepared myself as well as I was able to reply to the arguments brought forward, and on the 23d the Council met again. The attendance was full—13 out of 15 (the President being in the country, and Lee, about to go out, taking no part). Sabine's proposal was temperately brought forward by Lord Carnarvon, most violently supported by Mr Harrison, and Malcolm (a nurseryman), as violently opposed by Vigors, well argued by Loddiges and others, and finally put to the vote. On the [482] ballotting box being opened, there were found to be 14 balls, 7 for, and 7 against. Dr Henderson, who was in the chair, said it was just possible he may have put in a ball at first and another at last, and sent the ballotting box round again, when there were again 14 balls, though only 13 voted, upon which the chairman said he must request every member to turn up the cuff of his coat (two Earls being among those present),[15] when on the third time the voting came right, 6 for Sabine's plan, 7 against it.—Harrison immediately left the room in a rage, and Malcolm resigned his seat in the Council. Lord Carnarvon, on the contrary, when the meeting was over, came up to me, said that he was glad to hear I was to be proposed as Secretary, should be very happy to make my acquaintance, and invited me to dinner on a day he named. Sabine himself behaved very well towards me. I went the same evening to the Royal Institution, where I had a long conversation with him, to explain the part I had taken against his friends, which he said he was sorry for, and that he was sure I should rue the day when I saddled myself with Lindley;[16] but calling on him at his request two or three mornings after, he said his object in asking to see me was to express the pleasure he felt at the manner in which I had spoken to him on the previous Friday night, and to offer me any assistance in my secretaryship, an offer which he in the sequel fully acted up to.

Mr Knight, the President, came to town at the end of the month for the Anniversary meeting on the 1st May and, the organisation of the Society being now settled, I started on [483] the duties of Secretary, we heard no more of the bitter feuds, and the Council set heartily to work at the restoration of the Society. At first it seemed difficult—a habitual extravagance in minor details, a rapidly encreasing debt and falling off of support—bondholders clamorous for payment and no balance at the bankers—the coalmerchant, who had long been paid only in bonds and consequently added a few shillings per ton to his charges for coal, was now threatening an execution; it was clear that mere economising and reducing expenditure would be nothing unless we could restore credit and confidence—cash to the amount of £4000 to £5000 was immediately wanted, and applying for it out of doors was hopeless. I proposed, therefore, that we of the Council should privately advance it on 5½% bonds, which I felt convinced was good security. The proposal was agreed to. I advanced £2000, and other members supplied the rest—the coalmerchant and other troublesome creditors were at once paid off—bondholders, seeing that we could pay, changed their minds and kept their bonds, a few conciliatory words brought back several of the withdrawing members—a complimentary letter induced old Mr Rudge not only to withdraw his resignation but to send in his life-composition, a resolution to admit ladies to the fellowship gave us additional support, and we could seriously reduce the staff in town and the labourers in the garden without the appearance of being compelled to it by pecuniary distress. The byelaws of the Society had also been violently attacked in the stormy meetings, and we had promised to revise them—an apparently difficult undertaking, when so many different ideas prevailed about particular items as to promise much opposition. I undertook, however, to draw up [484] an entirely new set, which I had printed[17] and sent round to the Members of Council and to a few others who had been most clamorous about them, asking for their opinions, observations or objections—which, however, scarcely any one was at the trouble of sending in. These byelaws were discussed at two separate meetings. It appeared that there were two who were disposed to object to everything. I therefore first brought forward a few verbal points of no importance to be hotly discussed by the objectors, and on which, after long talk, I finally gave way, at which they were satisfied and allowed all the important parts to pass unchallenged. By these and other measures, perfect harmony was restored, and the Regent Street meetings became more and more frequented, their popularity much encreased by the new lady-Fellows, amongst whom Mrs Marriott and Mrs Lawrence—besides Lady Antrobus, as wife of a Fellow, contributed largely. All this however took up a great deal of my time. Nothing was resolved on without long consultations with Lindley, who devoted himself most zealously to the restoration of the Society, and I had often to secure the concurrence of some of the most steady supporters of the Society. I soon found that the honorary secretaryship was no sinecure.

Having once laid law wholly aside, various circumstances induced me to devote to botany any leisure left me by my father, my Uncle and the Horticultural Society. I became much interested in Wallich's distribution of the rich collections of the E. India company. I saw a great deal of him in his workshop in Frith Street or at Turnham Green, [485] where he had just taken a house very near Lindley's and, much taken with his hearty, cordial manner and kindly, honorable feelings, became sincerely attached to him, a friendship which I was proud to maintain to the end of his life. I saw much also of several botanists who came over to assist Wallich in the distribution of the natural orders which they had severally undertaken to elaborate, and first, Dr Graham of Edinburgh, who undertook to work up Wallich's Leguminosae, and I assisted in the sorting and distributing; subsequently, however, he never found time for the work, and after two or three years gave it up and returned the *unica*. Whilst he was in town, I met him, Brown and Wallich at Lindley's at Turnham Green, and the whole party walked over to Sion House, Lindley having obtained leave to take a party of gardeners to be shown the new hothouses by Forrest, the gardener. This was then a very great privilege, the Duke having given very strict orders that no one should be admitted on any pretext, and these were so rigidly enforced that Forrest was very nearly dismissed for having admitted the Duke's father-in-law, Earl Powis.[18] At the time these houses were regarded as a horticultural wonder, built at an expence of between thirty and forty thousand pounds.

Alphonse de Candolle arrived on the 22d April, and Kunth, sent by the Berlin Museum, on the 29th, and I spent all the time I could spare with them in Frith Street, helping in the sorting the families they had respectively undertaken, took them both to the Linnean Society club dinners and meetings, and to the Anniversary dinner on the [486] 24th; with them also to one of Lambert's overcrowded dinners. At this anniversary I was, for the first time, elected into the Linnean Council, and very regularly attended its meetings; also at this time I joined the Zoological Society, in the course of formation.[19] The greater part of my time was, however, taken up with the Horticultural Society's affairs, and it was only in early morning that I could work at the papers on Indian Labiatae, on Linums and some other genera, which I published in Wallich's *Plantae Asiaticae* or in Lindley's *Botanical Register*,[20] or at a very fine collection of Mexican Plants collected by Mr Graham. In the evenings, I was now generally out—twice a week as usual at my Uncle's, and occasionally at the Opera or at dinners and balls. At one of these dinners at

Mr Jellicoe's, I sat by Miss Kindersley, who, as ladies are apt to be when they take up a hobby, was most enthusiastic about Jacotot's new method of teaching, which was to supersede all others, and I was obliged to devote a morning to studying his book—his system being to teach the child everything a propos of everything, and make it teach itself as much as possible by comparisons in its own mind. On the *langues étrangères*, for instance, his general instruction was *Apprenez par coeur, repétez sans cesse et rapportez-y tout le reste.*[21]

Prof Lehmann of Hamburgh was here only for a few days early in June on his way home from Scotland, where he had been spending a fortnight. I introduced him to the Linnean Club dinners, etc.

In the middle of June, I was elected into the Athenaeum Club. They had just come in to their new building and [487] added 200 to their numbers towards meeting the expences. Of these, 100 were selected by the Committee as men of eminence in science, litterature or the arts, or as patrons, and I felt some pride in coming in as one of these 100, at the same time as R. Brown, John Crawfurd, and others of real eminence. The other hundred were elected by the club at large out of some 1100 or 1200 candidates, of whom lists were printed, and each member was to score off 100 names—two or three weeks were allowed for this, but I soon scored off mine, and sent the list in to avoid the somewhat scandalous jobbing and canvassing carried on by some, under the pretence of exchanging votes—some promising a couple of hundred votes, when they had only one hundred to give, etc.[22] This club has, however, been ever since a grand resource to me, and I have often made much use of its most valuable library of reference. When the time came for casting up the votes, after rejecting a number of unsigned or otherwise defective lists, it appeared that 1020 were sent in, and the scrutiny occupied 4 scrutators 6 days, working 9 to 10 hours each day. About the same time or rather later, I attended the meeting constituting the Geographical Society,[23] which I joined.

In the early part of July, my father's old friend, Admiral Tchitchagoff (the "terrible man with a terrible name" of Canning's ballad)[24] came over for a short time, and I was a good deal with him.

On the 14th July, with Alph. De Candolle, took the afternoon coach to Dorking to see the gardens about there, and particularly Mr Barclay's of Bury hill. Early the following morning, Mr Barclay sent his carriage for us, to drive us to [488] "his garden, a short distance from his house, in a very beautiful situation. The gardener, Mr Cameron, a Scotchman, was there when we arrived, and went over with us giving us specimens of everything we wished for. Mr Barclay himself soon joined us, the kindest old man that can be. He is above eighty, but strong and healthy; he seemed to have the greatest pleasure in doing anything he could for us, at the same time putting us perfectly at our ease. After taking what specimens we liked from his garden, we went to his house, in a very fine situation overlooking a large piece of water and a rich looking valley. He showed us a considerable collection of drawings of plants that had flowered in his garden and he and Mrs Barclay gave us a good luncheon, and we left these hospitable people much regretting that the shortness of De Candolle's stay prevented our remaining longer." Mr Barclay lent us his carriage to take us first to Mr Hope's and then back to Dorking, whence we returned to town by the afternoon coach—the streets looking dismal and gloomy, all the shops shut, being the day of the funeral of George IV.[25]

On the 20th July, the new byelaws were passed at the Horticultural Society without opposition—the last of the great measures which had been so much squabbled over. After settling various matters with Sabine, who has been throughout friendly and useful to me in setting Horticultural matters right—but I was now rather hurt at what he said about the Royal Society—my friends had rather pressed me to come forward as a candidate, and Brown undertook to propose me and get my certificate properly signed. Sabine [489] now told me that Brown had asked for his signature, which he said he should be most happy to give, but only on one condition, and that is that it should not be signed by Lindley. As I should not like to come in to the Society except on the recommendation of all my botanical friends, Fellows of the Society, independently of any quarrels amongst themselves, this refusal of Sabine's occasioned its being deferred and, on the disastrous election of the President the following November, the scientific Fellows were so disgusted that Brown recommended me to withdraw my certificate, and I never came forward again till more than thirty years later, when I was already President of the Linnean.[26]

On the 21st, I left town with Alph. De Candolle on a few days' visit into Wiltshire, chiefly to old Lambert's. Taking the afternoon coach, arrived at Salisbury at one o'clock in the morning, and then at ½ past 8 by the Bath coach, alighting "at 12 at the village of Codford, where Mr Lambert's servant was waiting for us, and we walked up to Boyton, a curious old-fashioned house, with gable ends all round, carved ceilings, irregular entrances on several sides, fine cut yew and hawthorn hedges, a real bowling-green, with formal terraces one above the other and bushy evergreen trees, some fine Pines, and particularly a P. Pallasii, and at the back a high row of trees with a dark walk underneath—a singular place, and beautiful from this old-fashioned singularity, though not presenting much idea of comfort.—A good many trees and good looking grounds in and immediately about the place, but, all round, [490] the country very dull and bare—rich cornfields—chalk downs, covered with rich sheepwalks, but a poor prospect for the eye, as all this part of Wiltshire seems to be. Found Mr Lambert as nervous and fidgetty and laughing as much as ever. Went with him to his garden, a hybrid between a kitchen and a flower garden, with an admixture of fruit—no great variety of plants, but a very neat green and hothouse. In the garden were some very fine plants of the Rheum Emodi. The sun being too hot for Mr Lambert, we returned to the house, where there soon arrived Mrs William Bennett (wife of Mr W. Bennett of the New Police Commission, and sister of Mr Lambert's late wife) with a little girl, her daughter. Soon after, Miss Lucy and Ann Bennett, daughters of Mr Bennett of Pyt house (MP for Wiltshire, and also a brother of the late Mrs Lambert)[27] two fine girls, particularly Miss Ann Bennett who appears excessively cheerful and pleasing.—Mr Selwyn, rector of Kilmarston, a great horticulturalist, arrived soon after, with Sir Christopher Cole of Glamorganshire, a good, stout John Bull of an old sailor. Lady Mary Cole, his wife, a horticultural amateur of the Ilchester family, and two Miss Talbots, her daughters by a former marriage, very pleasant, though no longer in their première jeunesse. Walked about or lounged with some or other of these till dinner time, when we were also joined by Col and Captn A'Court, two of the most agreable men, particularly the Col, a ci-devant militaire, brother of Lord Heytesbury and now living at his Lordship's place at Heytesbury—a country gentleman magistrate and horticulturist—also Mr John Bennett, brother to the two Miss Bennetts, a red-haired élégant, an angler, sportsman and [490]§ cigar-smoker, but withal well informed and agreable—on the whole a very pleasant party," though rather too much for poor, old, nervous Mr Lambert, who left the dinner table before the ladies, and soon after sent in a message to say that he was gone to bed—leaving the ladies much embarassed when the time came for breaking up.—Sir C. and Lady Mary Cole, who on a general invitation had expected to stay the night but now found that nothing was prepared for them, were taken to Heytesbury by the A'Courts, and Mrs W. Bennett alone remained. After she had retired, De Candolle and I remained alone, when down she came again, saying there were no sheets in her bed, the housekeeper was laid up and could do nothing, the upper-housemaid was in close attendance on Mr Lambert, and Mrs B.'s maid was at her wits end finding no one to help her—at last all got right and, as for De Candolle and myself we were made most comfortable and carefully attended to by the old butler.

Friday, 23d. "After breakfast, De Candolle and I, accompanied by a guide, walked over the downs, here and there clothed with stunted underwood, thence called *woods*, to gather the *Cirsium anglicum*, DC. at about three miles from Boyton, and thence on three more to the A'Courts at Heytesbury. . . . After partaking of an excellent luncheon, Col A'Court took us in his gig to Warminster, to see the gardens of Mr Phelps, a solicitor, and Mr Wheeler, a nurseryman—and returned to Boyton to dinner—where, besides the Bennetts of Pyt house and the A'Courts, were the well-known Dr and Mrs Fowler, altogether a most agreable evening."

[491] Saturday, 24. We (DC. and I) chartered a fly and, after about seventeen miles of dull uninteresting country, drove into the beautiful borders of Somersetshire to visit Sir Richard Hoare's place and gardens at Stourhead—where, however, the fine collection of Pelargoniums was now cut down for its annual[§] rest—thence to Longleat—and to the A'Courts at Heytesbury to dine and sleep—Mr Lambert and Mr John Bennett meeting us there.

Sunday, 25. After breakfast, Alph De Candolle left us, on his return to town and home, and soon after, "I took leave of the hospitable inhabitants of Heytesbury, to ride over with Mr John Bennett to Pyt house, his father (the MP.)'s place, Col A'Court having kindly lent me a horse. The way was entirely over the downs till we came to Fonthill woods, near to which is Pyt house, an elegantly built house, planned by Mr Bennett, who is very fond of architecture—well placed under an amphitheatre of trees, looking over a fertile and riant valley, in the bottom of which a small brook is dammed up into ponds so as to look like a river. Mr Bennett, the M.P., with his eldest daughter Lucy, were just getting into the carriage to go to Salisbury for the Assizes tomorrow, but Miss Anna Bennett was there to receive us. After a good luncheon, Mr J. Bennett and myself again mounted our horses, and spent three or four hours in visiting the ruins of Fonthill Abbey, in driving over the grounds amongst the thick woods, and in walking through the American gardens which, though now left to grow half wild, must make a great show in spring, when this multitude of large Rhododendrons, Azaleas, etc [492] are in full bloom. It was a gloomy, overcast but sultry day, without rain or wind, and the excessive stillness of these wilds and thickets, with their dark shades, gave one feelings of loneliness which, though calm and not without their charms for a time, end by producing too much melancholy, and I should fear ennui and misanthropy, if one were to live in such a place.

"Mr J. Bennett, his sister and myself dined and spent the evening together. Miss Anna B. is a beautifull girl, and so excessively cheerful and lively, with so much esprit and good feeling, that it was impossible not to be charmed with her, and I even let myself be persuaded to copy some verses into her album, which I had never done for any one. She is very accomplished, draws, sings, plays on the piano and writes verses. She has never been to town since she has been *out*, so that she is free from affectation. Miss Lucy Bennett, whom I only saw a very little of, is of a more quiet and reserved disposition. Another sister is married to Lord Charles Churchill, and the fourth, a little girl of ten, appears as if she would be, in beauty and cleverness, the very counterpart of Anna. Mr John Bennett is a Cantab and, as there is but little fortune amongst them, his Cambridge expenses leave but little for his sisters, who are thus obliged to reside entirely in the country, confining themselves to such amusements and gaieties as the neighbourhood affords."

Monday, 26. "Breakfasted again with these amiable Bennetts and returned on horseback over the downs to Boyton, quite captivated with the charms of Anna [493] Bennett* and roasted by the rays of the most scorching sun I have felt since Montpellier; took a hasty leave of Lambert with a glass of wine and a biscuit, and walked out to the road to catch the coach, but after waiting half an hour, discovered that I had missed them all three—therefore got Mr Lambert's man to carry my bag, and walked on four miles to Deptford Inn, where I took a post chaise to Salisbury, the sun burning as much as ever. At Salisbury, finding the London coaches did not pass till the evening, sauntered about the town and joined a party that was going into the Cathedral. Listened with much nonchalance to the guide's usual monotonous tale of the Counts and Bishops of old, whose mutilated statues lie upon as many heavy masses, presenting neither beauty to the eye nor interest to the

---

* Though they did keep me waiting for breakfast till 11 or 12 o'clock, and though the two girls at Lambert's amused themselves by changing the labels of his plants, for the fun of seeing their uncle hold forth on them, exhibiting the wrong plants as specimens.

imagination—strained my neck in admiring the beauties of the gothic
roof, wondered, at the bidding of the guide, at the weight the pillars had
to support, and after going round the whole without having learnt a single useful additional historical fact or stored my mind with a single new
form which might add to the numbers of the class of *beautiful*, returned
to the inn with the satisfaction of having idled away an hour and seen
Salisbury Cathedral, objects equally essential to attain.—Sat down to
write—ordered tea—and at ½ past 8 left Salisbury, alone in a six inside,
so that notwithstanding the excessive heat, spent a good night, arriving
in town at 8 in the morning, to breakfast with my father and mother—
both of them much oppressed with the heat."

[494]I found young De Candolle still in London for a few days, and
Gussone, the Sicilian botanist, come over; but now every one was, for
some days, quite taken up with the astounding news from Paris. The
famous *Ordonnances*,[28] issued on Monday morning, reached London on
the Wednesday; "they come like a thunderbolt, wholly unexpected by
any one, at home or abroad—very bold, if they have means to support
them—if not, most egregiously foolish and absurd," as I wrote at the
time. We were particularly interested, and soon intensely anxious, from
the fact of my sister Sarah being at the time with Countess Ludolf at
Paris. Ever since my sister Clara's death, the intimacy between Sarah
and the Countess had become very close. My sister was a great deal at
the Countess's, enjoyed much the kind of Society she met with there,
and at the same time was useful to her and, with the Countess's excessive amiability and kindness, did not mind her somewhat peremptory
fancies. One morning in April, for instance, when at my Uncle's, I got a
message from Sarah to say that the Countess wanted to see a boy in
whom she was interested, then at Downside College, an establishment
of Benedictine monks between Bath and Wells, and that she desired
Sarah and me to escort her there, and that I was to go and secure the
inside of the Bath mailcoach for that night.—Nothing would do but to
obey. I found the places vacant—we went down to Bath that night, partook of the monks' hospitality the next day—I had a bed in the convent—the ladies lodged themselves near, and the following evening we
again took the mail to town. Since that, [495] my sister had almost lived
at the Countess's, and on the 4th of May accompanied her to Paris—at
first for a few weeks, but the stay was prolonged for months, and now
we knew that Countess Ludolf, my sister and Mrs Scudamore—(whose
sister I afterwards married) were in the Hotel Bourbon in the Rue de
Rivoli, without any man in their party—Col Scudamore being at the

time in Herefordshire, having been called home on business. At first we had but little anxiety—on the Friday morning Count Ludolf heard from the Countess, but only up to Tuesday, when all was quiet, but as nothing dated Wednesday came from Paris, we got very uneasy; up to Saturday morning neither the Government nor any of the corps diplomatique received any accounts, no one had left Paris except a courrier of Rothschild's, who brought vague accounts of severe fighting, and in the course of the afternoon expresses brought to the evening papers dreadful news,[29] which threw us all into a state of the greatest anxiety, till the evening, when a letter from my sister, dated Wednesday evening, at length assured us of her safety; and the expresses in Monday morning's papers, "contained news from Paris up to Saturday afternoon, with all the details of the termination of the struggle, in Paris at least, by the complete victory of the Liberals, who had already restored order, and business going on as usual. What a number of events crowded in a few short days—it was but this day week that the Ordonnances issued in Paris, and already we have here the news of the complete overthrow of the Bourbons." My sister and Countess Ludolf, being close to the scene of action, were very much struck with the total absence of any [497][§] precautions taken against any outbreak which might have been expected, or effective resistance to it when it did occur. The Garde Royale, who would have been ready to fight to the last, were merely drawn up in the Jardin des Tuileries, and left to broil in the excessive heat the whole day of Wednesday, in perfect inactivity, and only drawn off after a couple of fourgons[§] had passed with the crown jewels, etc—at which they were no little indignant. If there had been anything like good generalship on that day, most people thought that the result would have been very different, and even the Ordonnances might have been made acceptable to a large part of the nation.

During the next fortnight, I was much occupied with some botanical papers I was writing[30]—with my Uncle, who took up the pen a-propos of the events at Paris[31]—at the Horticultural Society, doing the honors of the garden to some of our new Lady Fellows and others—with Mr Harvey of Moscow (who had married Lise Gordon), who was here for a short time—with Gussone, who gave me a good set of his Sicilian plants, and to whom I gave others from Montpellier. He had a thorough knowledge of Mediterranean plants, but did not care much for others. He was always, however, most accurate in all his observations and, though very quiet, of a most amiable and friendly disposition. Met also, at the Horticultural Garden and at Lindley's, Cruckshanks, the botanist just returned from Chile, from whence he had supplied Sir W. Hooker with many valuable specimens.

[498]In the middle of August, I went down into Wiltshire again, and staid two or three days with the Bennetts at Pythouse—a very pleasant party in the house, and I enjoyed myself much with the young ladies and others, though I had at once to get rid of all my previous reveries about Anna Bennett—rode out to see the curiosities of the neighbourhood, and paid a formal visit to Stonehenge, and thence went for a few days to Lord Carnarvon's at Highclere house, which I spent very pleasantly, Lord Carnarvon being very hospitable and attentive, and much to see in the beauties of the park and the neighbourhood. The then celebrated novelty of the hybrid Rhododendrons raised by Lord Carnarvon and his secretary, Mr Gowen, could not, however, at this season be duly appreciated. The party in the house chiefly a family one. The then Lord Porchester—the poet—with his newly married bride, a niece of the Duke of Norfolk's,[32] Lord C's two daughters and their husbands, Mr and Lady Emily Pusey and Mr and Lady Harriet Stapleton—Mr Gowen and the quondam governess, Miss Martin—besides Dr Wallich and the Marquess of Aylesbury.

Returned to town on the 25th with Dr Wallich, and occupied for two or three days in family as well as in Hort. Soc. arrangements, for various matters during my absence, in anticipation of a visit to Germany I had long promised myself. Some trouble also about my passport; a Foreign Office passport was then a very expensive and troublesome affair—and the Prussian Embassy had just received orders—in consequence of the French troubles—to [499] grant no passports. However, I succeeded in getting one for Hamburgh from the Hanseatic Consulate, for which the Prussia Minister granted their visa, and early in the morning of the 28th, embarked at the Tower Stairs in the *Sir Edward Banks* steamer for Hamburgh, a large and good vessel, and agreable companions—amongst others Count Moltke, the Danish Minister, and Mr Hardwicke, the police magistrate. The weather [was] at first fair, but the cabin the first night excessively close and hot, and the next morning the wind rising and the sea rolling sent most people to their berths. I, however, kept on deck and well. The next night passed Heligoland at 12, and then came on the most pouring rain; however, as we ascended the Elbe, the weather cleared up, and a bright sun showed off to advantage the Danish bank of the river, the pretty village of Dungenese, the grounds and gardens of Mr Bauer of Hamburgh, and the rich-looking Danish Altona (All-zü-nah of the Hamburghers) and by midday on Monday 30th lodged at the Hotel de Russie, on the Jungfraustieg, overlooking the Alster.

I had now the whole afternoon to perambulate the town, take my place for Berlin, change my money, etc, but here it took me a good half hour to understand the coinage, which I never knew any where in a state of such confusion as in this eminently commercial and business town. The banker, in exchange for your bill on London, gave you an order on his money-changer in so many *marks banco*, which are purely theoretical. The [500] money-changer converted them into *marks gross-courant*, in which, and in schillings (little more than pence), all current accounts, bills, etc, are made out, but these marks are also almost imaginary, for I never saw a coin representing a mark or any multiple of it. The currency was chiefly in *Drittels*, mostly Hanoverian or Westphalian silver coins, representing the third of an Imperial Kronenthaler, and passing at Hamburgh for rather less than two marks—with these were occasionally a few Prussian or Saxon dollars, Imperial Kronenthalers, or Danish Speciethalers, all of very different values, and the small change was a complete chaos of copper, silver or mixed metal pieces—Hamburgh schillings, Danish skillings, North German silbergroschen, gutegroschen, mariengroschen, etc, and their multiples, with all sorts of dies and impression, often no indication of their value and very often worn as smooth as our shillings and sixpences before 1814. In changing a drittel at the Café, the waiter would pull out a handful of these little bits of metal and give you a certain number, you trusting to his honesty and intelligence that it was all right, for he himself was not always certain whether one he gave was worth four or five schillings.

At 9 in the evening I left Hamburgh in one of the *beiwagens* of the *schnellpost* for Berlin.[33] "By all public conveyances—at least by all mails—in North Germany, they take an unlimited number of passengers—the first inscribed go in the carriage which runs through the whole way, and [501] those which this principal carriage will not hold are sent in as many additional carriages, called *beiwagens*, as are necessary, these beiwagens being furnished by the postmasters with the horses and changed every stage. They vary much in form and size; the number of persons changes also very frequently, so that it requires every stage a fresh combination to make the capacity of the vehicles exactly suit the number of the travellers they are to hold. In parting we were 16, 8 in the grosse wagen and four in each of two calèches, each carriage drawn by four horses, on account of the very bad first stages. . . . I was at first n. 13, but as previous passengers stopped and others were taken up I got rather higher, and with the ever-varying vehicles, I do not think I occupied the same place two stages during the whole journey.

"It was dark when we left Hamburgh, and the first two stages across a corner of Denmark to Boitzenburg are most detestable, the road sometimes full of large stones and deep holes that toss you about so as to break your bones, sometimes through a deep wet sand, in which the wheels are buried to the axle, but never long enough to allow you to get any sleep during the whole night from 9 in the evening till 6 in the morning that it took us to go these 7½ German, about 35 English miles."[34]

Tuesday, 31 Augt. "A little before Boitzenburg, we came to an excellent chaussée, and stopped at that town to take coffee. Here the passengers n. 1 to 8 were transferred to a very excellent carriage which goes all the way to Berlin, and the others, 9 to 16, were all put into one very good beiwagen, on the diligence principle, but only for one stage, after which the beiwageners were again put into calèches—indeed all [502] the way to Berlin changes of this sort occurred every stage.

"At Vellahn, at about ½ past 8, we found a kind of substantial breakfast set out. At Ludwigsburt we got a good dinner at about 1, at Kletzke a supper in the evening, and the next morning a coffee breakfast at Spandau at 6, with plenty of time to eat, drink and smoke every time[§] the horses were changed, yet upon the whole we travelled much quicker than I expected and much more agreably. Owing to the variety of arrangements, I got successively into company with the greater part of the inmates of the conveyance, and found them very civil and very well disposed to converse with me, though it was with great difficulty that I made myself understood, écorching their language in a manner which must have been grating to their ears. I was also much with two young Englishmen, a Mr Booth and a Mr Jones, who were in the steamboat with us, and are now going on a tour to Berlin, Leipzig, Dresden, Vienna, etc, both pleasant enough, though not very brilliant, and not understanding a syllable of German. The conducteur very civil, the postillions elegant, all in a neat uniform, with a horn slung en bandaulière, which they sound sometimes very well as they arrive at the stage, and on some other occasions.

"From Boitzenburg to Berlin the country is flat and uninteresting, the soil very sandy, in many places covered to a great extent with nothing but heath and pines, and these but meagre looking—here and there a little rising ground gives a pleasing view over the wooded parts, but in

general it both looks and is poor—but the new road from the Mecklenburg frontier, near Boitzenburg, is an excellent chaussée, begun [503] a
few years ago, and finished only near the end of last year. In the Grand-
duchy of Mecklenburg Schwerin it is about fifty feet wide, of which
about 8 on each side are occupied by a path, on one side for pedestrians,
on the other for horsemen. Trees are planted the whole way along, and
once or twice in the interval between each stage is a sort of circular plan-
tation, apparently intended to afford shade for horses to stop under to
take breath. Milestones are regularly planted every half German mile;
they are large, neat granite stones, with a stone seat on each side, and
often a little arbour to shade them—all of which looks very nice. In Prussia, which we enter near Tarnow, the road is rather broader and the side
paths and milestone are not there, but otherwise it is as in Mecklenburg.
The posthouses at every stage are large, new, handsome and commodious; in each is a passenger stube, for passengers to eat, drink and smoke,
all under certain regulations, which are hung up at each place. The turnpikes are all new, the gate à bascule opened and shut by means of a
string, pulled down from inside the house, this house a good-looking
building, much larger than we should conceive necessary. Direction
posts are put up at every crossroad, these as well as the turnpikes generally striped with the colours of the country, red, white and sky-blue in
Mecklenburg, black and white in Prussia"—all now superseded by railroads.

Wednesday, 1st Sept. "Arrived at Berlin at 9 in the morning, having
been 35 hours coming 37½ German, or 175 English miles, and deducting
the time and distance from Hamburgh to Boitzenburg, gives 140 miles
in 27 hours, or a little more than 5 miles an hour, including stoppages, as
the rate of North German [504] schnellpost (mailcoach) travelling. The
entrance to Berlin through the Thiergarten and Brandenburg gate and
along the Linden, a fine promenade sort of street, is very handsome, and
the number of fine palaces and palace-like buildings is what strikes one
most, as well as the broad streets, alignés au cordon, and at right angles.
Put up at the hotel de Russie, said to be, and apparently, the best inn,
and which I find very comfortable. . . . But going to bed in the evening,
much puzzled how to manage it, the bedstead the size of a small sofa,
one half occupied by an enormous eiderdon, the other by a quilt and
sheets, so laid as only to cover the legs. However, by undoubling these, I
just contrived to cover myself, and found the bed underneath soft and
comfortable enough, but do what I could, the covering was so small that
the least motion threw it off; to guard against this, I suppose it is that the

bedstead is so small as to leave you no room to move—the table d'hote dinners good, consisting of soup and five dishes, with a good lesson of patience between each."

I remained above a fortnight at Berlin, chiefly with botanists, and enjoying myself so much that I found it hard to leave. The following are extracts from my journal.

Wednesday, 1st Sept., day of my arrival—"called at Kunth's, and with him to Humboldt's, who however was absent at Potsdam (I was singularly unfortunate in missing Humboldt entirely. I called afterwards twice on him by appointment, but both times he had been suddenly sent for by the King, and twice he called on me whilst I was out), then to Ehrenberg's, [505] who received me with great civility—then back to Kunth's to dinner—remaining with him the whole evening (the dinners generally at 2 o'clock) examining Labiatae." I was much with Kunth during my stay at Berlin, often dining or breakfasting there, Madame Kunth a very amiable French bourgeoise.

Thursday, 2d. "Breakfasted at the hotel with the two Englishmen who had come with me in the schnellpost; neither will, I think, be much the wiser for their journey," as proved to be the case, for ten days later I wrote to my father, "I shall now stay here till the 16th, then go straight back to Hamburgh, as they appear to be burning and fighting at Brunswick—at Leipzig they are as bad. At Dresden they have burnt the Police Office, and were fighting all day on Friday. Some Englishmen who went there from here on Thursday returned last night, as they found the place 'too hot for them.' In short, Prussia alone seems exempt from this epidemic fever of destruction, which is spreading over Germany. At Hamburg all is settled; there it was little more than a quarrel between the Jews and the Christians, and was chiefly confined to a quarter inhabited by the lowest of the rabble."[35] A fortnight later, I wrote from Hamburg: "The riots here were nothing—in Saxony they have all ended in rejoicings, at having two Kings instead of one;[36] at Vienna the epidemic has not yet arrived, but when it does, serious consequences are apprehended. In Prussia there will be none, for what occurred at Berlin on Thursday night (the night I left it), and the next, was nothing but a publichouse [506] quarrel between some journeymen tailors, which collected a mob, some of whom were tipsy, and refused to disperse. This occasioned a number of arrests—some thought too many, and wanted them to be set free, which [was] the cause of the mob the next evening, consisting chiefly of lookers on, but they were eventually dispersed after a little resistance, during which a few were wounded, and then it all ended. These riotous times naturally encrease the number of *curieux* where there is any street quarrel, but at Berlin the King is so very much liked that political disturbance is, I think, impossible."[37]

Thursday, 2d Sept. "To Kunth's, and with him to the Botanical Garden at Schoneberg, about a mile from the town on the Leipzig road, which is bordered by little country houses and tea gardens. The Botanical garden is large and contains a great number of species, but is in very bad order. The old Palmhouse must have been magnificent when built, but is now old and shabby; another large hothouse is very handsome. There are especially a very fine Latania, a Pandanus, and a few others. The Orchideae also look very well. The other houses are extensive, but contain nothing remarkable. The director, Mr Otto, received me very well, and went over with us.—To the herbarium at the bottom of the garden. It consists chiefly of Willdenow's Herbarium, the Garden herbarium, the general Herbarium, and Sellow's. Willdenow's is arranged according to his *Species Plantarum*, and the specimens numbered, the others according to the natural orders—Sellow's Brasilian plants the most valuable,[38] from the beauty and number of specimens, as well as the number of species. Of these they sell duplicates to pay for paper and other petty expenses, a paltry business for [507] a Royal Museum; the whole however, is very well kept, by Chamisso and Schlechtendal, the latter a pleasant, gentlemanly young man, Chamisso (the poet and author of *Peter Schlemihl*)[39] an eccentric sort of personage, with his long, uncombed hair hanging over his shoulders, so as to make him look like an wild, uncombed bear; he is, however, evidently very clever, and has been round the world," in Kotzebue's expedition, of which he published so graphic an account. After seeing the man, it struck me as thoroughly characteristic of him; the passage in which, after dwelling on the straits and discomforts they were put to on board, he complains, amongst other things, that "we naturalists and extras were not allowed any attendance, no one to clean our boots, etc, and we were put to great shifts— some cleaned them themselves—I left them uncleaned the whole voyage."[40] "Leaving the garden, returned to town to dinner and then to work in Kunth's herbarium till night"—and for several successive days worked most mornings[§] at Kunth's till 12 or 1 o'clock.

Friday, 3d Sept. The afternoon and evening with Dr Spiker, the librarian of the Royal library, author of *Travels in England*, a good deal read— before dinner, went over the library with him, and after dinner with him out to Charlottenburg, to see the palace and park—"the garden and park well laid out, but want that neatness and care which would otherwise make it a real jardin anglais. It is also so very flat and in many places so swampy, and the water so stagnant and dirty, though it be on the banks [508] of the Spree, that I cannot so much admire it as if I had not just come from England. There is a fine monument here by Rauch of the late Queen,[41] represented lying down in a very quiet posture, though too little like death. It is in a sort of mausoleum, to the portico of which are four beautiful columns of a granite, remarkable for its exquisite polish, and inside are also some very fine marble columns. This Rauch was formerly a servant of the Queen's, and she perceiving in him a natural talent, sent him to Italy, where he acquired a considerable degree of perfection in his art." This statue first established that great reputation, which was still so much further developped by his subsequent works.

Saturday, 4th Sept. After an early breakfast, "to the Botanical Garden, where Mr Otto gave me as many specimens to dry as I had time to take; he was exceedingly civil and prevenant, notwithstanding that he had all the time to hear my bad German—he made me eat a sort of déjeuner à la fourchette, and offered me all sorts of things. . . . Dined at Sir Brook Taylor's, English envoy here, a very pleasant party, all men—several diplomats, Rauch the sculptor, Dr Spiker, Lord Albert Cunningham and others. Sir Brook very civil to me, placed me beside him à la place d'honneur, etc. Dinner well served, good wines, cuisine à l'Allemande, fine appartments, dinner served at ½ past 4, coffee, and all over by 6, when Dr Spiker and I went to the play at the Royal Theatre—in *Karl. XII. Koenig der Schweden*,[42] some good acting by Devisme as "Adam Brock immer lachend"—all over at 9, when to tea with Dr and Mde Spiker— after which time to write home, and to spread my plants gathered in the morning.

[509]The two following mornings spent at work in Kunth's herbarium[§] and again a few days later, two more mornings in the Royal herbarium, where I sorted out and determined Sello's very large collection of Brasilian Labiatae, of which I bought a set of above 80 species, at the rate of twelve thalers (about 36'/) per hundred, which is excessively dear, and on such an occasion as this the set might have been given to me—however, it is worth all the money to me." This is what I felt at the time, but I am happy to say that this fit of stinginess soon passed away, and the Royal Herbarium of Berlin, like all Botanical Establishments on the Continent, has ever since been most liberal to me, in the number of valuable specimens presented to me on various occasions, and in the readiness with which they have invariably complied with my applica-

tions for loans of specimens from their herbaria. Besides Sello's, I went through the Labiatae of Willdenow's and of the general herbarium, Schiede and Deppe's Mexican ones and others. Both Chamisso and Schlechtendal were regularly at work at their joint papers, published in the *Linnaea*[43]—and these were more really joint publications than most of those which go under the names of two authors. Instead of working up a distinct portion, the two sat opposite each other at the same table, and usually one examined, whilst the other committed to paper the result of the examination.

In the afternoons I generally did a little sightseeing, at the Museum of painting and antiques, etc—dined two or three times at Kunth's, but usually at the table d'hote, where [510] met several very agreable people and few, if any, commis voyageurs. Amongst others, made acquaintance with a Polish Austrian, Baron Bludowski, who appeared to belong to the Court, and to be a clever man, but a violent liberal. He gave me a letter to Madame Binder, wife of the Austrian Minister at Hamburgh, which procured me so much agreable society there. The Baron was to have come later to England, but he never turned up, and I have never heard anything more of him. In the evenings (usually 6 to 9 o'clock), I often went to the Opera or to the theatre. At the Opera, the prima donna was Mlle Heinefetter, "who has a fine voice, but not always up to her part and, although she sometimes acted well when excited by passions (being herself very passionate), yet at others she stood with her long arms hanging down, as if she did not know what to do with herself. She looks pretty enough, has black hair and eyes. She was the other day opposite to me at the table d'hote, when I took her for a French girl." At the theatre one evening, saw "Schlegel's translation of Shakespeare's *King Richard III*, in which the original is pretty closely followed, Devrienne, as King Richard, very much like Kean, particularly in the three first acts. His gait, his looks, the trembling of his hands, the drawing the plan of battle with his sword, etc, would make one almost think he must have studied Kean, though it is said he never saw him. Devrienne was, however, not quite up to the most energetic parts, and was very deficient in memory, the prompter being obliged to read every word, but these defects are said to have grown on him lately. He drinks, too, a great deal—like Kean." Several good comedies and farces, both at the Schauspielhaus, and the smaller Koenigstadt theatre.

[511]Thursday, 9th Sept. "After dinner to Chamisso's, to look through the Labiatae of his voyage, and again in the evening to join a small party there to tea and supper, where Chamisso showed off as a man of

genius—the disorderly room, the dense atmosphere of tobacco smoke, of a piece with his round jacket and long, wild, bushy hair, whilst his conversation was quite on a par with his writings, in prose or poetical, and his civility and prevenance everything that could be wished."

Friday, 10th Sept. "With Kunth to Dr Beuth's, director of the Royal Institute,[44] to whom I presented Maudslay's card he had given me for the purpose, Dr Beuth an odd-looking, half female kind of a person, but remarkably clever and with much esprit, as proved by the flourishing condition to which he had brought the Royal Institute, almost created by him. This establishment contains a school for the instruction of a limited number of the cleverest artisans in the several arts and sciences conducive to the improvement of manufactures, and also a very large collection of models of machinery, etc, beautifully executed, chiefly by the pupils—a chemical laboratory, models, busts, etc, for drawing from, and a great variety of articles useful for the purpose of the establishment. . . . After dinner, to the gasworks, to the director, Mr John Perks, whose perseverance through all the obstacles encountered in getting up so new an establishment in a foreign country has brought it into the most flourishing condition."

Saturday, 11th Sept. "To see the Parade, for which I got a good place, on a stand on the Opera house stairs, for five silbergroschen. The Parade was in honor of General Diebitsch, [512] consisting of the garrison of Berlin, that is three infantry regiments, three of cavalry, besides horse and foot artillery and Cadets, the tenue of the troops very fine, particularly that of the infantry, the King, Diebitsch and the Royal Princes on horseback with a numerous staff, the King a fine-looking man, remarkably well on horseback, Diebitsch a short, thick, stumpy body, looking anything but a great general,[45] the day beautiful, so that it was a fine sight—great crowds—indeed, Diebitsch's hotel is daily beset by a crowd when he is expected to go out."

Sunday, 12 Sept. "With Kunth, to the meeting of the Gartenbau Verein, or Horticultural Society, in the rooms of the Herbarium at Schoeneberg, announced for 12, but only began at 1. Otto, Chief Secretary, in the chair, Link being absent, about thirty or forty persons—very long, wordy procès-verbal of the last sitting read, then Schlechtendal gave the resumé of a paper and some books presented to the Society. Flowers and fruits exhibited, and the fruit tasted, and lots drawn for two pineapples and three Oleanders—a very fine Clethra in flower, also a Hedychium, some Angelonias, etc. The fruit consisted of melons, grapes and plums, all very middling. I was elected honorary member, and the diploma and the last number of their *Transactions* presented to me. After the meeting, about three or four and twenty adjourned to the inn at Schöneberg to dinner, served in the same style as the table d'hote, with the same long intervals between each dish. Each person pays, except the *Invités*. I was invited by Otto—but did not sit it out the whole time, not to lose the Opera."—In our English Linn. Soc. and other club dinners, the *Invités* had to pay like the others.

[513]Wednesday, 15th Sept. With Kunth, to Potsdam. Torrents of rain interrupted our visit to Sans Souci, with its "magnificent set of orange trees, rather irregularly arranged terraces, but after dinner the sky cleared up again, and we drove to the Pfauen Insel or Isle of Peacocks, about a mile lower down the Havel, a beautiful spot, laid out as a sort of private garden of the King's, with a very odd looking structure, where he sometimes spends a day or a night. Fintelmann, the gardener, cultivates this with great care, his nephew (he himself being gone to Hamburgh) went over with us.[46] The Dahlias are very fine, though they have none of our globe or Anemone-flowered, but the ordinary ones are fully as large as double, and as brilliant as ours. The hothouses are not remarkably rich, excepting in a splendid collection of Palms, lately bought by the King and brought by young Fintelmann from Paris. Amongst others, a splendid Latania, of which the leaves extend to above sixty feet. For these Palms, a very large house is building; they are now crowded into one that will but just hold them. Besides the plants, the Pfauen Insel also contains a menagerie in the style of our Zoological gardens, with a good variety of birds, monkeys and animals of the deer and gazelle tribes, also half a dozen very fine Llamas, singular animals, stinking most abominably, all very tame. The birds are under the care of a dwarf of about 20, and looking quite like a child."

Thursday, 16 Sept. The last day of my most enjoyable visit to Berlin, "spent the morning with Kunth and G.E.§ Gray of the British Museum (who is here on his way to Hamburgh), chiefly at the Natural History and Anatomical Museums, and [514] in leave-taking visits, etc,—very nearly detained by the want of quick communication with England. I had brought with me a letter of credit from Martin, Stone and Martin, on Anhalt u. Wagener, the principal bankers in Berlin, but when I presented it they said they had received no advice of it, and could not give me any money on it. Mentioning the matter to Sir Brook Taylor, he said that if Anhalt and Wagener would refer to him, he would set it all right, but still they would not give any money unless Sir Brook would countersign my bill. This I could not ask him to do, and there was no time to write to London." I find by the postmarks that letters were then from eight to ten days between Berlin and London. Fortunately, my friend Kunth advanced me the money I wanted, which I was enabled to return to him from Hamburgh.

From Berlin, I returned to Hamburgh, to attend the meeting of German Naturalists and Medical men "Versamlung Deutscher Naturforscher und AErtzte," the third annual meeting of this Association, upon the model of which was formed our British Association, which first met in 1831.[47] The German one originated chiefly with Professor Oken, and became immediately popular with German men of science, and well supported by the ruling authorities or Sovereigns of the different states where it assembled. The first meeting was at Berlin in 1828, the second at Heidelberg in 1829, and this, the third, in Hamburgh. Left Berlin on the 16th in the evening, arriving at Hamburgh in the morning of the 18th, "going over the same road I had come a fortnight before, and in the same manner, with this exception, that I was now [515] in the coupé, my companion in the coupé being an Englishman, of the name of Gibbings, a young tourist of the true English type, damning everything and everybody, who will go home from his six weeks' tour about as wise as he came, without having learned a word of German—in the interior, J.E. Gray and two German Professors and others."

Saturday, 18th Sept. "To the Hotel de Ville, to get my card of Mitglieder of the meeting, where, after I had made myself known, I had to sign my name, and was given a card to admit me to all the meetings of the assembly, cards of admission to some Museums, etc, a description of Hamburgh and the regulations of the meeting," proceedings upon which those of our Reception room were afterwards modelled—made some calls to present my letters, and "to the general meeting at the Borsen Halle, a large room with about four hundred seats, all numbered, with a corresponding number on each person's card of admission, thus designating the place each is to occupy at all these general meetings. The result is that people cannot get near those whom they know—you may be placed between Herr Apotheker this, and Herr Mediker that, from this or that little town of Germany, of neither of whom you have ever heard, any more than they of you. Besides, with their arrangements, they have contrived that the Hamburghers themselves have all got good places, and several foreigners, who cannot understand the speakers unless placed near enough to hear them well, are quite at the further corner of the room. They profess to give the tickets in the order in which the members have arrived, but this is not the case; besides that they have reserved a certain number [516] of places for distinguished persons, which they give in a manner not calculated to convince people of their impartiality. As for me, I am so far down that I cannot hear well, and shall not attend any more; the subjects treated today also were not very interesting to me—a speech on German astronomers, and another on animal magnetism.[48] The room was quite full and the gallery crowded with ladies. Left the room before the end; home to dress, and to dinner in the Apollons-Saale, where were all these naturalists and some of their wives and daughters—very difficult to get places, a great noise, bustle and confusion, and a very indifferent dinner. I, however, contrived to get a seat amongst some of the botanists, but for the most part it was very ill managed." After dinner to the play, in the new, handsome theatre—and afterwards to tea at Mde Binders, to whom Baron Bludowski had given me a letter, and spent a very agreable hour or two there the majority of the evenings during my stay at Hamburgh—she very amiable, and still young—her husband, the Austrian minister here, rather old, apparently clever and well informed, but an ennuyeux talker—their daughter, a lively, little, good-looking girl of 16 or 17, a brilliant musician and gracefull dancer—with rather more continental freedom than we are accustomed to see (fast young ladies were not yet the fashion in England). All received me very well, and became quite cordial—the family made up by an English widow staying with them.

Sunday, 19th. "The savans had a breakfast this morning at Booth's, the nurseryman of Flotbeck (Altona),[49] but I did not go, as I did not care to see the gardens in a crowd of three or four [517] hundred; so I spent the morning at Lehmann's, studying some Labiatae from Vahl's and Hornemann's herbaria which he had had sent from Copenhagen for the purpose. The dinner at the Apollons Saale not near so crowded as yesterday, and better arranged—the botanists got together to one table. After dinner to the play, then back to the Apollons Saale, where another room was lighted up, an orchestra provided, and a dance got up, with some naturalists' wives and daughters, and a few Hamburgh ladies. No toilettes—a dirty floor—the smoke of tobacco penetrating into the room, and everything looking more like a pothouse dance than a meeting of bonne société.

Monday, 20th Sept. "After breakfast, to the meeting of the botanical Section at Lehmann's from 10 till 2, which was much more interesting than their general meetings. About thirty persons present. Amongst others, Mertens of Bremen in the chair, Count Sternberg and Baron Jacquin from Vienna, Fischer of Petersburg, Agardh of Stockholm, Hornemann of Copenhagen, Horkel, Otto and Chamisso of Berlin, Wikström of Stockholm, Estreicher of Cracow, Hornschuch of Greifswald, Schubert of Warsaw, Frölich of Bozen, Presl of Prague, Fintelmann the Pfaueninsel gardener, etc,—communications by Sternberg, Jacquin, Mertens,[50] and others. Called on Prof Lichtenstein, the Berlin Zoologist, brother of Lichtenstein of Montpellier—dined at the Apollon-Saale—to the play— to tea at the Binders, and back to the Apollons Saale to dance—both the dinner and the dance rather better arranged and got up than yesterday, but not much better."

[518]Tuesday, 21st Sept. After the botanic section, "to the Botanic garden, where the Naturalists had a dejeuner, or cold collation, prepared for them in two tents. The garden is very prettily situated and laid out, and the day was fine, so that it was a very gay scene, though with too few ladies and too much champagne—the dinner at the Apollon Saale— the theatre—tea at the Binders, and then to dance as usual."

Wednesday, 22d Sept. "At the botanical section, a strong feeling of regret was expressed at the prospect of Dr Wallich having to return to India without having finished the distribution of the Indian collections and, on the proposition of Lehmann, it was resolved that a letter should be written from the Section to the East India Company, and an address to the King of England, with a view to the procuring a prolongation of his leave of absence. There were subsequent meetings of the botanists to settle the terms of the letter and address, and they were afterwards laid before a general meeting of the Association,[51] but there Oken and Lichtenstein objected that it was out of the province of the Association to interfere in the matter," and I believe that the affair was dropped, though a prolongation of Dr Wallich's leave of absence was obtained by other means.—This day, after the usual dinner, "to the Binders, and with them to spend the evening at the Slomans, a pleasant Dutch family living at about a mile from the town, the father and mother with a [519] son and two daughters, both rather pretty, and one a poet, all half English, at least in speaking—music and dancing till half past 11."

"The greater part of the Association are gone to Heligoland in a steamboat, hired by the town for the purpose of showing the savans the sea (quite a novelty to many of them). They go today, stay tomorrow, and come back the next day—today it pours of rain. I did not go because I have seen enough of the sea; besides, except Sternberg and Oken, scarcely any of the botanists are gone." They returned on the Friday night, having seen and felt quite enough of it, bad weather and a stormy return; out of 150 on board, only about ten were not thoroughly seasick.

Thursday, 23d. "After the botanical section, out to Mr Parish's at Nienstetten, on the Elbe below Altona, a very pretty drive over a very bad road, and to Booths' nursery and botanic garden at Flottbeck. Dined at Mr Struve's, the Russian Minister here (nearly related to Struve the Astronomer). Besides the family, M. and Mde Struve and their two daughters, one Mde de Bacharacht and her husband, Russian consul here, the other unmarried, the party consisted of the two Fischers, Fischer le végétal, the Petersburgh botanist, and Fischer l'animal, the Moscow zoologist, President of the Moscow Society of Naturalists, and Dr Mertens—after the dinner to the Binders to tea, and then to the dance."

Friday, 24th. "After the botanical section, out to the Booths' at Flottbeck where, between heavy showers, went over the arboretum with Jacquin and one of the Booths, and dined there, meeting Jacquin, Agardh, Otto, Wikström, [520] Estreicher, Bueck, Mertens and another—back to town to the play."

Saturday, 25th. The last day of the Association, "the botanical section well attended, and a letter to Wallich signed—a crowded dinner at the Apollons Saale, with good singing, all like the first day but better managed—to the theatre—to the Struves to tea, and then to the Apollons Saale, where the dancing was in the great room, upwards of a hundred ladies and between two and three hundred gentlemen, but no or very few toilettes, good music, very bad floor, pretty girls but very bad dancers."

Sunday, 26th Sept. "After breakfast, with the Binders to Wandsbeck about two miles from the town on the Lubeck road, *en partie de campagne* at Mde d'Ehrenstein's. M. d'Ehrenstein is a Holstein nobleman formerly in the Prussian service, in which his son is now. The father appears *très comme il faut*, Mde d'Ehrenstein, like so many ladies in this country, a little too fat, from the prevalent fashion of living to eat not eating to live. Wandsbeck is a little village, like tout autre, in the plains of the neighbourhood, and the d'Ehrensteins' house has nothing extraordinary. The Slomans came, and two or three young men. After a short walk, we had a substantial dejeuné dinatoire, then all walked out over a park belonging to a chateau now abandoned, and spent the morning with a great deal of gaiety. At ½ past 3 we took leave, and the Binders were kind enough to set me down at Hamm at the Senator Merck's, where I was asked to dinner, with a large party, consisting chiefly of the principal members of the botanical section (except the Swedes who left early this morning); besides M. de Struve, M. Fricke the general Secretary [521] of the Association, and a few others, altogether about forty persons. We sat down to dinner at ½ past 4, and the desert was served after 7. A profusion of dishes served in the German way, one after the other, with a long interval between each (the mehlspeise before the roast, etc). A great deal of wine, and altogether an excellent dinner, but so long as to be quite fatiguing. I left it still going on at ½ past 7, returning to town for the play."

I remained three days more, enjoying myself much at Hamburgh—the mornings at the botanical garden with Jacquin or with Fischer—or a botanical stroll along the Alster, gathering, amongst other things, the Cotula aurea, then new to me—the evenings at the play and at the Binders or Struves or both. Monday, 27th, "at a great dinner, given by Lehmann to the botanical section, now still farther diminished by the departure of Count Sternberg, Presl and others. Chamisso and the Booths were not invited, owing, it was said, to divers piques between them and Lehmann; besides the botanists, Lichtenstein, J.E. Gray and one or two other zoologists were there, in all about twenty. As yesterday, a great dinner, with plenty of dishes and a variety of wines—sat out to the end about 8 o'clock, then to the Struves', where met Fischer, who had been at another great dinner given by Syndicus von Siemers, to which I had been asked, but I had already promised Lehmann."

Wednesday, 29th. "Wound up with leavetaking visits, settling with Fischer, who like me was to leave the next morning, to meet him in the evening at the Struves to take leave, but Mozart's *Zauber-flöte* at the theatre lasted[§] much longer than usual, and it was too late for the Struves' tea." I had, however, just got [522] home when Fischer came in to say his plans were changed. Instead of leaving the next morning, he had proposed to Mlle Struve and had been accepted, and should remain a few days longer to make the necessary arrangements, and begged me, before I left the next day, to call on them. This I did, "found Fischer there and the family very happy in their morning toilettes, Madame Struve in her morning jacket (then called manteau de nuit, and perhaps what she had slept in), Mademoiselle the bride in her curlpapers. Without being very pretty she is good looking, and her amiability and character are very highly spoken of; indeed the whole family appears to me very delightful, so that it looks like an excellent match on both sides." Fischer himself, with his amiable manners and excellent qualities, secured to him the highest regard from the numerous friends he made in Germany and England as well as in Russia.

Thursday, 30th Sept. "Left Hamburgh at 1 o'clock in a very good steamboat for Harburg, a traversée of a little more than an hour. This is but a very small town, the houses very barn-looking, but with their high roofs, gable-ends and profusion of windows, very picturesque. After dinner, took a walk upon the rising ground above the town—the commencement of an immense extent of barren heaths as dreary as possible, the evening still, cold and cloudy, a few peasants about, silently occupied with the potato harvest, a burial ground at the edge and a distant view over a marshy plain, through which wind the several branches of the Elbe—a fine but melancholy scene. At 8 left Harburg in the Hannover post-Kutsche, rather a small, uncomfortable diligence, in which, moreover, I had a central place, and passed an indifferent night. The whole of the next day going a snail's pace, over dreary heaths, with here and there a [523] patch or two ploughed up and cultivated but without enclosure, the villages few and far between—the road sometimes good, but generally dry and sandy—the country unbroken by hills of any heighth, Celle, a small town where we dined, the only considerable place we went through. The same sandy heaths, with here and there a pine wood, last to the very gates of Hannover, where we arrived at about 6 o'clock, having gone 75 English miles in 22 hours, being very nearly 3½ miles an hour—just in time to see some pretty good comic acting in the curiously constructed theatre."

Saturday, 2d Oct. "Left Hannover at 7 in the morning, in the Cassel Schnellpost—the weather clear and beautiful though cold in the morning—the carriage very good and comfortable—my place in the cabriolet—the country fine—altogether a perfect contrast to my yesterday's dreary, uncomfortable journey. At first, on leaving Hannover, the same plain continues, though richer and less sandy, but soon after the first stage we got into a hilly country, and at Else entered a beautiful valley, in the midst of which is the small town of Ahlfeldt, with a picturesque two-towered church. In the next stage, crossed a high hill called the Hugel, commanding a very extensive view, and descended to the small town of Eimbeck, where we dined. From hence to Göttingen the road leads through a broad and rich valley, though not so picturesque as that of Ahlfeldt, through several large villages or small towns—amongst others Salzburg, where are very extensive saltworks with a most cumbersome apparatus at work, which I was told was pumping the water out of the mines, but certainly the enormous beams I saw in motion could not be necessary for that purpose. Got into Göttingen at 9 in the evening, by moonlight, the moon at its full, not a cloud to be seen, [524] ein recht fröhliches Abend, having enjoyed my journey more than any since I left England."

Sunday, 3d Oct. "Early in the morning to the botanical garden. Schrader, the Professor, was not up yet, but the Garten-Inspector, Fischer, received me very well, and I spent two or three hours with him, going over the garden and gathering a few specimens for drying. The garden is extensive, but irregularly scattered over a part of the ancient ditches and walls of the town. It is pretty well laid out for the purposes of the lectures at the University, having separate collections of medicinal plants, of fruits, vegetables, forage plants, oil plants, tinctorial plants, etc, besides a general collection arranged according to the Linnean system, and a part laid out for a Jussieuan collection, also collections of annuals, of grasses, of trees, etc; the houses are extensive, but oldfashioned, pretty well kept, but by no means handsome. The collection good in point of numbers, but nothing very extraordinary. Fisher appears to be an excellent fellow and very zealous; the garden is well supported, and the botanical lectures well attended. Göttingen a neat, good-looking town, but I could not stay to see anything but the garden, and started again for Cassel at ¼ before 12 in a calèche I hired for the purpose.

"The immediate environs of Göttingen, at least at this time of year, do not present anything very remarkable, though certainly the situation is good. The valley of the Seine, in which it lies, is here broad and not deep, which takes off from the heighth of the surrounding hills, and there is too much corn, without divisions or variety, to look well at this time of year; but after [525] ascending the hill on the way to Cassel, the view back is very fine, and further on, after passing through the little town of Dransfeld, the view down to the right and in front is truly magnificent, then a beautiful road winding down a deep valley, the picturesque town of Münden, the ascent to the other side, and again the noble view over the plain of Cassel was altogether finer than anything I have seen this long while. We have nothing of the kind in England. Münden pleased me particularly; the bricknogging mode of building and multitude of windows are excessively picturesque. It being also a fine Sunday afternoon, a great part of the population was walking on the roads in their best dresses, and the females are very pretty, very fine eyes and countenances that dart a look at you as you go by that pierces through and through. Stopped at Münden an hour to refresh the horses and to dine, and got to Cassel at six, having come at the rate of six miles an hour over a mountainous country but with a beautifully smooth road, the sun shining bright all day without being too hot, altogether fully as pleasant a day's journey as yesterday"—without any of the stoppages I had anticipated. I had carelessly left behind me at Berlin the passport I had had so much trouble in procuring in London, which might have occasioned great inconvenience during these times of rioting and disorder, but I found the Schnellpost officials readily satisfied with the explanation that I was a savant coming from the meeting, and in the hurry had left my passport behind, and though required at Münden and Cassel to show my papers, they were easily satisfied on my subscribing my *Werthe, Name und Charakter*, and [526] later on, on the Rhine, though cautions were stuck up in several parts of the steamer that no one was to be admitted on board unless his papers were *bien en règle*, no one ever asked me for mine.

Arrived in Cassel in time to go to the play, where *La Dame Blanche*, translated into German, was well given, "Anna, by Made Roller-Schweitzer, with fine black eyes ever rolling about, and a very expressive countenance, but not much taste in singing—the chorus girls ugly and awkward for the country, though they might do in London—the theatre full, some very pretty girls in the first boxes, but in general the Casselianes are not so pretty as those of Münden, and even at Hamburgh the theatre contained more beauty."

Monday, 4th Oct. "Walked out to Wilhelmshöhe, where I spent the whole morning admiring this truly magnificent spot, both naturally and artificially so. Cassel lies on a gentle eminence on one side of a broad, rich valley, watered by the Fulda and bordered by high hills. The palace of Wilhelmshöhe is quite at the foot of, or rather a little way up the hill, the whole side of which is occupied by the richly wooded park. A perfectly straight avenue of above two miles long connects it with the town. It is a very fine building, and from its situation much finer than any palace I have seen. Immediately above it on the top of the hill is a spring, the waters of which are collected in a large reservoir, enclosed in a massive structure, crowned by a high tower, with a colossal bronze statue at the top. From this chateau d'eau, especially from the tower, is the most magnificent view on all sides, particularly over the rich valley [527] or plain of Cassel, and from the reservoir the waters are let out three times a week over a number of cascades, jets d'eau, etc, contrived with a good deal of taste. There are also a number of pieces of water about the park and a few buildings scattered among the trees, without that gimcrack confusion we too often see in such parks—and what cannot but be admired is that this beautiful place, full of flowers, seats, and all sorts of things that would not a moment be left uninjured by the English public is here so completely open to every one that there are not even gates to it, merely posts with indications of the places where it is forbidden to go on the grass, or to approach too near to the private part at the back of the palace, which injunctions are strictly obeyed by the multitudes who make it the object of their promenades. The only fault to be found is that the park is too thick of trees—the greater part is a mere mass of wood, and the long, straight road bordered by large trees, though it looks well from the top of the hill, is rather tedious to go along. But one would not wish anything to be otherwise, either in the building or the site of the palace. The old part of Cassel is like a little dirty country town, but the new part, particularly the large Friedrichsplatz, may, for situation and style of building, rivalise with the first capitals in Europe—on a small scale, it is true—but as far as it goes, full of handsome palaces, museums, etc. At the play in the evening, very much amused by the farcical comedy, *Das Räuschen* (Drunkenness), capitally acted—a dark, drizzling night, and the town in complete darkness, because it is moonlight in the almanach, though *leider* not in the town—and no gas yet as in Berlin and Hannover."

[528]Tuesday, 5th Oct. "At ten in the morning left the beautiful little city of Cassel in the Frankfurt Eilwagen (idle waggon), a Frenchified edition of the Schnellposts (snail-posts) which contrives to go from 4½ to 5 miles an hour on the road. The country, though not so pretty as between Göttingen and Cassel, is still diversified, with a few very fine spots, but it begins to look and feel not a little wintery, and towards evening a drizzling rain made it rather uncomfortable—the road still very good, and the carriage also, though heavy and cumbersome, the Hessian postillons remarkably smart. Dined at Jesberg and had coffee at night at Marburg, both of them small towns, very prettily situated. Some of these places have, within the last few days, been the scene of some of these riots which are raging over the Continent, but without anything more serious than breaking a few windows or burning some of the papers of the toll houses, and now nothing is to be seen indicating unquiet, except here and there a piquet of troops on the bivouac, or a travelling bataillon met on the road."

Wednesday, 6th Oct. "Reached Frankfurt at about ½ past 10, 24½ hours to about 100 miles—about 4 miles an hour, including stoppages—spent the day in doing the sights of Frankfurt, and in the evening to the theatre to hear Mlle Schroeder-Devrient in Spontini's opera of *The Vestalian*."

Thursday, 7th Oct. "To Bethmann's Museum in the morning, to see Danneker's 'Ariadne,'[52] and after dinner steamed down to Mayence where, after clearing my things at the Custom house (for the third or fourth time after Berlin), to the theatre, a dull looking, excessively dark house, but excellent acting by Döring, a young man of 24, at first as the old Jew in a translation of Cumberland's *Jew*, and afterwards as the student in a capital farce, *Der Alte Student*."

[529]Friday, 8th, to Wednesday, 13 Oct. From Mayence, straight home to London, steaming down the Rhine, and from Rotterdam, by the bulky stoomboot *Batavier*, to the Thames. Stopped to sleep at Coblentz, Cologne, Nimeguen and Rotterdam, and nearly a whole day at Coblentz, in the exceedingly nice, small hotel of the day, the large, noisy hotels along the Rhine, of modern days, not being yet thought of. "Up to the fortress of Ehrenbreitstein, on the opposite bank. The fortifications of this place, all entirely new, are very strong, and at present considerable preparations are making for the reception of troops. The threatening aspect of affairs in the Netherlands,[53] and the strong disposition manifested by the French to seize any pretext for war, oblige the Germans to be on their guard, even supposing the King of Prussia should not think it advisable to send troops to the support of his brother of Holland, and a war with France would not be unpopular in Prussia, for they hate the French; it might also not be unsuccessful, for Prussia is now remarkably strong in a military point of view. This neighbourhood looks martial enough; the garrison of Mayence, Austrian and Prussian, is put au grand complet, and here drilling troops and warlike implements may be seen all over the town." Apparent precautions also taken to prevent surprises and riots, and street notices stuck up in the steamboats about stopping any travellers whose papers were not en règle—as for me, however, they either did not ask for my passport—or when they did, were quite satisfied with my telling them that I had forgotten it at Berlin, and was going straight home to London—where I arrived at 12 on the 13th, and after being detained four hours at the Custom-house, drove home in very good spirits, having much enjoyed my tour, and finding my father and mother [530] both very well and expecting my sister Sarah, who arrived a few days after with Countess Ludolf from their eventful visit to Paris.

November and December 1830 were months of great political excitement in London, though the routine of ordinary business, social intercourse, and the course of scientific societies, in which I now took an active part, were but very little affected by it. The Continental disturbances had had their *contrecoup* in England. The Whigs and Radicals, with their watchword, "Parliamentary Reform," succeeded in raising much outcry against the long-persistent Tory Government, and every now and then the police had a little tussle with street-rows, which I, however, never came across, much as I was about in the streets at all times of day. Exaggerated accounts of them were current in society, but they really appeared to be nothing more than threatening crowds, assembled in the principal West End streets, which the police had to disperse without actual bloodshed.[54] The first alarm was on the occasion of the Lord Mayor's day. The new King (William IV), who delighted in show, was to have gone in state to the city dinner, and great and costly preparations were made on the occasion. The previous day (Nov. 8), I went early to the city to see the Chamberlain, whom we knew, about admission to Countess Ludolf, with the Duchess of Berri (then in England), to see the Guildhall preparations, and to secure windows for ourselves—when I found all in great confusion, on the announcement that the Royal visit was postponed, the Lord Mayor (Key) having written to Peel to say that the public mind was in so excited a state that he could not answer for the ceremony passing off quietly. Much anger was expressed, [531] and excited groups collected in the streets this and the following day, and exaggerated reports of the rioting circulated in the clubs, but it all ended in nothing more than a few pickpocket rows on the evening of the 9th.[55] When Parliament met, the Duke of Wellington's speech, firmly resisting any reform in parliamentary representation, followed by a majority against ministers on Sir Henry Parnell's motion on the Civil list having shown that the position of the Tory administration was no longer tenable, they resigned, and Lord Grey and the Whigs were called in.[56] This, of course, much occupied all men's minds, but the immediate effect was not disturbance, but eager expectation, or intense anxiety about what was to follow. No one was more excited at the time than my uncle Jeremy Bentham. He had several times of late seen Brougham—then plain Mr Brougham, who entered a good deal into his law reform projects, giving him to understand that in this new Parliament he intended to devote himself to the task of procuring the abolition of the principal abuses of the law as exposed by Jery Bentham, and indeed that he should consider himself as his, Jeremy Bentham's mouthpiece in Parliament—and on the resignation of the Tory Cabinet, he wrote to assure my uncle that nothing in the new arrangements could affect him further than in giving him more influence in the house, as he should not accept any post in the new ministry.[57] My uncle's hopes were thus raised to the highest pitch, and Brougham was to have dined with him on the 23d—as my uncle expected to settle the plan of operations. In the mean time, however, Mr Brougham, the independent member, and still in the outer [532] [court] had, as represented in H.B.'s caricature, leaped over the inner bar and become Lord Brougham, Lord High Chancellor,[58] who sent an excuse to Jeremy Bentham for not coming to the dinner, and *never after came near him*[59]. The disappointment rankled deep in my uncle's mind, and was partly the cause of the criticisms on some of Broughams measures which he subsequently published under the title of *Lord Brougham displayed*,[60] though toned down in some respects from what he had originally written.

During these two months, I was a good deal occupied with the Horticultural Society's business—arranging for the distribution of the duplicates of the different collectors' herbaria which the Council had entrusted to me—settling the preliminaries of the fête at the gardens to be tried again next year, etc. Two Councils were also held of the Linnean Society, in which Robert Brown, from his long connection with the Society and the universal respect in which he was held by the members, naturally took the lead—but rather let it fall asleep; at the first Council, nearly the whole time was consumed by a long desultory conversation and discussion about the wording of an address to the new King on his accession. Brown brought in a proposed draft, to which the most unmeaning alterations were suggested—an *and* for an *or*, or one adulatory epithet for another, and these were warmly discussed, although not of the slightest importance, even if the address should ever be really read, which every one knew it would not be. At the second Council [533] I took upon myself to bring forward something more practically useful, and succeeded in getting measures adopted for diminishing the large amount of overdue arrears of subscription entered on the books. I also attended regularly the Linnean Society club dinners, and the evening meetings of the Linnean and Geographical Societies. On the 30th November, going down to the Royal Society to see Mr Barnard on Horticultural Society business, was induced to remain there till the ballot was over at the Anniversary meeting, which was very fully attended, and the greatest interest excited by the contest for the Presidency. The scientific Fellows of the Society had put forward Herschel, and a recommendation of him, signed by one hundred of the most eminent, had been published in the papers,[61] but some busybodies, who hoped to gain importance for themselves, had induced the Duke of Sussex to come forward. After the strongest canvass, chiefly by his Secretary, Mr Pettigrew, and Dr Bozzi Granville, who did not scruple to represent it as a measure which was supported by Royal influence, they succeeded in carrying the Duke, but only by a majority of 8—119 against 111 votes.

This was generally regarded as a death blow to the Society, and not one of the scientific Fellows attended the Anniversary dinner.

In Botany, I compleated my paper on Indian Labiatae for Wallich—worked up Chamisso's Labiatae and sent him the result,[62] and spent many a morning in Frith Street, [534] assisting Wallich in his distributions. On the 3d Nov., I spent the afternoon, and dined at Dr Burchell's at Fulham, his house full of the curiosities he had brought from his two great expeditions, to South Africa and to Brasil,[63] with the numerous cases containing the rich botanical collections he had made, which he had never unpacked, always waiting till he should have built a herbarium to contain them. This he never did; his Brazilian boxes remained unopened to the day of his death—it was only from his African collections that he had sent a few specimens to De Candolle for publication in his *Prodromus*, and that he afterwards sent me some Leguminosae, and a few others. He was, however, most friendly and hospitable, and I had several pleasant dinners at his house.

I continued occasionally assisting my father in his writings, but his energy was beginning to fail him. Early in December, he was one day thrown down in Cavendish Square by the pole of a carriage, and though not hurt was a good deal shaken, and Mr Copeland, the surgeon, a great friend of his, and enjoying great reputation, thought it adviseable to bleed him, notwithstanding his age. After that, his appetite began to fail and he got weaker. Dr Maton, however, whom we several times consulted, gave us no cause to be uneasy, and my father continued every now and then to dine with his old friend Count Woronzow, now very aged but unchanged. I accompanied my father there once or twice, meeting one day the Count's grandson, Sidney Herbert, then a young Oxonian, showing good promise of what he afterwards became.[64] [535] I was also much in society in the evenings, dining out with my sister, or at dancing parties, or at the play. One day, whilst my sister was at the Ludolfs' and I had a desperate cold, the Countess found that one of her dinner party of 14 could not come, and she could not bear to have the Duke of Sussex in a party of thirteen, so she sent to insist on my coming, which I was forced to do, bon gré, mal gré. Besides the Duke, there were the Rothschilds and some others, old Rothschild exceedingly amusing, but the Duke any thing but the affable, liberal mannered man his partisans in the Royal Society represented him to be—requiring the most punctual etiquette, and at dessert with the ladies at the table, smoking his cigar—then not [at] all general in men's parties, and unheard of before ladies.

At my uncle's, I continued my regular dinners once or twice a week, sitting often till past 12 writing from his dictation, or "marginalising" his MS; and on Christmas day he had my father, mother and sister, as well as myself, to dine "downstairs in the parlour"; my father seemed then to be improving, my uncle in high spirits, and it turned out a most happy family gathering, destined to be the last, but closing well a happy year of my life.

10

Death of His Father; Montpellier and Geneva, 1831

[536]The year 1831 brought about a reversal of the career entered upon the previous one. The death of my father and consequent loss to us of his pension (£1600 a year), and the growing uncertainty of my Uncle's arrangements as to the disposal of his property after his death, recalled to me the necessity of my following up a money-making profession. The year rose for me in Botany and set in Law.

The first two or three months passed like the latter ones of 1830— much of Horticultural Society's business, regular attendance at the Linnean Council and meetings, and frequent mornings at Wallich's distribution in Frith Street, besides Botany at home, and preparing my *Scrophularineae Indicae*.[1] Much in Society in the evenings, and my father still able to dine frequently with Count Woronzow. I was also a good deal taken up with Simon de Klustine, the younger brother of my friend who was killed in the Turkish war and of Anastasie, who was now married to M. de Circourt. Simon came over on the 2d Jany, and remained in London three or four months, during which time he was almost daily at our house, and engaged himself to my sister, an engagement, however, that was ultimately broken off. With him I made acquaintance with M. de Tourgueneff, who had been Ministre des Cultes at Petersburgh during Alexander's liberal days, but was now in a sort of disgrace. His brother, who had taken part in the conspiracy of 1825, was also here— under sentence of death.[2] At Countess Ludolf's I met, amongst others, Marshal Bourmont[3] and his three sons, [537] "the Marshal a short man, rather vulgar but by no means borné in appearance, his sons young dandies—the eldest rather vulgar but apparently very clever, the second more recherché, the third very young."[4] On the 22d Jany, "with my father and sister to a party at Mrs Denman's, on the occasion of her 84th birthday. Never saw her looking so well and so happy as she did there, surrounded by friends, and her son, the new Attorney General, by her side." When Queen Caroline's cause was so warmly advocated by Brougham, Denman and Lushington, most people[§] observed that these three men had thus foregone all future advance in their profession. No-one would have predicted that they could ever be severally at the head of it, as Lord High Chancellor, Chief Justice of the King's Bench and Judge of the High Admiralty Court, respectively. All three men of the greatest ability, and the two that we were intimate with, Denman and Lushington, as steady in character and sound in judgement as amiable in private life.

During this time, I added to my herbarium plants received from Gussone, and other correspondents abroad, and to my library, especially by the purchase of several good botanical works at the sale of the library of Mr Barclay of Bury Hill, but soon was very much occupied with the Registration Bill prepared by [   ], and of which a copy had been sent to my uncle, by the Commissioners on the law of Real property. Reading it over with my Uncle at one of my weekly dinners there, and noting some observations of his and discussing some points with him, he asked me to work out my notes in detail, a work to which, for the next six weeks, I [538] devoted almost every morning, from an early hour till 12, besides going over my MS with Jery Bentham—on one occasion for six consecutive hours—and at Lincoln's Inn with Mr Tyrrell, who had been the medium of communication with the Commissioners, and who urged me to get my observations printed, he undertaking to pay the expence, which, however, my uncle did not allow. Mr Tyrrell, however, took great pains in discussing various points with me, and when the pamphlet was printed, in the course of March, he purchased 100 copies for distribution.[5] I gave away a few—received a few compliments—and there the matter ended. No public notice taken, except an abusive review in the *Athenaeum*[6] and, in the excitement of Lord John's Reform Bill,[7] the Law Commissioners and their plans for the registration of deeds and other amendments of the law were laid aside.

But now I was much taken up with domestic arrangements. In the early part of the year, my father was much engaged in organising experiments, for which he had obtained the authority of the Navy

Board, on the influence of the shape of the hull of navigable vessels on their progression and direction. I had to assist him in some papers he wrote on the subject,[8] and his friend Maudslay, the Engineer, was preparing some models—but Maudslay was taken ill and died, and my father's own appetite and strength failed him, so as to give us serious cause of alarm. Early in April he had ceased to go out and had shut up his desk, and during the whole of that month he was evidently [539] sinking. I could seldom leave home, and the last fortnight his end was imminent. It was, however, only on the night of the 30th April (not 31 March, as stated by some mistake in my mother's life of him)[9] that he breathed his last, from pure exhaustion, without suffering or positive disease. This, of course, prevented my taking part in the Anniversary meeting of the Horticultural Society on the 1st May, and the greater part of that month was taken up with the arrangements consequent upon his death and the great reduction in our income. We succeeded in securing my mother's pension of £300 a year, disposed of our expensive house in Lower Connaught Place, taking a small one in Gloucester Street, Portman Square, sold off the greater portion of my father's general library, etc. My father had sold off a portion of the estate at Restinclières, and the purchase money was fortunately received and invested just before his death—but yet our means had become very much reduced.

Simon de Klustine remained in London, spending a good deal of time with us till my father's death; his engagement with my sister had given pleasure to my father who, in his will, left her the estate in South Russia, near Cherson, of which he had one sixth—three-sixths being the property of Admiral Mordwinoff, who directed the management and occasionally remitted small sums on account of income; but of late the Russian Government had made great claims for arrears of dues, and even my father's title to the share was becoming rather problematical, but Count Michel Woronzoff (afterwards Prince Woronzoff), who was in London at the time [540] of my father's illness and death, and showed himself exceedingly kind and friendly towards us, undertook the management of the business, and on his return to Russia succeeded in securing and selling my father's title to it, and remitted to my sister between £3000 and £4000 as the price. The marriage with Klustine, however, never took place. He left London early in May to see his mother at Geneva and to settle the preliminary money matters, etc, met with an accident on his way, the wheel of his carriage having gone over his foot, was laid up some time at Geneva, during which time a misunderstanding, which I never knew the rights of, took place, and the engagement was broken off.

Towards the end of May—without thinking much as yet of our future prospects—I resumed my botanical and horticultural occupations, often at Wallich's distributions in Frith Street, and early in June went with Wallich down to Highclere on a few days' visit to Lord Carnarvon's, where met a very agreable party; and the rest of June was much taken up with the Horticultural fête of the 22d,[10] which was so far successful that it was numerously attended, the weather all that could be wished, and the visitors pleased—but after all it brought in no great clear profit, entailed a great deal of trouble, and was scarcely *horticultural* enough to justify the high price at which the tickets were necessarily sold, so that it soon became evident that some other plan must be devised. The further consideration of future plans was, however, deferred till after the summer recess.

[541]The death of my father entailing the necessity of rather complicated arrangements with regard to the French property, now managed by my eldest sister and her husband M. de Chesnel, it was determined that I should go over to Montpellier for the purpose. I settled also to take Geneva on my way back, partly to make further acquaintance with the elder De Candolles and other scientific men there, partly at my younger sister's request to ascertain from the Klustines' friends the circumstances which brought about the rupture of her engagement. In connection with this subject, I called on Mrs Marcet, whom I had met at a dinner at the Longmans' the winter before the last. In the course of the conversation, she enquired whether I knew of any one going to Geneva who would join her in the journey, as it was the first time she was to make it with only her man and maid, without any one of her family— and upon my telling her that I was myself going to Montpellier, she immediately proposed that we should go as far as Paris together. The result was one of the most agreable journeys I ever made. Mrs Marcet, with all her eminence in science,[11] was no blue-stocking. She was remarkably well informed on a great variety of subjects, intelligent, quick and ready, without anything of pedantry; her conversation was delightful, whether scientific or on worldly questions, and none of that political excitement and exaggeration which, at this time, ladies who mixed much in the world indulged in. Indeed, after having been thus for six days in close intimacy with her, we parted without having ascertained to which side of the burning questions of the day our views tended respectively.

[542]We left London on the 20th July, embarking at the Tower Stairs in the morning on board the *Lord Melville* steamer, which landed us in the evening at Calais—we slept there, were detained till near midday the next day by Custom House formalities, carriage hire, etc, then posted on to Paris, stopping to sleep at Montreuil and at Beauvais, and arrived at the Hotel Mirabeau, Rue de la Paix, in the afternoon of the 23d. Here I only staid a couple of days (one a Sunday), necessary to secure my place in the malle-poste. Paris looked very dull, notwithstanding the preparation for the anniversary of the three "glorious days."[12] Two of our friends, the Abbé Longuemarre and M. Pons, on whom I called, gave a sad picture of the state of society, broken up by the revolution of the previous year. M. Pons, a true representative of the old school, received me[s] in the middle of the day in his dressing gown and slippers, taking his large bowl of café au lait in his bedroom window—full of compliments but hot with politics, on which he declaimed with the greatest energy. The Saturday of our arrival turned out a wet, disagreable afternoon—the streets nearly empty, not half a dozen gentlemen's carriages to be met. "But if there were few promeneurs, there were, en revanche, hundreds of men, women and children crying, 'V'la Messieurs, V'la le discours du Roi tel qu'il a été prononcé aujourd'hui à la Chambre des Deputés. V'la le superbe discours du Roi en faveur du peuple, le v'la pour deux sols,' enough to stun one. This famous discours, though it seems in general to have given here more satisfaction than dissatisfaction, will, I should think, be well [543] ridiculed abroad, for the very reason the French must like it. The King says, 'I have done this, I have done that,' as if he alone were governing the whole of Europe. The *Quotidienne* says, 'On fait dire au Roi à propos de la Pologne, "J'ai voulu."—C'est que vous avez voulu, et vous n'avez pas pu, n'est-ce pas?[13] Eh bien, il ne fallait pas le dire.' Looking over the papers I was much struck with the boldness with which the Carlists and Henricinquists speak their minds. The *Gazette du Midi* contains a long ode to Henri V, in which his return is anticipated as a matter of course."[14]

On the Sunday evening I went with Mrs Marcet to the Theatre de Madame, now rechristened Gymnase Dramatique, to see the admirable acting of Leontine Fay and Paul, and on Monday 25th, leaving Mrs Marcet for a few days longer at Paris, I took the malle-poste for Lyons—two nights and the intervening day with the following morning—the carriage comfortable, and "my only companion (there were only two inside places) a Parisian lady, still young and good-looking, going to see her son at St Etienne, well informed, not prudish, though I have no doubt strictly *virtuous*, a bonne voyageuse, not douillette, and therefore a most agreable travelling companion and, though she got rather unwell in the afternoon, I had on the whole very little trouble and much agré-ment from her, the more so as our Courrier was the most silent and inat-tentive one I ever met with."

Arrived at Lyons in the afternoon of the 27th, the first of the three anniversary fêtes being the *mourning* one—saw but few signs, except at Mâcon, where the national guard [544] with crape on their arms, were assembling for mass. Here there had been a bit of a riot early in the morning, owing to some Italian refugees[15] having quarrelled with some young men about a ball and killed one, but all was quiet when we passed through; at Lyons it was like a dull Sunday, with several shops shut—perhaps a few more tricolor flags than usual, but nothing more.

On arriving at Lyons, I immediately took my place in the malle-poste for Avignon, but I had no sooner left the Office than I found that the new steamboat would take me down in much less time, so returning to the post Office, I found them obliging enough to return my money and, sleeping at Lyons, started at 5 in the morning. Though eight years previ-ously I had much enjoyed the row down in an open boat (24 hours to Pont St Esprit), I now found this 12 hours steam to Avignon, about 200 miles, most delightful. "The beautifully diversified banks, vine-clad coteaux, rich meadows, and arable land interspersed with willows, mul-berries, Olives, Ashes, Alders, etc, thickly wooded mountains, precipi-tous rocks, and turretted promontories, towns and villages, chateaux and farms, following each other in such rapid succession, the mighty Alps on the one side, the Cevennes on the other, giving a general charac-ter of grandeur to the scene, the noble river itself broad, deep and rapid, without those dreary sandbanks which disfigure so many large streams, and the number and extreme elegance of the new suspension bridges gave me on the whole more pleasure perhaps [545] than the Rheingau last year. The clouds and rain had ceased, or rather I had left them far behind. The richness of the southern sky was not, it is true, to be enjoyed without the necessary drawback, the scorching rays of the sun, but on the other hand there was a good deal of wind. The steamboat is a good one, though not refined in the accomodation—the company of course much mixed; amongst them were a number of young Carlists, ex-offic-ers of the Guards now en demi-solde, or obliged to accept service under the new regime, and sent to a distance from Paris to join their regiments, or on other pretexts in order to get them out of the way during the three days. One gentleman wore a fleur-de-lys between two red ribbands, several were talking carlism, whilst others were singing "The Marseillaise"—no English except a Master-workman looking man who was talking engineering with the engineer of the boat.

"At Avignon, where I dined and remained till between 12 and 1 at night, all was in a bustle, this being the second or national fête. Tricolor flags, Mats de Cocagne, illuminations and fireworks, great crowds in the streets, chiefly artisans and peasants, and the garrison and national guards in uniform, both very numerous and enough to keep down any tumult—a great deal of singing revolutionary and republican airs—much more 'Vive la liberté!' than 'Vive le Roi!' and to the very great amusement of the young men, plenty of pétards being thrown about among the crowd, often wounding several, but upon the whole no serious accident or disorders.

"§By ½ past 12 when I left Avignon, all had subsided into the dead stillness of night, except here and there the drums of a military patrol— passed Nîmes at 5 in the morning. [546] There it appears things are not expected to go off so quietly, and the fêtes are put off till next Sunday, and arrived at Montpellier, at the Hotel du Midi, at ½ past 10, under a most scorching sun. . . . Dining with Gordon, went in the evening with him to the Esplanade to witness the fêtes of this, the third or military day.

"The state of Montpellier is very different from what it was on my last visit and, though there is no rioting, it is worse than I expected—a great many Carlists, still more Republicans, and few Juste-milicux[16] except the Autorités, and they without any influence or power. Zoé Granier, who had been Mayor, and Bérard, Farel, Vialars, etc, who were Adjoints and Conseillers municipaux, finding they had no controul over the ultra-liberals, gave in their resignation a few days ago, and have been succeeded by men without name, talent or influence. The Préfet, a M. Fumeron des Ardennes, who followed Louis XVIII to Ghent, and from ultra-royalism has taken to liberalism, is laughed at and hooted by all, as well as the Secrétaire Général, a man of low extraction, without any moyens. The General, M. de Solignac, is as bad in public affairs as he always was in private, and is ridiculed by all he has to command. He issued an order the other day that all the Officiers should go to mass— some refused—he put them aux arrêts—and threatened to order the regiment (the Génie) away in three days. They wrote a sort of protest, and he raised the arrêts. All police is at an end, and the authorities have no means of controling the people, who are quiet only because the Carlists keep aloof [547] and there is nothing at present to excite them to disorder. At the review this evening, the cry of 'Vive le Roi!' was attempted, but the soldiers answered 'Vive la Liberté!' and the whole evening every thing showed a complete disorganisation of social order and military discipline—the soldiers on guard were all drunk and were talking, singing, etc, in the ranks, or rather out of them, for they could not keep in. The Esplanade was illuminated and full of promeneurs to see the fireworks (which by the bye were completely manqués), and as all seemed of one mind, singing republican songs and crying 'Vive la Liberté!' there was no disorder. There were a good many tricolor flags and illuminations in the town, but it was evidently a rejoicing more of the populace than of any other class of society.

"Of our friends, but few are in town. Charles X's autorités all resigned immediately on the revolution of July and have dispersed in their respective country places.... Roger de Ginestous has gone headlong into the new system, whilst his old mother, who had gone mad for joy at the Bourbon restoration, has been driven yet more frantic at the sight of the hateful tricolor, and the poor old Count sees his last days embittered by the unfeeling conduct of his son."[17]

Lawyers were not to be hurried on at Montpellier any more than in other places, and it was three weeks before we could sign the acte de partage, by which, under certain conditions, the Restinclières estate was assigned to my sister. The time was spent partly with her, partly with my friends in town—often with Delile at the Botanical Garden, or with Farel visiting La Verune, La Valette, and other places of the neighbourhood; also with him made a two days excursion [548] to Le Vigan to see Mr Hammond,[18] a friend of my father's, now managing the mines of Cavaillac, which showed well the difficulties then existing (and indeed which may still exist) in taking advantages of rich natural resources in out of the way parts of France. I wrote at Le Vigan:

"The mines of Cavaillac, where I am now, are about a mile from Le Vigan, in a little plain above the town; they belong to a company consisting of Paulin Farel, Levat, Villebacq, Rech, Deshours, Verey, Felix Bouché and two others, who have obtained from Government the concession of all the mines (coal as well as iron) of the neighbourhood of Le Vigan,[19] and have set up steam engines (then quite new to the country) to pump out the water, which has at present inundated the collieries, the only mines as yet worked. The great abundance of iron ore of every kind seems to promise a great profit, whenever worked with the coal on the spot, but the difficulty of procuring machinery, there not being at this moment in France a single establishment where a steam engine can be ordered, the number of local prejudices to contend with, the inconveniences of detail in managing an establishment at Le Vigan by a board of directors at Montpellier (communications between the two towns then required two days), and that in a country where the people are wholly unused to speculations of the kind, will probably occasion the failure of this enterprise. . . . The works are now at a stand, owing to a shaft having broken, which could not be recast anywhere nearer than Vienne, on the Rhone. . . . Mr Hammond had just been there to order a new one, and there learnt that all the steamboats on the Rhone have English engines. Immense capital had been laid out in building near twenty steamboats with French engines [549] for the navigation of the river, but not one could be made to answer, till at last they sent for twelve English engines, with an Engineer for each, mounted them on as many boats, and are now succeeding in every respect and making a good deal of money."

I finally took leave of my sister on the 19th, had a very fatiguing night journey to Avignon, where I remained three days, entirely engrossed from morning till night in sorting Labiatae and taking specimens from Requien's herbarium; then a 24 hours' journey to Lyons in the three-inside malle-poste, with a Lyons' pâte-de-Gênes[20] manufacturer and a fat Polish General on his way from Malta to Paris—as thick as two ordinary men—the weather very hot and too much wind to have both glasses down made the night rather fatiguing. Remained two days at Lyons, going to the play as usual in the evenings, and spent one morning and dined with the Lajards at their country house about a mile from the town, Madame Lajard (my old flame Emma Dax) looking thin and unwell, but as kind and friendly as ever—with two spoiled and petulant children. The other morning, "to the Botanic Garden, where found Seringe, a little, oldish man, who has been hard at work making something of the Garden, small as it is, but its position and commanding view are delightful . . . ; looked through Seringe's Labiatae and Medicagos, and took a few specimens." On the Friday evening before leaving Lyons, "walked again up to the botanic garden where, on the esplanade at the top, a band of military music plays twice a week. The music was indifferent, but there were a good [550] many people—some ladies—many bonnes d'enfans and some females of a less reputable description, and a good many men; the situation, the manner in which the gardens are laid out, and the great number of at least well-dressed females made it a very fine sight.

"Embarked in the Geneva diligence at nine in the evening of the 28th August, fortunately in the coupé, for the weather was most sultry, and the night's journey was only comparatively pleasant, with three in the small coupé—comparatively, that is to say, in respect of those in the main body of the vehicle, who were packed as close as herrings in a barrel, one of the six being very stout, and another moderately so. The moon was at the full and splendidly brilliant, the diligence easy and now slow for a diligence, but the road a tedious succession of up and down. After, however, a good café-au-lait breakfast at 7 in the morning in the little village of Cerdon, came into a more interesting country, first crossed a high and well wooded mountain, then down to the lake town and beautifull little valley of Nantua—a succession of varied mountain, though not alpine, scenery. An hour and a half at Bellegard spent in dining and customhouse ceremonies gave me the opportunity of going down to the perte du Rhone, but found it much inferior in interest to what I expected, as there is at present so much water that it does not all lose itself—then walked up a tremendous hill under a scorching sun— and up and down, and round and round rock and hill till at last, after going through the fort de l'Ecluse, well suited to stop the way, *debouched* into the broad valley of the Rhone, and after two tiresome stages of roads cut straight over hill and dale, pitching in a deep hole or bolting over an [551] abrupt coteau rather than turn a few hundred yards to avoid the one or the other, entered the town of Geneva at eight in the evening—rather disappointed, I confess, at its first appearance, after the magnificent descriptions I had heard and read—but I shall probably think better of it tomorrow. This being the reign of liberty, the passports of all the passengers were examined no less than four times between Lyons and Geneva."

I spent a week at Geneva, a great deal with the De Candolles. I had met Auguste Pyrame at Seringe's at Lyons on passing through on one of my former journeys, but having seen so much of his son in England, I now became at once intimate with them all. There was something so genial and cordial in the elder De Candolle's manner, and his conversation was so agreable and lively, with so much esprit, that it was impossible not to be taken with him, independently of his being the first continental botanist of the day, with general scientific attainments, a most honorable character and warm heart. He was at this time of year in a little country house on the northern shore of the lake, about a mile and a half from the town on the Lausanne road. The morning after my arrival (Sunday, 28th August), I drove out to him; "found him laid up with the gout. He, however, as well as Madame de Candolle and Alphonse, received me in the most friendly manner. After a short visit, having promised to return to dinner, I drove on to Mrs Marcet's at Malany, a beautiful place with a park à l'Anglaise, about three miles higher up the lake on the same road. The park was planted by Dr Marcet, and is exceedingly [552] well kept up. . . . Calling also at M. Levat's, returned to M. De Candolle's by ½ past 4 to dinner. After dinner, walked out with Alphonse to Mr Saladin's, a propriétaire here who has built a very elegant house on a projecting hill very near the De Candolles and commanding one of the finest views of the neighbourhood over the lake backed by the Alps. He has a great passion for gardening, and especially for pineapples, which he has succeeded in bringing nearly to equal common pineapples in England. (One of De Candolle's papers is on the plants of this garden.)[21] After having admired as much as necessary à droite et à gauche, à tort et à travers, returned to De Candolle's to tea, where an intimate friend, Made Pictet, spent the evening, and two or three others called in."

Monday, 29th. After being introduced by Alphonse to the Reading Society, a flourishing institution or kind of club of three or four hundred members, who take in the principal French and German papers and periodicals, and have already a permanent library of some 30,000 volumes, went over to De Candolle's herbarium at his house in the Cour St Pierre, where found the Keeper, Mr Wydler, and began to work at the Labiatae—then a long and painful visit to the Klustines, on the unfortunate affair with my sister. To dinner at Mrs Marcet's at Malany, and with her to a small tea party at De Candolle's—about a dozen persons, amongst whom were Webb and Berthelot, the Canary island travellers, now preparing their Flora.[22] I had met Mr Webb previously at Lambert's in London. M. Berthelot, who had been ten years in the Canary islands, made himself very agreable, relating many curious adventures he had had in [553] visiting the caves in which the mummies of the Guanches are found.[23]

Tuesday, 30th. "With Alphonse to the Botanic Garden. It was established by M. de Candolle on his arrival here, on the site of an old promenade which had been entirely abandoned, since it had been the scene of some revolutionary horrors. It is large and very well laid out and, for the garden of a small town, contains a good many species. Attached to it is a building containing the commencement of a library, herbarium and other botanical collections, the building due to the munificence of some one who has kept his incognito. Spent the day at Labiatae in De Candolle's herbarium—out to dinner at De Candolle's, where met M. Duby, the author of the *Botanicon Gallicum*—and in the evening to a party at Made Pictet's, about a dozen people, rather *blueish*."

Wednesday, 31st. The whole morning in the herbarium and, after the table d'hôte dinner, "to a party at the Sismondis', at his country house about 1½ miles from the town, on the Savoy side (at Chêne). Between 30 and 40 people, amongst others Made Munier, a clever portrait painter, Miss Patty Smith (William Smith's eldest daughter) and several of the Genevese litterati. M. de Sismondi himself had not the appearance of a savant—he looks too mild and too active—but made himself very agreable. He was very busy about the Polish loan, the Polish gentleman who had come to negotiate it being there."

Thursday, 1st Sept. Early "to the herbarium, where Mr Wydler had promised to meet me, but *he could not find the key*; so had to return at the official hour, 11 to 4. At the table d'hote [554] dinner. Countess Guiccioli, Lord Byron's chère amie,[24] now at Geneva, usually dines there. She does not strike one as handsome, as the lower part of her face is broad, and her mouth rather large, but her eyes are fine, her hair of an auburn colour is also fine, and with a great deal of conceit she has something very attractive in her appearance. She joined in the conversation, which is generally only such as might be expected at a table d'hôte."

Friday, 2d Sept. "After my morning's work in the herbarium, dined at Mrs Marcet's to meet M. Prevost, chemist and physician, and to the De Candolles' to tea." Saturday, 3d. "At the herbarium, finished the preliminary arrangement of the Labiatae, and took notes of Medicago's, etc. Dined at De Candolle's, making the acquaintance of M. de la Rive, the physicist, a very genial man and a great friend of the De Candolles."

Sunday, 4th Sept. Took leave of my kind friends, who had made my visit to Geneva so agreable and profitable, and in this cold, wet wintery weather—a perfect contrast to the summery heat of the previous week, had a four-and-twenty hours' diligence to Lyons. Detained there, waiting for a place in the mail, till the Tuesday evening, spending my time chiefly with the Lajards, and the evenings at the theatre, and then three nights and intervening days in the two-inside malle-poste to Paris. The first night my companion was a M. de Fontenille, whom I had known as a Col of Chasseurs at Montauban but, being a Royalist, is now an ex, and retired to his estate near Moulins; he was making a tour in Italy, but driven home by choleraphobia and quarantines. After Moulins I was alone, which was all very comfortable at first, but as the day went on, "I began to find that perfect solitude [555] is not the most delightful, although I am generally so unsocial with fellow travellers. The first night was admirable, and in the morning, with the book I had, I got on very well, but in the afternoon my eyes were too tired to read, and I began to feel ennuyé and long for night, and when night came, though I slept a good deal, yet my bones began to feel sore, and I was heartily glad to escape from my case at five in the morning of Friday the 9th Sept." Rather distressing letters from home and consequent business took the greater part of the day, but in the evening I contrived to go to the Gymnase Dramatique (late Theatre de Madame) to see Jenny Colon's acting. "She is very pretty, and much improved since I saw her three years ago, but has not the *finesse* of Léontine Fay, nor quite the sentiment of Jenny Vertpré, but certainly comes next to these two."

I remained about three weeks at Paris, the mornings very frequently in Delessert's or in the Jardin des Plantes' herbaria, the evenings often at the theatre, and a good deal with Dr Henderson, who is at present on a visit to Paris—the town often disturbed with *émeutes* on the occasion of the Polish insurrection—and at the theatres, political allusions much taken up by the pit, chiefly critiques of the ministry and the *juste-milieu* system, which is very unpopular.

Sunday, 11 Sept. "After breakfast, to the Carrousel, where the King, accompanied by Marshalls Lobau and Soult and a small Etat-Major, reviewed a bataillon of each legion of the Garde Nationale, a regiment of infantry and one of cavalry, but the attendance of the Garde Nationale was very thin, and the King very coldly received. [556] The Queen and her family were at the balcony. The Duc de Nemours was with the King, a young blondin, certainly not appearing to have much *weight* to govern a set of turbulent burghers.[25] The review was very long. After the King had gone through the ranks, he had to wait an hour before the Garde Nationale were ready to *defile* before him. What a difference from the review I saw last year at Berlin!"

Monday, 12th. Availing myself of a ticket M. Benj. Delessert had given me yesterday, "went to the Chambre des Députés. After sitting for an hour after it was opened before the séance began, only heard the reading of uninteresting reports, no debate—the reading the procès-verbal a real farce worthy of Lincoln's Inn, only a few words of each page read in an inaudible voice. Left the Chambre at 3 to go to the Institut, where Humboldt presented his new work on some observations made in his Siberian journey; he made also some interesting remarks[§] on some extraordinary meteorological phenomena observed this year in the East of Europe[26]—saw Desfontaines, Mirbel, Auguste St Hilaire, etc."

Tuesday, 13th. "After spending the morning at Labiatae in Delessert's Herbarium, went with Guillemin to Benj. Delessert's at Passy to dinner—a beautiful place with a fine garden extending all the way down the hill, some fine green-and-hot-house plants, particularly a Carica Papaya in full flower, a very good collection of Dahlias, and some fine trees, amongst others of Celtis occidentalis, a beautiful Swiss cottage, etc. At dinner a party of about twenty, chiefly Deputies. I was most agreably seated between Humboldt and my friend Felix Bodin. Made Francois and Made Gabriel Delessert both very nice and agreable."

[557]Wednesday, 14th. "Spent an hour with Humboldt at his lodgings in the Rue du Colombier most agreably; he is full of conversation, and altogether one of the most delightful scientific men I ever knew—to Lointier's, with Dr Henderson and Felix Bodin whom I had asked to dine with me there, but did not find the dinner equal to the reputation of the place—then with Dr H. to the Opera—one act of *Guillaume Tell*, and a splendid ballet called *Manon Lescaut*, the dresses beautiful, and altogether producing a fine effect. The Dey of Algiers, who is almost always there,[27] seemed to enjoy it—a little man, just like his portraits, fat and squat, in green spectacles, bright eyes and a jovial face, without the appearance of any remarkable cleverness—his attendants grim, sour, lanthorn-jawed men with black beards and sournois look."

Thursday, 15th. Began my work at Labiatae, etc, at the Jardin des Plantes, "found out Adolphe Brongniart, and by his means got into the herbarium in the morning (it is only regularly open and attended by the aides-naturalistes for a couple of hours in the afternoon), and spent the day tête-à-tête with Lamark's daughter, who, having been left penniless at her father's death, has been placed there as a gluer of plants, almost out of charity."

Friday, 16th. "The day at Delessert's herbarium in the Rue Montmartre. The news received this morning of the taking of Warsaw a subject of great lamentation here,[28] and this evening, it is said, the mob has collected before the Ministère des Affaires Étrangères and are breaking Sebastiani's windows, but in this part of the town (Hotel des Étrangers, Rue Vivienne) all is quiet."

[558]Saturday, 17th. "Returning in the afternoon from the Jardin des Plantes to M. Delessert's, surprised to observe great crowds in the streets and about the Palais Royal—the gardens closed, the shops shut, and cavalry galloping about the streets. Learn that large groups collected in the Palais Royal, shouting 'Vive la Pologne!' and 'A bas les Ministres!' and had been driven out by the troops—the rappel beating

everywhere, and disquiet reigning in the town, although the number of rioters be so very small. Dined with Dr Henderson at the Café Hardy, and with him to the Gymnase. About eight o'clock, the loud shouting without announced the passing by of the 'Emeute.' But as the noise died away again directly, the representation went on, and none of the audience went out to see what was going on till the act was over—then a hard shower of rain had dispersed the crowd. When the play was over (it having left off before the last piece, several actors not having come on account of the tumult) going home along the boulevards they presented a melancholy scene—a dark, dismal, rainy night—all the lamps broken and the coffeehouses shut. Further on, some scaffolding boards and young trees scattered about showed the débris of a barricade that had been attempted. The mob had now dispersed, but there had been much scuffling. No one, however, appears to have been killed."

Sunday, 18th. "Today, at about one o'clock, attempts were again made to create a row by the crowds in the Palais Royal, upon which the yard and garden were again cleared and shut up. The mob, consisting of some twelve to fifteen hundred of the rabble, with a few well-dressed young men mixed with them, [559] proceeded up the Rue Vivienne to the Boulevard, shouting as usual, but there they soon dispersed and, though the whole day the streets were much crowded, the large bodies of troops which were patrolling in every direction kept them down, and the evening passed off quite quietly. In the evening, to Benjamin Delessert's at Passy—about a dozen people there, amongst others Villemain, the celebrated Professor. He read some poetry from a book that had just been presented to M. Delessert, but I did not so much like his manner as I had expected—there is something decided and brusque, and at the same time distrait about him that is at best rather odd—he is too violent, also, in the expression of his opinions—perhaps from being too much used to seeing himself taken as an authority."

Monday, 19th Sept. Going out to St Cloud on a commission for my sister, "everything in the morning was as usual, except perhaps more groups in the Palais Royal. Returning in the afternoon to the meeting of the Institut, saw large crowds collected at the Chambre des Députés, the Palais Royal Gardens again cleared, and the shops in the neighbourhood mostly shut. With Dr Henderson, round by the Place Vendome to the Café Hardy to dinner. Great crowds about, but as yet no rioting. After dinner on the Boulevards, a fine night and numbers of promeneurs, so that were it not for the troops that are every where about, we might fancy that Paris was restored to its usual calm—the Place de la

Bourse, it is true, covered with ill-looking groups, and it is said that a charge upon the populace has just taken place in the Palais Royal. Now, however, at nine o'clock, the crowd is gradually diminishing, and it seems that all will be quiet, but the alarm that all [560] these foolish riots create among the tradesmen is productive of the greatest commercial mischief. Aussi, all the respectable citizens reprobate them most vehemently, but the deputies and others of the opposition, instead of rallying round the ministry and helping them to repress the tumults, only make it the more difficult to do so, by attacking them for not doing it effectually."—The riots gradually disappeared, and even became the subject of ridicule, and not long after "Mademoiselle l'Émeute" appeared as one of the characters in a farce at the Théâtre du Palais Royal.

Tuesday, 20th Sept. "At seven in the morning, with Dr Henderson, Adolphe Brongniart and Guillemin to see M. Soulange-Bodin's Institut Horticole at Fromont, six leagues from Paris on the Fontainbleau road, in a very pretty situation just above the village of Ris, on a declivity extending to the banks of the Seine—the coteaux on the other side of the river covered with country houses and parks, backed by the Forêt de Senart—below, almost opposite Ris, a new suspension bridge over the river built by M. Aguado at his own expense. *Le public réconnaissant* wanted to hang him for *féodalisme*, and when the authorities wanted to call§ the bridge Pont Aguado, they announced their intention (at the revolution of last year) of hanging to the church steeple the maire, the curé and the tricolor flag. The mayor was, however, beforehand with them, and put up the flag alone, and afterwards they thought it scarcely worth while ascending again for the purpose of putting up the Mayor and the Curé. Now [561] this spirit has a good deal subsided. M. Soulange remains Mayor, and the bridge is to be called Pont Aguado. M. Soulange received us very well; he is a most active man, talking incessantly, and devoted to his pursuits. He has made a beautiful place of his park. His nursery of green-and-hothouse plants is extensive and kept with great order. A practice which he has carried to a very great extent, and with great success, is the *greffe herbacée*, grafting on the shoots of the year, which is particularly useful in enabling him to graft very young plants—cuttings and seedlings of the year—and thus giving means of a very extensive multiplication of choice varieties in a very short time, small space and little expense. Camellias in particular, also Magnolias, Azaleas, etc, have been thus multiplied by him to a very great extent. He has also been very successful in various other grafts, such as Cunninghamia upon Pinus balsamea, Pinus mugho upon P. sylvestris, Cupressus sinensis upon Taxodium distichum, Tomatoes upon Potatoes, etc; he also grafts Paeonia Moutan upon the roots of P. arborea and P. albiflora, to a great extent. Amongst trees, he has some fine Pinus's of various kinds, Juglans nigra, a great variety of Magnolias, etc. At breakfast (a substantial one at 12) were his whole family, his mother-in-law, wife, daughter and two sons, all good housewify kind of people."

Wednesday, 21st. Studying Labiatae at the Jardin. Thursday, 22d. Having a ticket for the Chambre des Deputés, went there "but a very little after 12, but found it already nearly full; [562] got a very bad place in the second row behind the bureaux, but soon after the séance opened, someone having gone away, got to the front row, where I saw almost as well as anywhere. The sitting began at 2 and was not over till 8, during which I had the advantage of hearing most of the best orators or remarkable men: Casimir Périer, Barthe and Soult, amongst the ministers, Dupin, Guizot, Felix Bodin, etc, on their side, Odillon Barrot, Lafitte, Lafayette, Mauguin, Tracy, Lamarque, etc, on the opposition. A very full meeting, plenty of tapage, violent speeches about nothing at all, interruptions, explosions, approbative and improbative, half a hundred members speaking and a whole hundred gesticulating at once, and the whole closed by an *appel nominal* and a *vote au scrutin*.[29] The Dey of Algiers, all the while directly opposite, appearing to take the greatest interest in a debate of which he did not understand a single word. The question before the house, or rather the no-question, being the attack upon ministers, which had been the subject of dispute, not debate, for the three previous days, and the immediate subject of the day being the question how they should put an end to the discussion. Most of the speeches were improvisés. By 3 or 4 o'clock, they settled by assis et levé that they closed the discussion, and the four remaining hours were spent in disputing *how* they should close it, whether by an ordre du jour simple, or by an ordre du jour motivé, in approbation of the ministers' conduct. When the majority of 221 for ministers was announced, the [563] coincidence of this number with that of the opposition to Polignac in the beginning of last year produced a good deal of sensation.[30]

"Of the several orators I heard, most of them certainly spoke well, without any of the hesitation or stammering observed so frequently amongst our speakers, but on the other hand there is a uniformity, a kind of singsong accentuation, which after a while gets tiresome, and a great deal of gesticulation. Casimir Perrier, Odillon Barrot, Guizot, Mauguin, Laurence, Barthe, Dupin, De Tracey, etc, all spoke well, Soult and Lafayette both of them feebly, particularly Soult, who is a better warrior than orator. Lafayette seems enfeebled by age. Barthe and Dupin spoke very lawyer-like, Felix Bodin wandered into general principles, but spoke distinctly. In general, when the French do improvise, they do it well, but their written speeches are a sad *verbiage* and *galimathias.*"

Remained another week at Paris, every morning in some of the herbaria—twice at Auguste St Hilaire's on the Quai de Béthune, an out-of-the-way quarter of Paris at the other end of the Ile St Louis; went through his rich collection of Brasilian Labiatae, of which he gave me two or three. He afterwards sent me over to England his whole set of Labiatae, with numerous specimens, which I described and returned faithfully, on the understanding that I was to have a complete set—which, however, I never received, either from him or from the herbarium of the Jardin, to which his collections were transferred after his death. Another pleasant morning was with old Desfontaines in his herbarium. In the evenings usually at one of [564] the theatres—one evening at the Passy subscription at Ranelagh, at the entrance of the Bois de Boulogne,[31] a very pleasing sight. Dined usually at one of the principal restaurants, with Dr Henderson or Sutton Sharpe—especially at the Café Hardy, then reckoned the best, also at its rival, the Café Riche, certainly rather inferior, so as to justify the saying, "Il faut être hardi pour diner chez Riche—il faut etre riche pour diner chez Hardy."

Left Paris by the Calais Diligence on the evening of the 28th, the two rival diligences (Lafitte's Co. and Rue Notre Dame des Victoires) keeping together the whole 24 hours, with 41 passengers between them, in a cloud of hot dust—from Calais by steam, in beautiful weather to London, reaching home on the evening of the 30th—48 hours from Paris, including a night's rest at Calais. I was now to be settled with my mother and younger sister in Gloucester Street, and had made up my mind to take seriously and steadily to the law, but there were still a few weeks of vacation. These were taken up a good deal by the engaging and removing to our new house, and by other family business consequent on my father's death—also Horticultural Society arrangements. On the 1st Nov., attended the Linnean Council and evening meeting, as well as the Horticultural. Dr (Sir William) Hooker was in town for a few days, and I was much with him, as well as with Lindley. A chest of Ceylon plants sent over by Macrae, before his death, to the Horticultural Society enabled us to select from duplicates a good set for Hooker and another for myself; but the great addition made to our herbaria [565] was that of Cuming's collection from Chile and Peru, from whence he had just returned. The number of duplicates enabled him to dispose of a dozen good sets, at £2.10.0 the hundred. Of these, Hooker undertook to dispose of ten sets, and Lambert and Brown each one, and it was settled that Hooker, Lambert and Brown should meet every morning at Cuming's, in Charlotte Street, from 7 to 10 o'clock, to make the selection. Hooker was, however, obliged to return to Glasgow, and I took his place, sometimes breakfasting at Lambert's at 6 in the morning before going to Cuming's, sometimes breakfasting after 10. It was settled that Hooker was to have the first selection of his own set, then Brown was to select his, then Lambert, and after that, the nine Hooker was to dispose of, and it was amusing to watch the different manner in which the several selections were made as each species turned up. The best specimen for Hooker was easily picked out, then came Brown in his careful, quiet manner, scrutinising the whole series before he had fixed upon the most instructive specimen, whilst Lambert, who at once cast his eye upon the most showy specimen with large leaves or numerous well dried flowers, watched with the most keen and anxious countenance their being handled by Brown, for fear his *fine specimen* should be taken from him. This selection took us some 17 or 18 mornings on and off, and I had for myself the first of Hooker's nine extra sets.

[566]On Friday, 18th Novr, I was called to the bar at Lincoln's Inn. The first and most important part of the ceremony was paying the bill for my call[32]—about £100—and signing a bond for £200 for the future payment of my annual dues, which was deposited with my certificate of bonos mores; then dined in Hall, and after dinner called up to the Benchers', instead of the barristers', table; went through the ridiculous farce of exercise reading, only differing from the previous exercises in having a foolscap sheet instead of a small quarto sheet of nonsense, supposed to be a case or answer, of which I had to read two or three words only; took two or three long oaths, unintelligibly read from a long slip of parchment held by us (myself and five others called at the same time) by the clerk who was afflicted with St. Vitas's dance—one oath understood to be that of allegiance, another, as far as I could make out, had something about the damnable doctrines of Popery. The Benchers then *published* us to the Bar, in a tone of voice which certainly no one could hear, and we followed them into the Council room, where we sat down to a handsome desert (which *we* pay for); a book was brought for us to sign our names—the Benchers drank our healths and left the room.—I went away almost immediately, but one or two others remained, with some friends they had invited to drink with them. The next morning I had another long string of oaths to take, in the Bail Courts in Westminster

hall—again renouncing the Pope, the Pretender and the Devil—ordered my wig, accepted a gown which my friend W. Carr gave me, and was thus regularly transformed into a Counsel learned in the law.

[567]I now settled regularly to my legal—still studies, not business—spending the mornings at Koe's, as his pupil, drawing bills and answers, etc, now and then sitting in court in my wig and gown, and for chambers took one room and half-time of a clerk at my friend George Lake Russell's chambers, but got no brief yet this year. I continued dining once or twice a week at my Uncle's, and had some trouble yet with the giving up the house in Lower Connaught Place and settling in Gloucester Street—for botany, obliged to limit myself to the early morning hours at Cuming's plants, etc, or to a little work at night or on Sundays—and even thought it necessary to give notice of resigning the secretaryship of the Horticultural Society next May. In evening society I partook but little, and that chiefly with my sister at the Ludolfs', where I first met Sir Harford Brydges and his son.[33]

11

Death of His Uncle;
Congress at Vienna, 1832

[568] The year 1832 brought about another change in my prospects and pursuits, though it did not finally settle them. By the death of my Uncle, notwithstanding the large deductions from his property occasioned by some of the dispositions of his will, my sisters and myself came into a considerable addition to our incomes,[1] and rendered us less dependent on my earnings; and other circumstances, especially my visit to the meeting at Vienna, tended to turn the balance in favour of botany versus law. In the first half of the year, however, I stuck pretty steadily to legal pursuits, in which my interest encreased, though it was some months before I got a brief. I spent most mornings, and some evenings, either at Lincoln's Inn, drawing, etc, in Koe's chambers, or reading in my own or at Lincoln's Inn or Westminster, sitting in Court in my wig and gown, to show that I was ready for briefs. This was tedious work, but I spent hours over Koe's bills, answers, interrogatories, cases, etc, with the more

satisfaction, as I found that my most complicated and long draughts were often finally settled with scarcely a single alteration. It was not till June that I got my first brief, as junior counsel with Koe, in a bankruptcy case on a question of partnership. I had had several days to wait in court for it to come on, at a time when I had to be much at Queen Square Place during my Uncle's last moments, and it finally came on, occupying the whole day next after his death. "Mr Montague was against us, occupying a long while in a rambling discussion that had nothing to do with the question. After Koe had spoken, I got up and cited some [569] cases and made a few observations, but I was so dreadfully nervous that I was obliged to cut my argument short,"[2] and Mr Montague in his reply, after discussing Koe's arguments, added that, as to the junior counsel, if he had not happened to know that it was the first time he had addressed the Court, he should have said that a more *preposterous* speech it had not been his fortune to hear during a long course of practice—which was by no means encouraging, and made me more than ever regret that my difficulty in speaking in public had not been met by a little school discipline or other such practical means.

With all this law, however, I never broke off from botany. In the early morning, and in the evenings when not socially engaged, and often returning home late at night, I worked in my herbarium—prepared papers on Stemodia, etc, for Lindley, and was especially engaged in the *Labiatarum Genera et Species*,[3] of which I now finished for press the first part. Occasionally, on my way to Lincoln's Inn, I would steal half an hour or an hour to describe specimens at Lambert's, the British Museum, or other herbaria, and I regularly attended the meetings of the Linnean Council and Society. I continued also the Horticultural Society's business, consenting to retain the Secretaryship another year—and this took me up rather more time in the early part of the year, owing to a severe illness of my friend Lindley's, following upon the loss of his eldest son, a fine little boy, whose lively disposition and active mind had promised great things. I had [570] considerable accessions to my herbarium, chiefly East Indian plants from Dr Wight, whose acquaintance I made during his visit to London this winter, and a very fine set of North American plants from Dr Schweinitz of Bethlehem, and I often sat up very late at night laying these in to my herbarium. I dined frequently at Count Ludolf's, and occasionally at Count (afterwards Prince) Woronzow's, meeting at both houses interesting foreigners. We had also a visit from M. Delpech, the eminent Montpellier surgeon, who came over partly to procure patients for his establishment for the cure of

spinal complaints, but chiefly to study the cholera, which broke out in
the autumn at Sunderland and Gateshead, then creating much alarm,
and this spring made its appearance in London, without, however, producing any disturbance beyond a few street-rows, especially in the Irish
quarters, where often considerable resistance was offered to the carrying off those attacked to the hospitals.

Jeremy Bentham's health now began to give us some anxiety. In the
last autumn he had had a slight cold, but in the early part of this year, as
he entered his 85th year, he retained his full vigour of mind, and on the
evenings that I dined with him—once or twice a week—he would often
dictate after dinner for a couple of hours, and always sat up till 11 or 12
in the evening. He was perfectly reconciled to my being at the bar, and
one day he had Richard Doane, his quondam amanuensis and now his
friend and manager, Edwin Chadwick, now staying in his house, nominally for the purpose of completing his *Constitutional Code*, and myself,
all three dine with him [571] in our wigs and gowns. He was also one
day much excited and highly pleased by having old Talleyrand one day
to dine and spend the evening with him. In the middle of February,
however, his cold and cough returned and pulled him down, and Monday 27th I dined with him, "to meet M. Sismondi, who appeared much
pleased, but my uncle was very weak from the effects of his cold, and
not having slept last night, was low and half asleep all the time, and did
not show to advantage." 3d March. "To Queen Square Place to dinner.
J.B. had been very unwell; he was part of yesterday in a state of half stu-
por, but having, by Dr Arnott's order later, a good dose of medicine,
was much better today, and though without appetite and weak, was
cheerful and well in appearance, and had me read to him after dinner."
On the 5th, however, "calling at Queen Square Place, found that J.B. was
seized last night with a return of fever and torpor in the stomach, and
had been in delirium ever since, which continued till this afternoon,
when, having had a warm bath, and a large blister on the nape of the
neck by Dr Arnott's order, he gradually became more tranquil, and at
length sank into a deep sleep, which lasted till 5 in the morning, and
when I returned home at ½ past 6 after sitting up with him, he appeared
much better, and to have got over all danger." Returning in the afternoon, found him quite revived and cheerful, though very weak—he was
able to sit up and even to eat a little at dinner, and I left him at half past
11 in a very promising condition, which continued to improve daily,
and on the 14th, "To Queen Square Place to dinner [572] when found
J.B. quite recovering his strength and appetite, and in very good spirits

about an article in the *Tatler* about him and Brougham, very well done and signed Junius Redivivus,[4] but not known by whom."

Wednesday, 21st March. "Fast day for the cholera, the town like a gloomy Sunday, all the shops shut, but people not in their Sunday clothes—mobs collected in the city, but no row as was expected—to dinner at Queen Square Place. J.B. very well, except a sort of fit he had at dinner affecting his speech, occasioned by his not having taken his medicine as usual, but on taking it that went off, and his appetite and strength appear to be completely restored." In the middle of April he had another cold which pulled him down, and though generally able to dine and sit up as usual, and one day walked briskly round his garden with me for half an hour, yet on the 2d May, dining there with Dr Southwood Smith, who now attended him, found him low and melancholy, doing and saying little, and very weak, but otherwise perfectly collected. 8th May. "J.B. in good spirits, but weak and thin, with very little appetite." 10th May. "Taking to him the proof of his Registration paper, printing in the Appendix to the 3d *Report* of the Real property Commissioners,[5] he was not well enough to attend to it." 15th May, "dining with him, found him better, and in high spirits at the return of the Whigs to power." 24th May, he was no longer able to sit up to dinner with us, and after that he very gradually sunk. In the early days of June he was still up, and to a certain degree sensible, then scarcely able to rise [573] at all and, lying half conscious in his bed, his brain appeared to retain a part of its wonted activity; he seemed to be feeling that his faculties were going but, trying to persuade himself that he was still able to recognise surrounding objects, he would go on for a length of time, repeating, "and there are the bedposts, the curtains, the chairs, the table, etc." On the 5th June, "he had become quite speechless and powerless; he did, however, appear to understand when told that the Reform Bill is carried,[6] and to feel pleasure at it, but did not recognise any one." On the 6th, "left him in the morning in the same state, but on returning in the afternoon, found him just expiring, and at half-past 5 he breathed his last, in the presence of Bowring, Doane, Chadwick and myself."

After my Uncle's death, I continued my legal occupations till the vacation, working much at Mr Koe's and reading in my own chambers, and had one more brief, but I soon relaxed a little, lingering rather longer at Wallich's distributions. I was also much taken up with the settlement of matters connected with my Uncle's property. By my grandfather's and father's wills, I was entitled to the whole of the Queen Square Place property, but my Uncle in his will left it in equal shares to my two

sisters and myself. I was advised, however, to adopt my Uncle's disposition, as though I should thereby get so much less myself, still it would
be better for us three together, and I therefore made arrangements for
purchasing my sisters' shares. I had [574] thus only to deal with Dr
Bowring, whom my Uncle had left sole executor, with uncontrolled
power to spend money upon editing and publishing a complete edition
of his works and his life. After much correspondence, I found Bowring's
views as to the way in which this was to be done so extravagant—and
his interpretation of the agreement upon which my Uncle had taken
shares in Owen's Lanark Mills so much against my interest in it, that
acting on the advice of my best legal friends, I filed a bill in Chancery for
the purpose of obtaining a reference from that Court. Bowring and
myself agreed at once that Mr Rolfe (afterwards Lord Cranworth)
should be the referee—and in the result I obtained a decision by which
we obtained from Lanark £10,000 instead of £7,000, which Bowring
would have accepted; but on the other hand it was impossible to control
the expenditure on the complete edition,[7] the publication of which
lasted some years, and at the final winding up resulted in a clear loss of
£6,000, whilst it might have been done, if not with profit, at any rate
with only a small loss.

Another business I had was the settling with Count Michel Woronzow (afterwards Prince Woronzow) the steps to be taken to secure to my
sister the value of the Russian property at Tchernaia Dolina, which my
father had left her, and which we had long thought would be ultimately
lost to us, from the difficulty of establishing my father's right under the
Russian laws. Count Woronzow, however, [575] kindly undertook it,
and returning to Russia after the death of his father, my father's old
friend, he there succeeded in selling it and obtaining for my sister
between £3,000 and £4,000. My elder sister's troubles at Montpellier
were also now beginning to cause us much anxiety.

Besides the study of law, I had a little practical experience of it on my
own account. In one of the narrow courts I went through on my way to
Lincoln's Inn, I had my pocket picked of a silk hankerchief. A passer-by
called my attention to it, and pointed out a young man running away
with it. I ran after him; he dodged me through several courts, and I just
came up to him when he bolted into a public house, where I found him
quietly standing at the counter with a glass of gin. There was a police-
man close by, to whom I gave him in charge. There was nothing found
upon him, but a grocer came up, producing[§] the handkerchief, which he
said the man threw down as he passed the corner of the shop. We all

went before a Magistrate, who I thought could have dealt with him summarily as the matter was so clear, but the law as it was then did not give him jurisdiction, and I was bound over to prosecute at the Clerkenwell sessions. The consequence was I had to waste a whole morning at Clerkenwell whilst the matter came before the Grand Jury, and again a day and a half at Sessions waiting for it to come on, and when it did come on, the grocer having given evidence that he saw the man throw down the handkerchief [576] which his, the grocer's, boy picked up and gave to him, the magistrate told the jury that the matter was so simple and clear that he need not trouble them with a detailed summary, and left the chair for a few minutes. Whilst he was away, the foreman of the jury, a wiseacre in his way, asked the grocer whether he picked up the handkerchief himself; the grocer said, "No, my boy picked it up and handed it to me." "And is your boy here to give evidence?" "No." "Then the evidence is incomplete and we must acquit him." And the culprit was at once let free, delighted at having spent a few days in comparative comfort in prison (for he was a rough of the lowest sort). When the magistrate came in again, presuming that the man had been sent to prison, [he] allowed the expences of prosecution as a matter of course, which, however, did not reimburse me all the actual expense I had been at, besides the loss of three days—and I promised myself never to prosecute a pickpocket again, especially when I found that my friend Philip Abbott had not long before had a much worse experience of the inconvenience of prosecuting. Another friend who knew better, having caught a pickpocket, gave him a good thrashing and let him go.

As summer came on, I paid some few days visits in the country, to the Culling Eardleys at Bedwell, and to the Carrs at Salden, and gradually gave a little more time to botany, but chiefly early in the morning and late at night, and I now first made acquaintance with Dr Royle, who arrived from India with large collections. The Horticultural [577] Society took up less time than last year. At the Linnean Society, Dr Wallich had secured the presentation to the Society of the East Indian Herbarium.[8] At a special meeting of the Council, we drew up a letter of thanks, and most of us members of Council accompanied the President, Lord Stanley, on the 26th June to the East India House, where Lord Stanley read the adress, to which Mr Ravenshaw, the Chairman of the Board, replied, following it up with a luncheon, when upon a hint of Wallich's, the Directors, delighted with the compliments paid to them by Lord Stanley, at once allowed £200 for paper on which to mount the specimens. Our Council named a Committee of myself and two others to settle matters of detail. We raised a subscription of £270 for the cases, etc, and the mounting, etc, was at once commenced and steadily proceeded with. I had originally compounded at the low rate, but had soon after given £10 on the subscription for the purchase of the Linnean library and collections and, on the present occasion, willingly came down with another £10. (Wallich's Assistant, Watson, sent out to Ceylon as Director of the Garden, on the recommendation of the Hort. Soc.)

I was now also printing my *Labiatarum Genera and Species*—corrected the last proof of the first part on the 15th of August, and by the 17th, before leaving England for Germany, procured a sufficient number of copies to distribute to my English and French friends and to take a few with me abroad.

[578]My friend Dr Wallich, being about to make a trip to Copenhagen to visit his family previous to his return to India, I agreed to accompany him, taking that opportunity of seeing something of Denmark, and with some idea of going on later to the meeting of Naturalists at Vienna—if nothing occurred to oblige its being again deferred. We accordingly went on board the *Sir Edward Banks* steamer for Hamburgh on the evening of Friday the 17th August, and starting at 4 in the morning, landed at Hamburgh in the morning of Monday the 20th. We had time that day to visit the Botanical Garden with Dr Lehmann and Mr Ohlendorf, the head gardener, who between them kept the garden in very good order, with considerable additions since I last saw it two years previously,[9] and at 6 p.m. left Hamburgh, in a calèche we had hired, for Lubeck, "where we arrived at about 7 in the morning of Tuesday, 21st, having gone with the same horses, with only an hour and a half's rest, a distance of 50 miles, over the most abominable road that can be conceived. It consists of a way originally traced over the sandy hills which separate the two towns and which had been subsequently paved, but the pavement having been suffered to fall completely out of repair, it is at once the heaviest for the horses, and the most trying for your carriage, your bones and your patience. At Oldenslohe, where we were above an hour in the middle of the night, had an opportunity of hearing the old-fashioned watchmen calling the hours, with quaint doggrel rhymes attached to each, ending with—*denn es ist (ein) Uhr geschlagen.*"

At Lubeck, we had time to go over this singular [579] quiet old town, with its "gable-ended houses, in the style of Hamburgh but more antiquated—the cathedral, a large, massive building without any elegance in its form, the interior columns plain and square, all whitewashed, the floor and furniture old and shabby, with a profusion of tasteless gingerbread-looking ornaments all awry, as is everything in the church, and an enormous clock, the centre of the dial plate representing a sun's face, with the eyeballs made to roll with the vibrations of the pendulum like a person squinting in the most horrible manner. The Marienkirche, a fine church inside, the tombs and accessories, particularly the organ, profusely but tastefully ornamented, and a complicated astronomical clock and calender, which must have cost much labour and is very ancient, having been originally built in 1405, though since repaired and altered. In the afternoon, a small steamer took us down the winding river through a flat but rather pleasing country to Travemunde, where we were transferred to the *Frederik den seite*, a fine Danish steamer with a Maudsley's 80-horse engine, rather large for the engine, but the accomodations good, although with no curtains to the bed places, so that we slept rather in public. We had on board, amongst others, Baron de Selby, the Danish Minister at the Hague, with eight or nine daughters, besides his wife and son. Left Travemunde at 7 in the evening and, with delightful weather and calm sea, passed the picturesque cliffs of Mönen early in the morning, and afterwards at a greater distance the hills of Flint. . . . (Vindbyeholt?), and at half past 12 anchored at the entrance of the port of Copenhagen."

Wednesday, 22d August. Landing at Copenhagen, the first business was to go through the board of health and [580] Customs. We had been rather afraid of the former, for the Danes were just now in great fear of the cholera, and very strict in their regulations, and we had left it rather bad at Lubeck, and Hamburg, though nearly free, was on the list of infected towns; but our captain had procured us fresh passports at Travemunde, and we passed safely with certificates of *ikke smitsot* (no contagious disorder). Dr Wallich was immediately taken possession of by his friends, and I got comfortable quarters at the Hotel d'Angleterre, a good hotel but rather dirty, with a large café and a few French and German papers, and plenty of Danske, which was all baragouin to me, and only made my mouth water; and wandering over the town in the afternoon, felt so dreadfully puzzled with the inscriptions on the shops that I bought a dictionary and went home to study, and it was not long before I could get on tolerably with the Danish papers, assisted by my former, but now almost forgotten, knowledge of the Swedish language.

Thursday, 23d Aug. "With Wallich and Professor Jacobson to the Botanical Garden, which is of some extent, in the middle of the town, and contained a good many plants, but in the most disorderly state. Whilst Hornemann, the Director of the garden, was engaged in a lecture, I went with Profr Jacobson to the round tower, containing a spiral inclined plane, up which Peter the Great drove to the top in a carriage and four—and to the University library, including a rich cabinet of Runic and Danish and Norwegian antiquities, which formed the nucleus of the celebrated Museum since established. After the lecture, spent the rest of the morning in Vahl's and Schumacher's [herbaria], [581] for the examination of which Hornemann gave me every facility. In the afternoon, with Wallich and Profr Jacobson to call on Prof. OErsted, the celebrated Astronomer and physicist. Found him a very agreable man, though with rather a hesitation in speaking, his countenance expressive of intelligence and vivacity, but with something of a wildness in it. He is in great favour here, and has conferred great benefits on his country, particularly in the establishment of a polytechnic school, of which he is director. Called also on Baron Nicolay, the Russian minister, from whom I met with the most cordial reception, and on Dr Wallich's sister, Mrs Cantour,[10] and in the evening to a supper (which they call tea) at her house, where the whole family were assembled. His relations are not rich nor high in rank, but warm in their feelings, and elated at seeing him again after a 25 years' absence. He had left them poor and young, to work his way in the medical service in the then Danish small settlement at Serampore, and now returned a celebrated scientific botanist, received with honor by the Danish sovereign, and courted by every one—and Dr Wallich himself was in extasies.—No loss in his family during his long absence, but only additions to it, his respectable father quietly enjoying the happiness thus conferred on his latter days and, as for his little old mother, it was a real pleasure to see the way in which Wallich went about with *mi gamel moder*, as he called her. The supper on this occasion was a most joyous as well as [582] a substantial one, and at its close I first witnessed a curious Danish bourgeois custom. On rising from table, every one shakes hands with each of the others, saying, or rather muttering, the words, *Wel bekommet*, which may be interpreted, *Much good may it do you."*

Friday, 24th. "Spent the whole morning in the herbarium, where verified the greater number of Vahl's Salviae, Schumacher's Guinea Labiatae, etc. Vahl's herbarium is rich in Spanish and Eastern plants, Schumacher's in European and garden ones, besides his Guinea collections, and Wallich's East Indian ones, and both these herbaria are in good order. Hornemann's, on the contrary, may be richer, but [is] in a state of great confusion. The library and other collections are very disorderly placed about the room, and indeed Hornemann's dress and manner show that he has been brought up under the influence of the genius of disorder, rather than of order. Wandering about the town in the afternoon, went over the quarter called the Nyiborg, a number of long parallel streets of low shabby one-storied houses, but broad, clean, and at this time of day nearly deserted. These are the habitations of mariners and other poor persons, who live under certain regulations, which make this class of dwellings one of the healthiest of the town, instead of the unhealthiest as it usually is. In the evening to a party at Prof. Jacobson's, where we had tea, pianoforte music, singing and a substantial supper (which, however, I am [583] told is only given at parties and not eaten every day), after which the usual *wel bekommet*."

Saturday, 25th. "This morning at the herbarium. Professor Schouw very attentive to me, and gave me a copy of Schumacher's *Beskrivelse* of Guinea plants, and I bought two others for friends at home, also a visit from old Lindegaard of Rosenborg, a most zealous horticulturist. Out to dinner at Christiansholm, Baron Nicolay's country seat, about five miles from the town along the seacoast. The Baron was formerly private Secretary to Count Michel Woronzow and afterwards Secretary to the Russian Embassy (I believe in England), and is now Russian minister here, with a family of three, just grown-up daughters and some children. The weather was splendid, the country home beautifully situated adjoining the King's Park, a noble forest covering some gentle rising ground, and so thick and so well situated as to assume the appearance of the entrance to a ridge of mountains. We dined in a sort of summer house, which opens on the sea. The air was calm, the sea close in as smooth as glass, whilst at a little distance there was just wind enough to enable a number of vessels to glide along. Opposite to us was the Swedish coast and town of Landscrona shining in the sun, higher up the island of Hoeen, and at a distance the Sound. Nothing could be finer or more enjoyable than this afternoon in the Baron's most friendly family party, to which were added his two secretaries. After dinner, walked to some artificial mounds, whence with a telescope we had a capital view of the Sound, and at the moment the Norway steamer just in the middle, between the Danish fortress of Elsineur and the Swedish church of Helsingborg opposite, the great beauty of this coast being due much to [584] the woods coming down to the seashore. Drove home along the coast, and to another supper and *wel bekommet* at Mr A. Wallich's, the Doctor's brother, who is an artist of considerable repute here, and first scene painter to the theatre."

Sunday, 26th. "Walked out to Frederiksberg, a Royal palace and park where the King now lives, about 2 miles from the town. The park is beautifully laid out, with a handsome building on the only hill so near to Copenhagen, and which is said to have been artificially raised higher than it was in order to give a better view of the town. The weather being tolerably good, I was enabled to enjoy the view, which is certainly fine. Returning to town, drove out to Baron Nicolay's at Christiansholm, and with him to a picnic dinner of a portion of the Corps diplomatique (I presume the Conservative portion, for the English and the French Ministers appear not to be on very intimate terms with the northern ones) at the Hermitage, a hunting box of the King's lent to them for the purpose, in the park of Frederiksgarde, just beyond Christiansholm. The party, made up on the reception of a turtle from England, consisted of the Russian, Prussian, Austrian, Swedish Ministers, some German Ministers, Consuls, Secretaires d'Ambassades, etc, in all about 25, the soup, etc, prepared by Count Katchinsky the Prussian Minister's excellent French cook, plenty of wines, and a thoroughly jolly party. It broke up at half-past six, and I walked back with Baron Nicolay to Christiansholm through the beautiful park. It is laid out on broken ground, and thickly covered with fine beech wood, interspersed [585] with rich and extensive pasturages, enlivened by the number of cattle and deer feeding. Returned late to town, too much fatigued for a farewell party at Wallich's sister's, to which I had been asked—having, moreover, seen the whole family in the morning."

Monday, 27th August. "After being kept an hour and a half at the police office with passport formalities, went with Hornemann to the Rosenborg, a royal garden, with an old palace, in the middle of the town. Here found old Lindegaard, the head gardener, a most zealous F.H.S., and Petersen his undergardener, who both showed me round. It is one of the principal fruit gardens for the King's table, and the grapes and pineapples in the houses are fine. One grapevine covers the interior of a house for a length of about eighty feet, and produces annually from 350 to 420 fine bunches. There are a great many grapes on walls out of doors, but this year, owing to the very bad season, none will ripen, except where they put frames in front. A new pine house on the model of the latest in England is almost finished, and well executed. In general, the garden is in good order, but they have a shocking climate to contend with. The ornamental part of the garden is a small public promenade, something in the style of the Tuileries.

"At 3 in the afternoon, embarked with Wallich for Lubeck, where we arrived at 2 p.m. on Tuesday, 28th, and at 6 set out again in a calèche for

Hamburg, taking this time the Schonberg road. This road is a German mile shorter than the one by Oldenslohe, and the first three-quarters of a (German) mile, there is a very good chaussée—just to show how easy [586] it would be to have a good road—but the rest of the way it is the most wretched that can be conceived, and is justly celebrated as the worst in Europe, being nothing but a broken-up pavement intermixed with the sandy bottom. At about 11 at night, near the village of Labentz, in attempting to avoid one of the worst places, the wheels on one side got upon a big stone, and on the other sank in the sand, and over we went. Our calèche was one without glass, but with leather curtains, closely buttoned together on all sides, except on that on which we fell, shutting us up completely. Wallich, who had been in a sound sleep, was undermost, and as I could not help falling upon him, he woke with an exclamation that all his bones were broken. With some difficulty I contrived to open the curtains, and we crept out, both unhurt, to see the horses with hanging heads, quietly enjoying their rest, and the great tall boor of a Pomeranian Kutscher, who at the first overturn only called out, 'Ach, mein Gott!' was standing stock still, looking on, apparently bewildered at what was next to be done. We sent him to the village to get assistance, and in a good half hour the calèche was set upon its wheels, and we drove on, stopping for some coffee at Schonberg, and arriving well jolted, bruised and battered at Hamburgh at 8 in the morning.

"I remained with Wallich a couple of days at Hamburgh—visited Booth's nursery at Flottbeck—studied Labiatae in Colemann's herbarium, which Lehmann had just bought—had a smoky dinner party at Lehmann's, got good letters for Vienna from the Binders, went two [587] evenings to the play with Wallich. Heavy rainy weather, and got very wet in the dirty streets of the town—but interested on meeting a funeral—that of an ordinary tradesman, but the undertaker's men, eight to carry the coffin and eight to relieve them, all wore little black gowns, something like our university gowns but narrower, and wigs exactly like our lawyers' wigs, but all the same colour, nearly white, and this, I am told, is the universal custom."

Saturday, 1st Sept. "Having seen Wallich embark for London last night, I slept today in the postwagen for Brunswick—a very indifferent vehicle, with the windows so low that one had to stoop much to see out of them, and not much to see—a long, tedious journey, crossing never-ending sandy heaths, along straight roads for miles and miles without a house or a cultivated spot, creeping slowly in the sand, with long stages and long stoppages at the end and in the middle of every stage, thirty-two hours for about 120 English miles, and heartily glad to land in the comfortable Hotel d'Angleterre."

Monday, 3d Sept. "Brunswick is an extensive old town, thinly inhabited, with broad, winding streets, some old-towered churches, and older houses—all awry, with upper stories overhanging, and crooked roofs, picturesque but dismal—there are, however, a good many newer and good-looking houses. The palace, now a heap of ruins, must have been[§] very fine, and one can scarcely conceive the spirit which induced the Brunswickers to destroy the pride of their town, which was a source of much benefit from the number of travellers who were induced to come this way to see it.[11] The country round about is very flat [588] and though the Harz mountains are at no great distance, I could not find an elevated spot sufficiently near to get a general view of the town. At 4 in the afternoon left Brunswick, in a well-hung Leipzig schnellpost, which drove pretty fairly for Germany, carrying us to Leipzig, 130 miles in 24 hours, and enabled me to make friends with two Professors, going like myself to the meeting at Vienna. 'Herr Medizinalrath Koehler aus Celle,' and 'Herr Doctor[§] Ziegler aus Hanover,' who were both most attentive to me, though they did smoke so steadily. At the Saxon frontier (the Saxons boasting that their quarantine regulations had entirely kept the cholera away from their country), our passports were closely examined, and as all but one in the coach had come from Hamburgh, Hannover, or other places officially declared healthy (though there is plenty of cholera at Hamburgh), we were allowed to pass, nothing showing that I had so lately been at Lubeck, for instance. One poor Lady, however, had been lately at Nordhausen, which is still on the official sick list (though there has been no case of cholera there for the last fortnight), was obliged to get out to perform ten days' quarantine; so would it have been with me, if I had not taken the precaution of changing my passport at Hamburgh."

Tuesday, Sept. 4. "Arriving at Leipzig, went to the play, which opened with a prologue on the occasion of the day, the anniversary of the publication of the constitution,[12] a boon which they do not seem to care much about, for as the prologue ended, with three 'lebehoch's' and flourishes of trumpets, the first for the Constitution and the second for the King were received with solemn silence, and there was only [589] some slight cheering at the third, for Saxony. The play was a translation of Boieldieu's *Jean de Paris*—pretty good, but too loud—a comic inn-keeper, a screaming princess, and a page out of tune, but much ensemble. After the play, walked about the streets, which were very brilliant, the illumination being very general, nothing however but rows of candles or plain lamps (wicks swimming in a saucer of tallow). The streets crowded and gay, all very quiet, here and there perhaps a little cheering before two or three brilliantly illuminated houses. One of these had four transparences, the first a candle with 1832 Geduld (Patience), the second a torch with 1835 Hoffnung (Hope), the third a flame with 1838 Freude (Joy), the fourth an expanded glory with 1841 Friede (Peace), an excellent specimen of the rapidity of German ideas," but this rapidity, little as it was, proved to be overestimated, for they had to wait not three, but thirty years more before the full expansion of their glory.[13]

Wednesday, 5th Sept. "Remained the day at Leipzig, chiefly with Professor Kunze, a most zealous botanist, whose Labiatae I looked over, getting from him specimens of several German species. With Herr Medizinal Rath Koeler (who, like myself, had planned to stay one day at Leipzig and two at Dresden) to Hofmeister's, a musicseller and a sort of bookseller, of whom I purchased Reichenbach's *Iconographia Exotica* and some other books. The town lies in a dead flat, part of it intersected by branches of the Elster and two other little rivers, along which, just out of the town, are some fine houses and pretty gardens. The inner part of the town [590] has a clean, gay and busy look, the streets not very narrow, though the houses are very high, the whole reminding me something of Paris. The great square is very fine. The houses have all very slanting roofs; in one, I counted six tiers of garret windows in the roof. In the evening, again to the play, *Er mengt sich in alles*, a little comedy taken partly from *Paul Pry*, which was really most admirably acted, and *Der alte Feldherr, or Kosciusko*,[14] a very short comedy, nothing in itself, but remarkable for a lament over the fate of Poland, rendered very fine by the appeance of Napoleon, exceedingly well represented with his Etat-major and by the singing of 'The Marseillaise,' which were all received with very great enthusiasm by a crowded house. There was also one chorus, a prayer of forgiveness by some Polish soldiers when they recognize Kosciusko, as he is endeavouring to stop their marauding, which really was one of the most beautiful pièces d'ensemble I ever heard."[15]

Thursday, 6th. In a very comfortable Eilwagen to Dresden, putting up at the Hotel de Saxe, "an excellent inn, with an excellent host," whence I wrote to my mother: "I must tell you, however, that it is dangerous not to hurry me home, for I never had so agreable a journey. A week or two of this is almost worth to me years of enjoyment. Since Brunswick, I have left bad roads, bad coaches, bad weather, and whatever bad can be found in this tour (which was, with all that, already one of pleasure) far behind me, and my course is now through a country of the greatest interest, with the most beautifull weather, though rather cold, and amongst a [591] people whose apathy and constant smoking I forget in the amusement of *baragouining* their language, and particularly from their prévenance to foreigners. At least I have nothing to complain of in my reception both from those who know me, and those who do not. Saxon politeness is proverbial in Germany and, as far as I see, not undeservedly so."

Reichenbach was absent, and there was no other botanist at Dresden, so I spent my two days there chiefly with my diligence friends, Herr Medicinalrath Koeler and Herr Doctor Ziegler, in visiting the celebrated picture gallery, then in the old building,[16] and other galleries and lions of the place—and the afternoons in the Grosse Garten, or the beautifully situated Findlater's, where after dinner, the upper and middling classes spend two or three hours taking tea or coffee and listening to good band, the ladies knitting all the time as perseveringly as the gentlemen smoked—a dull passetemps of which I soon had enough. Indifferent acting one evening in the shabby town theatre adjoining the Palace, but a capital farce the other evening (*Leichtsinn und Liebe*), in a wooden theatre in the Kaffee-garten at the Linksche Bad—the acting of some of the parts à mourir de rire.

Sunday, 9th Sept. "At 6 in the morning left Dresden in a voiturin's calèche, which I hired for Toeplitz for 7 thalers. The distance is but eight German, or about forty English miles, but the road is exceedingly hilly, and it took eleven hours including stoppages. The road lies, as far as the beautifully situated little town of Pirna, up the valley of the [592] Elbe, or rather the Dresden plain. There we leave the Elbe and the Saxon Switzerland on the left, and ascend, by an ill-laid out but otherwise good road, the ridge that separates Bohemia from Saxony. This ridge was formerly covered by a thick and widely extended forest, celebrated, under the name of the Bohemian forest, as the haunt of robbers and the scene of many a German romance. The wood is now, in a great many places, cut down and converted into arable land—still enough remains to make many parts exceedingly picturesque, and several ruined towers show the strength with which these marauders fortified themselves in their haunts. Before we came to the top, stopped at the Austrian frontier village, Peterswalden (a straggling village above a mile long), to rest the horses and to dine. Here my passport was examined, and the *outside* of my trunks looked at—for a couple of shillings kept the inquisitive eyes of the Officers from the inside. At the top of the ridge is a most splendid view over the mountains of Saxony and Galicia to the east, and of Bohemia to the south. Here is also a wild, desolate looking village of some twenty or thirty houses, called Jungferndorf, where there is not even a publickhouse, and yet there is a board over a door, marked Augustus Hiecke, Wappen-und Siegel-Graveur. Quite at the top is the village of Nollendorf, and at the edge all alone, as if in the wildnerness, the village church, from whence proceeded the chaunt of vespers, accompanied by an organ, producing a very singular effect in such a situation. The descent to Bohemia is steep and picturesque, and the situation of Toeplitz, where [593] I arrived at 5, pleased me much; the houses, chiefly inns and lodging houses, are neat and well built and very clean."—To the play, and next day took a carriage to Prague, arriving there at 8 in the evening, remaining there two days.

Tuesday, 11th Sept. "Prague is a very fine town, with a population of 120,000 and quite a city-like appearance. It is a very old one, and contains many very ancient buildings, and yet the streets are generally broad and well built. As usual in Germany, but here in particular, there is a great profusion of statues and ornaments. The insides of the principal churches are overloaded with them, and on each pier of the bridge, there is, on each side, a group representing some passage in the New Testament. Everything denotes a kind of idolatrous catholicism, and that, although the town has long been the chief seat of protestantism in this country. The town is also full of troops, and the K.K.[17] arms are, in some shape or another, on almost every other house. The people, too, are eminently aristocratic in their ideas, and their nobility are like so many petty sovereigns, but on the whole it is a noble place. The King's palace, in the Hradschin, on the hill on the left bank of the river, is an enormous building, and the view from it is beautiful. The archbishop's palace, museum, etc, adjoining, are also fine buildings, and in general the town is full of them. The play in the evening pretty good, in a good-looking house, very full, and a great many pretty girls, with which Prague seems to abound."

I failed in finding Count Sternberg, but found Presl in the Museum, where the botanical library, chiefly presented [594] by Count Sternberg, is very rich, as well as the collection of fossile vegetables. Looked over Haenke's Labiatae, and got specimens of some of them. To the churches, with Herr Medizinalrath Koehler, and in the evening of the 12th Sept. took the eilwagen for Vienna, where arrived early in the morning of the 14th, over a country generally uninteresting, but in [a] comfortable carriage on good roads. Put up at the Kaiserin von Œsterreich, the second-best hotel, the Erzherzog Karl being full—the accomodation good, the dinner (always *à la carte* here) indifferent, and slovenly served, and the waiting bad. No better, I am told, at the other hotels. After settling myself there, went out in seach of Baron Jacquin, whom I found already at his post in the University, preparing for the meeting next week, of which he is the President. He was very friendly, introduced me to Endlicher of Presburg and Hayne of Grâtz, who were already there, and when business was over, took me down to the Botanic Garden, where he resides. "This Garden is in very good order, and contains a very extensive collection of trees and shrubs. The hothouses, greenhouses and herbaceous plants are not so good, the latter still arranged according to the Linnean system, and very deficient both in extent and in interest. The most interesting specimens in the garden those of two new European plants, the Hungarian lilac, Syringa Josikaea in the arboretum, and several fine plants of the new Sicilian Stapelêa Gussoni in one of the houses, two of them now in flower. In the evening to the Opera, where Herold's *Zampa* was well acted."

[595]Saturday, 15th Sept. "At the University reception room met Count Sternberg and others, and in the afternoon with Pohl to the Brasilian Museum, taking a general view of the rich collections made at a considerable expense by the Emperor,[18] Pohl himself very friendly in his manner. At the Opera in the evening; Méhul's *Joseph* very stupid."

Sunday, 16th Sept. "Breakfasted at Jacquin's, meeting Zahlbruckner and two or three other botanists, and joined in the Garden by Visiani from Dalmatia. Out to dinner at M. v. Hammer's, the Orientalist (afterwards Hammer-Purgstall), to whom I had letters from the Binders. He lives at Döbling, a little village just beyond the suburbs properly so called, with a large family, consisting of his own wife and children, and his wife's father, mother and sisters, and their children. There was also a French Baron Pasquier, a lawyer, and two or three others. The Hammers all very amiable and civil to me. In the evening to the Leopoldstadts Theatre—an amusing farce, though rather too much of Vienna patois for me to enter into all the jokes."

Monday, 17th Sept. "Again to Jacquin's to breakfast, and with the gardener to Host's garden to gather his Mints to dry. Got about thirty of his species, most of them as much like each other as any two individuals of any one species, but Host himself thoroughly persuaded of their specific value, and very glad that I should carry away specimens to place them on record. Tried the public dinner prepared for the naturalists in the

Augarten, and in the evening to the Kaernthner Thor Theater, where the chief performance was a ballet, with a good display of Fanny Elssler's legs."

[596]Tuesday, 18th Sept. The first general meeting of the Versamlung Deutscher Naturforscher und AErzte, of which Association I prepared at the time some account, from which I make the following extract:[19]

"It had long been the wish of the promoters of the annual meetings of the German Naturalists that one of them should be held in the Austrian Capital, but it was generally believed that the Government of that country looked upon these Assemblies with a jealous eye, and endeavoured in every way to discourage them. Indeed it has been asserted repeatedly that no Professors from any part of the Austrian dominions could obtain leave to attend the meeting held at Heidelberg in 1829, so much did Prince Metternich fear, as it was stated, that under the name of science, politics might become the subject of discussion. But whatever foundation there may have originally been for these statements, the dispositions of the Emperor Francis and of his administration had certainly become much more libéral before the meeting at Hamburg in 1830, when the members were expressly invited to fix their next one at Vienna.

"This change has been attributed to the efforts of Count Sternberg, a Bohemian nobleman, well-known in the whole scientific world for his geological and botanical labours, and still more so in his own country for the liberal patriotism with which he devotes a considerable fortune and the influence of his high rank to the promotion of science in general, and especially to afford his own countrymen every [597] facility in its pursuit. Not only has he presented his splendid library of botanical and other works and collections in various branches of Natural History to the Museum of Prague, but he continues, at his own expence, to supply this library with the most important works now in the course of publication. It is to his representations that the removal of whatever misgivings Prince Metternich may have had on the effect of bringing together in the Austrian dominions so many men of various opinions on political matters is supposed to be owing, and certain it is that in the spring of 1830, both the Prince and his Imperial Master took up the cause of Naturalists, with so much interest as to determine on sending the abovementioned invitation. Accordingly, Baron Jacquin, Professor of Botany and Director of the Imperial Botanical Garden of Vienna, and Councillor Littrow, Professor of Astronomy at the University, received his Majesty's command to repair to Hamburg for that purpose. The universal satisfaction with which the invitation was accepted, and the assurances given by them and by Count Sternberg of the cordiality with which the naturalists would be received by the Imperial Government, seemed to afford every prospect that the Vienna meeting would be the most brilliant of any that had taken place since the institution of the Society.

"But long before the time fixed upon (September 1831) had arrived, various causes had intervened to frustrate these liberal intentions. Not only had the clouds which obscured the [598] political horizon of Germany, and the severe contests carrying on on its northern frontier obliged many of the most eminent men to give up all thoughts of leaving their homes, but a scourge which was then considered as far more fatal, the yet more dreaded than dreadful cholera, was fast encroaching on the Austrian dominions, and the fear that it would, before the day of meeting, have visited the capital itself, as indeed afterwards proved to be the case, rendered it necessary to defer the assembly till the following year, to which effect advertisements were inserted in the public journals.

"As the summer of 1832 advanced, the political ferment had in a great measure subsided, and although the cholera was as severe in the city of Vienna as it had been the previous autumn, yet it had lost many of its terrors. Cholerophobia and its attendant quarantines and restrictions were fast disappearing, and it was determined no longer to put off the intended meeting. Unfortunately, this determination was not sufficiently known in the more distant parts of the country, the supposed obstructions to travellers from quarantine regulations were much exaggerated and, above all, the panic into which so many were thrown by the singular course of the pestilence had not sufficiently abated to admit of so large a concourse of eminent men as there would otherwise have been. Even Oken, the founder of these meetings, has given way to cholerophobia and sent an excuse, and a special messenger sent to Munich to represent the real state of the case as to the salubrity of the town failed in§ persuading him to change his mind." [599] On seeing him afterwards at Munich, I found that that was not his only fear. The old man had shown himself to be an advanced liberal, and attaching great importance to his own political consequence, he imagined that the deputation to him was a trick of Metternich's to entrap him and put him in prison.

Arriving at Vienna a few days before the general meeting, the first business was to enter our names as members of the Association. For this there was no fee to pay. I believe some kind of introduction was necessary, but I was too well known to the President and other Officials to require it, and I received the accompanying ticket,[20] which was to secure free admission to all meetings of the Association, to the public Museums, etc, and to answer to the police as a carte de séjour. We also signed our names in lithographic ink.

"The day before the meeting, I tried the general dinner at the Augarten. This was once an Imperial garden, with a banqueting house for the use of the Imperial family, but since they have ceased to make use of it, it has been let to a restaurateur, with whom arrangements had been made for providing a dinner for us, at a fixed rate, during the time the meeting was to last. These common dinners for the members are usually a great convenience, as affording a good opportunity for making personal acquaintances, one of the chief objects of the Association. But in the present case two great inconveniences took much away from the advantages. The distance was considerable—about a mile and a half from the centre of the town, and the dinner was so long that [600] three or four hours of the best part of each day were thus thrown away—and when the dinner was well attended, the confusion of getting places was so great that it was very difficult for those whose pursuits were the same to contrive to be together. At Hamburgh, there was a botanical table, another for zoologists, for mineralogists, for medical men, etc, and although we there found it rather long to be two hours getting through five dishes, yet in the intervals, as we were all botanists together, we could converse on that subject nearly as well as when sitting in section in the morning. But at the Augarten we were obliged to be seated at half-past two (having left Vienna at two) in order to secure places. The soup was seldom brought till half-past three, and during that hour the botanist or zoologist, surrounded by physicians or geologists, with whom he had no rapports, had nothing to do but to dine on the bread and wine before him; and by six o'clock, when he got back to town, he had the satisfaction of finding that he was sacrificing four hours out of the few days he had ever been in Vienna to the most stupid of all dinners." So much indeed was said about dinner arrangements and the means of improving them, that amongst the numerous verses distributed, amongst others, were the following:

> Was wollen die Gelehrte aus der Ferne?
> Suchen sie den Lauf der Cometen, der Sterne?
> Forschen sie nach dem Gang der Flüsse?
> Oder andere Natureignisse?
> Oder suchen sie vielleicht gar den Stein der Weisen?
> O nein!—nur wo man am besten kann speisen.[21]

[601]Tuesday, 18th Sept. "At ten o'clock, to the first general meeting of the Association at the University, where the large hall was fitted up for our reception. It is a lofty and spacious room, richly decorated with a profusion of marble of various colours and fresco paintings. At the upper-end was an elevated platform, with three seats, for the president Baron Jacquin in the centre, the secretary Prof. Littrow on his right, and the left-hand one reserved for the several persons who should read papers at the meetings. Immediately in front of the chair was left an open space, on each side of which were chairs prepared for the most distinguished of the guests, and the rest of the hall was occupied by rows of chairs and benches for the meeting at large. Those to the right of the President were almost all occupied by Imperial Ministers and Officers of state, and other Noblemen and Gentlemen of rank. Amongst the foremost, sat Metternich himself who, during the whole of the meeting, paid the greatest attention to the proceedings, and who, adding the greatest affability to a noble carriage and handsome person and the manners of a perfect gentleman, won the hearts of all present. Being so very well informed on a great variety of subjects, he was enabled to enter into conversation with each of the savans relating to the particular objects of his pursuits—with me, for instance, he showed how well he was versed in our scientific societies, and the horticultural in particular—and thus putting every one in good humour with themselves [602] and bringing science into fashion, he did far more for its general encouragement, than if he had confined himself to an ostentatious display of splendid patronage. And his example was followed by nearly all those connected with the Administration, amongst whom the following were observed to be present at the general meetings: the Minister of the Interior and President of the Commission of Public Instruction Count Mittrowsky, the Minister of Police Count Sedlnitzky, the Hungarian Chancellor Count Rewitzky, the Minister of Finance Count Klebetsberg, the President of the Court of Accounts Baron Baldacci, the Governor of Gallicia Baron Krieg, the Captain Guardian of the Hungarian Crown Count Zichy Ferrari (Princess Metternich's father), the Hungarian Grand Chamberlain Count Nadasdy, the Empress's Grand Chamberlain Count Wurmbrand, the King of Hungary's Grand Chamberlain Count Hoyos, the Queen of Hungary's Grand Chamberlain Prince Odelscalchi, the Prelate Archbishop of Austria, the Probst of Kloster Neuburg, the Abbe der Schotten, General Mazzuchelly, the Vice-President of the Court of Justice Count Lobkowitz, the Keeper of the Crown Jewels Count Taafe, Baron Metzbourg, Count Collorado-Mansfeld, etc, and amongst foreigners, several

members of the Corps Diplomatique, Marshal Marmont, who is made much of here, and others. The members of the Association present now amounted to about 360, and some 300 visitors filled the back of the room." I was very well placed for watching the proceedings, being seated in the front row between Mr Hammer and M. de Montbel, who both of them made themselves very agreable.

The sitting was opened by a short speech from the President and the Secretary's formal Report, including the Official regulations, after which between two and three long hours were occupied [603] in the reading of technical papers totally unsuited to the occasion. To me the most interesting sight was that of the great man who had for so many years wielded the destinies of half Europe. He listened for an hour to Hofrath Burdach's dissertation on the pulsations of the heart, and another hour to Dr Wawruch's latin demonstration that the Israelites in the desert had the cholera morbus, besides half an hour to Dr Goeppert's account of the germination of plants, without showing the least ennui at the medical details, which made half the audience yawn, or drawing his lips to a smile when the learned Doctor argued that, as the Israelites eat vegetables because meat produced nausea, therefore this nausea was the cholera, whilst Marmont, at the Prince's side, had his hat before his face to conceal his smile, and further back many a suppressed laugh could be heard.[22]

"After the meeting we adjourned to the several sections to choose Presidents, Secretaries, and [conduct] other formal business. Our botanical section showed much thinner than had been hoped—cholerophobia kept away many foreigners who had intended to have come—scarcely any indeed were there, except Goeppert of Breslau and Estreicher of Cracow. Amongst Austrian botanists, besides Baron Jacquin and Count Sternberg, I observed Endlicher, Fenzel, Host, Pohl, Trattinick and Zahlbruckner of Vienna, Mikan and Presl of Prague, Hayne of Gratz, Biasoletto from Trieste, and Visiani from Dalmatia. In all we were forty-two. A long and tedious Augarten dinner, and afterwards to the Burg theatre, where I had a good view of the Emperor, Empress, and some of the Archdukes. The Emperor Francis and Metternich, side by side, a perfect contrast in appearance, Metternich tall and rather stout, with remarkably [604] noble features, and very recherché in his dress and manners, covered with stars and orders—the aged Emperor, with a long, thin countenance, sunken cheeks and a small quantity of white hair combed straight down, dressed in a plain black coat buttoned to the top, and not a single order or decoration. He has, however, something exceedingly benevolent in his countenance, and is said by all to be a most excellent man to his family and to his people. The Imperial party were received with much cheering as they entered their box."

Wednesday, 19th Sept. "Our sectional meeting having to submit to a sentimental paper of Trattinick's,[23] I went out to Dobling to breakfast at the Hammers', meeting there again the French Baron Pasquier and some other gentlemen and ladies, including a very handsome and amiable Hungarian girl, and after breakfast a large party of us walked up to Bottsleinsdorf, a house and park laid out quite in the English style by a Swedish gentleman, now dead, but his daughter and son-in-law, who live there, joined us, and we spent the whole morning going over their park and the adjoining Neuwaldegg (above Dornbach) Park, belonging to Prince Schwarzenberg. All these lie on the hills, or rather mountains, at the foot of which Vienna is situated, and afford the unique advantage of wild, wooded mountain scenery on one side, and on the other a splendid panoramic view of a large capital in a rich plain, bounded again at a distance by lofty mountains. Before us the Carpathian mountains, with the Presburg chain connecting them with the Schneeberg on the right, and on the left the lower mountains of Moravêa, [605] the Danube, full of islands, intersecting the plain at our feet, and on its banks rises the city of Vienna, with St Stephen's beautiful steeple in its centre, and round the ramparts a belt of promenade, being the ancient glacis, and around that again a broader belt of suburbs, all clean and well built, and all full of palaces and churches. It was one of the most beautiful views I ever saw. Returning to town, found that besides Trattinick's Amaryllis and Roses, Unger of Kitzbühel (afterwards of Grätz) had given the section a good paper on the attachment of Orobanche and Lathraea, and what seemed to have given more satisfaction, dinner invitations had been liberally distributed. After a good and quiet dinner at the 'Erzherzog Karl,' I spent the afternoon with Pohl, over his Brasilian Labiatae, and the evening at the Leopoldstadt minor theatre, where the opera of *Fra Diavolo* was very fairly got up."

Thursday, 20th Sept. "About forty of us, chiefly belonging to the botanical section, proceeded early in the morning in a number of Gesellschaftswagen, to the Imperial gardens of Schoenbrunn. They lie on the little stream Wien, about a mile from the extremity of the town, and adjoin the village of Hietzing. The park rises behind the palace, and on the top of the eminence is a sort of colonnade and arcade called the Gloriole, which from some points of view has a tolerably good effect, but from others looks unmeaning and rather ridiculous. The greater part of the garden is old-fashioned, French and formal, but rather more neatly kept than is usual in France. The hothouses are also old-fashioned, the specimens they contain generally fine, but little new [606] amongst them, with the exception of the Brasilian plants collected by Schott and a fine series of Aroideae in a new house built for them. We perambulated the grounds§ under the direction of Bredemeyer, the Director. Poor Schott, the head gardener, already known for his Brasilian expedition and for the study and care of the plants brought home by him, was still confined to his room by the remains of a severe attack of cholera. From the Imperial garden we adjourned to the almost adjoining one of Baron Hügel, at Hietzing, which, though small, contains by far the best collection in the country and kept in the best order. The Baron himself is a young man, much devoted to horticultural botany, who brought over from England some two years ago many of the choicest things then in cultivation, and is now absent on a tour through Egypt to India"[24] (afterwards extended to Australia). He was strongly attached to, engaged to be married to, Countess Zichy's daughter, when Prince Metternich, having lost his (2d or 3d) wife, paid his addresses to this lady,[25] whose mother at once broke off the engagement with Baron Huegel, and this, it is said, was the occasion of his starting on this distant expedition. The Baroness his mother and his sister (afterwards Countess Hardenberg) received us with great attention, and were particularly civil to me.—We sat down, some fifty of us, to a very good dinner at the principal Café at Hietzing, after which I left them to go to a party at the Hammers'."

Friday, 21st Sept. "Drove out to Baden, and a little way up the valley to the Archduke Charles's palace of Wallburg, [607] a romantically situated old chateau—to see Mlle Hauser, governess to the Archduke's daughters, and a great friend of our friends the Carrs. Her little pupil, Princess Marie (afterwards Queen of Naples) a nice little girl, showed me her dried plants, and seemed delighted to give me two or three specimens. The Archduke himself expressed a desire to see me, and on my being introduced, entered into a very friendly and kind conversation. With all his military reputation, he has in every respect the appearance of being, and is in reality, an excellent man, very fond of his family, and having every domestic quality. Dined with Mr Kochel and Mlle Hauser at the inn at Baden, and returned to town to spend the afternoon with Visiani, selecting from his Dalmatian plants—and to the Burg theatre, where *Der Müller und sein Kind*, a Volksdrama, or tragedy in low life, was pretty well acted, but a kind of play not to my taste."

Saturday 22d. To the Brasilian Museum, working at Pohl's Hyptises till the hour of the second general meeting of the Association, where after some speeches, the next year's meeting was fixed to take place at Breslau. Littrow, the Secretary, read us a lecture on not attending regularly at the Augarten dinners, but on trying it again today, found no improvement on the tediousness and waste of four of the best hours of the day. "In the evening (at half past seven) to Prince Metternich's party, to which he had invited the whole Association. The rooms were well lighted up and the Prince and Princess received us very graciously, the Princess a handsome woman with remarkably elegant manners, and [608] her mother, Countess Zichy, was très aimable.[26] Pozzo di Borgo, M. and Mde de Tatischeff, Prince Esterhazy, about half a dozen ladies and some fifty gentleman-looking persons, with above three hundred Naturforscher—many of them unshaved, with dirty cravats, and stinking of tobacco—others dressed out, but without knowing how to put on their clothes."

Sunday, 23 Sept. "At half-past seven to the Post, where were prepared a number of Eilwagens to convey us to Baden, each paying a florin (2 shillings), Baden paying the rest. By about 8 o'clock we were off, about 300 of us in 38 carriages, to the great amusement of the crowds who lined the streets to see us. By eleven we reached Baden, where the magistrates waited at the Casino door to receive us. After clearing off the dust we were covered with, we were shown into a room, where the chief Burgermeister (an apothecary of the town) made us a long speech, in which he told us that our visit opened a new *area* for the town. We then went in a body to Wallburg, and were presented to Archduke Charles, who received us very affably. After that we separated into different parties, and united again to pay our respects to Archduke Anthony in Baden itself, where we met with the same reception as at Wallburg, and were shown round his garden. He is very fond of gardening, and has a very good collection of fruit trees. Returning to the Casino, we sat down at half past three to an excellent dinner in a very handsome room. Opposite me was sitting Mlle Pichler, the first German novelist of the day.[27] She is something like Mrs Marcet in appearance, but is said to have been excessively plain when young; she has, however, something remarkably [609] brilliant in the expression of her eyes. By a little after 6 the dinner was over, and before seven we were off again in the order in which we came, not reaching town till past 10. When the dust was not too thick, the procession of 38 carriages, each with two large lamps, had a very fine effect. The day had been splendid, though cold in the morning and evening, and the whole went off very well. The expence is said to have been borne equally by the town of Baden and by the Archduke Anthony, who takes great interest in the meeting, though not so much as the Archduke John. The latter wished to preside the meeting, but the Emperor, who is jealous of his popularity, would not allow him, and the Archduke, in ill humour, went to spend the time of the meeting in Thyrin, which I regret much, as he would certainly have received us all very well."

Monday, 24th Sept. "Spent in the botanical section, working in the Brasilian Museum, and in a third trial of the Augarten dinner—afterwards to the Theater-an-der-Wien, another popular theatre—large and well shaped, but old and shabby looking. The play, *Herr Joseph und Frau Baberl*, à mourir de rire—the greater part in the Vienna patois, and from beginning to end excessively absurd, but very well acted."

Tuesday, 25th Sept. "At 8 in the morning, we started for Laxenburg, where the Emperor had us invited to a fête at his expence. We were about 420, in 88 [610] government, yellow carriages, eilwagens, postwagens and separatwagens, treble-bodied, double-bodied and single-bodied, drawn by above 250 horses, the postillons all in their best uniforms, and the Hofpost-director von Ottenfels and other Post-Officials heading the procession on horseback in full uniform. (I was with Baron Jacquin, the President, in his private open carriage.) We had to drive through immense crowds collected in the streets to see us, the wonderful procession of Naturmenschen, as they called us; and the road was covered with other carriages of persons going to see the fête prepared for us. Arriving at Laxenburg at about ten, we found nearly a hundred open court carriages, char-a-bancs, droschky's and calèches, with the court liveries waiting for us, and accordingly, as soon as we had all alighted, etc, we proceeded, the greater number of us, in these carriages, the remainder on foot, to go round the park under the guidance of M. Riedl, the head gardener and manager. He it was that laid out the grounds, which were originally a thick game forest, but which are now quite an English park. The situation is a perfect flat, but the Baden hills, extending to the Schoenberg mountains, are not far distant, and many very pretty openings are cut to show them in different points of view. At one end of the park is the Ritterburg, a partly ancient, but chiefly modern-antique castle, in an island surrounded by a very pretty piece of water. Here the Imperial standard was hoisted to receive us, and a number of boats, with watermen in full unifornm, were prepared for such of us [611] as might like to go on the water. The Burg itself is beautifully fitted up in the ancient style, but is rather too full of paintings, some

very indifferent, and other ornaments. Ameling's portait of the
Emperor,[28] and two portraits of two of the Empresses, copies of the productions of a Bavarian artist, are very good. In the gardens we saw nothing very remarkable. The Dahlias and, indeed, most of the flowers were
destroyed by the frost of the night before last, but the trees are generally
very fine. An Araucaria, planted in the open ground and covered up
every winter, is now about 15 feet high. Towards three o'clock, we proceeded to the palace, which is, as it were, a merely provisory one, the
Emperor considering that the first thing is to plant, the building can be
done at any time. Here a large tent or temporary room had been
erected—168 ft. by 60 inside, and the side walls at least 9 ft high, and as
it was all perfectly straight and well proportioned, beautifully fitted up,
and elegantly lighted by a number of candelabras and hanging lamps, it
looked very splendid. It was placed against the principal hall of the chateau, through which we entered it, down the perron steps. Count Wurmbrand, the Empress's chamberlain, did the honors and presided at the
central table, Jacquin the President at the right hand one, and Littrow
the secretary at the left hand one. On each side of Count Wurmbrand
were the Presidents of the different sections and myself, the Count having told us that the Empress had desired these places to be reserved for
us. Metternich was on Jacquin's right and the [612] rest were placed
indiscriminately, 75 down each side of each table, in all about 450. The
dinner was provided under the direction of an ancient, retired, celebrated traîteur, at 16 florins (32 shillings) a head, and was of the most
recherché cookery; the wines were served in great profusion, of the
Emperor's own cellar, and every thing was in truly imperial style. The
only thing that was wanting was the Emperor's presence. It was said he
was to have been there, and such is supposed to have been his intention,
as courriers were sent round to the different Archdukes to that effect,
but he found himself indisposed this morning, the orders were contradicted, and the Archdukes could not for etiquette come without him.
(This disappointment was said to be the result of the intrigues of Baron
Stifft, the Court physician, who did what he could to thwart the Association, out of jealousy of some of the principal medical men who formed
part of it.) Prince Metternich's and Count Wurmbrand's families and
others came round the tables to see us, and the steps leading down from
the hall were covered by two or three hundred spectators. Dinner concluded by about half-past seven, when we all returned to town in the
order in which we went out."

Wednesday, 26th Sept. "To the botanical section, where nothing particularly interesting, and then to the third and last general séance. This was opened by reading the minutes of the different sections, the most remarkable that of the Mineralogical section, owing to a proposition of Prince Metternich's. Leopold de Buch told me the story with great [613] enthusiasm. A number of geological maps variously coloured being exhibited, Prince Metternich asked whether the different colours represented the same thing in different maps, and being told that such was not the case but that each author coloured his maps according to his own fancy, he suggested the propriety of an universal language in this respect—that in all geological maps the same colours should represent the same formations—observing that questions of this kind were peculiarly the province of such meetings as this, which might thus be rendered really useful. He therefore proposed, and it was resolved, that M. de Buch be requested to prepare a scheme for colouring geological maps, to be submitted to next year's meeting at Breslau.[29] After the reading the protocols, two excessively stupid papers were read, then Littrow delivered, in a very feeling manner, a discours d'adieu. Stierling of Hamburg returned thanks, and the meeting separated after long-repeated cries of 'Long live the Emperor.' The dinner at the Augarten was much crowded, a number of healths were drunk with much noise, but none with so much enthusiasm as that of the Emperor, the band playing 'Gott erhalte Franz den Kaiser,'[30] which was sung in chorus by the whole company. After dinner to the Burg Theater, where the *Schoehmanlein*, a most amusing but highly absurd play, was well acted, especially by Costenoble."

Thursday, 27th Sept. "To breakfast at Jacquin's; went with him over the botanical gardens, and to Endlicher's to [614] go through his Labiatae. To dinner at Count Mitrowsky's 'Oberst Känzler und President des Comität des Studiums,' where we were forty, all belonging to the Association, and selected from different nationalities. Everything was in very grand style and most recherché. The desert service and ornaments covering the table (a custom then not yet introduced with us), lighted up by between three and four hundred wax candles, looked splendid. Strauss's band[31] was in one gallery, and in another a number of ladies to look at us. On our plates, under our napkins, we found each of us a silver medal, struck from the same dye as the bronze one the town of Vienna gives us, and the here annexed list of the guests, and of the wines handed round[32]—amongst others Gumpold-Kerichen of 1720. Of this, Count Mitrowsky told me that the Archbishop of Baden is always obliged to keep twenty small casks of old date in his cellar, and that this was from the oldest. M. de Mitrowsky is the most aristocratical of all the grandees here. He is said to have cut a man because he called in the morning in boots. He was, however, very civil to us, though proud of the fête he was giving us. The dinner was, indeed, the most brilliant and best got up one I have ever been at in any country. After it was over, went out to a small party at the Hammers' to take leave."

Friday, 28th Sept. "The whole morning (eight hours) at the Brasilian Museum, describing Pohl's Brasilian Hyptises; then to a grand dinner given by Prince Metternich to [615] forty of us. It was splendidly served, but not perhaps with quite as much *recherche* as Count Mitrowsky's. The Princess and her mother, Countess Zichy, dined with us, and were très aimables, as well as the Prince. The dinner being at the unusually late hour of 5, was not over in time enough to go to the play after it."

Saturday, 29th Sept. "A few hours early at the Brasilian Museum at Pohl's Hyptises, then with Pohl to the Imperial private garden adjoining the palace in town. It has extensive hot-houses, and a good collection of plants, but nothing remarkable. The Emperor used to work in it an hour or two daily, but now seldom goes into it. Leave-taking calls and packed up a number of specimens given for my herbarium, and out to dinner at Baron Hügel's place at Hietzing, where I was received by the Baroness his mother (he himself being as abovementioned in India), his brother and sister and her future husband Count Hardenberg, and two or three other gentlemen, all very civil and making much of me—of course a very pleasant dinner, thus closing my most enjoyable visit to Vienna, which I left at half-past nine in the evening for Munich by the Inspruck Eilwagen."

Sunday, 30th Sept. "Stopped to breakfast at Molk, and to sup at night at Linz—the road all the way beautiful, with splendid views of the hills on the other side of the Danube [616] on our right, and the mountains on the left. The day was very fine, and I was in the cabriolet, so that altogether this was a delightful day's journey."

Monday 1st Oct. "By daybreak we were at the foot of the Salzburg Alps, and rising gradually through a broken, varied and beautiful country, arrived at Salzburg at twelve o'clock. Here I remained the day, much struck with the picturesque beauty of the situation—though the town did not look inviting to live in, and the theatre, where I saw once more the German *Paul Pry. Er mengt sich in alles* is one of those which is so very bad as to be amusing once in the way, but would be very ennuyant if often visited."

Tuesday, 2d Oct. "All day again in the Eilwagen from six in the morning, gradually descending from the level of Salzburg to the monotonous plain of Munich, where arrived at 11 at night, to find the good hotels full, and at last got only a miserable bed in the Goldene Kreutz.

"Next morning, succeeded in getting good accomodation at the Hirsch, where I remained four days, chiefly with botanists. Martius, a most gentlemanly and amiable man, met me with great empressement. Dined with him to meet Hugo Mohl, Zuccarini and Schultes, went over the library, the botanical garden, etc, with him, and spent the two evenings when there was no theatre in his herbarium, selecting Labiatae, etc. In this town of 80,000 inhabitants, even in the present fête time, they cannot keep up theatrical representations every night, beer drinking being the chief [617] amusement both of the rich and poor. Spent one morning with Zuccarini and his long coat at the library, going over Brasilian Labiatae, and breakfasted another morning with Schultes and his Labiatae—both intelligent and well informed men, and very attentive to me, notwithstanding the quantity of beer they daily swallow down in true Bavarian style."

Saturday, 6th Oct. "My last day here, called on the veteran Oken, whom I found a little old man, as shabby and dirty as could well be, but very civil to me. Packed up and sent off a box of botanical treasures given or lent to me here (I had already sent one from Vienna), and in the afternoon, to see the preparations for the Octoberfest in the Theresien Wiede, a large burnt up meadow with booths, mats de cocagne, etc, and already about a thousand persons walking about or drinking beer. The fête itself is put off for a few days to await the expected arrival of a Greek deputation. The evening at Martius's to take leave, looking through his Medicago's, etc, to the last."

Sunday, 7th Oct. "Left Munich at six in the morning, in the eilwagen for the Rhine—four hours in the afternoon at the large, dull town of Augsburg, where, it being now fair time, there is more animation than usual, the peasant women many of them very pretty and their variety of dress curious. Monday, 8th, at four in the morning, an hour's stoppage at Ulm to exchange our Bavarian carriage and conducteur for Wurtemberg ones, the blue postillons for yellow, and the blue and white posts for black and brick red, [618] arriving at four in the morning of Tuesday 9th at Carlsruhe, where spent the day in this singular town, with eighteen straight drives in the forest and fourteen streets all radiating from the central palace. In the castle garden observed many rare trees of remarkably fine growth, the largest Sophora Japonica I ever saw—also very fine specimens of Ginkgo, of Liquidambar, Quercus fastigiata, Q. aegylops, etc, several American Oaks, Gleditsias, Platanus, a very fine bush of Zanthoxylum fraxinifolium, etc, and the native trees also of a remarkably fine growth. After dinner, a beautiful walk through the woods and to the hills at the east of the town, and afterwards to the play. Not a large theatre, but one of the most elegant I have seen—good Orchestra and Chorus, as usual in Germany, but the chorus girls younger and prettier than they usually are. In *Fra Diavolo*, Haizinger acted the part, and Mde Fischer, from the Josephstadt Theater of Vienna, that of Zerlina, Mde Haizinger, as the English lady, very amusing, and the whole pleased me more than that opera had done yet."

Wednesday, 10th Oct. "Leaving Carlsruhe at half past six, and passing only within sight of Heidelberg, had the whole afternoon and evening at Mannheim—straight, right-angled streets, with a palace, an old red brick mass of buildings, as dreary and desolate-looking as can be imagined, with a garden containing some fine trees, but deserted and abandoned looking—in short, I cannot see anything to justify Mannheim's reputation for beauty—and no theatre tonight."

[619]Thursday, 11th Oct. "At ½ past 7 again in the Eilwagen, and through the Palatinate, arriving at Mainz in the afternoon, in time to dine and go to the play, in the same dark, dismal theatre where I was two years ago, and by chance in the same box, and, like on that occasion, by the side of a very entertaining girl, the daughter of a Colonel. A good farce, in which Cornelius and Döring acted well, and a most laughable comic ballet."

Friday, 12th. "Down the Rhine in the small steamboat to Cologne, and Saturday 13th, by *extrapost* to Aix la Chapelle. I had too much luggage for the Prussian *Schnellpost*, and no time to wait for it to come after me by the *Fahrpost*, but posting—or as they call it by extrapost—you always find carriages—small calèches—but have to change every stage, and they are not always good. The heavy rains of last night had made the roads so heavy that I was glad soon to get on the pavé, fatiguing on the road. At Aix la Chapelle the hotels good, and for the first time these two months I had the enjoyment of sleeping in a bed in which I could turn and stretch without finding myself quite uncovered."

Sunday, 14th. "Left Aix la Chapelle at 9 in the morning in the coupé of the Belgian diligence, travelling slowly on paved roads through a beautiful country; stopped to dinner at Liège, and arrived at Brussels at 8 in the morning of Monday, 15th. To the botanical garden, a non-public day, but strangers admitted on payment of 15 centimes (3d). The hot and green houses are as I had heard, splendid for the country, but there is not money enough to keep up the collection of plants as it ought to be. [620] The garden belongs to a Society who are aided by 6000 florins (£500) from Government, and as much from the town annually, but as there are 9000 florins a year interest to pay on money borrowed for building, there remain but 3000 fl. for current expences, so they are obliged to sell plants, the contributions from the members themselves being but very small. Only eight men are kept, and besides the immense extent of glass, there are about eighteen acres of garden. But little of this is laid out botanically, and that little not with much taste, notwithstanding the beautiful situation they had to work upon. All the contrivances for raising water, etc, are very good, and the gardener appears zealous and careful, but the botanists are all gone with the Dutch. This botanical garden was in the centre of the field of battle in September 1830.[33] The Dutch were there stationed and during four days kept up a continual exchange of firing with the inhabitants of the town below—but each party kept at so cautious a distance from the other that, though half the glass of the houses was broken and the garden was full of troops, there were but two men killed during the whole time. Brussels is more animated than I had expected, although the chambers are not now sitting. There are, it is true, a great many empty houses, but there is also a great deal of building going on. The people seem all eager for war, and make a great bustle in their preparations—soldiers, gun-carriages, ammunition, waggons, etc, are marching or driving about in every direction, and plenty of argumentation and political talking going on—but au reste the town is quiet. At the reading room, got a sight of the English papers for [621] the first time since Hamburgh, and in the evening at the play, a rather stupid, long melodrame, L'Abbaye aux bois, and a pretty good, but excessively ridiculous comic ballet."

Tuesday, 16th Oct. "Walked out to the Royal country seat, Lachen, but all I could see was the front elevation of the Palace—no admission to the grounds in this land of liberty. It is only in barbarous, despotic countries, such as Prussia, Austria, Denmark, Bavaria, etc, that all the Imperial, Royal, Grand Ducal, Electoral, etc, parks are open to the public. Under a Citizen King,[34] all is as aristocratically closed as the closest private estate. However in walking out there, I had the satisfaction of passing the young Queen, who was driving into town, and in the afternoon I saw the King, reviewing a batallion of infantry on its way to the frontier—a set of raw recruits, who have not yet learnt even to march together. They defiled before the King quite *à la debandade*. A pretty prospect His Majesty has before him, the having to defend his throne with a set of fellows who will swagger away now, but when it comes to the fighting, they have not the power, nor the desire, to make use of any weapons but their legs. In the evening to the play, and at 10 o'clock in the Calais diligence. Some hours delay the next afternoon at Lille, arriving at Calais at two in the afternoon of Friday afternoon—a tedious afternoon there, and a poor performance at the theatre—crossed over the next morning, with what was then reckoned a good passage of three hours to Dover—again there to the play before the London mail started, which landed me in the smoky, foggy metropolis at 6 in the morning."

[622]Saturday, 20th Oct. My mother and sister all well at home. At the Horticultural Society, parcels of plants and botanical letters awaiting for me from Fischer of Petersburgh, Besser of Podolia, Brydges from Valparaiso, Schlechtendahl of Halle, Gussone of Naples, etc. At Lincoln's Inn, found I was two days too late to secure some good briefs. However I set to work steadily, and for the next five or six weeks was every day some hours at Lincoln's Inn, either at Koe's chambers, working at equity, bills, answers, opinions, etc, or in my wig and gown showing myself in Court—generally an hour's botany before breakfast in the morning, and two or three hours in the evening, when not engaged at dinners, etc—attending also in the afternoon, before going home, to Horticultural Society business. Towards the end of November, however, letters came from my sister de Chesnel, from Montpellier, with the sad news of her husband's cruel desertion, carrying off her little boy, and leaving her destitute and in the greatest distress,[35] making it almost necessary for my mother to go to her. This was a severe trial for my mother at her age, having thought herself settled for the remainder of her life, now to undertake so long a journey; however she determined to go, and accordingly in the afternoon of the 2d Decr, I started with her; posting to Dover, crossed over to Calais early in the morning, hired a carriage at Regnolles, and continued posting night and day, stopping only 24 hours at Paris, and thence on to Chalons, leaving the carriage there, [623] and down the Saone by steamboat to Lyons. Here the Lajards (Mad Lajard my old flame Emma Dax) were most attentive, and our friends, two young Calvières, going down the Rhone in the steamer the next morning, took charge of my mother, and I returned to Chalons, posted thence night and day to Calais, stopping only another 24 hours at Paris, and reaching London at 7 in the morning of the 17th Decr.

Here I found great excitement with the elections. I had been much pressed to go down to vote for South Hampshire by intimate friends belonging to both parties, and, as of the four candidates I thought one of each party were the two best, I thought I might be excused voting at all. However the Committees urged me so strongly to go that I took the Portsmouth mail that night—went to my friend Mr Goodrich's, who drove me over to my polling place at Fareham, where I voted for Lord Palmerston and one of the Conservatives;[36] called to see such of our old friends who were still in the Dock Yard, dined with Goodrich and returned to town by the next night coach—the outside loaded with tipsy sailors and women they had picked up who had stuck to them, and we had all night the pleasure of hearing the language of the last degree of depravity and grossness. In town, I had again only one day—to vote for Middlesex—to settle much business connected with my Uncle's affairs—to get my friend Russell to hold a consent brief for me—and in the afternoon of the 21st started with my sister Sarah to spend Christmas with her friends, the Scudamores, in Herefordshire. Stopped to sleep at Oxford, and arrived at Kentchurch late in the evening of the 22.

12

Marriage; and Botany at Last, 1833–34

[624] The year 1833 finally settled the course of my future life. I married, and after some months, finding that there was little likelihood of our having any family, that my wife's wishes were very moderate, that our income was sufficient to enable us to live comfortably, though not luxuriously, and that I need not toil for our support, I determined to give up the law, and to devote myself entirely to botany.

The year began well for me. I had been spending the Christmas with my sister at her friends, the Scudamores', at Kentchurch in Herefordshire, on the borders of Monmouthshire, an old but recently almost rebuilt manor-house which had been in the family since the days of Owen Glendower,[1] with whom they had been connected. A large deer-park in a beautiful situation in the valley of the Monnow and rising up the side of Garway hill, but at that time rather out of the way of the world. The nearest post-offices, the nearest butchers, etc, were at Hereford or Abergavenny, each about fourteen miles distant—the only public communication with which was a market cart twice a week and a coach three times a week. This coach left the Scudamores' letter bag at an inn two and a half miles from Kentchurch, and also their supply of such provisions as they did not [625] raise on the estate, and as the coach left Hereford for Abergavenny about an hour before the mailcoach from London came in, the London letters were often three or four days in reaching Kentchurch. The road to the two towns was tolerably fair, and they could be reached in the Scudamores' carriage in two hours, but there were four turnpikes to pay going to Hereford, five going to Abergavenny, and one of the trusts being wholly insolvent, some miles of the road were maintained at the expence of the parish. The legal administration of the parishes was in a primitive state—very few magistrates for the petty sessions, and some of them wholly incompetent; of the parish overseers and road surveyors, two at least could neither read nor write, and religious matters were not much better off. The Welsh parson who held Kentchurch and another parish could just mumble through two or three services on a Sunday, without ever troubling himself about his parishioners on other days; if he was asked to dinner at the Court, as soon as dinner was over, he liked to adjourn, not to the drawing-room, but to the housekeeper's room. Parochial schools were few and far between, and the schoolmasters or mistresses of a very inferior description, and most of the surrounding parishes—small and numerous on the Herefordshire side, few and very large in the wild [626] but beautiful hilly country down the Monnow to Monmouth—were in the same neglected state. All that has, however, since that time undergone a great alteration. Post Offices, Railroads and other modern improvements have civilised the country, though perhaps at the expense of some enjoyments, whilst a better class of clergymen, schoolmasters, etc, have come in, with improved churches and schoolhouses.

The Christmas party at Kentchurch consisted of Col and Mrs Scudamore and her father, Sir Harford Jones Brydges and his son and daughter[2]—and, for a couple of days, Mr Clive of Whitfield, M.P. for Hereford. Spent the time very pleasantly, and on New Year's day 1833, proposed to, and was accepted by, Miss Brydges. It was settled, however, that the wedding was not to take place till April, after the expiration of the mourning for the late Lady Brydges.

(I had gone thus far when, seeing that my wife's failing health rendered it very unlikely she would take any interest in these notes, which at first amused her, and all others for whom I wrote them being now dead and gone, I ceased writing them, in order to interfere as little as possible with the *Genera Plantarum*, of which I was just beginning the Monocotyledons. If, since these are published, I occasionally take to these Memoranda again,[3] it is [627] simply from a certain pleasure I feel in living over again, as it were, in recollection, the happy times of fifty years back.)

We (my sister and myself) remained about ten days more with the Scudamores, spending two days at Mr Clive's at Whitfield, from whence we went a large party to the Hereford County Ball. On the 9th and 10th returned to town (stopping to sleep at Cheltenham) and resumed pretty close attendance at Lincoln's Inn, generally in Koe's chambers, working still as a pupil, drawing bills, etc, but sometimes sitting in court in my wig and gown, or reading in my own chambers, continuing, however, in the mornings my botanical pursuits—distributed and sent abroad to various correspondents duplicate specimens, and worked hard at Labiatae. Received from Auguste St Hilaire the whole of his fine collection of Brasilian Labiatae, often with numerous duplicates, which [I] described and scrupulously returned the whole, he promising to send me a compleat set (which he never did); spent a morning at Burchell's, looking over his Cape Labiatae, of which got a set—also his Cape Orchideae for Lindley—his Brasilian ones never yet unpacked.[4] The evenings often out at dinner, etc, and in the mornings, sometimes interrupted law to attend [628] Linnean Council, or on Hort. Soc. business—also having got possession of my Uncle's house in Queen Square Place, had to make arrangements for the alterations in the house, previous to moving there. The Brydges also came to town for a fortnight, and I was often with them—though generally only after my morning at Lincoln's Inn—but on one of these occasional absences, I lost an intending client. In March went down for a couple of days (including a Sunday) to the Nightingales' beautiful place at Embley, near Romsey; they are great friends of the Brydges, and Mrs Nightingale, knowing that I was engaged to Miss B., invited me down to meet her—the first of many most agreeable visits I have paid to this place.[5]—Florence Nightingale and her sister were then quite little girls.

Sunday, 24th March, left town to spend the fortnight at Kentchurch necessary to get my marriage licence, and sleeping at Witney, arrived there on the Monday. I had been expected on the Saturday, but such was the state of affairs of the post Office then that a letter posted in town on the Thursday never reached Kentchurch till after my arrival on Monday. Before leaving town, I was able to send off to the printers a batch of my Labiatae, including Hyptises—and I took down with me to Kentchurch matter for continuing the work, to which, however, I did not do much. On the 9th April, Countess Ludolf and my sister Sarah came down to be present at my marriage, and on the 11th we were married in Kentchurch [629] Church—the only persons present besides the Brydges, the Scudamores, Css Ludolf and my sister, being Mr and Col Clive from Whitfield and Mr (afterwards Dr) Sewell, who married us— all very quiet—no display of presents, which was not yet the fashion— and after the breakfast, my wife and myself posted to Sir Harford's place, Boultibrooke, near Presteign, which he lent us for the "honeymoon." Here we spent nine or ten days, enjoying the beautiful country when weather permitted, but term time calling me to town, we left on the 20th, spending a couple of days on our way at Mr Andrew Knight's at Downton Castle, where were only the Knights themselves and some of their connections, old Mr Knight in good health and spirits— absorbed in pears and potatoes. He went over his garden with me, "which is certainly in very bad order, notwithstanding all the experiments he carries on. His peaches are very fine, but in general, to an ordinary observer, his garden does not do much credit to the President of the Horticultural Society."[6] After church (Sunday 21st), enjoyed much the walk through the beautiful grounds. Amongst those here was the Knight's eldest daughter, Mrs Stackhouse Acton, with whom laid the foundations of a long and lasting intimacy[7]—her husband Mr Stackhouse "has for many years lost the use of all his limbs from creeping paralysis, and is quite blind, so that he is obliged to lie all day on his couch and to be always fed, but he is remarkably cheerful and has a well stored mind. He was in Russia in his [630] younger days, so that we had a good deal of conversation about common friends."

Left Downton Castle on Monday 22d, and stopping at Oxford to sleep, breakfasted the next morning with Mr Sewell, at his rooms in Exeter College, walked with him over Magdalen and Christchurch meadows, and went on to town in the afternoon, settling for the present in Manchester Street. Here spent rather more than three months, very busy in the endeavour to combine law, botany and society. I generally spent the best part of the day, and often the evening, at Lincoln's Inn, either in Koe's chambers, equity, drawing, or reading in my own chambers, or sitting in Court in my wig and gown. In botany I worked at home before breakfast, and often till late in the evening—sometimes also for an hour or two at the Horticultural Society's rooms before going to Lincoln's Inn; finished the 2d part of my *Labiatarum Genera et Species*, which was published in the end of June, and corrected the last proofs of the 3d part before leaving town at the end of July; worked up also Royle's Sileneae;[8] distributed duplicates of Douglas's Californian, etc, plants; and [worked] at some minor botanical papers. I had, however, during these three months various interruptions. In Society we gave up all idea of keeping up with a few great people I had become acquainted with, as that would have led us to more expence than I could afford, but saw much of our own, more intimate, friends, dining out very frequently, and having often small parties to dinner at home. Sir Harford was in town for some weeks, [631] my sister Sarah was staying at Countess Ludolf's—and we were necessarily much with both. We went down to Salden in Buckinghamshire to stay a day with our friends the Carrs on the 25th June, leaving my wife in town, chiefly with her father. I went down for a couple of days with Lindley and Royle to attend the meeting of the British Association at Cambridge, where my friend Richard Russell had prepared rooms for me in Caius College, of which he was[§] a Fellow.

Arriving at 8 in the evening, went to the general meeting in the Senate House, which was numerously attended, the proceedings rather differently conducted from what I had seen in the two German meetings I had attended. When I went in, "Mr Taylor was reading a geological report,[9] Sedgwick in the chair, and near him were sitting the most distinguished of the scientific men assembled, amongst whom I observed Buckland, Murchison and Greenough, Geologists; Herschel, Airey, Dalton, Brewster, Rennie, Brunel, Davies-Gilbert, Whewell, etc. Behind them, a splendid array of ladies, and in front, many hundred men, collegians and foreigners. After the paper was read, a discussion arose in which, besides the above-mentioned geologists, Phillips of York and others took part, and occupied till past 11, when the meeting broke up."

Wednesday, 26th. "To a grand breakfast at Corpus College, where we were about 200—and with Lindley and Royle to their rooms in the splendid new buildings of St Johns[10]—then to the Natural History section—not many botanists. Of those I knew [I] saw (besides Lindley and Royle) Henslow, Burchell, Agardh, [632] Edward Forster, Sabine, D. Don, etc, and amongst Zoologists, Col Sykes, Curtis, Dr Jennings, Gray of the British Museum, etc. Here papers chiefly Zoological were read till 1, when went to the general meeting. Report on Mathematics by Dr Peacock, an interesting paper on physiological Botany by Lindley, and an interminable one on hydraulic Architecture by Rennie.[11] At 4, to a grand dinner in Trinity Hall, where we were about 400. Besides the people mentioned above, I observed Lords Fitzwilliam, Northampton, Cavendish, Adair, etc, Mr Spring Rice and others, and at the table near me, Profr Ritchie, Dr Daubeny, Mr Jordan, etc. The dinner was excellent, toasts drank with great noise, but none so well received as Herschell's.[12] At 8 left the hall, and after taking coffee in the Senate House, adjourned to our several sections. In the Natural History section, the topics were almost entirely Zoological." Here also I was requested to prepare a report on Systematic Botany for the next meeting of the Association, which, however, I never presented till forty years later at the meeting at Belfast.[13] "A little after 10, went to see the fireworks to be let off from the banks of the Cam just opposite the lawn of King's, where we were invited to see them, but from a caprice of Thackeray, the Provost, the immense crowd that gathered at the gate were at first let in slowly, one by one, and then the gate was shut entirely; the crowd got very thick, the ladies fainting, etc, and after waiting till past 11, all that Sedgwick could obtain for us was an entrance by the stable gate, which as soon as opened, we kept open, and rushed in with or [633] without tickets. The fireworks were half over, but what we did see were very good—bright and without failures, the evening very beautiful, although the moon too bright. After they were over, returned to Caius College with Russell, had my things taken to the Bull, and at a little before 1, left in the mail, and arrived in town early in the morning of the 27th."

Some time was taken up by discussion with Bowring as my Uncle's Executor. I succeeded in saving some two or three thousand pounds which he was giving up from neglecting to look into the deed of Lanark Company, in which my Uncle had invested £10,000; but for the publication of the complete edition of Mr Bentham's works, he had left to Bowring the uncontrouled disposal of an indefinite sum—and by expensive stereotyping and the large sums paid to editors,[14] the whole publication resulted in a dead loss of between five and six thousand pounds.

In May, I went out of the Linnean Council, but the Horticultural Society's affairs occasioned frequent interruptions to my law duties. We had three Exhibitions at the Garden, all three successful and well attended, but giving much trouble in their organising, which mostly fell upon Lindley, but also took up much of my time. During this period, I had much pleasure in becoming acquainted with Dr Torrey of New York, who was over here for two or three weeks. We had him to meet a few friends at dinner, and I saw him occasionally at the Horticultural [634]

Rooms or at his own lodgings, giving him Californian and South of France plants, and receiving North American ones from him.

In the end of July, after winding up as much as possible my own private affairs and those of the Horticultural Society, undertook a journey to the South of France, chiefly for the purpose of introducing my wife to my mother and elder sister, and assisting the latter in her family arrangements. Taking our caleche, which proved a very comfortable travelling carriage, we embarked at the Tower stairs in the evening of the 31st July for Calais, where the following morning was taken up with customhouse clearing, etc, and in the afternoon, started post for Paris—the slowest posting of any road in France, and from the crowds of English just now going abroad, the horses tired and lazy—stopped to sleep at Montreuil and Beauvais, and arrived at Paris at the Hotel Windsor at ½ past 4 on the 3d August. Here we remained four days—chiefly showing the lions to my wife. On the Sunday, after attending at the Ambassador's chapel, went out to the "grandes eaux" at Versailles. On the Monday, I went to the meeting of the Academie des Sciences at the Institut, and the following day, Adolphe Brongniart went with us over the Ménageries and galleries at the Jardin des Plantes, and in the evening of Wednesday, 7th, started for Montpellier, travelling all night the first night, and generally lying by for a few hours in the middle of each day on account of the great heat. Instead of the usual road by Lyons which I knew so well, we determined to go straight through the centre of France, although [635] there were no post horses the whole way—by Nevers, Moulins, Clermont, St Chely to Mende—Clermont beautifully situated but inside wretchedly filthy. At Mende, the greater part of the day with Mr Prost, the botanical Post Office director, whom I found as active as when I was with him ten years before;[15] gave him some plants I had brought with me. From Mende, we were obliged to take voiturin horses, and had to stop to sleep twice, at Florac and Anduze—the latter a rich, silk-producing town, where we were taken to what was said to be the best hotel, but proved the most wretched—the bugs swarmed in the furniture (beds, tables, chairs, etc), on the walls, worse than in any place I ever was in, except perhaps the valley of Andorra, and Calatifima in Sicily—and arrived at length in the afternoon of Friday 16th Augt at Restinclières—where found my mother very well, my niece Adèle much improved—my sister very anxious, and suffering from fear.

Barring two or three excursions, we remained with my sister at Restinclières or at the Hotel du Midi at Montpellier till the beginning of

November. In her tedious and painful lawsuit with her husband, my sister, with the assistance of several kind and excellent Montpellier friends, had been successful in every particular. The courts, both at première instance and on appeal, had given her the exclusive control over her property, and the sole guardianship and custody of both her children. The daughter was with her, but M. de Chesnel, when he left her last autumn, had carried off the boy, whom he refused to give up. They were now, as we learned, at Toulouse, and as a means of [636] getting hold of the boy, our lawyers advised that I should get M. de C. arrested for the heavy debt he owed me. I determined, therefore, to go myself to Toulouse, and Mrs B. accompanied me. Provided with the necessary papers for procuring the arrest, we left Montpellier on the 3d Sept. and, posting all night, arrived at Toulouse early on the 4th, and with the assistance of our excellent friend Dr Russell, put the papers at once into the hands of legal officials, but innumerable difficulties occurred. At first, M. de C. could not be found, and when his residence was ascertained, he took care to remain within doors except on Sundays. I had also great difficulty in getting good legal advice, the lawyers being mostly absent during this vacation time, so that after waiting till the 26th, and taking all possible steps, we had to leave Toulouse without having really effected§ any thing. During this time, we were much with Dr Russell. The Courtois (bankers) also gave us a dinner party, and lent us their box at the theatre, of which we availed ourselves two or three times. We also spent two nights and the intervening Sunday at Montauban, where I took my wife to see the Maison Collet, where we spent 13 months in 1818–19, and the neighbouring village and mill of Albarèdes, the scene of my first regular herborisations, where I began collecting and drying specimens for my herbarium. The weather, as well as the surrounding country beautiful, and the promenade in the afternoon crowded, the band of the regiment in garrison playing, and the elegance of the still picturesque dresses, and the real beauty of the grisettes made it a very gay scene. During this stay at Toulouse, I had no opportunity of seeing any botanist. We went once to the Botanic [637] Garden, which was in better order than when I saw it last as to weeds, but the collection of plants is poor and badly named. Left Toulouse in the afternoon of the 26th, and stopping to sleep at Carcassone and Pezenas, got back to Restinclières on the 28th.

Our next excursion was intended to be to Genoa and the Riviera, for which we started on the 9th Oct. Staid half a day at Nîmes to show Sarah the Antiquities, and two nights at Avignon. Failed in meeting my friend Requien, but found Audibert at his house—well, hearty and zealous as usual. We took advantage of the intervening day to visit Vaucluse, a much easier excursion than it used to be, and got an excellent dinner at the new Hotel Petrarque. Went on on the 12th to Aix, on Sunday the 13th to Marseilles, where in the beautiful afternoon and evening, "the Allée de Meilhac was crowded, as indeed every street in the town, all in their Sunday's best, enjoying themselves, altogether a busy and a merry scene, without the disgusting filth and drunkenness on similar occasions in our own country." The next day we took a boat round to the mouth of the Huveaune and walked up to the Chateau Borely,[16] "went over this princely palace, originally built by a rich merchant for his mistress but, dying before it was made over to her, it devolved on his children, and is now in the possession of his son in law, M. de Panisse. The rooms are splendidly furnished, and there are many very valuable pictures, especially some Murillos and Vandykes. The view from the terrace of the first floor is the finest that can be conceived." On the 15th, walked up to [638] "the botanical garden, about a mile from the town, a small garden, and a very poor collection, with some trees which would be fine if they were not so miserably hacked, to torture them into the artificial form they give to their mulberries and olives." Met in the town our old friends the Partouneaux's, who were on their way from their country house near here to pay a visit. My great friend Tonin staid to dine with us, and the following day we "drove out to Montredon, rather a collection of *Bastides* than a village, about five miles from Marseilles on the sea coast, to General Partouneaux's country house in the midst of a fine wood at the foot of the wild, arid rocks of Montredon, a singular but very beautiful situation, very characteristic of the country. Here spent a happy morning with Madame Partouneaux, who is still the same kind and excellent person she always was. The General is getting rather old and fidgetty, but they are living happily and comfortably, spending alternately a few months here, at Menton, and at Foseovitz, their estate near Nice."

From Marseilles, we had intended going by steam to Genoa, and I had actually taken our places in the steamboat of the 16th and gone through the passport and other formalities, when a letter from my sister obliged us at once to go back to Montpellier, forfeiting part of the fares I had paid. A M. Parmentier had made a very advantageous offer for the purchase of the estate of Restinclières, to which my sister had sent a written acceptation, which I signed as guarantor before I left Montpellier the other day, but now it appeared there were a number of formalities which required immediate attention, and my sister's legal adviser, M. Charles Durand, was absent [639] for his holiday, at Rodez. We therefore returned at once to Montpellier (stopping to sleep at Aix and Nimes), and settled to go to Rodez to see M. Durand. There is no post road there, so I took the coupé of the diligence, Sarah having preferred going with me and roughing it to waiting for me at Restinclières. We started in the morning of the 20th—had a couple of hours and a disgusting bourgeois table d'hote dinner at the prettily situated town of Lodève, then all night crossing the bare, dreary, raised rocky plateau of the Larzac—had to wait nearly the whole day in the prettily situated town of Milhaud, on the banks of the Tarn, which runs in a deep valley like many others in these raised plateaus of central France, and in the morning of the 23d ascended from the valley of the Aveyron to the town of Rodez, which is small and generally ill-built, but in a pretty country, and the tower of the Cathedral is richly and beautifully ornamented. Here I soon settled matters with M. Durand, but we were detained two days before we could get places in the diligence, and in these two days the south wind was so very violent that we were obliged to remain in doors at the hotel. In the evening of the 25th, left Rodez, and again two nights on the road, but with only a short stoppage at Milhaud, and crossing the dreary Larzac by day instead of by night, arrived at Montpellier early in the morning of the 27th. Detained a few days at Restinclières, awaiting the arrival at Montpellier of M. Durand and M. Parmentier, then a few days at the Hotel du Midi (where my mother and sister joined us), settling all the details of the sale with some difficulties, and at length definitively signed the agreement on [640] the 8th Novr, and started the same afternoon on our return home. During this stay at Montpellier, I did nothing in botany, except spending one morning at the Jardin des Plantes, breakfasting with Delile and going with him over the garden, which he keeps in fair order, but offers nothing much noteworthy.

Leaving Montpellier on the 8th, stopped to sleep at Nimes, and the next morning to Avignon; here we staid the rest of the day, and got on the next as far as Montelimart, the bitter cold *vent de bize* so very violent that we had not courage to face it more than these few hours. It abated fortunately on the third day. We stopped two nights at Lyons, spending the intervening day in shopping and visiting the botanic garden in a dense fog, and dining at the Lajards'. Madame Lajard (my old flame, Emma Dax) very blooming, and much happier with her good husband and two fine (spoiled) children than she ever would have been with me.

Proceeding by Chalons and Auxerre, arrived at Paris at the Hotel Mirabeau in the evening of the 19th Nov. Here we remained a week, during
which I was three or four mornings at the Jardin des Plantes with
Adrien de Jussieu, Adolphe Brongniart, etc, meeting also Jean Gay,[17] or
at Delessert's herbarium with Guillemin and Perrottet. With Belanger
went over and named his Persian and Indian Labiatae, in the expectation of getting a set, but he finally excused himself as having few if any
duplicates, and much later when he offered me a set, it was under conditions which I could not accept.[18] From Boué, I purchased two complete sets of his Sinai and Syrian plants, [641] verified Kunth's and other
Salvias in the Museum herbarium, and it was also on this occasion, I
believe, rather than in 1831, that A. de Jussieu introduced me to his venerable father, Antoine Laurent. I have lost the original notes made on
this interview, but I well recollect the kind and affable manner in which
he received me. Nearly blind himself, he had a specimen of Salvia I
wished to verify in his herbarium got out for my inspection, and [he]
gave me much good advice on the prosecution of my botanical studies;
he especially insisted on the importance of well studying species in
order to form good ideas of genera.

We necessarily spent much of the week in sight-seeing and shopping,
and went several evenings to the play—to the Français, where saw Mlle
Mars in *Les Enfans d'Edouard*; "she is grown fat, and looks old, but is still
remarkably good; the house was crowded." At the Gymnase, Made Volnys (Léontine Fay), who, "though not quite so pretty as she was, is yet a
very charming actress." At the Italian Opera, the *Gazza Ladra* exceedingly well got up; Grisi as Ninetta, Ivanhoff as Fabricio, and Tamburini
as Fernando. At the Grand Opera, the *Muette de Portici* noisy as usual,
and the brilliancy of the dresses much gone off, but still a very good
opera. Left Paris in the morning of the 27th Nov., stopping to sleep at
Grandvilliers and Montreuil; kept nearly two days at Calais by the high
wind; crossed to Dover on the 1st Decr in a four hours' passage, and on
the 2d posted up to London, where my sister Sarah met us at dinner at
our house in Gloucester Street, she still staying with Countess Ludolf at
Norwood, where she returned after dinner.

[642]It now became absolutely necessary for me to fix my choice for
my future career between law and botany; the experience of the last season had shown how vain it would be to attempt to continue the combining the two with any chance of ultimate real success in either. My
friends strongly advised me to stick to the law, which certainly had
some attractions for me. I got much interested in the unravelling of intri-

cate complications in cases of successions, or of knotty legal questions, the draughts of bills, etc, and legal opinions I drew up for my master Mr Koe met with his full approbation, and he often adopted them without alteration, and I felt that I had abilities for the work, which might ultimately be the means of my securing a good income as equity draftsman and conveyancer; but I should first have to get through a more or less lengthened period of tedious waiting with little to do, the last season had only brought me two insignificant consent briefs, and I lost two briefs at least by non-attendance at chambers at times when I ought to have been there—and in the end I never could have risen to distinction. As a barrister I was certain to fail, owing to my constitutional inability to speak well and, although I flattered myself that I had great powers when I had time to mature my thoughts, yet I entirely failed in the readiness to come to a right conclusion, which is so essential for judicial purposes. In botany, on the other hand, I had already made for myself a name, at least on the Continent, and [643] was being well received by naturalists in my own country. It is true that there was yet no prospect of deriving any pecuniary profit; all was direct expenditure, but I already saw that there was very little chance of our having any family to support, my income, though not large, was sufficient to maintain us in comfort in that moderate sphere in which my wife showed herself as contented, as I was myself, and taking all these circumstances into consideration, I had already, before we went abroad, almost determined to give up law for botany; and now, on our return, further communications with foreign correspondents, the number of botanical works and specimens which I found waiting for me on my reaching home, finally decided the question, and I immediately gave up my chambers, refused a couple of briefs which were offered me, sold my technical law books, gave away my wig and gown, and determined on adopting botany as the great business of my future life, a determination which I never, during the long period of my subsequent career, had on any occasion any reason to repent of.

The three weeks that intervened between this and Christmas were spent chiefly in botany, working hard at my Labiatae, and sorting, etc, the plants received during my absence or brought with me from Paris; prepared also and sent to press, for the Horticultural *Transactions*, a paper on some of Douglas's plants.[19] Some time taken up also with the Horticultural business meetings of the Society, and of the Council. My sister Sarah [was] still staying with Countess Ludolf at Norwood, but came several times to see [644] us, and we drove out once to see them there, and on the 23d we started to spend Christmas with the Scud-amores in Herefordshire, stopping to sleep at Northleach and arrived at Kentchurch on the 24th, meeting there, besides the Scudamores, my wife's father and brother. The last day of the year we went with the Scudamores to Mr Clive's at Whitfield to attend the Hereford ball, the weather generally wet, though not cold.

1834

After a most enjoyable three or four weeks' Christmas and New Year's visit to the Scudamores, we left them on the 17th Jany and, not a little impeded by the heavy floods which converted the Wye, Severn and other rivers into broad lakes, stopped to sleep at Witney, and got into town in the evening of the 18th. Here, the next six months were devoted chiefly to botany. Besides the ordinary day work, I often got an hour's work before breakfast, and again (when not socially engaged), another hour or so in the evening; finished and published two more parts of my *Labialarum Genera et Species*, which, as I advanced, gave more and more trouble as the materials received from various sources encreased. I also prepared for Wight and Arnott's Flora an account of East Indian Labia-tae, which, however, was never published, the work having stopped with the first volume—the plants, moreover, being all included in my *Labiatarum Genera et Species*. I also [645] worked up a Monograph of Hydrophylleae, which I gave in for the Linnean *Transactions* on the 13th June[20]—sorting and distributing of duplicates and laying in plants in my herbarium also took me up a good deal of time.

On the 30th Jany, we finally moved from Gloucester Street to my late Uncle's house in Queen Square Place, in which I had made considerable necessary alterations, and which we now found exceedingly comfort-able, very quiet, in a rather large garden. Here we had frequently friends to dinner, in small parties, usually limited to ten, rarely twelve—not many foreigners, chiefly M. Marin, who in 1824 when I was in Paris was tutor to young Prince Gagarin, and now superintendent of Prince Gagarin's Industrial Establishments in Russia and on a two or three weeks' visit to England for the purpose of studying English Manufac-tures—M. and Made Dunant of Geneva, M. Dunant a great friend of the De Candolles, very fond of Botany and already owner of an extensive herbarium—Count Jennison, the Bavarian Minister, a most agreable, well informed, gentlemanly man, dined with us frequently—Dr Gillies

from Scotland, two or three times—and we very frequently dined out—
amongst others, at Mr Lawrence the surgeon's, the only medical man
whom Jeremy Bentham would really listen to, and husband of Mrs
Lawrence, one of our first Lady Fellows of the Horticultural Society. In
disgrace with Hospital Officials in his earlier days on account of the radical ideas he introduced in his inaugural Addresses, [646] he afterwards,
in Reform days, got Baroneted, and was father of the present Sir Trevor
Lawrence—then a little boy.[21] Sir Harford and Mr Brydges were a good
deal in town this season, as well as Mr Scudamore, and we were of
course much with them. Mrs Scudamore was for a fortnight an inmate
of our house. On the 25th June, I attended King William's Levee, where I
was presented by Sir Harford Brydges, at the same time as Mr Robert
Phillips of Herefordshire. It was a thin Levee, but the uniforms enlivened the scene. In the throne-room itself, where the Corps Diplomatique
are allowed to remain the whole time, we were passed through so
quickly that I could scarcely see anything. When the Chamberlain
announced my name, he did [it] so inaudibly that the King called out,
"*Mr Who?*" When my name being repeated and I knelt down, the King
put forward the back of his broad, flabby hand, and said in a loud voice,
"*You must kiss it.*" These being all the words his gracious Majesty said to
me, and with the pleasure of having had to pay twenty guineas for my
court dress (which I never used again) was all I got by my presentation.
On the 1st July, my wife and my sister Sarah, with Mrs Scudamore, went
to the grand Musical Festival at Westminster Abbey, for which the lady
had come to town. I could not get a fourth ticket for myself.

The Trades Union Procession of the 21 April had been the cause of
anxiety and uneasiness, but excellent precautions were taken, and a
large show of troops prepared, and whatever may have been the original intention, all went off quietly—the procession was [647] not interfered with, except that they were not admitted en masse at the Home
Office—the petition was not received, and had to be carried out by a
back door.[22] I watched the procession from the Athenaeum—the men
marched orderly by, five abreast at the rate of from 180 to 200 per
minute, the Committees with blue or red scarfs, the others with a bit of
red ribbon in their button holes, all very quiet in the midst of a large
crowd of spectators—the whole taking 2½ hours to go by, giving the
total number nearly 30,000.

§Much time [was] taken up in the course of my legal arrangements
with Bowring about Jeremy Bentham's affairs, and a change in my solicitor. Mr Bramley, the senior partner who had managed for me, died, and

his partner, Mr Cardale, [was] too much of an Irvinite for me to trust him,[23] and I transferred my business to Mr Robert Henry Jones, whom I had known for some years and was a quiet solicitor, who chiefly managed the business of a few gentlemen like myself. I employed him to my great satisfaction so long as he lived, getting accounts regularly settled every Xmas, which I could never do with Bramley and Cardale—and now that I left them, Cardale was furious, threatened legal proceedings, and swelled out his long-standing account enormously—and by advice I found it better to pay at once some fifty pounds more than the proper charge than to undergo any tedious legal proceedings.

[648]The Horticultural Society occupied much of my time. We had three very successful Exhibitions, in fine weather, and very well attended by the upper and paying classes—thus beginning to show clear gains towards the reducing our debt. I had several times to do the honors of the garden to foreigners and others, but to no Royal personages this year,[*] except the Duchess of Kent, who came down with her brother Prince Ferdinand, who is a great horticultural amateur and went over with much interest, and came to our next Exhibition, but the Duchess seemed not to know or care any thing about the matter.

At the Linnean Anniversary Dinner, 24th May, a subscription was proposed for a portrait of Robert Brown, to be taken by a first rate artist and presented by the Society, and from which each subscriber was to have a good line engraving. The proposal was most readily taken up by those present, a certain number were requested to act as a Committee, with Mr Bicheno the Secretary and myself at the head, and to us two the business was ultimately left. After seeing Mr Brown, we agreed with Pickersgill to paint the portrait, which he undertook with great zeal, accepting a reduction from his usual price; and relying upon the apparent readiness of subscribers to come forward, we entrusted Mr Fox with the engraving.[25] All this took time. Mr Bicheno emigrated to New South Wales, and the whole responsibility ultimately devolved upon me; the portrait and engraving were excellent, but upon winding up accounts, they involved me in an ultimate net loss of about £200, which, with [649] a loss of between £15 and £20 on Wallich's portrait,[26] made me thenceforth very shy in supporting or managing portrait testimonials.

---

[*]My pen here came to grief after more than 28 years' constant and exclusive use (Nov. 1883).[24]

Saturday, 31 May. A general meeting of the Zoological Society summoned to determine a point on which the Council of the Society were
divided. I had joined the Society from the first, and although Zoology
was not my department of Science, I felt interested in its progress and
had been asked to join the Council—but I was aware that some of those
whose oversanguine expectations had so nearly ruined the Horticultural Society were now very influential in the Zoological Council, and
that moreover the bitter hostilities between parties, so very prejudicial
to any Society, were now very rampant in the Zoological. I declined taking any active part, but attended the meeting for the purpose of learning
what was really doing, without any idea of coming forward with any
ideas of my own. The Society, like many other Natural History Associations which had come into existence of late years, had amongst its principal objects the meeting to hear and discuss papers, and their
publication, which individual authors had not the means of doing. Specimens illustrating the papers accompanied them, others were presented
for the purpose of exhibition, and very frequently because their owners
did not know what else to do with them, and an association could better
afford to keep them than individuals. Thus collections were formed
which, as they grew, took the name of Museums, without any definite
idea of what they might ultimately [650] lead to. The Zoological Society
was in this respect in exceptional circumstances, the establishment of
the Zoological Gardens, containing a collection of living animals, which
so far exceeded in interest as well as in every other respect the old
menageries of Exeter Change and the Tower, attracted vast numbers of
paying visitors, the receipts of the Society encreased rapidly, and at this
time they had already a capital of some thousands on hand; and the
same sanguine minds which had relied on a steady and unlimited
encrease of the Horticultural Society's receipts now relied on a similar
encrease of those of the Zoological, and the Council was readily persuaded that the time was come for adding to the collection of live animals a Museum for preserved skins and skeletons on a grand scale,
without a moment's reflection that the one would always be a source of
income, whilst the Museum would be pure expenditure, for no one
would care to pay for seeing a collection of stuffed animals when one
which would always be far superior could always be seen for nothing at
the British Museum. The Council therefore, as it would appear, determined without hesitation to have a Museum on a large scale; but a bitter
feud arose as to the details, and the Council became nearly equally
divided between two plans, advocated on each side with great violence,

and resolved upon calling this meeting to settle their disputes. The meeting was largely attended,[27] when it was explained to us that the two plans between [651] which we had to decide was whether we should build a Museum in the Garden, at an immediate outlay of between £15,000 and £20,000 towards a plan, the total estimate for which amounted to £50,000, or purchase Anglesea House, then on sale, and convert it into a Museum, at an expence of £30,000. Then, as to the means of meeting this gigantic outlay, we were told that the Society had accumulated a capital of about £4,000, that they had more or less definite, or vague, promises or expectations of nearly as much more. On hearing this, the prospect of such an expenditure with such small means appeared to me so absolutely ruinous that, although I had no time to consult with any one, I thought that with my Horticultural Society experience it was my duty to protest against it, and I moved as an amendment to the proposals brought forward that, on the face of the statement made, the Society was not in a position to accede to either proposal. Mr Daniel, Secretary of the Royal Institution, which had been barely saved from ruin by similar extravagation founded on similar expectations, rose to second my amendment, though I was personally unacquainted with him, and had had no previous communication, and after a good deal of discussion, my amendment was rejected by a majority of 83 to 50, and the proposal to purchase Anglesea House carried by 76 to 39. The next day (Sunday) the Zoological Gardens were much crowded in the afternoon, and I had a great deal of argument to go through about the previous day's proceedings, but, as a result, I [652] learned a few days later that the Council thought it unwise to proceed in the face of so large an unprepared minority, and gave up their plans. Some year later, with an improved Council, the Museum was definitively abandoned, the collections made over to the British Museum, and still later the Society, under the able management of Dr Sclater, has been brought into the state of steadily encreasing prosperity it now enjoys.

On the 26th July, we started on a tour into Switzerland and north Italy. Having had our britzka refitted for travelling, we slept that night at Dover, crossed over the next day to Calais, posted on to Brussels, stopping to sleep at Ypres and Ghent, by a much more cheerful and prettier, richly cultivated country than the usual dreary Paris road by Boulogne and Montreuil. At Brussels we remained a couple of days, seeing sights, etc, and to the theatre to which Sir Robert Adair had sent us his box. Did not hear of any botanist to call on, and the Botanic Garden remains in pretty much the same desolate state I saw it in after the disorders of 1831. Stopping half a day at Aix la Chapelle and again at Cologne, we remained the whole of the 5th of August at Bonn to see Nees von Esenbeck and the Garden. Went early up to the Chateau de Poppendorf, where found Nees von Esenbeck, a miserable looking, little old German, who moreover was not well, and had his face [653] all plastered up, so that he looked like anything but the gay Lothario he gave himself out as. Not being able to leave his room, he gave me an order on Sinning, the head Gardener or Curator, to show me the garden, etc. We both of us went up to the Museum of Natural History, which is very young, but very well arranged. Sinning was at dinner, so we settled to return after our dinner to go over the garden with him, but a very heavy thunderstorm lasting all the afternoon and evening prevented our going out again.

After Bonn, stayed a day at Wiesbaden, and two at Frankfort, to see the botanists there. Spent the mornings at the Senkenbergian Natural History Museum, very rich in African animals, etc, brought by Ruppell. Ruppell himself, just returned from Abyssinia,[28] proved very agreable and particularly civil to me. With him and his friend Dr Fresenius, botanical keeper of the Museum, went through his Abyssinian Labiatae. Leaving Frankfort, went on by Darmstadt, Heidelberg, Carlsruhe, Baden, Schaffhausen, Berne and Lausanne to Geneva, stopping only half days or single days where necessary to see the sights, arriving in the evening of the 24th August at Geneva, where we took up our quarters in the Hotel des Bergues, now just opened, the first of the large hotels since built in Geneva. Here we remained (with the exception of the Chamouny and Bex excursion) till the 10th Sept., enjoying much the scientific and literary Society, which was at this time particularly good. I spent most mornings in De Candolle's herbarium, chiefly at his Labiatae, and [654] the evenings frequently with our kind, excellent friends the De Candolles, sometimes dining with them, often at tea, either at their house, or meeting them at their friends'. Auguste Pyrame was still in full vigour, working in the morning in his study or library, in which were the books he most consulted, whilst a private back staircase gave him access to his herbarium overhead without his being disturbed by those who came to consult the herbarium. He never worked after 4 p.m., when he retired (in summer) to his little country place on the lake, dined usually at 5, and spent the evening in society, which he so thoroughly enjoyed, and in which he always made himself so remarkably agreable. Madame De Candolle, always the same kind, amiable and excellent lady I had always found her, did the honors in her quiet way, most admirable. Their son, my friend Alfonse, had married since I last saw him; his wife (Mlle Kunkler) handsome, clever and well informed, though no botanist, had been partially educated at Paris, of which she had adopted much of the manners, and seemed in some measure a contrast to her quiet, unexcitable husband, but she eventually proved a most valuable acquisition to the domestic circle. They kept up a separate establishment on the second floor of the house in the Cour St Pierre, where the old De Candolles occupied the first floor, with the excrescence at the back form-ing De Candolle's study, with the herbarium over it—a quasi living together, so common on the Continent, so rare with us. The house was the old family one, in which Auguste Pyrame often showed the window out of which his father, then Syndic of Old Geneva, had to escape in his dress coat, wig and sword, from the fury of the revolutionary mob of 1794.[29] [655] Madame Alphonse's young baby was, of course, the pet of the whole circle, and I have rarely seen a domestic union to all appear-ance so happy as that now exemplified in the De Candolle family.—At the De Candolles', met Prof. Moris of Turin, very busy with his *Flora Sardoa*, and whom we afterwards saw more of at Turin, M. and Mde de Saussure, M. and Mde Louis Pictet (the entomologist), several Martins and Prevosts. We dined one day at Mrs Marcet's beautiful place at Mala-gny, an hour's drive from Geneva, Mrs Marcet as kind, agreable and cheerful as ever; met there the De Candolles, Sismondis, and others, and one day drove out to Chene to the Sismondis' weekly evening tea—a large party, chiefly foreigners, many English, amongst others, surprised to find Countess Guiccioli, Lord Byron's mistress, who did not appear to us remarkably prepossessing. Miss Smith (Patty Smith, the eldest of the family) was staying here with the Sismondis, and made herself very agreable.

The Chamouny excursion occupied six very pleasant days, up by St Gervais and down to Martigny and Bex by the Col de Balme—the means of conveyance still very primitive. Near Bex, spent a very pleas-ant afternoon and evening tea with M. Charpentier, Director of the Salt-works here, who has been much in the Pyrenees, and studied much the natural history; he sent for M. Thomas, the then chief Swiss dried plant seller, from whose catalogue I selected several. On the 10th Sept., finally left Geneva, stopping a day at Bex to dine and tea with the Charpentiers. M. Charpentier took us to the curious bains de Lavange, with the hot spring embedded in the deep Rhone. [656] M. Charpentier had a consid-erable herbarium and collection of mineralogic specimens from the Pyrenees, etc. I looked over and named his Salvias; from thence we went on over the Simplon—the road but just passable, having been almost washed away by violent storms a fortnight or three weeks since, and arrived at Milan on the 21st Sept.

Here we remained two or three days, besides about a week spent on the lake of Como, chiefly at Cadenabbia, which we much enjoyed. At Milan, I found no botanists. Lady Davy was there, as usual very friendly, active and agreable; she took Mrs Bentham out driving, sent us her box at the Scala, etc. She was very anxious that, immediately on our return home, I should call on her father and mother in Portland Place[30] and report on our having left her in good health and spirits. I did so, but found that they had both died (I believe within a day or two of each other), and their remains removed to their last home that day. On our return from Como to Milan, we made a little detour by Monza to see the Imperial and Royal Garden there. "The Director, Mr Rossi, received us very civilly, but being old and not speaking French, he sent Mr Manetti, the head of the botanic portion of the garden, to show us over. The garden, altogether containing about 25 acres, is divided into Exotic Garden, Jardin Anglais, American Garden, Fruit Garden and Kitchen Garden, the three former more specially under M. Manetti, who is a very zealous man, now translating into Italian, without much prospect of success, the elementary horticultural and botanical works of Lindley and others, in the hopes of spreading the taste in [657] Italy.[31] He also gives a course of lectures to the gardeners and apprentices. The garden contains much, considering the difficulties of communications, and also that the climate is so much inferior to that of the lake of Como, but to those used to English Gardens, the collection is poor. The Jardin Anglais is pretty well laid out, and from the tower is a splendid view of the plain of Lombardy. The palace itself is a very handsome and large building, but the furniture not splendid. The Viceroy (Archduke Rainier) is at present at Vienna."

Leaving Milan on the 1st Oct. for Pavia, after turning off to see the Chartreuse, getting early to Pavia, went to see Professor Moretti, and with him over the botanical garden, which does not contain much but has some good plants, especially economical ones. There was also a fine littaea geminiflora in flower. Being induced by Professor Moretti to stay the rest of the day at Pavia, went to the Cabinet of Natural History, which has a little of many things, but not much of any, and after dinner returned to Prof. Moretti's and looked over with him the Labiatae of Bosc's herbarium (which he had bought); he gave me some specimens of good things from Oliver's eastern journeys[32] and from Carolina, on which the professor laid little store, for he seemed to care for very little except Italian plants.

From Pavia, went on to Genoa, staying there a couple of days, and thence by the beautifull corniche round to Mentone. This was not yet the resort of English; there were no large hotels, but the place looked so very pretty and quiet, and the [658] Hotel de Turin so clean and comfortable, that my wife determined to remain there rather than at Nice, whilst I went over to Montpellier for a few days to see my mother and sister, who had pressed me to come, as much on business as for pleasure, a three days' journey and as much back, by the quickest mail carriages or diligences then going. Got back to Mentone on the 16th; found my wife had been comfortable—the host of the Hotel de Turin had been very attentive, and went out occasionally to shoot little birds for her roast at dinner. Bathilde Partouneaux, the youngest of the General's three sons, was settled here; he had entered the financial career when the revolution of 1830 made the whole family quit the public service. Bathilde soon after married into the Tringua family living at Mentone, and here he had settled down into a routine life, not unfrequent in the South, lounging about the Cafés, etc, without any particular occupation. He and his wife, as well as the Tringuas, were very friendly to my wife,§ walked out with her, and spent a good deal of time with her, but never once asked her to dinner, which I was told was not much the custom amongst Italians—perhaps from their dinner hour being 12 o'clock, or from the few servants they kept, certainly not from uncivility.

Left Mentone on the 17th Oct. and, spending a couple of days at Nice, crossed the Col de Tende, a locality celebrated since the days of Allioni as the station of a number of rare or unique plants of limited areas[33]— but the season now too far advanced to find them in [659] flower. On to Turin, where detained a couple of days, Professor Moris being absent, the first of which, however, we went over the botanic garden at the Chateau de Valentin, rich in European and alpine plants, but poor in other things. It is laid out according to the natural system and has some pretty good houses. The following day spent chiefly with Prof. Moris at the Garden herbarium, which contains, besides the original garden herbarium, Balbis's, many with Sprengel's authentic names[34] and Moris's own. He gave me a number of good Sardinian plants. From Turin we went by Chambery to Geneva, crossing the Mont Cenis in a tourmente, with such violent gusts of wind and snow that two or three times going up, the postboy begged us to put down the head of the carriage, which resisted the wind too much. About the post-house on the top, where we had intended to sleep, the scene was most wretched and desolate, and we were right glad to get down to Lanslebourg a little after dark, where the inns were so full of travellers waiting for the fury of the weather to abate that we had the greatest difficulty in getting a bed, and those who came after us got none at all. However we got off early in the morning, and were in the comfortable Hotel des Bergues at Geneva in the evening of the 26th.

Remained four or five days at Geneva, chiefly with the De Candolles, who are now all settled in their winter quarters in the Cour St Pierre, and was chiefly occupied in finishing up the determination of his Labiatae as far as published and taking notes on others.[35] One afternoon at the Felix Dunants', whose Labiatae I also went through, and on the 30th finally left Geneva, going by Orbes over the Jura to Besançon, for the purpose of meeting the de Circourts. Since the breaking off the match between [660] Simon de Klustine and my sister Sarah, there had been a coolness between the two families, which, considering our long intimacy, both much regretted, and now Anastasie de Klustine (now Madame de Circourt) arranged with M. de Candolle to put an end to it. The Circourts were at present on a small property of his not far from Besançon, and it was settled that we should go that way home, and they would come to Besançon to meet us. Stopping accordingly at Orbe to sleep, we crossed the Jura, and got in to Besançon in a dense fog in the evening of the 1st Nov. Spent Sunday the 2d there, dining and spending the whole day with the Circourts, "who were so exceedingly friendly, renewing the old intimacy and talking over old stories. Madame de Circourt (Anastasie) was much affected, and appeared much to grieve the breaking off her intercourse[§] with Sarah, to whom she still expresses great affection. She is now in good health, and strong, and improved in looks, and certainly her esprit deserves much of the admiration it has met with[§], and which made Bonstetten (in his letter to Zschokke, printed as introduction to the *Creole*) call her a second De Stael, especially in esprit.[36] M. de C. has lost a great deal of the cringing civility he had, but talks too much, and in particular breaks out now and then into an ennuyeux declamatory style, which to me, at least, appears overbearing and tiresome. In all other respects, he is very well." This overtalking in both of them encreased in after years, even in their brilliant days of the Rue des Saussaies and the Celle St Cloud.

From Besançon, we had five long, weary days of posting by [661] Langres, Rheims, Laon and Arras, the weather at first cold and foggy, then better, but the country at this time of year most dull and uninteresting, the road carried Roman fashion in a perfectly strait line for miles and tens of miles, over hill and down dale, without ever the slightest deviation to avoid a steep patch—at first thick and clayey, then chiefly the old-fashioned pavé—the last day to Arras posting nearly 100 miles over the granite pavé almost wore the tire off our wheels. At Arras, stopped to have to breakfast with Th. Le Blanc,[37] who was in garrison there. On to Calais on the 9th, and after a good passage to Dover, and as usual a tedious Custom House, got to Rochester to sleep, and finally home on Tuesday, 11th November—1834.

List of Abbreviations

The following abbreviations will be found in the notes and appendices below:

GB   George Bentham
JB   Jeremy Bentham
MLC   Mary Louise Bentham de Chesnel
MSB   Mary Sophia Bentham
SB   Samuel Bentham

BAAS   British Association for the Advancement of Science
BL   British Library
HSL   Horticultural Society of London
LSL   Linnean Society of London
RBGK   Royal Botanic Gardens, Kew
RHS   Royal Horticultural Society
UCL   University College London

ABF   *Archives biographiques françaises*
AC   J. and J.A. Venn, *Alumni Cantabrigienses*
ADB   *Allgemeine deutsche Biographie*
AO   J. Foster, *Alumni Oxonienses*
BBA   *British Biographical Archive*
BPBK   *Burke's Genealogical and Heraldic History of the Peerage, Baronage, and Knightage*
BLG   *Burke's Landed Gentry*
BLKO   *Biographisches Lexikon des Kaiserthums Œsterreich*
BNB   J.H. Barnhart, *Biographical Notes upon Botanists*
C   G.E. Cockayne and V. Gibbs, *Complete Peerage*

CJB	*Correspondence of Jeremy Bentham*, in
CW	*The Collected Works of Jeremy Bentham*
D	R. Desmond, *Dictionary of British and Irish Botanists and Horticulturists*
DAB	*Dictionary of American Biography*
DBA	*Deutsches biographisches Archiv*
DBF	*Dictionnaire de biographie française*
DBL	*Dansk biografisk Leksikon*
DCF	*Dictionnaire des comédiens français*
DHBS	*Dictionnaire historique et biographique de la Suisse*
DNB	*Dictionary of National Biography*
DPF	H. Lyonnet, *Dictionnaire des parlementaires français*
DSB	*Dictionary of Scientific Biography*
EB	*Encyclopaedia Britannica*, 11th ed.
EUI	*Enciclopedia universal ilustrada*
G	*New Grove Dictionary of Music and Musicians* (1980)
GDU	P. Larousse, *Grand dictionnaire universel du dix-neuvième siècle*
Life	MSB, *Life of Sir Samuel Bentham*
LP	*Les préfets du 11 ventôse an VIII au 4 septembre 1870*, ed. R. Bargeton, et al
MEB	F. Boase, *Modern English Biography*
MERSH	*Modern Encyclopedia of Russian and Soviet History*
NDB	*Neue deutsche Biographie*
PD	Hansard's *Parliamentary Debates*
PP	*Parliamentary Papers*
T	R.G. Thorne, ed., *The House of Commons, 1790–1820*
TL2	F.A. Stafleu and R.S. Cowan, *Taxonomic Literature*, 2nd ed. (1976–92)
Works	*The Works of Jeremy Bentham* (1843)
WWBMP	*Who's Who of British Members of Parliament*

Notes

Chapter 1

1 For details of the Bentham family, see the Introduction, x–xi above. The Minories is a street in the City of London, named for the convent, formerly located outside Aldgate, of the Poor Clares (Minoresses), nuns of the second order of St Francis (the Friars Minor).

2 By May of 1763 Jeremiah Bentham's family had moved from Crutched Friars Street to a house at Queen Square, Westminster, which was at first rented, and then purchased at the end of 1764 or early 1765.

3 It was, in fact, in 1791 that SB returned home, spending three weeks in Paris en route; see xvii above, and his letters to JB, from Paris and from London, of 3 and 26 May, *CJB*, IV, 273–7 and 300.

4 See xx above. Among the works of George Fordyce (1736–1802) were several studies of fever, all issued in London: *Dissertation on Simple Fever* (1794), followed by a five-part *Dissertation* on other aspects of the subject (1795, 1798, 1799, 1802 and 1803); he also published *Elements of Agriculture and Vegetation . . . to Which Is Added an Appendix, for the Use of Practical Farmers* (Edinburgh: n.p., 1765), and various studies on anatomy and chemistry; see *Bibliotheca Britannica*, I, 377.

5 Some of these are preserved in JB, *Works*, X, 6–15.

6 GB's own performance on his fourth birthday, 22 September 1804, was a note to his father, written with carefully formed letters: "My dear Papa / I love you very much, to-day I am four years old. / George Bentham." (MS at LSL.)

7 Timber for shipbuilding was in short supply in England, and the government mistakenly believed that Russia would agree to SB's undertaking the construction of several ships of war, either at St Petersburg or on the Black Sea; see MSB, *Life*, 235–46, and Morriss, *The Royal Dockyards*, 214.

8 MSB's letters to JB, of 7–8 and 9 August 1805, *CJB*, VII, 313–22, identify the governess as a Miss Engleheart, some of the young men as Messrs Clason, Gibbs, Heard, Stuckie and Upsal, and the captain of the vessel as Robson. SB's principal assistant was Joseph Helby, "quartermaster in the Portsmouth dockyard" (*Life*, 236, 245).

9 GB's letters to his uncle from St Petersburg are preserved in the collection of the LSL. Dated 18 July, 10 October, 17 November and 25 December 1806 and 1 April 1806 [*sic* for 1807], they are in *CJB*, VII, 351, 384, 390, 391 and 338. The children all use "wooden rakes," and are studying music; GB and Sam are learning Latin, and are to begin "Carpenters work." The plans for their greenhouse (drawn by young Sam) and the progress in its construction are also reported. Their projected indoor gardening activities are more fully described in a letter from MSB and SB to JB of 19 August 1806, ibid., 358–60.

10 The earliest journal in the Kew collection, a small notebook bound in red leather, was a farewell present from Mme Necludoff to GB on his leaving Russia, the dedication dated 14 August 1807.

11 SB had discovered on his arrival in Russia that the government had no intention of allowing him to construct warships for the British Navy. He did manage to purchase timber, however, and there were some negotiations about his remaining in the Emperor's service, but the alliance of Alexander and Napoleon against England by the Treaty of Tilsit, 7 July 1807, necessitated his departure. During his visit, he had undertaken the construction of a panopticon at the mouth of the Okhta river, near St Peterburg, which was to accommodate a school of the practical arts and professions; see MSB and SB to JB of 19 August, and SB to JB of 10 October 1806, *CJB*, VII, 358, 384–6.

12 MSB reports that SB finally had to take command of the ship: "One stormy day she was about to be run ashore on a Danish island, when he at last ventured to interfere. The commander, to his credit, admitted the truth of his observations, and put the vessel under his direction; the sails were altered to his wish, and the corvette escaped. . . . At length he thought it prudent to steer for Carlscrona, the nearest port friendly to England, instead of Stockholm, the commander having had orders to land him at any place in Sweden which he might select." (*Life*, 247.) SB took the opportunity of inspecting the great naval arsenal at Carlscrona, "the only naval establishment in the Baltic which [he] had not previously visited" (ibid., 248).

13 "[SB's] kind acquaintances at Carlscrona had given him letters of introduction to the landed proprietors whose estates were situated on his route. This was fortunate; for when half way between that town and Gothenburg, his travelling coach, an English one, broke down, he learnt that he was within half a dozen miles of . . . the residence of a proprietor . . . where there was an

establishment of English workmen, for the works needed on the estate. . . . His carriage was well repaired; and during the three days requisite for the work, they were entertained in the most hospitable and friendly manner by the Major." (*Life*, 248)

14 Now called Frognall Lane. John James Park, *The Topography and Natural History of Hampstead* (London: White, Cochrane; and Nichols, Son and Bentley, 1814), 125–6, gives the following description: "The name of the Manor Farm is now appropriated to that portion of [the demesne lands] which is situate south of West-End lane. The old Manor-house, however, stood on the north side of the lane, on the site, it is said, of a modern residence now in the occupation of Sir Samuel Bentham. . . . In modern times the estate has been denominated Hall Oak Farm, and the house above-mentioned, which was built upon the site of the old manor house, is still so called, though lett separately from the demesnes on which it stands, and not having above two acres of land attached to it. . . . I am informed by Sir Samuel Bentham, that a handsome old pollard, still standing in his pleasure ground, is the particular oak-tree which he has always understood to have given its name to the manor farm."

15 SB may well have had grounds for thinking that the Russian expedition had been organized in part, at least, to keep him "out of the way" (letter to JB, 19 Aug. 1806, *CJB*, VII, 363). He discovered when he returned to England that, on the recommendation of the Commissioners of Naval Revision, the position of Inspector-General had been abolished, and that he, as Civil Architect and Engineer, and his assistants had been transferred to the Navy Office. He had also to accept a junior seat on the Navy Board, where his proposals met with little success, and he ceased regularly to attend. In November of 1812 his second office was abolished and he was retired on a pension of £1500 per year; see Morriss, 213–15. SB subsequently issued a pamphlet, in which he described all the improvements effected during his tenure: *Services Rendered in the Civil Department of the Navy* (London, 1813).

16 The earliest reference to this estate, in GB's "Diary MSS, 1807–11," RBGK, is a description of a journey from Berry Lodge to London in October of 1810.

17 See Introduction, xviii–xix above.

18 GB's Diary, RBGK, notes that on 17 August 1813, his uncle, accompanied by James Mill and his son John, arrived at Berry Lodge for a visit, "having travelled about the West of England." On 19 August, he records that "Papa, John and I went to Ryde." The observations on John Stuart Mill, which follow in the text, were probably prompted by the fact that, at the time of writing, in 1867, Mill was a well-known public figure and at the height of his parliamentary career.

19 John Churchill, 1st Duke of Marlborough (1650–1722), the most famous general of his day, was the great-great-grandfather of Lady Spencer's husband, George John, 2nd Earl Spencer (1758–1834).

20 Napoleon's army crossed into Russia in June and entered Moscow on 14 September 1812. The Russians set fire to the city shortly thereafter, and Napoleon's retreat began on 19 October.

21 A St Petersburg newspaper, founded in 1812. The translations have not been located.

22 Alexander I, Emperor of Russia (1777–1825), personally led his forces in the invasion of France; the Austrian troops were commanded by Karl Philipp von Schwarzenberg (1771–1820). With the Prussian army, under Gebhard Leberecht von Blücher (1742–1819), they entered Paris on 31 March 1814. Napoleon finally abdicated unconditionally on 6 April.

23 By 52 George III, c. 144 (1813), JB was granted £23,000 compensation for the cancellation of the Panopticon agreement with the Treasury (*Works, XI,* 106). Cf. GB's note at 184 above.

24 The Russian Emperor Alexander, accompanied by his sister Catherine, Duchess of Oldenberg (1788–1819), and Friedrich Wilhelm III, King of Prussia (1770–1840), were visiting England after the victory over the French. They had expressed a desire to see the British fleet and arsenal at Portsmouth, and were received by the Prince Regent and naval dignitaries, beginning on 23 June. See *The Times,* 29 June 1814, 2.

25 W. Kingston, Master of the Millwrights at the dockyard, gave up his office to them for the night. The Benthams observed the events of 22, 23, and 24 June 1814, shaking hands with "the Royals" on the 24th (GB's Diary, RBGK). The Master of the Wood Mills was, as GB mentions above, James Burr. With Simon Goodrich, Burr and Kingston had helped SB prepare his account of *Services Rendered;* see n15 above.

26 The elaborate preparations for the celebration of the peace are described in "The Grand Jubilee," *The Times,* 19 June 1814, 3. The main event took place on 1 August; see ibid., 2 Aug., 2–3, and 3 Aug., 3. The London house of the Spencer family is in St James's Street.

27 The eldest son of George III, Prince Regent with full royal powers from 1812 until he became King in 1820, was unpopular because of his dissolute habits and his callous treatment of the Princess Caroline, his wife.

28 Pavel Vasil'evich Chichagov (1767–1849) was Commander of the army of the Danube and the Black Sea fleet during the French campaign against Russia. He was severely censured for having failed to prevent Napoleon from crossing the Berezina river during the retreat from Moscow, left Russia as a result in 1814, and never returned. In 1799 he had married Eliza-

beth Proby, daughter of the Commissioner of the Chatham dockyard, and would have liked to settle in England, since his two daughters were attending an English school (their mother having died in 1811). His views of the Russian government are reflected in his letters to JB; see, e.g., *CJB*, VII, 489, 495, 498–500.

29 Legislation regulating the registration and movement of aliens in England had begun during the French Revolution, and continued into the nineteenth century. The Alien Act, 43 George III, c. 155 (1803), was replaced by 54 George III, c. 155 (19 July 1814), and again by 55 George III, c. 54 (12 May 1815), but many restrictions upon foreign residents remained, and violations were punishable by deportation.

30 The parliamentarian George Canning (1770–1827) was also an author of occasional poems; see, e.g., his *Poetical Works . . . Comprising the Whole of His Satires, Odes, Songs and Other Poems* (London: Limbird, 1823). The following poem, however, seems not to have been one of his.

31 A copy of the reprint is pasted in at this point. The ballad appeared on page 2 of the *Courier* of 23 June 1814.

Chapter 2

1 The feast of St Louis (1214–70), King Louis IX of France, is on 25 August.

2 A later diary, at RBGK, records GB's nostalgic visit to this house on 22 September 1857.

3 Napoleon had embarked for Elba at Fréjus, the scene of his earlier triumphant return from Egypt, on 29 April 1814. On 1 March 1815, he landed at Golfe-Juan, near Antibes.

4 Marshal Michel Ney (1769–1815) was said to have told Louis XVIII that he would bring Napoleon back to Paris in an iron cage (or that Napoleon deserved to be so confined because he had abused his liberty); but then, noting the mood of the country and the soldiers, Ney declared his allegiance to the Emperor at Lons-le-Saulnier on 14 March.

5 Louis XVIII fled north early on 20 March, and Napoleon entered Paris the same evening.

6 In 1803 the government of Napoleon had suddenly begun to treat the English residents and tourists in Verdun as prisoners of war. One of the unfortunate visitors, James Henry Lawrence (1773–1840), who managed to escape after several years, described their plight in *A Picture of Verdun; or, The English Detained in France; Their Arrestation, Detention at Fontainebleau and Valenciennes, Confinement at Verdun, Incarceration at Bitsche. . . . List of Those*

Who Have Been Permitted to Leave or Who Have Escaped out of France. . . . 2 vols.
(London: Hookham, 1810).

7 Louis Philippe, comte de Ségur (1753–1830), had resumed his position as
Master of Ceremonies at Napoleon's court, and become a member of the
Chamber of Peers.

8 The "chouans," named for one of their original leaders, Jean Cottereau, dit
Chouan (1767–94), were Royalist revolutionaries in the West of France, active
during the first French revolution and thereafter.

9 Blücher's army was routed by Napoleon's forces at Ligny on 16 June 1815,
but two days later the Emperor was decisively defeated at Waterloo. An
announcement of the loss was read by the Minister of the Interior in the
Chamber of Peers on the 21st; see *Archives parlementaires de 1787 à 1860*, 2^e
sér., 14, 498.

10 Napoleon returned to Paris on 21 June, abdicating in favour of his son on the
22nd. Ordered to leave by the Commissioners appointed by the Chambers,
he moved on the 25th to La Malmaison for four days and then departed for
Rochefort early on the 29th. He passed by Tours just before midnight on the
30th, briefly visiting with the Prefect, the comte de Cassagnes de Beaufort de
Miramon (1778–1816), his former Chamberlain; see Gilbert Martineau,
Napoléon se rend aux Anglais (Paris: Hachette, 1969), 95. Landor apparently
wrote to correct a similar version of the story that had appeared in William
Howitt's *Homes and Haunts of the Most Eminent British Poets*, 2 vols. (London:
Bentley, 1847). The letter was quoted in the 3rd edition (1857): "I had called
to pay my respects to Count Miramon, the prefect. The sentinel said, 'Sir, the
prefect does not receive on this evening.' I then walked along the esplanade,
and had taken two or three turns, when I saw a man in a grey coat, buttoned
under the chin, although the weather was hot, trot up to the prefect's gate.
The sentinel presented arms; the rider leapt from his horse, leaving him
loose. A servant, whom I had not seen, galloped up, took the horse, entered
the gate, and it was closed. The figure and the reception struck me at once.
The day but one after I called on the prefect. After a few words, letting him
know when I called before, and that I was not admitted, I said, 'I was master
of a secret too valuable to communicate.' He laid his hand on mine, and said,
'It could not be in better keeping.' Shortly afterwards news was brought of
Buonaparte's attempt to escape at Rochefort." (London and New York: Rout-
ledge, 1877, 590.) See also Robert Henry Super, *Walter Savage Landor: A Biography* (New York: New York University Press, 1954), 132–3.

11 Debate and voting on the draft constitution took place on 6 and 7 July;
see *Archives parlementaires*, 2e sér., 14, 614–24. The Allies entered Paris on the
7th.

12 Landor seems to have published neither his poem celebrating the King's second restoration, nor that included here on his earlier second exile to Ghent, at the time of Napoleon's return from Elba. For the following version, in which punctuation has been regularized, and the translation with comments below, I am indebted to Professor Wallace McLeod of Victoria College, University of Toronto:

To the King, a second time in exile

I did not bring any choice flowers of Pindus [i.e. of the Muses] to you [i.e., I did not write any poetry for you], O Louis, at the time when France was celebrating the return of [its] king. As everybody knows, all alone, in my own breast, I repressed my joys. [It was] enough for me to bear in mind how many [joys] were present in your [breast]. "Exile," I said, "has given [him] these things, that good luck could never give. Often called by his people, lo, he is home! Lo, he comes home, now that tyranny has been overthrown and driven from the realm! Lo, he comes home, the only saviour for his own people and for his neighbours!" But O, ye gods! Tell me, when could freedom or peace ever please Frenchmen, if it was free from bloodshed? But, O, ye gods! Tell me, when could freedom or peace ever please Frenchmen, if it was free from bloodshed? The nation dares to say that its crimes were committed by the few. Stupid! What can be greater than this very crime? Simply because of it, so many thousand people [are] intimidated by the three hundred blades of the presiding (?) leader. Because of it, the pale-faced exile has trodden down the ashes of [your] father. (But I am talking nonsense. Can there be any traitor who has a homeland?) Because of this, while he was fleeing over the Russian steppes [literally, Scythian fields], conspicuous on his racing steed, he shouted, "Stop those who are running away!" In whatever other land you choose, may you take your rest, and may loyalty in the hearts of the deserving not continue to be the sole criterion for establishing guilt. May the weapons of his citizens, and the courage of his forebears, and the love of his people, attend the aging king. But would that you might go home, may you go home, after Britain has won the war; and may your whole nation be rebuilt according to your example.

It is not certain whether the repetition of lines 9–10 as 11–12 appeared in the original or is merely a mistake of the copyist; no artistic purpose is served by anaphora in this context, however.

The author's Latin is not flawless. In line 6, the letter "a" in the word "daret" is long by nature; but the line will not scan unless it is short. The imperative of the verb "dico" is (irregularly) "dic," and not, as here, "dice" (10, 12). At least in more recent times, the interjection in lines 9 and 11 is spelled "pro" rather than "proh." "Considicus," in line 16, seems not to exist.

13 A fragmentary journal of this trip north and their stay in Paris, covering the period 14 July to 25 September 1815, is at RBGK.

14 Jules Paul Pasquier (1774–1858) was Prefect of Sarthe, at Le Mans, from 22 April 1814 to 22 March 1815. Reinstated on 17 July after the Hundred Days, he was arrested by the Prussians and imprisoned at Magdebourg from 20 August to 27 September 1815.

15 For the highlights of the Napoleonic collection, see Jean Chatelain, *Dominique Vivant Denon et le Louvre de Napoléon* (Paris: Perrin, 1973), 301–5. Louis XVIII returned many of the treasures; for example, the Belvedere Apollo, a Greek statue probably of the 4th century B.C., and the Laocoon, dating from the 1st century B.C., are now again in the Vatican museum, and the Medici Aphrodite, of the early 3rd century B.C., is in the Uffizi Gallery, Florence.

16 Boileau's unflattering picture of the capital is in "Satire VI" (1666), *Oeuvres complètes* (Paris: Gallimard, 1966), 34–7.

17 "Trims dogs and cats; makes house calls."

18 The four bronze horses of St Mark's basilica, Venice, temporarily adorned the Arc de Triomphe du Carrousel, opposite the Louvre.

19 The battle at Leipzig, a decisive victory for the Allied forces over Napoleon, had taken place 16–19 October 1813, the 18th being the day of the heaviest fighting.

20 "Get going!" "I'm off!" A less detailed account of this event of 27 August 1815 is in GB's journal, RBGK.

21 Armand Emmanuel du Plessis, duc de Richelieu (1766–1822), had gone to Russia at the time of the French Revolution, served there against the Turks, and been appointed Governor of the Euxine provinces. He was made Prime Minister of France, with the Foreign Affairs portfolio, in September 1815, and his close relations with the Emperor Alexander helped lighten the burden of the army of occupation. Andrault, comte de Langeron (1763–1831), and Joseph Élisabeth Roger, comte de Damas (1765–1823), were also émigré soldiers in the Turkish wars and old associates of SB; see Introduction, xvii above and *CJB*, IV, 203, 222.

22 Ségur was the author of such varied works as *Histoire des principaux événements du règne de F. Guillaume II, roi de Prusse, et Tableau politique de l'Europe depuis 1786 jusqu'en 1796*, 3 vols. (Paris: Buisson, 1800), and *Contes, fables, chansons et vers* (Paris: Buisson, 1801).

23 Geneviève Adélaïde, daughter of the philosopher Claude Adrien Helvétius

(1715–71), had married Antoine Henri, comte d'Andlau, in 1772. One of their two daughters, Anne Catherine, married Nicolas François Camille, comte d'Orglandes, ca. 1791; the other, Henriette Geneviève, became the wife of Louis Lepeletier, marquis de Rosanbo, in 1798. It was, in fact, Anne Catherine's daughter, Zélie d'Orglandes, who married Louis Geoffroy, comte de Chateaubriand, nephew of the poet and statesman, on 8 October 1811. The medallion of Helvétius is probably that described in H. Jouin, *Notice historique et analytique des peintures . . . exposés au palais du Trocadéro* (1879): "No. 539. Claude-Adrien Helvétius, Miniature sur ivoire de forme ovale; haut 0m, 055, large 0m, 065. Par Marolle." (I am very grateful to Professor D.W. Smith for this reference.)

24 A group of army officers attended the Comédie Française and raised a commotion to prevent the performance, because Mlle Mars had been a great friend of Napoleon. They insisted that she cry "Vive le roi!" She is reported to have won them over by saying, "You want me to say 'Vive le roi'? Well, I've said it." (*GDU*, under Mars.)

25 Antoine Marie de Chamans, comte de Lavalette (1769–1830), resumed his former position as Director-General of the Postal Service and Councillor of State during the Hundred Days. Condemned to death for high treason, he managed to escape from the Conciergerie, disguised in his wife's clothes, on 20 December 1815, and eventually made his way to Bavaria. He was subsequently pardoned and allowed to return to France in 1822.

26 Condemned as traitors for having given their allegiance to Napoleon during the Hundred Days, General Charles Labedoyère (b. 1786) was executed on 19 August and Marshal Ney on 7 December 1815.

27 Charles Maurice de Talleyrand-Périgord (1754–1838) had held important positions in every régime since the 1780s, when, during Louis XVI's reign, he was "agent général" of the French clergy and Bishop of Autun. He was a deputy of the clergy to the Estates General in 1789 and a commissioner on various constitutional and financial commissions. Under the Directory he was Minister of Foreign Affairs, helped Napoleon to power and served for a time on his Council of State. He worked on the transition from the Empire to the restoration of the Bourbon dynasty in 1814, and became Foreign Minister. Resisting the Emperor during the Hundred Days, he intrigued both left and right under the restored Louis XVIII and subsequently Charles X, and was made Ambassador to London on the accession of his friend, the duc d'Orléans, as Louis Philippe I in 1830. For a contemporary view, see "Camelions," *The Times*, 1 Nov. 1815, 4.

28 Armand de Chastenet, marquis de Puységur (1751–1825) was a disciple of Franz Mesmer, popularizer of the theory and practice of "animal magnetism," hypnosis.

29 See letters from SB and MSB to JB of 17 and 20 March 1816, *CJB*, VIII, 515–17.

30 Alexander von Humboldt (1769–1859) and Aimé Bonpland (1773–1858) had travelled extensively in South America and Mexico over a five-year period, 1799–1804. Their discoveries in various branches of science were published in a monumental work of many parts, whose general title was *Voyage aux régions équinoxiales du Nouveau Continent* (Paris, 1805–34).

31 A fragmentary five-folio account of the journey from Arcueil to Orléans is in GB's "Diary MSS, 1812–17," RBGK.

32 The Prefect of Loiret at this time was Alexandre Daniel, baron de Talleyrand-Périgord (1776–1839).

33 On 16 May 1806 the British Government had declared the coast of the Continent, from Brest to the Elbe, under blockade. Napoleon responded with the Berlin decree of 21 November, which imposed a blockade upon England and closed the Continent to British ships and goods. When Britain demanded that any ship trading with France first land in England and pay transit duty, he replied with the Milan decrees of 23 November and 17 December 1807, ordering the seizure of any vessel that had touched at a British port, or any that had submitted to British legislation.

34 The château of Chanteloup had been built by Marie Anne de la Trémoille, princesse des Ursins (1642–1722). Chaptal acquired the estate and established a beet-sugar factory there during the Empire. The property was sold in 1823 and the château pulled down.

35 Marc René Marie de Voyer de Paulmy, comte d'Argenson (1771–1842), had married the widowed princesse Sophie de Broglie in 1795, thus becoming the stepfather of Achille Charles Léonce Victor, duc de Broglie (1785–1870). D'Argenson was very interested in engineering and agricultural improvements on the family estate at Les Ormes-Saint-Martin, in Poitou.

36 "Four plagues give this country pain: Decazes, Richelieu, clemency and the rain." Richelieu who was both Prime Minister and Minister of Foreign Affairs from 26 September 1815, seemed too moderate to the "Ultras." He was, however, less liberal than duc Elie Decazes (1780–1860), who, having opposed Napoleon on his return from Elba, became Minister of Police of the restored Louis XVIII in August, drawing criticism by his lenient treatment of Bonapartists under the law of 18 October, and for the passing of an amnesty law of 12 January 1816.

37 The *Flore françoise* (1779) of Jean-Baptiste Lamarck (1744–1829) was continued by Augustin Pryamus de Candolle (1771–1841) in a third edition, 5 vols. (Paris: Agasse [and Desray], 1805–15).

38 William Townsend Aiton (1766–1849) had succeeded his father, William, as chief gardener of the Royal Gardens at Kew, in 1793. William Forsyth

(1737–1804) was head of the Chelsea Physic Garden from 1771, and of the gardens of St James's and Kensington from 1784.

39 The Duke of Wellington's campaign to get the French out of Spain had begun in 1812. After fighting through the Pyrenees in the winter of 1813–14, his efforts culminated in the battle of Toulouse, against the forces of Marshal Nicolas Soult (1769–1851), on 10 and 11 April 1814. The advance guard of the Allied armies had already entered Paris on 31 March, and Napoleon abdicated on 6 April. The messengers dispatched on the following day apparently did not reach Wellington and Soult until the 12th. See "The Battle of Toulouse," *The Times*, 12 May 1814, 3.

40 See "29° Bulletin de la Grande Armée" (3 Dec. 1812), *Le Moniteur Universel*, 17 Dec. 1812, 1391. General Louis Partouneaux (1770–1835) was accused of having abandoned his regiment to try to save himself.

41 "Tonin" later became Sub-Prefect of Yonne, at Tonnerre; see 323 above.

42 GB's diary indicates that he visited with Félix Courtois during a brief stay in Toulouse, 27 June to 1 July 1859.

43 Richard Norris Russell (1809–96); see 419 above.

44 Richard Archdall (ca. 1746–1824) was a former Member of Parliament from Ireland. According to MSB, he was accompanied by his daughter, see her letter to JB of 3–9 August 1818, *CJB*, IX, 238 and n.

45 Given the great detail in the following account, it seems likely that GB was using copies of the reports of the sittings, such as those described on 46 above. The story appears in the *Dictionnaire de biographie française*, vol. XIV, cols. 1422–6, under the name of the victim, Antoine Bernardin Fualdès, and has been the subject of several monographs, e.g., Armand Praviel, *L'Assassinat de M. Fualdès* (Paris: Perrin, 1922), and Edmond Locard, *Le Magistrat assassiné* (Paris: Éditions de la Flamme d'or, 1954).

46 Bernard Charles Bastide-Grammont (Fualdès' godson), and Joseph Jausion (Bastide-Grammont's brother-in-law, an exchange-broker), both, according to rumour, in debt to Fualdès.

47 All were found in the house of Bancal, reputed to be a haven for smugglers and prostitutes.

48 Bancal, who apparently committed suicide with verdigris on 15 May 1817.

49 The following year, 1818.

50 On 3 June 1818.

Chapter 3

1 For more detail of the circumstances surrounding the move to Montauban, see a letter from SB to JB, of 11 May–18 June 1818, *CJB*, IX, 197–204.

2 Isaac Bénédict Prévost (1755–1819) believed in continuity in the natural order, as GB's diary entry for 24 June 1818 illustrates: "[T]o the philosophy lesson. M. P. showed some examples of combinations of sulphur with metals, but it must always be in certain proportions. . . . [S]ome things combine more intimately than others so as to make almost a regular scale from the maximum of combinations to simple cohesion, like the scale of progression from man the most perfect animal to the trees, which are the most removed; a propos to that M. P. made once an observation of a body that he doubted whether was an animal or a plant—took a globule that grows on purslane leaves, put it in water—in the microscope the globule swelled by degrees and in a few minutes got 7 or 8 little animalcules seemingly burst out and began moving with great vivacity in the water. [A]fter some time they got more quiet and at last stationary; each one threw out a stalk like a plant." For more detail about GB's studies at this period, see a letter from SB to JB, of 4 December 1818, *CJB*, IX, 291–2.

3 "Un médecin soutenait à Fontenelle que le café était un poison lent. 'Oui-dà, dit le philosophe en souriant; il y a plus de quatre-vingts ans que j'en prends tous les jours.' Voilà ce qu'on appelle une preuve sans réplique." (*Fontenelliana, ou Recueil des bons mots, réponses ingénieuses, pensées fines et délicates de Fontenelle, par C . . . d'Av . . .* [Paris: Marchand, an IX, 1801], 112; no source given.)

4 Benoît Daniel Émilien Frossard (1802–81), fifth son of Benjamin Sigismond, Professor at the College of Montauban, was later an evangelical pastor and educator at Bagnères-de-Bigorre. Co-founder of the Société Ramond for the exploration and study of the Pyrenees, he was its President until his death.

5 Manuel María Cambronero (1765–1834) had been head of the Justice Department during the reign of Napoleon's brother, Joseph Bonaparte, 1808–13. For more detail about him, and Tomás Rodríguez Burón, mentioned below, see *CJB*, IX, 237, 251 and *passim*.

6 Alain René Lesage, *Histoire de Gil Blas de Santillane* (in French, 1715–35), was translated into Spanish as *Aventuras de Gil Blas de Santillana* by José Francisco de Isla, 4 vols. (Madrid: Gonzalez, 1787–88).

7 *Nouveau Dictionnaire d'histoire naturelle, appliquée aux arts, à l'agriculture et à l'économie rurale et domestique, par une société de naturalistes et d'agriculteurs*, 36 vols. (Paris: Deterville, 1816–19) was issued alphabetically, in three-volume sets; contributors included Bosc, Chaptal, Huzard, Olivier, Parmentier and Thouin.

8 Augustin Pyramus de Candolle, *Regni vegetabilis systema naturale*, 2 vols. (Paris: Treuttel and Würtz, 1818–21). In his address "On the Recent Progress and Present State of Systematic Botany," delivered to the annual meeting of

the BAAS at Belfast in 1874, GB did not mention this work, but specified that during these years in France he studied de Candolle's *Théorie élémentaire de la botanique* (Paris: Deterville, 1813), as well as de Candolle and Lamarck's *Flore française*, 3rd ed.; see *Report of the BAAS* (1874) (London: BAAS, 1875), 27, and 36n37 above.

9 The poet Jean Jacques Lefranc, marquis de Pompignan (1709–84), was the adversary of the philosophes, attacking them in a speech to the Académie Française in 1759. Voltaire responded with many satiric verses, among them a series entitled "L'assemblée des monosyllabes" (1760), and "Chanson en l'honneur de maître Lefranc de Pompignan ..." (1761); in *Oeuvres complètes*, 52 vols. (Paris: Garnier, 1877–85), X, 560–4, and 567–8, respectively.

10 On 16 September 1819; the certificate of marriage is in "Benthamiana," RBGK.

11 Under the regime of separate property, provided for in Articles 1536–9 of the French *Code civil* (1804), a married woman could hold property in her own name, but she was not free to mortgage or dispose of it without her husband's consent or, failing that, a court decision. In English law, an unmarried woman could hold property and inherit directly, but until the passing of the Married Women's Property Acts of 1870 and 1882 (33 & 34 Victoria, c. 93, and 45 & 46 Victoria, c. 75), the property of a married women belonged, in law, to her husband. It was, possible, nevertheless, in equity, to settle property upon her for her own use, under the management of a trustee responsible for seeing that the terms of the trust were properly carried out. Only about one woman in ten, however, enjoyed this arrangement. See Lee Holcombe, *Wives and Property* (Toronto: University of Toronto Press, 1983), esp. 38–43.

12 A diary of this trip, 8 October to 17 November 1819, from which the following account is taken, is at RBGK.

13 The entry for 11 October, for example, contains such comments.

14 GB is referring to his visits to Trieste in May of 1837 and to Odessa in September of 1846.

15 Though the *Dictionnaire de biographie française* gives the birth date of Jean Baptiste Suzanne d'Albertas as 1747, GB is quite specific in the diary entry for 26 October that M. Albertas is eighty-two years of age. His father was assassinated on 14 July 1790 by Anicet Martel, the son of a former schoolmaster of Gémenos, who had been dismissed for improper conduct.

16 Marshal Guillaume Marie Anne Brune (b. 1763), loyal to Napoleon during the Hundred Days and responsible for repressing royalist ardour in the South, had resigned after the second Restoration in 1815, and was on his way to Paris when he was assassinated by the Avignon mob on 2 August 1815.

17 The château of Le Parc, still in existence, dates from the sixteenth century. It

served as a hunting lodge for the Montmorency family, who were the royal governors of the province of Languedoc, and for Armand de Bourbon, prince de Conti (1629–66), who made Pézenas the cultural centre of the area.

18 "If God lived on earth he would live in Béziers . . . so that he might be crucified a second time."

19 The following account and quotations derive from a diary, begun on 10 February 1820; MS at RBGK.

20 On 29 January 1820.

21 Louis Pierre Louvel, a saddler who wished to exterminate the Bourbons, assassinated Charles Ferdinand, duc de Berry (b. 1778), second son of the duc d'Artois (later Charles X), on 13 February 1820.

22 See 34n36 above. Decazes, a favourite of Louis XVIII, had become President of the Council in November 1819, but fell from power in February 1820 as a result of the assassination of the duc de Berry.

23 A Spanish military revolt in January 1820 resulted in the capture of Ferdinand VII, who had ruled from 1814, and in the forced restoration of the Constitution of 1812. An amnesty for political refugees was declared, some of whom had served during the reign of Joseph Bonaparte; see note 5 above. Attempts at constitutional government between this time and 1823 were destined, however, to have little success.

24 Fire insurance, which had been an experiment as early as 1787, was successfully inaugurated during the Restoration. The Société d'Assurance Mutuelle de la Ville de Paris, founded by royal ordinance in 1816, was followed in 1819 by the Compagnie d'Assurances Générales, and, on 11 February 1820, by the Compagnie Royale (vie et incendie), which later became known as La Nationale. It is perhaps to the promotional efforts of this last company that GB is referring.

25 For Richard Doane (1805–48), see *CJB*, IX, 338–9 and *passim*. He later edited JB's *Constitutional Code* and *Principles of Judicial Procedure*; in *Works*, IX, and II, 1–188, respectively.

26 GB is referring to the comments he wrote in his diary on the events of 2 June 1820, Mill's first day with the family: "Went early with JM to Toulouse; on the road he conversed much in French on the crops, the country he has passed—though he has been but a fortnight in France and had learned but a month or 6 weeks before from Richard. [G]ave him an algebra sum that I had not been able to do, which he resolved in a few minutes."

27 J.S. Mill stayed with the Benthams until mid-April of the following year. GB was living at Restinclières during the first few months of 1821, while Mill was in Montpellier, a fact that probably accounts for GB's remembering that the visit lasted only seven or eight months. Mill's "Journal and Notebook of a

Year in France" are in *Collected Works*, XXVI (Toronto: University of Toronto Press, 1988), 1–143. Describing the formative influences in his life, Mill later wrote that he "owed [one] of the fortunate circumstances in [his] education, a year's residence in France," to [the Benthams], to whom he was "indebted . . . for much instruction, and for an almost parental interest in [his] improvement." He characterized Lady Bentham as "a woman of strong will and decided character, much general knowledge, and great practical good sense . . .; she was the ruling spirit of the household, as she deserved, and was well qualified, to be." (*Autobiography*, *Collected Works*, I [Toronto: University of Toronto Press, 1981], 57–8; see also "Journal," *Collected Works*, XXVI, 44). Lady Bentham was, without doubt, a contributing factor to Mill's views about the capability of women.

28 GB correctly said above that Mill joined them on 2 June, "after [their] return from [their] second journey."

29 This quotation derives from GB's diary entry for 24 April 1820, RBGK.

30 The diary account ends with their arrival at Montpellier. GB presumably based it on his journal-letters from the first part of the trip, which, with the exception of that of 25 April (MS at LSL), do not survive. The rest of the journey is described in six letters to his mother at Pompignan, dated 29 April to 15 May 1820 (also at LSL).

31 The history of the château of Restinclières, which dates from the time of Louis XIII, is given in Albert Leenhardt, *Quelques Belles Résidences des environs de Montpellier*, 2 vols. (Montpellier: Causse, Graille et Castelnau, 1931–32), II, 151–61.

32 According to the *Dictionnaire de biographie française*, the Ginkgo biloba was sent to Antoine Gouan by Sir Joseph Banks. The official description of the tree in the Jardin des Plantes of Montpellier reads: "Planté par Gouan en 1795. Greffé rameaux femelles par Delile en 1830. Première fructification 1835."

33 In GB's letter of 12 May 1820, from Le Vigan, the General's name is given as Boussairolles, that of an old Montpellier family.

34 GB's diary, at RBGK, which resumes on 1 June and continues to 10 November 1820, records that the move into Toulouse took place on 25 June. MLC's daughter, Adèle, was born on 7 July.

35 The diary entry for 26 June reports that he had just received Stewart's "Dissertation: Exhibiting the Progress of Metaphysical, Ethical, and Political Philosophy," in translation, i.e., the first volume of *Histoire abrégée des sciences métaphysiques, morales et politiques, depuis la renaissance des lettres. Traduite de l'anglais de Dugald Stewart, et précédée par un discours préliminaire par J.A. Buchon*, 3 vols. (Paris: Levrault, 1820–23). He was not impressed by Buchon's

"Discours préliminaire," describing it as having "some good ideas, clothed in a number of useless words." On the 27th he recorded his opinion that "Dugald Stewart's preface seems better; in criticizing D'Alembert's Encyclopedical table, he brings forth several ideas which seem to coincide remarkably with some of my Uncle's *Chrestomathia*. Went on with the translation of this work." GB had been studying d'Alembert's "Explication détaillée du systême des connoissances humaines," and "Systême figuré des connoissances humaines," *Encyclopédie, ou Dictionnaire raisonné des sciences, des arts et des métiers* (Paris: Briasson, et al., 1751), I, xlvii–li and [liii], and had probably read the whole of his "Discours préliminaire," ibid., i–xlv.

36 The diary entry for 27 June 1820 also records that he read Jean Baptiste Lamarck's *Système analytique des connaissances positives de l'homme, restreintes à celles qui proviennent directement ou indirectement de l'observation* (Paris: chez l'auteur, au Jardin du roi, et chez A. Belin, 1820); for the quotation, see the 1830 ed. (Paris: Germer Baillière), 9–10.

37 From 14 August to 17 September. Cf. J.S. Mill's account, *Collected Works*, XXVI, 65–101; Mill was also with them on the excursion to Bayonne.

38 GB's next extensive visit to the Pyrenees was with his friends George Arnott, Urbain Audibert and Esprit Requien in 1825; see 215–33 above. His later visits were from August to early October of 1839 and July to mid-September of 1859.

39 Henri de Bourbon, duc de Bordeaux (later comte de Chambord), son of the assassinated duc de Berry, was born on 29 September 1820.

40 Ange Jean Michel Bonaventure Dax, marquis d'Axat (1767–1847), was Mayor of Montpellier from the Restoration to the Revolution of 1830. His wife, Anastasie, and her sister, Pulchérie, marquise de Calvière, were the daughters of François Emmanuel Guignard, comte de Saint-Priest (1735–1821), diplomat and statesman, Ambassador at Constantinople, 1768–85, and Guillelmine Constance de Ludolf (b. 1752), daughter of the chargé d'affaires from Naples to the Porte.

41 Martin Heinrich Karl Lichtenstein (1780–1857) spent several years as doctor and tutor in the house of the Dutch Governor of the Cape Colony, travelling and collecting specimens in his spare time. His experiences were recorded in *Reisen im südlichen Afrika in dem Jahren 1803, 1804, 1805, 1806*, 2 vols. (Berlin: Salfeld, 1811–12).

42 The popular term for an alcoholic drink taken first thing in the morning.

43 Article 745 of the *Code civil* (1804) required as a general principle that parents leave their property to their children of both sexes equally. More specific rules about amounts of property disposable by gift or by will, the "quotité disponible," were spelled out in Articles 913–19.

44 The ultra-conservative majority government of Jean Baptiste Séraphin Joseph, comte de Villele (1773–1854), passed the "Loi sur les substitutions," Bulletin 90, no. 3028 (17 May 1826).

45 Two articles by GB entitled "Sketches of Manners in the South of France. I. The Roussillonnais; and II. The Republic of Andorra" appeared in the *London Magazine*, 7 (Jan. and Feb. 1827), 19–25 and 145–51. The original manuscript of the third article, from which the following is copied, is at RBGK. Founded in 1820, the periodical was acquired in 1825 by Henry Southern (1799–1853), a Benthamite and sub-editor of the *Westminster Review*. In April of 1828 Southern sold it to Charles Knight, and it ceased publication in June 1829. See Josephine Bauer, *The London Magazine, 1820–1829* (Copenhagen: Rosenkilde and Bagger, 1953), esp. 144–52 and 243–5.

46 Both steam navigation and railways were somewhat slower to develop in France than in England. By the time of the French naval expedition to Algiers in May of 1830, there were only seven steamships in a fleet of 104 vessels. A very few, short rail lines were built in France in the late 1820s and 1830s, one running from Alais to Beaucaire, in 1833. The development of a general railway system followed the passing of legislation in 1842.

47 Flooding of the Rhône through the Camargue area, a recurring problem, was particularly severe in 1840 and again in 1841 (Les Bouches-du-Rhône, *Encyclopédie départementale*, 7 [1928], 413–14).

48 Louis IX, St Louis, constructed the harbour of Aiguesmortes, the point of departure for his crusades in 1248 and 1270.

49 The castle of Tarascon, first built in 1291 on the site of a Roman fortification, had been reconstructed early in the sixteenth century.

50 Presumably one of the towers of the papal palace at Avignon.

51 The French chemists Joseph Bienaimé Caventou (1795–1877) and Pierre Joseph Pelletier (1788–1842) published their discovery that year in "Recherches scientifiques sur les quinquinas," *Annales de Chimie et de Physique*, 2nd ser., 15 (1820), 289–318 and 337–65.

52 A secret benevolent and social society, established in England and Ireland in the first half of the eighteenth century. The name "Independent Order of Oddfellows" was adopted in 1813 at a convention in Manchester.

53 Théodore Leblanc was apparently a friend from the Montpellier area; see also 437n37.

54 Count Mikhail Alekseevich Pushkin and his brother Sergei were condemned to death for having attempted to counterfeit the new banknotes introduced in Russia in October 1772, but the sentences were commuted. Sergei went to prison, and Mikhail was exiled to Siberia, where SB met his family on arriving at Tobolsk in January 1782 (MSB, *Life*, 44).

55 SB apparently had three natural daughters, two with Maria Burton of
   Bishops Stortford (see J.R. Dinwiddy, "Bentham's Letters to Herbert Koe,"
   Bentham Newsletter, no. 2 [Mar. 1979], 39), and Elizabeth Gordon, of whose
   mother nothing is known. Elizabeth did not, in fact, accompany the
   Benthams to Russia, but followed shortly after their departure (*CJB*, VII, 323,
   330, 331). Three letters from her, one a copy, are in the collection of the LSL.
   The first, to SB, is dated 15 January 1813, and describes her experiences during the Napoleonic invasion of Russia (published in the *Linnean*, 3 [Aug.
   1987], 10–12). A copy by GB of a letter to him, in French, dated 7 October
   1826, is in his letter to MLC of 20 November 1826, ff. 73–5. The third, also in
   French to GB, is dated 23 April 1827. As well as recommending a young Russian who was soon to visit France, she describes her young family, a son,
   George, and a daughter, Elizabeth (Lise), GB's god-daughter.
56 See 371, 414, and 424 above.
57 Honoré Édouard Delon (b. 1792) was a Bonapartist lieutenant at Saumur,
   who had been arrested on 24 December 1821 for plotting against the Bourbon
   régime, but succeeded in escaping towards the Spanish border.
58 Quoted from a letter to JB of 27 November 1822; MS at LSL.

Chapter 4

1 This and all subsequent quotations in the chapter derive from journal-letters
   sent to GB's parents and eldest sister at Restinclières; MSS at LSL.
2 The Swiss jurist Pierre Étienne Louis Dumont (1759–1829) had published the
   following redactions of JB's work: *Traités de législation civile et pénale*, 3 vols.
   (Paris: Bossange, *et al.*, 1802), 2nd ed. (ibid., 1820); *Théorie des peines et des
   récompenses*, 2 vols. (1811), 2nd ed. (Paris: Bossange and Masson, 1818); *Tactique des assemblées législatives*, 2 vols. (1816), 2nd ed. (Paris: Bossange frères,
   1822); and *Traité des preuves judiciaires*, 2 vols. (Paris: Bossange frères, 1823).
3 See 12 above.
4 See 27 above.
5 The Bourbon government, with a disaffected army on its hands, determined
   on a mission, commanded by Louis Antoine de Bourbon, duc d'Angoulême
   (1775–1844), to reestablish Ferdinand VII on the throne of Spain. The French
   invasion occurred in April 1823, and the army remained in Spain until September 1828.
6 In the course of a debate on the intervention in Spain on 26 February 1823, a
   republican deputy, Jacques Antoine Manuel (1775–1827), was deemed to
   have expressed approval of early revolutionary excesses and the death of

Louis XVI. By a vote on the 27th, he was excluded from the Chamber for the remainder of the session, but declined to comply, returning to subsequent meetings. On 4 March, he refused to obey the President's order to retire, and when the National Guard would not agree to remove him, the police escorted him from the Chamber; see *Le Constitutionnel*, 27 Feb., 2–4, 28 Feb., 1–2, 4 Mar., 2 and 6, and 5 Mar. 1823, 2–3.

7 Joanna Baillie (1762–1851), the dramatist and poet, and her sister Agnes (1760–1861), friends of the Benthams from the time of their residence in Hampstead, 1807–14.

8 The "reprobates," as GB later notes, was JB's nickname for his two amanuenses, Richard Doane and John Colls.

9 The ambassador from Tripoli was Hassuna D'Ghies (b. ca. 1791); see JB, *Works*, VIII, 555 and X, 534; JB, *Constitutional Code*, I, ed. F. Rosen and J.H. Burns (Oxford: Clarendon Press, 1983), xv–xvi; and JB, *Securities against Misrule and Other Constitutional Writings for Tripoli and Greece*, ed. Philip Schofield (Oxford: Clarendon Press, 1990), xv–xxxvi. John Bowring (1792–1872) had been a friend of JB's since 1820; see *Works*, X, 516.

10 Beginning in 1801, Joseph Lancaster (1778–1838) developed a method for imparting the rudiments of reading, writing and arithmetic to large numbers of poor children by using older children as monitors and teachers of small classes of the younger pupils. His system was introduced into France, and was very popular there until the government of Charles X put all education under the control of the Church in April of 1824.

11 The Longman publishing firm was headed at this time by Thomas Norton Longman (1771–1842). He and his wife Mary (b. ca. 1781) had seven children, of whom four, according to GB's letter, were present at this party: the eldest and second sons, Thomas and Charles, and two of the daughters, Louisa and Fanny. For more detail about the estate, named Mount Grove, see Richard Cooper, "Thomas Norton Longman's House and Garden," *Camden History Review*, 13 (1985), 6–11. Red Lion Hill, so called for the public house mentioned above by GB, was later named Rosslyn Hill, to commemorate the local residence of a Lord Chancellor, Alexander Wedderburn, Earl of Rosslyn (1733–1805).

12 In fact, the family of Herbert Koe, JB's solicitor and GB's later mentor.

13 Joseph Paxton (1801–65), gardener and architect to the Duke of Devonshire, erected a splendid conservatory at Chatsworth between 1836 and 1840, and designed the Great Exhibition building of 1851.

14 Thomas William Coke (1754–1842) encouraged his tenants to undertake agricultural improvements by personal investment and the granting of long leases. He enhanced the quality of the land on his estate at Holkham, thus

increasing wheat production, and improved the breeds and the methods of rearing sheep, cattle and pigs. He put on shows to popularize the new ideas, attracting large gatherings of farmers, aristocrats and reformers. See A.M.W. Stirling, *Coke of Norfolk and His Friends*, 2 vols. (London and New York: Lane, 1908), I, 251–305, and R.C.A. Parker, "Coke of Norfolk and the Agrarian Revolution," *Economic History Review*, 2nd ser., 8, no. 2 (1955), 156–66.

15 The tread wheel was a kind of squirrel cage in which convicts walked, originally to no purpose, but subsequently to provide power for grinding grain. Introduced into prisons in 1818, it was hailed by some as a useful improvement in methods of punishment, and condemned by others as inhuman torture; see, e.g., J.S. Mill, "Atrocities of the Tread Wheel," *Globe and Traveller*, 3 Oct. 1823, 3; in *Newspaper Writings, Collected Works*, XXII (Toronto: University of Toronto Press, 1986), 67–70.

16 For centuries, hunting for game had been restricted, by a property qualification, to the landed gentry, and penalties for poaching were severe. The Night Poaching Act (57 George III, c. 90, 10 July 1817) had introduced even more stringent regulations, stipulating, for example, transportation for seven years as the penalty for hunting, armed, at night (§1). Game was, however, regularly stolen, and found a thriving open market. By the 1820s, the situation had reached a crisis, reformers pointing to the cruelty and immorality of the laws and the exorbitant number of the poor and hungry in the jails. For a discussion of the complex problem, see Peter Munsche, *Gentlemen and Poachers, the English Game Laws 1671–1831* (Cambridge: Cambridge University Press, 1981).

17 Sir James Edward Smith (1759–1828) had purchased Linnaeus' collections in 1784; see Andrew Thomas Gage and William Thomas Stearn, *A Bicentenary History of the Linnean Society of London* (London: Academic Press, 1988), 5, 176–81, and Margot Walker, *Sir James Edward Smith 1759–1828, First President of the Linnean Society of London* (London: Linnean Society, 1988).

18 Thomas William Coke had three daughters by his first marriage, the second of whom, Anne Margaret (1779–1843), was the widow of Thomas, Viscount Anson (1767–1818). Their daughter, Anne Margaret (1796–1882), had married Archibald John Primrose, 4th Earl of Rosebery in 1819. Coke's third daughter, Elizabeth Wilhelmina (1795–1873), had, in fact, married John Spencer-Stanhope on 5 December 1822. Early that year Coke had married Anne Amelia Keppel (1803–44). The "three-month old" was Thomas William, born 26 December 1822 (d. 1909), the first of five sons and a daughter of this second marriage. A family genealogy is in an appendix to Stirling, *Coke of Norfolk*, II, 499–535.

19 The question of whether the law should be changed to allow members of the

Roman Catholic faith to hold office was a problem of long standing, and one of the sources of discontent in Ireland. Catholics were prevented from entering Parliament or the civil service by being unable to swear to the Test Act, which rejected transubstantiation. This particular debate, which occurred on Thursday, 17 (not 15) April, is recorded in *PD*, n.s., vol. 8, cols. 1070–1106, and in *The Times*, 18 Apr. 1823, 2–3. Some of the details that GB provides are not mentioned, as the reports of the day were not *verbatim*.

20 The speech of Sir Francis Burdett (1770–1844) is in *PD*, n.s., vol. 8, cols. 1071–8; William Conyngham Plunket (1764–1854), the Attorney-General for Ireland, at the conclusion of the debate would move for the House to resolve into a committee to "consider the state of the laws by which oaths or declarations are required to be taken or made as qualifications for the enjoyment of offices, or for the exercise of civil functions, so far as the same may affect his majesty's Catholic subjects, and whether it would be expedient . . . to alter or modify the same . . ." (ibid., cols. 1108–9). The portion of Plunket's earlier speech, of 25 February 1813, quoted by Burdett, is ibid., 1st ser., vol. 24, cols. 816–17.

21 The speech of George Grenville, Baron Nugent (1788–1850), is ibid., n.s., vol. 8, col. 1078.

22 George Canning had earlier been an active supporter of Catholic emancipation, and was being accused of having abandoned the cause in order to be accepted into the Cabinet, in November 1822, as Secretary of State for Foreign Affairs. His refutation of Burdett is ibid., cols. 1078, 1079–81.

23 The speeches by George Tierney, Charles Williams Wynn, Robert Peel (1788–1850) and Archibald Hamilton are ibid., cols. 1081–9, 1094–5.

24 The speech by Henry Peter Brougham (1788–1868) and Canning's outburst are ibid., cols., 1089–91.

25 The appeal by the Speaker, Charles Manners Sutton (1780–1845), to Peel, and the exchange between the latter and Brougham are not reported in *PD*.

26 E.g., Tierney, at col. 1093.

27 Canning's, Henry Bankes' and Williams Wynn's observations are in cols. 1094–6; Arthur Onslow's part is not recorded.

28 Canning's statement is in col. 1098 and Brougham's final observations are in cols. 1099–1102. Plunket's motion was defeated and the matter was "adjourned till this day six months," i.e., dropped, at least for the time being. Catholic emancipation was finally implemented by 10 George IV, c. 7 (1829).

29 The House of Commons had traditionally met in St Stephen's Chapel in the precincts of the palace at Westminster. On 16 October 1834, all the buildings of the palace, except Westminster Hall, were destroyed by fire. The new

Houses of Parliament, designed by Sir Charles Barry, were begun in 1840 and completed in 1867.

30 See *PD*, n.s., vol. 9, cols. 30–4.

31 The account is ibid., cols. 34–69 and in *The Times*, 6 May 1823, 2–3, which includes more detail. The parliamentary inquiry resulted from the handling by Sheriff Charles Thorpe of the trial of those accused of assault against the Lord Lieutenant, Marquess Richard Colley Wellesley, at the Dublin Theatre on 14 December 1822. The sheriff was alleged to have packed the jury with members of the Dublin corporation, who effectively threw out the bills of indictment against the rioters. An account of the trial, of 2 January, is in "Conspiracy against the Lord Lieutenant," *The Times*, 7 Jan. 1823, 3.

32 The testimony of Benjamin Ricky is reported in *PD*, vol. 9, cols. 34–40, followed by that of Terence O'Reilly, cols. 40–6, and Dillon (or William) Macnamara, cols. 46–50.

33 John McConnell, in col. 52.

34 This last remark was, in fact, made by the previous witness, Peter Tomlinson, in col. 51.

35 The story about the witness William Poole is not reported in *PD*, but is in *The Times*, 6 May 1823, 3.

36 Not reported. The inquiry into Thorpe's conduct continued until 27 May, but the session ended without any action being taken.

37 In fact, two days later, on 7 May; see "Anniversary Meeting of the Bible Society," *The Times*, 8 May 1823, 3.

38 Henry Ryder (1777–1836), evangelical Bishop of Gloucester, 1815–24, brother of Dudley Ryder, Earl of Harrowby (1762–1847).

39 A major earthquake occurred in Syria in mid-November of 1822; reported in *The Times*, 18 Jan. 1823, 2.

40 Franz Joseph Gall (1758–1828) and Johann Caspar Spurzheim (1776–1832) had published their theories about phrenology in *Anatomie et physiologie du système nerveux en général, et du cerveau en particulier; avec des observations sur la possibilité de reconnoître plusieurs dispositions intellectuelles et morales de l'homme et des animaux, par la configuration de leurs têtes*. 4 vols., plus 1 vol. of plates and atlas (Paris: Schoell, 1810–19).

41 Sir Joseph Banks (1743–1820) had accompanied Captain James Cook (1728–79) on his first voyage around the world, August 1768 to June 1771. They sailed westward to South America, rounded Cape Horn, visited Tahiti, New Zealand and Australia, and returned to England via the Cape of Good Hope. Banks left to Robert Brown (1773–1858), who had served as his librarian, £200 a year for life, and the use of his house, library and herbarium, with a reversion to the British Museum. In 1827 Brown transferred the herbarium

and library to the Museum, where he was appointed Keeper of the botanical collections, a position he retained until his death.

42 Major-General Thomas Hardwicke (1757–1835) had collected plants, mammals, birds, and drawings of the last, during his service with the East India Company, bequeathing them to the British Museum on his death; see *The History of the Natural History Collections . . . of the British Museum*, 2 vols. (London: British Museum, 1904–12), II, 169. The "other birds" may have belonged to the George Caley collection; see Gage and Stearn, *Bicentenary History*, 175.

43 This was part of a series presented by Francis Hamilton Buchanan (1762–1829) at no fewer than thirty-one meetings, beginning in May 1821, under the general title "Commentary on the *Hortus [indicus] malabaricus*," of Hendrik Adriaan van Rheede tot Draakestein (1637–91); see Gage and Stearn, *Bicentenary History*, 156.

44 Joseph Julien Ghislain Parmentier (1775–1852), Belgian botanist and horticulturist, who introduced many new plants from England into his garden at Enghien.

45 Archibald Menzies (1754–1842) had been surgeon and naturalist with Captain George Vancouver (1758–98) on a voyage of exploration, April 1791 to October 1795. Sailing round the Cape of Good Hope, they visited Tahiti and the Sandwich Islands (Hawaii), then explored the coast of North America as far north as Nootka Sound, and south to San Francisco, returning to England via Cape Horn.

46 This part of Menzies' collection was bequeathed to the Edinburgh Botanical Garden.

47 The Chelsea Physic Garden was established in 1676 by the Apothecaries' Company on land they had leased with the intention of building a boathouse for their state barge. In 1681 the first greenhouse and stove in England were built here, and in 1683 the first cedar trees to grow in the country were planted. Sir Hans Sloane (1660–1753), who was Lord of the Manor, gave the land to the Apothecaries' Company on condition that they maintain it to the glory of God in his natural works, and that they give 2000 dried plants to the Royal Society at the rate of 50 per annum. Philip Miller (1691–1771) was in charge of the Garden from 1722 to 1770, and William Anderson (1766–1846) assumed the position in 1816.

48 JB's preferred term for "before breakfast."

49 *The Oxford Dictionary of English Place Names* (1960) indicates that the names "Chelsea" and "Battersea" derive from words meaning "Landing place for chalk or limestone," and "Beaduric's island."

50 Charles Thomas Longley (1794–1868), Archbishop of Canterbury from 1862 until his death.

51 Vauxhall Bridge, the first iron bridge over the Thames in London, was opened in 1816. Waterloo Bridge, the work of the engineer John Rennie and the contractors Joliffe and Banks, was completed the following year.

52 For William Townsend Aiton, see 36n38.

53 Uncharacteristically, GB seems to be confusing the Parmentier identifed in n44 above with Antoine Augustin Parmentier (1737–1813), the French chemist and agronomist, author of such works as *Recherches sur les végétaux nourrissants . . . avec de nouvelles observations sur la culture des pommes de terre* (Paris: Imprimerie royale, 1781).

54 The practice of tracing out the boundaries of a parish by striking them at certain points with rods, or by some other means, in the presence of witnesses.

55 From 1759 the British Museum had been located in Montagu House, situated in what is now the forecourt of the present Museum in Great Russell Street. Prospective visitors usually applied for tickets of admission to view the treasures, from Monday to Friday, between 10 and 4 o'clock, when they were shown round in parties of no more than five persons. The King's Library, the large east wing built to house the library of George III, which came into the Museum's possession in 1823, was begun in that year and completed in 1827.

56 The Portland (formerly Barberini) vase, dating from about the 1st century A.D., is a fine example of cameo glass, with a design of white, opaque glass on a blue background. It was purchased by the Duke of Portland in 1790; a Wedgwood copy, made that year, is in the Victoria and Albert Museum.

57 It was presumably on his first voyage in search of the North West passage, 1819–20, that William Edward Parry (1790–1855) collected this specimen.

58 The oversupply of grain in the British market, with consequent low prices and hardship for farmers, had been a problem ever since the conclusion of the peace in 1815; see Alexander Brady, *William Huskisson and Liberal Reform, an Essay on the Changes in Economic Policy in the Twenties of the Nineteenth Century*, 2nd ed. (London: Cass, 1967), chapter 3, "The Corn Laws," 41–72.

59 See Louis Simond, *Journal of a Tour and Residence in Great Britain during the Years 1810 and 1811, by a French Traveller*, 2 vols. (Edinburgh: Constable; London: Longman, et al., 1815), I, 9.

60 Vauxhall pleasure gardens, first laid out in 1661, added "Royal" to their name in 1822 as a result of the active patronage of George IV.

61 GB describes the Cosmorama as an exhibition of "a number of paintings that we look at through a pane of glass, that is, so many dramas in miniature. This is the best way of creating illusion, but they were most of them indifferently done. There were views of Mont Blanc, 2 of Versailles, 1 in Spain, 1 in Mexico, two or three in the Andes, 1 of Cairo, 1 of Thebes, 2 of Palmyra, and

some other cities in Asia and Africa, on the whole, scarcely worth the 2 shillings. . . ." (Entry for 24 May 1823.)

62 From 1795 the Anniversary Meeting of the LSL was held on 24 May, "which
was taken to be the birthday of Linnaeus according to the New Style Calen-
dar," though the date, in fact, should have been calculated as 23 May (Gage
and Stearn, *Bicentenary History*, 17).

63 Samuel Goodenough (1743–1827), Vice-President of the Society, had been
Bishop of Carlisle since 1808.

64 George Spencer-Churchill (1766–1840), 5th Duke of Marlborough, had
depleted his finances by spending extravagant sums on his gardens and his
library, at White Knights, near Reading.

65 A full-size equestrian portrait of King Charles I by Anthony Van Dyck
(1599–1641).

66 Henry Richard Greville (1779–1853), 3rd Earl Brooke of Warwick Castle and
Earl of Warwick.

67 Guy de Beauchamp (ca. 1273–1315), 10th Earl of Warwick.

68 A Greek marble vase, dating from the end of the 4th century, B.C., excavated
in 1770, and purchased by George Greville (1746–1816), 2nd Earl Brooke of
Warwick Castle and Earl of Warwick.

69 JB had been very impressed by a work of Matthew Davenport Hill (1792–
1872), *Public Education. Plans for the Government and Liberal Instruction of Boys
in Large Numbers, As Practised at Hazelwood School* (London: Knight, 1822),
which described the educational theory and practice of his brother, Rowland
Hill (1795–1879). In about 1803, their father, Thomas Wright Hill (1763–1851),
had established Hill Top School on the outskirts of Birmingham, where his
sons were first pupils and then teachers. In 1819 the school was renamed
Hazlewood and moved to new quarters, Rowland Hill becoming the director, assisted by his mother, Sarah, his brothers Arthur, Edwin and Frederic
and his sister Caroline. The publicity provided by the publication of the
eldest brother and the genuine merit of the program made the school very
successful.

70 The postal service had been viewed by government as a money-making venture, and rates, originally settled by an Act of 1711, had risen steadily
between 1797 and 1812. Charges were based on distance, for a single piece of
letter paper, folded and sealed. A second (or third) piece of paper or any
enclosure incurred a double (or triple) charge. Prices ranged from 4d. for
delivery within a 15-mile range to 1/1d. for 300–400 miles and 1d. extra for
every additional 100 miles thereafter, and there was an array of further regulations and costs. For instance, an extra halfpenny was exacted for a letter
going to Scotland, and 1/2d. was the cost of the English portion for a letter

going to France. (See GB's note, 189 above.) For an unskilled labourer, whose daily rate of pay might be 1/ to 1/6d., postage was virtually prohibitive, and the public used every possible means to evade payment. In 1837 Rowland Hill's pamphlet *Post Office Reform, Its Importance and Practicability* (London: privately printed) demonstrated that revenue could actually be raised by instituting a more efficient system. He advocated the uniform charge of a penny for every letter of half an ounce in weight, prepayment, and the use of adhesive postage stamps. The scheme was adopted in January of 1840, and gradually succeeded in overcoming the many bureaucratic objections that were raised against it. See Frank Staff, *The Penny Post 1680–1918* (London: Lutterworth, 1964), chapter 4, 71–95.

71 Jedediah Strutt (1762–97), the original partner of Richard Arkwright (1731–92) in the cotton-spinning business, had passed the concern on to his three sons, William (1756–1830), George Benson (1761–1841) and Joseph (1765–1844). They provided housing, schools, and an infirmary for their workpeople. William's only son, Edward (1801–80), who later had a distinguished career in public life (and whom GB erroneously calls Lord Derby as well as Lord Belper), was at this time studying at Trinity College, Cambridge. William, the engineering partner, built the first fire-proof buildings at Belper. This was but one of the interests he shared with SB. For more on the achievements of this remarkable family in its manufacturing and philanthropic enterprises, see R.S. Fitton and A.P. Wadsworth, *The Strutts and the Arkwrights, 1758–1830* (Manchester: Manchester University Press, 1958), esp. 169–91.

72 The collection is described in *Catalogue of Paintings, Drawings, Marbles, Bronzes, &c. &c. in the Collection of Mr. Joseph Strutt* (Derby: privately printed, 1827 and 1835).

73 Charles Sylvester, a civil engineer, was the author of *The Philosophy of Domestic Economy, As Exemplified in the Mode of Warming, Ventilating, Washing, Drying, and Cooking, and in Various Arrangements Contributing to the Comfort and Convenience of Domestic Life, Adopted in the Derbyshire General Infirmary, and More Recently . . . in Several Other Public Buildings* (London: Longman, et al., 1819).

74 The first rail of George Stephenson's Darlington to Stockton railway was, in fact, laid on 23 May 1823, and the line was opened for traffic on 27 September 1825. It was followed by the Liverpool and Manchester Railway, inaugurated on 15 September 1830.

75 On the death of Elizabeth I in 1603, James VI of Scotland, whose great-grandmother was a daughter of Henry VII, succeeded to the throne of England as James I.

76 See Homer, *The Odyssey* (Greek and English), trans. A.T. Murray, 2 vols.

(London: Heinemann; New York: Putnam's Sons, 1919), I, 311, 317–19, 323 (bk. IX, 110–15, 215–25, 287–300).

77 Mrs Morton (b. ca. 1730) was presumably the mother both of Mrs Ibbetson, wife of Henry Ibbetson of St Anthony's, Northumberland, and of Frances, wife of Thomas William Carr of Hampstead. Mrs Ibbetson's daughter, Isabella Grace, married Cuthbert Ellison (1783–1860) in 1804, and died in 1860. Her daughter, Isabella Caroline (1805–53), married George John Venables-Vernon, 5th baron Vernon (1803–66) in 1824.

78 James IV was, in fact, killed at the battle of Flodden Field in 1513.

79 John Charles Wallop, 3rd Earl of Portsmouth (1767–1853), was mentally unfit to manage his own affairs, and from 1790 his property had been in the hands of four trustees, the most influential of whom being the family solicitor, Charles Hanson. In 1814, after the death of his first wife, the Earl married Hanson's daughter, Mary Ann. Mr Alder, ostensibly a doctor, but in fact the young Countess's lover, joined the ménage, which moved about the country, purportedly seeking healthy situations and medical advice. An action aimed at ending the Earl's mistreatment by his keepers occupied the House of Lords from 10 to 28 February 1823. It was found that he had been of unsound mind from 1 January 1809, and his second marriage was dissolved. For details, see *A Genuine Report of the Proceedings on the Portsmouth Case, under a Commission Issued by His Majesty* [*to Enquire into the Sanity of the Earl of Portsmouth*] (London: Duncombe, [1823]), or *The Times*, 12–15, 17–21, 24–8 Feb. all 3, and 1 Mar. 1823, 2–3.

80 A reference to the regulation of the shape of wheels for the protection of the roads in §1 of the most recent of the Turnpike Acts, 4 George IV, c. 95 (19 July 1823).

Chapter 5

1 Macadamization consisted of putting down successive layers of stones of nearly uniform size, each layer being allowed to consolidate under the pressure of traffic before the next was applied. The method had first been described in a pamphlet in 1816, and had recently been studied by government; see John Loudon McAdam (1756–1836), *Remarks on the Present System of Road-Making, Eighth Edition, Carefully Revised, with an Appendix, and Report from the Select Committee of the House of Commons, June 1823, with Extracts from the Evidence* (London: Longman, et al., 1824).

2 This and all subsequent quotations in the chapter derive from GB's journal-letters to his family; MSS at LSL.

3 The monument to commemorate the Scottish soldiers who fell in the wars against Napoleon was begun in 1824 but never completed for lack of funds.

4 A provision of the Copyright Act, 54 George III, c. 156 (1814).

5 Eliza Fletcher (1770–1858) was the wife of the barrister Archibald Fletcher (1745–1828), and a hostess for the Edinburgh Whig circle. Her eldest daughter, Elizabeth (b. 1794), was married to William Taylor II, proprietor of collieries in Ayrshire. She had two younger daughters, Margaret (b. 1798) and Mary (b. 1802), and two sons, the younger of whom was Angus (b. 1799); see also 161 above and n10 below.

6 In 1814 McVey Napier (1776–1847) had undertaken to organize the production of a series of supplementary articles to the *Encyclopedia Britannica* (1771) that would present the most advanced views on each subject. The *Supplement to the Fourth, Fifth and Sixth Editions of the Encyclopedia Britannica* appeared first as fascicles, and was finally completed in six volumes (Edinburgh: Constable, 1824).

7 Only two of the papers of which abstracts were read at the meeting of 17 June 1823 appear to have been later published in full: David Brewster (1781–1868), "Description of Hopeite, a New Mineral from Altenberg near Aix-la-Chapelle," *Transactions of the Royal Society of Edinburgh*, 10 (1826), 107–11, and Robert Knox (1791–1862), "Observations on the Comparative Anatomy of the Eye," ibid., 43–78.

8 Jacob Perkins (1766–1849), American-born inventor, was experimenting at this time with high-pressure steam boilers and engines. By 1827 he perfected a boiler and single-cylinder engine using steam at 800 lbs. per cubic inch, and that same year constructed a compound steam engine, with pressure at 1400 lbs.

9 Public libraries had been established in France by a decree of the Convention Nationale, session of 28 January 1794; see *Le Moniteur Universel*, repr. (Paris: Plon, 1858–63), 19, 334–5. Each department had a central library in its chief town, and there were many municipalities with their own collections.

10 Accompanied by her sisters Harriet and Sophy, Maria Edgeworth was in Scotland at this time, primarily in order to visit Sir Walter Scott; see her *Life and Letters*, ed. A.J.C. Hare, 2 vols. (London: Arnold, 1894), II, 93–119. Eliza Fletcher's impressions of Maria and her account of the party are in the *Autobiography of Mrs. Fletcher*, ed. Mary Fletcher Richardson, 2nd ed. (Edinburgh: Edmonston and Douglas, 1875), 156–7. Angus Fletcher, whose career in sculpture was just beginning, later moved to London. Among his works exhibited at the Royal Academy were marble busts of the Duke of Argyll (1831) and of Charles Dickens (1839).

11 A novel by Henry Mackenzie (1745–1831), entitled *The Man of Feeling* (Lon-

don: Cadell, 1771), was a popular sentimental work in the style of Laurence Sterne.

12 Robert Liston (1742–1836) had been British Ambassador to the United States, 1796–1804.

13 The *Oxford English Dictionary*, quoting J. Robertson, *Agriculture in Perth* (1799) gives the following definition: "A Scotch acre commonly = 6084 sq. yards. If the differences of inches were narrowly attended to in making the Scotch chain, a Scotch acre would be equal to 6150.7 sq. yards." An English acre had been fixed by statute at 4840 sq. yards.

14 Captain Basil Hall had been in the East Indies, 1812–15, and on Lord Amherst's mission to China, 1816–17 (see 281n3 above). Sent to South America in August of 1820, Hall was stationed at Valparaiso, spent two years exploring the western coast, and returned to England in the spring of 1823. He had met William Effingham Lawrence (1781–1841), a merchant and shipper, friend of JB, who stopped at Rio, June to November 1822, on his way to settle in Australia; see also *CJB*, IX, 279–80, 382.

15 Magdalene De Lancey Harvey (d. 1822) wrote an account of her experience caring for her first husband, later edited by B.R. Ward, *A Week at Waterloo in 1815* (London: Murray, 1906).

16 In 1785 James Hutton (1726–97), an Edinburgh geologist, lectured and published a pamphlet expounding his theory of the "System of the Earth." From examination of sedimentary rocks composed of fossils and the products of erosion, he concluded that they had originally been at the bottom of an ocean, and over time subject to consolidation and to upheaval to their present positions by the force of an internal fire existing beneath the earth's crust. Abraham Gottlob Werner (1749–1817), originator of an alternative theory about the earth's origin, believed that it had once been enveloped in a universal ocean, from which all existing rocks were precipitates. The receding of the water had occurred in five stages, producing the various classes of rocks, the latter two named volcanic and alluvial. Experiments performed by Sir James Hall had given support to Hutton's theory of consolidation through the process of heat.

17 GB presumably should have said that three nineteens and *three* fifteens were the equivalent of 102 years.

18 *Galignani's Messenger* was an English newspaper, published in Paris from 1814, composed of excerpts from the London and Paris papers.

19 During the previous year major reforms in the commercial and navigation regulations had been introduced, in five statutes, 3 George IV, cc. 41–5 (24 June 1822). In the Liverpool ministry formed in August of that year, F.J. Robinson (Lord Goderich), who had worked for these changes, was appointed

Chancellor of the Exchequer, and in April 1823, William Huskisson became President of the Board of Trade. Several further measures for the expansion of freer trade were introduced: e.g., a Scotch linen manufacture Bill, removing restrictions on that industry in Scotland (3 & 4 George IV, c. 40, 1823); in 1824, a Warehousing Bill, which allowed foreign merchants to deposit and remove their goods from warehouses in Britain without duty (4 George IV, c. 24), a Reciprocity Duties Bill, which proposed that duties should be equal on goods carried in British ships or in ships of those foreign countries that would adopt the same principle (c. 77), and the repeal of the Spitalfields Acts, which had provided special protection for the silk trade (c. 66); see Brady, *William Huskisson and Liberal Reform*, chapter 4, "The First Breaches in the Old Commercial System," esp. 89–99. These initiatives had the desired effect of increasing British trade, particularly, over time, that of silks exported to France (ibid., 102–6). GB is probably thinking of the commercial treaty between England and France of 1860 as a later step forward; reported in *The Times*, 3 Oct. 1860, 8.

20 A line of inland navigation, partly natural, partly artificial, from Inverness to Glasgow. Begun in 1803, it was opened in 1822, only two-thirds finished, and was completed in the years 1843–47.

21 William Jackson Hooker (1785–1865) was the son of Joseph Hooker, a Norwich merchant, and his wife Lydia. In 1815 William married Maria Turner, eldest of the twelve children of Dawson Turner, a banker as well as a botanist and antiquarian, and his wife Mary. By 1823 William and Maria had four children: William Dawson, Joseph Dalton (1817–1911), Maria and Elizabeth. A fifth, Mary Harriet, would be born in 1825. Maria Turner Hooker's sister, mentioned below as being sixteen years of age, might be Hannah Sarah (1808–82) or Harriet (1806–69). For both families, see Mea Allen, *The Hookers of Kew, 1785–1911* (London: Joseph, 1967).

22 "To wait for one who ne'er comes by / To be in bed and sleepless lie / To serve and not to satisfy, / Are reasons three to make one die." The verse was a development of the line from act IV, sc. i of Giordano Bruno's comedy, *Candelaio* (1582): "Aspettare e non venire è cosa da morire."

23 See Walter Scott, *The Lady of the Lake* (1810), canto first, stanzas xxvi–xxvii; in the Riverside ed. (Boston and New York: Houghton Mifflin, 1900), 161–2.

24 GB is probably referring to the two elder sons of Robert Owen (1771–1858), the industrialist and socialist, i.e., Robert Dale (1801–77) and William (1802–42), who assisted their father in the management of the cotton mills at New Lanark. In 1824 William would accompany his father to the American community of New Harmony, Indiana, and Robert Dale would join them in 1825.

25 In 1813 JB had invested in a quarry and masonry business, conducted by

James Grellier, which declared bankruptcy in 1817; see *CJB*, VIII, 218, 515–16 and IX, 8, 268.

26 Investing the remaining £10,000 in Owen's enterprise, JB had become a partner with, in fact, five others: William Allen, Joseph Foster and John Walker, three wealthy Quaker philanthropists; Joseph Fox, a dissenting dentist; and Michael Gibbs, Alderman, later Lord Mayor of London.

27 Owen, a Scottish mill-owner devoted to reform, had constructed a model factory town at New Lanark, in accordance with his views outlined in four essays, entitled *A New View of Society; or, Essays on the Principle of the Formation of Human Character, and the Application of Principle to Practice* (London: Cadell and Davies, 1813) and in his *Report to the County of Lanark, of a Plan for Relieving Public Distress, and Removing Discontent, by Giving Permanent, Productive Employment to the Poor and Working Classes* (Glasgow: Wardlaw and Cunninghame; Edinburgh: Constable, et al.; London: Longman, et al., 1821). The schools, particularly, became a show place for educators. They were described by Robert Dale Owen in *An Outline of the System of Education at New Lanark* (Glasgow: Wardlaw and Cunninghame, 1824).

28 In 1820 Henry Peter Brougham had introduced into the Commons a Parish School Bill, which would have put the curriculum in the hands of the parish clergy and required that teachers be regular communicants of the Anglican Church; see M.G. Jones, *The Charity School Movement* (London: Cass, 1964), 330.

29 In Robert Owen, *Report to the County of Lanark*, 27–8.

30 Archibald James Hamilton (1793–1834), laird of Dalzell and Orbiston, a philanthropic Scottish landlord, had joined Owen and others the previous year (1822) in forming the British and Foreign Philanthropic Society to initiate productive communities all over the country. He had offered an estate at Motherwell, near Lanark, as a site for one of these, but the total subscription never exceeded £55,000 and the scheme had to be dropped. Hamilton, in collaboration with Abram Combe of Edinburgh, later started an experimental community at Orbiston; see J.F.C. Harrison, *Robert Owen and the Owenites in Britain and America* (Cambridge, Mass.: Harvard University Press, 1969), 26–30.

31 In Hamilton one could visit the ruins of Cadzow Castle, as well as Hamilton Palace, famous for its splendid picture gallery.

32 Housed in its own special building, opened in 1808, the Hunterian Museum contained the general and anatomical collection of Dr William Hunter (1718–83), which he had bequeathed to the University of Glasgow on his death.

33 This plan was not pursued.

34 After the prohibition of clandestine marriages by Lord Hardwicke's Act, 26

George II, c. 33 (1753), English persons who wished to marry secretly had to leave the country, and as the nearest and most convenient spot north of the Scottish border, Gretna Green became a popular refuge for couples wishing to take advantage of Scottish law, under which it was sufficient to declare one's intent to marry, before witnesses. Any person could officiate at the ceremony, though it was apparently the blacksmith who was frequently called upon. This situation continued until the passage of 19 & 20 Victoria, c. 97 (1856), which stipulated that after 1 December 1856 all irregular marriages entered into in Scotland would be declared invalid unless one of the parties had been a resident for twenty-one days.

35 The museum at Keswick was established in 1780 by Peter Crosthwaite, and his son Daniel (ca. 1776–1847) succeeded him as director. The guide, Hutton, has not been further identified.

36 The cairn was, rather, in memory of Dunmail who, according to tradition, was defeated and killed by Edmund I (ca. 922–46 A.D.) in the year 946; see, e.g., the account in one of the most popular of the guide books by Thomas West, *A Guide to the Lakes, in Cumberland, Westmoreland, and Lancashire*, 11th ed. (Kendal: Pennington, 1821), 83.

37 The family name *Scitamineae* (no longer in use) is generally attributed to Robert Brown, *Prodromus florae Novae Hollandiae* (London: Johnson, 1810), 305, but is, in fact, one of the small number of natural families recognized by Linnaeus. *Cannae* Jussieu and *Amomeae* Jussieu were included in *Scitamineae*. *Monandria* is not a family name, but Class 1 of Linnaeus' Sexual Sytem of Classification, which includes *Scitamineae*, along with other very distinct families. [Note by Desmond Meikle.]

38 The article referred to is probably that by John Lindsay, "Account of the Germination and Raising of Ferns from the Seed," *Transactions of the Linnean Society of London*, 2 (1794), 93–100.

39 Prince Gagarin was very interested in agricultural improvements on his estates in Russia, and he studied the most up-to-date methods on his trips to France. See also 94 above.

40 *Flora; oder, Allgemeine botanische Zeitung*, founded in 1818 in Regensburg (Ratisbon) by D.H. Hoppe (1760–1846) and C.F. Hornschuch (1793–1850), with the collaboration of C.G. Nees von Esenbeck (1776–1858).

41 William Allen's only child, Mary, married Cornelius Hanbury in 1822, and died after childbirth on 17 May 1823; see *Life of William Allen, with Selections from His Correspondence*, 3 vols. (London: Gilpin, 1836–47), II, 222, 347–42.

42 A journal-letter from Paris, covering the period 16 to 23 August 1823, is at LSL.

43 A braking device attached to the wheels of horse-drawn carriages.

44 The son and daughter of the duchesse de Berry: Henri Charles Ferdinand, duc de Bordeaux (1820–83), heir to the throne, and his sister, Louise Marie Thérèse d'Artois, "Mademoiselle" (1819–64), a year older. See 61n21 and 70n39 above. Their governess was Joséphine de Gontaut-Biron (b. 1773), lady-in-waiting to their mother.

45 The review of troops was conducted by Louis XVIII's brother, the comte d'Artois, in honour of George IV's brother, Ernest Augustus, Duke of Cumberland (1771–1851), who spent several days in Paris, before continuing on a visit to Germany; see *Le Constitutionnel*, 19 and 23 Aug. 1823, both 4.

Chapter 6

1 Fifteen letters for this period, dated 26 February to 8 April 1824, are at LSL, but others must not have been preserved, as some quotations have not been located. For background to the journey, see the Introduction, xxviii–xxix above.

2 Having demonstrated in 1796 that a vaccine of cowpox lymph was protective against smallpox, Edward Jenner (1749–1823) published his findings two years later as *An Inquiry into the Causes and Effects of the Variolae Vaccinae* (London: printed for the author, 1798), and the technique of vaccination slowly gained acceptance from that time.

3 As is confirmed in GB's letters, one of these was Elizabeth Gordon; see 94–5n55 above.

4 The entry in the journal-letter for 15 March 1824 indicates that GB is referring specifically to an article in the *Journal des Débats* of that day, on Adam Smith's *Wealth of Nations* (1776), and on Canning and Huskisson's free trade initiatives.

5 Robert Owen attacked traditional marriage and the family as narrow, tyrannical institutions, and fostered the ideal of an extended community as the proper object of loyalty. He did not advocate indiscriminate sexual relations, but marriage based on affection, with birth control and the possibility of divorce as parts of the social arrangements in a more moral world; see J.F.C. Harrison, *Robert Owen and the Owenites in Britain and America*, 59–62. Frances (Fanny) Wright D'Arusmont (1795–1852), a pioneer feminist, had visited the United States, 1818–20, and published *Views of Society and Manners in America* (London: Longman, et al., 1821), which had attracted the attention and the friendship of JB (*Works*, VIII, 515, and X, 526–7). She and her sister Camilla spent three years in Paris, Fanny becoming the protégée of Lafayette during this time, and then they

returned to the U.S. in 1825, where Fanny founded the colony of Nashoba, West Tennessee, on Owenite principles, to be a free home for ex-slaves. Both sisters entered into unfortunate marriages, Camilla in 1827, and Fanny in 1831. See A.J.G. Perkins and Theresa Wolfson, *Fanny Wright* (Philadelphia: Porcupine Press, 1972), esp. 188–207.

6 The herbarium, but not the correspondence, is at RBGK.

7 The name given in J.J. Roemer and J.A. Schultes, *Caroli a Linné Systema vegetabilium*, 16th ed., 7 vols. (Stuttgart: Cotta, 1817–30), IV, 248; see F.A. Stafleu and R.S. Cowan, *Taxonomic Literature*, 2nd ed. (Utrecht: Bohn, Scheltema and Holkema, et al., 1976–92), IV, no. 9408. [Note by Desmond Meikle.]

8 SB died, in fact, on 30 April 1831.

9 Her friendship with Augustin Pyramus de Candolle is documented in *L'Europe de 1830, vue à travers la correspondance d'Augustin Pyramus de Candolle et de madame de Circourt*, ed. Roger de Candolle (Geneva: Jullien, 1966).

10 The following account of a three-months' botanizing journey in southwestern France was composed from journal-letters, some of which are apparently no longer extant. One letter, covering the period 31 May to 6 June 1825, is at RBGK; another nine, dated 25 May to 9 August, are at LSL. GB had already used his letters to write the lively "Notice sur un voyage botanique fait dans les Pyrénées pendant l'été de 1825," *Catalogue des plantes indigènes des Pyrénées et du Bas Languedoc* (Paris: Huzard, 1826), 15–55, from which some of the episodes are taken.

11 See GB, *Catalogue*, 100.

12 As a result of the uprising of 1820 (see 61–2n23 and 101n5 above), Ferdinand VII had been compelled to swear allegiance to the Constitution of 1812, but did everything he could to undermine its operation and the authority of the Cortes, which tried unsuccessfully to reconcile constitutional liberty with monarchy. By 1822, the liberal party had discovered that it could govern only on absolute lines, Ferdinand was in the power of his ministers, and the country was in chaos. The duc d'Angoulême's army, which had entered the country in April of 1823 had succeeded in restoring Ferdinand to power by 1 October.

13 The botanic garden at Valencia was established in 1802 under the aegis of José Antonio Cavanilles (1745–1804), Professor of Botany and Director of the garden at Madrid.

14 GB visited southwestern France and Spain again in September and October of 1859.

15 General Francisco Espoz y Mina (1781–1836) led the forces of the Constitutional Cortes of Spain against the invading French army until 1 November 1823, when he was obliged to surrender at Barcelona. Joaquín Ibañez Eroles (1785–1825), member of a triumvirate regency established at La Seo d'Urgel,

which represented the authority of Ferdinand VII, was, in fact, waging a civil war against his former comrade, Mina. Eroles was believed to have had mixed feelings about the foreign invasion in support of the King.

16 A net-like head covering.

17 The article in question, which GB also refers to in "The Republic of Andorra," *London Magazine*, 7 (Feb. 1827), 145, is "Notice sur la république d'Andorre," *Revue Encyclopédique*, 17 (Feb. 1823), 221–7, signed "A.L."

18 See Philippe Picot de Lapeyrouse (1744–1818), *Supplément à l'Histoire abrégée des plantes des Pyrénées* (Toulouse: Bellegarigue, 1818), 27; corrected by GB in his *Catalogue*, 113.

Chapter 7

1 See 34 above. Documents relating to this dispute are in the the Archives départementales de l'Hérault, 7 S, 107.

2 This and subsequent quotations in the chapter derive from journal-letters for the period, addressed to his sister MLC at Restinclières, the first dated 11 August 1826; MSS at LSL.

3 John Neal (1793–1876) had been called to the Maryland bar in 1820, but he was chiefly interested in writing, and between 1818 and his departure for England at the end of 1823 had published a verse tragedy and five novels. His next novel, *Brother Jonathan; or, The New Englanders*, 3 vols. (Edinburgh: Blackwood, 1825), was a financial failure in Britain. Though drawing praise for "superb descriptions of New England wrestling matches and quilting frolics," it was criticized for dwelling at length on the "adventures of profligates, misanthropes, maniacs, liars and louts" (quoted from the *British Critic*, 2 [July 1826], 406, in Benjamin Lease, *That Wild Fellow John Neal* [Chicago and London: University of Chicago Press, 1972], 59). Neal contributed pieces on American literature, fine arts, politics and society to such various periodicals as *Blackwood's Edinburgh Magazine*, the *European Magazine and London Review*, the *London Magazine*, the *New Monthly Magazine*, and the *Westminster Review*; a list of his articles is in Lease, 207–9. For his work on JB's projects, see nn 5, 6 and 9 below.

4 For the problems of the London Greek Committee, see 252–5 above. John Bowring had been editor of the *Westminster Review*, the organ of the Radicals sponsored by JB, since its foundation in 1824.

5 In his autobiography, *Wandering Recollections of a Somewhat Busy Life* (Boston: Roberts, 1869), 285–6, Neal reports (and GB's remarks below make his claim plausible) that Bowring had offered him 200 guineas to translate part of JB's

Traités de législation, in order to increase his English audience. Neal completed one volume and asked for some money, which was not forthcoming. An earlier dispute had arisen when Bowring inserted a comment in an article by Neal, making him appear critical of American writing; in "United States," *Westminster Review,* 5 (Jan. 1826), 173–201. The interpolated passage, "exaggeration . . . the character of American literature," is on 194. Neal evened the score by giving details about Bowring's role in the Greek scandals in "Dr. Bowring," *Knickerbocker's Monthly,* 2 (Nov. 1833), 358, and by his full description of their dealings in *Wandering Recollections,* 273–90.

6 JB was working on codes in constitutional, civil, penal and procedural law. One volume of the *Constitutional Code* would be published in 1830, but the projects would all remain incomplete; see "Editorial Introduction," *Constitutional Code,* I, ed. F. Rosen and J.H. Burns (Oxford: Clarendon Press, 1983), esp. xi–xiii, xxvii–xxxix.

7 Entry for 14 April 1827, the day of Neal's departure for France. The novel that he had failed to sell in London is probably *Rachel Dyer: A North American Story,* which was published after his return to the U.S. (Portland, Me.: Shirley and Hyde, 1828); see Lease, *That Wild Fellow John Neal,* 60–1.

8 Neal practised law, lectured, and, from 1828–29, edited the *Yankee,* of Portland, continued as the *Yankee and Boston Literary Gazette,* and later merged into the *New-England Galaxy.* He served briefly again as editor of the latter in 1835, and of *The Portland Transcript* in 1848. His financial success, however, largely resulted from investment in granite quarries in Maine.

9 *Principles of Legislation: From the MS. of Jeremy Bentham . . . by M. Dumont, . . . Translated from the Second Corrected and Enlarged Edition, with Notes and a Biographical Notice of Jeremy Bentham and of M. Dumont. By John Neal* (Boston: Wells and Lilly; New York: Carvill, 1830). This was the work originally commissioned by Bowring. Neal's account of his experiences in JB's household is in the Introduction, 41–55.

10 Horatio (Horace) Smith (1779–1849), *Brambletye House; or, Cavaliers and Roundheads,* 3 vols. (London: Colburn, 1826), connected with a ruined mansion in Ashdown Forest, Sussex, was a romance in imitation of those of Walter Scott.

11 See 371 above. Emma Dax had married Claude Saint-Hilaire, baron Lajard, a senior government administrator in Lyon.

12 The successful three-act comedy, *Paul Pry,* by John Poole (1786?–1872), had first opened at the Haymarket Theatre on 13 September 1825; reviewed in *Examiner,* 18 Sept. 1825, 592–3.

13 See 120 above.

14 See 254n41 above.

15 In GB's *Catalogue*, "Préface," 5–14, and "Notice sur un voyage botanique," 15–55.

16 George Arnott Walker Arnott (1799–1868), the Scottish botanist, had worked for a time in the Paris herbaria. His paper, "Nouvelle disposition méthodique des espèces de mousses exactement connues," read on 18 March 1825, at a meeting of the Société d'Histoire Naturelle de Paris, was first published in their *Mémoires*, 2 (1825), 249–320, and then in pamphlet form (Paris: Tastu, 1825). GB's copy of the latter is at RBGK.

17 Louis Auguste Guillaume Bosc (1759–1828) was the principal editor of the *Nouveau dictionnaire d'histoire naturelle*, 24 vols., 1803–4, the *Annales d'Agriculture Française*, 1811–28, the *Encyclopédie de Panckoucke*, 1813–21, and wrote a great many of the articles.

18 Lady Maria Frances Margaret Lindsay (1783–1850), JB's tenant and next-door neighbour, wife of James Lindsay (1783–1869), later 24th Earl of Crawford and 7th Earl of Balcarres; see *CJB*, VIII, 314.

19 Four bills designed to consolidate the laws relating to offences against property had been drafted at this time. They appear in *PP* in their latest version as: "A Bill for Repealing Statutes in England Relative to Larceny, Malicious Injuries to Property, and to Remedies against the Hundred" (13 Mar. 1827), *PP*, 1826–27, 1, 217–31; "A Bill . . . Relative to Larceny and Other Offences Connected Therewith" (25 May 1827), ibid., 137–60; "A Bill . . . Relative to Malicious Injuries to Property" (25 May 1827), ibid., 201–14; "A Bill . . . Relative to Remedies against the Hundred" (30 May 1827), ibid., 175–83. Robert Peel sent JB draft versions of three of them on 2 September 1826; the accompanying letter is at UCL, 11b, 215–16. The four would pass as 7 & 8 George IV, cc. 27, 29, 30 and 31, respectively (21 June 1827).

20 In "Ministers Collectively: Statistic Function," chapter 9, §vii, *Constitutional Code*, I, ed. F. Rosen and J.H. Burns, 218–67.

21 JB's criticisms of the English law were frequently directed against its exposition and defence in William Blackstone's *Commentaries on the Laws of England*, 4 vols. (Oxford: Clarendon Press, 1765–69).

22 JB's *Constitutional Code* was being translated by Antonio Puig y Blanch (1775–1840), a Spanish philologist and politician. See also 252n30 above.

23 See 285, 312–14n57 above.

24 John Sims (1749–1831) was editor of *Curtis's Botanical Magazine*, 1801–26. Sir William Hooker assumed the editorship in 1827 and served until 1865. John Lindley (1799–1865) wrote the majority of the articles in *Edwards's Botanical Register* from 1825; he was officially editor, 1829–47.

25 See 77n45 above.

26 A Benthamite term, meaning "beautify."

27 From 1777 to 1803, Alleyne Fitzherbert, Baron St Helens (1753–1839), had served as British minister in various European capitals: Brussels, Paris, St Petersburg, the Hague and Madrid. He had known SB during his period as envoy to the Empress Catherine, 1783–87.

28 After studying at Edinburgh University, Robert Liston was appointed tutor to the sons of the statesman and philosopher Sir Gilbert Elliot (1722–77), and spent the years 1764–66 with Gilbert (1751–1814) and Hugh (1752–1830) in Paris. When Hugh Elliot later became a diplomat, Liston served as his private secretary, in Munich and Regensburg, and then in Berlin, 1777–82, where SB made his acquaintance during a visit to that city in November 1779; see *CJB*, II, 326–7. In 1783 Liston moved to Madrid as Secretary, and was raised to the rank of Ambassador in 1788. After a series of important diplomatic posts, he officially retired from the service in 1821.

29 See 162–4 above.

30 The movement for a union among the former Spanish colonies in Central and South America was organized to resist any attempt by Spain or other European power to interfere with their newly won independence. In June of 1826, the Congress of Panama, including representatives from Colombia, Guatemala, Mexico and Peru, signed a treaty of union and perpetual confederation, which the governments of the last three states subsequently refused to ratify.

31 In the fall of 1826, an investigation began into the handling of the money that had been raised by issues of bonds to provide material support for the Greeks in their struggle for independence from Turkey, which had begun in 1821. The first bond issue was launched in February 1824, the second a year later, January–February 1825; see G.F. Bartle, "Bowring and the Greek Loans of 1824 and 1825," *Balkan Studies*, 3 (1962), 61–74. For JB's involvement in Greek affairs, see F. Rosen, *Bentham, Byron, and Greece* (Oxford: Clarendon Press, 1992); the loan scandal is treated in chapter 13.

32 Two deputies, Andreas Louriottis and Ioannis Orlandos, had entered into negotiations with the London Greek Committee, concerning the first bond issue, early in 1824. When relations with Bowring deteriorated, they tried unsuccessfully to enlist JB's help against him; see Rosen, *Bentham, Byron and Greece*, chapter 6. After the second loan had failed to provide the money immediately necessary to the Greek government, another deputy, Georgiou Spaniolakes, came to England in 1825, with instructions to investigate the conduct of his two colleagues.

33 The banking house of J. and S. Ricardo.

34 Charles François Antoine, baron Lallemand (1774–1839), a former general, who had lived in the United States after Napoleon's defeat.

35 John Bowring, "The Greek Committee," *Westminster Review*, 6 (July 1826), 113–33; this article was his defence against the call for the investigation of the dealings of the London Greek Committee.

36 A full account of the meeting of the bondholders on 23 October, and of the report, is in *The Times*, 24 Oct. 1826, 2–3. The chairman was Leicester Stanhope (1784–1862), who had played a major role in the English effort to help the Greek cause; see Rosen, *Bentham, Byron, and Greece*, chapter 8.

37 Letters from Louriottis, defending himself against the accusations of misconduct, are in *The Times*, 25 and 30 Oct. and 1 Nov. 1826, all 2. For examples of self-defence on the part of those accused with Bowring, see ibid., 31 Oct., 1 Nov., both 2, and 4 Nov., 3.

38 John Bowring had been arrested in early October 1822, as he was about to return from France to England, and detained in solitary confinement for two weeks in a Boulogne prison. The ostensible offence was that he was carrying a diplomatic dispatch from the Portuguese Ambassador at Paris to his Portuguese counterpart at London, without the authority of the French government, and thus was in breach of the law governing the Post Office. According to his letter to Canning, the Foreign Secretary, Bowring was suspected of having been engaged in a plot with French radicals to rescue some young political offenders. No formal charge was ever laid, and he was ultimately released, but the incident provoked much criticism of the despotic and high-handed methods of the French government; see *Examiner*, 13 and 20 Oct. and 3 Nov. 1822, 645, 665 and 693, and Bowring, *Details of the Arrest, Imprisonment and Liberation, of an Englishman, by the Bourbon Government of France* (London: Hunter, Wilson, 1823).

39 A paraphrase, rather than an exact quotation, of Bowring's statement in his letter of defence, dated 1 November 1826; in *The Times*, 3 Nov., 3.

40 William Burton, a London stockbroker, held some bonds in trust for Luriottis' English secretary, George Lee (Bartle, "Bowring and the Greek Loans," 72).

41 The two frigates contracted for in the United States and the steamships under construction in the Thames were to have made up a naval expedition, led by the British admiral, Thomas, Lord Cochrane (1775–1860). He arrived in Greece in March 1827 with a single ship, and tried unsuccessfully to organize the Greek navy. See "The Greek Frigates," *Examiner*, 12 Nov. 1826, 722; and, for a more sympathetic treatment of the engineer's problems, "Mr. Galloway and the Greek Steam Engines," ibid., 31 Dec. 1826, 836–7.

42 The Carr family had a house in Bloomsbury Square as well as an estate at Hampstead.

43 The letter from the French botanist Jean Baptiste Antoine Guillemin (1796–

1842), dated 11 November 1826, had been forwarded from Edinburgh by George Arnott, and did not reach London until the first week of December; the original is in Bentham Correspondence, no. 1682, RBGK. The brief notice of GB's *Catalogue* in the *Bulletin des Sciences Naturelles et de Géologie*, 10 (1827), 260–1, is signed "R.", and may have been written by Achille Richard (1794–1852), a regular contributor like Guillemin, or by the general editor of the botanical section, François Vincent Raspail (1794–1878). This periodical formed section II of the *Bulletin Universel des Sciences et de l'Industrie*, which appeared from 1824–31, under the general editorship of baron André Férussac (1786–1835). There appears to have been no report on GB's *Catalogue* by the Académie des Sciences.

44 John Dundas Cochrane's travels are described in *Narrative of a Pedestrian Journey through Russia and Siberian Tartary, from the Frontiers of China to the Frozen Sea and Kamtchatka, Performed during the Years 1820, 1821, 1822, and 1823*, 2 vols. (London: Murray, 1824). Though the journal-letter reads "Colombia," GB here, incorrectly, wrote "British Columbia." Cochrane died in 1825 in Valencia, now Venezuela.

45 During a visit to Paris, September–October 1825, JB stayed at the Grand Hôtel, Place Vendôme.

46 See n19 above. The following quotation is from the entry for 18 November.

47 A copy of GB's letter to Robert Peel of 27 November 1826, and his "Observations on the Bill for Consolidating the Laws Relating to Larceny," are in BL Add. MSS, 33,546, ff. 81–99. GB seems to have copied Peel's letter of 17 January, which follows, *verbatim* from the journal-letter to his sister.

48 JB had been in correspondence with Peel about the new bills, and the property code mentioned below (n55), and had sent him an account of GB's background and talents, dated 2 February 1827; in BL Add. MSS, 40,391, ff. 192–3. This document presumably prompted Peel's reply of 3 February, quoted here; in UCL, 11b, 253.

49 The extract was taken from *A Letter to the Members of the Different Circuits by A.H.* (London, 1826), privately distributed, by Anthony Hammond (1758–1838). Peel's response, which follows, appeared first in *The Times*, 10 Feb. 1827, 3. On the 12th, the *Morning Chronicle* reprinted, on page 1, Hammond's statement, the introductory comment critical of it, which GB quotes, and Peel's letter.

50 See "Report from the Select Committee on the Criminal Law of England" (2 Apr. 1824), *PP*, 1824, 4, 39–405; the quoted resolution is on 41.

51 On 6 April 1827, James Archibald Stuart-Wortley-Mackenzie, Lord Wharncliffe (1776–1845), moved that the House of Lords consider in committee a bill to amend the game laws; *PD*, n.s., vol. 17, col. 268.

52 Cf. Maria Edgeworth's account of a New Year's party at the Carrs' five years earlier, in *Maria Edgeworth: Letters from England 1813–1844*, ed. C. Colvin (Oxford: Clarendon Press, 1971), 300–14.

53 For criticism of the Duke, see "Promotion in the Army," and "Memoir of the Duke of York," *Morning Chronicle*, 5 and 6 Jan. 1827, 2 and 2–3, respectively. The account of the following events near St James's Palace is in "Ceremony of the Remains of His Royal Highness the Duke of York Lying in State," ibid., 19 Jan. 1827, 2–3.

54 Próspero Herrera was serving as agent in London of the state of Guatemala, which had declared its independence from Spain in September 1821. He presumably provided JB with copies of the speeches and the manifesto of his cousin, del Valle, mentioned in n56 below.

55 JB, "Bentham on Humphreys' *Property Code*," *Westminster Review*, 6 (Oct. 1826), 446–507, reviewed *Observations on the Actual State of the English Laws of Real Property, with the Outlines of a Code* (London: Murray, 1826), by James Humphreys (d. 1830). The October number of the *Westminster* did not appear until mid-January 1827. GB feared that his uncle's unintelligible writing, which Bowring had not dared to edit sufficiently, would bring the radical review into further disrepute.

56 Herrera had probably given JB a copy of *Discursos de José del Valle en el Congreso Federal de Centro-América de 1826*, 7 pts. (Guatemala: Imprenta de la Unión, 1826). These speeches, delivered by José Cecilio del Valle (1771–1834), a leader of the Guatemalan independence movement, between 7 April and 29 June 1826, to the National Congress of the new Central American republics, dealt with issues of sovereignty and non-intervention, the injustice of military courts, and the need for an assessment of the area's natural resources, through an expedition led by someone like Alexander von Humboldt; see Louis E. Bumgartner, *José del Valle of Central America* (Durham, N.C.: Duke University Press, 1963), 253.

57 Del Valle had gone to Mexico City in July 1822 to serve as a deputy from Guatemala to the Mexican Congress. In August, the self-proclaimed Emperor, Agustín Itúrbide (1783–1824), who feared a conspiracy, imprisoned fourteen of the deputies, including del Valle (whose name was, in fact, not on the list of suspects). In February 1823, after six months in jail, he was suddenly invited by the Emperor to become Secretary of Foreign and Domestic Affairs, a post which he occupied until Itúrbide's abdication and departure in March. At the end of the year del Valle returned to Guatamala City. See Bumgartner, *José del Valle*, 189–205. The description of his experience was part of the protest he published in pamphlet form against the election of Manuel José Arce to the Presidency of Guatemala; "Manifiesto a la

Nación Guatemalana, 20 de Mayo de 1825. Alegato Autobiografico. Documentos Justificativos," in *Obra Escogida*, ed. M.G. Laguardia (Caracas: Arte, 1982), 23–53.

58 The review of GB's *Catalogue*, by the French naturalist J.B.G.M. Bory de Saint-Vincent (1778–1846), is in the *Revue Encyclopédique*, 32 (Nov. 1826), 437–8.

59 J.M.L. Dufour (1780–1865), a surgeon with the French army in Spain, 1808–14, had spent much of his time botanizing, and published *Lettres à M. Palassou . . . sur les excursions tentées vers les montagnes maudites des Pyrénées*, with his friend Bory de Saint-Vincent's *Voyage souterrain, ou Description du plateau de Saint-Pierre de Maestricht et de ses vastes cryptes* (Paris: Ponthieu, 1821).

60 *Article Eight of the Westminster Review No. XII for October, 1826, on Mr. Humphreys' Observations on the English Law of Real Property* (London: Hansard, 1827).

61 The following letters, from James Humphreys to JB and JB's reply, are copied from GB's journal-letter to MLC at LSL. The original of the former and a copy of the latter are in UCL, 11b, 237 and 239, respectively.

62 Humphreys, *A Letter to E.B. Sugden, Esq., in Reply to His Remarks on the Alterations Proposed by James Humphreys . . . in the English Laws of Real Property* (London: Murray, 1827); Edward Burtenshaw Sugden (1781–1875), *A Letter to James Humphreys, Esq., on His Proposal to Repeal the Laws of Real Property, and Substitute a New Code* (1826) 3rd ed. (London: Clarke, 1827).

63 In 1825, a liaison of the actor Edmund Kean (1787–1833) with the wife of Robert Albion Cox, a banker and alderman of the City of London, had resulted in a court case, and Kean's having to pay £800 in damages, after which he went to America to escape public disapproval. He reappeared at Drury Lane as Shylock on 8 January 1827. The actress Maria Foote (1797?–1867), on the other hand, drew much sympathy because she had been jilted by a Colonel Berkeley, by whom she had two children.

64 Elizabeth Isabella Spence (1768–1832), whose mother (née Fordyce) was a first cousin of MSB's father, was the author of such works as *Helen Sinclair, a Novel*, 2 vols. (London: Cadell and Davies, 1799), *Summer Excursions through Parts of Oxfordshire . . . and South Wales*, 2 vols. (London: Longman et al., 1809) and *Dame Rebecca Berry; or, Court Scenes in the Reign of Charles the Second*, 3 vols. (London: Longman, et al., 1827).

65 Probably some preliminary printing of items in SB's *Naval Papers*, which would be published the following year; see 312–14n57 above.

66 Established in 1799, the Royal Institution aimed at enlisting the help of science to raise the standard of living among the poor, i.e., to make philanthropy scientific. Research would promote new inventions, workmen would be taught how to use them, and the improving landlords, the

founders and patrons, would both support and profit from the undertaking. A scientific lecture theatre was opened at 21 Albemarle Street in 1801, and serious and scientific lectures, as well as more popular ones for ladies, began on a regular basis; see Gwendy Caroe, *The Royal Institution* (London: Murray, 1985), 1–18.

67 Arthur de Capell Brooke (1791–1858) published two works on his Lapland travels, which contained much new information: *A Winter in Lapland and Sweden, with Various Observations Relating to Finmark and Its Inhabitants, Made during a Residence at Hammerfest, Near the North Cape* (London: Murray, 1827), with a companion volume, containing the engravings to which GB refers, *Winter Sketches in Lapland, or, Illustrations of a Journey from Alten, on the Shores of the Polar Sea, in 69°55′ N.L., through Norwegian, Russian, and Swedish Lapland to Tornea, at the Entrance to the Gulf of Bothnia, Intended to Exhibit a Complete View of the Mode of Travelling with Reindeer, the Most Striking Incidents That Occurred during the Journey, and the General Character of the Scenery of Lapland and Sweden* (London: Rodwell, and Arch, 1827).

68 William Bentham's grandfather was Edward (d. 1774), whose father, Bryan (d. 1748), was a brother of JB's grandfather, Jeremiah (1684/5–1741) (*CJB*, I, xxxviii–xxxix).

69 George Bentham (1787–1862), a naval Captain, "one of the sons of the late General [W.] Bentham of Canterbury." GB and his father later dined at Mr William Bentham's, in Gower Street, and met the young man and his fiancée, Miss Parker (journal entry for 17 May 1827).

70 These initials were the signature of the caricaturist John Doyle (1797–1868), but the cartoon that GB describes in the journal-letter entry for 21 March 1827 cannot have been by Doyle, whose earliest work of this kind dates from 1829: "Canning and Eldon are each sitting at one end of a highly ornamented boat on which is inscribed 'The Cabinet Cock Boat.' This boat has no stern but two heads; at Canning's end floats the flag of Catholic Supremacy; at Eldon's that of Protestant Ascendancy; the two ministers in their shirts are rowing with all their might, puffing and blowing and pulling away in opposite directions."

71 William Allen (see 203n41 above) married Mrs Grizell Birkbeck, a long-time friend, on 14 March 1827; see *Life of William Allen*, 3 vols. (London: Gilpin, 1846–47), II, 437 and III, 207–8.

72 GB's *Outline of a New System of Logic, with a Critical Examination of Dr. Whately's "Elements of Logic"* (London: Hunt and Clarke, 1827); its appearance was announced in the *Morning Chronicle*, 26 Mar. 1827, 1. This work has been reissued in the Nineteenth-Century British Philosophy Series (Bristol: Thoemmes, 1990).

73 In the "Historical Register" section, part III of *New Monthly Magazine and Literary Journal*, 21 (May 1827), 212.

74 T.W. Carr was not alone in this opinion. John Stuart Mill, who had just produced "Whately's *Elements of Logic*," *Westminster Review*, 9 (Jan. 1828), 137–72, was apparently asked by Bowring to review GB's work, and replied as follows: "I do not think that Mr. G.B.'s book affords any proof of want of talent—far from it—but many of haste, and want of due deliberation. This mistake was, as it seems to me, that of supposing that he was qualified to write on such a subject as Logic after two or three months' study, or that so young a logician was capable of maintaining so high a ground as that of a critic upon Whately. The consequences of his mistake have been twofold: first of all, he has produced nothing but minute criticism, which even when most just, is particularly annoying to the person criticized when so much stress appears to be laid upon it. This minute criticism is often just, sometimes very acute, but frequently, also, if I am not mistaken, altogether groundless. Instead of this, a good critic on Whately should have laid down as a standard of comparison, the best existing or the best conceivable *exposition of the science*, & examined how far Whately's book possesses the properties which should belong to *that*. In the second place, Mr. George Bentham seems not to be aware, that Dr Whately is a far greater master of the science than *he* is, & that the public will think the disproportion still greater than it is. It would therefore have been wiser in him not to have assumed the tone of undisputed & indisputable superiority over Whately, which marks the greater part of his critique. . . . I have put this more strongly, and enlarged upon it more fully, to you, than I should in the W.R. But I should think it wrong, in noticing the book, not to say something of this sort." (10 Mar. 1828, *Earlier Letters*, *Collected Works*, XII [Toronto: University of Toronto Press, 1963], 23–4.) No notice of GB's *Logic* ever appeared in the *Westminster Review*.

75 Notice of the bankruptcy of the booksellers Henry Leigh Hunt (1784–1859) and Charles Cowden Clarke (1787–1877), York Street, Covent Garden, is in *The Times*, 18 Apr. 1829, 2.

76 William Hamilton (1788–1856), "Recent Publications on Logical Science," *Edinburgh Review*, 57 (Apr. 1833), 194–238; GB's work is mentioned briefly on 199 and 205, and included in the general criticism of all the volumes under review on 200.

77 Between pages 393 and 394, GB inserted two sheets with pasted-on clippings from the *Athenaeum* on this controversy. The discussion was prompted by the publication of *An Essay on the New Analytic of Logical Forms* (Edinburgh: Sutherland and Knox; London: Simpkin, Marshall, 1850) by Thomas Spencer

Baynes (1823–87). The work gave a full exposition of Sir William Hamilton's doctrine of the quantification of the predicate as a new form of the syllogism. William Warlow's first letter to the editor (n.d.), in the *Athenaeum*, of 21 Dec. 1850, 1351, pointed out that GB had already advanced the doctrine in chapters 8 and 9 of his *Outline*. Baynes replied with a letter (n.d.), published in the *Athenaeum*, 1 Feb. 1851, 146, in which he denied that GB appreciated it as a scientific principle, and *"only doubtfully allowed it in a single instance"* (*Outline*, 134–5). In Baynes' view, GB had not employed "the quantification of the predicate to explain the true logical value of propositions, the true relation of their terms, or [applied] it with any consistency to simplify the doctrine of their conversion," as had Sir William Hamilton. A letter from the correspondent, "J.B." (1 Feb.), *Athenaeum*, 8 Feb., 173, suggesting that GB's position was closer to that of William Thomson (1819–90), then tutor in logic at Queen's College, Oxford, than to that of Hamilton, brought both Thomson and Hamilton into the discussion. Thomson explained the views he had published in his *Outline of the Laws of Thought* (London: Pickering; Oxford: Graham, 1842) in a letter (19 Feb.), *Athenaeum*, 22 Feb., 227–8, to which Hamilton replied (n.d.), ibid., 1 Mar., 253, and Thomson responded (4 Mar.), ibid., 277. GB was virtually ignored in these letters, Hamilton deeming it "unnecessary to say anything" to the "other animadversions on [the] doctrine which have lately appeared," based on "misapprehension." Further comments from "J.B." (3 Mar.), and from Warlow (n.d.), followed by an editorial note bringing the discussion to an end, are ibid., 8 Mar. 1851, 277. Yet another editorial note, 22 Mar. 1851, 333, indicated that Warlow had sent in a further comment, which the *Athenaeum* declined to publish, as "an admission of Mr. Warlow's rejoinder would re-entitle all the rest." For an explanation of the discredited doctrine, see H.W.B. Joseph, *An Introduction to Logic*, 2nd ed. (Oxford: Clarendon Press, 1916), 222–8.

78 William Stanley Jevons (1835–82) investigated the controversy when preparing to publish his *Elementary Lessons in Logic: Deductive and Inductive* (London: Macmillan, 1870), part III of which dealt with the syllogism. His letter to GB, of 30 June 1869, is in Bentham Correspondence, no. 2096, RBGK.

79 Herbert Spencer (1820–1903), "The Study of Sociology. IX. The Bias of Patriotism," *Contemporary Review*, 21 (Mar. 1873), 475–502. Reviewing what had been done in Britain in the abstract sciences, Spencer remarked: "The doctrine of the quantification of the predicate, set forth in 1827 by Mr. George Bentham, and again set forth under a numerical form by Professor De Morgan, is a doctrine supplementary to that of Aristotle; and the recognition of it has made it easier than before to see that Deductive Logic is a science of the relations implied by the inclusions, exclusions, and overlappings of classes.*

[*footnote:*] Most readers of logic will, I suppose, be surprised on missing from the above sentence, the name of Sir W. Hamilton. They will not be more surprised than I was myself on recently learning that Mr. George Bentham's work, *Outline of a New System of Logic*, was published six years before the earliest of Sir W. Hamilton's logical writings, and that Sir W. Hamilton reviewed it. The case adds another to the multitudinous ones in which the world credits the wrong man; and persists in crediting him in defiance of the evidence." (489–90.) Baynes replied the following month, in "Mr. Herbert Spencer on Sir Wm. Hamilton and the Quantification of the Predicate," *Contemporary Review* (Apr. 1873), 796–8, and Jevons responded with "Who Discovered the Quantification of the Predicate?" ibid. (May 1873), 821–4, in which he ruled in favour of GB: "I should like to explain that neither by . . . correspondence [with Baynes], nor by any subsequent inquiry, have I been led to abandon my strong opinion that Mr. George Bentham, the present distinguished President of the Linnaean Society, is substantially the first discoverer of this logical principle, so far as its discovery can be said to be due to British philosophers of the present century" (821). A copy of this article is included in GB's "Autobiography," with the pages of clippings from the *Athenaeum*, before page 394.

80 The menagerie of Edward Cross had been housed at the Exeter Change since 1773. When the building was demolished in 1829, the animals were moved to the King's Mews, on the site now occupied by the National Gallery, and then in 1831 to the Surrey Zoological Gardens, rather than to the Regent's Park Gardens of the Zoological Society, which had opened in 1828.

81 John ("Jack") Ketch was the common executioner, 1663?-86, his name being given to the hangman in the Punchinello play introduced into England after his death.

82 A copy of JB's letter to Robert Peel, the Home Secretary, of 26 March 1827, accompanying GB's *Logic* is in UCL, 11b, 263, with Peel's acknowledgment of 29 March 264.

83 Peel made this proposal on 27 March 1827; *PD*, n.s., vol. 17, cols. 91–2, 94.

84 On 17 February 1827, Lord Liverpool suffered a stroke that ended his administration and his political career. George Canning appeared as the obvious successor, and on 10 April was asked by the King to form a government, including all the existing ministers, with the difficult question of Catholic emancipation remaining open. Half the previous Tory cabinet and many holding government office immediately resigned, leaving Canning in need of the support of the Whigs to form a coalition government, an alliance of the liberal members of both parties. Henry Brougham was influential in the negotiations, though he was not given a Cabinet post, as the King would not

tolerate his presence in government after his connections with the Queen and their daughter.

85 JB's letter to the editor is in *Globe and Traveller*, 18 Apr. 1827, 2; a portion appeared in the *Morning Chronicle*, 19 Apr., 4, under the heading, "Prophecy Regarding Mr. Canning." The comment on JB's style has not been located in *John Bull*.

86 The engineer Marc Isambard Brunel (1769–1849) constructed the first underwater tunnel in history, from Rotherhithe to Wapping, between 1825 and 1842. It is still in use as part of the Metropolitan Line of the London Underground.

87 The diving bell was not fully practicable until 1778, when the innovative British engineer John Smeaton (1724–92) fitted it with an air pump.

88 The origins of this new institution are described in Hugh Hale Bellot, *University College London 1826–1926* (London: University of London Press, 1929), 1–59. JB subscribed to shares, but took no active part in the organization; nonetheless, "only in a naively literal sense is it true that Bentham was not among the founders of University College. In spirit the institution was, and in important respects still is, Bentham's college." (W.L. Twining, "Law," in *The University of London and the World of Learning, 1836–1986*, ed. F.M.L. Thompson [London and Ronceverte: Hambledon, 1990], 86–7.) The activities of 30 April 1827, are described in *The Times* and *Morning Chronicle*, both 1 May 1827, Supplement, 3, and 3, respectively.

89 In 1824 and 1825 there was a proliferation of new joint stock companies for an almost infinite variety of purposes. The *Monthly Repository of Theology and General Literature*, a Unitarian periodical, felt duty-bound to make the public aware of the extent of the "extravagance . . . [unequalled] since the infamous South-Sea bubble of 1720." From February to December 1825, it published a list of almost 750 of these schemes; ibid., 20, 119–23, 188–90, 247–8, 382–3, 501–4, 636–7 and 755–6. See also *The Times*, 31 Oct. 1825, 3, and, for a satirical treatment, "General Cooling Company," ibid., 26 July 1825, 3.

90 For an example of such an attack, see "The Cockney University and the Chimney Sweepers," *John Bull*, 6 May 1827, 142–3.

91 According to the letter of thanks from William Courtenay, dated 17 Apr. 1827, in UCL, 11b, 290, JB had sent him a copy of his *Summary View of the Plan of a Judicatory, under the Name of the Court of Lords' Delegates* (Westminster, 1808).

92 On 1 May 1827, at the first meeting of Parliament after the appointment of the new administration, explanations for resignations were offered: Peel's speech is in *PD*, n.s., vol. 17, cols. 393–412; Canning's reply is in cols. 428–39; Dawson's is in cols. 418–21, and Burdett's, cols. 412–16.

93 The following day, 2 May, Lords Eldon, Wellington, and Melville explained themselves; ibid., cols. 450–4, 454–67, and 483–5, respectively.

94 The National Guard was abolished by the Villèle ministry, after anti-government demonstrations during a review by the King, Charles X, and jeering at Villèle himself by one legion of troops as they marched past the Ministry of Finance; see "Ordonnance du roi qui licencie la garde nationale de Paris" (29 April), *Le Moniteur Universel*, 1827, 617.

95 The three families were related: the wives of Sir Richard Croft, the accoucheur (d. 1818), and of Dr Matthew Baillie (1761–1823) were the twin sisters of Thomas Denman.

96 See n6 above.

97 "George Bentham, Esq., Montpellier" was admitted as a non-resident member of the Society at a meeting of 12 December 1826 ("Historical Register," part III of *New Monthly Magazine*, 21 [May 1827], 204).

Chapter 8

1 Almack's Assembly Rooms, in King Street, St James's, had been designed in 1765 by Robert Mylne, and named for the first proprietor, William Almack (d. 1781). "A voucher of admission to a weekly ball was 'the seventh heaven of the fashionable world.'" Ladies of high rank strictly controlled the guest lists and standards of dress at these events, whose popularity began to decline in about 1835. (*London Encyclopaedia*.)

2 George Granville Leveson-Gower, 2nd Marquess of Stafford (1758–1833), husband of Elizabeth, Marchioness of Stafford and Countess of Sutherland (1765–1839), had been the English Ambassador in Paris, May 1790 to September 1792, where SB had met them during his visit in the spring of 1791 (see Introduction, xvii above).

3 William Pitt, Lord Amherst (1773–1857), was sent as British envoy to Peking in 1816 to plead the case of English merchants at Canton who felt that they were being unjustly treated, but he failed even to secure an audience with the Emperor, because of irreconcilable differences relating to protocol.

4 At the Westminster election held on 2 July 1818, the successful candidates for the two seats were Sir Samuel Romilly and Sir Francis Burdett; Sir Murray Maxwell (1775–1831) ran narrowly behind the latter; *The Times*, 3 July 1818, 2.

5 All quotations in this chapter derive from GB's journal-letters of the period; MSS at LSL.

6 Probably at the home of Dorian Magens (ca. 1762–1849), former M.P., and author on currency and banking.

7 Almack had bequeathed his premises to a niece, wife of a Mr Willis, and both names were apparently used for the rooms, where the Caledonian Ball was held on Monday, 14 May 1827.

8 The Duke of Clarence would succeed to the throne as William IV on the death of his brother, George IV, on 26 June 1830.

9 The object of this institution was "to support and educate the children of soldiers, sailors and mariners, natives of Scotland, who have died or been disabled in the service of their country, and of indigent Scotch parents, resident in London, and not entitled to parochial relief" (*The Times*, 18 May 1827, 4).

10 GB was hoping to be able to marry Laura Carr.

11 The Metropolitan Police Act, 10 George IV, c. 44 (19 June 1829), among other provisions, established a single, paid police force of "bobbies" for Westminster and other specified parishes, to replace the local night watch and constables.

12 "Saints" was the nickname for the Evangelical members of Parliament who stood for high moral standards, and particularly advocated the total abolition of slavery. Nicholas Van Sittart (1766–1851) returned to the new cabinet in the same office, of Chancellor of the Duchy of Lancaster, i.e., as a minister without portfolio. The other six who had resigned were Lords Bathurst, Eldon, Melville, Wellington and Westmoreland, and Robert Peel; see 274n84.

13 Introduced into the House of Lords on 25 May 1827, by Frederick John Robinson, Viscount Goderich (1782–1859), *PD*, n.s., vol. 17, cols. 984–99, "A Bill for Granting Duties of Customs on Corn," 7 & 8 George IV (29 Mar. 1827), *PP*, 1826–27, 1, 413–18, provided that the duties to be paid on foreign grain and the price in England at which they were to be levied would be the same whether the grain was imported directly into the market from abroad or had been previously warehoused in bond. Fearing that the warehousing system might become a vehicle for fraud, the Duke of Wellington moved, in Committee, on 1 June, that no foreign grain should be taken out of bond until the price had reached a certain level, thus, in effect, establishing a prohibitory principle that the bill was designed to remove; *PD*, n.s., vol. 17, cols. 1096–8.

14 Nikolai Mikhailovich Karamzin (1766–1826), *Istoriia gosudarstva Rossiiskago*, 11 vols. (St Petersburg: printed Gretcha, 1818–24); a twelfth volume, ed. D.N. Bludov (1785–1864), was published in 1829.

15 The notice by the botanist Jacques Étienne Gay (1786–1864), quoted here in full, is in *Flora; oder, Allgemeine botanische Zeitung*, 10th year, I (14 Jan. 1827), 29.

16 See the account in H.R. Fletcher, *The Story of the Royal Horticultural Society*,

1804–1968 (London: RHS, 1969), 84–5, and *The Times*, 25 June 1827, Supplement, 3.

17 The first lady Fellows were admitted in 1830; see 331 above.

18 Having been Prime Minister for only four months, George Canning died on 8 August 1827, and was succeeded by Lord Goderich.

19 George IV's private collection of pictures, particularly rich in Flemish and Dutch masters, was on display at the British Institution Gallery, 52 Pall Mall. The National Gallery had been established in 1824, the nucleus of the collection being thirty-eight pictures, purchased by the government from the estate of the Russian-born merchant and philanthropist John Julius Angerstein (1735–1823), and sixteen others, donated by Sir George Beaumont. They were housed in Angerstein's house in Pall Mall, until a building for the Gallery was constructed on the north side of Trafalgar Square, 1832–38.

20 Philip Parker King (1793–1856) made an extensive survey of the coast of Australia, 1817–22.

21 James John Gordon Bremer (1786–1850) was sent in 1824 on the first attempt to settle Australia's north coast. The colony of Fort Dundas, established on Melville island, lasted only until 1829; see J.J. Eddy, *Britain and the Australian Colonies, 1818–31* (Oxford: Clarendon Press, 1969), 235–6.

22 GB continues: "If I have courage I shall speak to Morton at Edinburgh [about the possibility of marrying his sister Laura] (which is really my great motive for going this journey). . . ."

23 See 154n3 above.

24 A fire that broke out on 15 November 1824 had destroyed much of the High Street in Edinburgh; see *The Times*, 20 Nov. 1824, 3, and 22 Nov. 2.

25 See 323–4 above.

26 See 309 and n41 above.

27 See 162–4 above.

28 The Grand Signior was the title of the Sultan of Turkey, at this time Mahmud II (1785–1839). In 1826 Britain, France and Russia had unsuccessfully tried to pressure him to agree to their mediating a settlement of the conflict between Turkey and Greece. In June of 1827, having captured Athens, the Sultan issued a strong statement of his independence, which led to the signing of the Treaty of London by the three powers on 6 July, to force his compliance with their terms. In effect, the allies threatened to recognize Greece as an independent state, and to prevent further deployment of Turkish military personnel and supplies in the Morea, if Turkey failed to agree to mediation. The Sultan delayed giving his answer until the middle of September, by which time the Egyptian fleet had arrived to reinforce his own. The situation culminated in the unplanned naval battle of Navarino, in which the Turko-

Egyptian navy was destroyed. See *Annual Register of World Events*, 1827, 306–23, and 310 above.

29 See 158–9, 165 above.

30 Adèle was the name of MLC's daughter, born in 1820; see 68n34 above.

31 Mary Queen of Scots and her husband, the Earl of Bothwell, were outnumbered by the forces of the confederate lords in June 1567, and the Queen agreed to be taken into custody so that Bothwell and his followers might go free. She was imprisoned in the island castle of Lochleven until 2 May 1568, when she escaped. Her forces were subsequently defeated at the battle of Langside, after which she fled to England, hoping for the protection of Elizabeth I.

32 Thomas Graham II (1752–1819), of Kinross House, left his estate to whichever of his two co-heiresses first produced a son. This proved to be his younger daughter, Helen, who married Sir James Montgomery (1766–1839) in 1816. The birth date of their eldest son, Graham Graham-Montgomery, is given as 1823.

33 Cannobie Lea and Netherby Hall are place names in the ballad "Lochinvar"; in Walter Scott, *Minstrelsy of the Scottish Border* (1802) (repr. London: Murray, 1869), 298–9.

34 In Scott's novel *Waverley; or 'Tis Sixty Years Since*, chapter 69, the hero, Waverley, pays a visit to Fergus McIvor, before his execution in Carlisle Castle.

35 If Morton Carr had given him any encouragement about marrying his sister Laura, GB would have returned to the Carr family's country estate.

36 As GB tries to temper his early assessment of Colls, he omits the fact that in 1844 Colls published *Utilitarianism Unmasked*, a personal attack against JB himself in an attempt to discredit his philosophical ideas. For an explanation of Colls's motives, see Stephen Conway, "J.F. Colls, M.A. Gathercole, and *Utilitarianism Unmasked*: A Neglected Episode in the Anglican Response to Bentham," *Journal of Ecclesiastical History*, 45 (July 1994), 435–47.

37 Probably Francis Seymour Larpent (1776–1845), from 1821 a Commissioner, and from 1826 Chairman, of the Board of Audit of the public accounts. At this time, SB was being consulted about the finances of the Navy; see 314 above.

38 JB's first letter to Brougham, recommending Bowring, dated 13 September 1827, is at UCL, Brougham MS, 26,000; Brougham's reply, in which he apparently made much of Bowring's role in the Greek scandal, has not survived. JB later tried again, on 1 January 1828, Brougham MS, 26,003, but the chair of Literature was awarded to the Rev. Thomas Dale (1797–1870); see Chester W. New, *The Life of Henry Brougham to 1830* (Oxford: Clarendon Press, 1961), 377–8.

39 JB's letter of 20 September is in Brougham MSS, 26,001, and part of
Brougham's answer of 22 September 1827 is in JB, *Works*, X, 574–5. Brougham
described the plan that he would undertake in the following session of
Parliament; see his speech on the state of the courts of common law (7 Feb.
1828), *PD*, n.s., vol. 18, cols. 127–247. For a detailed discussion of Brougham's
proposals, see New, *Life of Henry Brougham*, chapter 21, 390–401.

40 JB's delight at his disciple's apparent willingness to be coached is reflected in
his letters to Brougham of 24 September (Brougham MSS, 26,002), 9 October,
and 30 November 1827 (*Works*, X, 575–6).

41 W.J. Hooker was appointed to the chair of Botany and Vegetable Physiology,
but gave it up, as GB asserts, partly because a satisfactory income was not
guaranteed, and partly because of a decision of the Council that it could not
afford a botanic garden. John Lindley subsequently received the appointment before the University opened in October 1828; see Bellot, *University
College London*, 38–40.

42 In the *Statement by the Council of the University of London, Explanatory of Its
Nature and Objects* (London: printed Taylor, 1827), issued in July, an
announcement was made that "An Hospital capable of containing a sufficient number of patients to afford opportunities of Clinical Practice, both
medical and surgical, and of illustrative Lectures, will be provided, as being
an essential requisite of a Medical School . . ." (55). The University hospital,
temporarily postponed, finally opened in November 1834.

43 Under the *Deed of Settlement of the University of London* (London: printed
Hughes, 1826), 3, the proprietors had to raise a minimum of £150,000, and
there were difficulties in getting even that amount paid down. The outlays for
the land and the building ate into the resources, and the salaries offered the
professors were consequently small; Bellot, *University College London*, 47–53.

44 See 121 above.

45 Sir Hans Sloane's collections, which included those of his friend, the naturalist and antiquarian William Courten (1642–1702), were acquired by the
nation in 1753, and formed the basis of the botanical, zoological and geological treasures of the British Museum. Gradually they had been supplemented
by various other gifts and purchases; see *The History of the Natural Collections
. . . of the British Museum*, 2 vols. (London: British Museum, 1904–12).

46 By mid-October 1827, Britain, France and Russia had succeeded in getting
Greece to agree to an armistice, and on the 20th, in a show of strength,
English, French and Russian vessels sailed unopposed into the port of
Navarino, where the Turko-Egyptian fleet was moored. On being asked to
move, a Turkish vessel opened fire without warning, igniting an excessively
bloody battle that virtually destroyed the Sultan's forces.

47 See "Important News from Greece: Destruction of the Turkish Fleet," and "Lord Mayor's Day," *Examiner*, Sunday, 11 Nov. 1827, 710–11 and 709, respectively.

48 In the course of the engagement, the French frigate "Armide," under the command of Gaud Amable Hugon (1783–1862), long sustained the fire of five Egyptian ships without serious injury. None of the ships of the Triple Alliance was, in fact, lost.

49 In May of 1672 the English and French fleets did combine in an engagement against ships of the Dutch navy, off Southwold Bay in Suffolk. The Dutch fleet suffered least in the fierce battle, and was able to establish its authority in the North Sea; see Maurice Ashley, *Charles II, the Man and the Statesman* (London: Weidenfeld and Nicolson, 1971), 178–9.

50 John Charles Herries (1778–1855), as Chancellor of the Exchequer, lived next door to the Prime Minister in Downing Street.

51 As well as being in trouble as a result of the battle of Navarino, Lord Goderich had failed to make a harmonious unit out of the Whigs and Tories in his cabinet, and particularly had not been able to keep the peace between Herries and Huskisson over the chairmanship of the Finance Committee. Goderich resigned on 8 January 1828, and Wellington became Prime Minister on the 26th.

52 For the speeches of Lord Goderich on 11 February 1828, in the Lords, and of Huskisson and Herries on 18 February, in the Commons, see *PD*, n.s., vol. 18, cols. 272–83, 463–87 and 487–507, respectively.

53 When members of Parliament, unpaid at this time, were given cabinet positions, they became paid appointees under the Crown, and by-elections were held in their constituencies, in which they were usually returned unopposed. Having accepted the post of Colonial Secretary, Huskisson was having to explain to his constituents in Liverpool why he had accepted office in the new Tory cabinet with men who had been so opposed to the liberal policies that he had pursued in Canning's administration; see *The Times*, 7 Feb. 1828, 2; Huskisson's long speech follows, on 3.

54 For Brougham's speech see note 39 above; his praise of the judges is in cols. 137–40.

55 Brougham later paid tribute to his mentor, however, in the Introduction to the version published after JB's death; see *Speeches of Henry Lord Brougham*, 4 vols. (Edinburgh: Black, et al.; London: Knight, 1838), II, 289–98.

56 Two commissions, one on the common law and a second on real property, were established on 29 February 1828; *PD*, n.s., vol. 18, esp. cols. 833–4, 922–3. Peel's praise of JB is in col. 894.

57 Though the title implies a collection, only one essay, "Efficiency of the Maté-

riel," appeared in *Naval Essays; or, Essays on the Management of Public Concerns, as Exemplified in the Naval Department, Considered as a Branch of the Business of Warfare* (London: Longman, et al., 1828); see MSB, *Life*, 313. This same year, Longman also published two volumes of SB's *Naval Papers and Documents Referred to in Naval Essays*. Volume 1 contained correspondence relating to improvements made in the dock yards, on experimental vessels, contracts for naval stores, etc. Volume 2 largely comprised reprints of SB's earlier pamphlets on naval subjects. The "observations," mentioned by GB, included a letter of 7 March 1828, "on the subject of the transport service, in which, among other suggestions, he remarked more particularly that in times of peace, if, instead of having vessels for any transport or packet service, vessels of war were, instead of lying in ordinary, to be employed for services of all kinds, the annual saving would amount to about £200,000" (MSB, *Life*, 315). SB had expected to be called to testify before the Finance Committee, but, according to MSB, he was not summoned because the chairman of the Committee, Sir Henry Parnell (1776–1842), disagreed fundamentally with SB's view, submitted in a letter of 13 April 1828, that "savings might be effected by manufacturing a great variety of articles on Government account, instead of procuring them in a manufactured state" (ibid.). This disagreement would ultimately prompt SB's pamphlet, mentioned at 327n6 below.

58 See 100n2 above. Dumont's latest production was the single volume, *De l'organisation judiciaire et de la codification* (Paris: H. Bossange, 1828).

59 For the parallel of Montesquieu and Bentham, see *Oeuvres de Bentham*, 3 vols. (Brussels: Hamann, 1830), III, 78–81, chapter 33, "Passages de *L'Esprit des lois* relatifs à l'organisation judiciaire."

60 Reviewed at length in the *Athenaeum*, 18 Apr. 1828, 394–5. The interpolated song was the "Air with Variations," by the violinist Jacques Pierre Joseph Rode (1774–1830), which had become a repertory piece for voice.

61 The account of the experience and the discoveries of David Douglas (1798–1834) was finally published as *Journal Kept by David Douglas during His Travels in North America, 1823–1827* (London: RHS, 1914); it has more recently been issued as *Douglas of the Forests: The North American Journals of David Douglas* (Edinbugh: Harris, 1979).

62 Douglas sailed again for North America in the autumn of 1829, spent three years in California, and two more on the Fraser River; he was killed by a wild boar during a visit to Hawaii in July of 1834.

63 See Gage and Stearn, *A Bicentenary History of the Linnean Society of London*, 41–2.

64 See 249–50 above.

65 Félix Bodin (1795–1837) was presumably doing archival research for his

Résumé de l'histoire d'Angleterre (1824), 6th ed. (Paris: Lecointe and Pougin, 1835), which continued the narrative to the reign of Charles I.

66 J. Lindley, "*Benthamia,*" *Edwards's Botanical Register*, 19 (1 May 1833), t. 1579, previously named by J.G.C. Lehmann, "*Amsinckia,*" *Delectus seminum quae in horto hamburgensium botanico e collectione anni 1831 mutuae commutatione offeruntur*, 1 (1831), 7.

67 See 122 and n47 above.

68 In 1829 the original asking price for the collection was £5000, but the executors finally agreed to accept 3000 guineas, which was raised partly by subscription from the members, partly by a loan, the final payment being made in 1835; see Gage and Stearn, *Bicentenary History*, 35–6.

69 9 George IV, c. 63 (Local Acts).

70 Cf. the following account with that in *The Times*, 23 June 1828, 7.

71 The German botanist Karl Friedrich von Ledebour (1786–1851) published an account of this journey the following year, entitled *Reise durch das Altai-Gebirge und die soongorische Kirgisen-Steppe*, 2 vols. (Berlin: Reimer, 1829–30).

72 The Council was apparently not satisfied that any of the applicants for the professorship in French was sufficiently versed in literature, and appointed Pierre François Merlet (1785–1866), the author of grammar texts, as professor of the language only; Bellot, *University College London*, 44–5.

73 In February of 1828, Russia declared war upon Turkey in her own right, justifying this move with claims that Turkey had provoked hostilities between Russia and Persia, closed the Bosphorus illegally, seized cargoes, and imprisoned Russian nationals; see "Declaration," *The Times*, 29 Mar. 1828, 2.

74 GB's supposition about the year seems correct. The baron Ange Hyacinthe Maxence de Damas (1785–1862), related to SB's friend, the comte Damas, who had served in the army of Catherine the Great (see Introduction, xvii above), was appointed tutor of the duc de Bordeaux on 22 April 1828.

Chapter 9

1 Nathaniel Wallich (1786–1854), a Danish-born physician and botanist, had been Superintendent of the Botanic Garden at Calcutta since 1817. For more on his collections, see Ray Desmond, *The India Museum, 1801–1879* (London: Her Majesty's Stationery Office, 1982), 52–3.

2 James George Watson, later Superintendent of the Peradeniya Botanic Gardens in Ceylon; see also 388 above.

3 GB, "*Hosackia bicolor, Lophanthus anisatus, Stachys germanica* var. *pubescens;* Conspectus of the Tribes of the Labiatae," and "*Lepechinia spicata, Phlomis*

floccosa; Conspectus of Labiatae Continued," *Edwards's Botanical Register*, 15 (1829), pl. 1257, 1282, 1289, 1292 and 1300.

4 Wife of Wilhelm Konstantin, Count Ludolf (d. 1839), Ambassador from the Kingdom of the Two Sicilies. He was the uncle of Anastasie Saint-Priest Dax, mother of GB's "flame," Emma. Maria Edgeworth gives the following account of the Ambassador and his wife (who must have been much younger than her husband) in a letter to Mrs Ruxton of 2 November 1821: "He is ambassador from Naples—a very agreeable man—not more of a dip-lomatist than is quite becoming . . . not literary but travelled. . . . He was *of* the Empress Catherine's famous journey to the Crimea and saw the wooden villages and canvas painted houses prepared. . . . Countess Ludolf is a Gre-cian lady—from the Corfu—but nothing Grecian about her—more like a lit-tle Frenchwoman—with pretty artificial flowers in her cap—talking a vast deal but saying nothing." (*Letters from England, 1813–1844*, ed. Christina Colvin [Oxford: Clarendon Press, 1971], 253.)

5 This remark and the evidence at 417 and n3 above suggests that GB is proba-bly writing in 1879 at this point. Volume 19 of his diaries, at RBGK, runs from 1 June 1874 to 31 December 1880; volume 20, from 1 January 1881 to August 1883, a year before his death.

6 The most notable of these was SB's *Financial Reform Scrutinized, in a Letter to Sir Henry Parnell, Bart., M.P.* (London: Hatchard, 1830); see also 314n57 above. Replying to Parnell's *Financial Reform* (London: Murray, 1830), SB not only dealt with the economics of manufacturing by government, but also made suggestions for more efficient accounting procedures, including "that great oversight in regard to finance—the taking *no* account of the value of interest on monies expended in public works" (MSB, *Life*, 316).

7 GB's "Synopsis of the Genera and Species of Indian Labiatae" is in Nathaniel Wallich, *Plantae asiaticae rariores*, 3 vols. (London: Treuttel and Würtz, 1830–32), I, 28–31, 58–68; II, 12–19. His article *"Medicago denticulata, M. minima"* is in W.J. Hooker, et al., *Supplement to the English Botany of the Late Sir J.E. Smith and Mr. Sowerby*, I (London: J.D.C. and C.E. Sowerby, 1831), pl. 2634, 2635. The artist James de Carle Sowerby (1787–1871) pro-vided most of the illustrations for the continuation of the work on which his father, artist and publisher James Sowerby (1757–1822), had collabo-rated with Smith.

8 The Argyll Rooms in Regent Street and the English Opera House in the Strand were destroyed by fire on the nights of 5–6 and 15–16 February, respectively; see *The Times*, 6 and 16 Feb. 1830, both 3. It may well be these events that are referred to in MSB's "Memoir of . . . Sir Samuel Bentham," at 76: "On the occasion of some extensive conflagrations in the metropolis, Sir

Samuel contrived an application of the same fire-extinguishing works he had devised for the dockyards. His plan was presented to Sir Robert Peel, but he was of opinion that the "public mind was not yet ripe" for such an application of the water-works."

9   On 9 March, Joseph Hume accused the Attorney-General, James Scarlett (1769–1844), of ridiculing JB in a speech introducing a new bill for improving the administration of justice in Wales. Scarlett utterly denied the charge, adding that, though he was not personally acquainted with JB, he held him in the highest respect; see *PD*, n.s., vol. 23, cols. 69–70.

10 Scarlett's disparaging comments on the French judicial establishment are in the speech mentioned in n9, ibid., cols. 59–61.

11 Founded in 1804, The Horticultural Society of London, though successful in its principal aims, was by this time financially "In the Doldrums," as its historian, Harold R. Fletcher, entitles the chapter dealing with the period. See *The Story of the Royal Horticultural Society, 1804–1968* (London: RHS, 1969), 113–16, where the contribution of the Secretary, Joseph Sabine (1770–1837), to the development and the difficulties of the Society is outlined.

12 The problems arising from the conduct of John Turner, the paid Assistant Secretary, are described ibid., 116–20.

13 A letter to the editor, probably written by C.H. Bellenden Ker (ibid., 120), in *The Times*, 15 Jan. 1830, 2, called attention to the irregular financial situation of the Society.

14 On 19 January 1830, Robert Gordon and seven other Fellows gave notice of their intention to move for an enquiry. A committee of thirteen was established, with Gordon as Chairman, at the meeting of 2 February; *The Times*, 21 Jan. 1830, 2 and 3 Feb., 3.

15 Henry George Herbert, Earl of Carnarvon (1772–1833) and William Legge, Earl of Dartmouth (1784–1853) were members of Council of the HSL.

16 The triumphant Lindley was given a dual appointment, as Assistant Secretary to the Society and to the Garden, with a salary of £300 per annum; see Fletcher, *Story*, 125.

17 GB, "By-Laws of the Horticultural Society of London," in *Charter and By-Laws of the Horticultural Society of London* (London: HSL [printed Nicol], 1830).

18 Edward Clive, Earl of Powis, was the father of Charlotte Florentina, wife of Hugh Percy, Duke of Northumberland, owner of Syon House. The botanic garden would be opened to the public in 1837.

19 The Zoological Society, founded in 1826, was granted its charter of incorporation in 1829. The following year questions were raised about the management and expenses of the Treasurer, Joseph Sabine, as a result of the difficulties at the HSL; see *The Times*, 2 Apr. 1830, 4, and 4 May, 1.

20 See n7 above, and GB, "*Linum mexicanum*," *Edwards's Botanical Register*, 16 (1830), pl. 1326.

21 The educator Jean Joseph Jacotot (1770–1840) frequently repeated his principles in the course of his exposition; see, e.g., *Enseignement universel. Langue étrangère* (1824), 6th ed. (Paris: Mansut, 1838), 30–3.

22 As an example of the canvassing that went on during the second phase of the election, see John Stuart Mill's letter to John Bowring of 19 June 1830, soliciting a vote for (among others) William Ogle Carr, "who is strongly recommended by Mr George Bentham" (J.S. Mill, *Additional Letters, Collected Works*, XXXII [Toronto: University of Toronto Press, 1991], 11).

23 The aims of the Society and a list of the founding members are given in *The Times*, 15 June 1830, 4.

24 See 12–15 above.

25 The state funeral for the King, who had died on 26 June, took place on 14 July; see *The Times*, 15 July 1830, 4.

26 For the 1830 election of the Royal Society of London, see 361 above. GB became a Fellow on 27 November 1862.

27 John Bennett (1773–1852), M.P. for Wiltshire, was, in fact, the husband of Aylmer Bourke Lambert's late sister, Lucy. William Bennett's wife, Lucy's sister-in-law, was Ellen (née Gore).

28 On 25 July, Charles X, claiming a power of personal government granted by the constitutional Charter of 1814, issued four repressive ordinances, which dissolved the recently elected Chamber of Deputies, put drastic restrictions on the liberty of the press, reduced the number of electors and the number of Deputies, and announced new elections (Bulletin 367, nos. 15135–8 [25 July 1830]); see *The Times*, 28 July, 2–3. Three days of revolution followed, on 27, 28 and 29 July. On the 31st, Louis Philippe, duc d'Orléans, accepted the liberals' offer to be Lieutenant-General of the realm, and then, on 7 August, became King.

29 See, e.g., the *Courier*, 31 July 1830, 2 and 3.

30 The diary entries for these two weeks indicate that he was working at Mexican plants, and at labiatae, for his "monograph," *Labiatarum genera et species*, 3 vols. (London: Ridgway, 1832–36).

31 JB's immediate response to the revolution was a letter, "Bentham to the French People" (August 1830); in *Works*, XI, 56–8.

32 Henry John George Herbert, Viscount Porchester (1800–49), son of the Earl of Carnarvon, was the author of such works as *The Moor; a Poem in Six Cantos* (London: Knight, 1825) and *Don Pedro, King of Castile; a Tragedy*, (London: Colburn, 1828). On 4 August 1830, he had married Henrietta Anne, daughter of Lord Henry Howard-Molyneux-Howard, and niece of Bernard Edward Howard, Duke of Norfolk.

33 The quotations that follow, with the exception of those mentioned in n35, derive from GB's diary for the period, at RBGK.

34 The length of a "German" mile varied in different states, but where GB was travelling it was roughly the equivalent of five English miles.

35 Quoted from a letter to SB, dated 12 September 1830, from Berlin; the following quotation is from a letter dated 21 September, from Hamburg; MSS at LSL.

36 Friedrich August I, King of Saxony (1750–1827), had been succeeded by his brother Anton (1755–1836), to the great disappointment of his people, who had been expecting a more liberal regime under the King's nephew, Prince Friedrich Augustus (1797–1854). In 1830 rioting against Anton's repressive policies occurred in Leipzig and Dresden, with positive results. The Prince was made co-regent with his uncle, and a constitution promised. It was promulgated the following year, on 4 September 1831. See also 394 above.

37 The King of Prussia, Friedrich Wilhelm III (1770–1840), was popular for his efforts, following the Napoleonic wars, to promote religious tolerance at home and peace in Europe.

38 Friedrich Sellow (1789–1831) did important botanical exploration in Brazil and Uruguay, 1814–31.

39 Adelbert von Chamisso (1781–1838) was from a French noble family of the Champagne region that fled eastward from the Revolution in 1792, and ultimately settled in Prussia. He was the author of *Peter Schlemihls wundersame Geschichte* (Nuremberg: Schrag, 1814), the story of a man who sold his shadow to the Devil and subsequently refused to give up his soul to get it back. The tale had appeared in English as *Peter Schlemihl . . . with Plates by George Cruikshank*, trans. John Bowring (London: Whittaker, 1823).

40 Chamisso had served as the naturalist on the voyage financed by Nikolai Petrovich Rumiantsev (or Romanzoff) (1754–1826), and had contributed scientific observations, constituting the third volume of Otto von Kotzebue's, *Entdeckungs-Reise in die Süd-See und nach der Berings Strasse*, 3 vols. (Weimar: Hoffman, 1821); in English, 3 vols. (London: Longman, et al., 1821). Chamisso's full account appeared as *Reise um die Welt*, vols. I–II of *Werke* (Leipzig: Weidmann, 1836). GB's summary quotation, from the Journal (Tagebuch), is in *A Voyage around the World with the Romanzov Exploring Expedition in the Years 1815–1818 in the Brig Rurik, Captain Otto von Kotzebue*, trans. and ed. Henry Kratz (Honolulu: University of Hawaii Press, 1986), 23.

41 The statue of the popular Queen Luise, who died in 1810, was commissioned by the King the following year. It was the first of many monuments to public figures, such as Luther, Kant and Frederick the Great, by the sculptor Daniel Christian Rauch (1777–1857).

42 This play was a translation of *Charles XII: An Historical Drama in Two Acts*, by

James Robinson Planché (1796–1880). It had been first performed in London on 11 November 1828, at Drury Lane Theatre, with John Liston (1776?–1846) in the role of the comic character Adam Brock; see Planché, *Recollections and Reflections*, 2 vols. (London: Tinsley, 1872), I, 147–8.

43 Chamisso and Diederich Franz von Schlechtendal (1794–1866), the editor of *Linnaea*, were probably working on the next instalment of their series, "Plantarum mexicanarum a cel. viris Schiede et Deppe collectarum recensio brevis," *Linnaea*, 5 (1830), 72–174, 206–36, 554–625; 6 (1831), 22–64, 352–84 and 385–430. They also collaborated at this time to produce another series, "De plantis in expeditione speculatoria Romanzoffiana observatis," ibid., beginning in 2 (1827), to which GB would contribute "Labiatae," 6 (1831), 76–82. See Günther Schmid, *Chamisso als Naturforscher: Eine Bibliographie* (Leipzig: Koehler, 1942), 59–73.

44 In 1821 Christian Peter Wilhelm Beuth (1781–1853) founded this school, which in 1827 became the "Technical Institute."

45 The princes with the King were probably Karl Friedrich Wilhelm IV (1795–1861), the heir to the throne; Wilhelm, later Kaiser Wilhelm I of Germany (1797–1888); and Karl (1801–83). Hans Karl Friedrich Anton Diebitsch-Sabalkanski (1785–1831), the Russian Field Marshal, had been Quartermaster General of the combined Russian-Prussian forces against Napoleon. In the previous year he had successfully conducted the Russo-Turkish war, which ended with the Treaty of Adrianople on 28 August 1829.

46 Joachim Anton Ferdinand Fintelmann (1774–1863) had already gone to the meeting of the Deutscher Naturforscher, which that year was being held in Hamburg; see 350–4 above. His nephew, Gustav Adolf (1803–71), would later succeed to the post of Head Gardener of the Pfaueninsel.

47 The Gesellschaft Deutscher Naturforscher und Ärtzte, whose conference GB was attending, had, in fact, held its first meeting at Leipzig in 1822, but had only begun to publish reports of the annual gatherings from 1828. A brief history of the Association, its by-laws, and accounts of the early meetings are given in the tenth anniversary volume, *Bericht über die Versammlung Deutscher Naturforscher und Ärtzte in Wien in September 1832*, ed. J.F. von Jacquin and J.J. Littrow (Vienna: Beck, 1832), 1–21. Personal acquaintance among scientists was a primary aim of the organization, membership being open to all authors on scientific and medical subjects (doctoral dissertations excepted). It was a loosely constituted group, with no formal membership procedures. Its original organizers, Lorenz Oken (1779–1851) of Jena being the prime mover, were trying to create an association with a broad base, beyond the boundaries of any university. The venue for the annual September meeting changed each year, and an Administrative Officer and Secretary, based in the chosen town or city, were responsible for the arrangements. From an original

membership of 13 in 1822, the Assocation grew very quickly, and there were over 400 participants at the Hamburg meeting in 1830. For its influence on the development of an Association of scientists in England, see *Gentlemen of Science: Early Correspondence of the British Association for the Advancement of Science*, ed. J. Morrell and A. Thackray (London: Royal Historical Society, 1984), esp. 23, 33–5, 38–9, 46.

48 Friedrich Georg Wilhelm Struve (1793–1864) spoke on relations between German astronomy and that in other countries, and Dr J. Wendt, Professor of Medicine at Breslau, on hypnosis; *Bericht*, 32.

49 The Scottish nurseryman James Booth (1770–1814) had established a business at Flottbeck in 1795, and his sons, James Godfrey (1794–1871) and John Richmond (1799–1847), carried it on together until 1828, when the latter assumed full control. He and his brother George Booth (1804–66) were registered as botanists at the Hamburg meeting.

50 Count Kaspar Sternberg (1761–1838) spoke on fossil flora, Baron Joseph Franz von Jacquin (1766–1839) introduced *Syringa Josikaea*, and Professor Franz Karl Mertens (1764–1831) reported on the state of studies in algolology; *Bericht*, 40–1.

51 The proposal and discussion in the Botanical Section and the reaction at the final General Meeting on 25 September are reported in *Bericht*, 48, 51 and 58–9.

52 The statue of Ariadne with a panther (1814), by Johann Heinrich Dannecker (1758–1841), was purchased by the Frankfurt banker Simon Moritz Bethmann (1768–1826) and displayed in a temple, specially constructed for it in the family garden beside his art museum.

53 In the wake of the July Revolution in France, Belgium, which had been part of the Kingdom of the Netherlands since the settlement of 1815, protested against the autocratic regime of William I, King of Holland (1772–1843) with an uprising in Brussels. The rebels enjoyed considerable success, prompting a conference of European powers; see 375n25 and 413n33 below.

54 See *The Times*, 9 Nov. 1830, 3.

55 See ibid., 10 Nov. 1830, 3.

56 The Duke of Wellington declared against further reform in his speech of 2 November, on the Address in answer to the King's speech, *PD*, 3rd ser., vol. 1, cols. 52–3. On 15 November, Sir Henry Parnell's motion for an inquiry into the details of the expenditures in the civil list was successful, ibid., cols., 525–32, 548, and Wellington resigned the following day. In the ensuing Whig administration, under Charles, Earl Grey (1764–1845), Henry Brougham became Lord Chancellor; see New, *Life of Henry Brougham to 1830*, 414–18.

57 This letter has not been preserved.

58 Neither of the two caricatures created by "H.B." (John Doyle) at this time corresponds to GB's description. The first, issued 23 November 1830, entitled "The Coquet, or a Political Courtship," depicts Brougham as a shy maiden, replying to Grey, who is offering him out the Chancellor's wig, "Ah! dont ask me? – you know I said *twice over* I wouldn't take anything." The second, issued 27 November 1830, entitled "Samson and Dalilah [*sic*]," presents Lady Holland and Lords Grey and Durham as three conspirators, preparing to put the Chancellor's robes on Brougham as he sleeps. Lord Grey is saying, "Hush! How 'astonished' he'll be when he awakes!" Both are in *Political Sketches, &c., by H.B.*, I (London: McLean, 1830), under date.

59 In UCL, 174 118, is a letter from Brougham, of Sunday morning, 21 November 1830, thanking JB for his of the previous day "about Chancery shop, etc" (not extant), and asking him to name a time for their dining together. JB's reply, with an invitation for Tuesday, 23 November, is in Brougham MSS, 26,006, and in *Works*, XI, 62. Brougham's "excuse" has not been preserved.

60 *Lord Brougham Displayed, Including 1. Boa Constrictor*, alias *Helluo Curiarum; II. Observations on the Bankruptcy Court Bill, Now Ripened into an Act* (1832); in *Works*, V, 549–612.

61 A recommendation of the distinguished astronomer John Frederick William Herschel (1792–1871), by scientific colleagues of the Royal Society, was published several times before the meeting; see *The Times*, 25, 29 and 30 Nov., and for an account of the election, 1 Dec. 1830, all 3.

62 See n43 above.

63 William John Burchell (1781–1863) travelled in South Africa, 1811–16, where he collected more than 63,000 natural history objects. He described this trip in *Travels in the Interior of Southern Africa*, 2 vols. (London: Longman, et al., 1822–24). From 1825–29 he explored in Brazil, and collected some 15,000 species of plants. A short account, "Mr. Burchell's Brazilian Journey," based on two letters, of 25 April 1828 and October 1830, appeared in volume 2 of W.J. Hooker's *Botanical Miscellany* (1831), 128–33.

64 See 312 above. Sidney Herbert (1810–61), a conscientious parliamentarian and cabinet minister, would give his full support to Florence Nightingale's mission during the Crimean war, and lead the subsequent movement for army reform.

Chapter 10

1 Later published as *Scrophularineae indicae: A Synopsis of the East Indian Scrophularineae Contained in the Collections Presented by the East India Company to*

the Linnean Society of London, and in Those of Mr Royle and Others; with Some General Observations on Affinities and Sub-Divisions of the Order (London: Ridgway, 1835).

2 Alexander Turgenev (1783–1845), having been forced to leave government service, devoted his time to searching in foreign archives for documents relating to Russia, which he published as *Historica Russiae monumenta* (St Petersburg: Pratzi, 1841–2). His brother Nicolas (1789–1871) had been a member of the diplomatic corps, was implicated in the plot of upper-class youth against the Emperor Alexander in 1825, and was condemned to death *in absentia* for treason.

3 Louis Auguste Victor, comte de Bourmont (1773–1846), had been relieved of his command in Algeria by the new government of Louis Philippe, to whom he refused to give allegiance.

4 All the quotations in this chapter derive from GB's diary for the period, at RBGK.

5 GB, *Observations on the Registration Bill* (London: Ridgway, 1831).

6 The review, in which GB is accused of inadequate exposition and defence of his uncle's ideas, appeared in the *London Literary Gazette* 12 Mar. 1831, 167–8. According to his diary for that day, GB read it at the Athenaeum Club.

7 The first attempt at parliamentary reform, "A Bill to Amend the Representation of the People in England and Wales," *PP*, 1830–1, II, 197–218, was introduced in the Commons on 1 March 1831, by Lord John Russell (1792–1878), who was largely responsible for its framing. Its aim was to make representation more equitable, particularly of large towns, by abolishing many small boroughs and redistributing seats. It also extended the franchise based on the rates, the most significant provision being that male householders in boroughs rated at £10 or over would become electors. It was defeated in Committee on 21 April, and Parliament was dissolved, but the reformers were returned at the June election in even larger numbers; see E.L. Woodward, *The Age of Reform, 1815–1870* (Oxford: Clarendon Press, 1938), 77–83.

8 These papers apparently remained unpublished. SB's work in progress at this time is described in MSB, *Life*, 318–21.

9 SB's death date is given as 31 May 1831, ibid., 321.

10 See the account in *The Times*, 24 June 1831, 3.

11 Jane Marcet (1769–1858) was a Swiss-born writer of popular works on scientific subjects from 1806, of which the best known is probably *Conversations on Political Economy* (London: Longman, et al., 1816).

12 The three days of revolution in the previous year, 27 to 29 July 1830.

13 An uprising of Poland against Russia, inspired by the French Revolution of July, had begun on 29 November 1830, and received much popular support

in France, though no assistance from the government. In his speech at the opening of the Chambers on 23 July 1831, with reference to Poland, Louis Philippe said: "J'ai voulu arrêter l'effusion du sang, préserver le midi de l'Europe du fléau de la contagion que la guerre propage et surtout assurer à la Pologne . . . cette nationalité qui a résisté au temps et à ses vicissitudes"; reported in *La Quotidienne,* 24 July 1831, 2, with an editorial comment, critical of the ministry's attitude, on the preceding page. See also 376 above.

14 Henri V was the name given by the royalists to the legitimate heir to the throne, the duc de Bordeaux. Charles X, in an unsuccessful attempt to save the crown for the Bourbons, had abdicated in his favour on 2 August 1830, and then taken the boy with him to Edinburgh. The ode in the Marseilles paper, *Gazette du Midi,* has not been located.

15 The popular revolution in the states of central Italy, begun in February 1831, was put down by the end of March, and many of the participants were forced into exile.

16 The phrase represented the official position of the government of Louis Philippe, suggesting a conciliatory and moderate policy, avoiding extremes at both right and left.

17 Paul Joseph Marie Roger, marquis de Ginestous (1797–1884), of an old aristocratic family in Languedoc, at Vigan, was won over to the idea of constitutional government under the July monarchy. He became Colonel of the National Guard of the town, then Mayor, and was a member of the General Council of the department of Gard, 1831–34. His father, Jean François, comte de Ginestous (1751–1834), was a retired cavalry officer, whose pension was cut off in 1831 because he actively disapproved of the new regime. His mother, comtesse Marie Louise (1764–1841), had been a member of the salons of Versailles before the 1789 Revolution, and was mentally unbalanced for a period of time by the horrors of 1792 that she had witnessed. (H. Vergnette de Lamotte, *Histoire de la maison de Ginestous* [1975].)

18 Probably Charles Hamond, formerly of Hamond and Hill, steam-engine-boiler manufacturers of Wapping (*CJB,* IX, 280).

19 The coal mines at Cavaillac and Sumène and the coal and iron mines at Le Vigan were purchased in 1826 by a consortium which, according to the deed of sale, consisted of Paul Deshours-Farel, Odon Rech, Samuel Véret, Antoine David Levat, Zoé Guillaume Granier and Félix Bouché, all of Montpellier; Jules Deshours of Calviac and Renaud de Vilbak apparently became partners subsequently. Relevant documents (including a description of the mines) and correspondence are in the Archives départementales de l'Hérault, sous-série 1E (Archives de familles), 291, 294, 297 and 298.

20 A popular variety of pasta, originally manufactured in Genoa.

21 A.P. De Candolle, "Note sur quelques plantes observées en fleurs au mois de jan. 1828 dans la serre de M. Saladin, à Pregny," *Mémoires de la Société de Physique et d'Histoire Naturelle de Genève*, 4 (1828), 85–90, and in pamphlet form (Geneva: Barbezat and Delarue, 1828).

22 Sabin Berthelot (1794–1880) and Philip Barker Webb (1793–1854) had explored together in the Canary islands, 1828–30, and were preparing their *Histoire naturelle des Iles Canaries*, 9 vols. (Paris: Béthune, 1836–50), of which the third volume, in three parts, was devoted to botany.

23 The Guanches were aboriginal people in the western Canary islands, of early Stone Age culture at the beginning of the 15th century when they were first encountered by conquering Spaniards.

24 The Countess Teresa Guiccioli (1801–73) was Lord Byron's companion in Italy, from 1819 until his departure for Greece in July 1823. She later published a eulogistic memoir, *My Recollections of Lord Byron*, 2 vols. (London: Bentley, 1869).

25 See 359n53 above. As a result of a meeting of the five principal European powers at London, Belgium was declared an independent state on 7 February 1831. Louis Philippe's second son, the duc de Nemours (1814–96), was chosen King of the Belgians at this time, but his father yielded to hostile pressure from the other European powers and stopped the appointment.

26 Alexander von Humboldt published the findings of his journey as *Fragmens de géologie et de climatologie asiatiques*, 2 vols. (Paris: Gide, 1831).

27 Hussein-Pacha (1767–1838) had been Dey of Algiers from March 1818. In June of 1830 the French government, largely to divert attention from its own unpopularity, had launched a military campaign to put a stop to the piracy and slavery practised by Algiers. By 5 July 1830, the French army was in control, and the Dey went into exile, moving at first to Paris and finally settling at Alexandria.

28 The Polish revolution ended with the fall of Warsaw to the Russian armies on 7 September, 1831; see *Le Constitutionnel*, 17 Sept., 1. Accounts of the resulting popular disturbances are ibid., 18, 19 and 20 Sept., 1, 3, and 4, respectively.

29 For an account, see *Archives parlementaires*, 2nd ser., 70, 38–73.

30 In the November 1827 elections, the number of liberal members in the Chamber of Deputies increased significantly, to about two-fifths, and the conservative Villèle ministry was succeeded by that of the vicomte de Martignac, which introduced more moderate measures. Concerned by the trend, Charles X, in 1829, appointed an ultra-conservative ministry, under Prince Jules de Polignac (1780–1847), a move that only increased liberal opposition. In the reply to the King's address at the opening of the session in March 1830,

a protest by 221 deputies demanded that ministers be made responsible to the majority in the Chambers; see the *Moniteur*, 17 and 20 Mar. 1830, 303 and 315. The King subsequently dissolved the session and announced new elections.

31 Named for a similar pleasure ground in Chelsea, Ranelagh opened in 1774, and remained a popular spot for dancing and theatre until the site was expropriated in 1854.

32 Inserted, unnumbered, between pages 566 and 567, are the itemized bill of £95/7/10 for GB's call to the bar, and the receipt issued by the official of Lincoln's Inn, dated 18 November 1831.

33 Harford Jones Brydges (1764–1847), in the service of the East India Company, became a successful scholar of oriental languages. He served as minister plenipotentiary to the court of Persia, 1807–11, and on his appointment was created 1st Baronet Boultibrook. His son, Harford James Jones-Brydges (1808–91), was educated at Oxford, and would later be Sheriff of Radnorshire. See also 416 above.

Chapter 11

1 By his will, dated 30 May 1832, JB appointed John Bowring his executor, giving to him, out of the proceeds from the sale of JB's interest in the New Lanark Company, "the sum of two thousand pounds sterling to be laid out . . . in the publication of a Complete Collection of all my works and the completion of such of them as are not yet published and moreover so much as in his judgement shall be a sufficient remuneration for the person or persons by whom the service of Editorship shall be performed." To GB was left the "freehold estates which consist of a Hollow square Edifice which with the land within it is called Bell Yard and of part of my dwellinghouse and garden. . . ." The "leashold property consisting of my estates at and near Queen Square Place held under the Dean and Chapter of Westminster part comprized in a lease in which I am sole lessee and other part in another lease in which I was a lessee jointly with my late brother" was left in equal shares to GB, MLC and Sarah Bentham. (Public Record Office, Prob11/1801, 4, 5.)

2 The quotations in this chapter, unless otherwise indicated below, are taken from GB's diary for the period, at RBGK.

3 GB, "*Stemodia chilensis*, Including a Synopsis of the Genus," *Edwards's Botanical Register*, 17 (1831–2), pl. 1470; "*Scutellaria alpina* var. *lupulina*, Including a Synopsis of the Genus; *Coleus aromaticus*," ibid., 18 (1832), pl. 1493, 1520; *Labiatarum genera et species; or, A Description of the Genera and Species of Plants*

of the Order Labiatae; with Their General History, Characters, Affinities, and Geographical Distribution, 3 vols. (London: Ridgway, 1832–36), of which part A, 1–60, appeared in August 1832.

4 William Bridges Adams ("Junius Redivivus") (1797–1872), "Lord Brougham and Mr. Bentham," *Tatler,* 9 and 10 Mar. 1832, 233–4 and 237–8.

5 JB's "Outline of a Plan of a General Register of Real Property" first appeared in the Appendix to the *Third Report* of the Real Property Commissioners, *PP,* 1831–32, 23, 431–50; in *Works,* V, 417–35.

6 The third version of the Reform Bill, introduced in December 1831, was ultimately successful because the Whigs persuaded the King to agree to create a number of peers sufficient to assure its acceptance, though the threat was never actually carried out. Passing a third reading in the Lords on 4 June 1832, the Bill was enacted as 2 & 3 William IV, c. 45 (7 June 1832).

7 Robert Monsey Rolfe concluded that it had not been JB's intention to limit the expenditure on the edition to the £2000 mentioned in the will, and that editors might be paid the whole amount of a fair remuneration over and above that sum; "Award in the suit of George Bentham, *v.* J. Bowring, *in re* Jeremy Bentham's Will, 1835," 9 Feb. 1835; copy in BL, Add. MSS, 33,553, ff. 72–3.

8 The extensive collections made by John Forbes Royle (1799–1858), naturalist of the East India Company, would also be turned over to the LSL and incorporated into the Wallich Herbarium in 1836. With other of the Society's Asian collections, they were transferred to RBGK in 1913; see Desmond, *The India Museum,* 53.

9 See 352 above.

10 Nanine Cantor (1782–1867), whose son, Theodor Edvard (1809–60), followed in his uncle Wallich's footsteps as a physician and botanist for the East India Company.

11 Cf. 344 above. Brunswick was the only German state where serious destruction occurred in the wake of the French revolution of 1830. Duke Karl II, a tyrannical ruler of the old school, promised the populace assembled at his gate on 6 September that he would comply with their demands: remove the canon he had recently posted about the town; recognize a parliament; remain in the state rather than go abroad, and not send his money out of the country. When he reneged the following day, the palace was almost completely destroyed by a fire, started in the rear wing, where the people were able to gain entry; see *The Times,* 14 Sept. 1830, 3.

12 See 344 above.

13 GB is referring to the unification and rise to power of Germany, which began when Otto von Bismarck (1815–98) became Prime Minister in September of 1862.

14 Tadeusz Andrej Bonaventura Kosciuszko (1746–1817), a Polish patriot, was the military commander of the popular insurrection at Cracow in 1794 against the Russian army, which was backing the pro-Russian, conservative forces in the government of Poland at the time.

15 The last two sentences in this quotation and the quotation in the following paragraph derive from GB's letter to his mother, from Dresden, dated 7 September 1832; MS at LSL.

16 GB is presumably referring to the original parts of the Zwinger palace, which dated from 1711. A new wing to house the famous collection of pictures was begun in 1847.

17 The abbreviation is of "kaiserlich" and "königlich," i.e., imperial and royal, referring to the Austrian empire constituted in 1804, and the kingdoms of Bohemia, Hungary, etc., within it, ruled by the house of Habsburg.

18 In 1817 the youngest daughter of the Austrian Emperor Franz I, married the Portuguese Crown Prince Dom Pedro and moved to Brazil. As the Princess Leopoldine was an avid amateur of natural history, Austria sent a team of scientists and artists to explore and document her new country in honour of the marriage.

19 The draft account, from which the following quotations derive, is in "Benthamiana," RBGK.

20 His admission ticket and an information sheet for the members are included, unnumbered by GB, between pages 599 and 600 of the text.

21 "These foreign scholars, gathered from afar, / They aim to chart the comets, or a star? / To trace the course of rivers, or to find / The source of nature's wonders, for mankind? / Or do they seek perhaps, to make it known, / Of ancient alchemists, the magic stone? / Oh no, [their quest is that of all us sinners;] / They want to know who serves the first-class dinners!"

22 This paragraph and the description of the Emperor and Clemens, Prince Metternich (1773–1859) in the following paragraph are summarized from GB's letter to his mother of 18 September 1832, from Vienna; MS at LSL. The speeches mentioned, by Karl Friedrich Burdach (1776–1847), Andreas Johann Wawruch (1782–1842), and Heinrich Robert Goeppert (1800–84), are reported in *Bericht über die Versammlung deutscher Naturforscher und Ärtzte in Wien im September 1832*, ed. J.F. Jacquin and J.J. Littrow (Vienna: Beck, 1832), 54–7.

23 The paper by Leopold Trattinik (1764–1849) on aesthetical aspects of botany, and another by Franz Joseph Unger (1800–70), mentioned below, are both reported in *Bericht* (1832), 107.

24 This paragraph is quoted from the draft account, in "Benthamiana," RBGK, which ends at this point in the narrative. The subsequent details are taken from the diary.

25 In 1831 Prince Metternich married his third wife, Melanie von Zichy-Ferraris (1805–54).

26 The Princess' impressions of this evening are recorded in "Journal de la princesse Mélanie" (1832), *Mémoires, documents et écrits divers, laissés par le prince Metternich*, 8 vols. (Paris: Plon, 1880–84), V, 249–50. Her experience at the opening meeting on the 18th of September, at Laxenburg on the 25th, and at the dinner she gave on the 28th, are also ibid., 248–9, 251–2; see 407–8 and 410 above.

27 Karoline Pichler (1769–1843), poet and novelist, whose salon was the literary centre of Vienna, was particularly known for her historical romances, such as *Die Belagerung Wiens (The Siege of Vienna)*, 3 vols. (Vienna: Pichler, 1824) and *Die Schweden in Prag (The Swedes in Prague)* (ibid., 1827). Her *Sämtliche Werke* ultimately filled 60 volumes (ibid., 1820–45).

28 The portrait of the Emperor Franz, in full imperial regalia, painted in 1832 by Friedrich von Amerling (1803–87), is considered to be one of the artist's finest works. One of the other portraits referred to is presumably that of the fourth Empress, Karolina Augusta (1792–1873), painted after her marriage in 1816 by the Bavarian artist Joseph Stieler (1781–1858).

29 Metternich's suggestion that both the terminology for species of rocks and the colouring for geological maps be standardized is reported in *Bericht* (1832), 120. The following year, at Breslau, Leopold von Buch submitted a draft proposal, mentioned in *Bericht* (1833), ed. J. Wendt and A.W. Otto (Breslau: printed Grafs, Bart, 1834), 49. At the next meeting, in Stuttgart, a sample of his scheme was submitted to members; *Bericht*, ed. C.V. Kielmeyer and G. Jäger (Stuttgart: Metzler, 1835), 89. According to the report of the Bonn meeting in 1835, in *Isis, oder Encyclopädische Zeitung*, 9, 1836, cols. 708–9, a committee was struck to study the suggestion, and the matter was quietly dropped, the reports of subsequent years containing no mention of it.

30 The full text of what is described as a "beloved folk song," written by Lorenz Leopold Haschka (1749–1827), is given in *Bericht* (1832), 84. It was sung to a tune by Joseph Haydn, first performed in Vienna in February 1797, and incorporated that year into his "Emperor" String Quartet, Opus 76, no. 3.

31 Presumably that of the popular Viennese conductor Johann Strauss (1804–49).

32 The guest and wine lists, unnumbered by GB, appear between pages 613 and 614 of the text.

33 See 359n53 above. The situation remained precarious into 1832, as the Dutch were very unwilling to accept the terms of Belgium's independence, though British and French forces were insisting on their compliance.

34 Leopold of Saxe-Coburg (1790–1865) had been proclaimed King of the Belgians on 21 July 1831. On 9 August 1832, he had married Louise Marie d'Orléans (1812–50), daughter of Louis Philippe.

35 In 1826 MLC had been "induced to return to her husband, who she vainly hoped had reformed his ways" (see 68 and 234 above) and she gave birth to a son, Théodore, the following year. Both her children would unfortunately predecease her: Adèle in 1844 and Théodore in 1857.

36 GB was entitled to vote in South Hampshire because his family had retained a farm near Alverstoke when they disposed of their country home, Berry Lodge; see 132 and 291 above. Henry John Temple, Lord Palmerston (1784–1865) had been Secretary of State for Foreign Affairs in the Whig administration of Lord Grey since November 1830. The two Conservative candidates were the sitting member, John Willis Fleming, and Sir George Thomas Staunton (1781–1859), a writer on China, East Indian administrator, and M.P. Staunton was returned second to Lord Palmerston in this election; Fleming would regain the seat in 1835.

Chapter 12

1 Owen Glendower (1359?–1416?), a Welsh rebel during the reign of Henry IV.

2 Sir Harford Jones Brydges and his wife Sarah (d. 1832) had two daughters as well as a son; see 382n33 above. On 23 October 1822, the elder, Laura (d. 1863), had married John Lucy Scudamore (1798–1875), an army Colonel. Sarah, the middle child (ca. 1806–81), became GB's wife.

3 GB's diary indicates that he began work on the Monocotyledons, part II of volume III of his and J.D. Hooker's *Genera Plantarum*, on 1 September 1879; it was published on 14 April 1883. His wife died on 15 July 1881. See Introduction, xxxvi–xxxvii above. The handwriting from here to the end of the narrative suggests that GB had grown very frail by this time.

4 Auguste de Saint-Hilaire (1799–1853) had acquired remarkable collections during his six years of exploration in Brazil, 1816–22. For Burchell, see 362n63 above.

5 William Edward Nightingale (1794–1874) and his wife Frances (1788–1880), parents of Florence Nightingale, purchased the estate of Embley Park in Hampshire in 1825, and used it as a winter home; see Cecil Woodham-Smith, *Florence Nightingale, 1820–1910* (London: Constable, 1968), 5–6.

6 The quotations in this chapter all derive from GB's diary for the period, at RBGK.

7 Frances Stackhouse Acton (1793–1881), daughter of T.A. Knight, was a skil-

ful botanical draughtswoman, who shared in her father's experiments, and contributed the biographical section to *A Selection from the Physiological and Horticultural Papers Published in the Transactions of the Royal and Horticultural Societies by the Late Thomas Andrew Knight, to Which Is Prefixed a Sketch of His Life*, [ed. George Bentham] (London: Longman, *et al.*, 1841).

8 GB, "Sileneae," was the first of three contributions to the work by John Forbes Royle, *Illustrations of the Botany and Other Branches of the Natural History of the Himalayan Mountains*, 11 parts in 2 vols. (London: Allen, 1833–40), I, 79–81 (June 1834); GB would later contribute "Leguminosae" (April 1835) and "Boraginaceae" (May 1836), ibid., 197–200 and 305–6, respectively. Among "minor botanical papers," mentioned below, GB is presumably referring to his "*Collomia coccinea*, 'Epitome' of Polemoniaceae," *Edwards's Botanical Register*, 19 (1833), pl. 1622. He would also, in this same year, publish "Account of Indian Labiatae, in the Collection of J.F. Royle," *Botanical Miscellany*, ed. W.J. Hooker, 3 (1833), 370–84.

9 John Taylor (1779–1863), "Report of the State of Knowledge Respecting Mineral Veins," in *Report of the Third Meeting of the British Association for the Advancement of Science* (1833) (London: Murray, 1834), 1–25.

10 New Court, in the Tudor Gothic style, with a covered bridge over the Cam, was added to St John's College, 1826–31.

11 George Peacock (1791–1858), "Report on the Recent Progress and Present State of Certain Branches of Analysis"; John Lindley, "On the Principal Questions at Present Debated in the Philosophy of Botany"; George Rennie (1791–1866), "Report on the Progress and Present State of Our Knowledge of Hydraulic Architecture as a Branch of Engineering"; *Report of the Third Meeting*, 185–352, 27–57, and 153–84, respectively.

12 A demonstration of continuing support from the scientific community; see 361 above.

13 GB, "On the Recent Progress and Present State of Systematic Botany," delivered at the Annual Meeting, Belfast, 24 August 1874; in *Report of the British Association for the Advancement of Science* (1874) (London: BAAS, 1875), 27–54.

14 Bowring himself received the lion's share of the money. Others involved were his friend John Hill Burton (1809–81), who contributed numerous "notes and elucidations" to the edition; Richard Doane, who prepared the *Constitutional Code*, IX; Richard Smith (fl. 1825–35), who prepared the *Principles of Penal Law*, I, 365–580; and Southwood Smith (1788–1861), who edited *Chrestomathia*, VIII, 1–191.

15 See 96–7 above.

16 Louis Borelli, a wealthy Marseille merchant, began construction of this palace in the 1750s. It was completed by his son, Louis Joseph Denis Borelli

(1731–84), who acquired the rich picture collection. His niece and heir, Louise Jeanne Marie, wife of Pierre Léandre de Mark de Tripoli, comte de Panisse-Passis, sold it in 1856 to the city of Marseille.

17 The botanist's forenames were, in fact, Jacques Étienne.

18 The letter from Charles Paulus Bélanger (1805–81), dated 24 April 1834, is in Bentham correspondence, no. 201, RBGK. The conditions laid down were as follows: "1. Toutes les labiées que je vous enverrai . . . porteront un nom qui sera le mien. Je désire que vous adoptiez ce nom pour toutes les espèces nouvelles, à moins que ce nom appartienne deja à une autre espèce du meme genre, ou qu'il blesse les loix admises pour la nomenclature. Dans ce cas vous lui consacrerez le nom que vous jugerez convenable avec mes initiales comme parrains en auteurs de l'espèce. 2. Vous aurez la complaisance de m'envoyer dans le plus court délai, un choix de quatre des plus belles espèces nouvelles ou genres nouveaux de cette collection, avec leur description, et dessin analytique aussi grossierement fait que vous voudrez. Ce choix m'est indispensable pour les planches que j'ai à faire exécuter de suite. 3. Vous m'obligerez de m'envoyer aussitot votre travail terminé, mes liabiées *sans en excepter une seule*. 4. Vous aurez soin de n'alterer les échantillons qu'autant que cela sera necessaire à vos etudes."

19 GB, "Report of Some of the More Remarkable Hardy Ornamental Plants Raised in the Horticultural Society's Garden from Seeds Received from Mr David Douglas in the Years 1831, 1832, 1833," *Transactions of the Horticultural Society*, 2nd ser., 1 (1834), 403–14, 476–81; part I, read 21 January, 1834; part II read 17 June 1834.

20 GB, "Review of the Order of Hydrophylleae," *Transactions of the Linnean Society*, 17 (1837), 267–82, read 17 June 1834; this section of volume 17 was, in fact, published in 1835.

21 William Lawrence (1783–1867) had been accused by contemporary theologians of attempting to undermine religion in his course of lectures, *On the Physiology, Zoology, and Natural History of Man* (London: Callow, 1819). He was created a baronet on 30 April 1867. His son, James John Trevor Lawrence (1831–1913), would be President of the Royal Horticultural Society, 1885–1913.

22 The London branch of the Grand National Consolidated Trades Union, founded in 1834 under the influence of Robert Owen, was marching to present a petition requesting the remission of the recent conviction to seven years' transportation of six Dorsetshire agricultural labourers for having administered illegal oaths to other labourers. The Home Secretary, Lord Melbourne, transmitted a message that he refused to receive it because of the manner of the presentation; see *The Times*, 21 and 22 Apr. 1834, 3 and 6, respectively.

23 John Bate Cardale (1802–77) retired from the law in 1834 to lead a dissenting congregation that indulged in glossolalia. He was a follower of the charistmatic preacher, Edward Irving (1792–1834), who had been expelled from the Presbyterian church the previous year for allowing such practices.

24 This pen, with other Bentham memorabilia, is preserved at RBGK.

25 The portrait of Robert Brown, by Henry William Pickersgill (1782–1875), is at the LSL. An engraving was made by Charles Fox (1794–1849).

26 The portrait of Nathaniel Wallich, by John Lucas (1807–74), is also at the LSL.

27 No account of this contentious issue seems to have appeared in the daily or weekly press.

28 The German naturalist Eduard Rüppell (1794–1884) had been exploring in Abyssinia since February 1833; his account was published as *Reise in Abyssinien*, 2 vols. (Frankfurt: printed Schmerber, 1838–40). The collections from all his journeys were gifted to the Frankfurt museum and library.

29 Alphonse de Candolle had married Laura Kunkler in 1832 and their daughter, Valentine, was born the following year. Augustin de Candolle (1736–1820), the father of Augustin Pyramus, was twice elected First Syndic of Geneva, in 1785 and 1789.

30 Lady Davy was the daughter of Mr and Mrs Charles Kerr, of an Irish family, originally from Kelso.

31 Copies of the Italian translations, by Giuseppe Manetti (fl. 1831–58), of the following works by John Lindley are at the Royal Horticultural Society: *An Outline of the First Principles of Botany* (London: Longman, et al., 1830), *Principi fondamentali di botanica* (Monza: Corbetta, 1834); *An Outline of the First Principles of Horticulture* (London: Longman, et al., 1832), *Principi fondamentali di orticoltura* (Monza: Corbetta, 1833).

32 Guillaume Antoine Olivier (1756–1814), a French zoologist and botanist, travelled and collected extensively in the countries of the Middle East, 1792–98.

33 GB is referring to the work of the botanist Carlo Allioni (1728–1804), *Flora pedemontana*, 3 vols. (Turin: Briolus, 1785).

34 Presumably meaning that the identifications were written by the botanist K.P.J. Sprengel (1766–1833) himself, as distinct from specimens given a Sprengel name by someone else.

35 Answering a letter from Anastasie de Circourt of 31 October, Augustin Pyramus de Candolle wrote on 5 November 1834: "J'avais bien reçu votre bonne lettre mais j'avais tardé d'y répondre voulant vous annoncer en même temps l'arrivée de Bentham. Je l'ai beaucoup vu pendant les quelques jours qu'il nous a donnés et sa conversation m'a valu presqu'un voyage à Londres par tous les détails qu'il m'a donnés sur la gent botanique de ce pays-là. Il tra-

vaille beaucoup et bien. Par la suite je ne doute pas qu'il ne prenne une influence considérable et heureuse sur la direction de la botanique anglaise."
(*L'Europe de 1830*, ed. Roger de Candolle, 80.) In subsequent years, de Candolle would be very grateful for GB's considerable contributions to his great
Prodromus systematis naturalis regni vegetabilis, expressing his appreciation to
Mme de Circourt on 25 November 1839: "Le brave Bentham est excellent
pour moi. Il m'a donné un excellent morceau pour le volume que j'imprime
et m'en promet de plus importants encore pour les suivants. Je n'ai de possibilité d'achever mon entreprise qu'en appendant ainsi ma vie à celle de mes
amis. Heureusement qu'il s'en trouve quelques uns qui veulent bien me
faire le cadeau le plus précieux de tous, savoir de quelques années de leur
vie. Aucun ne me rend dans ce genre autant de service que l'excellent
Bentham. . . ." (Ibid., 170; GB's contributions, 1838–64, are listed in F.A.
Stafleu and R.S. Cowan, *Taxonomic Literature*, 2nd ed. [1976–92], I, 173.)

36 In a prefatory letter to a tale by his friend Johann Heinrich Daniel Zschokke
(1771–1848), *Der Creole; eine Erzählung* (1830), the writer Charles Victor de
Bonstetten (1745–1832) praised Anastasie de Circourt, who was a favourite
in the salons of Geneva; see *Zschokkes Werke*, 5 vols., ed. Hans Bodmer (Berlin: Bong, 1900), V, 8–9.

37 An entry in GB's journal-letter to his sister of 1 August 1827, reports that he
had received a letter from Théodore Leblanc, their Montpellier friend, who
was delighted now to be in Paris. "He is lodged close to the Ecole Militaire
where he has every facility for drawing hussards & horses & whatever other
military models he pleases. He says he intends painting a picture for the
Salon." During a subsequent visit to London, November–December 1834, he
painted GB's portrait, now at the LSL and reproduced in this volume. In
March 1835 Leblanc married GB's sister, Sarah, and died at the end of 1837 of
a wound suffered in Algeria (GB's diary entry for 16 December 1837).

APPENDIX A

Textual Emendations

The following is a list of slips of the pen and other textual errors that have been silently emended in the text. The page and line numbers at the left margin are keyed to the text above. The form found in the manuscript is given first, followed by the corrected version in square brackets.

3.6	have [has]		43.4	any [no]
11.25	Alexand [Alexander]		44.15	piece [peace]
11.36	extempory [extemporary]		49.20	he [her]
17.8	and [in]		50.1	ad [at]
17.15	was [were]		51.30	us [use]
18.5	with with [with]		53.12	concerts [concertos]
19.16	propriétaire [proprié- taires]		58.7	ground [gown]
			58.13	rock [rocks]
21.34	remained—then [remained. Then]		62.26	pleased [please]
			66.11	too [two]
22.2	extacy—after [extacy. After]		67.14	and [in]
			68.14	bread [bred]
23.7–8	on one [no one]		68.15	know [known]
23.39	Louvres [Louvre]		70.9	and and [and]
28.6	from [for]		74.2	eminents [eminence]
8.10	Dictionnaires [Diction- naire]		78.11	appurtenancies [appurte- nances]
34.26	heard [heart]		82.31	therefore was therefore [therefore was]
36.14	scenere [scenery]			
36.28	it a a [it as a]		83.33	own [on]
38.4	we [were]		87.20	althoug [although]
38.37	at bring [of bringing]		91.19	Beacaire [Beaucaire]

92.30   evening [evenings]
93.5   difficult [difficulty]
105.9   even amongst those [even those]
106.37 of [for]
111.2   done [down]
116.21 a [as]
117.26 no [know]
118.20 and that they [and they]
122.10 exlusive [exclusive]
124.13 followng [following]
133.25 knowing [knocking]
137.7   months. [months?]
138.10 acending [ascending]
146.10 in [on]
146.38 heterogenous [heterogeneous]
147.32 there [their]
147.40 irregularly [irregular]
157.13 on [one]
160.6   goal [gaol]
165.23 certainly [certain]
167.21 sceen [scene]
172.31 not not [not]
176.11 Toward [Towered]
189.1   leavin [leaving]
209.36 converted to in [converted in]
214.11 overcome [overcame]
216.31 an [and]
217.3   doube [double]
219.7   tune. The [tune, the]
221.26 boads [boards]
222.11 afford [afforded]
225.18 so [saw]
225.26 course [coarse]
226.18 waste [waist]
229.25 soverign [sovereign]
231.8   back [sack]
241.14 enable [enabled]

242.24 —and arriving [—arriving]
245.32 who were all [who all]
251.10 time before me [time before]
256.22 series [serious]
263.17 born [borne]
264.33-4 readily, and and [readily, and]
275.7   down to to [down to]
275.25 muids [muid]
275.32 on [one]
278.7   sit.' [sit?']
278.37 live [leave]
280.9   bud [but]
287.16 case [cases]
288.24 favourably [favourable]
288.33 dale [day]
292.34 gest [gesture]
295.38 one. [one?]
297.5   there [their]
298.21 past [passed]
306.34-5 man Driving [man, driving]
308.7   born [borne]
309.28 collected [collect]
314.18 gread [great]
316.7   and Again [and again]
317.35 title [titled]
319.18 bill [bills]
322.19 not [now]
324.6   Italy. M. [Italy, M.]
330.19 write [right]
331.26 several [separate]
333.8   *cesse* et . . . reste [*cesse et . . . reste*]
333.21 afford [avoid]
335.29 brother the the [brother to the]
338.25 he [her]

340.34   births [berths]
340.35   night—passed [night passed]
341.10   currant [current]
345.31   wer [were]
346.7   colums [columns]
348.7   Mr [Dr]
348.25   infantry. The [infantry, the]
348.30   expectd [expected]
352.5   garden [gardener]
355.12   there a a [there a]
356.15   an [and]
358.36   here [hear]
360.19   pickpoket [pickpocket]
365.34   succeeding [succeeded]
367.15   disclaimed [declaimed]
371.3   established [establishment]
372.21   ell [dale]
374.6   mile [miles]
374.21   general [generally]
376.7   of [a]

377.23   past [passed]
388.35   est [es]
390.38   contrary, which may [contrary, may]
391.35   opposite. The [opposite, the]
394.27   list though [list (though]
395.24   tier [tiers]
396.23   voiturin [voiturin's]
397.38   Koehel [Koehler]
406.38   lamp [lamps]
409.29   belong [belonging]
410.13   over time [over in time]
412.17   desert [deserted]
414.33   Chalons. Leaving [Chalons, leaving]
417.22   looking out [looking over]
418.10   which were [which was]
425.33   Countess as Ludolf [Countess Ludolf]
435.30   first in which [first of which]
436.34   appear [appears]

APPENDIX B

Textual Variants and Notes

In the following selection of textual variants and notes, page and line numbers at the left are keyed to the text above, where they are indicated by a "§". One or more cancelled words are enclosed in angled brackets. When a structure has been altered, the version in the text is indicated by the first . . . last words (or more, if necessary for sense), ending with a "]", followed by the cancelled version; for example, at 4.20, the text reads: "to take a part in her father's writings", the cancelled version being "to assist her father in his writings".

3.1	[*written on a half-sheet of paper, bound in as a preface; in pencil, below*: 1823, p. 139; 1824, p. 300; 1826, p. 340; 1827, p. 374; 1828, p. 453]
3.14	the \<eighteenth\> century
3.16	some \<freehold\> property
3.18	freehold partly \<copyhold\> under
3.22	in \<1831\> [*the year of GB's father's death*] when
4.6	absence \<paid a visit\> to
4.18	beautiful . . . hand] beautiful clearly legible hand
4.20	to . . . writings] to assist her father in his writings
4.35	write . . . reading] write very early—reading
4.36	we \<were taught\> to
6.40	limestone? [*word interlined; space left below for name*]
7.13	after a long] after \<above\> a \<fortnig\> long
7.30	before the \<war sent\>
7.33	till the \<spring\> of
8.27–8	suffered \<very few\> interruptions during the \<whole time\>.
8.33	[*superscript; space left for correction*]
8.34	The . . . abroad.] [*footnote written sideways in the margin*]
10.16–17	to . . . humiliation.] to the entry of the Allies into Paris.

11.1   to . . . honours] to do the honours

11.14   [*two consecutive pages so numbered by GB*]

14.28   [*next two lines, in reprint, joined to stanza above; break here, for sense, as in* Courier]

15.23   were <such a> contrast

15.26   little <disappointment> when

16.16   quite <at home> with

16.39   mathematician . . . thoroughly] mathematician and Greek and Latin scholar, thoroughly

18.40   game <which abounded in that country>.

20.2   confusion in the <country>.

20.2   The . . . France] The <numerous> English <spread over the> in France

20.34   some <English> acquaintance

21.19   in a letter sent] in one of his published letters sent

21.21   when <the Emperor> changed

21.34   remnants of the <army> dispersed

24.29   and <did not extend so> were

25.5   The <fine> trees

26.17   been <broken> up

30.25   also the <worthy> librarian

31.21   encampment <where we were sent> free

31.22   <At> Etampes

33.18   now <dismantled of all> quite

34.8   on the <Chevaliers de la> Table

37.22   the <Gironde> at

39.8   the . . . considerably] the English were considerably

39.10   they . . . retreat] they would have been compelled to retreat

39.11   battle . . . armistice] battle were it not for the armistice

40.5   and <often> the

41.20   <Dinners were also frequent although> [*paragraph*] For

44.20   any <man> I

45.12   [sic *for 64*]

45.15   and . . . friends [*written sideways in the margin*]

45.37   [sic *for 65*]

46.24   25th <April> and

47.23   named <Bach> and

47.29   Bach <Meissonier> and

48.13   or . . . deed] or who had taken a direct part in the deed

49.35   <In> the

49.36   a <winter> at

50.26   Mr <Ellison> received

50.27–8   to . . . week.] to call on Col. Coehorn for some explanations.

50.28–30 This . . . declined] These were indignantly refused. Mr Ellison
         insisted and finally declined

50.32–7   which . . . had therefore] [*addition written sideways in the margin*]

51.21   courses <and worked hard at home early and late>—the

52.23   ladies of <many> Spanish

53.18   in <the summer> May

53.19   the <collecting of> plants

54.33   that [*uncancelled*:] events took

56.33   with <no> signs

56.40   drying. The] drying. [*cancelled*:] I also paid a visit to M. Gouan,
         the once celebrated botanist and correspondent of Linnaeus,
         long Professor of Botany and Director of the Botanical Garden, and
         since his retirement living in a small house in the vicinity, in a small
         botanic garden of his own. He had long been blind and was now
         some years over 80, but was every day out in the garden and made
         a point of feeling his favorite Ginkgo biloba. [*marginal note*:
         "That was later"; *cf. 65 below*]

59.5   [*footnote written on an unnumbered slip, bound in opposite this paragraph,
         with the marginal comment*: "The Queen at Aix."]

60.10   [*footnote pasted on over the bottom half of pages 87 and 88 is clearly related
         to the loan to his brother-in-law, though not keyed in the text*]

60.10   and <still contrived to persua[de]>

63.14   was <shortly after> cut

63.23   his <quickness> in

74.1   [*footnote written on an unnumbered slip of paper, inserted between
         pages 106 and 107*]

76.37   one of <the other children was far away, and the third, anxious
         to sell the bit of meadow which the father had left to him could not
         do so without the consent of the others> the

91.16   very [*uncancelled*] pleasant in [*correct word in pencil above in GB's
         wife's hand*]

97.23   working <steadily> as

97.27   elt <thoroughly> satisfied

100.37   first <day> of

101.23   and . . . exceeded] <perhaps was still greater>

112.14   [sic *for 9th*]

112.40 his <eldest> daughter

113.37 [sic *for 17th*]

122.18 town <and at the annual dinner of the Horticultural Society on the 20th> and

122.19 Secretary <and on the 24th, on the invitation of Sir James Smith at the Linnean anniversary dinner, but my journal of that week, contained in a letter with much private matter has not been preserved>. In [*see entry at 132.33 below*]

129.13 [*footnote written sideways in the margin*]

132.33 north, <but as above mentioned the letter giving the details of all that I saw and did this last week has not been preserved> dining [*marginal note*: "Has been since found."]

134.36 [*on a half-sheet of paper, unnumbered by GB, bound in between pages 189 and 190*]

135.31 and 136.20   [*incorrectly numbered by GB*]

146.12 monuments, <amongst them was one of Lord Colchester's brothers who was buried here,> but

173.1 taught to <believe> the

175.16 mother <staying> with

189.32 [sic *for 17th*]

190.17 [sic *for 18th*]

193.19 be a <great> talker

193.23 up <Snowdon> a

194.37 walk <out> in

196.6 must be <enormous>.

196.18 wind <and> tide

204.6 but the <Inspecteur was> in

207.35 readily <find> conveyances

210.39 shipment to <London> and

215.24 beauty <almost> apparently

220.34 Pyrenees <establishing>

221.9 it is <occupied>

223.4 our own <bread> or

225.39 in the <evening>.

230.7 but <rain> came

232.23 night <surprised> us

237.25 but <to my surprise> not

246.32 it is <only> those

247.36–248.4   Bowring . . . again. [*passage circled in pencil, possibly for excision?*]

248.21   devoted . . . at] devoted four or five mornings in the week at

251.7   to the <Monthly> Magazine

256.20   A . . . hesitation. [*footnote a later addition, written sideways in the margin*]

256.29   15th <Nov.>, one [Nov. *is, however, correct*]

267.31   year <and as you have probably never seen one any more than myself, I shall endeavour to give you a sketch of it> (the

269.16   17th [sic *for 18th*]

271.4   noticed; <but few> copies

284.36   quoted. <The rooms excessively crowded> My

286.16   [*two consecutive pages so numbered by GB*]

287.16   Lapeyrouse's <specimens> are

288.8   [*cancelled paragraph follows:*] The Horticultural Society, as was the practice with scientific Societies generally, had every year an Anniversary dinner, at which they prided themselves, as characteristic of their special pursuits, on having as rich and varied a dessert of fruit as they could muster. But at these dinners ladies were not admitted, so it was resolved to substitute for them an annual fête at [417] their Turnham Green gardens.

288.25   began to <arrive> at

293.9   [sic *for 18th*]

294.40   [sic *for 22nd*]

300.32   more <interesting> at

301.1   all <towns>

305.23   [*two consecutive pages so numbered by GB*]

310.36   [sic *for 18th*]

311.8   [sic *for 18th*]

316.11   conceived. <(My father and sisters with the Maxwells had to pay fourteen guineas for a small box in the third tier.)>

319.13   [sic *for Tuesday*]

320.16   on <money> is

321.22   upon the <fruit> with

322.6   cleared. <De Candolle and I remained to the end when we went across to Lindley's to sleep.> Upon

323.34   [sic *for 471*]

324.17   [sic *for 472*]

327.34   me to <procure for> him . . . details <from France> as

329.15   next <few> days

329.36   defalcation <an Assistant> Secretary

335.30   [*two consecutive pages so numbered by GB*]

336.20   for its <winter> rest
339.19   [*no. 496 omitted by GB*]
339.25   couple of <waggons> had
342.22   smoke <at> every <stage>
345.35   worked <every> morning
346.30   herbarium [*uncancelled*:] and then three <in the Royal herbarium
         where> and again
349.30   [sic *for J.E.*]
354.24   lasted <too long>
364.8   Lushington <every one> observed
367.13   me <in bed> in
369.15   <At> By
375.38   interesting <observations> on
378.22   authorities <intended calling> the
386.39   up, <saying>
394.8   been <a> very fine <one>
394.19   Herr <Professor> Ziegler
400.31   in <his object>
405.6   perambulated the <garden> under
419.19   of which he <is> a
422.21   really <advanced> any
428.38   <Besides the> time
435.20   wife <but did>
436.27   breaking off <the intimacy> with
436.30   has <received>

APPENDIX C

Index of Plant Names

Index of Persons and Works Cited

- "By-Laws of the Horticultural Society of London." In *Charter and By-Laws of the Horticultural Society of London*. London: HSL (printed Nicol), 1830, 11–29: xxxiii–xxxiv, 331
- *Catalogue des plantes indigènes des Pyrénées et du Bas Languedoc, avec des notes et des observations sur les espèces nouvelles ou peu connues; précédé d'une notice sur un voyage botanique fait dans les Pyrénées pendant l'été de 1825*. Paris: Huzard, 1826: xxx, xxxix, 213nn10–11, 233n18, 234, 239–40n15, 243, 255–6, 265, 286–7
- "*Collomia coccinea*, 'Epitome' of Polemoniaceae," *Edwards's Botanical Register*, 19 (1833), pl. 1622: 419n8
- "De plantis in expeditione speculatoria Romanzoffiana observatis: Labiatae," *Linnaea*, 6 (1831), 76–82: 347n43, 362
- trans. *Essai sur la nomenclature et la classification des principales branches d'art-et-science, ouvrage extrait de "Chrestomathia" de Jérémie Bentham*. Paris: Bossange frères, 1823: xxviii, xxxi, xliv n13, 61, 69, 97–100, 241
- "The Fair of Beaucaire." Printed at 77–91 above: xxxix, xli, 77
- and J.D. Hooker, q.v. *Genera plantarum ad exemplaria imprimis in herbariis kewensibus servata definita*. 3 vols. London: Reeve, Williams and Norgate, 1862–83: ix n1, xxxvii, xl, 417
- "*Hosackia bicolor, Lophanthus anisatus, Stachys germanica* var. *pubescens*; Conspectus of the Tribes of the Labiatae," *Edwards's Botanical Register*, 15 (1829), pl. 1257, 1282, 1289: 326n3
- *Labiatarum genera et species: or, A Description of the Genera and Species of Plants of the Order Labiatae; with Their General History, Characters, Affinities, and Geographical Distribution*. 3 vols. London: Ridgway, 1832–36: 339n30, 383n3, 388, 418–19, 426–7
- "*Lepechinia spicata, Phlomis floccosa*; Conspectus of Labiatae Continued," *Edwards's Botanical Register*, 15 (1829), pl. 1292, 1300: 326n3
- "*Linum mexicanum*," *Edwards's Botanical Register*, 16 (1830), pl. 1326: 332n20
- "*Medicago denticulata, M. minima*." In W.J. Hooker, et al., *Supplement to the English Botany of the Late Sir J.E. Smith and Mr. Sowerby*, I. London: J.D.C. and C.E. Sowerby, 1831, pl. 2634, 2635: 327n7
- *Observations on the Registration Bill Now Pending before the House of Commons, Addressed to the Commissioners on the Law of Real Property*. London: Ridgway, 1831: 364n5
- "On the Recent Progress and Present State of Systematic Botany," Delivered at the Annual Meeting, Belfast, 24 August 1874. In *Report of the British Association for the Advancement of Science* (1874). London: BAAS, 1875, 27–54: 53n8, 420n13
- *Outline of a New System of Logic, with a Critical Examination of Dr. Whately's "Elements of Logic"*. London: Hunt and Clarke, 1827. Reissued in the Nineteenth-

tion, Proposed to Be Set on Foot, under the Name of the Chrestomathic Day School (1816). In *Works*, ed. Southwood Smith, q.v., VIII, 1–191. In *CW*, ed. M.J. Smith and W.H. Burston. Oxford: Clarendon Press, 1983: xxviii, xxxi, xliii, n13, 61, 69n35, 92, 97–9, 420n14

- "A Commentary on Mr. Humphreys' Real Property Code," *Westminster Review*, 6 (Oct. 1826), 446–507. In *Works*, V, 387–416: 265–6n55
- *Constitutional Code*, I (1830). In *Works*, IX, ed. Richard Doane. In *CW*, ed. F. Rosen and J.H. Burns. Oxford: Clarendon Press, 1983: 63n25, 104, 236n6, 244n20, 248n22, 250, 384, 420n14
- *De l'organisation judiciaire et de la codification*, ed. P.É.L. Dumont. Paris: H. Bossange, 1828: 314n58
- *A Fragment on Government* (1776). In *Works*, I, 220–95. In *CW*, *A Comment on the Commentaries and A Fragment on Government*. Ed. J.H. Burns and H.L.A. Hart. London: Athlone Press, 1977, 391–551: xiii n14
- *An Introduction to the Principles of Morals and Legislation* (printed 1780; published 1789). In *Works*, I, 1–154. In *CW*, ed. J.H. Burns and H.L.A. Hart (1970); repr. with intro. by F. Rosen. Oxford: Clarendon Press, 1996: xiii n14
- Letter to the editor, *Globe and Traveller*, 18 Apr. 1827, 2: 274n85
  Lord Brougham Displayed, Including 1. Boa Constrictor, alias Helluo Curiarum; II. Observations on the Bankruptcy Court Bill, Now Ripened into an Act (1832). In *Works*, V, 549–612: 361n60
- "Outline of a Plan of a General Register of Real Property." In Appendix to the Third Report of the Real Property Commissioners, *PP*, 1831–32, 23, 431–50. In *Works*, V, 417–35: 385n5
- *Panopticon; or, The Inspection-House: Containing the Idea of a New Principle of Construction Applicable to Any Sort of Establishment, in Which Persons of Any Description Are to Be Kept under Inspection; . . . in a Series of Letters, Written in the Year 1787, from Crecheff in White Russia, to a Friend in England* (1791). In *Works*, IV, 37–66: xvi, xvii n29, n31, 236
- *Panopticon Postscript; Part I. Containing Further Particulars and Alterations Relative to the Plan of Construction Originally Proposed; Principally Adapted to the Purpose of a Panopticon Penitentiary-House* (1791). In *Works*, IV, 67–121: xvi, xvii n29, n31, 236
- *Panopticon Postscript; Part II. Containing a Plan of Management for a Panopticon Penitentiary-House* (1791). In *Works*, IV, 121–72: xvi, xvii n29, n31, 236
- *Principles of Judicial Procedure*. Ed. Richard Doane. In *Works*, II, 1–188: 63n25
- trans. John Neal. *Principles of Legislation; from the MS of Jeremy Bentham . . . by M. Dumont . . . Translated from the Second Corrected and Enlarged Edition, with Notes and a Biographical Notice of Jeremy Bentham and of M. Dumont*. Boston: Wells and Lilly, 1830: 237n9

Chichagov, Catherine, later comtesse Eugène du Bouzet. Younger daughter of the following: 12n28, 100

Chichagov, Elizabeth (née Proby; d. 1811). Wife of the following: 12n28

Chichagov, Pavel Vasil'evich (1767–1849; *MERSH*). Russian Admiral; Minister of Marine, 1807: 12n28, 27, 100–1, 120, 323, 333

Chiron (M.). GB's tutor: 16–17, 23–4, 28

Chrestien, André Jean (1758–1840; *DBF*). Physician: 211–12

Churchill, John, 1st Duke of Marlborough (1650–1722; *DNB*). English general: 9n19

Churchill. *See also* Spencer-Churchill

Cinti-Damoreau (Cinthie), Laure (née Monthalant; 1801–63; *G*). French soprano: 101

Circourt, Adolphe Marie Pierre, comte de (1801–79; *DBF*). French diplomat: 213, 324, 363, 436

Circourt, Anastasie, comtesse de (née Klustine; 1808–63). Wife of the above: 211–13n9, 233, 281, 286, 324, 363, 436n35

Clarence, Duchess of. *See* Adelaide

Clarence, Duke of. *See* William IV

Clarke, Charles Cowden (1787–1877, *DNB*). Author, publisher and bookseller: 271n75

Clason, Francis Lewis (d. 1818; *CJB*, VII): 5n8

Cleghorn, Mr. Farmer: 156

Clive, Archer, Rev. (1800–78; *BLG*). Son of Edward Bolton and Harriet, below: 417–18

Clive, Edward, 1st Earl of Powis (1754–1839; *C*): 332n18

Clive, Edward Bolton (ca. 1765–1845; *BLG*). M.P. for Hereford City, 1826–45: 416–18

Clive, Harriet (née Archer). Wife of the above from 1790: 417–18

Cochrane, John Dundas (1780–1825; *DNB*). Pedestrian traveller: 256n44

Cochrane, Mrs. Wife of the above: 256

Cochrane, Thomas, 10th Earl of Dundonald (1775–1860; *DNB*). Admiral; styled Lord Cochrane until 1831: 240, 252–4n41

Cockburn, Sir George (1772–1853; *DNB*). Admiral. M.P. for Plymouth, 1828; junior Lord of the Admiralty, 1818–30: 295

Coder, Joseph (1778–1841; *DBF*). French pharmacist and botanist: 220

Coehorn, family: 50

Coigny, Augustin Louis Joseph Casimir Gustave de Franquetot, marquis de (1788–1865; *DBF*): 170

Coigny, Henrietta Dundas, marquise de (née Dalrymple-Hamilton; b. ca. 1801). Wife of the above from 1822: 170

banking family; industrialist, philanthropist, botanist: 240–1, 375–7, 425

Delessert, Julie Élisabeth Sophie (née Gautier; d. 1877). Wife of François Marie, above: 376

Delessert, Valentine (née de Laborde). Wife of Abraham Gabriel, above: 376

Delile, Alire Raffeneau (1778–1850; TL2). French botanist and physician; from 1829 Professor of Botany and Natural History and Director of the Jardin des Plantes, Montpellier: 57, 65n32, 93–4, 96, 211, 370, 424

Delon, Honoré Édouard (b. 1792; DBF). Bonapartist lieutenant: 95n57

Delpech, Jacques Mathieu (1777–1832; DBF). Professor of Surgery, Montpellier: 211, 383–4

Denman, Elizabeth (née Brodie; b. ca. 1747). Mother of the following: 278n95, 281, 364

Denman, Thomas, 1st Baron (1779–1854; DNB). Lawyer and politician; Lord Chief Justice, 1832–50: 278n95, 364

Denmark, King of. See Frederik VI

Deppe, Ferdinand (d. 1861; BNB). German botanist: 347

Desfontaines, René Louiche (1750–1833; TL2). French botanist: 204, 375, 380

Deshours, Jules, of Calviac: 370n19

Deshours-Farel, Paulin. Montpellier manufacturer and entrepreneur; Mayor, 1832–33: 73, 77, 82–7, 99, 369–70n19

Destutt de Tracy, Alexandre César Victor Charles, comte (1781–1864; DBF). French parlementarian: 379

Destutt de Tracy, Antoine Louis Claude, comte (1754–1836; DBF). Eléments d'idéologie. 5 pts. in 4 vols. Paris: Didot l'aîné, et al., 1801–15: 61

Devisme. Comic actor; probably of the family of Anne Pierre Jacques De Vismes du Valgay (1745–1819; ABF), author and theatrical administrator: 346

Devonshire, Duke of. See Cavendish

Devrient, Daniel Louis (Ludwig) (1784–1832; NDB). German actor: 347

D'Ghies, Hassuna (b. ca. 1791). Ambassador from Tripoli: 104n9, 135

Dictionnaire d'histoire naturelle. See Nouveau dictionnaire . . .

Dictionnaire des girouettes, ou Nos Contemporains peints d'après eux-mêmes. [Ed. A. Eymery, et al.] Paris: Eymery, 1815: 28

Didone. See Purcell

Diebitsch-Sabalkanski, Hans Karl Friedrich Anton (1785–1831; NDB). Prussian-born Russian Field Marshal: 348n45

Doane, Richard (1805–48; CJB, IX). Amanuensis and secretary to JB, 1819–31; barrister from 1830: 63n25, 97–8, 104n8, 108–10, 235, 237, 243–4, 267, 272, 279–80, 318, 320, 384–5

Don, David (1800–41; TL2). Botanist: 120–1, 133, 158, 240, 310, 419–20n14

Don Quixote. See Cervantes

Elliot, Hugh (1752–1830; *DNB*). Diplomat; English Ambassador to Prussia, 1777–82: 251n28

Ellis, Mr, of Edinburgh: 302

Ellison, Isabella Grace (née Ibbetson; d. 1860): 149n77

Ellison, Thomas. Rector of Kilamery: 50–1

Elssler, Fanni (1812–84; *BLKO*). Austrian dancer: 399

Encontre, Daniel (1762–1818; *DBF*). Professor of Theology, Montauban: 51

Encyclopaedia Britannica (1771). *Supplement to the Fourth, Fifth and Sixth Editions of the Encyclopaedia Britannica* (issued in fascicles from 1816). Ed. Macvey Napier, q.v. 6 vols. Edinburgh: Constable, 1824: 159n6

Endlicher, Stephan Ladislaus (1804–49; *TL2*). Austrian botanist: 398, 403, 409

Les Enfants d'Édouard. See Delavigne

Engelheart, Miss (*CJB*, VII). Governess: 5n8

Er mengt sich in Alles. See Jünger

Ernest Augustus, Duke of Cumberland (1771–1851; *DNB*). Fifth son of George III: 207n45, 321

Eroles. *See* Ibañez

Espoz y Mina, Francisco (1781–1836; *EUI*). Spanish guerilla general: 221–2n15

Esterhazy von Galantha, Maria Theresia, Princess (née von Thurn und Taxis; b. 1794). Wife of the following: 321

Esterhazy von Galantha, Paul Anton, Prince (1786–1866; *BLKO*). Austrian Ambassador to London, 1815–42: 406

Estreicher, Alojzy Rafal (1786–1852; *Polski Slownik Biograficzny*). Polish botanist: 352–3, 403

Euclid (fl. ca. 300 B.C.): 17

Evans, Mr. Tutor: 294

Falck, Anton Reinhard, Baron (1777–1843; *Biographisch Woordenboek der Nederlanden*). Dutch diplomat: 296

Falla, William (1761–1830; *D*). Nurseryman at Gateshead: 148, 150–1

Fane, John, 10th Earl of Westmoreland (1759–1841; *C*). Lord Privy Seal, 1798–1806, 1807–27: 285n12

Farel. *See* Deshours-Farel

Farr, Mr and Mrs. Relatives of George Arnott, q.v.: 304–5

Farren, William (1786–1861; *DNB*). English actor: 294

Fay, Jeanne Louise Baron ("Léontine") (1810–76; *DCF*). French actress; married Volnys, q.v., in 1832: 99, 367, 375, 425

Fellowes, Robert (1771–1847; *DNB*). Physician and philanthropist: 309

Fenzl, Eduard (1808–79; *TL2*). Austrian botanist: 403

Gowen, James Robert (d. 1862; *D*). Horticulturist: 340

Graham, George Edward (1771–1831; *T*). M.P. for Kinross-shire, 1819–20, 1826–30: 299

Graham, Miss, of Garbraid: 299

Graham, Robert (1786–1845; *DNB*). Physician; Regius Professor of Botany, Edinburgh, 1820–45: 158, 301–2, 325, 332

Graham, Thomas II (1752–1819; *T*). M.P. for Kinross-shire, 1811–12, 1818–19. *See also* Montgomery: 305n32

Granier, Guillaume Zoé (1788–1856; *DBF*). Mayor of Montpellier, October 1830–July 1831: 369–70n19

Grant, Charles II, 1st Baron Glenelg (1778–1866; *T*). President of the Board of Trade, September 1827–June 1828: 119, 293

Granville, Augustus Bozzi (1783–1872; *DNB*). Physician and Italian patriot: 361

Graves, Mr. Guest of William Allen, q.v.: 202

Gray, Asa (1810–88; *TL2*). American botanist: ix–x n2, xix n38

Gray, John Edward (1800–75; *DNB*). British zoologist: 349–50, 354, 419

Greenough, George Bellas (1778–1855; *DSB*). Geographer and geologist: 419

Gregson, William (1790–1863; *MEB*). Private Secretary to Sir Robert Peel; drafted bills for Home Office from 1820: 259 61

Grenville, George, 2nd Baron Nugent (1788–1850; *T*). M.P. for Aylesbury, 1812–32, 1847–50: 114n21

Greville, George, 2nd Earl Brooke of Warwick Castle and Earl of Warwick (1746–1816; *C*): 139n68

Greville, Henry Richard, 3rd Earl Brooke of Warwick Castle and Earl of Warwick (1779–1853; *C*): 137

Greville, Robert Kaye (1794–1866; *TL2*). Scottish botanist: 173, 201, 302

– *British Cryptogamic Flora. See Scottish . . .*

– *Flora edinensis; or, A Description of Plants Growing Near Edinburgh, Arranged According to the Linnaean System: with a Concise Introduction to the Natural Orders of the Class Cryptogamia, and Illustrative Plates.* Edinburgh: printed for Blackwood, 1824: 173

– *Scottish Cryptogamic Flora; or, Coloured Figures and Descriptions of Cryptogamic Plants, Belonging Chiefly to the Order "Fungi"; and Intended to Serve As a Continuation of English Botany.* 6 vols. in 3. Edinburgh: printed for Maclachlan and Stewart, 1823–28: 173

– and George Arnott Walker Arnott. "Tentamen methodi muscorum; or, A New Arrangement of the Genera of Mosses, with Characters, and Observations on their Distribution, History, and Structure," *Memoirs of the Wernerian Natural History Society,* 4 (I), 5 (I) and 5 (II) (Aug. 1822, May 1824, and Jan. 1826), 109–50, [42]–89 and 442–74, respectively: 173

– *Public Education. Plans for the Government and Liberal Instruction of Boys in Large Numbers; as Practised at Hazelwood School*. London: Knight, 1822: 141n69

Hill, Rowland (1795–1879; *DNB*). Educator. Established the penny postage, 1840: 140–2n69

Hill, Sarah (née Lea). Mother of the above; wife of the following: 141n69

Hill, Thomas Wright (1763–1851; *DNB*). Schoolmaster and founder of Hill Top School, Birmingham, 1803: 141n69

Hoare, Richard Colt, 2nd Baronet (1758–1838; *DNB*). Traveller; historian of Wiltshire: 336

Hobhouse, John Cam, 1st Baron Broughton (1786–1869; *T*). M.P. for Westminster, 1820–33: 252–5, 259–61, 277

Hocquart, Louis Mathieu (1760–1843; *DPF*). Toulouse magistrate: 40

Hocquart, Mlle. Daughter of the above: 40

Hoffmeister (Hofmeister), Franz Anton (1754–1812; *NDB*). Composer and music publisher: 395

Holdsworth, Arthur Howe (probably) (1780–1860; *T*). M.P. and inventor: 269

Hone, William (1780–1842; *DNB*). *The Man in the Moon* (1820; 20 eds.): 267

Hooke, Nathaniel (1664–1738; *DNB*). *The Roman History, from the Building of Rome to the Ruin of the Commonwealth*. 4 vols. London: Bettenham, 1738–71: 30

Homer (ca. 700 B.C.). *The Odyssey* (Greek and English). Trans. A.T. Murray. 2 vols. London: Heinemann; New York: Putnam's Sons, 1919: 148n76

Hooker, Elizabeth (1820–98). Daughter of William Jackson, below: 175–6n21, 298, 300

Hooker, Joseph (1754–1845). Norwich merchant; father of William Jackson: 175n21, 300

Hooker, Sir Joseph Dalton (1817–1911; *TL2*). Botanist; second son of William Jackson: ix–x, xlviii n56, 175n21, 298, 300

– *Life and Letters of Sir Joseph Dalton Hooker*. Ed. Leonard Huxley. 2 vols. London: Murray, 1918: ix–x n2, xxxvii n54

Hooker, Lydia (née Vincent; 1759–1829). Mother of William Jackson: 175–6n21, 300

Hooker, Maria (née Turner; 1797–1872). Wife of William Jackson: 175–6n21, 190, 298, 300

Hooker, Maria (1819–89). Daughter of William Jackson: 175–6n21, 298, 300

Hooker, Mary Harriet (1825–41). Daughter of William Jackson: 175n21, 298, 300

Hooker, William Dawson (1816–40). Eldest son of the following: 175n21, 298, 300

Hooker, Sir William Jackson (1785–1865; *TL2*). Regius Professor of Botany, Glasgow University from 1820; first Director of RBGK, 1841: xxx, xxxv, 133, 173–6n21, 182, 188, 189–90, 201, 210, 213–14, 249–50, 298–300, 309–10n41, 340, 380–1

Landor, Julia (née Thuillier; b. ca. 1794). Wife of the following from 1811: 21, 23

Landor, Walter Savage (1775–1864; *DNB*). English writer: 21–3n10, n12

– "Ad regem iterum exulem." Printed at 22n above

Langeron, Andrault, comte de (1763–1831; *GDU*). French general: 26n21

Lansdowne, Lord. *See* Petty; Petty-Fitzmaurice

Lapeyrouse, Isidore Thérèse Gérard Picot, baron de (b. 1776). French botanist; son of the following: 233–4, 287

Lapeyrouse, Philippe Picot, baron de (1744–1818; *TL2*). French botanist: 219, 233–4n18, 287

– *Histoire abrégée des plantes des Pyrénées, et itinéraire des botanistes dans ces montagnes.* Toulouse: Bellegarrigue, 1813: 219, 233

– *Supplément à l'Histoire abrégée des plantes des Pyrénées.* Toulouse: Bellegarrigue, 1818: 219n18, 233

Laplace, Pierre Simon, marquis de (1749–1827; *DSB*). French mathematician, astronomer and physicist. "Leçons de mathématiques professées à l'École Normale en 1795." In *Séances de l'École Normale* (an VIII [1799–1800]), 1–6, *passim.* In *Oeuvres complètes.* 14 vols. Paris: Gauthier-Villars, 1878–1912, XIV, 10–177: 17

La Roche de Fontenilles, Honoré, marquis de (fl. 1806–36; *ABF*): 371

Larpent, Francis Seymour (probably) (1776–1845; *DNB*): 308n37, 316

Larpent, Seymour. Possibly a nephew of the above: 249

Lauderdale, Earl of. *See* Maitland

Laurence, Justin (1794–1863; *DPF*). French parliamentarian: 379

Lavalette, Antoine Marie Chamans, comte de (1769–1830; *GDU*). Councillor of State: 27n25, 28

Lavigne (M.). French educator: 104

Lawrence, James John Trevor (1831–1913; *BBA*). Son of the two following: 428n21

Lawrence, Louisa (née Senior). Wife of William, below: xxxiv, 331, 428

Lawrence, William (1783–1867; *DNB*). Surgeon: 428n21

– *On the Physiology, Zoology, and Natural History of Man.* London: Callow, 1819: 428n21

Lawrence, William Beach (1800–81; *DAB*). American diplomat and jurist: 318

Lawrence, William Effingham (1781–1841; *Australian Dictionary of Biography*). Merchant and shipper: 166n14

Le Blanc, Théodore, Captain (d. 1837). GB's brother-in-law: 93n53, 437n37

Ledebour, Karl Friedrich von (1786–1851; *TL2*). German botanist: 322n71

Lee, George. Secretary to William Burton, q.v.: 254n40

Lee, James (1715–95; *DNB*). Established nursery at Hammersmith. His son, James (1754–1824; *D*) in charge from 1814. *See also* Kennedy: xvi, xliv n22, 122

Lee, John (ca. 1805–99; *D*). Son of James (1754–1824): 330

Lefèbvre-Desnouettes, Charles, comte (1773–1822; *GDU*). French general: 19

Legendre, Adrien Marie (1752–1833; *DSB*). *Éléments de géométrie*. Paris: Firmin Didot, 1794: 17

Legge, William, 4th Earl of Dartmouth (1784–1853; *C*): 330n15

Lehmann, Johann Georg Christian (1792–1860; *TL2*). German physician and botanist: 333, 351–2, 354, 388, 393

– "Amsinckia," *Delectus seminum quae in horto hamburgensium botanico e collectione anni 1831 mutuae commutatione offeruntur*, I (1831), 7: 319n66

Leichtsinn und Liebe: 396

Leinster. *See* Fitzgerald

Leopold I (of Belgium) (1790–1865; *EB*). Ruled from 1831: 321, 413–14n34

Lesage, Alain René (1668–1747; *GDU*). *Histoire de Gil Blas de Santillane*. 4 vols. Paris: Ribou, 1715–35; in Spanish, trans. J.F. de Isla. 4 vols. Madrid: Gonzalez, 1787–88: 52n6

Levat, Antoine David. Montpellier investor: 370n19

Levat, Jean David (probably). Montpellier banker and merchant: 73

Leveson-Gower, Elizabeth, 2nd Marchioness of Stafford and Countess of Sutherland (1765–1839; *C*): 280–1n2

Levesque, Pierre Charles (1737–1812; *GDU*). *Histoire de Russie*. 5 vols. Paris: Bure, 1782: 30

Lichtenstein (M.), of Montpellier. Brother of the following: 73–4, 354

Lichtenstein, Martin Heinrich Karl (1780–1857; *ADB*). Prussian zoologist: 73n41, 352, 354

Lindegaard, Peter (1758–1832; *DBL*). Danish horticulturist: 391–2

Lindley, John (1799–1865; *TL2*). Professor of Botany, University of London, 1828–60: xxxiii, 122, 133, 239, 249n24, 295–6, 308–9n41, 316–19, 322, 325–32n16, 334, 339, 380, 383, 417, 419–20

– "Benthamia," *Edwards's Botanical Register*, 19 (1 May 1833), pl. 1579: 319n66

– "On the Principal Questions at Present Debated in the Philosophy of Botany." In *Report of the Third Meeting of the British Association for the Advancement of Science* (1833). London: Murray, 1834, 27–57: 419n11

– *An Outline of the First Principles of Botany*. London: Longman, et al., 1830; in Italian, *Principi fondamentali di botanica*. Trans. Giuseppe Manetti, q.v. Monza: Corbetta, 1834: 434n31

– *An Outline of the First Principles of Horticulture*. London: Longman, et al., 1832; in Italian, *Principi fondamentali di orticoltura*. Trans. Giuseppe Manetti, q.v. Monza: Corbetta, 1833: 434n31

Lindley, Mrs (née Freestone). Wife of John, above, from 1823: 308

Lindley (d. 1832). Son of the above: 383

Lindsay, John (fl. 1750–88; *D*). "Account of the Germination and Raising of Ferns

O'Reilly, Terence. Witness: 117n32

Orglandes, Anne Catherine, comtesse d' (née d'Andlau; 1773–1855). Grand-daughter of Helvétius. *See also* Chateaubriand: 27n23, 101

Orglandes, Mathilde d'. Daughter of the above: 101

Orlandos, Ioannis. Greek deputy: 252–4n32

Osterman-Tolstoi, Countess, and her niece, Olga. Presumably relatives of the Russian military commander, Count Aleksandr Ivanovich Osterman-Tolstoi (1770–1857): 209

Ottenfeld (Otto von Ottenfeld), Maximilien von (1777–1858; *BLKO*). Reformer of the Austrian postal system: 407

Otto, Christoph Friedrich (1783–1856; *TL2*). Director of the Schönberg Horticultural School, 1823–43: 346, 348–9, 352–3

Owen, Robert (1771–1858; *DNB*). Industrialist and socialist: xxx, 184–5n24, nn26–7, 187–8n30, 203, 210n5, 386

– *A New View of Society; or, Essays on the Principle of the Formation of Human Character, and the Application of Principle to Practice.* London: Cadell and Davies, 1813: 184n27, 187

– *Report to the County of Lanark, of a Plan for Relieving Public Distress, and Removing Discontent, by Giving Permanent, Productive Employment, to the Poor and Working Classes.* Glasgow: Wardlaw and Cunninghame; Edinburgh: Contable, et al.; London: Longman, et al., 1821: 184n27, 187n29

Owen, Robert Dale (1801–77; *DNB*). Eldest son of the above; publicist and author: 184n24, n27

Owen, William (1802–42). Second son of Robert Owen: 184n24

Pagès (M.). Employee at Restinclières: 75

Paley, Thomas (b. 1803; *AO*). Called to the bar, Lincoln's Inn, 1828: 264

Palmerston, Lord. *See* Temple

Panisse-Passis, Pierre Léandre de Mark de Tripoli, comte de (1770–1842; Bouches-du-Rhône, *Encyclopédie départementale*, 11 [1913], 378): 423n16

Parish, John (1742–1829; *ADB*). Scottish-born Hamburg merchant: 353

Parkes, Joseph (1796–1865; *DNB*). Solicitor and politician: 314

– *A History of the Court of Chancery; with Practical Remarks on the Recent Commission, Report, and Evidence, and on the Means of Improving the Administration of Justice in the English Courts of Equity.* London: Longman, et al., 1828: 314

Parmentier, Antoine Augustin (1737–1813). French agronomist: 127n53

Parmentier, Joseph Julien Ghislain (1775–1852; *TL2*). Belgian botanist and horticulturist: 122n44, 127–8n53, 423–4

Parnell, Henry Brooke, 1st Baron Congleton (1776–1842; *T*). M.P. for Queen's Co., 1802, 1806–32: 327n6, 360n56

Puzzi, Giacinta (née Toso; *G*). Italian soprano: 293

Quéraus, curé de: 221–3
Quin, Edwin Richard Windham Wyndham-, 3rd Earl of Dunraven and Mount
    Earl (1812–71; *DNB*). Styled Viscount Adare, 1824–50: 420
La Quotidienne. Article of 24 July 1831, 2: 367

"R." (Achille Richard, q.v., or François Vincent Raspail [1791–1878; *TL2*]). Notice
    of GB's *Catalogue des plantes indigènes des Pyrénées*, *Bulletin des Sciences Naturel-
    les et de Géologie*, 10 (1827), 260–1: 255n43
Rainer, family. Tyrolese singers: 288–9, 321
Rainer, Viceroy. *See* Habsburg
The Rambler: 179
Ramond de Carbonnières, Louis François Élisabeth, baron (1753–1829; *TL2*).
    French botanist and mineralogist: 256
Raphael (Raffaelo Sanzio) (1483–1520; *EB*). Italian painter: 24
Rapin-Thoyras, Paul de (1661–1725; *GDU*). *The History of England as Well Ecclesi-
    astical as Civil* (in French, from 1724). Trans. N. Tindal. 28 vols. London: Knap-
    ton, 1726–47: 30
Rauch, Christian Daniel (1777–1857; *EB*). German sculptor: 346n41
Das Räuschchen. See Bretzner
Raupach, Ernst Benjamin Salomo (1784–1852; *ADB*). *Der Müller und sein Kind*.
    Leipzig: Reclam, n.d.: 405
Ravenshaw, John Goldsborough (1777–1840; *Dictionary of Indian Biography*).
    Chairman of the Court of Directors of the East India Company, 1832: 387
Réaumur, René Antoine Ferchault de (1683–1757; *DSB*). Physicist and naturalist:
    61
Rech, Odon. Montpellier investor: 370n19
Reeve, John (1799–1838; *DNB*). English actor: 294
Reichenbach, Heinrich Gottlieb Ludwig (1793–1879; *TL2*). German botanist: 396
– *Iconographia botanica exotica*. 3 vols. Leipzig: Hofmeister, 1827–30: 395
The Rencontre. See Planché
Rennie, George (1791–1866; *DNB*). "Report on the Progress and Present State of
    Our Knowledge of Hydraulic Architecture As a Branch of Engineering." In
    Report of the Third Meeting of the British Association for the Advancement of Science
    (1833). London: Murray, 1834, 153–84: 420n11
Requien, Esprit (1788–1851; *TL2*). French botanist: xxx, 210, 213–20, 323, 423
Requien, Mme. Mother of the above: 213–14
Reviczky, Adam, Count (1786–1862; *BLKO*). Austrian statesman: 402
Revue Encyclopédique: 61, 255, 265, 318

Russell, Richard Norris (1809–96; *AC*). Son of the following: 44n43, 68–9, 419–20
Russell, William Thomas (b. 1776). Irish physician, living at Toulouse: 44, 68–9, 422
Russell, William. Eldest son of the above: 44, 68–9
Ryder, Dudley, 1st Earl of Harrowby (1762–1847; *DNB*). Statesman: 118–19n38
Ryder, Henry (1777–1836; *DNB*). Brother of the above; Bishop of Gloucester, 1815–24: 118–19n38

Sabine, Joseph (1770–1837; *TL2*). English barrister and horticulturist; Secretary of the HSL, 1816–30: xxxiii, 121–2, 133, 196, 239, 295–6, 317, 327–30n11, 332n19, 334, 419
Sablukov, Nikolai Aleksandrovich (1776–1848; *MERSH*). Russian general: 285–6
St Albans. *See* Beauclerk
St Avet, Mme de: 35
Saint-Chamans, Louis Marie Joseph de (1779–1824; *LP*). Prefect of Haute-Garonne, at Toulouse, from March 1817: 40
Saint-Cricq, Pierre Laurent Barthélemy, comte de (1772–1854; *DPF*). Director of French customs from 1815: 204
Saint Guilhem: 220
St Helens, Lord. *See* Fitzherbert
Saint-Hilaire, Auguste François César Prouvençal de (1779–1853; *TL2*). French traveller and botanist: 375, 380, 417n4
St Joseph: 93
St Louis. *See* Louis IX
Saint-Priest, Armand Emmanuel Charles Guignard, comte de (1782–1863; *GDU*). Brother of Mesdames Dax and Calvière, q.v.; French diplomat: 95
Saladin, Jean François, dit Saladin de Montrepos (1754–1836; *DHBS*): 373n21
Salzmann, Philipp (1781–1851; *TL2*). German botanist and collector; physician at Montpellier: 214
Saussure, Mme de. Wife of the following: 433
Saussure, Nicolas Théodore de (1767–1845; *TL2*). Swiss botanist and chemist: 433
Sauvages, François Boissier de (1706–67; *GDU*). French physician and botanist: xii
Saxony, King of. *See* Anton; Friedrich Augustus II
Say, Jean Baptiste Léon (1767–1832; *GDU*). French economist: xvii, 27–8
Scarlett, James, Baron Abinger (1769–1844; *DNB*). Barrister; Attorney-General, 1827–28 and 1829–30: 319, 327nn9–10
Scarsdale, Lord: *See* Curzon
Schiede, Christian Julius Wilhelm (1798–1836; *TL2*). German botanist and traveller: 347

Schernsward, Major. Swedish landowner: 6–7n13

Schlechtendal, Diederich Franz Leonhard von (1794–1866; *TL2*). German botanist. *See also* Chamisso: 345, 347–8n43, 414

Schlegel, August Wilhelm von (1767–1845; *EB*). German author, and translator of
Shakespeare, q.v.: 347

Schott, Heinrich Wilhelm (1794–1865; *TL2*). Austrian botanist: 405

Schotten, abbé der, 402

Schouw, Joachim Frederik (1789–1852; *TL2*). Professor of Botany, Copenhagen,
from 1820: 391

Schrader, Heinrich Adolf (1767–1836; *TL2*). Professor of Botany, Göttingen: 356

Schröder-Devrient, Wilhelmine (1804–60; *G*). German soprano: 358

Schubert (Szubert), Michael (Mikael) (1787–1860; *TL2*). Professor of Botany and
Director of the botanical garden, Warsaw: 352

Schuhmännlein: 409

Schultes, Julius Hermann (1804–40; *BLKO*). Physician at Munich: 411

Schumacher, [Heinrich] Christian Friedrich (1757–1830; *TL2*). Danish botanist
and physician: 390–1

– *Beskrivelse äf Guineiske Planter*. Copenhagen: Popp, 1827: 391

Schwarzenberg, Karl Philipp, Prince von (1771–1820; *EB*). Austrian diplomat
and general: 10n22

Schweinitz, Lewis David von (1780–1835; *TL2*). American botanist: 383

Sclater, Philip Lutley (1829–1913; *BBA*). Secretary, Zoological Society of London,
from 1859: 431

Scott, John, 1st Earl of Eldon (1751–1838; *DNB*). Lord Chancellor, 1801–Apr.
1827: 269n70, 278n93, 285n12

Scott, Sir Walter (1771–1832; *DNB*). Scottish novelist and poet: 159, 164–5

– *Lady of the Lake*. Edinburgh: Ballantyne, 1810: 179–81n23

– *Minstrelsy of the Scottish Border*. 3 vols. Kelso: Ballantyne, 1802: 306n33

– *Rob Roy*. 3 vols. Edinburgh: Constable, 1818: 179

– *Waverley; or, 'Tis Sixty Years Since*. 3 vols. Edinburgh: Constable; London,
Longman, et al., 1814: 306n34

Scribe, Augustin Eugène (1791–1861; *GDU*), and Anne Honoré Joseph Duveyrier
("Mélesville") (1787–1865: *DBF*). *Valérie, ou La Jeune Aveugle*. Paris: Ladvocat,
1822: 101

Scudamore, John Lucy (1798–1875; *BLG*). Husband of the following; GB's
brother-in-law: 338–9, 415–18n2, 427–8

Scudamore, Sarah Laura (née Brydges; d. 1863). Wife of the above from 1822;
GB's sister-in-law: 338–9, 415–18n2, 427–8

Sébastiani, François Horace Bastien, comte de (1772–1851; *GDU*). French Minister of Foreign Affairs from November 1830: 376

Sedgwick, Adam (1785–1873; *DSB*). Professor of Geology, Cambridge, 1818–73: 419–20

Sedlnitzky, Joseph, Count (1778–1855; *BLKO*). Minister of Police, Vienna, from 1817: 402

Ségur, Louis Philippe, comte de (1753–1830; *GDU*). Deputy, Councillor of State and author: xvii, xlv n23, 20n7, 26–7n22, 209

Selby, Charles Borre, Baron (1778–1849; *DBL*). Danish diplomat: 389

Selby, Mme. Wife of the above: 389

Sellow, Friedrich (1789–1831; *TL2*). Prussian gardener and botanical explorer: 345–6n38

Selwyn, Mr. Rector of Kilmarston: 335

Seo d'Urgel, Bishop of: 229

Seringe, Nicolas Charles (1776–1858; *TL2*). Professor of Botany and Director of the botanical garden, Lyon: 235, 323, 371

Sewell, William (1804–74; *AO*). Fellow, Exeter College, 1827–74; Dean, 1839: 418

Shakespeare, William (1564–1616; *DNB*): *Othello*: 267

– *Richard III*; in German, *König Richard der Dritte*, part IX.I of *Shakespeare's dramatische Werke*. Trans. A.W. von Schlegel, q.v. Berlin: Unger, 1810: 347

Shannon, family: 40

Sharpe, Sutton (1797–1843). Barrister and law reformer: 380

Shepherd, John (1764–1836; *TL2*). British botanist; first Curator of the Liverpool botanic garden, 1802–36: 196–7

Sheridan, Richard Brinsley Butler (1751–1816; *DNB*). *A Trip to Scarborough*. Dublin: Company of Booksellers, 1781: 140

Sheridan, Misses: 284

Shore, John, 1st Baron Teignmouth (1751–1834; *C*). Governor-General of India, 1792–97: 118–19

Sibthorp, John (1758–96; *TL2*). Professor of Botany and Director of the botanical garden, Oxford, 1783–95: 134

– *Flora graeca*. 10 vols. Ed. J.E. Smith (vols. I–VII) and John Lindley (vols. VIII–X). London: Taylor, 1806–40: 134

Siemers, Georg Johann Heinrich II (1794–after 1879; *DBA*). Syndicus of Hamburg: 354

Simond, Louis (1767–1831; *GDU*). *Journal of a Tour and Residence in Great Britain during the Years 1810 and 1811, by a French Traveller*. 2 vols. Edinburgh: Constable; London: Longman, et al., 1815: 131n59

Sims, John (1749–1831; *TL2*). British botanist; editor of *Curtis's Botanical Magazine*, q.v., 1801–26: 249

Sinclair, Sir John (1754–1835; *DNB*). Statistician and agricultural improver: 159

Sinning, Wilhelm (1792–1874; *TL2*). German horticulturist and botanist: 432

Viceroy, at Monza. *See* Rainer Joseph von Habsburg

Vigors, Nicholas Aylward (1785–1840; *DNB*). Irish zoologist and politician: 330

Vilback, Renaud de. Investor: 370n19

Villèle, Barbe Ombline Mélanie Panon-Desbassayns, comtesse de (1781–1855; J. Fourcassié, *Villèle* [1954]). Wife of the following from 1799: 242

Villèle, Jean Baptiste Séraphin Joseph, comte de (1773–1854; *GDU*). French statesman: 77n44, 209, 278n94, 505n30

Villemain, Abel François (1790–1870; *GDU*). Professor of French literature, Sorbonne, 1816–30: 377

Villeneuve, Louis, comte de (1768–1851; *GDU*). French agriculturist: xxvi, 64–5

Visiani, Roberto de (1800–78; *TL2*). Italian-born botanist and physician: 398, 403, 405

"Vive Henri quatre!": 27

Volnys, Claude François Charles, dit (ca. 1803–ca. 1893; *DCF*). French actor; husband of Léontine Fay, q.v., from 1832: 425

Voltaire, François Marie Arouet (1694–1778; *GDU*): 54n9

– "L'Assemblée des monosyllabes, les Pour, les Que, les Qui, les Quoi, les Oui et les Non" (1760), "Poésies mélées," nos. 218–23. In *Oeuvres complètes de Voltaire*. Paris: Garnier, 1877, X, 560–4: 54n9

– "Chanson en l'honneur de maître Lefranc de Pompignan, et de révérend père en dieu, son frère, l'évêque du Puy, lesquels ont été comparés dans un discours public à Moïse et à Aaron" (1761), "Poésies mélées," no. 229. Ibid., 567–8: 54n9

Vorontsov, Mikhail Semenovich, Prince (1782–1856; *MERSH*). Commander of the Russian corps of occupation in France 1815–18; from 1823, Governor-General of the "New Russia": 14, 26, 106, 274–5, 365, 383, 386, 391

Vorontsov, Semen Romanovich, Count (1744–1832; *MERSH*). Russian Ambassador to London, 1784–1806: 26, 245, 255, 256n, 312, 362–3, 386

Walker, Miss. Relative of George Arnott, q.v.: 304

Wallich, Aron (Arnold) Wulff (1779–1845; *DBL*). Danish painter; brother of Nathaniel, below: 391–2

Wallich, Hanne (née Jacobson; 1757–1839; *DBL*). Mother of the following: 390, 392

Wallich, Nathaniel (b. Nathan Wulff) (1786–1854; *TL2*). Danish-born botanist: xxxiii, 325–6n1, 332, 340, 352–3, 362–3, 366, 385, 387–93n8, 429n26

– *Plantae asiaticae rariores; or, Descriptions and Figures of a Select Number of Unpublished East Indian Plants*. 3 vols. London; Paris; Strasburg: Treuttel and Würtz, 1830–32: 327n7, 332